A History of Eastern Europe 1918 to the Present

A History of Eastern Europe 1918 to the Present

Modernisation, Ideology and Nationality

Ian D. Armour

BLOOMSBURY ACADEMIC
LONDON • NEW YORK • OXFORD • NEW DELHI • SYDNEY

BLOOMSBURY ACADEMIC
Bloomsbury Publishing Plc
50 Bedford Square, London, WC1B 3DP, UK
1385 Broadway, New York, NY 10018, USA
29 Earlsfort Terrace, Dublin 2, Ireland

BLOOMSBURY, BLOOMSBURY ACADEMIC and the Diana logo are
trademarks of Bloomsbury Publishing Plc

First published in Great Britain 2021

A catalogue record for this book is available from the British Library.

A catalog record for this book is available from the Library of Congress.
Names: Armour, Ian D., author.
Title: A history of Eastern Europe: modernisation, ideology and
nationality / Ian D. Armour.
Identifiers: LCCN 2020050388 (print) | LCCN 2020050389 (ebook) | ISBN
9781472508614 (paperback) | ISBN 9781472510365 (hardback) | ISBN
9781472511973 (ebook) | ISBN 9781472508652 (epub)
Subjects: LCSH: Europe, Eastern–History–1918-1945–Textbooks. | Europe,
Eastern—History–1945—Textbooks.
Classification: LCC DJK49 .A76 2021 (print) | LCC DJK49 (ebook) | DDC
947.0009/04–dc23
LC record available at https://lccn.loc.gov/2020050388
LC ebook record available at https://lccn.loc.gov/2020050389

ISBN: HB: 978-1-4725-1036-5
PB: 978-1-4725-0861-4
ePDF: 978-1-4725-1197-3
eBook: 978-1-4725-0865-2

Typeset by Deanta Global Publishing Services, Chennai, India
Printed and bound in Great Britain

To find out more about our authors and books visit www.bloomsbury.com
and sign up for our newsletters.

Contents

Maps

Preface

This book makes no great claim to originality. Like most books intended for students and the general reader, it has been built on foundations laid by others. In addition, my own specialism lies in nineteenth-century rather than twentieth-century East European history. What knowledge and understanding of twentieth-century Eastern Europe I possess have been acquired through teaching the subject for many years, through travel in the region, and through the area's continuing relevance to understanding European and world history in general. As a non-specialist, I can only hope that my approach to this subject will offer the reader a fresh look; certainly this book can hardly claim to be the last word on the subject.

I have been much influenced by the work of Robin Okey, whose general history was one of the pioneering treatments of Eastern Europe and a rich source of thematic insights. Another trailblazer is the late Gale Stokes, the utility of whose conceptualisation of twentieth-century Eastern Europe as a laboratory for rival ideologies struck me as soon as I read his brilliant account of 1989. I am also indebted to Mark Wheeler, then at the School of Slavonic and East European Studies (SSEES), who recruited me in 1993 as a teaching assistant on his course 'Quest for Modernity', covering the history of Eastern Europe from 1740 to the present. Not only did I inherit this course from Mark and teach it at SSEES myself for another couple of years, but its content and structure formed the basis for courses on twentieth-century Eastern Europe that I subsequently offered at Staffordshire University and at MacEwan University in Alberta. The present work is in many respects the book I wish I had already written while I was teaching several iterations of this course. It is also intended as a sequel to my *History of Eastern Europe 1740–1918* (2nd edition, 2012).

I am extremely grateful to Frances Arnold, then of Bloomsbury Academic, who invited me to undertake this project, and to a succession of Bloomsbury editors since, notably Emily Drewe and Abigail Lane, for shepherding it through to completion with encouragement and immense patience. I am also grateful to Bloomsbury's external readers, who were kind enough to be cruel in pointing out the deficiencies of the first draft; the final version has undoubtedly benefited from a trawl through more recent literature suggested by both of them.

It is a truism that one learns history most effectively by teaching it, and this is no less true in my case. I owe a profound if unquantifiable debt to the generation of students, in both Britain and Canada, who have taken my courses on various aspects of East European history. In some cases I have learned just as much from them as they have from me. I hope that students in particular will find this book of some use in understanding a subject of continuing relevance to contemporary affairs.

Ian D. Armour
Stoke, Devon
7 April 2020

Introduction

The premise of this book is that, even in the twenty-first century, after Europe has been 're-united' under generally democratic political systems and free market economies, Eastern Europe remains distinct from Western Europe. The reasons for this continuing difference can only be understood with reference to the region's tortured twentieth-century history.

What makes Eastern Europe different to this day is the fact that much of it has remained economically, socially and politically 'backward' in comparison with Western Europe, even if some of the differences are markedly less obvious now than, say, in 1989. Admittedly the whole concept of backwardness is problematic, and laden with Western-centred values; and at a time when West European societies show every propensity for succumbing to retrograde tendencies like neo-fascism, racism and a general intolerance of difference, it is clearly important not to be too judgmental. Nevertheless I propose using the concept of backwardness in the absence of some less freighted term.

Largely agrarian at the outset of the twentieth century and during the interwar period, Eastern Europe has been consistently less developed than the West, and decades of subjection to the ostensibly modernising influence of communism, ironically, only widened this gap. The region has been the testing ground for a succession of large-scale political experiments: liberal democracy, authoritarian regimes, fascism and finally communism. It has been the plaything of regional hegemons and their rivals: Germany and Russia in the first half of the century, Russia and the West during the Cold War and, sadly, since the start of the Putin era in 1999. The result is that, even today, and although some East European societies have done much to close the gap, much of the region still feels different. The economic legacies of the communist command economy have been only partially overcome; in some countries political institutions remain – or have become – shockingly authoritarian, with some, such as Belarus, never having left the Soviet-style system of control at all; and aggressive nationalism and open racism are still respectable, indeed positively encouraged in some quarters. The region is also in many respects uncomfortably wedged between the European Union and a revived, authoritarian Russia, as became painfully clear during the Russo-Ukrainian war of 2014–15.

Definitions

Delineating Eastern Europe is more complicated than one might think. As one study put it, 'the wit of man has not yet devised for this area any term which is not objectionable on grounds either of accuracy or of euphony'.[1] Nevertheless, a start must be made somewhere.

The Polish historian Oscar Halecki defined Eastern Europe as 'the region between the Holy Roman Empire, or the Teutonic and Romance nations, on the one hand, and Eurasian Russia, i.e. those Eastern Slavs who found themselves in certain periods of history outside the European community, on the other hand. In other words, it is that large and important part of Europe of which the Byzantine Empire only . . . is duly considered in general historiography . . . all the other countries of that region are usually treated on the margin either of Western European history, if they are Catholic, or of Russian history, if they are Orthodox or Slavic or both.'[2] This may be complicated enough for those unfamiliar with the Holy Roman and Byzantine Empires of the middle ages. It may also be unduly simplistic, in that Halecki, a patriotic Pole, is possibly too anxious to draw a distinction between East European peoples and 'Eurasian Russia'.[3]

The utility of Halecki's definition, however, is its elasticity. Some peoples, 'in certain periods', vanished from history, or were at the very least marginalised from a West European perspective, because they were subsumed within great multinational empires. Such peoples became subjects, often unwilling subjects, of the Tsar of Russia, the King of Prussia, the Habsburg Monarchy, the Polish-Lithuanian Commonwealth before its disappearance at the end of the eighteenth century and, in the Balkans, the Muslim-ruled Ottoman Empire. The key point is that an entire region existed for centuries, and continues to exist, between Russia and what we still think of as Western Europe; yet the peoples of this huge area never properly 'belonged' either to Russia or to 'the West'. It is one of the arguments of the companion volume to this book that the separate, distinct regional identity of Eastern Europe was forged in the century and a half or so before the end of the First World War, long before the concept of Eastern Europe became common parlance.[4] The distinction became even more marked in the twentieth century, and remains striking to the present day.

In a purely geographical sense the term 'Eastern Europe' has always had a certain currency. It was only with the collapse of the old multinational states at the end of the First World War, however, and the establishment of a raft of new or enlarged successor states, that the concept of Eastern Europe as a distinct region became common. This was partly a matter of the new states' identifiability on the map. It was also a function of Western perceptions of these states as politically inexperienced, economically vulnerable and culturally

[1]   Macartney, C.A. and Palmer, A.W., 1962, *Independent Eastern Europe: A History*, London and Basingstoke, v.
[2]   Halecki, O., 1962, *The Limits and Divisions of European History*, Notre Dame, IN, 118–19.
[3]   Longworth, P., 1992, *The Making of Eastern Europe*, Basingstoke, 9, note 9.
[4]   Armour, I.D., 2012, *A History of Eastern Europe 1740-1918: Empires, Nations and Modernisation*, 2nd edn, London, 1.

inferior; certainly examples of this sort of 'East Europeanism' abound in the interwar period. But the inhabitants of the region shared these perceptions to some extent, and showed every consciousness of wanting to overcome them.

For the purposes of this book, 'Eastern Europe' will be defined as those countries that either already existed, or were newly created, or became independent in 1918, plus those west of the Caucasus which have emerged from the wreckage of the former Soviet Union and former Yugoslavia since 1991. On a north-south axis this runs from Finland to Greece, and on an east-west axis from Austria and the former Communist East Germany to Belarus and the Ukraine. It includes the 'lands between' of the interwar period, but also those societies under Soviet or Yugoslav jurisdiction between 1945 and 1991, but now independent.

In addition, the creation since the late nineteenth century of sizeable and often vocal East European diasporas, particularly in Western Europe and North America, has complicated this definition, with waves of migration following the upheavals of 1918, 1945 and 1989. Not only has migration shaped the demography of Eastern Europe itself, but émigré communities have continued to play a role in the region's fate, whether as lobbyists with their host countries, contributors of remittances to families back in the 'old country', or as returning participants in East European politics. The wider world has in turn been shaped by these successive displacements of East Europeans, not least the huge Jewish diaspora triggered by the rise of Nazism. As Steven Beller reminds us, 'Central Europe is elsewhere'.[5]

Themes

The main themes of the book, reflected in the sub-title, are the comparative backwardness of the region, and how this has driven strategies for modernisation; the way in which the region has been used as a sort of giant test tube for political experimentation; and the enduring strength of nationalism in the region, which has survived decades of communism only to re-emerge in many respects more virulent than before. All three of these themes remain relevant to understanding Eastern Europe today: the region is still 'behind' the West; it is still wrestling with the legacies of communism and the fact that it was one of the battlegrounds of the Cold War; and it is arguably even more bedevilled by nationality disputes than Western Europe, not least because of the continuing malign influence of Russia in the countries forming what Russians still refer to as the 'near abroad'.

[5] Beller, S., 2005, 'Commentary: Central Europe Is Elsewhere', *Austrian History Yearbook*, XXXVI, 208.

Modernisation. Students of Eastern Europe should be aware that the debate about modernisation is by no means open and shut. In our own time the whole concept of economic development and growth as necessary for the prosperity of human societies has been derided, especially on the green wing of the political spectrum, as inimical to larger environmental concerns. For most of the twentieth century, however, this attitude would have been incomprehensible to most people wherever they lived, and East Europeans were no exception. From the time of Peter the Great, rulers and elites in Eastern Europe strove to emulate what they perceived to be superior Western models of organisation and economic management. This was primarily about strengthening the state, especially in military terms; rarely, and then only tangentially, was it about bettering the lot of the state's inhabitants. The onset of industrialisation, beginning in Britain in the eighteenth century but spreading to Western Europe by the early nineteenth, only heightened East Europeans' sense of inferiority, and the nineteenth century was distinguished by efforts to modernise of varying determination or fitfulness by the Habsburg Monarchy, the Russian and Ottoman Empires, and the emerging Balkan states.

Eastern Europe's trajectory in the twentieth century was equally dominated by the drive to modernise. Modernisation took two forms, economic and political. Economic modernisation revolved around the promotion of industrialisation, the improvement of infrastructure, education, and other attributes of modernity. The attraction of communism for East Europeans, as elsewhere in the twentieth century, was precisely its apparent ability – illusory as it transpired – to kick-start or further modernisation.

Political modernisation has proved rather trickier, and is still a work in progress in Eastern Europe. In the interwar period the vogue for liberal democracy proved short-lived, country after country succumbed to dictatorship, and significant numbers of East European intellectuals, at least, surrendered to the delusion that modernisation might as plausibly be delivered through authoritarian or even fascist modes of governance. Communism, as mentioned, was by definition a modernising ideology, but it was by no means democratic, whatever its advocates' claims. Only in the period after 1989 has political pluralism, otherwise known as liberal democracy, made a comeback, with mixed if encouraging results to date. The essential point about such political experimentation, however, is that its longer-term purpose has been the modernisation of East European societies. In the twenty-first century, the debate about modernisation has even shifted to cultural terrain, with issues such as gender equality and toleration of alternative sexuality coming to the fore; here, too, Eastern Europe often feels behind the curve, although Russia's record in this respect is even worse.

Ideology. Closely linked to the preoccupation with modernisation has been the way in which Eastern Europe has served as a sort of laboratory for political ideologies generally.[6] Liberal democracy, conservative authoritarianism, fascism, communism – all have been promoted and, in many cases, imposed on the region's peoples. In this respect, it is true, East Europeans' experience in the twentieth century does not differ significantly from that of West Europeans and the rest of the world; the Cold War alone amply demonstrates how global this competition between ideologies has become. Nevertheless, Eastern Europe offers a fascinating example of successive attempts at mass transformation, across an entire region and affecting radically different societies: almost universal adoption of liberal democratic institutions after 1918; an equally comprehensive slide into authoritarian rule in the next two decades; the blanket imposition of communism in 1944–8; and finally the abrupt, if messy and incomplete, transition to political pluralism in 1989 and after.

The history of Eastern Europe since the First World War therefore serves as an introduction to conceptual thinking. What were the strengths but also the weaknesses of liberal democracy, which in the past had, as it has now, plenty of contemptuous enemies, not the least of them the current presidents of both the Russian Federation and the United States? What is the difference between conservative authoritarianism and fascism, which is vital to understanding the interwar period and the Second World War? What exactly did communism mean to the millions of East Europeans who, however deludedly and briefly, subscribed to its tenets with such fanaticism, and why were communists such determined enemies of social democrats? How, in societies which for much of the twentieth century were by no means universally literate or politically mobilised, do we gauge the extent to which such political creeds commanded allegiance?

Nationalism. Finally, nationalism is an enduring theme in the history of Eastern Europe; and although it is essentially a political ideology like communism, fascism and liberal democracy, its importance in this story arguably warrants separate consideration.

To recap the rudiments of nationalism from this book's companion volume, nationalism can be defined as a modern ideology, originating in Western Europe in the eighteenth century (although the dating of this remains disputed), and which holds, in Peter Alter's succinct formulation, 'the nation and the sovereign nation-state to be crucial indwelling values.'[7] The term 'nation' itself can be conceived in a political sense, as all inhabitants of a particular state; but 'nation' can also be understood in a cultural sense, as all those who share certain cultural attributes, such as language, religion, common history and so on. Throughout the nineteenth century these political and cultural meanings

[6] Stokes, G., 2012, *The Walls Came Tumbling Down: Collapse and Rebirth in Eastern Europe,* 2nd edn, Oxford, 3.
[7] Alter, P., 1989, *Nationalism,* London, 8. For a general discussion of nationalism's origins and its definition, see Armour, *A History of Eastern Europe 1740-1918,* 4–6, 36–9.

of 'nation', never mutually exclusive, tended to converge: political nationalists came to assume that the nation should also be culturally homogeneous, while cultural nationalists increasingly sought a political home – a state – for their nation.[8] The 'unification' of Italians and Germans in 'nation-states', in the mid-nineteenth century, became a template for comparable aspirations on the part of East Europeans, and much turmoil and bloodshed flowed from this.

In the twentieth century East European nationalism can be said to have reached its apogee, although the story is by no means over yet. The First World War saw the collapse of Eastern Europe's multinational states and their replacement by so-called successor states, very few of which were truly 'nation-states', in the sense that their borders included only one ethnicity or 'nation'. On the contrary, the countries of the 'new Europe' were for the most part multinational themselves, and this fact is key to understanding the horrors of the twentieth century. Nationalism embittered relations between the new states, as well as the domestic politics of countries laden with aggrieved national minorities. It furnished the great powers with justification and pretexts for intervention in the region, and in the case of Nazi Germany it was the ostensible reason for territorial expansion and the renewed outbreak of war in 1939. Nationalism occasioned a veritable bloodbath of 'ethnic cleansing' and score settling both during and at the close of the Second World War, including the mass murder of Europe's Jews, most of whom were done to death in Eastern Europe. It remained a potent, if officially unacknowledged, undercurrent in the communist period, breaking through the surface in revolts such as Hungary's in 1956, and in the late communist period became more respectable as 'national communism'. And the history of the region since the revolutions of 1989 has shown that democratic politics means nationalist politics and, in some cases, most notoriously that of the former Yugoslavia, this has meant nationalist war as well. The extent to which nationalism and its manipulation by political leaders can destabilise and impoverish the entire region, with incalculable consequences for the rest of Europe, remains a live issue at time of writing.

Organisation

Given the large number of states and peoples involved, an attempt to treat each country individually would be impractical, although some countries figure prominently at certain points. The structure of this book therefore offers a

[8]   Vick, B., 2006, 'Language and Nation: National Identity and the Civic-Ethnic Typology', in T. Baycroft and M. Hewitson (eds), *What Is A Nation? Europe 1789-1914*, Oxford and New York, 155–70.

mix of chronological and thematic treatment. It includes a section on the 'prehistory' of the twentieth century, in other words the early twentieth-century background down to the close of the First World War. The book then falls naturally into three main sections: the interwar period, climaxing in the Second World War; the communist period; and 1989 and 'post-communism'.

Given the sheer size of the canvas attempted, no effort has been made to chart systematically the complex historiography of the subject. The attentive reader will, however, glean something of the range and diversity of the debate among historians from the occasional note, and from the extensive bibliography.

PART I

The prehistory of twentieth-century Eastern Europe

1

The making of 'Eastern Europe'

Just as we cannot understand the present without a knowledge of the past, so too every history has its 'prehistory'. This chapter describes Eastern Europe at the outset of the twentieth century, at a point when profound changes already lay behind the region, but when the cataclysms of the twentieth century were still to come. This involves a brief survey of the physical and human geography, the peoples of Eastern Europe and their environment. It involves a summary of economic and social conditions, and how these shaped domestic political developments. Finally, it involves a tour of the international political landscape, the empires and other states and their relationships with one another. Although much of this terrain is covered in this book's predecessor, some sort of recapitulation of these aspects seems in order. The chapter concludes with a necessarily brutal analysis of the origins of the First World War, which had their ostensible locus, at least, in Eastern Europe.[1]

Physical and human geography

Whatever common characteristics Eastern Europe might possess, they are not to be found in its physical geography. The region ranges from the Arctic taiga of Finland and European Russia, across a vast swathe of boreal forest, the North German Plain and the steppe grasslands of Russia and Hungary, to the mountain ranges of the Carpathians, the Alps and the Balkans, taking in rich river valleys and huge alluvial plains at the mouths of the Vistula, Danube and Dnieper, and narrower mountain gorges throughout the Balkan Peninsula. Eastern Europe includes some of the most fertile land in the world, but it also features rocky, barren landscapes like the Greek archipelago and the limestone karst of the Adriatic littoral. It remains to this day a region rich in natural resources, arable and mineral, one reason among others for the near-continual conflict which has shaped its history.

The human geography is even more complex. The peoples of Eastern Europe are numerous, and divide into at least ten main language groups, living in

---

[1] On the origins of the First World War, see Armour, I.D., 2012, *A History of Eastern Europe 1740-1918: Empires, Nations and Modernisation*, 2nd edn, London, 238–40; for the physical and human geography, 15–19.

Map 1 Languages of Eastern Europe.

1914 under the rule of only eleven sovereign states.[2] Long before the twentieth century, as a result of migration, conquest and displacement, these peoples had become in many areas inextricably intermixed, to a far greater extent than the peoples of Western Europe. Revolts against Ottoman rule in the Balkans, and the emergence of nation-states there, had begun to undo this intermixture of peoples, by forcing out unwanted ethnic or confessional groups; but this early form of 'ethnic cleansing' was far from completed, and the continuing

[2] The Ottoman Empire, Greece, Bulgaria, Serbia, Montenegro, Albania, Romania, the Russian Empire, the German Empire, and Austria-Hungary; Italy after 1912 ruled the largely Greek-speaking islands of the Dodecanese.

complexity of the population in almost all the states of the region was a source of as yet unresolved tensions. The 'great departure' of mass emigration, most of it to the Americas, accelerated after 1880, prompting concerns among rulers about population loss, but did not materially alter the ethnic balance in Eastern Europe itself.[3]

In addition, populations were divided vertically as well as horizontally. It was not uncommon, even in the twentieth century, for towns to be of a different ethnicity than the people in the surrounding countryside. An example was the largely Polish-speaking city of Vilnius, which in 1918 was anchored in a sea of Belorussian-speaking peasants. Yet towns were themselves multinational: Vilnius hosted German-speakers and Yiddish-speaking Jews, as well as a small but growing number of Lithuanians; it had only just shed its upper crust of Russian administrators, servants of the defunct tsarist regime. Across the region the spread of education meant that long-dominant urban ethnicities were being infiltrated by a trickle of literate peasants, or the literate sons and daughters of peasants.

Until the nineteenth century most of Eastern Europe was profoundly agrarian; in other words the vast majority of the population lived largely on and off the land, with small urban centres and little in the way of industry. The picture changed in the century preceding 1914, but even at the beginning of the twentieth century, due to the uneven spread of industrialisation, much of the huge mineral and non-agricultural richness of the region remained unexploited. On the eve of the First World War there were serious concentrations of industry in metropolitan Austria and Hungary, in Bohemia and Silesia, in Russian Poland and the Baltic provinces of Russia, and in the Donbass region of what is now eastern Ukraine.

Language alone, in Eastern Europe as elsewhere, was no firm guide to ethnic identity, and not just because many East Europeans to this day have, of necessity, a working knowledge of more than one language. Individuals might pass their childhood speaking one language, but receive their education in another, or acquire a second tongue due to migration to a town or elsewhere. Pressure to assimilate into the culture of the dominant ethnicity, in some countries, resulted in sizeable minorities of recent 'converts'; in interwar Hungary, for instance, nearly 7 per cent of the population were German speakers, quite apart from the large number of Hungarian citizens of German origin. In addition, recent work on transnational history reminds us that regional identities remained important in many parts of Eastern Europe, especially in borderlands like Upper Silesia and Macedonia, which often retained 'a distinct mixture of cultures and

---

[3]   Zahra, T., 2017, *The Great Departure: Mass Migration from Eastern Europe and the Making of the Free World*, reprint edn, New York, 5.

languages', including what linguists call 'continuous dialects' shaped by the everyday use of several languages.[4]

Of the ten main language groups, the *Greeks* were among the longest-established inhabitants of the region. They were also one of the most geographically dispersed groups, with settlements stretching back to antiquity on the shores of Asia Minor and the northern littoral of the Black Sea, in the Caucasus and the Levant as well as the territory of present-day Greece. As late as 1922 the largest Greek urban centre was not Athens, but Smyrna (İzmir) on the west coast of Anatolia. Many Anatolian Greeks, the so-called Karamanli Greeks, did not even speak Greek; the only thing that set them apart from their fellow Turkish-speakers was their Orthodox religion.

Hardly less venerable than the Greeks, in terms of the antiquity of their presence, were the *Albanians*. Crowded into the mountains of the Western Balkans by the arrival of newcomers like the Slavs, the Albanians had spread outwards again following the Ottoman conquest, since the conversion of many Albanians to Islam gave them upward as well as lateral mobility. While a minority of Albanians remained Catholics, the Muslim majority became the general factotums of Ottoman rule, serving as soldiers, administrators and ministers, when they were not feuding among themselves or setting up as semi-independent warlords. From 1913 Albanians even had their own nation-state, although it would be an optimist who claimed to 'rule' the new Albania, and large numbers of Albanians continue as minorities in neighbouring states to this day.

Ancient, too, given their alleged descent from the Roman colonists of Dacia, were the *Romanians*, speakers of a Latin-based tongue heavily influenced by Slavic, Turkish and other languages. At the turn of the twentieth century Romanians were still divided between the newly united kingdom of Romania, the Hungarian half of the Habsburg Monarchy, the Bukovina, an Austrian province at the tail-end of the Carpathians, and the Russian province of Bessarabia. Independent Romania had a native landowning class, whereas the Romanians of Hungarian Transylvania, the Bukovina and Bessarabia were largely peasant.

On the other side of the Balkans, *Italians* were Eastern Europe's other Romance language speakers, concentrated in the coastal towns of Croatia, the Istrian Peninsula, and in large numbers in the port of Trieste and its hinterland, and in the South Tyrol, all still Habsburg provinces.

In the north, the two *Baltic* peoples, Latvians (or Letts) and Lithuanians, were also among the longest-established inhabitants of Eastern Europe, with a presence on the shores of the Baltic Sea dating back to 2000 BC, and speaking

---

[4]   Ther, P., 2013, 'Caught in Between: Border Regions in Modern Europe', in O. Bartov and E.D. Weitz (eds), *Shatterzone of Empires: Coexistence and Violence in the German, Habsburg, Russian and Ottoman Borderlands*, Bloomington, IN, 485–7.

Indo-European languages related to one another but distinct from any other language family. In the early twentieth century, both Latvians and Lithuanians were peasant peoples of the Russian Empire, only beginning to develop an educated class and, with it, a sense of national consciousness. Other Baltic peoples, like the pagan Prussians and Curonians, had suffered extinction during the northern crusades of the middle ages, but bequeathed their names to the territories they had inhabited, Prussia and Courland.

The *Finno-Ugrian* language family, distinctive in Europe in that it is not Indo-European, included two groups related, but separated by centuries of historical development as well as physical distance. On the shores of the eastern Baltic lived Finns and their close linguistic relatives, Estonians, both indigenous to the region since antiquity, both, like the Baltic peoples, long subsumed within the Russian Empire. Finland at least enjoyed a partial autonomy and a set of codified privileges under tsarism, whereas the Estonians, like the Latvians and Lithuanians, were still overwhelmingly peasant. Far to the south, the Magyars, or ethnic Hungarians, had arrived in Eastern Europe much later, settling in the Pannonian Plain in the ninth century; they remained the dominant element in the Kingdom of Hungary, itself a multinational unit within the Habsburg Monarchy.

The *Slavonic*-speaking peoples, who as migrants into the Roman Empire were relative latecomers to Eastern Europe, constitute by far the most numerous language group. The East Slavs are the Russians, the Belorussians or White Russians, and the Ukrainians. The West Slavs are the Poles, Czechs and Slovaks. The South Slavs are the present-day Bulgarians, Macedonians, Serbs, Montenegrins, Croats, Slovenes and Bosnian Muslims (today rather misleadingly called Bosniaks, and descended from converts to Islam after the Ottoman conquest). Linguistically, however, there are only three main South Slav languages: Bulgarian, Slovene and what used to be called 'Serbo-Croatian'. Macedonians or, to adopt a more precise terminology, Macedonian Slavs, speak a variant of Bulgarian, rather akin to the differences between Bavarian German and High German. Serbs, Montenegrins, Bosnian Muslims and Croats all speak dialectical variants of Serbo-Croatian, with the principal difference being that Croats and most Bosnian Muslims use a Latin alphabet, whereas Serbs, Montenegrins and a minority of Bosnian Muslims use a Cyrillic alphabet, as do Bulgarian-speakers. Since the break-up of the former Yugoslavia, however, it has become politically impossible to justify the existence of 'Serbo-Croatian', and its speakers now habitually refer to their variants as Croatian, Serbian and Bosnian.

Among the Slavonic-speaking peoples mention should also be made of much smaller groups which, by the early twentieth century, were already in danger of dying out. In East Prussia there was a minority of Kashubians, while in Silesia scattered pockets of Sorbs were still to be found.

Germans today are far less numerous in Eastern Europe than they have been historically, and at the start of the twentieth century they were scattered across the region, the result of migration back and forth since the middle ages. Predominant in the new German Empire and the Austrian crownlands of the Habsburg Monarchy, they were elsewhere a sizeable, often preponderant, element in many urban centres for most of the nineteenth century, and were also settled as agriculturalists in substantial pockets, such as the Saxons of Habsburg Transylvania. By 1900 the numbers of Germans in large cities like Prague and Budapest had shrunk in comparison, as the numbers of educated, urban Czech- and Hungarian-speakers increased; but across Eastern Europe ethnic Germans were still a strong presence. In the Baltic provinces of Russia, Germans were not only the majority of town dwellers, but they formed the local landowning aristocracy; the roll-call of imperial Russia's diplomatic corps in 1914 was full of Baltic German names. The presence of substantial German minorities in so many East European successor states, after the First World War, was a recipe for political instability and worse.

Ethnic *Turks* arrived in the Balkans from the fifteenth century onward as Ottoman conquerors, and settled as soldiers, administrators, landowners and merchants.[5] The emergence of the Balkan nation-states in the nineteenth century, however, and the protracted rolling-back of the Ottoman imperium, meant that Muslims of all ethnicities were no longer welcome, and their extermination or expulsion from Balkan Christian societies was the usual concomitant. At the outset of the twentieth century this process was far from complete, although the ferocious Balkan Wars of 1912–13, which virtually eliminated Ottoman rule in the Peninsula, advanced this 'ethnic cleansing' considerably. Of the 2.3 million Muslims living in the Ottoman Balkans in 1912, it is estimated that some 632,000 died during the wars; some 414,000 fled or were expelled to Ottoman territory.[6] Despite the persecution to which they were exposed, however, on the eve of the First World War some ethnic Turks remained in Montenegro, Serbia, Bulgaria and Greece.

One special group of Turkic ethnicity is formed by the Crimean Tatars. They were deported en masse to Siberia in the Stalinist period, but since the break-up of the Soviet Union some 250,000 of them are estimated to have returned to the Crimea, their status currently at risk in the ongoing dispute between Russia and the Ukraine.

Jews were a ubiquitous minority across Eastern Europe, although they were especially numerous in Russian Poland and the other parts of western Russia

---

[5] A distinction must be drawn here between 'ethnic Turk' and 'Ottoman', although the Ottomans were undoubtedly Turkish in origin. Because being Muslim was the key to upward mobility in the Ottoman Empire, the Ottoman elite over time was drawn from multiple ethnicities, and by the late Ottoman period 'Ottoman' could not be equated with 'Turkish'. See Armour, *A History of Eastern Europe*, 77.

[6] McCarthy, J., 2001, *The Ottoman Peoples and the End of Empire*, London and New York, 92.

designated as the 'Pale of Settlement', to which in theory Russian Jews were still confined; in Habsburg Galicia; in Moldavia in Romania; and in urban centres generally. Many Jews scraped a precarious living as tradesmen, artisans and moneylenders, and as a result their lot was little better than that of the Christian or Muslim societies which hosted them. In the nineteenth century, however, Jews had been accorded civil liberties, including freedom of movement, in many countries, and with this the numbers of urban, educated and even wealthy Jews expanded exponentially. By the turn of the century Jews were almost 9 per cent of the population of Vienna, and were a million strong in Budapest, which anti-Semites dubbed 'Judapest'. Jews were disproportionately represented in certain professions, especially medicine, journalism and the law; they played a leading role in the arts; and notoriously, they were unfairly identified with the evils of finance capital. Long discriminated against and in most societies only recently emancipated, Jews no matter how assimilated faced continuing prejudice; as the founder of psychoanalysis, Sigmund Freud, commented in 1908, 'if my name were Oberhuber, my innovations would have encountered far less resistance, despite everything.'[7] In tsarist Russia anti-Semitic prejudice took the form of periodic state-tolerated violence against Jews, or pogroms, a factor which encouraged successive waves of Jewish emigration to Western Europe, the Ottoman Middle East and the Americas. Even in Central Europe the rise of political anti-Semitism prompted the Hungarian German Jewish journalist, Theodor Herzl, to found a Zionist Organisation in 1897 to promote the foundation of a Jewish homeland in Palestine. For most East European Jews, however, emigration was not an option; assimilated or otherwise, they remained a part of the societies they lived in, despite their separate identity.

Finally, mention should be made of Eastern Europe's most downtrodden people, the *Roma* or Gypsies. Scattered across the region since the middle ages, with large numbers in Romania and Hungary in particular, Roma like the majority of Europeans were of Indo-European origin, but their frequently alien appearance, and the itinerant lifestyle forced on them by the hostility of the host societies, meant that they barely survived by peddling, tinkering, horse-trading, music-making and other lowly occupations. Roma in the first half of the twentieth century, an age of increasingly respectable racial nationalism, faced an uncertain future wherever they were; that future turned lethal during the Second World War, when Roma, like Jews, were targeted for extermination. In the post-war communist period, East European regimes officially dedicated to building social equality nevertheless continued to marginalise their Roma minorities. It is one of the more scandalous aspects of the present-day European Union, to which many East European countries now belong, that the prospects of the Roma are not much brighter in the twenty-first century.

---

[7] Quoted in Gay, P., 1978, *Freud, Jews and Other Germans: Masters and Victims in Modernist Culture*, Oxford, New York, Toronto and Melbourne, 76–7.

Socio-economic conditions

In socio-economic terms the salient fact about Eastern Europe even at the turn of the twentieth century, setting it apart from much of Western if not Southern Europe, was its largely agrarian nature. The majority of the population was made up of peasants, who still lived on and off the land. Land ownership, by contrast, in the Russian, German and Habsburg empires was largely confined to the nobility, although by the early twentieth century there was also a growing number of peasant proprietors or smallholders. In the independent Balkan states the peasant smallholder class was predominant, since these societies' noble landowners had for the most part been expropriated and driven out centuries before by the Ottoman conquest, and as the Ottoman imperium was rolled back in the nineteenth century land had been distributed among the Christian peasants. Only in Romania was there a native Christian landowning nobility; in Bosnia-Hercegovina, a province of the Habsburg Monarchy until 1918, there remained a sizeable number of Muslim landowners.

In this agrarian environment towns had historically remained small, and the number of urban middle-class people was correspondingly limited. On the other hand, industrialisation had started to transform the economic landscape in the nineteenth century. It was well under way in German Silesia before mid-century, struck roots in parts of the Habsburg Monarchy from the 1850s, and spread to the Russian Empire from about 1890, particularly in the Polish and Baltic provinces and the big urban centres of European Russia, as well as in the mineral-rich Donbass region of what is now the Ukraine. This growth of industry not only created a new class of industrial workers, who played a significant political role in Russia in 1905 and again in 1917, but also intensified urbanisation and with it an increase in the middle class. Economic modernisation, patchy though it was, had thus made East European societies more variegated, and more prone to political stress. The rising middle class were vocal supporters of constitutional government and further economic development; the old artisan class of handicraft workers were everywhere feeling the pinch as their livelihoods were undermined by the spread of industrial processes; and the new industrial proletariat showed a natural interest in socialism and even revolution as a remedy for poor living conditions. In the countryside peasant smallholders demonstrated an increasing political consciousness, while the huge mass of landless or insufficiently landed peasants remained a potentially explosive revolutionary force.

Population figures for the entire region are hard to come by, although we do know that numbers had been rising throughout the nineteenth century, further intensifying social tensions and the pressure on governments to modernise. The population of the Russian Empire west of the Ural Mountains, commonly known as European Russia, was 95.4 million as of the first state census in

1897; 51 per cent of these were ethnic Russians.[8] The Habsburg Monarchy, at the time of its last pre-war census in 1910, numbered 51.39 million, of which 28.5 million inhabited 'Austria', 20.8 million the Kingdom of Hungary, and 1.9 million the recently annexed province of Bosnia-Hercegovina.[9] It is hard to give clear figures for the German Empire's share of Eastern Europe, but suffice it to say that out of a total population in 1910 of 65 million one in ten subjects of the King of Prussia, or 2.4 million, were Poles.[10] Matters were most confusing in the Balkans, where borders were shifting right up to 1914, with attendant fluctuations in population and a residual problem, in the wake of the Balkan Wars of 1912–13, with simply counting the number of refugees. In so far as can be ascertained, the population of the Balkan states in the year given for each country was roughly as follows: Romania, 6.9 million (1910); Serbia, 2.9 (1910); Montenegro, 212,000 (1911); Bulgaria, 4.3 (1910); Greece, 4.8 (1913); Albania, 800,000 (1913).[11]

Of the social strata within Eastern Europe's population, *peasants* were by far the most numerous class. Even after the First World War, when firmer numbers become available, peasants of one sort or another still constituted 60.6 per cent of the population of Poland, 55.7 per cent of Hungary's, 78.9 per cent of the new Yugoslavia's, 78.9 per cent of Romania's, and so on.[12] Only interwar Czechoslovakia had more population in its towns than in the countryside. Emancipated everywhere, including Russia, by the mid-nineteenth century, the condition of country folk varied widely, but was more likely than not to be one of extreme poverty and immiseration. At the top of the scale were the smallholders, peasants who owned their own land, some of them in sufficient quantities to be considered affluent. Far more peasant proprietors, however, owned scarcely enough land to get by on; and as population increased the tendency of such peasant farmers was to subdivide their land among their offspring, thus making subsistence more difficult for more peasants. At the bottom of the heap were landless peasants, forced to hire their labour out to landowners, whether noble or smallholder, and condemned to a miserable, often peripatetic, existence, because they were dependent on trudging from estate to estate in search of work. For the vast majority of such unfortunates the only imaginable solution to their problems was to acquire more land; only a minority was able to take the more drastic option of emigrating, although

---

[8] Crampton, R. and Crampton, B., 1996, *Atlas of Eastern Europe in the Twentieth Century*, London and New York, 13.

[9] Crampton and Crampton, *Atlas of Eastern Europe*, 9.

[10] Porter, I. and Armour, I.D., 1991, *Imperial Germany 1890-1918*, London and New York, 21, 29.

[11] Crampton and Crampton, *Atlas of Eastern Europe*, 47; Jelavich, B., 1983, *History of the Balkans*, vol. 2: *The Twentieth Century*, Cambridge, 101; Clogg, R., 1992, *A Concise History of Greece*, Cambridge, 83; Palairet, M., 1997, *The Balkan Economies c. 1800-1914: Evolution without Development*, Cambridge, 20.

[12] Rothschild, J., 1974, *East Central Europe between the Two World Wars*, Seattle, WA, 39, 167, 270, 285.

millions did so in the decades after 1890. Interestingly, up to a third of emigrants returned, many if not all having made their fortune in the 'new world'. Here, in the 'land hunger' of millions of poor or landless peasants, was a fertile source of social and political unrest, whether in the form of inchoate uprisings like that in Romania in 1907, or more directed revolutionary violence, as in Russia's revolutions, both in 1905 and 1917.

The *noble landowning class*, across Eastern Europe, was also in trouble, if not to such an existential extent. Nobles divided into two sub-strata, the more numerous gentry and the titled aristocracy or magnates. Gentry status depended as much on possession of a patent of nobility as on actual land ownership; and indeed, in the course of the nineteenth century many nobles, in part because peasant emancipation had deprived them of free labour, were forced off their land entirely. Nobles in such a position were perforce town dwellers: they turned to the professions, or politics, or the arts for a livelihood. Landless nobles were especially numerous in Hungary, and the lands of the Polish partitions, but their numbers were rising in late imperial Russia as well, their predicament classically illustrated in Anton Chekhov's play *The Cherry Orchard* (1904).

At the very top, however, the magnate class of large landowners grew even wealthier in the nineteenth century, largely because of their ability to buy out the impoverished gentry who could not make ends meet. Despite the agricultural depression and accompanying fall in farm prices, which distinguished the last quarter of the century, therefore, the biggest noble landowners were cushioned against hard times, and in the Habsburg Monarchy and the German Empire they used their privileged political position to safeguard their incomes by maintaining high tariffs against foreign grain imports. As a result the very wealthiest led lives of seemingly limitless luxury. In the Kingdom of Hungary, in 1895, 0.2 per cent of landowners, fewer than 2,000 individuals, with estates of more than a thousand cadastral acres, owned 32.3 per cent of all land; 15.4 per cent of land was in the hands the 0.8 per cent who owned estates of between a hundred and one thousand acres. Nearly 50 per cent of Hungarian land was owned by a mere 1 per cent of landowners. In Prussia, in 1912, Count Guido Henckel von Donnersmarck, owner of estates in Russia and Austria-Hungary as well as Prussia, counted as the second wealthiest man in the kingdom, with a worth of fifteen million marks. The economic and political influence of such 'bread lords' was still considerable on the eve of the First World War; and while in Russia the Bolshevik Revolution of 1917 led to the expropriation of the entire landowning class, in Eastern and Central Europe the economic, if not political, power of this class survived into the interwar period.

As mentioned, the spread of industrialisation and the increase in the size of towns carried with it a rise in the numbers of the urban middle class. It was the broad middle class which provided the most articulate and determined advocates of modernisation, both economic and political. Yet the term 'middle class' itself requires qualification; it would be more accurate to speak of 'middle classes'. At the top in terms of income and, potentially, political influence stood the upper middle class. This included industrialists, merchants, bankers and anyone else whose income put them on a par financially, if not socially, with the landed gentry and aristocracy. The number of such plutocrats was necessarily fewer in East European societies than in the more industrialised West; but by the turn of the century even Russia had its share of native millionaires.

Next in rank came the middle middle class, sometimes referred to as the professional middle class or, in German, the *Bildungsbürgertum*: lawyers, academics, bureaucrats and other officials, businessmen and merchants who, by virtue of their education and material attainments, enjoyed a comfortable existence without being fabulously wealthy. At the bottom of the scale came the lower middle class, also known as the petty bourgeoisie or, again in German but more confusingly, the *Mittelstand* (literally the middle class). Lower middle class East Europeans, as elsewhere, led a rather more precarious existence, deriving their livelihood from running small shops and businesses, petty officialdom, and a variety of craft skills which put them, in good times, materially above the factory working class but, in bad times, potentially below them.

These differentiations in the composition of the middle class had political consequences. The upper middle class – where it existed; in the peasant societies of the Balkans there were even fewer of this class than elsewhere in the region – tended to be conservative and to identify with the interests of the state. The middle middle class hosted a wider variety of political tendencies. This was the class which, throughout the nineteenth century, had been the standard-bearers of liberalism; but the broad middle class was also the classic carrier of nationalism, and by the twentieth century it was abundantly clear that for many East Europeans nationalist values trumped liberal ones. The Hungarian Liberal Party of István Tisza, which held power until 1905, before returning to office in 1910 as the Party of Work, was an example of this, even if the fact that much of its leadership, like Tisza, was gentry, illustrated another aspect of the middle class, at least in Hungary and the Polish lands, namely its tendency to ape gentry values. In other respects, however, middle-class intellectuals could be politically radical. Their education as well as their privileged position made some individuals more alive to the misery of the masses, whether in countryside or town, and thus more likely to gravitate towards socialism, whether social democratic or revolutionary. Nationalism caused other middle-class individuals to veer rightwards, even to espouse so-called scientific racism; the leader of the National Democrats in tsarist Russia, Roman Dmowski, was a good example of this unpleasant tendency.

This capacity for radicalisation to either left or right was if anything even more pronounced in the lower middle class. Precisely because of its more marginal economic position, this class was historically more likely to embrace extreme political solutions: republicanism, socialism, even anarchism on the left; ultra-nationalism, racism and anti-Semitism on the right. The Christian Social movement in *fin-de-siècle* Austria, led by the charismatic mayor of Vienna, Karl Lueger, was an early expression of this demagogic populism of the right, appealing to the anxieties of the 'little man' with a shrewd mix of welfarism, hostility to the capitalist elite, and selective anti-Semitism. The fascist movements of the interwar period owed much of their early support to just such aggrieved members of the petty bourgeoisie.

The emerging industrial working class of Eastern Europe was, as elsewhere, the ideal matrix for revolutionary socialism. As the events of 1917 in Russia demonstrated, the factory proletariat not only had real grievances about the conditions in which it worked and lived, but was ideologically motivated as well. It was significant that, as in 1905, the impetus to revolution in 1917 found plenty of support in Russia's western provinces where industrialisation had sunk deepest roots, among the new factory workers of the Baltic provinces, Russian Poland and the Ukraine. Felix Dzerzhinsky, first leader of the *Cheka*, the Bolshevik dictatorship's dreaded revolutionary police force, was a Russian Pole. Yet we should beware of labelling an entire class as politically uniform. To begin with, and depending which state they lived in, the industrial working class inclined just as much, if not more, towards social democracy than violent revolutionary socialism. It was not until the First World War, for instance, that the Social Democratic Party of Germany, the SPD, split into moderate and radical factions, out of which, in 1918, emerged the German Communist Party. When the Russian Social Democratic Workers' Party split into two factions in 1903, it was the more moderate faction, the Mensheviks, which was the larger; Vladimir Lenin's Bolsheviks, despite their name, were decidedly outnumbered. And beyond this it is worth remembering that, at any given point, such socialist movements hardly spoke for all members of the industrial working class, most of whom did not belong to any political party at all.

One other phenomenon peculiarly strong in Eastern Europe was peasantism, often called populism. Peasant-based parties sprang up in these overwhelmingly agrarian societies in the late nineteenth century, and expressed the radicalism of the rural masses in an age when no other political movement, whether gentry-based or middle class or urban Marxist socialist, convincingly represented peasant interests. The politics of many peasantist movements seemed initially socialist, in that they favoured cooperative self-help organisations like credit associations and land banks; and the destitution of millions of landless agricultural labourers, whose numbers persisted into the twentieth century, made this class in particular a potentially revolutionary force. The peasant smallholder's desire to farm his own land, however, and if possible to increase his holding, made him an unlikely convert to Marxism. Peasants, too, were more likely to be intensely religious, to have socially conservative values, to be hostile to urban dwellers generally, and to see themselves by contrast as the true nation. By the turn of the twentieth century, and despite the limitations of restrictive political systems, a number of peasantist parties had appeared: the Radical Party in Serbia, the Croatian Peasant Party, the Bulgarian Agrarian National Union, and – the largest of them all – the Socialist Revolutionary Party in Russia. The democratic franchises adopted across the region at the end of the First World War meant that peasantism was destined to play a much larger role in the interwar period.

A final aspect of Eastern Europe's social character worth stressing, and which continues to be relevant to this day, is religion. Historically Eastern Europe has been split between Roman Catholicism and Orthodoxy since the region's inhabitants were first converted to Christianity, since some peoples were proselytised from Rome and others from Greek Orthodox Constantinople. A religious and cultural fault-line thus runs through the region from the Adriatic to the Russo-Finnish border. Croats, some Albanians, Hungarians, Czechs, Slovaks, Poles and the Baltic peoples all belonged, initially, to the Roman Catholic world, and employ to this day a Latin-based alphabet. Greeks, Serbs and Montenegrins, Bulgarians, Romanians, Ukrainians, Belorussians and Russians all followed the Orthodox rite and used Greek-based or Cyrillic alphabets; only the Romanians later, in the nineteenth century, switched to a Latin-based alphabet. A final wrinkle in Catholic-Orthodox relations was introduced in the sixteenth century by the emergence of the Uniate or Greek Catholic Church: Orthodox communities, among western Ukrainians and the Romanian population of the Habsburg Monarchy, who followed the Orthodox rite while acknowledging the spiritual leadership of the Pope in Rome. In the middle ages, the conquest of the Balkans by the Ottoman Turks injected Islam into the confessional mix. Numbers of ethnic Turks settled in south-eastern Europe, and while many of these had been forced out of the newly independent Balkan states by the end of the nineteenth century, there also remained sizeable minorities of Slavs, in Bosnia and Bulgaria, who were descended from converts to Islam, as well as the majority of Albanians. Jewish immigration into Eastern Europe dates back at least to the middle ages, when some Christian rulers invited in Jews fleeing persecution in Western Europe. By the start of the twentieth century the Jewish population of tsarist Russia was, at over five million, one of the largest in Europe, with the majority still legally confined to the Pale of Settlement, comprising Russian Poland, Belarus, the Ukraine and Bessarabia. In the Balkans another legacy of Ottoman rule, with its even-handed treatment of monotheistic religions, was the arrival from the late middle ages of substantial numbers of Jews, again fleeing persecution in the West. The Protestant Reformation of the sixteenth century also left its mark on Eastern Europe. Lutheranism, apart from being the majority religion of Prussian Germans, was well-represented among the Baltic peoples, Estonians and Finns. Calvinism, originally successful among the Poles and Hungarians but rolled back long ago by Catholic counter-offensives, retained a bastion of followers in eastern Hungary.

The secular mind-set that many in the twenty-first century take for granted, despite abundant evidence that religious values can still be a powerful motivator, should not blind us to the importance of religion in Eastern Europe throughout the twentieth century. The cultural chasm between Catholic and Orthodox, Lutheran and Catholic, Christian and Muslim, Christian and Jew remained profound and, for most East Europeans, unbridgeable. This made the presence of religious minorities a constant irritant to governments: the Prussian government regarded its Catholic Polish population as inherently disloyal, as did tsarist Russia, whose mistreatment of its Jewish population was even harsher. Most Serbs, Croats and Bosnian Muslims, divided by religion, were never able to sink their differences in a common, Yugoslav identity; during the Second World War this antagonism tipped over into genocide, and even in the 1990s Yugoslavs of no particular religious belief nevertheless fell back on national allegiances in part defined by religious history, in the name of which war was waged, atrocities committed, and the Yugoslav state torn asunder. In the case of Eastern Europe's Jews, the addition of racial nationalism made age-old religious prejudice all the deadlier, and during the Nazi imperium of the Second World War many East Europeans proved all too enthusiastic assistants in the murder of the Jewish population. Nor did the imposition on East European societies of communism, an avowedly atheist political ideology, do much to eradicate religion. On the contrary, the communist period demonstrates the futility of assailing people's most deeply rooted beliefs. In many societies the church, or simply the private religious principles of individuals, proved immune to the regimes' anti-religious message, and in the late communist period it was in many cases religious communities which provided the inspiration for dissidence if not outright resistance.

The international landscape

In terms of political geography Eastern Europe until 1912 was still divided into only nine sovereign states; Italy acquired the Dodecanese Islands in 1912 and an eleventh, Albania, was created in 1913. All these states were constitutional monarchies by 1908, the year in which the Ottoman Sultan Abdul Hamid II was forced to accept representative institutions by the Young Turk Revolution. Even Tsar Nicholas II of Russia, by the October Manifesto of 1905, legalised political parties and their representation by election to a state Duma or parliament, although Russia remained a constitutional halfway house down to 1917, with the Tsar determined to ignore the Duma as far as possible. The emperors William II of Germany and Francis Joseph of Austria-

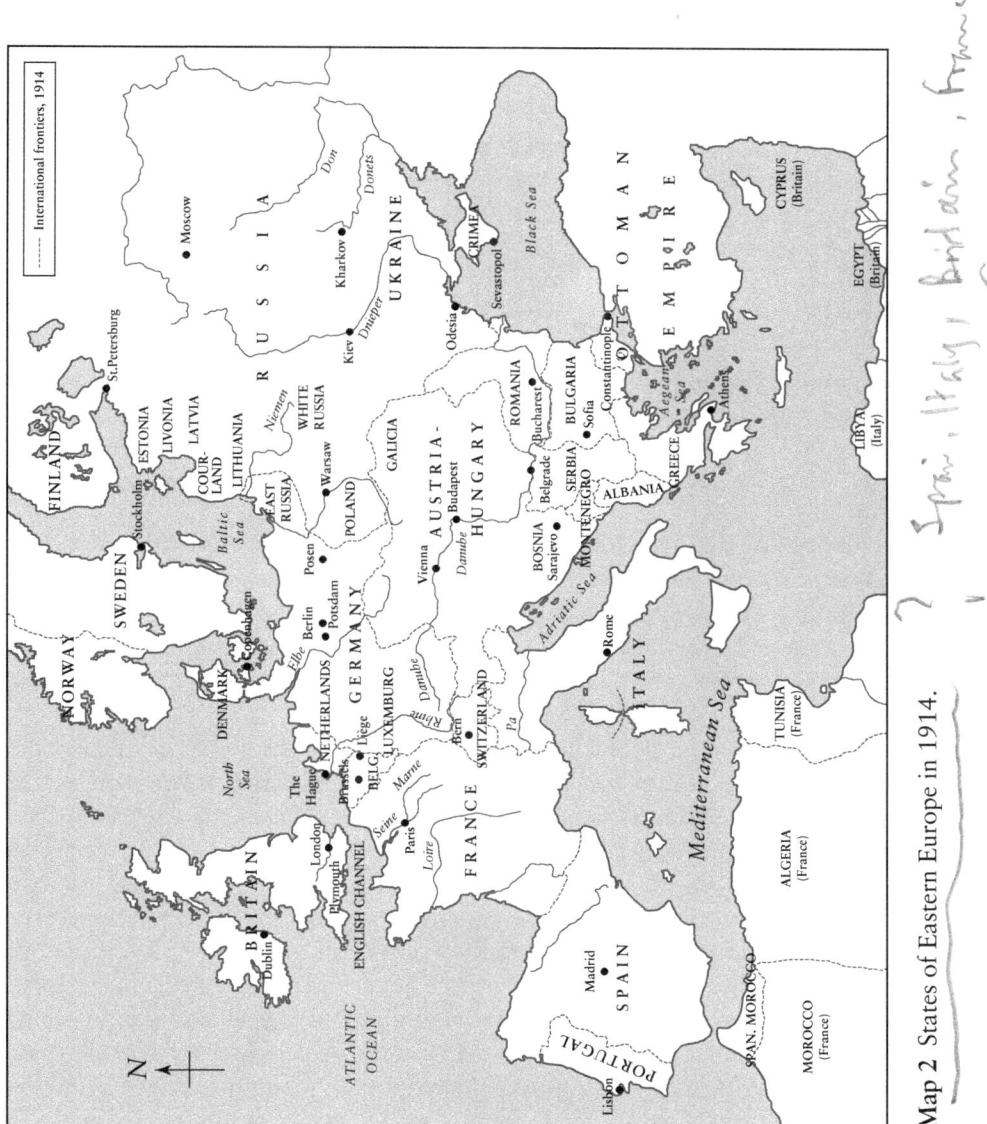

Map 2 States of Eastern Europe in 1914.

Hungary, by contrast, abided by much more solidly entrenched constitutional restraints, even if in foreign policy they, or to be more exact their chosen ministers, enjoyed much greater freedom of movement. Constitutionally the Habsburg Monarchy was unique: Francis Joseph after 1867 ruled over what was called the Dual Monarchy of Austria-Hungary, two separate states, each with its own government and parliament, conjoined at the top by the monarch and a trio of 'joint' ministers responsible for external relations. After 1878 the monarchy also administered Bosnia-Hercegovina, an Ottoman province which was not formally annexed until 1908. The Balkan states were also constitutional monarchies, with party systems, representative assemblies and cabinet government, although it is fair to say that some countries were more constitutional than others. Serbia had only returned to genuine constitutional rule following a bloody revolution in 1903, which saw the extermination of the Obrenović dynasty and a return to competitive party politics. Tiny Montenegro, with a population of less than 200,000, was granted a constitution in 1905, but Prince Nikola, who proclaimed himself king in 1910, ruled more by fiat and force of personality than by consent. Prince William of Wied, nominated Prince of Albania by the great powers, spent six months trying to gain control of his fractious and tribally riven new country before giving up in despair in September 1914.

The creation of Albania, virtually at the behest of the great powers, was characteristic of international relations in Eastern Europe before the First World War. At the outset of the nineteenth century the region had been divided between four huge multinational states, and although the decline of Ottoman rule in the Balkans saw the emergence of new states there, as of 1914 it was still the great powers who called the shots, or tried to.

What changed in the intervening century was the nature of the relationship between states, great or small. Put simply, industrialisation became the key to state power. A relatively small but industrialised Prussia, by the 1860s, had defeated the much bigger but less advanced Habsburg Monarchy and muscled it out of German affairs to create the German Empire. This new, 'united' Germany, an even greater industrial and hence military power, in turn presented a potential threat to Russia, and indeed every other great power in Europe. To put it another way, the pressure on governments and ruling elites to modernise, in order to remain competitive or simply to survive as states, intensified throughout the century. Reeling from military defeats and territorial losses, the Habsburg Monarchy strove to modernise its economy, promoted industrial development and finally accepted the need for constitutional government in the 1860s. By the late 1880s Tsar Alexander III, not the brightest of autocrats, appreciated that, without kick-starting Russia's industrialisation, his huge empire could not hope to engage in war with Germany without risking defeat and possibly even partition. Even the Ottoman Sultans, or to be more precise their ablest advisers, were conscious of the need to reform administrative structures and tax collection, improve infrastructure and make some appeal, however confused, to the residual loyalty of their multitudinous subjects, otherwise their realms threatened to melt away beneath them.

Modernisation, as suggested in the Introduction, can be understood in two ways, economic and political. Under economic comes the spread of industrial modes of production, the creation of efficient infrastructure and communications, and the emergence of large-scale capital formation in the shape of banks and reliable media of exchange. A sub-aspect of economic modernisation, appreciated by most East European rulers since the eighteenth century, was the expansion of education, since modernisation depended on a trained bureaucracy and an educated workforce. Under political modernisation comes the establishment of constitutional government, implying at least some restraint on monarchical power, the rule of law, some form of representative institutions, if not full democracy, and a competitive party system.

By these indices the German Empire was by far the most modern as well as the most powerful state in the region, whose industrial production by the turn of the century was beginning to outstrip that of Great Britain. Germany's East Prussian provinces, with the exception of Silesia, were still largely agrarian, but its economy as a whole, as well as its total population of 65 million in 1910, made it a natural regional hegemon. With an army whose peacetime strength by 1913 stood at 782,000 men, but which fully mobilised would number 2,398,000, Germany was feared by its potential rivals, Russia, France and Britain, and seen as an essential prop by its ally since 1879, Austria-Hungary.

The Habsburg Monarchy, for all its persistent weaknesses, was undoubtedly the next most modern economy, in that industrialisation had taken firm root in both halves of the empire, even if parts of each remained profoundly agrarian. Much of the industry revolved around the processing of agricultural produce, but the Monarchy nevertheless exported industrial manufactures, mainly to the Balkans. The weaknesses, however, were undeniable. Militarily the Monarchy was the second weakest of the great powers, with a peacetime army in 1912 of 391,000. More seriously the very multinational composition of Austria-Hungary meant that its foreign policy was inevitably dictated by the ethnicity shared between some of its peoples and the neighbouring states of Italy, Serbia and Romania. In the Balkans the Monarchy feared the growth of Russian influence, and as a result it was fatally reliant on Germany for support; and by the occupation and later annexation of Bosnia, Austria-Hungary ensured itself the lasting enmity of Serb nationalists on both sides of its borders.

The Russian Empire, though embarked on a government-led industrialisation programme since about 1890, was, if not yet modern, formidable by virtue of its size, population and industrial potential. Humiliatingly defeated in 1904–5 by the smaller but more industrialised Japan, and as a consequence tipped into a year of revolutionary chaos, the tsarist autocracy grudgingly conceded a measure of political modernisation; but its focus remained on regaining lost prestige as a great power. Subvented by the loans of its ally France, Russia by 1914 was making great strides in the improvement of its military capacity, especially its European railway network. It was this aspect of Russia's modernisation which, by the spring of 1914, increasingly preoccupied the imperial German government; in this sense the war which broke out in the summer can be seen as essentially a clash of Eastern Europe's two rival hegemons.

The Ottoman Empire never really caught up in the modernisation stakes, although the extent to which the regime of Abdul Hamid II (1876–1909) improved the empire's infrastructure should not be overlooked. But it was a case of too little, too late. Frustrated by the slow pace of change, as well as the loss of two provinces in 1908, when Bosnia was annexed by Austria-Hungary and the already autonomous Bulgaria proclaimed full independence, modernisers in the Ottoman bureaucracy and army led the so-called Young Turk Revolution. This forced Abdul Hamid to restore the mothballed constitution of 1876, and the government that subsequently assumed power set about implementing wide-ranging reforms. Ironically, this movement to forestall the Ottoman Empire's decline only hastened its further partition. Italy, encouraged by the Empire's evident weakness, launched a successful war of aggression in 1911–12 for Tripolitania and the Dodecanese Islands. In 1912 a newly formed Balkan League of Serbia, Montenegro, Greece and Bulgaria took advantage of the Italian war to stage its own attack. The rollback of the Ottoman imperium in the Balkans in 1912–13 set the scene for the outbreak of the First World War, in that it left the Habsburg Monarchy, as most of its policy-makers perceived the situation, confronting an enlarged and potentially dangerous Serbia.

This culmination of generations of Austro-Serbian antagonism is a fitting point at which to stress the importance of nationalism, and nationality issues, in complicating the international scene, as well as the internal politics of individual states.

Nationalism in the course of the nineteenth century had proved to be one of the great solvents and disruptors of stable government in Eastern Europe. The preoccupation of a minority in all societies early in the century, with the spread of literacy the number of nationalists had undoubtedly risen across the region by the turn of the twentieth century. While it is equally plain, as recent research has reminded us, that rival allegiances like dynastic loyalty or religion continued to sway millions of East Europeans, and that we must not underestimate the persistence of what has been called 'national indifference', the reluctance of many to be pigeonholed as belonging to a particular nationality, there still can be no denying the prominence of nationalism as a widespread, mass phenomenon by 1914. Even Russians were becoming nationalist in increasing numbers by this point.

What was, and is, nationalism? Most historians would accept that, historically, the ideology or political concept of nationalism is a product of relatively recent times, being first coherently conceptualised and articulated in Europe in the late-eighteenth century. It is equally accepted that the roots of this sense of national identity go back much further, in some cases to at least the middle ages, but that it is only in the period leading up to the French Revolution of 1789 that we find significant numbers of Europeans proclaiming their commitment to it. However we date its origins, nationalism can best be defined as a belief that one's nation is the most important thing in the universe, and that loyalty to this collective identity called the nation is the ultimate, transcendental value. What constitutes a nation is still a matter for debate, but the commonly accepted consensus for some time now is that the concept can be understood in two principal ways, politically and culturally, even if neither of these concepts is exclusive of the other. A political, or civic, nation is that which is equated with a state or other political unit; in other words all inhabitants of a given state, say France, constitute the nation. A cultural, or ethnic, nation, by contrast, can most easily be understood as all those who share certain cultural attributes, such as language, ethnicity, history, religion and so on; hence, all those who speak German can be considered as the German nation. These two concepts, as said, were never mutually exclusive, and in fact converged in the course of the nineteenth century. Adherents of the political nationalism associated with revolutionary France in the 1790s, for instance, quite quickly showed a concern that members of the French nation ought also to be able to speak French, and to share other cultural traits. Most explosively, those who thought of their nation initially in purely cultural terms soon started to articulate the belief that their nation should also have its own political home, in short, an independent, sovereign state. The 'unification' stories of nineteenth-century Italians and Germans provide the classic examples of this aspiration, even if much of the practical work towards a united Italy and Germany was done by traditional state action rather than by nationalists. The example, however, was catching, and in Eastern Europe in particular one nation after another 'awakened', and some at least of its partisans started clamouring for a state of their own.

The break-up of Eastern Europe's multinational empires at the end of the First World War cannot be understood without appreciating the subversive and in the end explosive contribution made by nationalism. One of these empires, the Ottoman, lost territory in the Balkans repeatedly to emerging 'nation-states': Greece, Romania, Serbia, Montenegro, Bulgaria and Albania all were formed from the wreckage. The penultimate stage in this dismemberment was the Balkan Wars of 1912–13, when an alliance of Greece, Serbia, Montenegro and Bulgaria mopped up most of the remaining Ottoman territory in south-eastern Europe inhabited by their fellow nationals. Bulgaria, dissatisfied with its share of Macedonia, then waged war against its former allies and lost, ceding territory to Romania and the Ottomans as well as Greece and Serbia. In all these conflicts the justification of the aggressors was that they were liberating fellow nationals and 'nation-building'. The reality, as ever, was that these unifications were achieved through diplomacy, war and the actions of states, and that territorial aggrandisement was as much a motive as nationalism; only thus can we explain the fact that Serbia, for instance, in 1913 took over territory inhabited by Albanians, Macedonian Slavs and other non-Serbs. But the official line was that this was the triumph of nationalism.

The threat nationalism posed the Habsburg, Romanov and Hohenzollern empires was just as latent. The newly unified Germany was, in the eyes of German nationalists, a 'nation-state', even if it never included all German speakers; yet Germany was also home to a substantial Polish minority, in addition to Frenchmen, Alsatians and Danes, and by 1914 Prussian Poles had experienced generations of discrimination in cultural matters, as well as attempts to expropriate Polish-owned estates.

The Russian Empire was every bit as multinational as the Habsburg or Ottoman realms, and it was obvious long before the start of the century that Poles in particular were unwilling and disaffected subjects, even if no longer willing to revolt against Russian rule; that the rise of national consciousness among Ukrainians, Balts, Estonians and even Belorussians was producing friction; and that even historically privileged minorities like the Finns and the Baltic Germans were aggrieved over their treatment by the Russian state, not least because tsarist governments by the early twentieth century reflected an increasing ethnic Russian nationalism, typified by the minorities policy of Piotr Stolypin, prime minister from 1906 to 1911.

As for the Habsburg Monarchy, its reputation by the turn of the century for chronic, bitter nationality disputes, in both its constituent 'halves', was such that observers, anticipating its break-up, spoke of a 'Monarchy on short notice'.[13] In the Austrian half, Czechs squabbled with Germans, Slovenes with Germans and Italians, and Poles with Ruthenes (the Ukrainian speakers of Habsburg Galicia). In 1914, when the Monarchy took the momentous decision to go to war, the Austrian Reichsrat was not even in session, having been prorogued earlier in the year due to intractable nationality disputes. In the Kingdom of Hungary the Magyar ruling elite's stranglehold on the machinery of state meant that, with the exception of the Croats, who had a certain constitutional identity within the country, minorities were almost unrepresented in parliament, and a decades-long policy of Magyarisation only served further to alienate all the non-Magyar peoples. The Magyars' own nationalism frequently exacerbated

---

[13] Bridge, F.R., 1972, *From Sadowa to Sarajevo: The Foreign Policy of Austria-Hungary 1866-1914*, London, 252–3.

Hungary's relationship with Austria and even with the monarch himself, and in 1905–6 there was an almighty constitutional crisis over the question of a more distinct Hungarian army, which Francis Joseph flatly refused to countenance. The result was a short-lived coalition government in Hungary (1906–11), led by the Independence Party and notionally committed to secession.

Finally, nationalism affected international relations both generally and in terms of specific potential flashpoints. Across Europe the sense that nations, or 'races', had certain fundamentally opposed interests was becoming commonplace, and Eastern Europe was no exception. The nationalism driving the expansionism of the Balkan states has already been mentioned, and the Balkan Wars had already contributed to a serious heightening of tensions and instability by 1914. Politicians and generals and rulers, like William II of Germany among others, spoke casually about the coming conflicts between 'Teuton and Slav'. Even the least accountable of governments, that of imperial Russia, felt increasingly obliged to take account of public opinion in conducting foreign policy, and feared being seen as weak. Most obviously, nationalism was what impelled the nineteen-year-old Bosnian Serb, Gavrilo Princip, and his fellow conspirators to assassinate the Archduke Francis Ferdinand at Sarajevo on 28 June 1914, since in a nationalist's eye Austria-Hungary's continued possession of Bosnia was an affront to Serb national feeling. Nationalism also motivated the Black Hand, the Belgrade-based secret society which supported the conspirators with weapons, training and safe-conduct back into Bosnia, regardless of the effect this was likely to have on relations with the Habsburg Monarchy. Nationalism stiffened the resolve of the Serbian government not to accept the terms of the Austro-Hungarian ultimatum of 23 July, demanding the involvement of Habsburg officials in a criminal investigation to be conducted on Serbian soil, and despite the fact that official Serbia was not behind the assassination. Finally, the Monarchy's own reaction to Sarajevo was driven by what might be called 'anti-nationalism': in response to what they took to be the existential threat posed by Serb nationalism, the Monarchy's leaders resolved to take some form of military action against Serbia. In doing so, they helped unleash a general European war, and brought the whole house of cards down on themselves.

This is not the place for a general discussion of the origins of the First World War. Suffice it to say that the immediate locus of the conflict, the Sarajevo assassination, was an East European one. The Austro-Serbian antagonism was seemingly irreducible, and the Balkan Wars exacerbated the relationship, in that the Monarchy's leaders concluded that, after the Ottoman Empire, Austria-Hungary was next in line to be attacked. Yet Vienna's desire to 'eliminate Serbia as a political power factor in the Balkans', to quote Francis Joseph's letter to the Kaiser on 2 July, need not necessarily have produced a general war, had not the German government, for reasons of its own, shown the Monarchy a green light.[14] Sarajevo, for Germany no less than for Austria-Hungary, was a pretext for war, not its cause. The real origins of the war lie beyond the long-standing Austro-Russian rivalry in the Balkans. They lie in the fact of a powerful Germany, increasingly seeking a greater role in the Near and Middle East, and a rapidly industrialising Russia, which by 1914 was within sight of becoming the superpower its size and economic potential promised. The German government brooded on Russian growth, and decided to act before it was too late to act at all. The Russian government feared its vulnerability to Germany's more industrialised might, and the apparent possibility of German domination of the Straits, Russia's economic windpipe to the West. This clash of regional hegemons was at the root of the war's origins, and their conflict was to become the defining logic of Eastern Europe's tragedy in the twentieth century.

---

[14] Quoted in Bridge, *From Sadowa to Sarajevo*, 369.

2

Melting-pot

Eastern Europe in the First World War

If war is, as R.J. Crampton puts it, 'the midwife of all modern epochs', then the First World War delivered the most monstrous and painful birth of the twentieth century.[1] In terms of state boundaries the end of the war saw the literal making of Eastern Europe, when the multinational empires all disappeared and were replaced by the 'successor states'. This geopolitical cataclysm was preceded by four years of unprecedented bloodshed and loss of life, widespread physical destruction across the region, food shortages and economic dislocation, resulting in social and political unrest, and ultimately revolution and territorial break-up. Even after the formal end of hostilities between the main combatants in November 1918, political turmoil and physical conflict continued in Eastern Europe for some time to come.

There was nothing inevitable about these outcomes, but the fact of war undoubtedly made them more likely. Initially the peoples of the multinational empires responded loyally to the conflict, and hundreds of thousands died in battle, or endured hardship on the 'home front', simply because to defy the authority of the state was unthinkable. The fact that it took nearly three years of war for the Russian Empire to crumble, or that the multiple peoples of the Habsburg Monarchy put up with more than four years of suffering, is a reminder of the residual power of custom and the limitations of nationalism. Nevertheless, as the cost of the fighting mounted, in both human and economic terms, ties of dynastic loyalty and fears of adverse consequences for disobedience weakened, until people proved capable of imagining the hitherto unimaginable, and pre-war aspirations for mere autonomy metamorphosed into demands for outright independence. Of equal if not greater importance, however, was sheer war-weariness: the majority of East Europeans, long before 1918, were probably sick of loss and privation, and yearned only for peace and the cessation of want.

The war was thus the culminating stimulus to European nationalisms generally, and Eastern Europe was no different in this regard. Germans and Magyars on one side, Russians and Serbs on the other, saw the conflict as one of national defence and survival. The governments of those states with

---

[1] Crampton, R.J., 1997, *Eastern Europe in the Twentieth Century – And After*, 2nd edn, London, 6.

fellow nationals in the Habsburg Monarchy – Italy, Serbia and Romania – certainly hoped to expand at their enemy's expense. Among the subject nationalities of multinational states the picture is more complex. Some nationalists right from the start saw the war as an opportunity to fight for independence; but for most of their co-nationals this was hardly imaginable. In any case until a very late stage in the war it was not the policy of the Allied powers to dismember the multinationals, not least because Russia was on the Allied side until November 1917. It was not until the entry of the United States into the war on the Allied side, and President Woodrow Wilson's proclamation of 'national self-determination' as one of the causes the Allies should be fighting for, that a time bomb was laid under Eastern Europe's multinational states. The leaders of nationalities across the region were thereby encouraged to think that national liberation and statehood were practical possibilities.

In addition to the activation of nationalism as a force for dissolution and state-building, however, the war produced yet another profound complication with the second, Bolshevik revolution in Russia in November 1917, and the emergence of the world's first communist state. This bizarre development, inconceivable without Russia's catastrophic involvement in the war in the first place, not only took Russia out of the conflict, but accelerated the former Empire's disintegration, as nationalist revolutions among non-Russian peoples sought to escape Russian rule, and communist dictatorship, while they still could. But the survival of Communist Russia, formally renamed the Union of Soviet Socialist Republics (USSR) in 1922, meant that the hearth of the world Communist movement was next door to interwar Eastern Europe. This had ominous implications for the future.

The course of the war

The events of the First World War in Eastern Europe are so complex that it helps to see the conflict chronologically, in four main stages. A preliminary stage, already discussed, preceded the war itself, when in 1912–13 the rolling back of the Ottoman Empire in the Balkans contributed to the destabilisation of relations between the great powers. As a result of the Balkan wars, all the Balkan nation-states, with the exception of the new Albania, took over new national minorities, a fact which played its role after 1914. Crucially, the government of the Habsburg Monarchy saw the enlarged Serbia as an imminent threat, and it was Vienna's reaction to this perceived menace, after the Sarajevo assassination, which triggered the crisis leading to general war in August 1914.

1. Expansion and intensification 1914–17

The first phase can be seen as one in which the war expanded and intensified, until the whole region was involved. The Austro-Serbian conflict, though the ostensible occasion for the war, was almost immediately overshadowed by the clash of the great powers. While the main thrust of Germany's initial offensive was against France, in the east German strategy counted on holding Russia at bay. This strategy reckoned without Austria-Hungary's vainglorious chief of the general staff, General Franz Conrad von Hötzendorf, who was obsessed with attacking Serbia first, regardless of the obviously greater threat from Russia. Due to the astonishing lack of Austro-German coordination in pre-war planning, each of these allies assumed the other would launch his main offensive against Russia. The result was near disaster: Russian forces, mobilising far faster than anticipated, rolled into both East Prussia and Galicia, catching the Central Powers unawares. But whereas the Germans successfully contained the Russians' advance and inflicted a stinging defeat on them at Tannenberg, the Habsburg Monarchy's forces were fatally divided between a Serbian and a Galician front. In the south, invading Austro-Hungarian forces were humiliatingly expelled from Serbia within two weeks before the end of August, with a loss of 28,000 men; a second invasion attempt, in November, failed just as ignominiously. In the north, most of Galicia was overrun by the Russians, with Lemberg falling on 2 September, the strategic fortress of Przemyśl invested and 100,000 dead, 220,000 wounded and 100,000 taken prisoner. It was only the Russians' even greater defeat in East Prussia, at the hands of Germany, which saved the Monarchy from a full-scale invasion of central Hungary. By the end of 1914 Austria-Hungary's army had lost nearly a million men, and was 'nearly eliminated as a fighting force'.[2]

Although both sides had fought one another to a standstill by the end of the year and, as on the Western Front, a period of stalemate and trench warfare ensued, the war in Eastern Europe was more fluid, with greater fluctuations in the front line. In May 1915 a new German offensive around Gorlice, designed largely to take the pressure off the Habsburg Monarchy, drove Russia's forces hundreds of miles eastward, with the result that the whole of Russian Poland, together with much of Belorussia and the Baltic provinces, was German-occupied by September. In the summer of 1916, however, Russia's general A.A. Brusilov mounted a final offensive, which pushed the Central Powers westward again by some fifty miles before coming to an exhausted halt. The total territory fought over, as well as the amount of physical destruction and dislocation of population, was thus far greater in Eastern Europe than in the west.

---

[2] Herwig, H.H., 1997, *The First World War: Germany and Austria-Hungary 1914-1918*, London, 119.

The entry of the Ottoman Empire into the war on the Austro-German side, in October 1914, had fateful consequences for Serbia and Russia especially, even if it seemed at first a liability for the Central Powers. The Young Turk regime hoped to reverse the territorial losses of the Balkan Wars, and its very participation in the conflict necessarily diverted Allied resources, in particular British and Russian ones, to the Middle East and the Caucasus, as well as prompting the abortive Gallipoli campaign to gain control of the Straits. The Allies' failure to force the Straits and knock the Ottomans out of the war meant that landlocked Serbia was even more cut off from potential assistance, and in late 1915 a joint offensive by the Central Powers, joined by Bulgaria, finally conquered and partitioned Serbia, whose government and army survived a nightmare retreat through the mountains of Albania before finding refuge on the Allied-held island of Corfù. Outlying parts of Serbia were handed over to Bulgaria and, notionally, Albania, while the core of the country was subjected to military occupation by Austria-Hungary. Tiny Montenegro, which had joined the war on Serbia's side in August 1914, and whose small army was subordinated to Serbian command from then on, shared a similar fate: King Nikola and most of his government fled in December 1915, and the forces remaining in Montenegro capitulated to Austria-Hungary in January 1916.

An additional effect of the Gallipoli campaign was to throw the internal politics of Greece into turmoil, since it set the pro-German King, Constantine I, at loggerheads with the Liberal Party of Eleftherios Venizelos, which demanded entry into the war in order to achieve Greek nationalists' *Megali Idea* or 'Big Idea' of acquiring Greek-inhabited territory in Asia Minor. In October 1915 Allied forces landed at Salonika, in what was still a neutral state; by August 1916 Greece was split between the king's government at Athens and a rival, pro-Allied government under Venizelos at Salonika. In the end Allied pressure forced Constantine to leave the country in June 1917, and Greece formally entered the war on the Allied side.

Next to Serbia it was Russia which suffered the most drastic consequences of Ottoman entry into the war. Closure of the Straits to Russian and other Allied shipping effectively subjected Russia to economic blockade, since this Ottoman-controlled waterway was Russia's principal conduit to the outside world. Manpower shortages in the countryside due to the military call-up, the inadequacies of Russia's transport infrastructure and the general dysfunctionality of the tsarist regime did the rest: by 1915 this huge grain-producing economy was already facing serious shortages of food and raw materials, with disastrous effects on morale and internal social stability. The preconditions were being set in place for some sort of violent political revolution which, without the war's malign influence, would have been much harder to imagine.

The further expansion of the war with the entry on the Allied side of first Italy, in May 1915, and then Romania, in August 1916, had especially ominous implications for the Habsburg Monarchy, since both states explicitly aimed to acquire Habsburg territory inhabited by co-nationals. Both had been peacetime allies of the Central Powers, but territorial and nationalist aspirations now took precedence. Fighting on the Italian front, in particularly harsh, mountainous terrain, was soon locked into the same futile stalemate as elsewhere in the First World War; the spectacularly successful Caporetto offensive of the Central Powers in October 1917, while a humiliating reverse for Italian arms, nevertheless failed to knock Italy out of the war. Romania's opportunistic entry into the hostilities was prompted by the seeming success of the Brusilov offensive; yet the breaking-off of what proved to be Russia's last hurrah left the incompetently led Romanian army vulnerable to counter-attack by the Central Powers. A German-led offensive occupied Bucharest in December 1916, and forced the Romanian government to sue for an armistice. At no stage of either Italian or Romanian entry did the Habsburg Monarchy seriously contemplate buying these states' neutrality by the cession of territory.

Finally, Albania, without any clearly established government or boundaries in 1914, was kept in a state of anarchy by the war. Factions of Albanians supported by both sides claimed power, but the fluctuations of the conflict made Albania 'everybody's battleground'.[3] An Allied agreement of April 1915 assigned the north of the country to Serbia and Montenegro, the central portion to Italy, and the south to Greece; the defeat of Serbia and Montenegro, however, led to a mosaic of competing occupations, with Austria-Hungary and Bulgaria taking over the north-central and eastern parts, Greece and France occupying the south, and Italy taking over from Greece by mid-1917. Suffice it to say that the Albanians played little role in determining their own fate.

Two general points are worth stressing with regard to this initial phase of the war in Eastern Europe. Firstly, although nationalism can hardly be said to have started this general European conflict (leaving aside the obviously nationalist motivations of the Sarajevo assassins), the continuation and bitterness of hostilities was increasingly determined by national emotions on both sides. First of all, in some countries the war was portrayed by government, the press, intellectuals and patriotic bodies of all sorts as one of national defence. If, to paraphrase the nineteenth-century Italian nationalist Giuseppe Mazzini, the concept of the nation was one requiring blood-sacrifice, then the First World War provided ample provender for all nationalisms. Certainly the Serbian, Romanian and Italian governments and their publics saw their war as one of national liberation; so too, in reverse, did the Bulgarian government and people. In addition, the great powers were also aware that the fact of war opened up the future of the whole of Eastern Europe, in that the prospects of territorial conquest required some disposition of the peoples inhabiting those territories.

[3]   Vickers, A., 1997, *The Albanians: A Modern History*, revised edn, London and New York, 88.

This was particularly obvious with regard to the Polish question, and the fact that Poles were fighting in three separate armies, on both sides. Whereas the territory of the former Polish-Lithuanian Commonwealth had remained conveniently divided up between Russia, the Habsburg Monarchy and Prussia/ Germany throughout the nineteenth century, the Central Powers' occupation of the whole of Russian Poland by 1915 raised the prospect of a revived Polish state, as long as it was firmly under German or Austro-Hungarian control. In what was increasingly depicted as a war of nations, however, the Central Powers had to present this resurrected Poland in a way calculated to elicit the approval of Poles. The German and Austro-Hungarian governments accordingly announced, in November 1916, plans for the foundation of a kingdom of Poland, a move cynically intended by the German high command to rally all Poles around the Central Powers' cause. The matter was not, however, so clear to the Poles themselves, and right from the start of the war some opted for the Central Powers, while others put their trust in the Allies. What cannot be denied is that the war posed this Polish question in acute form; and for the Poles, read every other people in Eastern Europe.

Secondly, with each state's declaration of war, and the involvement of the whole region, the fact of war opened up hitherto unimaginable vistas for nationalists. Not only were subject nationalities, like the Poles, torn as to how loyal they should be to their respective rulers, even if most individuals, especially those in military service, had no option but to obey their respective states. The governments of multinational states had good reason, or thought they did, to worry about such subjects' allegiance.

As if in confirmation of such misgivings, right from the start a handful of individuals chose to use the war to work for outright national independence. Thus, Thomas G. Masaryk, a Czech academic and nationalist politician, fled the Habsburg Monarchy on the declaration of war to lobby Allied governments, and the Slovak émigré community, for their support in creating an independent Czechoslovakian state. Similarly, a number of South Slav politicians, notably the Croats Ante Trumbić and Frano Supilo, set up a Yugoslav Committee, eventually based in London, to argue for the union of the Habsburg Monarchy's South Slav peoples with Serbia and Montenegro – a Yugoslavia. Józef Piłsudski, a Russian-Polish nationalist leader who saw Russia as the Poles' greatest enemy, backed the opposite side even before the war, when he emigrated to Austria-Hungary and, on the outbreak of hostilities, received permission to raise a Polish Riflemen's Union to fight on the Central Powers' side for a revived Poland. Most East European nationalists, of course, did not have this option, one way or the other; indeed, not only did members of minorities face potential treason charges for expressing such ideas, but millions of individuals had no choice but to serve and, if necessary, to die on the front line. Nor did the Allied governments, to begin with, show any enthusiasm for the radical restructuring of Eastern Europe which the nationalist exiles demanded. Russia for obvious reasons resisted its own dismemberment. Britain and France saw the break-up of the Habsburg Monarchy as too dangerous for international stability, although that did not stop them promising bits of the Monarchy to Italy, and then to Romania, as an inducement for these countries to join them. Italy, while keen on its own territorial aggrandisement at Austria-Hungary's expense, was equally averse to seeing the whole of Central Europe put up for grabs, with unforeseeable consequences.

2. The Russian revolutions 1917–18

The second stage of the war saw Russia slide into revolutionary chaos, the end of the tsarist regime, and the country's gradual collapse as a serious combatant, culminating in takeover by the extreme left-wing Bolsheviks and dictatorship. The longer-term consequences of these developments for Eastern Europe and the wider world were profound.

By late 1916 Russia was militarily exhausted and economically crippled, largely thanks to the sheer incompetence of the tsarist government. Nicholas II's semi-autocracy prosecuted the war disastrously, although it is worth noting that the extent to which Russia had industrialised, by 1914, meant that militarily Russia was no pushover. Yet Russian generalship, with few exceptions, was poor; and this deficit in leadership was compounded when, in September 1915, Nicholas insisted on taking personal command of the army in the field. This not only separated the tsar physically from his ministers; it henceforward associated the dynasty itself with military failure and national humiliation. In addition Russia's casualties were, like all the major combatants', heavy, and affected millions of families across the empire. Economically the blockade of the Straits strangled Russia, leading to food and other shortages, and long before revolution occurred it was clear that war-weariness was the dominant mood among the people and, more importantly, the rank-and-file of the army. The conflict was, if anything, even more unpopular among Russia's national minorities, whose commitment to suffering and dying for a state they saw as an oppressor was never high.

In these circumstances, the focus of Russia's first revolution, early in 1917, was the political parties represented in the Duma, supported by unrest at popular level. As the war went from bad to worse the patriotic, middle-class elements in the assembly grew increasingly critical of the government's mismanagement of the conflict. Fearful that Russia was going to lose the war and cease being a great power, the liberal Constitutional Democrats or Kadets started calling on the tsar to abdicate. It was the tsar's attempt to dissolve the Duma, in early March 1917, that triggered violent revolution: the defiance of the Duma parties was backed by workers' strikes and demonstrations in Petrograd and Moscow and, crucially, by the army and navy units stationed in the capital. The tsar's generals persuaded him to abdicate on 15 March. As in 1905, much of the popular unrest in the Western provinces was among national minorities like the Poles, Latvians and Lithuanians.

The avowed aim of the middle-class liberals and other progressives who formed the Provisional Government was to continue the war while transforming Russia into a modern, pluralist society. This attempt at a liberal democratic revolution was hailed with acclaim by liberals in the West, like President Wilson; but it fatally undermined the Provisional Government's chances of survival from the start. The intention of successfully prosecuting the war immediately alienated much of the government's support at street level and in the armed forces, the officer corps excepted. A final offensive against the Central Powers, mounted in July 1917, was an abject failure, leaving the army on the brink of disintegration. The failure to embrace land reform speedily lost the support of millions of peasants; and the delay in holding elections for a constituent assembly until November 1917 deprived the government of its last shreds of legitimacy. The exploitation of this situation by Lenin's Bolsheviks, and their subsequent seizure of power in November 1917, followed logically if not inevitably from these failures.

Before the Provisional Government fell, however, it initiated a transformation in the position of Russia's national minorities which rapidly threatened to get out of hand. Instead of regarding the nationalism of non-Russians as inherently revolutionary, like its tsarist predecessor, the Provisional Government at least professed to recognise the right of national minorities to some form of democratic self-determination. On 9 April 1917, it issued an epochal declaration that 'the purpose of free Russia [is] not domination over other peoples, . . . but the establishment of a permanent peace on the basis of the self-determination of peoples'.[4] As a result, the government called for the dissolution of Russia's opponent, the Habsburg Monarchy; it recognised Masaryk as spokesman for the Czechoslovak movement, and permitted him to recruit a Czech Legion from among Czech prisoners of war in Russia. This later became a decisive force in the creation of an independent Czechoslovakia. The Provisional Government also announced that it supported the formation of an independent Polish state. In response other national minorities started forming representative bodies and demanding greater autonomy within Russia. As early as March 1917, a Ukrainian national council, the *Rada*, was formed to push for genuine autonomy. When the Provisional Government failed to respond, the *Rada* proclaimed autonomy in June and formed its own government. By this point the Russian nationalists in the Provisional Government were regretting their own liberalism, but it was too late. By the

---

[4]   Quoted in Chernev, B., 2011, 'The Brest-Litovsk Moment: Self-Determination Discourse in Eastern Europe before Wilsonianism', *Diplomacy & Statecraft*, XXII, #3, September, 372.

time the Bolsheviks took power, Russia was already fragmenting, as some of its constituent peoples took matters into their own hands.

Once in power, Lenin's first priority was to stifle democratic opposition, and much of the apparatus of dictatorship and terror usually associated with Stalin's regime was in fact put into place at the very outset of Bolshevik rule; this in itself was yet further cause for leaders of national minorities – those, at least, who were not themselves committed Bolsheviks – to start considering secession and full independence. Yet there was a paradox at the heart of Bolshevik policy regarding national minorities: in theory Lenin and his government supported the principle of self-determination. True, the Bolsheviks hoped that, given the right to choose for themselves, the non-Russian minorities would opt for socialist fraternity; but for the moment, given their shaky hold on power, the Bolsheviks were ready to make a virtue of necessity. Lenin accordingly accepted Finland's declaration of independence on 6 December 1917. Between December 1917 and March 1918, Lithuania, Ukraine, Estonia, Latvia, Bessarabia and Belarus all proclaimed their independence, although the extent to which these proclamations could be made reality varied widely, and was conditional upon the presence of German occupation troops to back them up.

Lenin's second priority, however, was to sue for an armistice with the Central Powers and conclude peace as soon as possible. This pariah regime, committed to a radical reordering of economy and society regarded with horror by every other government in the world, had enemies aplenty at home, and could not afford to have enemies abroad. The result was the punitive Treaty of Brest-Litovsk, signed between Communist Russia and the Central Powers on 3 March 1918. A separate treaty had already been signed on 9 February between the Central Powers and the newly independent Ukraine.

Brest-Litovsk represented the first formal stage in the break-up of the former Russian Empire and the emergence of interwar Eastern Europe. German and Austro-Hungarian forces already occupied substantial parts of western Russia, and the German government seized the opportunity to carve out a dominant position for Germany in the region; this was the high-water mark in imperial Germany's drive for European hegemony. Finland and the Ukraine, the latter as the so-called Hetmanate of the Ukrainian National Republic, were recognised in separate treaties by the Central Powers as independent states, although the intention of the German government was that both would be firmly under German control. The re-united components of Poland, now recognised as a (puppet) Kingdom of Poland, as well as the former Russian provinces of Lithuania and Courland, were to be incorporated into Germany. The former Russian provinces of Livonia and Estland were set up as protectorates dominated by the German element in their population. The territory of present-day Belarus, despite attempts since March 1917 by a Belorussian National Committee in Minsk to assert some form of autonomy against first the Russian Provisional Government and then the Bolsheviks, was simply divided between

German-controlled Poland and Russia. Brest-Litovsk demonstrated the true extent of Germany's aims in the East: the entire region was to serve as imperial Germany's economic hinterland. Only Germany's final defeat in the West, late in 1918, prevented this dream of regional hegemony from being realised. The fact that Germany lost the war in the end, however, meant that the whole Brest-Litovsk settlement unravelled within months since, as a precondition for agreeing the armistice of 11 November, the Allies insisted that Germany annulled the treaty. The former Russian borderlands remained in a state of flux and chaos well beyond 1918.

3. US entry 1917–18

The third stage of the war, overlapping with the second, began with the entry into the conflict of the United States. As with the Bolshevik Revolution, American participation transformed the strategic situation, in that it promised to tip the balance decisively in the Allies' favour. It also profoundly altered the war's political character, because President Wilson presented the United States' war aims as radically different from those of the European powers. Wilson did this, moreover, precisely to issue a counter-blast to the siren allure of communism, which the war threatened to make increasingly attractive to the peoples of Europe and the world. Wilson saw the causes of the war in a lack of democratic accountability on all sides; governments more accountable to their electorates for policy, including foreign policy, were less likely in this view to go to war in the first place. In addition, just as individuals had rights so too, in Wilson's liberal democratic world view, did nations, and it was the denial of this right to national self-determination, in Wilson's opinion, which was another major cause of war in 1914.

Wilson's Fourteen Points, announced to Congress on 8 January 1918, thus depicted the extension of democratic governance, and the establishment of a League of Nations for arbitrating disputes between states, as principal war aims. While the Fourteen Points did not explicitly mention national self-determination, Point 13 called for the establishment of an independent Polish state, and Point 10 demanded that the other peoples of the Habsburg Monarchy be given 'the freest opportunity of autonomous development'.[5]

The Fourteen Points fatally undermined the multinational empires of Eastern Europe. Up to this point the Allied powers had not been committed to the break-up of the Habsburg Monarchy, let alone Germany or their former ally, Russia, although as far as the Ottoman Empire was concerned Britain and France had already agreed on the carving up of the Ottoman Middle East.

---

[5]   Quoted in Macartney, C.A. and Palmer, A.W., 1962, *Independent Eastern Europe: A History*, London and Basingstoke, 81.

The Fourteen Points, however, forced the logic of supporting break-up on the Allied governments; and by the late summer of 1918 Britain, France and Italy had all committed themselves to the dissolution of the Habsburg Monarchy. In addition to the likely annexation of Habsburg territory by Italy and Romania, the creation of an independent Poland, the union of Czechs and Slovaks in a single state, and the union of the South Slavs in some form of Yugoslav state under Serbian leadership were all regarded as foregone conclusions.

4. The collapse of the Central Powers, 1918

The fourth and final phase of the war saw the defeat of Germany and its allies Austria-Hungary, the Ottoman Empire and Bulgaria. This was despite the substantial reprieve afforded the Central Powers by the earlier collapse of Russia and the imposition of Brest-Litovsk, and was very much a consequence of American entry on the opposite side. By early 1918 food shortages in German and Austro-Hungarian cities were causing genuine distress, strikes and mass demonstrations in favour of peace. By the late spring, when Germany's last offensive on the Western Front ground to a halt, it was clear that defeat was only a matter of time. With the army undernourished and exhausted thanks to the economic blockade, German forces started yielding ground in the West, yet come the autumn the Germans still occupied French and Belgian soil. It was developments in Eastern Europe which broke the nerve of the German high command and convinced it to sue for an armistice.

The first state to collapse was Bulgaria, facing a newly invigorated Allied offensive from Salonika. On 28 September the Bulgarian government sued for peace. By the terms of this armistice the Bulgarian government withdrew from occupied Greek and Serbian territory, and allowed Allied troops into Bulgaria for an assault on the remaining Central Powers. It was this news which prompted the German high command finally to seek peace terms; but the subsequent negotiations with the Allies took another month and a half to resolve, one of the principal reasons for the German revolution of 9 November, the deposition of the Emperor William II, and the proclamation of the German Republic, followed by the armistice of 11 November.

In the meantime, Germany's other partners had also collapsed. The Ottoman government sued for peace and signed an armistice at Mudros on 30 October; by its terms the Ottoman army was required to retreat to the Empire's 1914 borders. The precise nature of the territorial losses to be imposed on the Ottomans was put off to the peace conference.

The Habsburg Monarchy was equally anxious to negotiate peace terms, not least to avert disintegration; the Hungarian government, however, obstinately refused to entertain any idea of territorial concessions, and while the common ministerial council squabbled, the mood among the Monarchy's war-weary peoples became increasingly volatile. Long before an armistice could even be negotiated the various peoples of the Monarchy took matters, as in Russia earlier, into their own hands.

The Poles already had the nucleus of a government to hand, in the shape of the German-controlled 'Regency Council' set up in 1917; now, as Germany drifted towards its own revolution, this Council assumed real powers. Early in October the Poles of Habsburg Galicia set up their own National Council, and it was the decision of these two bodies to amalgamate, in mid-November, which called the new Polish state into being, the first independent Poland since 1795. The boundaries of this new state, however, were still very much undecided, not just in relation to Germany and Austria-Hungary, but even more so in relation to Russia, where the Bolshevik regime was already reclaiming territory lost to the Central Powers, and the non-Polish inhabitants of the Russian borderlands had claims of their own.

In the Bohemian crownlands, the diets of the three provinces of Bohemia, Moravia and Silesia separately declared independence from the Monarchy on 14 October, and united to proclaim a Czech Republic on 28 October. This entity then joined forces with the Slovak National Council, newly emerged in neighbouring Hungary, to proclaim a Czechoslovak Republic, with Thomas Masaryk invited back from exile to act as president. Further justification for Czechoslovak union was claimed on the basis of the Pittsburgh Agreement of 30 May 1918 with representatives of the sizeable Slovak community in the United States.

Among the South Slavs, representatives from the Austrian *Reichsrat* and Croatia formed a National Council of Croats, Serbs and Slovenes at Zagreb on 19 October. It was this body which proclaimed independence and then invited Serbia, as the only actor in the region with an army at its disposal, to assume control of these Habsburg lands, prior to proclaiming the Kingdom of Serbs, Croats and Slovenes on 1 December; the fundamental agreement on this union (although little else) had been reached between the Serbian government and the Yugoslav Committee, representing South Slavs in exile, at Corfù in July 1917. Meanwhile, in November 1918, Montenegro was effectively forced into joining Serbia, and King Nikola deposed.

Finally, Romania re-entered the war on 10 November, the same day that its German army of occupation started to withdraw. Anticipating this, Romanian political leaders in the Bukovina, Transylvania and the Banat formed national councils and demanded union with Romania. So too did the comparable body in Russian Bessarabia, which since the Russian revolutions had been maintaining a precarious existence as the Moldavian Democratic Federated Republic. Italy waited until the armistice with Austria was signed on 3 November before overrunning much more than the territories promised it in 1915: the South Tyrol, Trieste and its hinterland, the Istrian Peninsula, most of the Dalmatian and Montenegrin coastline, and virtually the whole of Albania.

Faced with this falling away of territories and peoples, the twin centres of power in the Habsburg Monarchy also collapsed. Revolutions in both Vienna and Budapest forced the Emperor Charles to renounce his executive authority and go into exile, left-leaning provisional governments were formed in both capitals, and separate Austrian and Hungarian republics were proclaimed in November. The Habsburg Monarchy as a state had ceased to exist.

The impact of the war on East European societies

Most people's images of the First World War remain dominated by the horrors of trench warfare on the Western Front. The Eastern Front, by contrast, is relatively unfamiliar, although conditions there were just as horrific, and the 'butcher's bill', in terms of military casualties, was just as brutal. In addition, the fighting in Eastern Europe was more fluid than in the West, ranged over a far wider theatre of operations, from the Baltic to Gallipoli, and thus arguably affected far more of the civilian population. Here, if anywhere, was the principal difference between East and West: the mass impact in terms of death and displacement on civilians was far higher in Eastern Europe, and often deliberate. In this respect the war in the East was a harbinger of the even greater horrors of the Second World War. Thomas Masaryk, surveying the post-war scene, described Eastern Europe as a 'laboratory atop a mass graveyard'.[6]

The military casualties alone were shocking, and match anything on the Western Front. Russia suffered some 2.3 million dead, and an estimated 4.9 million wounded; Austria-Hungary, 1.1 million dead and 3.6 million wounded; Germany, whose fighting was of course on both fronts, lost 2 million dead and 4.2 million wounded. Among the smaller combatants the casualty rate, though numerically nowhere near as high, was proportionately even higher: Serbia, with a pre-war population of 1.8 million, lost 250,000 military dead and 133,000 wounded.

It is when civilian deaths are added to these figures, however, that the true impact of the war on Eastern Europe becomes apparent. In addition to its 408,000 military casualties, for instance, Serbia suffered an estimated 450,000 civilian deaths as a result of enemy action, displacement and disease; many civilian as well as military deaths were caused by a typhoid epidemic in 1915. Something like 22 per cent of Serbia's population in 1914 did not survive the war. Some 1.5 million civilians died in the Russian Empire, 467,000 in the Habsburg Monarchy; 430,000 in Romania. The fighting itself caused mass

---

[6] Quoted in Baron, N. and Gatrell, P., 2004, 'Introduction', in N. Baron and P. Gatrell (eds), *Homelands: War, Population and Statehood in Eastern Europe and Russia 1918-1924*, London, 3.

dislocation and hundreds of thousands of refugees, some of them forcibly displaced by their own government as an impediment to the prosecution of the war. The tsarist authorities, for example, regarded all of the Empire's non-Russian minorities as potential traitors, and deported some 250,000 Germans, Jews, Roma and others from the Western provinces. Jews in particular were targeted from the first days of the war, with summary executions, forcible evacuation and no provision for support behind the front; and the Jewish population of Habsburg Galicia was similarly mistreated by the Russians during their temporary occupation of the province. The Habsburg government, for its part, treated Galicia's Polish but especially its Ruthene population as collaborators and, on reconquering Galicia, randomly executed between 25,000 and 30,000 civilians in 'the bloodiest massacre of civilians perpetrated within Europe during 1914', and deported thousands more to internment camps in Lower Austria.[7] In these conditions of upheaval and mutual suspicion, ethnic minorities in disputed areas started turning on one another, especially in the closing stages of the war, when territory seemed up for grabs. In short, the longer the war went on the more a sort of ethnic cleansing tended to become part of the logic of events since, in Niall Ferguson's words, 'it was understood early on that war spelt the dissolution of the old order of multi-ethnic empires and ethnically mixed communities'.[8]

The economic impact of the war on East European societies was no less catastrophic. The disruption of trade and normal lines of supply, the growing shortage of foodstuffs and other essential materials, the removal through conscription of millions of men from normal economic activity, not to mention the longer-term economic consequences of their death or disablement, were all disastrous in themselves. But the First World War as a whole is distinguished for the fact that it was the first general European war to be waged economically in a concerted fashion. Governments on both sides were acutely aware that they needed to mobilise the entire strength of their societies, and to put every economic resource into the struggle; by implication, this meant that the enemy's economy was just as much a target as its armed forces. Hence, both sides resorted to economic blockade in order to cripple each other; by extension, the infliction of economic suffering on the enemy's entire population was seen as a vital necessity, regardless of the fall-out in terms of starvation, malnutrition, vulnerability to disease and death.

In this economic warfare the Central Powers, Russia and the Balkan states were the principal victims. Germany's submarine warfare against Allied shipping was far eclipsed in efficacy by the Allied interdiction of global trade with Germany and its allies; and by 1916–17, known in Germany as the 'turnip

[7] Watson, A., 2014, *Ring of Steel: Germany and Austria-Hungary at War 1914-1918*, London, 148.
[8] Ferguson, N., 2006, *The War of the World: Twentieth-Century Conflict and the Descent of the West*, London, 136.

winter' because people were reduced to eating crops normally reserved for livestock, the dearth of foodstuffs was causing genuine hardship in Central Europe. Russia was similarly affected by Ottoman entry into the war and the closure of the Straits to Allied shipping. Real shortages and the low level of nutrition led to labour unrest, food strikes and an enhanced revolutionary mood in Russia by early 1917, and in German and Austrian cities by early 1918. In both cases such hardship on the domestic front eventually had a predictable effect on troop morale.

Finally, the war left a toxic psychological legacy, 'a new logic of violence' which in the post-war period affected domestic politics no less than international relations.[9] Not only did fighting and political upheaval continue in Eastern Europe long after 1918, but the brutalisation of millions meant that distinctions between civilians and combatants remained blurred, suspect groups within societies were more likely to be targeted, and population displacement and even extermination were more easily imaginable. The role of such experiences in radicalising sizeable numbers of East Europeans seems likely, if unquantifiable. In particular the lengthy occupation of Eastern Europe by some 2–3 million German troops during the war meant that 'durable impressions' of the region as a sort of natural field for German economic and political hegemony were formed, and passed on to the post-war generation.[10] This was a development with ominous implications for the future.

[9] Gerwarth, R., 2017, *The Vanquished: Why the First World War Failed to End 1917-1923*, London, 254.
[10] Liulevicius, V.G., 2000, *War Land on the Eastern Front: Culture, National Identity and German Occupation in World War I*, Cambridge, 14.

3

A new Europe? The peace settlement 1918–23

The immediate political consequences of the war, the collapse of multinational empires and the general redrawing of international boundaries, have already been sketched above. This chapter describes the extremely untidy way in which a peace settlement was reached, a process which extended over several years, and which in many parts of Eastern Europe involved yet further fighting and deaths.

Historians, and their students, are apt to refer to the Paris peace settlement, the series of five treaties concluded in 1919–20 between the Allies and their defeated enemies, as if it somehow conjured the new Eastern Europe into being. In reality, the proceedings at Paris did not literally create the successor states, for these had already emerged at the end of the war. For the most part, however, these were states with shakily established governments, varying powers of enforcement at their disposal, and borders as yet not internationally agreed upon. The situation on the ground, moreover, remained chaotic for months and even years afterwards, with conflicting claims to territory, different forces in control, continuing attempts at revolution and, in some cases, continuing armed conflict. The self-imposed task of the great powers at the Paris conference – Britain, France, Italy and the United States – was therefore, by dictating terms to the defeated, to define the borders of both the defeated and those states which profited from their defeat. Because of the multiplicity of conflicting claims, the 'Big Four' took it upon themselves to adjudicate, and the new states were obliged to accept this mediation. This was a mammoth task, with a far greater range of territories and claims to resolve, in Europe and the wider world, than at any previous international conference. The peacemakers have often been criticised for getting it wrong. Their inability to resolve certain problems, and their creation of entirely new ones, could be said to have sown the seeds of future conflict. On the other hand, in Eastern Europe in particular the odds against satisfying all conflicting claims were impossibly high. What is remarkable about the settlement is how much actually was settled. The Eastern Europe that we know today was in broad outlines created at this point.

Map 3 States of Eastern Europe by 1923.

A new Europe?

The New Europe was a periodical published in Britain from 1916 to 1920 by R.W. Seton-Watson and others, devoted to lobbying for the reordering of Eastern Europe. As we have seen, the collapse of the old Europe was the essential precondition for this reordering. Literally new were the republics of Austria, Hungary, Czechoslovakia, Poland, Finland, Estonia, Latvia and Lithuania, and the Kingdom of the Serbs, Croats and Slovenes (only formally renamed Yugoslavia in 1929). Romania expanded at the expense of the former Habsburg and Romanov empires; Greece at the expense of Bulgaria and the Ottoman Empire. Bulgaria survived in diminished form. The Ottoman Empire, last survivor of the old multinational order, was pushed into revolution by the peace settlement, and as a result the borders imposed on it in 1920 had to be drastically revised in 1923, by which point it had become the Republic of Turkey. Albania was the one state whose very existence hinged on the decisions taken in Paris; eventually it was Italy's need to trade its influence there for concessions elsewhere, and the weakness of Greece and Yugoslavia, which preserved Albanian independence. Bolshevik Russia, embroiled in its hideous civil war in 1918–21, was the one great power completely excluded from the peace settlement. As a result of the Russian civil war two potential new states, the Ukraine and Belarus, remained stillborn and were eventually reconquered by the Bolsheviks. The borders of what became the Soviet Union could not be settled until 1921, and were only provisionally accepted by the Communist regime. This meant that the Soviet Union, together with Germany, Hungary and Bulgaria, was one of the so-called revisionist states throughout the interwar period.

The Paris peace conference convened in January 1919, at which point discussion of much of the nitty-gritty concerning Eastern Europe was immediately delegated to various committees, who spent the following months hearing evidence from the new governments as well as from acknowledged experts on the history, geography and ethnography of the region. We can debate the use, if any, to which these committees' recommendations were put by the great powers, but certainly the peacemakers had access to a formidable array of expert opinion. As far as implementing the peace treaties was concerned, there was a two-way leverage: the new states, especially if militarily weak, relied on the great powers to settle their borders for them; the great powers, however, relied on the governments of the successor states to implement the decisions taken in Paris, since at the end of a long war none of the great powers was willing to deploy their own forces in Eastern Europe. A special aspect of the Paris peace settlement was the role envisaged for the new League of Nations which, it was hoped, would act as guarantor for the new order, as well as a court of appeal for resolving outstanding disputes and averting future conflict.

During the peace conference, moreover, events in Eastern Europe were hardly standing still, and indeed threatened even more alarming change. Civil war was already raging in Russia, with the Allied powers for a period supporting the 'Whites' or anti-Communist forces; and although the British, French, American and other forces landed in parts of Russia did not actively partake in the fighting, they nevertheless provided important logistical back-up for the Whites, thus prolonging what was already a vicious ideological conflict. Yet Allied governments felt they had no choice, given the extent of left-wing unrest in their own countries, and the perceived danger of communism spreading across war-torn Europe.

Allied jumpiness about the perils of letting communism survive in Russia was only intensified by events in Central and Eastern Europe itself. January 1919 saw the abortive left-wing uprising of the Spartacist League in Berlin, capital of defeated Germany. The Spartacists, led by Rosa Luxemburg and Karl Liebknecht, dissident Social Democrats who had opposed the war, had just decided to launch a German Communist Party, and found themselves pressured by their even more radical supporters to declare the deposition of the moderate, social democratic government of the new republic. Rapidly and ruthlessly put down by the government with the enthusiastic assistance of the German army and a variety of right-wing paramilitary organisations, the so-called *Freikorps*, this incident nevertheless seemed to show Germany's vulnerability to Communist subversion.

Nor was this vulnerability confined to Germany. In Finland a civil war broke out within a month of the proclamation of independence, and from January to May 1918 fighting swayed back and forth between the nationalist Civil Guards, in the north of the country, defending the government of Pehr Evind Svinhufvud, and the left-wing Red Guards, who formed a revolutionary counter-government under Kullervo Manner and temporarily took control of Helsinki and the south. The Civil Guards, led by the former tsarist general Carl Gustav Mannerheim, profited from the assistance of the German army, and when Mannerheim's forces eventually reconquered Helsinki in May there was a brief but vicious bloodbath. Apart from those killed in the fighting, some 10,000 Red Guards were summarily executed at the end of the conflict, and thousands more died of starvation and ill-treatment in government camps. Overall 36,000 people, 1 per cent of the population, are thought to have died.

In the new Baltic states of Estonia, Latvia and Lithuania, the proclamation of independence, notional while a victorious Germany was still in control of the region, approached reality as soon as Germany collapsed. Yet Baltic independence was immediately complicated by the presence next door of Bolshevik Russia, which on 13 November 1918 repudiated the terms of the Brest-Litovsk treaty, and proclaimed the 'liberation' of the Baltic peoples from 'German imperialism'. The Bolsheviks' attempted re-conquest of the Baltic states was aided by significant numbers of native Baltic communists. Not only had Latvians been particularly prominent in the Bolshevik Revolution, the Latvian Jakums Vācietis commanded the Red Army, and there were already embryonic Communist movements in Estonia and Lithuania. Between mid-November 1918 and January 1919 Bolshevik forces steadily advanced across all three states, and Soviet republics were declared. Fighting continued into the spring between the newly established governments and these communist forces. The survival of the new states was helped by the continuing presence in each country of units of the German wartime army of occupation, and at the request of the Allied powers Germany postponed withdrawal of its troops until the new governments were secure. In addition the Baltic Germans, a sizeable minority in all three states, sided overwhelmingly with the new national governments, at least for the interim. They raised volunteers from Germany itself, all eager to defend fellow Germans against communism; this was the genesis of several of the *Freikorps* units which in the post-war period were to bedevil Germany's internal politics. Finally, the Baltic governments could rely on the somewhat suspect support of Russian anti-Bolshevik elements based in the area, even if these Whites hoped eventually to restore the Russian Empire or some form of Russian-dominated state, which would include the former Baltic provinces. With the additional help of Finnish volunteers in Estonia, British naval units in the Baltic and their own coordinated efforts, the Baltic states had regained control of their territory by mid-1919. In Latvia and Lithuania Red Army units were driven out by the Polish army, which then in October 1920 occupied the largely Polish-speaking city of Vilnius, despite its historic status as the capital of medieval Lithuania, and the largely non-Polish character of the peasantry in the surrounding countryside.

Even more alarming than the seesaw of events in the Baltic was the progressive destabilisation of Hungary in the winter of 1918–19, which led to the proclamation in March of a Hungarian Soviet Republic. Ironically this startling development was in part due to Allied decisions. The left-leaning coalition that proclaimed the first Hungarian Republic in 1918, under Count Mihály Károlyi, struggled throughout to maintain its grip on the country, at a time when Hungary was still subject to Allied blockade, and was threatened by the loss of territory on all sides to the successor states of Czechoslovakia, Romania and Yugoslavia. Károlyi, a well-meaning aristocrat who attempted to distribute his own estates to the bemused peasants who farmed the land, hoped that the establishment of a democratic system in Hungary would win it favourable treatment at the Paris peace conference, and like virtually all members of the Hungarian political elite he proceeded from the assumption that the territorial integrity of historic Hungary could be preserved, as long as the non-Magyar minorities were assured full political rights and equality of treatment. In line with this assumption Károlyi appointed the young sociologist Oszkár Jászi minister for nationalities, with the brief of forging some sort of arrangement with the non-Magyars. Károlyi's government was doomed to disappointment. Even as the new cabinet was taking office, 'national councils' were being formed among Hungary's Slovaks, Romanians, Croats and Serbs, which refused to recognise Budapest's jurisdiction, and in short order appealed to the authority of the relevant successor state. In the north the new Czechoslovakia was empowered by Paris to occupy most of Slovakia, and the Hungarian government was ordered by Paris to fall back. Croatia and a large wedge of southern Hungary were taken over by what became the new Yugoslavia. Transylvanian Romanians announced their union with Romania on 10 November 1918, and within days Romanian troops had entered the province. The Banat, the territory between Transylvania and eastern Croatia, remained a subject of dispute between Romania and Yugoslavia for months to come; this was one of those issues entrusted for resolution to the Paris conference, which divided the Banat along roughly ethnic lines.

The Károlyi government's weakness vis-à-vis the Allied powers contributed to a rapid falling-off of popular support. When, on 20 March 1919, the great powers insisted on complete compliance with the territorial demands of Hungary's neighbours, the cabinet resigned, unwilling to accept the odium of signing away so much. It was replaced by a coalition led by Hungary's new Communist party, founded in the fall of 1918 by Béla Kun, a former prisoner of war in Russia who had converted to communism while there. The Hungarian Communist party was not large in numbers, and could take power only in alliance with the Social Democrats, although it made a noise out of all proportion to its real strength, and immediately proclaimed a Hungarian Soviet Republic and a 'dictatorship of the proletariat', the nationalisation of industry (including cafés), the confiscation of private property and much else that bore little relation to reality. The assumption of the Hungarian communists was that, as Kun put it, 'the victory of communism will not stop at the borders of Hungary, it will be worldwide'.[1] However unlikely, this was inflammatory, and the alarm raised on the nationalist right and centre by the new regime was hardly allayed by the fact that Kun and several other members of his cabinet were Jewish. More important for the temporary success of Kun's regime was the fact that virtually all shades of political opinion in Hungary were vehemently opposed to the cession of Hungarian territory. Kun's government, which pledged to resist territorial annexations, thus won the support of such unlikely groups as the officer corps of the former Austro-Hungarian army.

Two factors, however, doomed the Hungarian Soviet Republic from the start. The first was its underlying military weakness: despite a hasty recall of the Hungarian units of the former Habsburg army, there was simply not enough force at the regime's disposal. Secondly, support for this ostensibly radical regime among non-communists, who comprised the vast majority of

[1] Quoted in Low, A.D., 1963, *The Hungarian Soviet Republic and the Paris Peace Conference*, Philadelphia, PA, 40.

Hungarians, was solely dependent on its ability to reverse Hungary's territorial losses. Initially the regime had some slight successes, at least in Slovakia against a disorganised enemy. The Soviet Republic had nothing, however, to match either the Romanian army in the east, or the Serbian army in the south; and when the Romanians launched an invasion of Hungary, the regime collapsed. The Soviet Republic also dug its own grave by failing to copy Lenin's tactics in Russia, and winning over the Hungarian peasantry by promising wholesale land redistribution. Instead, Kun proclaimed the nationalisation of land, as a result of which the furious peasantry played a key role in bringing the regime down by blocking food supplies to urban areas. In the end Kun was chased out by the Romanian army, fleeing Budapest on 1 August. In the wake of the Romanians came a White reaction led by Miklós Horthy, an aristocrat and admiral of the Austro-Hungarian navy, who had formed a counter-revolutionary force at Szeged in southern Hungary. Horthy and his supporters instituted a counter-terror, shot several thousand left-wingers and other opponents, and proclaimed the restoration of the Kingdom of Hungary (although not the Habsburg dynasty), which meant that Horthy assumed the position of regent. The Horthy government also restored the pre-1918 electoral system, including a suffrage weighted in favour of the landed nobility and the wealthy. To the dismay of Horthy and Hungarian nationalists, however, the interlude of the Soviet Republic had the disastrous effect, as far as the Paris peace conference was concerned, of legitimising the blatant land grabs made by Romania, Czechoslovakia and Yugoslavia. As a result Hungary, like Germany, remained an aggrieved and revisionist society throughout the interwar period, yearning for the recovery of the lost territories, and regardless of the fact that the majority of the inhabitants of those territories were non-Magyars.

Two further complications were added to the peacemakers' agenda in 1919 with consequences far outlasting the conference itself. One was set in motion by Britain, France and the United States in May, when they authorised Greece to land occupation forces provisionally at the largely Greek-speaking port of Smyrna, on the Anatolian mainland of the Ottoman Empire. This was a reaction by the three powers to Italy's unilateral occupation of Ottoman territory to the south, with the implied threat to take Smyrna as well, and was symptomatic of how far the Allies' own interests in the Ottoman Empire clashed. By the terms of the armistice imposed on it in 1918, the Ottoman government agreed to Allied zones of occupation and influence, including British forces at Constantinople and the Straits, French forces in south-eastern Anatolia, and Italian forces in Cilicia; despite this, Italy felt that it was being unfairly frozen out. Now Greece was encouraged to establish a physical presence in Asia Minor, which its government took as carte blanche to pursue Greek nationalism's century-old *Megali Idea*, the 'great idea' of a restored Greek Byzantine empire. Within months, however, this provoked a Turkish nationalist backlash, revolution in the Ottoman Empire, and a bitter Greco-Turkish war.

The second complication arose out of the unresolved boundary issues between Italy and the new Yugoslavia. By the secret Treaty of London of 1915, by which the Allies bought Italy's entry into the war, Italy was promised the Habsburg territories of Trentino, South Tyrol, the port of Trieste, the Istrian Peninsula, the counties of Gorizia and Gradiska, and much of the Dalmatian coastline, including the port of Zara (Zadar) and its hinterland. The problem with these provisions, as South Slav leaders were quick to point out when they learned the details, was that they involved transferring large numbers of South Slavs to Italian rule (as well as ethnic Germans in Trentino and South Tyrol). Although Trieste was mainly Italian-speaking, the majority of the population of its hinterland was Slovene; and while there was a sizeable Italian-speaking minority in much of Istria and Dalmatia, the majority in these areas was Croat. Italy's reasons for seeking these territories were strategic, rather than ethnic. Conspicuously absent from the territories promised was the Italian-speaking port of Fiume (Rijeka) in Croatia; yet to Italian nationalists it too was part of 'Italia irredenta' or unreclaimed Italy. In the autumn of 1918, as the Habsburg Monarchy collapsed, Italy quickly sent troops to consolidate its hold on the territories promised it, but by this time both the Yugoslav Committee and the authorities representing the soon to be proclaimed Kingdom of Serbs, Croats and Slovenes protested vehemently against this flagrant disregard for the principle of national self-determination.

At Paris the Yugoslavs found a vocal sponsor in President Wilson, whose advocacy of their cause led to a temporary walk-out by the Italian delegation and nearly wrecked the conference. Italian nationalist opinion was stoked to boiling-point by this confrontation. It was in this febrile atmosphere, in September 1919, that Fiume was seized by a paramilitary expedition led by the flamboyant poet and war hero, Gabriele D'Annunzio. D'Annunzio's forces, acting independently of the Italian government, proclaimed Fiume a self-governing 'Regency of the Carnaro', and spent the next fifteen months defying the great powers' insistence that the port be handed over to Yugoslavia. In this period the international balance of forces gradually changed in Italy's favour: President Wilson, already obliged to accept innumerable grubby compromises in order to agree peace terms with the other great powers, fell ill in the last months of his term of office and abandoned the Yugoslavs' cause; and Britain and France had never been such warm supporters. As a result Italy and Yugoslavia, in the Treaty of Rapallo of 12 November 1920, were finally able to agree a common border, with Yugoslavia, by now on its own, forced to accept the abandonment to Italy of the territories promised in 1915. Fiume was not part of the deal; instead, a Free City of Fiume was set up by the new League of Nations, formally independent of both states and protected by the League. In December 1920 the Italian government, acting on behalf of the Paris peace conference, forcibly removed D'Annunzio and his supporters. When, however, the new Fascist government of Benito Mussolini annexed the city in September 1923, Yugoslavia was obliged to accept this fait accompli.

A final complication affecting the peace negotiations in Paris was the extraordinarily complex and rapidly shifting dispute over the borders of the new Poland, which were not resolved until 1921, and which decided the fate of both Belarus and the short-lived independent Ukraine. As of November 1918 the territory controlled by the Polish government comprised the core of Prussian Poland, western Galicia, and those parts of Russian Poland occupied by the German army. Beyond that, however, everything was up for grabs, and was disputed by Germany; the new governments of Czechoslovakia, Hungary and Lithuania; a Belarusan state proclaimed in March 1918 but leading a shadowy, underground existence within what the Soviets called the Lithuanian-Belarusan Soviet Socialist Republic; the Western Ukrainian National Republic proclaimed in Lviv (Lemberg); the Ukrainian National Republic, or Dnieper Ukraine, notionally based at Kiev; and, most ominously, the Bolshevik regime in Russia. German troops no sooner started retreating from Eastern Europe, under the terms of the armistice, than units of the Red Army began advancing westwards to reclaim former Russian territory. At the same time, competing non-Russian authorities and armed forces were springing up, anxious to forestall a Communist takeover by claiming territory themselves. Polish leaders were divided between those, like Roman Dmowski's National Democrats, who sought to consolidate an ethnically homogeneous Polish state, albeit one including territories such as Lithuania, western Ukraine and Belarus, which had belonged to the old Polish-Lithuanian Commonwealth, and which could, in their eyes, be Polonised; and those, like Piłsudski, who dreamed of taking advantage of the civil war in Russia to carve out 'an extensive East European federation' stretching from the Baltic states to the Ukraine, a re-creation of the Commonwealth but with added security.[2]

This issue of how big, and where, the new Poland should be depended in turn on the shifting fortunes of the Russian civil war, which was largely decided in the Ukraine. The Ukrainian National Republic proclaimed in Kiev on 19 December 1918, under the military leadership of Symon Petliura, was barely two months in charge before it was chased out by the Red Army in February 1919; in its place the Bolsheviks set up a Ukrainian Soviet Socialist Republic. This Communist regime, however, promptly alienated its own base: when the thousands of Ukrainian peasants who had flocked to the Red Army's standard, anticipating a Lenin-like re-distribution of land, learned that the new Soviet Republic intended nationalising the land instead, they swiftly turned against the Reds. Ukraine in the summer of 1919 descended into a chaos of rival armies, with White forces under General Anton Denikin, supported by the Allies and the Petliurists, chasing the Soviets out of Kiev in August, while self-styled 'anarchist' peasant armies under Matvii Hryhoriiv and Nestor Makhno

[2]   Lukowski, J. and Zawadzki, H., 2001, *A Concise History of Poland*, Cambridge and New York, 200.

defied the authority of both Reds and Whites in much of south-central and south-eastern Ukraine. The White forces across Russia, however, were too disunited and did not command enough support, and by December 1919 the Reds were on the offensive, gradually regaining control of Dnieper Ukraine and retaking Kiev in February 1920.

At this point Piłsudski and the advocates of a greater, 'Jagellonian' Poland prevailed: by the Treaty of Warsaw, in April 1920, Poland recognised Ukrainian independence and joined forces with Petliura in an invasion of Dnieper Ukraine. The Polish-Soviet War (1920–1) was brief but fiercely fought, and fluctuated dramatically. The Polish-Petliurist offensive drove the Soviets out of Kiev yet again on 7 May 1920, but support for the Ukrainian nationalists was weaker than anticipated, while their cause was tarnished, among both Ukrainians and ethnic Russians, by association with the Catholic Poles. For a few, tense weeks, as the Soviets rolled Polish-Ukrainian forces back almost to Warsaw by August 1920, it looked as if the export of world revolution along Communist lines was actually to become a reality. In the end, however, the nationalism of Poles at least proved far stronger than their potential attraction to communism, which in turn was identified with the traditional enemy, Russia. Helped by the programme issued by a government of national defence which promised, among other things, to prioritise land reform, and by the belatedly re-discovered military flair of Piłsudski, the Polish army counter-attacked and inflicted a number of decisive defeats on the Soviets in August and September. More than a million people are estimated to have died in the territory of present-day Ukraine in 1918–20. At the subsequent peace treaty signed at Riga, on 18 March 1921, Lenin's regime was obliged to accept a frontier with Poland which assigned to the latter much of the former Russian borderlands, including about half of present-day Belarus and a substantial slice of present-day Ukraine, as well as confirming Polish possession of eastern Galicia, the short-lived Western Ukrainian National Republic. These so-called *kresy*, although formerly part of the old Commonwealth, proved a serious liability for interwar Poland, both as a source of domestic instability and as the object of Soviet revisionism. With non-Polish minorities amounting to about 30 per cent of its population, interwar Poland was 'too westerly to be a federation, but not westerly enough to remain a national state.'[3]

The peace settlement

Meanwhile, at Paris the great powers attempted to achieve some sort of order on the map. Despite all the obstacles posed by their own conflicting interests,

[3] Snyder, T., 2003, *The Reconstruction of Nations: Poland, Ukraine, Lithuania, Belarus 1569-1999*, New Haven, CT and London, 68.

the rival claims of East European governments and peoples, and the distractions of outside events as described above, the negotiators concluded five separate treaties in 1919 and 1920.

The Treaty of Versailles, signed by Germany under duress on 28 June 1919, has traditionally drawn most attention, but there is no denying its importance in the shaping of Eastern Europe, or the trouble it stored up for the future. Most contentious, and bitterly resented by Germans of all political persuasions, were the provisions of Versailles stipulating the cession to the successor states of territories containing German-speaking populations. This included the so-called Polish corridor or West Prussia, between the main part of Germany and East Prussia; this was territory originally seized from Poland–Lithuania in the eighteenth century, and represented a total population loss of 3.5 million, mostly Polish-speaking, although about one million were German speakers. The port of Danzig, which Poland claimed on strategic grounds but which was overwhelmingly German-speaking, was made a Free City, its autonomous status guaranteed by the new League of Nations, but its foreign relations and its customs regime administered by Poland. In addition the German-speaking city of Memel (Klaipėda) was handed over to Lithuania, as the only serviceable port for this new state. Three areas, where the German-speaking population was intermixed with Polish speakers, were made the subjects of an unprecedented procedure, in deference to the principle of national self-determination: it was proposed that plebiscites should be held in Upper Silesia and the areas around Marienwerder and Allenstein in southern East Prussia. In the case of the latter two, the inhabitants voted overwhelmingly to remain in Germany; in the Upper Silesian plebiscite, held under League of Nations auspices in 1921 they divided more or less evenly between the two countries, with a regional autonomy on both sides. Most controversially, the German-speaking areas of Bohemia and Moravia, collectively if erroneously referred to as the Sudetenland, were assigned on strategic as well as economic grounds to Czechoslovakia; and Germany was expressly forbidden by the treaty to effect political union, or *Anschluß*, with the new Austrian Republic, which was also almost entirely ethnic German in population.

No aspect of the Paris peace settlement, with the possible exception of reparations, was so controversial as this obvious denial of the right of self-determination to ethnic Germans. To some extent the territorial cessions to Poland and Czechoslovakia were strategic; both states were seen by the Allies as potential counterweights to any resurgence in German power, as well as useful bulwarks against the threat of communism from Russia. Apart from the equally undeniable fact that most of the area ceded to Poland was inhabited by Poles, however, it is worth pointing out, firstly, that the Sudetenland and Austria were not 'lost' by Germany, since, despite their historic inclusion in the Holy Roman Empire, they had never belonged to the German nation-state created in 1871. Secondly, after four years of war to defeat Germany, none of the Allies was inclined to reward it with extra territory and resources, as well as a population increase, in the Sudetenland and Austria, of some eleven million people. A great deal of the problem with Versailles was a matter of perception. Another reason why these 'losses' smarted so much among patriotic Germans was that, psychologically, most Germans felt they had won the war in Eastern Europe, at least in so far as this was represented by the Treaty of Brest-Litovsk. Finally, a sense of cultural humiliation also played a role: the cession of territory inhabited by German speakers, and seen as historically German, to states identified with peoples, like the Czechs, Poles and Lithuanians, habitually seen by Germans as culturally inferior, was galling in the extreme. Here was a situation ready-made for exploitation by German nationalists, especially ultra-nationalists like Adolf Hitler.

The Treaty of Saint-Germain was signed by Austria on 10 September 1919. St. Germain, like Versailles, explicitly forbade an Austro-German *Anschluß*, even though the governments of both countries argued for it. Also resented was the treatment of the new, democratic Austrian Republic as legally responsible for a war unleashed by a completely different regime, the old Habsburg Monarchy, a factor which, as with Germany, was held by the Allies to justify the levying of financial reparations. Saint-Germain also formalised Austria's borders with the surrounding successor states and the transfer of territory to Italy, Czechoslovakia, Poland, Romania and Yugoslavia. In one respect Austria actually gained territory on the basis of ethnic composition: the strip of territory known as the Burgenland was ceded by Hungary, but minus the city of Sopron.

Bulgaria was penalised in the Treaty of Neuilly, on 27 November 1919, by the loss of all the territories which it had acquired during the war. In addition it was forced to cede Thrace, which it had held since 1913, to Greece, and with it access to the Aegean Sea. Bulgaria did not suffer the sort of territorial losses inflicted on Hungary, but in all, some one million Bulgarian-speakers were left outside the Bulgarian state, most of them in Yugoslavia and Greece. This ensured, if nothing else, that the 'Macedonian question' would continue to poison relations between these Balkan states for the next twenty years, with literally deadly consequences.

As far as Hungary was concerned, a definitive peace settlement was delayed by the interlude of the Hungarian Soviet Republic and the subsequent internal turmoil in Hungary. The Treaty of Trianon, when it was signed on 4 June 1920, created the most embittered society in Europe after Germany. By the treaty's provisions Hungary lost two-thirds of its pre-1918 territory, excluding Croatia, and about two-fifths of its pre-war population. Although most of the people thus transferred to Romanian, Yugoslav and Czechoslovakian rule were undoubtedly ethnic Romanians, South Slavs and Slovaks, with them went about a third of all ethnic Hungarians or Magyars. In Romania alone, whose takeover of Transylvania was confirmed by Trianon, there were now some 1.3 million Magyar speakers; an estimated 634,000 were stranded in Czechoslovakia, and 382,000 in Yugoslavia. As with the Germans, Hungarians in the interwar period burned with resentment at this dismemberment of historic Hungary. Revision of Trianon became an article of faith with all shades of political opinion, and fatefully influenced Hungary's foreign policy.

Finally, the Treaty of Sèvres was concluded with the Ottoman Empire on 10 August 1920. This assigned eastern Thrace to Greece, as well as confirming the provisional occupation by Greece of the region around Smyrna on the Anatolian coast. Like much of the Levant, Smyrna and its hinterland had been Greek-inhabited since antiquity, and the city had a larger Greek population than Athens, as well as a sizeable Armenian quarter. Nevertheless the fact that it was also inhabited by ethnic Turks, and was seen by Turks as an integral part of their own heartland, the Anatolian Peninsula, was the trigger for a Turkish nationalist backlash; this was intensified by the initial perpetration of atrocities against the Turkish population when the Greeks first occupied Smyrna. Although the government of Sultan Mehmet VI had little choice but to sign the treaty, a substantial body of opinion, especially in the officer corps of the army, and led by the successful wartime general Mustafa Kemal, favoured resistance to the peace terms. As a result the treaty with the Ottomans was the first part of the Paris peace settlement to unravel.

In the year before Sèvres was signed fighting had already become endemic between the Greek occupation forces and Turkish troops loyal to Kemal, who was acting in defiance of the Ottoman government. By April 1920 a rival nationalist government under Kemal had emerged at Ankara in the Anatolian interior, and it became clear that the sultan in Constantinople was powerless to enforce the terms of the treaty. In response, the royalist-dominated government which came to power in Greece in November 1920 could not resist the temptation to launch an all-out offensive against the Turks in March 1921, in hopes of realising the *Megali Idea*. The result was what Greeks still refer to as 'the catastrophe'. Despite an initial Greek advance almost to Ankara, Mustafa Kemal's forces counter-attacked in August 1922 and pushed the Greeks literally into the sea. Smyrna, in September, became the scene of a panic-stricken evacuation, in which some 30,000 Christians, Greek and Armenian, were massacred, and two and a half millennia of Greek presence in Asia Minor were brought to an end.

The subsequent revision forced on Greece by the new Turkish Republic, in the Treaty of Lausanne on 24 July 1923, re-established Turkish possession of eastern Thrace, a border which has survived to the present day. More significant was Lausanne's provision for the first internationally agreed transfer of national minorities. Some 1.1 million Greeks, with the exception of those living in Istanbul (as Constantinople was now renamed by the Turks), were expelled from Asia Minor alone; an unknown number of people, possibly as many as 500,000, remained unaccounted for and probably perished. Since

Bulgaria and the Soviet Union were joint signatories of Lausanne, an additional 100,000 Greeks were forced out of Bulgaria and Russia. In return, 380,000 ethnic Turks were deported from Greece, including the Greek islands, to Turkey. Many of the Greeks thus forcibly re-settled, from communities some of which stretched back to antiquity, did not even speak Greek; the sole criterion for being classified as Greek was adherence to the Greek Orthodox religion. The absorption of these refugees imposed severe strains on an impoverished Greece for decades to come. Similarly, many of the ethnic Turks transferred, on the basis of their Muslim religion, spoke no Turkish. Lausanne was the first time such a forced population exchange had been internationally ratified, and despite the relatively humane way in which the exchange was effected it can be regarded as setting an ominous precedent for the brutal agendas of the fascist dictatorships, and the even more extensive expulsions which took place in Eastern Europe after 1945, not to mention 'ethnic cleansing' in the former Yugoslavia in the 1990s.

In view of these complications, the Paris peace settlement clearly fell a long way short of the pious aspiration voiced by President Wilson to his fellow peacemakers, in March 1919, that 'We must not give our enemies even an impression of injustice'.[4] Such a platitude was likely to elicit hollow laughter from Germans, Hungarians and others. Yet the settlement also achieved national self-determination and formal statehood for many other East Europeans. The truth was that Eastern Europe was too complex and intermixed a region to be easily boiled down into discrete, ethnically homogeneous nation-states. In addition, as the French prime minister Georges Clemenceau reminded Wilson in reply, 'Some deviations from the principle of self-determination are inevitable, otherwise the principle itself cannot be safeguarded'.[5]

That said, it must be acknowledged that the balance of national self-determination in Eastern Europe was improved by the settlement. It has been calculated that, before the First World War, national minorities made up something like 50 per cent of the population of Eastern Europe; after 1919 this percentage was 25 per cent. In other words more people now lived in a state which they felt 'belonged' to them, even if an estimated 25–30 million were still left as minorities in one state or the other. To what extent this made for harmony was conjectural; it certainly did not take adequately into account the larger number of people who still did not readily fit into a particular national category. The replacement of old nationalist grievances with new ones was guaranteed to bedevil the domestic politics and the international relations of interwar Eastern Europe.

---

[4] Conversation between Wilson, Clemenceau, Lloyd George and Orlando, 27 March 1919, in Adamthwaite, A., 1980, *The Lost Peace: International Relations in Europe 1918-1939*, London, document 3, 24.
[5] Adamthwaite, *The Lost Peace*, 27.

Two factors in theory promised to mitigate the negative consequences of these new grievances. Firstly, virtually all of the new successor states, with the significant exceptions of Hungary and the Soviet Union, started as democratic polities. Whether republics or constitutional monarchies, they all adopted constitutions with universal manhood suffrage and relatively transparent representative mechanisms in place. This vogue for political pluralism owed something to American involvement in the war and the peace settlement: since Wilson had thrown the weight of the United States behind the cause of liberal democracy, the popular response had been unmistakably enthusiastic, despite the rival attractions of communism in Russia, and political leaders were quick to respond to this. And constitutional democracies, it was imagined, would be more mindful of the rights of aggrieved national minorities, as well as issues of social justice.

Secondly, thanks to Wilson's determined sponsorship of the League of Nations, the world's first-ever organisation for mediating international disputes, it was hoped that governments henceforth would be obliged to play by a different rule-book when it came to dealing with national minorities. One harbinger of the new order was the holding of plebiscites to decide the fate of disputed territories. The first plebiscites were held under the supervision of the great powers, but later they were run by the League itself, and they produced some unexpected results. In Upper Silesia, although the majority of the population spoke some form of Polish, while some stubbornly described themselves as 'Silesian', the vote in 1921 nevertheless was in favour of staying in Germany. In Carinthia, the Slovene majority opted in 1920 to stay with Austria rather than join the new Yugoslavia, probably for economic reasons. And a final pillar of the new order was represented by a series of minority rights protection treaties. At the insistence of the great powers, one of these was signed between each of the new states and the great powers in the course of 1919–20. According to each treaty, minorities were guaranteed the exercise of their language, especially with regard to education, legal representation and the like. The minorities were not themselves parties to the treaties, and any grievances they might have about perceived abuse of their rights could only be taken up if a member-state of the League of Nations Council agreed to do so. Despite the limited reach of these treaties the new states, with the exception of Czechoslovakia, signed them only reluctantly, regarding them as an infringement of sovereignty, and thereafter sought to evade compliance, accusing the Western powers of hypocrisy in not granting similar rights to their own minorities. Evasion turned out to be all too easy, since neither the treaties nor the League of Nations charter made any provision for the enforcement of minority rights. Here was a potent mix for future trouble.

PART II
Pig in the middle

4

Problems of the interwar period

Despite the suffering of the First World War, the new order fashioned in Eastern Europe seemed to offer a better future. The political order established in almost every state across the region was taken by many to represent the triumph of liberal democracy, and an at least partial realisation of the principle of national self-determination. Country after country adopted a constitution with universal manhood suffrage or something close to it; mass-based political parties arose, competing in free elections; and the guarantee of minority rights offered by the League of Nations would, it was hoped, iron out any remaining wrinkles in the smooth functioning of these pluralist polities. The successor states of Eastern Europe seemed to embody the assumption underlying so much progressive political thinking of the nineteenth century about 'the nexus between nationalism and democracy'.[1] The political twins, liberalism and nationalism, walked hand in hand, and this region of democratic 'nation-states' represented a liberation from centuries of misgovernment by multinational empires, as well as an alternative to the siren call of revolutionary communism.

In reality, this sense of triumph was illusory, and liberal democracy in Eastern Europe, as in the rest of the continent, did not last very long. The new states suffered from multiple problems, domestic and external, economic as well as political. Politics in Eastern Europe turned out to be exceptionally fractious and unconstructive, and in some countries was punctuated by flashes of horrifying violence. Extremist revolutionary movements, from both left and right, threatened the existing political order, and demonstrated that liberal democracy had effective ideological competition. The result was that, before a decade was out, several countries had slid into dictatorship or some form of authoritarian rule, and this trend continued into the 1930s. Eastern Europe was not unique in this respect. On the contrary, the failure of liberal democracy was a general phenomenon of interwar Europe; but the region was especially liable to succumb to authoritarianism because of its proximity to the communist Soviet Union. The coming to power of the National Socialist Party in Germany in 1933 only accelerated an already existing trend. Eastern Europe in the 1930s was caught between the two millstones of communism and Nazism, and in this bleak situation liberal democracy's chances of survival were slim. It should be stressed, however, that the competition to undermine democracy was not

---

[1] Okey, R., 1982, *Eastern Europe 1740-1980: From Feudalism to Communism*, London, 157.

simply an opposition between communism and fascism. Fascist movements in Eastern Europe, as elsewhere, were not the sole alternative on the right, and indeed never attained power anywhere in Eastern Europe before the Second World War. The real opposition to liberal democracy, on the right, was rather from what can be called conservative authoritarianism.

This chapter looks at the reasons for the failure of liberal democracy in Eastern Europe in this period. The initial democratic promise of the early post-war years will be treated first. As suggested, the reasons for the turn towards authoritarian or non-democratic rule were indigenous as well as external. There were economic factors at work, as well as problems with what might be called political culture. And the fact that most of the East European states were in fact multinational, rather than genuine nation-states inhabited by one ethnicity, played a special role in making the exercise of pluralist politics exceptionally difficult.

The story suggests parallels with more recent developments. After the revolutions of 1989, it was assumed for some time that liberal democracy had made a decisive comeback in Eastern Europe, and that the exercise of democratic rights, the introduction of market economies, and East European societies' integration into wider international communities like the European Union would be irreversible. Three decades later, however, the external threat from a resurgent and non-democratic Russia seems to be mounting, and democracy itself seems in peril in several countries. As in the interwar period, celebrating the triumph of liberal democracy might be premature.

The false dawn of liberal democracy

Constitutional government was no novelty in Eastern Europe, since by 1914 every state in the region, even Russia, was a constitutional monarchy. Apart from the fact of constitutionality, however, the situation had varied widely. The problem was in the nature of representative institutions, and the extent to which legislatures were able to restrain the actions of monarchs and their ministers, if at all. Some countries might be described as constitutional, but not parliamentary, in that the monarch appointed the government, and ministers, who were primarily responsible to the monarch, were not members of the legislature, even though the latter's consent was also required for the passing of laws. This described the situation in the German Empire (including the kingdom of Prussia), the Austrian half of the Habsburg Monarchy, Bulgaria and Russia.

In other countries the relationship between crown and legislature approached the parliamentary, in that ministers were appointed by the monarch, but responsible to both him and the legislature, of which ministers were also members, effectively requiring them to command a parliamentary majority. This in theory was the situation in the Hungarian half of the Habsburg Monarchy, Serbia, Romania and Greece. The catch in all cases was in the extent and nature of the suffrage by which the legislature was elected, and the way in which the electoral process was manipulated. Elections to the German federal Reichstag, the Austrian Reichsrat, and the national assemblies of Russia, Bulgaria and Greece was by universal manhood suffrage; in Prussia, Serbia, Romania and Hungary it was restricted according to tax paid (and in Romania according to literacy), which limited the electorate substantially. In addition, elections in Romania, Hungary, Bulgaria and Greece were notorious for corruption and violence. Montenegro was in a class of its own: the constitution of 1905 left real power to the monarch, and provided for an assembly partly elected by open vote, and partly appointed by the monarch. In short, constitutionality and liberal democracy were two quite separate things.

ditto
Russia

By the end of the First World War, however, the stock of liberal democracy had risen appreciably, and political leaders across Eastern Europe were anxious to demonstrate their adherence to liberal democratic values. This had much to do with the clarion call issued by President Wilson, who so confidently asserted that democracy was the only way to control the actions of monarchs and elites and thus ensure international harmony, and whose Fourteen Points, with their implicit equation of democracy with national self-determination, endorsed the aspirations of nationalists generally. America's military and financial clout at the end of the war was such that allies and enemies alike felt they must pay at least lip service to Wilsonian ideals. We should not, however, conclude that this wholesale conversion to liberal democratic values was invariably for show. The nationalist takeovers in many states at the end of the war commanded undoubted popular support. Several revolutions, as in Germany, Austria and Hungary, brought left-wing but democratically minded parties to power; and there was a sense, however illusory, of popular control and a break with the old order. Leaders like Thomas Masaryk in Czechoslovakia and Mihály Károlyi in Hungary sincerely hoped to follow democratic models, precisely because they felt that communism, the alternative ideology after 1917, was likely to prove the reverse of democratic, for all its talk of proletarian control.

With few exceptions, then, the constitutional arrangements reached in East European countries in the immediate post-war period were, on paper, models of democracy, whether monarchical or republican. Germany, Austria, Finland, Estonia, Latvia, Lithuania, Poland, Czechoslovakia and Albania were all republics; Hungary started as a republic in 1918–19, but under the Horthy reaction reverted to monarchy, albeit without a king. Romania, Greece, Bulgaria, Italy and Yugoslavia remained monarchies, the latter by prior agreement under Serbia's Karađorđević dynasty. The constitution of what, in Russia in 1922, became the Union of Soviet Socialist Republics (USSR or Soviet Union), represented a special case. Although the Communist Party exerted an iron dictatorship over the entire Soviet Union, the federal structure adopted was an explicit acknowledgement of the existence of nationalities, and with time the mere existence of the Soviet Socialist Republics of the Ukraine and Belarus, for example, helped to reinforce a sense of national identity, and in some cases to create one where it had hardly existed before.

The crucial ingredient in how genuinely democratic polities in Eastern Europe functioned was the suffrage and how it was exercised, because a broad, secret suffrage made mass-based political parties possible, in some East European societies for the first time. In this respect the initial facts were promising. Germany, Austria, Czechoslovakia, Poland, Finland and the three Baltic states led by adopting universal adult suffrage; in other words women as well as men received the vote. This represented a major social as well as political change, especially in the former kingdom of Prussia, where the three-class suffrage had severely limited the electorate down to 1918. In all these countries, too, voting was by proportional representation, which meant that the composition of national assemblies was bound to reflect the diversity of political opinion in the electorate fairly accurately. In the Balkan countries the enfranchisement of women was a step too far; but Romania, Yugoslavia, Bulgaria and Greece all nevertheless adopted or retained universal manhood suffrage, usually for those aged twenty-one or over, and in most cases with voting by secret ballot in a system of proportional representation. Even Romania went from a highly restrictive, indirect suffrage, based on tax-paying capacity and literacy, to this new norm, although it is worth noting that the Romanian constitution of 1923 also copied an electoral innovation from Italy's Acerbo Law of 1922, whereby the party winning the most votes in an election was automatically awarded half the seats in the legislature, with the other half apportioned according to the popular vote; designed to avoid weak government, this became an excuse for electoral manipulation and was termed 'mimic democracy'.[2]

Three countries stood out as exceptions to this general democratisation. In Hungary things literally went backward: in 1922 the universal manhood suffrage introduced by the first republic was abolished, and the restricted franchise of 1913 was restored, with open balloting in rural constituencies. This ensured that interwar Hungary remained dominated by the landowning nobility and the upper middle class, although paradoxically women aged thirty or over were enfranchised after 1920. In Albania elections to the national assembly were supposed to be by direct, secret ballot, but conditions remained so lawless and chaotic that the first general election was not held until April 1921, by which point the country was firmly under Italian influence. In the Soviet Union, where the Communist Party was the sole political party permitted after March 1921, it would be more accurate to speak of anti-democratisation.

[2] Crampton, R.J., 1997, *Eastern Europe in the Twentieth Century – and After*, 2nd edn, London, 110–11.

The central committee of the party controlled the entire apparatus of state, and in 1919 this took administrative form in the political bureau or politburo. Each politburo member controlled a specific ministry, and even within the party election of officials gradually ceased. Only in the realm of nationalities policy, as we shall see, did something like an independent decision-making process evolve, although this did not last beyond the 1920s.

With the exception of the USSR, the most obvious consequence of constitutional government, expanded suffrage and relatively free elections was a proliferation of mass-based political parties. Down to the First World War politics had largely been the preserve of the upper and middle classes, with parties representing the peasant masses and the industrial working class few in number; only in the German Empire at federal level, the Austrian half of the Habsburg Monarchy after 1907, and in Serbia and Bulgaria, were mass-based parties possible. Now, for the first time, in some countries, million-strong 'populist' or peasant-based movements sprang up or, where they already existed in embryo, exploded in membership and voter share. Social democratic and even communist parties emerged, although due to the prevailing fear of communism most of the latter were soon banned. Thus the Croatian People's Peasant Party, under the franchise obtaining in pre-war Hungary, never won more than three parliamentary seats in the Croatian diet, out of eighty-eight, despite having a membership by 1914 of 10–15,000. In post-war Yugoslavia, with universal manhood suffrage, the Croatian Republican Peasant Party, as it was initially called, swept the board; by 1923 it was the biggest single party representing Croats, with well over a million members and about 80 per cent of the Croat popular vote, and was the second biggest faction in the Yugoslav parliament, with seventy seats out of 311.

Similarly, in Romania the Peasant Party, founded in 1918, immediately emerged as the dominant voice of the rural masses, triumphing in the relatively uncontrolled elections of late 1919 and briefly taking office in coalition with the Transylvanian Nationalist Party. Dismissed by King Ferdinand in March 1920 at the urging of the landowning class and the parties of the traditional elite, the Peasant Party merged with the Transylvanian Nationalists in 1926 to form the National Peasant Party, but remained frozen out of power until after the king's death in 1927. By late 1928, however, it was becoming impossible to ignore the genuine mass support for the NPP, and when it was finally entrusted by a weak regency with power again, under Iuliu Maniu, it took an overwhelming 78 per cent of the popular vote in the elections of December 1928. Had it not been for the residual powers wielded by the crown, which enabled King Carol II to dismiss Maniu's government in 1930, the NPP would have governed uninterrupted throughout this period.

In Bulgaria the Bulgarian Agrarian National Union, denied effective representation before the war, was a political force to be reckoned with after it. In the elections of August 1919 BANU won 31 per cent of the vote, with its main rival the newly formed Bulgarian Communist Party, another beneficiary of universal manhood suffrage, with 28 per cent. Under a reasonably open electoral system, BANU under Alexander Stamboliski governed until 1923; what brought Stamboliski down, and led to his gruesome death following a military *coup d'état*, was not his lack of mass support but the poisonous cocktail of adverse factors militating against democratic government in Bulgaria in the first place.

Peasantist parties like BANU, or the Croatian and Romanian peasant parties, did not just represent peasants. They tended to be strongly nationalist, and indeed to identify their peasant constituents as embodying the nation itself, 'rooted' in the soil and unpolluted by modernity and the cosmopolitanism of the city. One peasantist leader, for instance, proudly claimed that he had never set foot in a café. Yet the appeal to national values, often accompanied by overt racism or anti-Semitism, meant that peasantist parties had a potential reach beyond the peasant masses, and were capable of allying with urban-based parties. Peasantist parties were also strongly religious, again seeing themselves as defenders of the traditional moral values represented by the national church. In the case of the Slovak People's Party, the leadership itself consisted of Catholic clerics, first the founder Father Andrej Hlinka, and then his successor Monsignor Jozef Tiso.

In principle, Eastern Europe's new democracies should also have benefited from free elections conducted fairly and without undue pressure brought to bear on voters by special interests. In reality, the difficulties experienced by mass-based parties, like the National Peasants in Romania, or BANU, reflected the extent to which traditional institutions and elites continued to fear political pluralism. This affected the details of constitution-making right at the start of the interwar period. The powers exercised by monarchs like Ferdinand of Romania, Alexander of Yugoslavia and Boris III of Bulgaria remained considerable, and reflected a general sense that, in an uncertain world, there still needed to be a strong executive authority in case of emergency. As a result the monarchs in Eastern Europe could still appoint and dismiss cabinets at will, a fact which enabled them to deny office, at least for some of the time, to parties with an obvious popular mandate. The formerly dominant parties, representing landowners and the wealthy urban middle classes, were usually the beneficiaries of this monarchical reluctance, since they were still on the scene and proved all too adept at manipulating the electoral system to their own advantage, if given the chance. The military, or rather the officer corps of a country's armed forces, was another factor inimical to democracy, since monarchs or would-be strongmen could usually appeal to it for support. All in all one of the most obvious weaknesses of democracy in Eastern Europe was the manipulability and fragility of the electoral process itself. In the hands of an unscrupulous ruler or ministry, voters could still be intimidated, opponents harassed, results falsified and legitimacy denied. The new mass-based parties themselves compounded the problem by their naïvety and extremism, both in and out of office. Thus, even when Stjepan Radić of the Croatian Peasant Party was taken on as a minister in 1925, having abandoned the formal republicanism which had excluded the CPP from consideration for office, he made himself so obnoxious to his Serb ministerial colleagues, apostrophising them as 'gangsters' and 'swine', that he was out of office again within months.[3] Alexander Stamboliski in power was almost as ruthless and exclusionary as the political opponents who eventually toppled him. Across the region the habits of democratic governance, in particular acceptance of the right to disagree, proved difficult to acquire.

Two factors, linked to the post-war international settlement, supposedly enhanced liberal democracy's credibility and staying power in Eastern Europe, but in practice turned out to be woefully inadequate. The first was the existence of the minority protection treaties imposed on the new states of the region. These were all modelled on the treaty with Poland, signed on 28 June 1919. Once Poland had signed, Romania, Czechoslovakia, Yugoslavia and Greece all followed suit. Austria, Hungary, Bulgaria and the Ottoman Empire had identical treaties incorporated into the peace settlements forced on them; the three Baltic states, not formally recognised in 1919, acceded to the same terms by binding declarations in 1921–2. The Polish treaty stipulated that all citizens of the new state, 'without distinction of birth, nationality, language, race or religion', were entitled to certain basic rights, such as equality before the law, the free private use of their own language, access to justice in the courts in their own language, and private religious and education institutions in their own language. Article 9 of the Polish treaty also, with unhelpful vagueness, required the state to provide primary-level instruction in the minority language in areas where 'a considerable proportion' of the population spoke that language.[4]

Minority rights were guaranteed by the League of Nations; but since the treaty was one between states, the Council of the League could only act on complaints of abuse if a member-state of the League brought this up. The treaty was notably vague as to what action the League might take in order to uphold a minority's complaint.

The minority protection treaties represented notional protection for the estimated twenty to twenty-five million East Europeans who, after 1918, found themselves living in a state dominated by a nationality which was not their own. Unfortunately this system laboured under two defects. Firstly, the treaties were signed under bitter protest from all the new nation-states, whether victors or vanquished in the late war. The new states resented the fact such treaties

[3] Biondich, M., 2000, *Stjepan Radić, the Croatian Peasant Party and the Politics of Mass Mobilization 1904-1928*, Toronto, Buffalo, NY and London, 208–19.
[4] 'The Polish Minority Treaty', in Macartney, C.A., 1968 [1934], *National States and National Minorities*, New York, App. I, 511, 513.

were imposed only on them: the great powers made it clear that they saw no need to accept similar protection rights for their own minorities, or for colonial peoples living under their rule. Moreover, all of the new successor states saw themselves as 'national' states, regardless of the clear demographic evidence that almost all of them were multinational in composition. Thus, to sign such a treaty was an implicit denial of each state's self-image and an affront to its national pride. As a consequence, virtually none of the successor states, with the exception of Czechoslovakia, took its obligations towards minorities seriously, and most of them did everything they could to avoid compliance. Secondly, the treaties contained no obvious mechanism for enforcing minority rights in cases of abuse. A minority could petition the League for redress, but any action depended on a League member-state taking up the minority's cause; it also depended on agreement between the states making up the League, and even then the League's own charter was strikingly unclear as to what then should be done about the matter. The result was that the whole concept of minority protection was discredited, while the existence of formal international agreements, guaranteeing rights, ensured that minority grievances remained an issue.

The other factor theoretically underpinning liberal democracy in Eastern Europe was the patronage of the Western democracies themselves, under the benevolent aegis of the League of Nations. To begin with, everyone had high hopes of this Western connection: the big democracies, it was reasoned, would protect the little ones, not only from the revisionist states of Germany, Hungary and Bulgaria, but also from communist Russia. In reality this was a broken reed. The United States, whose president had made liberal democracy and national self-determination the pillars of his peace policy, in the end did not even guarantee the peace settlement: due to Wilson's political ineptitude, as well as a still strong public antipathy to involvement in European affairs, Congress never ratified the Treaty of Versailles, nor did the United States join the League of Nations, Wilson's especial project. As a result the most powerful victor state had no formal stake in upholding the new order, in Western or in Eastern Europe. Instead, France and Britain were left as the only two major powers committed to enforcing the Paris peace, as well as upholding democratic values; yet in the post-war period these two great powers did not agree on much. France accordingly assumed the role of enforcer of Versailles, but also that of protector of East European democracy. In reality this was more about France's security than Eastern Europe's. The defensive alliance system known as the 'Little Entente', a condominium of Czechoslovakia, Romania and Yugoslavia formed in 1920–1 and in theory overseen by France, was designed to reassure the signatories against Hungarian revisionism, while also acting as a restraint on German aggression, and a bulwark against communist subversion from the Soviet Union. The Little Entente even went so far as to set up a permanent council and secretariat in 1933, and held regular talks on military cooperation. In practice the Little Entente was vitiated from its inception by the non-participation of Poland, which had an outstanding border dispute with Czechoslovakia over Teschen (Pol: Cieszyn; Cz: Těšín). It was also no proof against the revival of Germany under Hitler, and after 1933 it became painfully obvious that France's guarantee of its allies' security was worth very little. The whole edifice rested on a paradox: while the East European states believed France would protect them, the French government saw the arrangement as a means of ensuring its own security against Germany.

The decline and fall of liberal democracy in Eastern Europe

Despite the seeming triumph of liberal democratic institutions and values in the immediate post-war period, their weak roots soon became apparent. The basic chronology of democratic breakdown can be rehearsed briefly.

Hungary, as we have seen, never recovered from the episode of the Soviet Republic, in that from 1919 Horthy's regency, while in form a parliamentary system with a cabinet answerable to both the regent and the representative assembly, was in fact an oligarchy, the restrictive electoral rules of which ensured the dominance of the landed nobility and the wealthy.

In Romania a combination of the king's power of appointing cabinets and the tradition of electoral manipulation, aided by the electoral law of 1923, which rewarded the majority party with extra seats, made democratic politics a sickly growth from the start. With the brief exception of the National Peasant Party government of 1928–30, politics in Romania remained dominated by the parties of the traditional elites who, in turn, were blatantly manipulated by King Carol II after his return to the throne in 1930. It was not until 1938 that Carol openly suspended the constitution and governed by royal dictatorship, only to be supplanted in 1940 by the military dictatorship of General Ion Antonescu.

Greece emerged from the turmoil of its war with Turkey in 1922 under a revolutionary committee which abolished the monarchy in 1924, before being shouldered aside by a military dictatorship the same year; another military coup restored democratic politics in 1926, and even held the first general election using a system of proportional representation. This did not, however, hinder subsequent governments, starting with that of the veteran nationalist Eleftherios Venizelos, from implementing the same sort of electoral manipulation as in Romania, whereby the party which won the largest share of the popular vote then awarded itself an overwhelming majority of the seats in parliament. The impact of the Depression made this shaky system shakier still. In 1933 Venizelos lost power to the People's Party of Panayis Tsaldaris; but Venizelos' supporters, unable to accept this result, launched two unsuccessful coups in 1933 and 1935. Although the People's Party entrenched itself in power by holding elections in 1935 under martial law, which gave it a supermajority, this was not enough to prevent a growing royalist reaction. In October yet another military coup abolished the republic, and held a rigged referendum on the restoration of the monarchy; King George II duly returned to Greece in 1935, but was happy to appoint General Ioannis Metaxas in April 1936 as effective military strongman.

Albania's politics was exceptionally faction-ridden and violent. Following contested elections in 1923 Prime Minister Ahmed Zogu was lucky to survive an assassination attempt in February 1924, and a dramatic shoot-out between his supporters and the would-be assassin in the parliament building itself. Zogu was then ousted in June 1924 by his arch-rival, Bishop Fan Noli, only to storm back to power in December 1924. In 1928 he eventually dispensed with the pretence of parliamentary politics and had himself crowned King Zog I, before being driven out in 1939 by the Italian takeover of the entire country.

On the periphery but still exercising an important role in Eastern Europe, Italy lurched towards authoritarianism in October 1922 with the appointment as prime minister of Benito Mussolini, leader of the Italian Fascist Party. It was not until 1925 that, with the acquiescence of King Victor Emanuele III, the instruments of a full fascist dictatorship were put in place, but thereafter Italy played a malign role in the region, both as the aspiring regional hegemon but also, and in some respects more significantly, as a model for subsequent authoritarian takeovers in Eastern Europe.

Lithuania and, more seriously, Poland both succumbed to authoritarian rule in 1926, as will be discussed in Chapter 6.

After a decade of parliamentary squabbling in the Kingdom of Serbs, Croats and Slovenes, largely rooted in the non-federal structure of the country and the resulting discontent of national minorities, matters came to a head in June 1928, when a Montenegrin deputy fatally wounded the Croatian Peasant Party leader Stjepan Radić, on the floor of the national assembly. In response, King Alexander suspended the constitution and proclaimed a royal dictatorship in January 1929. Only on Alexander's assassination, in 1934, was something like free parliamentary politics allowed to resume.

In the 1930s, following the Nazis' assumption of power in Germany and in an atmosphere of increased fear of both Germany and Soviet Russia, the trend towards authoritarian rule increased.

Bulgaria, which had already seen Stamboliski's government toppled in a violent coup in 1923, finally saw the imposition of a formal dictatorship by Boris III in 1934. In the same year Estonia and Latvia were taken over by right-wing, authoritarian regimes In Austria the Christian Social chancellor Engelbert Dollfuß suspended the constitution in June 1934, and proclaimed a so-called *Ständestaat* or corporatist state where, instead of an elected parliament, appointed bodies based on occupation would advise government; this regime, sometimes referred to as 'Austro-fascist' or 'clerico-fascist', reflecting its links with the Catholic Church, survived down to annexation by Hitler in 1938. Only in Finland and Czechoslovakia did liberal democracy survive, and in the latter only until the end of the 1930s. In Finland, despite the bitterness of the civil war of 1918, left and right learned to live with one another, and coalition governments remained the norm. Czechoslovakia overcame divisions between Czechs and Slovaks and, more famously, the discontent of its national minorities of Germans, Hungarians and Ruthenes to function throughout the interwar period as a democracy, even if the nationalism of Slovaks was never wholly appeased.

Why this striking retreat of liberal democracy? While bearing in mind that the collapse was hardly confined to Eastern Europe in this period – by the outbreak of the Second World War democracy in Western Europe was confined to eight countries in Western Europe and Scandinavia – the handicaps under which East European societies laboured were arguably greater. These handicaps were both internal, in the sense of being peculiar to the region, and external, being the product of geopolitical forces beyond East Europeans' control. The internal problems can be summarised broadly as socio-economic, political and national in nature.

Internal factors

In socio-economic terms most of Eastern Europe started the post-war period profoundly disadvantaged. These were weak, still largely agrarian economies, and with the exception of the Soviet Union, where the landowning and middle classes vanished almost overnight, the class divisions characterising Eastern Europe before the First World War had hardly gone away. Hungary, Poland and Romania remained societies where the nobility owned a disproportionate share of the arable land, and although mass peasant enfranchisement meant that land redistribution in some form or other was very much on the political agenda, in Hungary and Romania in particular large numbers of landless agricultural labourers continued to live in grinding poverty; Gyula Illyés's *People of the Puszta* (1936) describes conditions in the Hungarian plains referred to with some justice as 'feudal'. In several of the successor states, for instance in the Baltic states, in the Slovak part of Czechoslovakia, in parts of northern Yugoslavia, and in Romania's newly acquired Transylvania, dispossessing noble landowners of an alien ethnicity, and distributing their estates among the peasantry, proved a popular policy. In Austria, Poland and the Balkan states there was already a sizeable peasant smallholder class, the representation of whose interests was the natural preoccupation of peasantist parties. As a result of the spread of industrialisation the urban middle class was also growing in numbers, particularly in Austria, Czechoslovakia, Hungary

noble

and Poland. So too was the industrial proletariat, whose radicalisation through communism was what the traditional elites and the middle class feared most. Despite industrialisation, however, and with the exceptions of Czechoslovakia and Austria, East European societies remained primary producer economies, dependent on the export of foodstuffs to earn hard currency, and tied like most of the world in this period to the more developed West.

The region's economic backwardness was only compounded by the effect of the First World War and the very creation of the East European successor states. Four years of war caused immense material destruction, the strangulation of normal economic life by blockade and the withering or outright breakdown of economic ties with the rest of the world, shortages of raw materials as well as manpower, and the dislocation of industry forced to retool for wartime production, and then obliged to do the same yet again for peacetime. Then, with the collapse and physical partition of the region's great empires – Russia, Austria-Hungary, the German Empire and the Ottoman Empire – new borders sprang up overnight between a multiplicity of new states. This fact alone acted from the start as a drag on economic life, because the old empires, whatever their faults, had acted as giant free trade zones, with no internal barriers. To give just one example: any goods exported after 1918 from the new Czechoslovakia via the nearest Mediterranean port, Trieste, now had to cross two new sets of customs tariffs, on the Austrian and Italian borders, even before reaching the outside world and any further destination. All across the region similar barriers went up, cutting manufacturers and primary producers alike off from long-established markets as well as suppliers of raw materials, trapping primary produce in its country of origin and, because of the resulting glut on the market, slashing prices. The natural if mistaken reaction of most of the new governments to this situation was to raise tariffs on imported goods, in order to protect what trade and industry they had; the result, however, was a near breakdown in trade across the region. There was an attempt, when the Treaty of Saint-Germain with Austria was drawn up at the Paris peace conference, to preserve some of the economic advantages of the defunct Habsburg Monarchy for the successor states: Article 222 of this treaty specifically permitted Austria to arrange a customs union with Hungary and Czechoslovakia, if all three states agreed to this. None of the states concerned could agree, however, and the opportunity was lost.

There were other obstacles to economic reconstruction and regional trade, physical and non-physical. Poland, for instance, inherited three different types of railway gauge, since it took over territories formerly in Germany, Russia and Austria-Hungary. Currencies became instantly valueless with the disappearance of the former empires. The entire region's traditional money market, the Vienna bourse, fell apart overnight. In the absence of stable currencies and access to credit, governments were tempted to print money, which led to rampant inflation. Most governments also pursued the nationalisation of assets, referred to as 'nostrification' or 'making things ours'. This involved the takeover of government buildings, railways and other assets; but what was a property windfall for the confiscating government was a loss for the former owner government or its successor. The land reforms undertaken in so many countries were an additional source of economic retardation. However essential politically, appropriating large, reasonably efficient estates and parcelling them out among millions of smallholders was economically a mistake, since one of the keys to agricultural efficiency was larger, rather than smaller units, whereas most of the new owners were not capable of the requisite level of capital investment. By the end of the 1920s crop yields and grain exports were down considerably in comparison to the pre-war period; only the three Baltic states bucked this trend by restructuring their agriculture in favour of pig and dairy exports. One of the inevitable results of land redistribution was that, despite gradual industrialisation, the re-allotment of so much land kept large numbers of peasants in the countryside; something like 40 per cent of land was redistributed in Romania, for example, and 25 per cent in Yugoslavia. There was also a steady rise in population throughout the interwar period, which may have been due to the increased availability of land, as well as the fact that the United States, in the 1920s, stopped accepting large numbers of immigrants, thus closing off one of the traditional means of escaping East European rural poverty. This led to an increase in the sub-division of small farms, and the spread of a mere subsistence economy for millions of people. Eastern Europe, it seemed, was stuck in a poverty trap.

In the course of the 1920s, the East European economies recovered to some extent. This was partly due to the natural effort required for reconstruction, and despite the difficulties of access to foreign capital. Loans on the international money market, not just in Europe but increasingly, of necessity, on Wall Street in the United States, eventually became available; one of the economic turning points for Austria, for instance, was Chancellor Ignaz Seipel's success in persuading foreign governments to sanction a major loan in 1922, in return for greater fiscal discipline by the Austrian government, such as not simply printing money to pay its way. By the mid-1920s, currencies had been stabilised in most countries. Trade gradually revived, as manufacturers and producers reconnected with old markets or found new ones, and a series of bilateral commercial treaties brought tariffs down. By 1926, it was estimated that production across the region was back to its pre-war level, and in the countryside there was a modest degree of capitalisation taking place, resulting in greater efficiency. This was partly due to the spread of the cooperative movement, which proved popular and provided much of the capital small producers needed to survive as well as to market their produce. Overall prospects, if not exactly rosy, were looking up.

Then disaster struck, in the form of the Great Depression, a catastrophe originating entirely outside the region. The Wall Street crash of October

1929 took some time to affect Central and Eastern Europe, in terms of the impact on the banking and credit system; Weimar Germany's great crisis, for instance, began with the failure of Austria's leading bank, the *Creditanstalt*, in the spring of 1931. But the banking crisis was preceded by a marked slump in agricultural prices worldwide, beginning in 1928 and caused by an exceptionally large global harvest; this affected the economies of Eastern Europe disproportionately. The greatest blow, however, came from 1931 on, through the calling in of foreign loans. Throughout the 1920s East European governments, businesses and landowners had incurred rising levels of debt, which made the entire region dangerously vulnerable to any sudden downturn in the global markets. Most of this debt was owed to American banks, and when these failed, ripples were felt around the world, bankrupting not only landowners and businesses, but governments as well. There was an immediate slump in incomes and industrial production: agricultural income in Poland, for example, went down by 50 per cent; industrial output in Czechoslovakia, the most advanced economy in the region, shrank by 40 per cent. Trade shrivelled up, with exports across the region down by three-fifths, and by 1935 estimated to be a sixth of the 1913 level. Unemployment soared: in Czechoslovakia over 16 per cent of the workforce was out of work at one point, with the German-inhabited Sudetenland accounting for half the unemployed in the entire country; this had ominous implications for the political affiliations of this already aggrieved minority. In response to the slump in trade, countries scurried to set up protective tariffs again. Czechoslovakia, which had better trading prospects than most, found itself forced to abrogate its trade treaty with Hungary, with the effect of denying Hungarian grain producers one of their most important markets.

As in the rest of Europe in the interwar period, not to mention our own day, the political effect of this economic tailspin on already weak economies was dire. Most notoriously, Germans under the shadow of the Depression reached for political extremes: in the elections of 1930 and 1932 a large number of voters concluded that the evils of capitalism had been conclusively proven, and turned leftwards to the German Communist Party; an even larger share of the electorate stampeded rightwards into the arms of Hitler's National Socialists, and by January 1933 the sense of near-insoluble crisis, and the perceived threat of a communist revolution, induced president Paul von Hindenburg to appoint Hitler chancellor. Elsewhere in Central and Eastern Europe the already discernible trend towards conservative authoritarianism, as well as the appeal of radical nationalist or fascist movements, was on the rise. More than any other single factor, the desperate economic state of the region was a principal reason for the failure of liberal democracy in this period.

There were also peculiarly political reasons for the slide into authoritarianism and even fascism. Again, these reasons were hardly unique to East European societies; indeed, what might be called the malaise of liberal democracy was a general European phenomenon, and had its origins in the relative novelty of mass democracy itself. Among the traditional elites and intellectuals everywhere there was a revulsion building up against the 'mass society' resulting from nineteenth-century industrialisation. Mass education, a mass press, mass political participation: all were deemed by some to lower cultural levels, impair political decision-making and degrade society as a whole. Even before the First World War there were calls to backtrack from ever-widening democratisation; what mass societies really needed, according to political philosophers like the German Carl Schmitt, was not personal freedom but authority and order. The mass hatreds unleashed by the First World War, and above all the spectre of the Russian Revolution, deepened this anti-democratic unease: societies facing the existential threat of communism, it was argued, could not afford to dissipate their energies in parliamentary squabbling. Democracy, with what Benito Mussolini called its 'spirit of collective irresponsibility', imperilled the unity and hence the very existence of the nation.[5]

In addition to these general European obstacles to political pluralism were others more peculiar to Central as well as Eastern Europe. Germany's Weimar Republic, above all, laboured from its birth under a perception that liberal democracy had been somehow imposed on a defeated Germany by the victorious Allies, and that this Western implant was alien to German political culture. This view of democracy as a victors' club was only reinforced by Germany's exclusion from the League of Nations until 1926. Hungarians, accustomed as they were to think of themselves as boasting a constitution of comparable antiquity to Britain's, were equally resentful at being treated as one of the parties 'guilty' of the First World War, and this resentment did little to recommend the Western model, even in a Hungary now shorn of national minorities. The minority protection treaties, as seen, were much resented, because imposed in the name of democratic accountability on the East European successor states alone, by great powers who admitted no such restrictions on their own sovereignty; the whiff of hypocrisy was heightened by the survival, and indeed expansion of the British and French colonial empires. Finally, the existence after 1917 of communism as an alternative, rival ideology offered a standing critique of liberal democracy as a species of con job, perpetrated on the working class by capitalists and the bourgeoisie; and the proliferation of communist parties across the region, whether banned or not, was testimony to the potential appeal of this critique, especially under the impact of the Depression. Political pluralism was under fire from both right and left.

There was clearly a problem with the political culture of East European societies in the interwar period. Apart from the Soviet Union, where liberal

---

[5] Quoted in Mazower, M., 1998, *Dark Continent: Europe's Twentieth Century*, London, 14.

democracy was unthinkable, most East European governments proved all too ready, and without resorting to dictatorship, to engage in electoral corruption and intimidation, to place difficulties in the way of legitimate opposition, and to view opposition itself as somehow illegitimate. Many East European societies before 1914 had acquired the habit of political pluralism only imperfectly, if at all; and as has often been remarked, democracy, like all habits, has to be learned. Perhaps the problems facing Eastern Europe in this period were simply too many, and too complex, to expect fully functioning democracy to take root. It might even be said that some countries suffered from too much democracy. Poland's system of proportional representation, for example, spawned a bewildering variety of political parties. By 1925 there were ninety-two parties legally registered in Poland, of which only thirty-two actually won seats in the *Sejm*, or national assembly. Between 1920 and 1926 Poland was governed by fourteen separate ministries, all of them coalitions, the composition of which often took weeks or months. Once formed, most governments could effect little in terms of legislation, because of the difficulty of securing agreement, not only of opposition parties, but of coalition partners. Left-wing parties opposed wage control; peasantist parties opposed the regulation of prices, especially of agricultural produce; nationalist parties opposed land redistribution in Poland's eastern provinces, as a threat to Poland's control of them; national minority parties clamoured for greater local autonomy. Marshal Piłsudski's military coup of 1926 was mounted precisely to impose a unity, in the face of external threats, which seemed otherwise unobtainable; and at least initially it appeared that many Poles, tired of endless squabbling, welcomed the coming of a strongman.

The final weakness of liberal democracy in this period could be described as national, because it was rooted in the existence of sizeable minorities in so many new states. The figures are instructive. Despite the general reduction in the numbers of national minorities, most of the successor states were multinational. Minorities made up over 34 per cent of Czechoslovakia's population of 13.6 million in 1921: 23.3 per cent German, 5.5 per cent Magyar, 3.4 per cent Ruthene, as well as Polish and Jewish. Two-thirds, or 65.5 per cent, belonged to a fictional ethnicity which the Czechoslovakian census office stubbornly insisted on calling 'Czechoslovaks'. In so far as can be calculated, this broke down into 17 per cent Slovaks, and about 48 per cent Czechs. The numbers had not shifted much by the time of the 1930 census.

Poland's population of 27 million in 1921 consisted of 69.2 per cent Poles; by 1931 this percentage had shrunk to 68.9 per cent. By contrast in 1921, 14.3 per cent of the population was Ukrainian. In 1921 this included Ruthenes, a new category only introduced in 1930 for political reasons, since counting Ruthenes separately reduced the number of Ukrainians. In addition, 7.8 per cent of the population identified themselves as Jewish, 3.9 per cent as Belorussian, and 3.9 per cent as German. Again, figures were not much different in 1930.

A third of Polish citizens either did not consider themselves Poles or were not Polish speakers.

Romania was in a similar position to Poland, in that almost 30 per cent of the post-1918 population consisted of national minorities. Pre-war Romania had also included minorities such as Jews and Bulgarians, but 92 per cent of its people were ethnic Romanian. The post-war kingdom was a kaleidoscope of ethnicities: 71.9 per cent Romanian, 7.9 per cent Magyar, 4.1 per cent German, 4.0 per cent Jewish, 3.1 per cent Ukrainian, 2.3 per cent Russian, 2 per cent Bulgarian – not to mention smaller numbers of Turks, Tatars, Roma and others.

Yugoslavia represented arguably the most complex mix of all. As in Czechoslovakia, Yugoslavia's census policy throughout the interwar period lumped Serbs, Croats, Macedonian Slavs and Bosnian Muslims together as a single, artificial ethnicity, 'Serbocroat'; this not only occluded the separate cultural identities of Serbs and Croats, but flatly ignored the fact that Macedonians spoke a language more akin to Bulgarian. In so far as these ethnicities can be disentangled, it has been estimated that Yugoslavia in 1921 contained 43 per cent Serbs, 23 per cent Croats, 8.5 per cent Slovenes, 6 per cent Bosnian Muslims, 5 per cent Macedonians, 4.2 per cent Germans, 3.9 per cent Magyars, and 3.6 per cent Albanians, not to mention Romanians, Turks, Roma and Slovaks.

In the remainder of the region the intermingling of peoples was not so pronounced, but posed potentially just as great a problem. Finland on gaining independence had a Swedish-speaking minority of over 10 per cent. Estonia in 1922 was 12.4 per cent Russian and 1.7 per cent German; Latvia in 1920, 7.8 per cent Russian, 5.2 per cent Jewish, 3.6 per cent German, 3.4 per Belorussian and 1.2 per cent Lithuanian; Lithuania about 9 per cent Russian, 7.3 per cent Jewish and 3.2 per cent Polish. Austria's population of 6.5 million in 1919 was overwhelmingly German, including some 220,000 Jews, although the country still harboured some Czechs and Slovenes. Hungary in 1920 was almost as homogeneous, with 89.8 per cent of its population Magyar; there was still, however, a significant ethnic German minority of 7.8 per cent, and Jews, whichever language they spoke, accounted for 6.7 per cent of the population. Bulgaria in 1920 was 83.4 per cent Bulgarian-speaking, but still contained 11.2 per cent Turks, 1.3 per cent Roma and 1 per cent Greeks. Albania's population of 1 million in 1930 was 92 per cent Albanian, although Greeks, Vlachs and Turks made up the rest. Finally, Greece after the catastrophe of 1922 was 'one of the most ethnically homogeneous countries in the Balkans', despite the (disputed) continuation of minorities of Macedonian Slavs, Muslim Turks, Vlachs and Albanians.[6]

---

[6] Clogg, R., 1992, *A Concise History of Greece*, Cambridge and New York, 106.

Tensions, both domestic and international, arose from the multinational composition of the successor states. These were states whose leaders and dominant nationalities for the most part saw themselves as having founded nation-states, and whose constitutions proudly asserted this, speaking, for instance, in the name of 'the Estonian people', or 'the Polish nation', or 'the Czecho-Slovak nation'.[7] The new states' constitutions, moreover, were almost all determinedly centralised and unitary in structure, as if to emphasise the monolithic, national character of the state, with few if any concessions made to the concepts of autonomy or regional identity; the autonomous areas of Carpatho-Ruthenia in Czechoslovakia, Memel in Lithuania, Upper Silesia and the Åland Islands in Finland, were rare exceptions to this rule.

Yet these pretensions were belied by the demographic reality. The result for the dominant nationalities was to prompt something like an identity crisis. Not only did the 'national' character of the state have to be loudly and repeatedly affirmed through ostentatious ceremonial, the creation of new national symbols and the celebration of the 'national' culture and history, but a nagging concern over the security of the nation fuelled authoritarian tendencies on the part of nationalists and conservatives generally. At its worst this fear for the integrity of the nation tipped over into paranoia, which provided a powerful extra ingredient for the cocktail of fears and emotion which swelled the ranks of native fascist movements. Even without the stimulus of a local fascist movement, however, right-wingers needed little excuse to claim that liberal democracy, in such circumstances, was a luxury they could not afford. States also in some cases attempted to alter the demographic balance by resettlement. The Polish government encouraged ethnic Poles to migrate to Galicia and Volhynia to reduce the overwhelmingly Ukrainian population of these provinces. The Serb-dominated Yugoslav government sent Serbs to 'reclaim' Kosovo.

For national minorities, a lively sense of grievance at being stranded in an 'alien' state led to years of sullen resentment, non-cooperation with the authorities, non-participation in the political system and, in some cases, violent resistance. The Sudeten Germans, for instance, at first flatly refused to accept their incorporation into the new Czechoslovakia, proclaiming an independent 'German Bohemia' in October 1918, which lasted all of six weeks. For some time after their takeover by the Prague authorities the Germans in Czechoslovakia boycotted the national parliament in a policy termed 'negativism'. Germans in Poland, the Baltic states, Romania and Yugoslavia were equally hostile to their new states, as were the Magyar minorities in Czechoslovakia, Yugoslavia and Romania. A significant number of Macedonian Slavs, unhappy at being denied union with Bulgaria, joined the Internal Macedonian Revolutionary Organisation (IMRO) and resorted to terrorism, attacking and assassinating

---

[7]   Quoted in Macartney, *National States and National Minorities*, 209.

not only Yugoslav government officials and politicians, but also the leaders of their own 'national' state, Bulgaria. It was IMRO which was responsible for destabilising relations between Bulgaria and Yugoslavia in the immediate post-war period; and after the Bulgarian prime minister Stamboliski had the temerity in 1922 to sign the Convention of Niš with Yugoslavia, promising to limit IMRO's activities, IMRO members kidnapped him, tortured him to death, cut off the hands that had signed the convention, and despatched his head to IMRO headquarters in a biscuit tin. Even supposedly privileged minorities, technically part of the dominant 'nationality', like the Croats in Yugoslavia or the Slovaks in Czechoslovakia, were dissatisfied with the centralised structure of the state and the absence of regional autonomy. The result was a growing sentiment in both the Slovak People's Party and the Croatian Peasant Party in favour of independence.

The presence of national minorities could thus pose a direct threat to the state, and this in itself could be taken as a pretext for dispensing with democratic accountability. In Yugoslavia the rancorous ill will generated among Croats over the lack of meaningful autonomy led to constant vitriolic attacks on the government in the national assembly by the Croatian Peasant Party leader, Stjepan Radić. In June 1928 a Montenegrin Serb deputy responded to these personalities by pulling a revolver out of his pocket and spraying the opposition benches with bullets; Radić's brother died on the spot, and Radić himself some weeks later, prompting King Alexander to suspend the constitution of 1921 and implement a royal dictatorship in 1929. The breakdown of parliamentary government in Yugoslavia led to the formation in 1929 of a Croatian ultra-nationalist terrorist organisation, the *Ustaše* (literally, 'insurgents'), committed to winning outright independence. Five years later King Alexander himself fell victim to an assassin's bullets, when a member of IMRO, with *Ustaše* backing, shot him in the streets of Marseille at the start of a state visit to France. National minority grievances, in short, posed a lethal threat to heads of state themselves. In Poland Ukrainian nationalism, and dissatisfaction with the denial of political rights after the coup of 1926, prompted the formation in Vienna in 1930 of the Organisation of Ukrainian Nationalists (OUN) under Ievhen Konovalets. Terrorist outrages by the OUN in turn deepened the authoritarianism of the Polish dictatorship, which felt obliged to mount a self-defeating 'pacification' campaign against the OUN in 1931.

Political violence could also be perpetrated in the name of the dominant nationality. In December 1922 the newly elected president of the Polish Republic, Gabriel Narutowicz, was elected, in part with the support of representatives of the national minorities in the *Sejm*. Shortly after Narutowicz was assassinated by Eligiusz Niewiadomski, a right-wing nationalist outraged at the idea that minorities should wield such influence in the new Polish 'nation-state'. The rise in 1920s Romania of radical nationalist, anti-Semitic and eventually fascist violence was in direct response to the increased prominence of national minorities, especially Jews, in the 'unified' Romania. Governments from Romania to Poland to Yugoslavia used the existence of nationalist terrorist movements like IMRO, the OUN and the *Ustaše* to restrict civil liberties, suspend constitutions and govern by decree. Liberal democracy, in such conditions, was the loser.

In this dismal picture of liberal democratic failure the two shining exceptions were Finland and Czechoslovakia. The former's ability to remain a functioning democracy seems at first sight all the more surprising, in view of the brief but bitter civil war of 1918. Finland, moreover, also had to cope with a sizeable Swedish-speaking minority, although many of these Swedish speakers were Finns who acquired Swedish to achieve upward mobility, since until independence Swedish was very much the language of the social elite in Finland. Only in the Åland Islands were Swedish speakers monolingual, and the granting of autonomy to these islands defused Swedish nationalism handily. At any rate Finns, despite their century-long subordination to autocratic Russia, were probably better equipped than any other people in the region to make political pluralism work. For centuries before incorporation in Russia in 1809, Finland had belonged to Sweden, and had sent representatives to the Swedish *Riksdag*. Even after 1809 the Grand Duchy had been granted autonomy and a separate constitutional status, and its four-estates *Riksdag* had even legislated universal suffrage in 1906; it was the tsarist regime's efforts to restrict these liberties which provided the most powerful stimulus to Finnish nationalism. In the interwar period the principal political division was between Whites and Reds, but despite or perhaps because of the proximity of the Soviet Union Finland's socialists, apart from splitting into two separate parties, remained a moderate lot. It was the anti-communism of Finnish nationalists, if anything, and especially their covert support for fellow Finns stranded in Soviet Karelia, which threatened to destabilise the country in 1929–30, when the proto-fascist Lapua movement attained a short-lived prominence, beating up left-wingers and talking up the possibility of a dictatorship. In the end, however, the Lapua movement failed to generate widespread support, even after regrouping as a formal political party, the People's Patriotic Movement; nor were potential strongmen like General Mannerheim willing to respond to calls for dictatorship. In short, Finland's survival as a democracy owed much to the essential moderation of both nationalists and socialists; 'the general thrust of Finnish politics was towards inclusivity and solidarity.'[8]

Czechoslovakia presents a more complicated picture: it was beset with national minority problems, suffered seriously from the Depression, and thanks to its comparatively high level of industrialisation possessed one of the

---

[8]   Kirby, D., 2011, 'A Scandinavian Erratic amidst the Ruins of Empire: The Finnish Case 1918-44', in R. Haynes and M. Rady (eds), *In the Shadow of Hitler: Personalities of the Right in Central and Eastern Europe*, London and New York, 149.

largest Communist parties in the region. Yet precisely because Czechoslovakia started its independent existence with a relatively long-established industrial base, and hence had a numerous middle class as well as a sizeable industrial working class, it perhaps benefited from this social diversity, demonstrated greater social cohesion, and was able to translate this into a more consensual political style than elsewhere in Eastern Europe. It probably helped that the former Czech crownlands of the Habsburg Monarchy had experience of constitutional government and a progressive widening of political rights, culminating in the enactment of universal male suffrage in 1907. Several generations of Czech politicians, like the first president, Thomas Masaryk, had grown up in this atmosphere, even if this pre-1914 period had also been notorious for the acerbity of Czech-German nationality disputes. The Slovaks, by contrast, had been second-class subjects of the Kingdom of Hungary, with its more agrarian economy, its restricted suffrage and its denial of adequate political representation to non-Magyars. This may explain the continuing loyalty of so many Slovaks in the interwar period to the ultra-nationalist and politically authoritarian Slovak People's Party. Certainly Slovaks, despite being counted officially as part of the dominant 'Czechoslovak' people, represented part of Czechoslovakia's national minority problem: instead of the federal autonomy they had been led to expect, they found themselves subjected to unitary government from Prague, with insufficient control as they saw it over their own affairs.

It was for its other national minorities, however, that Czechoslovakia became internationally notorious. Sub-Cartpathian Ruthenes, Magyars and above all Sudeten Germans were all unwilling citizens of the new state. Yet even here Czechoslovakia attained a limited success, up to a certain point. In the first few years of independence, Masaryk and his advisers, the so-called *Hrad* (castle) group, tended to assume the role of informal directors of political decision-making. There also evolved an equally informal, but effective, habit of consultation between the five main parties in the national assembly, the *pětka* or group of five. In a system based on proportional representation and unavoidable coalition governments, this system worked well in ironing out differences beforehand. Most interestingly, the cooperation of the national minorities was also achieved for a while. In part this was because the very openness of the system eventually persuaded even the Sudeten Germans that they had something to gain from participation. By the late 1920s governments in which all the main national groups were represented – Czechs, Slovaks and Germans – had become another feature of the political scene.

What upset this developing consensus and cooperation, after 1931, was the impact of the Depression, followed by the rise of Nazism in neighbouring Germany. This is a story best reserved for a subsequent chapter; suffice it to say that the twin impact of economic downturn, which entailed mass unemployment, especially among Sudeten Germans, and Nazism effectively put an end to Czechoslovakian Germans' willingness to accept the Czechoslovak state. A similar effect was discernible among Czechoslovakia's Magyars after 1933: as Nazi Germany's economic and political preponderance became more and more undeniable, the Magyar minority's hopes of deliverance and reunion with the Hungarian state rose. In a climate of rising international tension and nationalist excitation the fact that Czechoslovakia continued to be a functioning democracy, with a respectable record in its dealings with national minorities, counted for nothing. It was a supreme irony that the one East European state, Finland apart, which was still a democracy by 1938 should have been the first to fall victim to fascist aggression.

External factors

The East European successor states' record as liberal democracies was increasingly at the mercy of external factors over which they had no control. The external threat started with what might be called the 'security deficit': the 'provisionality of the East European settlement', in Robin Okey's words, due to the withdrawal of the United States and the weakness of France and Britain.[9] Eastern Europe, in these conditions, constituted a power vacuum, with both Germany and Russia temporarily eclipsed as regional hegemons. The successor states remained economically and militarily weak, divided among themselves and prey to domestic conflicts, not least because of their multinational composition. France's sponsorship of the 'Little Entente', as mentioned, was an inadequate guarantee of regional stability, and hence of domestic harmony. Added to this was an endemic fear of communism, which was all too easily fostered among nationalists and the right, despite the obvious weaknesses of native Communist parties, rooted in the relative scarcity of communists. The turn towards authoritarianism, whether in Poland, or Greece, or Bulgaria, or the Baltic states, was undoubtedly accelerated by this general sense of insecurity.

Added to this was the encouragement set by example. Italy, under Mussolini's fascist dictatorship from 1925, had aspirations to play the role of regional hegemon in the Balkans, as well as in Austria, and Mussolini's open contempt for what he termed the 'deserted temple' of liberal democracy did much to embolden authoritarians elsewhere; Hungary's proto-fascist prime minister from 1932 to 1936, Gyula Gömbös, was an avowed admirer of Mussolini. In the 1920s, however, fascist Italy's foreign policy in Eastern Europe was relatively cautious, and confined itself to temporarily occupying Corfù in 1922, permanently seizing Fiume the same year, and claiming Albania as a sphere

---

[9]   Okey, *Eastern Europe*, 168.

of influence. Mussolini's regime also had a vested interest in destabilising Yugoslavia, and covertly supported the Croatian *Ustaše* after its formation, providing them with a base and training facilities on Italian soil. The Italian government, with the Hungarian, was also complicit in the successful plot between IMRO and the *Ustaše* to assassinate King Alexander.

The decisive blow to the fortunes of liberal democracy in Eastern Europe was dealt by the ascent to power of Hitler's National Socialists in Germany. The Nazi dictatorship almost immediately pushed East European governments towards authoritarian rule, either in emulation of Germany or – in the case of Austria – in self-defence against the possibility of German aggression. To begin with, Hitler was cautious, confining himself in 1933 to leaving the League of Nations and withdrawing from the World Disarmament Conference, both ominous signals. It was not until 1935 that the Nazi regime openly repudiated the restrictions placed on its rearmament by the Treaty of Versailles. Yet, as the Nazi economic recovery gathered pace, in part stimulated by rearmament itself, Germany's natural pull as Eastern Europe's economic hegemon began to assert itself. Economic self-interest, accentuated by the impact of the Depression, impelled the successor states towards increased trade links with Germany; and the Nazi government, anxious to avoid the disaster of the First World War and to secure Eastern Europe in advance as an economic hinterland for its expansionist aims, was eager to respond. This economic preponderance was accelerated by the minimal interest of both Britain and France in intensifying trade links with the region. Hopes of territorial revisionism were additional motives for Hungary and Bulgaria to gravitate towards Germany, and fear of the communist Soviet Union was an equally pressing reason for almost everyone else.

There were multiple reasons for the failure of liberal democracy in Eastern Europe in the interwar period. None of these was inherently overwhelming on its own, but the cumulative effect of all combined was fatal. Economic backwardness, combined with a lack of experience with political pluralism, made the East European democracies fragile to begin with, liable to succumb to internal divisions, especially given the pervasive and understandable fear of communist subversion. Economic depression, however temporary, followed by the rise of a revived Germany and the continued strengthening of the Soviet Union, accelerated the drift towards authoritarianism and dictatorship.

5

Test tube of ideologies

Communism

One of the enduring themes of Eastern Europe's twentieth-century history was the region's fate as a test tube for rival ideologies. Having surveyed the failure of liberal democracy, it remains to examine liberal democracy's principal rivals in the interwar period: communism, conservative authoritarianism and fascism. In addition to being inimical to liberal democracy, these three ideologies were in competition with one another, even if conservative authoritarians and fascists shared some common ground, and could in certain circumstances make common cause.

Of these three ideologies communism has had by far the greatest impact on East European societies, since it was imposed on most of the region after the Second World War. This chapter confines itself to explaining communism's relatively limited role in the interwar period. The spectre of communism was used by the Right to scare the masses, while its modest appeal was rooted in the social conditions of the region, as well as in the fact that it could nowhere be put into practice outside the Soviet Union.

Communism is a radical variant of Marxist socialism, and as the designation of a specific ideological programme the term only became common currency after the Bolshevik revolution of 1917. Socialism, the root ideology from which communism grew, stresses the common human condition and the brotherhood of man, and sees society as a collective, as opposed to a mere aggregate of autonomous individuals. By definition, socialism opposes liberalism, which attaches importance to individual rights and freedoms, including the freedom to pursue one's own economic interests. Socialism also, by definition, opposes the conservative elements in society, which seek to preserve the old order and the privileges of established elites. Finally, socialism at least in theory opposes nationalism, that other ideological product of the nineteenth century, which saw the nation as the most important focus of loyalty.

Like all socialisms, communism is also based on the concepts of equality and sharing. It aims to achieve social equality or classlessness through the confiscation of the means of economic production, the liberation of workers from exploitation by capitalism, and the redistribution of wealth, a vision which still has a powerful resonance with present-day opponents of globalisation and 'neo-liberalism'. Communism was also, in theory, an ideology which had no truck with nationalism. In the eyes of Marxists like Lenin nationalism was

1848 Marx's & Engels' 'Communist Manifesto'!

a 'bourgeois trick', designed to distract the masses from their true socialist interests.[1] Yet paradoxically Russia's communists also supported the principle of national self-determination: having observed the strength of nationalism during the First World War, the Bolshevik regime concluded that it stood a better chance of disarming the nationalism of minorities within the Soviet Union, and weakening the USSR's multinational neighbours, if it acknowledged the fact of nationality, and within the Soviet Union at least granted 'the "forms" of nationhood'.[2] And whereas many socialist movements eventually resigned themselves to working within the political systems in which they found themselves, and became social democrats, committed to achieving socialism by parliamentary means, communism as it evolved in the twentieth century took a more direct and violent route to power. Communists also proved unwilling to relinquish that power once achieved, with disastrous consequences for the societies they controlled.

In the strategy pursued by Lenin's Bolsheviks, the industrial working class or proletariat was key to the success of communism, since it was only through the muscle and mass of a 'proletarian revolution' that power could be seized and retained. In this scenario the peasantry did not figure, since in Lenin's view peasants were innately self-interested and capitalist, even though Lenin was cunning enough to buy the Russian peasants' acquiescence in his 1917 coup by promising them land redistribution. Lenin's peculiar vision was also focused on dictatorship from the start, and in this sense communism as it was implemented in the Soviet Union, under both Lenin and his fearsome successor Joseph Stalin, was not only anti-democratic but thoroughly deserves the epithet 'totalitarian'. Certainly, Soviet communism aimed at a total control of the population through one-party rule, state terror and the fullest possible indoctrination of the Party membership if not the broad mass of the people.

This term 'totalitarianism', popularised by political scientists in the 1950s and often applied to the fascist as well as the communist dictatorships of the twentieth century, fell out of use on the ground that no regime, short of George Orwell's imagined dystopia in *Nineteen Eighty-Four*, can ever achieve total control; the term can also lead unwary students to conflate fascism and communism, since both types of dictatorship practised totalitarian methods. Nevertheless there is a case for rehabilitating the totalitarian label, since the aspiration to absolute control was clearly present. Votaries of communism, no less than of fascism, explicitly voiced their conviction that they alone possessed the answers to the world's problems, exhibiting a black-and-white mindset and a ruthless determination to crush opposition. Where communism differed from fascism was in ideological content. The core value of fascism, as we shall see,

---

[1] Quoted in Martin, T., 2001, *The Affirmative Action Empire: Nations and Nationalism in the Soviet Union 1923-1939*, Ithaca, NY and London, 4.
[2] Martin, *The Affirmative Action Empire*, 2–3.

was intolerant nationalism. Communism, by contrast, and despite its similar methods of repression, remained an ideology committed at least in theory to eliminating social inequality and economic want. Yet the rigidity and fanaticism with which communism's adherents pursued their utopian goal, and their conviction, inherited from Karl Marx himself, that theirs was a truly 'scientific' socialism, because based on a correct understanding of economics and history, was a form of what Gale Stokes memorably called 'hyperrationalism'.[3] Society, the economy, even human nature could be perfected, and those who got in the way of this noble enterprise deserved to be crushed.

In the trajectory of Soviet communism, which became the avatar of East European communism, there should be no doubt that Stalinism evolved out of Leninism. Both the fanatical commitment to the ideology, and the readiness to use state terror to crush opposition, were features of Lenin's regime and were merely amplified over a greater time span under Stalin's. Anyone doubting this should consult Lenin's savage exhortations to 'Hang the bloodsucker kulaks' during the Russian civil war, and his advice to subordinates that 'the more members of the bourgeoisie and clergy we manage to shoot, the better.'[4] Some, sympathetic to the progressive intentions of communism, have suggested that such excesses were the product of civil war and that, had Lenin not died in 1924, communism would eventually have become more benign, that Stalin perverted the whole communist experiment so that it no longer deserved to be considered communism. Such wishful thinkers should examine the evidence.

A word of caution is, however, in order. We now know so much about the horrors of Stalinist Russia – the mass purges, the show trials, the Gulag, the millions of deaths – that the genuine idealism of the communist experiment in the twentieth century is easily overlooked. What François Furet terms 'the universal spell of October' was prepared by the wartime privations and radicalisation of millions of Europeans, including the peasant masses of Eastern Europe.[5] The Bolshevik Revolution then electrified industrial workers, peasants and middle-class intellectuals alike with its promise of a classless, socially just future. Lenin's takeover in 1917 undoubtedly enjoyed mass, if not majority, support initially; later, as the regime battled to survive the civil war, it was still borne up by millions of Red Army volunteers. And in the early years of the Russian Revolution idealistic socialists from around the world migrated to the Soviet Union, eager to help 'build socialism'. The parents of Czechoslovakia's reforming communist leader of 1968, Alexander Dubček, in 1925 took their young family to the deserts of Soviet Tashkent to assist in this

[3]   Stokes, S., 2012, *The Walls Came Tumbling Down: Collapse and Rebirth in Eastern Europe*, 2nd edn, Oxford, 3.
[4]   Lenin to V.V. Kuraev, Ye. B. Bosh, A.E. Minkin, 11 August 1918; Document 24 in Pipes, R. (ed.), 1996, *The Unknown Lenin: From the Secret Archive*, New Haven, CT and London, 50.
[5]   Furet, F., 1999, *The Passing of an Illusion: The Idea of Communism in the Twentieth Century*, trans. Deborah Furet, Chicago, IL and London, 62.

project; as Dubček, who spent his formative years in Soviet Russia, recalled, 'Everything looked simple: a victorious working man's revolution was rising in Russia, the dream of social justice put into practice. Now it was all good souls' task to give that endeavour their support – complete, immediate, and unselfish.'[6]

This idealism and sense of revolutionary opportunity prompted the founding of communist parties around the world in 1917–21, and Eastern Europe was no exception. As we have seen, however, expectations of socialist revolution in Eastern Europe proved unrealistic, as evidenced by the failure of the Spartacist uprising in Berlin in January 1919, of the Hungarian Soviet Republic the same year, and the abortive communist putsch in Bulgaria in 1921. Thereafter East European Communist parties struggled to build up any sort of mass following, not least because governments one after the other banned them outright, and persecuted signs of communist activity relentlessly. Thus, Hungary and Poland both declared communism illegal as early as 1919; Yugoslavia in 1921; Bulgaria, Romania and Estonia in 1924. In Hungary by the 1930s the Communist Party had only some 2,000 members; in Romania the number never exceeded 5,000. Only in Czechoslovakia, with its relatively large industrial workforce, did communism not only remain legal but, initially, flourish, with 350,000 members in 1921. After that its numbers went into a steep decline; but the reasons for this are to be sought in the general handicaps under which communism operated in the region as a whole.

East European communism's weaknesses in this period can be ascribed in part to the political geography of the region, and the peculiarly unfavourable socio-economic conditions, but in part also to the nature of communism itself, and in particular the way in which it was organised and controlled.

Among communism's general disabilities must first of all be counted the overwhelmingly agrarian nature of the region. There was a paradox inherent in this situation, one which Lenin in 1917 had spotted: the sheer poverty and sense of grievance among the rural masses, especially their land hunger, made them potentially a revolutionary force, and it was this force which the Bolsheviks temporarily harnessed with their tactical promise of land redistribution, so contrary to their longer-term goal of collectivisation of agriculture. Lenin singled out the Hungarian Soviet Republic's failure to do the same in 1919, and the subsequent alienation of the peasantry, as the Hungarian Communists' greatest mistake. Communist parties did pick up some support among certain poor tenant farmers, because of communism's advocacy of national self-determination. Thus, in countries where there was still a peasantry of a different nationality to the landowner class, for instance in eastern Poland, with Polish landowners but Ukrainian or Belorussian peasants, or in Transylvania, with Hungarian landowners but Romanian peasants, or in eastern Slovakia, with

---

[6] Dubcek, A., 1993, *Hope Dies Last: The Autobiography of Alexander Dubcek*, edited & translated by Jiri Hochman, London, 10.

Ruthene and Hungarian peasants, Communist parties tended to attract voters where legal, and covert support if illegal. Yet on the face of it peasants made unlikely recruits for communism, and whatever limited appeal the ideology had was further eroded with the onset of Soviet collectivisation in the late 1920s. While little was known, at the time, of the huge scale of death and suffering unleashed in Russia, the fact that collectivisation was happening at all was enough: millions of East European peasants, if they had not sensed this already, could see that communism and peasant interests were mutually exclusive.

Communism also suffered by association with the Soviet Union generally. This negative effect took two forms. Firstly, the Bolshevik Revolution inspired such horror in the minds of conservatives and liberals alike that East European governments were quick to crack down on Communist activity, and needed little excuse to proscribe communist parties. Given that communists aimed to overturn the entire economic, social and political order, governments and elites had every reason for this neuralgic reaction. The result was that East European communists were almost everywhere forced into what George Schöpflin calls the 'ghetto of illegality'.[7] Communists operated furtively, in tightly controlled cells of a few individuals intent on subverting potentially useful organisations like trade unions and other political parties by 'entryism', but whose own rigid discipline and hierarchical command structure did not prevent them being penetrated by police informers. Such conditions bred a conspiratorial, even paranoid mindset; they also encouraged 'a propensity for authoritarianism and contempt for debate and discussion.'[8] Above all, illegality and marginality fostered an inward-looking obsession with doctrinal purity, and perpetual conflict within the movement, hence ensuring that East European communists remained on the fringes and powerless.

The second negative effect of association with the Soviet Union was what has to be called the Sovietisation of East European communism. From a very early stage in the interwar period communist parties were effectively subordinated to the Soviet Party, and this was generally known. The roots of this iron control by Moscow went back to the fiasco of the Hungarian Soviet Republic, which led to the formation of the Communist International, or Comintern, in 1919. Comintern's purpose was to ensure the survival of the Russian Communist regime by imposing the greatest possible uniformity and discipline on foreign communist parties. The fate of the Hungarian Soviet Republic, which in Lenin's view foundered because it failed to follow Moscow's advice, simply reinforced this message. The second Comintern congress in 1920 laid down twenty-one conditions, which had to be fulfilled before a political organisation could call itself communist. Communist parties were to have nothing to do with

[7]   Schöpflin, G., 1993, *Politics in Eastern Europe 1945-1992*, Oxford, 46.
[8]   Schöpflin, *Politics in Eastern Europe*, 47.

social democratic parties and parliamentary politics, except for purposes of revolution. They were to win peasant support, crucial in Eastern Europe, by at least offering land redistribution; Béla Kun's fatal mistake, according to Lenin, had been not to do this. Above all, communist parties were expected to practise 'democratic centralism': all communist parties were to follow the line set by the Comintern, in other words the Soviet Communist Party leadership. This rigid control undoubtedly ensured discipline; but it also helped limit communism's appeal, since it made it impossible for communist parties to identify with the national interest of their respective countries. On the contrary, East European communists were expected to subordinate their own countries' interests to the interests of the Soviet Union, the 'motherland' of socialism.

The disastrous effects of 'democratic centralism' were soon apparent. For some years, into the early 1920s, the Soviet leadership persisted in believing that world revolution was just around the corner and that, fearful of the Soviet Union as the hearth of revolution, 'capitalist' powers were conspiring to attack it. With the twin objects of forestalling attack and fomenting revolution, the Soviet regime was thus capable of commanding futile attempts at revolution like the failed German miners' uprising of 1921. Most catastrophically, in its annoyance at the Bulgarian Communist Party's passivity during the coup which toppled Stambolisky in June 1923, Moscow virtually ordered the Bulgarian Party to stage an uprising in September, despite its complete lack of military training or preparation for a coup. Thanks to government spies the uprising was snuffed out almost as soon as it began, its leaders arrested and martial law imposed; the Tsankov government used the failed uprising as an excuse for its turn towards authoritarianism, banning the Communist Party outright in April 1924, confiscating its property and ejecting its eight MPs from parliament. In response Bulgarian communists resorted to genuine extremism in April 1925, detonating a giant bomb in Sofia's Sveta Nedelya cathedral, which killed 120 people but narrowly missed Tsar Boris III. The predictable result was an orgy of anti-communist repression, during which up to 6,000 people, some entirely innocent, were detained, and many arbitrarily executed; Bulgarian communism's ranks were decimated for a generation, with many of its leaders, like Georgi Dimitrov, surviving only as refugees in the Soviet Union.

Moscow's leaden hand had similar consequences for other East European parties. Not least of their problems was that the Soviet Party kept changing its line, which meant that communist parties everywhere had constantly to follow suit. In 1923, in part because of the Bulgarian fiasco, in part because of the domestic compromise forced on the Soviets themselves by economic reality, which had led to the mixture of socialist control and free market represented by the New Economic Policy (NEP) of 1921, the Soviets decided to recognise the agrarian reality of Eastern Europe, and tried to forge a worker-peasant alliance in the shape of the Peasants' International, or Krestintern. Krestintern was intended to reach out to the peasant masses, by inviting the region's peasantist parties to affiliate with it. This was not a striking success, since most peasantist parties saw the basic antagonism of interests involved. The few that did affiliate briefly with Krestintern, like Radić's Croatian Peasant Party, did so largely for tactical reasons, in the CPP's case to force Yugoslavia's Serb-dominated government to compromise. By the late 1920s Krestintern was dead in the water, effectively abandoned by the Soviets as a strategy. Instead, from 1928 renewed emphasis was put on 'proletarian revolution', with both peasantists and social democrats denounced in equal terms. In 1935, finally awakening to the threat of fascism, Stalin switched to a policy of promoting the so-called popular front, an alliance of communists with other left-leaning parties; but after years of vituperation directed at social democrats and others as 'social fascists', for working within 'capitalist' political systems, this sudden stress on cooperation strained credulity. Finally, in August 1939 Soviet communism performed the most dizzying somersault yet by concluding the Nazi-Soviet Pact; overnight, communists had to justify the unjustifiable, an alliance with Hitler's Germany. This proved a leap of faith too far for some, and across Europe many members left the Party entirely at this point.

Long before 1939 East European communist parties had discovered the penalty for not adhering rigidly to the Moscow line. The Polish Party was subjected from its founding to continuous interference from the Soviets, reflecting a fundamental Russian mistrust of Poles, but which had the side-effect of reducing membership, in some regions of Poland by as much as 80 per cent. The Poles had the temerity to argue with Comintern, claiming they were better able to determine strategy in their own country; they further earned Stalin's enmity by siding with Leon Trotsky during the Soviet leadership struggles of the mid-1920s. In 1925 Comintern replaced the entire Polish Party leadership with one willing to initiate a self-defeating campaign of violence against the Polish state. In 1938, having purged and executed thirty out of thirty-seven top Polish communists unfortunate enough to find themselves in the Soviet Union at the time, Comintern finally shut the Polish Party down altogether. It was not reconstituted until 1941, when the Soviet Union was attacked by Nazi Germany, at which point the services even of Polish communists were suddenly deemed useful.

A similar, equally unwelcome independence of mind was shown by the Communist Party of Czechoslovakia (CPCS), the largest in the region. Under Bohumír Šmeral the CPCS, which could function legally, welcomed social democrats as members, showed 'gradualist' leanings towards working within the parliamentary system, and as a consequence became a truly mass movement. It was precisely this openness which attracted the disapproval of Comintern, which in 1928 denounced the CPCS as 'the worst section of the International'. When Comintern in 1929 imposed the 'Muscovite' Klement Gottwald as leader, the Party split, and membership fell to a mere 30,000 by

1930. Sovietisation also meant a sudden drop in electoral support in 1929, proving that subservience to Moscow was hardly an asset.[9]

Even the Great Depression, which to millions worldwide seemed to demonstrate the failure of both capitalism and democracy, and which undoubtedly boosted the fortunes of communism temporarily in more developed countries like Germany, could not reverse the negative image of the ideology in Eastern Europe. Stalin's collectivisation drive from 1928, coupled with Comintern's constant interference and manipulation and the bewildering changes in the Moscow line, left the East European peasant masses suspicious if not positively hostile. The one development which bade fair to make communism look attractive by comparison was the rise of Nazism to power in Germany in 1933; but the sudden reversal of Soviet policy represented by the call for a popular front did not work very well. After years of mutual antagonism, communists and social democrats found it hard to cooperate, not least because such cooperation always had to be on Moscow's terms.

To complete the mistrust of communism, the mass purges of the Soviet Communist Party, beginning in 1936 and reaching their peak in 1938, also affected East European communists directly. Because communist parties were proscribed in so many countries, there were many East European communists sheltering in the USSR, and they too were swept up in the purges, it being especially easy to accuse them of being agents of Western imperialism, fascism and so on. A whole generation of Polish, Hungarian, Yugoslav and other communists disappeared into the camps or were summarily executed; among the victims was Béla Kun, leader of the short-lived Hungarian Soviet Republic. An equally grim fate overtook Party members in individual Soviet republics, whose national identity, encouraged by the Soviet government in the 1920s, made them doubly suspect in the paranoid 1930s, which saw a mass liquidation of Ukrainian and Belorussian communists and intelligentsia. Those lucky enough to survive the purges were thoroughly cowed, and tended to remain terrified loyalists henceforth. Those who, like Josip Broz, the Yugoslav Communist otherwise known as Tito, either returned to their native country in time to avoid being purged, or who had never left it, learned to see things from a different perspective, and imbibed a rather more critical attitude to the Soviets. Such independent-minded individuals were the forerunners of what, in the post-1945 period, became known as 'national communism'.

---

[9] Quoted in Schöpflin, *Politics in Eastern Europe*, 52.

6

Test tube of ideologies
Conservative authoritarianism

Aspects of conservative authoritarianism have already been touched on in analysing the failure of liberal democracy. However, it is worth defining conservative authoritarianism in its East European context more precisely. Not only is the distinction between conservative authoritarianism and fascism an important one, which even today too many students ignore, but the various non-democratic regimes which emerged in interwar Eastern Europe were conservative authoritarian, not fascist. The two fascist powers, Fascist Italy from 1925 and National Socialist Germany from 1933, undoubtedly played a role in the region; but in Eastern Europe no native fascist movement exercised power before the Second World War.

The confusion is understandable, since conservative authoritarians shared certain values and enemies with fascists. Both were nationalist, contemptuous of liberal democracy, and bitterly hostile to the Left, especially communism. There remained, however, a fundamental difference: conservative authoritarians were, by definition, anxious to conserve the existing order or, in some cases, to return to a previously existing order, whereas fascists were radicals, who saw themselves as nationalist revolutionaries, committed to a complete reordering of society. Thus, across Europe in this period the two groups could make common cause, as did the nationalists under General Francisco Franco during the Spanish Civil War of 1936–9; as a result their opponents, especially those on the Left, understandably but mistakenly tended to lump them all together as 'fascist'. Yet the fact remains that conservative authoritarians and fascists had very different goals, which meant that conflict between them was always likely.

The term 'authoritarian' is also ambiguous, since strictly speaking it can describe regimes of both Right and Left: any government which insists on imposing its own authority, to the exclusion of potential rivals for power, is authoritarian. Stalin's rule in the Soviet Union was nothing if not authoritarian, to the point of what is also called 'totalitarian'; but this was an authoritarianism of the Left. By contrast, the other authoritarian governments which emerged in the interwar period were of the Right, many of them precisely in reaction to communism.

It is this abhorrence of communism as an existential threat which gives us a clue to the appeal of conservative authoritarianism, especially in East European countries neighbouring the Soviet Union. Not all conservatives, after all, were anti-democratic; on the contrary, in the course of the nineteenth-century conservatives generally had come to accept constitutional systems and an ever-widening mass participation in politics. Even before 1914, however, there was a rearguard tendency to deplore the advent of mass politics, and in the conditions of perceived crisis at the end of the First World War there was a pronounced shift rightward. Many on the Right, especially in the traditional elites, retreated into a sort of authoritarian bunker, and it is here that the distinction drawn between the conservative right and the radical right becomes crucial. Conservative authoritarians tended to include monarchs, many of whom were willing to act as figureheads for undemocratic regimes, if they did not actively lead them, as did Alexander of Yugoslavia and Carol II of Romania. They included the landed nobility, which in countries like Hungary or Romania had long exercised a political, as well as an economic and social influence. They included the 'national' church, whether Roman Catholic, Lutheran or Greek Orthodox, and which was also a substantial landowner. They included the armed forces, or at least their officer corps. And they included the upper middle class: manufacturers, bankers and businessmen, in short those with a lot to lose from any revolution. Martin Blinkhorn describes the authoritarianism of such groups as 'limited pluralism': essentially illiberal, they could accept a limited party system as long as they dominated it, but preferred as little politics as possible.[1] Instead of participatory democracy, some authoritarians favoured 'corporatism', a society organised not according to political parties or social classes, but by appointed 'corporations' or – to use a medieval term – 'estates', representing occupational groups. In no sense were such corporations designed to function as truly representative elective bodies, since democracy in this world view was simply not needed; on the contrary, given the communist threat, permitting too much mass involvement in decision-making was positively dangerous.

The dilemma of conservative authoritarians in the interwar period was that the threat was coming not just from the Left, in the shape of communism, but also from the radical right, in the shape of Europe's plethora of fascist movements. Conservatives rightly saw fascism as inimical to their own privileged world, since the nationalist revolution yearned for by fascists envisaged a nation 'without classes and castes', as Hitler put it in 1934.[2] Thus, conservative authoritarians in power preferred to keep the radical right at arm's length, and even when, in specific circumstances, the two groups were driven to make common cause, as for instance with the appointment of Hitler

---

[1] Blinkhorn, M., 1990, 'Introduction: Allies, Rivals or Antagonists? Fascists and Conservatives in Modern Europe', in M. Blinkhorn (ed.), *Fascists and Conservatives: The Radical Right and the Establishment in Twentieth-Century Europe*, London, 4–5.

[2] Speech to Hitler Youth, September 1934, in the Nazi propaganda film by Riefenstahl, L., 2001 [1935], *Triumph of the Will: Triumph des Willens: das Dokument vom Reichsparteitag 1934*, Bloomington, IL.

as chancellor by President Paul von Hindenburg in January 1933, this always involved an element of supping with the devil. This was also one of the reasons why native fascist movements in Eastern Europe were in a sense redundant in this period: given the largely agrarian nature of East European societies, and the ease with which conservative authoritarians maintained or achieved dominance, fascists were literally not needed to fend off the threat from the Left. As a result East European fascist movements remained radical, and on the fringes politically.

It is worth examining six of these conservative authoritarian regimes, because each in its way illustrates the distinction just drawn between them and fascism.

Hungary. The regency of Admiral Horthy in Hungary ruled by consent of a reconstituted parliament. Yet this parliamentary system operated under the same restricted suffrage as before the war, ensuring that power remained with the nobility and the wealthy; Count István Bethlen, the aristocratic leader of the Unified Party who served as Horthy's prime minister from 1921 to 1931, was typical of this traditional elite. Horthy, on taking power in 1919, had been supported by many on the nationalist radical right, including proto-fascists like Captain Gyula Gömbös, leader of the counter-revolutionary Hungarian National Defence Union (*MOVE*), which organised resistance to Kun's Soviet Republic, and the founder in 1923 of his own explicitly anti-Semitic Party of Racial Defence. The regency also drew support from both the Catholic and Calvinist churches, whose increasing emphasis on Christian values 'went hand-in-hand with a more exclusionary nationalism', and which later lent itself easily enough to outright persecution of the Jews.[3] Horthy himself, however, a noble who believed in constitutional government and the rule of law, albeit within a narrow framework, was hardly a fascist, and indeed regarded radical right-wingers like Gömbös with some disdain. The Horthy government, despite initially flirting with anti-Semitism, discouraged attempts in the early 1920s to enact anti-Semitic legislation; it also tried to suppress Hungary's main fascist movement, the Arrow Cross, after its formation in 1935, and kept its leader, Ferenc Szálasi, in prison for much of the late 1930s.

Two factors, however, edged the Horthy regime further rightwards in the 1930s. The economic tailspin of the Depression prompted Bethlen's resignation in 1931, and in 1932 Horthy felt obliged to appoint Gömbös prime minister. The latter, though something of a frustrated fascist, displayed the true populist touch, forming the first cabinet in Hungary's history without a single aristocrat, renaming the government party the National Unity Party and dramatically broadening its membership, and appealing to the masses with a National Work Plan and attempts at land reform which the Horthyist old guard found

[3] Hanebrink, P.A., 2006, *In Defense of Christian Hungary: Religion, Nationalism and Antisemitism 1890-1944*, Ithaca, NY, 2.

alarming. In return, Gömbös toned down his anti-Semitism and was forced to abandon radical land redistribution. Before his death in 1936, however, Gömbös had transformed the ruling party, in the elections of 1935 bringing in a significant number of radical nationalists like himself. The second factor pushing Hungary rightwards was the international scene: Horthy's regime was frankly revisionist, and its policy of cosying up to Hitler's Germany eventually paid off in territorial gains between 1938 and 1941. The quid pro quo for Germany support, however, was twofold: anti-Semitic legislation, stripping Jews of citizenship rights, was passed in 1938–9 thanks to the more radical parliament elected in 1935; and an even more terrible price awaited Hungary when it was pressured into Hitler's war against the Soviet Union in 1941.

Austria. Austria between 1934 and 1938 presents the peculiar case of an authoritarian Catholic regime, which has been labelled 'Austro-fascist' or 'clerico-fascist', neither of which terms is entirely satisfactory. From its birth in 1918 the First Austrian Republic was a weak, divided society, arguably the most economically handicapped of all the successor states. Cut off by new boundaries from former markets and supplies of foodstuffs and raw materials, burdened by reparations and the redundant bureaucracy of the former empire, this rump state of six million Germans struggled to evolve a national identity of its own, yet was forbidden by treaty from union with Germany. The capital, with a third of the population, was a large head on a tiny body; and 'Red' Vienna, which tended to vote social democrat, was deeply divided from the pious, conservative provinces. The dominant force throughout the 1920s was the Christian Social Party, which stood for strong Catholic values, tempered by social welfare policies designed to limit socialism's appeal to the masses. After 1917 fear of communism intensified this concern among Christian Social leaders like Monsignor Ignaz Seipel, chancellor for much of the 1920s; this increasingly brought out an authoritarian, anti-democratic tendency already detectable in the writings of Christian Social theorists like Othmar Spann. Such thinkers were also attracted to corporatism, the idea that, instead of relying on corruptible political parties, a state could be run by consultation with appointed corporations or estates representing occupational groups. Seipel, from 1928, campaigned for what he called 'True Democracy', which in fact meant an authoritarian, corporatist state. This rightward drift was reinforced by the Depression, and the resulting polarisation of Austrian society between left-wing and right-wing paramilitaries; the right-wing *Heimwehr* or 'home guard', originally formed in 1918 to patrol Austria's new borders and forestall a communist takeover, effectively functioned as the 'paramilitary wing of the Christian Social Party'.[4] In an atmosphere of sporadic street violence between

---

[4]   Lewis, J., 1990, 'Conservatives and Fascists in Austria 1918-34', in M. Blinkhorn (ed.), *Fascists and Conservatives: The Radical Right and the Establishment in Twentieth Century Europe*, London, 108.

left and right, Seipel played to a conservative backlash against the Left, praising the *Heimwehr* for wanting to 'liberate democracy from party rule.'[5]

Seipel's successor, Engelbert Dollfuß, like him an advocate of corporatism, in March 1934 went one better and simply suspended parliament and civil liberties, outlawed both the social democratic and communist parties, launched a pro-government 'non-party', the Fatherland Front, and in May 1934 proclaimed a new, corporatist constitution. This so-called *Ständestaat* or 'state of estates', which described itself as a 'Christian-German federal state on a corporative basis', was a dictatorship in all but name; of the seven unelected corporations planned to 'advise' the government, only two were ever set up.[6] Dollfuß in July 1934 succumbed to an attempted coup by Austria's real fascists, the local branch of the German Nazi Party, who stormed the federal chancellery and mortally wounded the chancellor in a shoot-out with police. Seemingly staged without Hitler's approval, the putsch failed when the *Heimwehr* rallied around the government, and when Mussolini's Italy, at this point still seeing Austria as within its sphere of influence, mobilised in support of continuing Austrian independence, forcing Hitler to disown the plotters. Dollfuß's successor, Kurt von Schuschnigg, was able to carry on; but within a year the logic of the international scene had changed. Italy's invasion of Ethiopia in 1935 drove Mussolini towards alliance with Nazi Germany, and this circumstance worked against the survival of the *Ständestaat*.

Poland. In Poland authoritarianism took on a peculiar form, in that the dictatorship proclaimed in May 1926 was ostensibly committed to holding Poland together as a multinational state, and its principal figure, Marshal Józef Piłsudski, was originally of the Left. Of noble background, Piłsudski before the war was a leader of the Polish Socialist Party in Russia, and had engaged in terrorism against the tsarist state in 1905. Yet Piłsudski was always more nationalist than socialist, admitting late in life that for him socialism had always been primarily a tool for overthrowing Russian rule. Piłsudski's record in raising a Polish legion on the side of the Central Powers, during the war, gave him military experience of a kind as well as immense prestige, consolidated by his role in building the new Poland. Piłsudski's nationalism was also peculiar: perhaps conditioned by his gentry origins, as well as by his socialism, he harked back to the old Polish-Lithuanian Commonwealth as a 'group of nations', living in harmony in the same state. For Piłsudski, according to Piotr S. Wandycz, 'the concept of the state transcended ethnic nationality'; and it was Piłsudski who, in the war with Soviet Russia, insisted on annexing the *kresy*, the frontierlands of the old Commonwealth, with their mixed, largely non-Polish

5   Quoted in Jedlicka, L., 1966, 'The Austrian Heimwehr', *Journal of Contemporary History*, I, no. 1, April, 133.
6   Quoted in Jelavich, B., 1987, *Modern Austria: Empire and Republic 1815-1986*, Cambridge, 202–3.

population.[7] Piłsudski acted as interim head of state until 1922, before refusing to campaign for the presidency on the ground that the office was dangerously lacking in power. When, in May 1926, the Marshal stepped in, backed by those elements of the army loyal to him, together with the Left and the trade unions, he proclaimed a government of *Sanacja*, or cleansing, posing as being above party politics, committed to ridding Poland of corruption and strong enough to defend the nation against external threats. The new regime did in fact draw support, at least initially, from a wide spectrum of Polish society, including the national minorities, who hoped for a federal restructuring of the state.

Once in power, however, Piłsudski turned out to have no programme other than to 'bring a bit of order and honesty' to government.[8] Piłsudski himself was not interested in holding office, except for being minister of war and commander-in-chief; instead he ruled through his 'trusties', most of them army officers. The 'colonels', as they were often described, occupied most of the ministerial and top administrative posts. The problem encountered by the *Sanacja* regime was that it proved rather difficult to govern without a coherent ideology or agenda, beyond merely holding power. This regime was not exactly right-wing; certainly it was not intent on governing in the interests of the gentry or big business. Nor was it anxious to embark on anything radical like further land redistribution, or a constitutional devolution of authority. At the same time, *Sanacja* was hardly totalitarian: political parties opposed to the government continued to be legal, and the *Sejm* continued to sit. The only major political change was the amendment of the constitution to empower the president, another of Piłsudski's 'trusties', to dissolve parliament and rule by decree if necessary, as well as to shape the budget. After a couple of years *Sanacja* abandoned the pretence of being non-political and founded the unsubtly named Non-Party Bloc for Cooperation with the Government or *BBWR*. This was not a conspicuous success at the polls, gaining only a quarter of the popular vote and 122 seats in the *Sejm* out of 444 in the elections of March 1928. Gradually the Piłsudski regime became more authoritarian, not least because the effects of the Depression from 1930 onwards made the Left bolder in demonstrations and strikes, leading to government repression, while on the Right the national democrats or *Endecja* were bitterly critical of *Sanacja*'s stewardship of the national interest. In addition, the positive relationship with the minorities had long since soured, as it became obvious that, for all its inclusive rhetoric, *Sanacja* would not abandon Poland's centralised structure for federalism. This was especially true of the Ukrainians of East Galicia, among whom discontent boiled over into sabotage and terrorism in the summer of

[7] Wandycz, P.S., 1990, 'Poland's Place in Europe in the Concepts of Piłsudski and Dmowski', *East European Politics & Societies*, IV/3, Fall, 459.
[8] Quoted in Andreski, S., 1981, 'Poland', in S.J. Woolf (ed.), *Fascism in Europe*, London and New York, 174.

1930; the brutal 'pacification' of the region by the Polish army only made things worse, ensuring that conditions approaching guerrilla warfare persisted for the rest of the decade. In November 1930 elections were more forcibly conducted, the government interned large numbers of the opposition, and the BBWR finally obtained a majority; yet even in these controlled conditions over half the popular vote still went to the regime's opponents, whether Left or Right.

When Piłsudski died in 1935, he was succeeded by a collective leadership of unimaginative army officers, even more inclined to repress dissent. A new constitution in 1935 neutered the *Sejm* by abolishing proportional representation, halving the number of deputies, and assigning the selection of all parliamentary candidates to the government; in response the opposition parties boycotted the elections in 1935 and again in 1938. The more hard line among the 'colonels', grouped around Marshal Edward Rydż-Smigły, and troubled by the government's lack of a coherent ideology, in 1937 launched a new pro-government party, the Camp of National Unity (*OZON*). Driven to spell out what the colonels stood for, *OZON* insensibly emulated the nationalist rhetoric of *Endecja*, toyed with bizarre plans for founding a Polish colonial empire, and indulged in increasingly overt anti-Semitism. As early as 1936 the *Sanacja* prime minister, General Felicjan Sławoj-Składkowski, publicly endorsed *Endecja*'s claim that Jews had too much economic influence; the government also took up the idea of encouraging Jewish emigration. By 1938 the regime was putting up posters echoing Nazi Germany's boycott of Jewish businesses five years earlier: 'Buy only in Polish shops!'[9] Shortly after the government published its 'Theses on the Jewish Question', which concluded that Poland's 2.2 million Jews were 'weakening' its national development, and were basically unassimilable; in the circumstances, forced emigration was 'the only proper method' for resolving the problem.[10] In short, by the time of the German invasion in 1939 Poland had the reputation of being, next to Romania and Germany itself, one of the most anti-Semitic regimes in Europe. It was a far cry from Piłsudski's initial stress on the virtues of a multinational commonwealth, and showed how easy it was for an authoritarian government to turn to xenophobic nationalism in its quest for legitimacy.

Romania. The turn towards conservative authoritarianism in Romania was in many respects the predictable consequence of the situation already described, whereby the traditional elite retained its hold on power throughout the 1920s, with the brief exception of the National Peasant Party government of 1928–30. At the same time the fractured nature of Romanian society in this newly enlarged state, coupled with the political system's entrenched corruption, called

---

[9] Wynot, E.D., 1971, '"A Necessary Cruelty": The Emergence of Official Anti-Semitism in Poland 1936-39', *American Historical Review*, LXXVI, #4, October, 1047.

[10] Quoted in Wynot, '"A Necessary Cruelty"', 1051.

forth serious tensions and the rise of a radical right in the shape of Romania's native fascist movement, the Iron Guard. The swing towards authoritarianism was both a cause of and a reaction to these internal tensions, compounded by the role of the monarch and, increasingly after 1933, foreign policy pressures.

The personality of Carol II, who unexpectedly returned to claim the throne in 1930, was key to subsequent developments. Carol's scandalous lifestyle, and in particular his long-standing liaison with the Jewish actress Elena Magda Lupescu, made him seem an unacceptable successor to King Ferdinand, and Carol was persuaded to renounce the throne in 1926. When Ferdinand died in 1927 a regency was appointed for Carol's infant son Michael. Carol's decision to return was initially supported by the Maniu government, on condition that he respect the constitution, and end his relationship with Lupescu. The King accepted these conditions, but promptly reneged on the deal as soon as he was back, prompting the resignation of the cabinet and the splitting of the main parties into rival factions, depending on who was willing to serve Carol. From 1930 to 1938 Carol governed with what has been termed the 'semblance of legality'.[11] His favoured method of ruling was to play rival parties off against one another, trading access to office for legislation and policies approved by the monarch; in the process the whole concept of political pluralism was further discredited, while Carol's personal cronies, including Lupescu, enriched themselves. Carol increasingly saw himself as embodying a sort of monarchical populism, stressing his identification with the nation as well as Romanian Orthodoxy. This also seemed to be why the King initially tolerated, and even appeared to encourage, the rise of the Iron Guard, as a sort of foil to the mainstream parties. Two factors, however, eventually turned Carol against the Iron Guard. The latter's virulent anti-Semitism was an aspect of their ideology Carol had been prepared to overlook; but their especial hatred for the King's Jewish mistress became hard to ignore. Secondly, the Iron Guard's identification with Nazi Germany, and the open support accorded them by Hitler, clashed with Carol's view of France and Britain as Romania's natural protectors. When elections in December 1937 did not return the pliant Liberal government Carol had hoped for, he briefly appointed a government led by the tiny, explicitly anti-Semitic National Christian Party, whose sole idea of governing was a series of measures depriving Jews of citizenship. Faced with widespread disapproval of this government at home and abroad, and in an atmosphere of mounting violence by the Iron Guard, Carol finally suspended the constitution in February 1938 and appointed a government of royal placemen.

The whole purpose of this royal dictatorship was to head off the rise of the Iron Guard, who had achieved an alarming 15 per cent of the vote in the previous election. The new minister of the interior, Armand Călinescu, was given carte

[11] Bucur, M., 2007, 'Carol II of Romania', in B.J. Fischer (ed.), *Balkan Strongmen: Dictators and Authoritarian Rulers of Southeast Europe*, West Lafayette, IN, 99.

blanche to crack down on the guardists, and the fascist leader, Corneliu Zelea Codreanu, was arrested; in November Codreanu and thirteen other guardists were murdered on government orders. In December 1938 Carol sanctioned the formation of a pro-government party, the Front of National Rebirth; yet at the same time the other political parties were allowed to continue functioning. Carol's dictatorship, in short, was weaker than it appeared, and the Iron Guard continued to create mayhem under new, more radical leadership. In the end it was the ascendancy of Nazi Germany which finished Carol: bereft of the Western powers' support, obliged to make obeisance to Hitler as the lesser of two evils following the Nazi-Soviet Pact of August 1939, Carol in the summer of 1940 was forced to cede Bessarabia to the Soviet Union, Southern Dobrudja to Bulgaria, and north Transylvania to Hungary, as well as to admit the Iron Guard leader, Horia Sima, into the cabinet. Hoping to maintain his hold on power by co-opting the Romanian army, Carol invited General Ion Antonescu to form a government; but it was Antonescu, a genuine military strongman, who forced the by now deeply unpopular Carol to abdicate. The king went into exile in September 1940, with enraged guardists taking pot-shots at the royal train as it left the station. The Antonescu regime, which lasted until 1944 and took Romania into the Second World War on the side of Nazi Germany, was briefly in coalition with the Iron Guard but, as we shall see, there remained irreconcilable differences between a conservative authoritarian like Antonescu and the fascist Iron Guard.

Yugoslavia. Many of the intractable problems that beset interwar Yugoslavia, leading to the proclamation of the royal dictatorship in January 1929, have already been described. Yugoslavia was arguably the most ethnographically complex of the successor states, yet the kingdom was dominated from the outset by the Serbs, and despite his best intentions King Alexander, head of Serbia's Karađorđević dynasty, personally embodied this preponderance, and the contradictions inherent in the creation of a South Slav state. From its inception Yugoslavia was founded on the pretence that Serbs, Croats and Slovenes, despite the clear linguistic and confessional differences between them, constituted a single, 'three-named' nation. This ideology of Yugoslavism was sincerely subscribed to by some individuals among all three peoples; yet the centralised constitution and de facto domination of the state by Serbs belied the aspiration behind Yugoslavism. Alexander, as a result of the antagonisms culminating in Radić's assassination in 1928, despaired of parliamentary politics and decided that the root cause of conflict was the nationalism of Yugoslavia's constituent peoples; eliminate or suppress this, the king reasoned, and a genuinely Yugoslav identity would emerge. In 1929 the Kingdom of Serbs, Croats and Slovenes was formally re-named Yugoslavia, and the country was divided up into nine *banovine* or administrative governorships named after geographical features, thus abolishing national labels like 'Serbia' and 'Croatia'. In 1931, a new constitution was promulgated, according to which voting was by open ballot, and parties based on national identity were forbidden to compete. As in Poland and Romania, an official, government-sponsored Yugoslav Unity Party was founded, which in the elections of November 1931 predictably gained every seat in the national assembly.

As authoritarian regimes went, Alexander's dictatorship was less vicious and murderous than King Carol's in Romania, but it was considerably harsher than Piłsudski's in Poland: those protesting were either imprisoned, or forced into exile, and the small fry of all parties, especially the banned Communist Party, were treated badly in prison. The most serious consequence of Alexander's attempt to create a Yugoslav identity by royal fiat, however, was not just that it failed, but that it positively exacerbated the nationalist antagonisms of Yugoslavia's peoples. Even Serbs were unhappy, since the attempted erasure of identities affected them as much as anyone else, even if they still seemed dominant to the other peoples. As for non-Serbs, the dictatorship gave extra motive to extremists in all camps, especially the Croats and Macedonians. It was in direct response to the royal dictatorship that Ante Pavelić, a parliamentary deputy of the ultra-nationalist Party of Rights, fled to Fascist Italy to found the *Ustaša* movement, committed to achieving Croatia's liberation from Yugoslavia by violent means. And it was the Macedonian terrorist movement IMRO, with *Ustaša* assistance and the covert backing of Mussolini, which effected the murder of Alexander himself at Marseille in October 1934. Clearly the differences between conservative authoritarianism and native fascism could have literally lethal consequences.

Under Alexander's milder brother, Prince Paul, who led the regency on behalf of Alexander's underage heir Peter, the royal dictatorship was effectively abandoned, although constitutionally still in force. Political prisoners were released, party political activity was tolerated, elections could be contested, and the press was freed from most constraints. The prime minister from 1935 to 1939, Milan Stojadinović, was appointed ostensibly as the man who could somehow reconcile Croats to the Yugoslav state; in practice he showed no interest in a federal restructuring, and arguably worsened Serbo-Croat relations by signing a concordat with the Vatican, which had to be withdrawn following violent protests against it by the Serbs. Stojadinović's strong suit was his sensible economic policy, and it was for economic reasons that Yugoslavia gravitated steadily towards the Axis powers, especially Germany; a trade agreement in 1936 provided a much-needed boost for Yugoslav exports. Stojadinović has often been depicted as having fascist leanings. He undoubtedly enjoyed good relations with Hitler and Mussolini, indulged in a certain aping of fascist mannerisms, for instance allowing himself to be addressed as 'leader', and founding a green-shirted youth movement. Yet Stojadinović still presided, under Prince Paul, over a quasi-parliamentary elective system; he was not anti-Semitic, nor was he an integral, racist nationalist; and in the end he was dismissed in February 1939 to make way for a government more determined to reach political accommodation with the Croats. It was the government of Dragiša Cvetković which, in August 1939, concluded the *Sporazum* or agreement, by which Croatia received autonomous status within the kingdom, as well an enlargement of territory to include part of Bosnia. This settlement, while it partially met Croatian grievances, satisfied no one else; and the Yugoslavia which faced the Nazi invasion in 1941 was one which commanded strikingly little allegiance from any of its peoples other than the Serbs.

Greece. Greece under General Ioannis Metaxas offers the peculiar phenomenon of a regime which was essentially conservative authoritarian but which, like Franco's in Spain, aped fascist mannerisms. Metaxas, a career soldier who by 1936 led the small, right-wing Freethinkers' Party, owed his appointment as caretaker prime minister in April 1936 to King George II, himself brought back to the throne by a sort of military coup against the republic, and who found it impossible to arbitrate a stable government from among Greece's mainstream parties. Metaxas held dismissive views of party politics generally, and in August 1936 persuaded the king to suspend the constitution, on the ground that the threat from communism made a parliamentary system impracticable. Metaxas was also convinced that his unruly, individualistic compatriots needed the discipline of strong government, and to assist them in this he promoted the first-ever grammar of demotic, or spoken, Greek, as opposed to the classical Greek favoured by the elite. The Metaxas regime also talked up a so-called third Hellenic civilization, which would be based on the values of ancient Greece as well as those of the Greek Orthodox Church. Metaxas posed as the 'First Peasant', founded a National Youth Organisation which has been described as 'a pale imitation of the Hitler Youth', and accepted straight-arm salutes, fascist-style, from his supporters.[12] Yet the Metaxas dictatorship was motivated more by a blend of nationalism and religion than any racist ideology; and it found the ultimate reason for dissociating itself from fascism, when Greece was attacked by Italy in October 1940. Successfully repelling this invasion was General Metaxas' main preoccupation until his sudden death in January 1941, shortly before Greece faced the far more serious threat of Nazi Germany.

Authoritarian regimes were in place, as already noted, in Bulgaria and all the Baltic states by 1934. In each case, however, the justification for non-democratic government was fear of communism, mistrust of parliamentary politics, a conservative nationalism and a desire to keep the extreme right out of power, rather than fascism.

---

[12] Clogg, R., 1992, *A Concise History of Greece*, Cambridge, 118.

7

Test tube of ideologies

Fascism

'Fascism' is a much-debated term; indeed, there is still an ongoing, if decreasingly relevant, discussion among scholars as to whether we can even talk about such a thing as generic fascism, that is, a group of characteristics which all so-called fascist movements share. The discussion here starts from the assumption that such a set of shared characteristics can be identified, both historically with reference to the interwar fascist movements, and in terms of contemporary, modern-day politics. In short, fascism can be defined and, as an ideology with identifiable traits and causes, its history in the specific context of Eastern Europe gives it a decided topicality.

Part of the confusion surrounding fascism stems from the fact that fascists themselves, from the founding of the Italian Fascist Party in 1919, denied any similarities or parallels between the various movements that we now identify as 'fascist'; as Mussolini famously said of the Italian variant in 1928, 'Fascism is not goods for export.'[1] It was in fact natural that movements rooted, above all else, in a hypertrophied nationalism should repudiate any suggestion that they were not unique; indeed, and unlike communism, the concept of an 'international fascism' is something of a contradiction in terms. By the end of the 1920s, moreover, a bewildering variety of movements across Europe were being identified as fascist, and it took time for the common traits between them to become apparent. Compounding the confusion was a tendency among observers to latch onto what have been called the 'fascist negations': it was clear that fascists had a visceral hatred of communism, liberalism and the old elites, but it seemed less clear what they were positively for. As a result it was common, down to the Second World War and beyond, to deny that fascism even constituted a coherent ideology. Anyone who has tried to read Adolf Hitler's turgid autobiography *Mein Kampf* will sympathise with this position; the same can be said for the mystical, obscurantist rantings of Ferenc Szálasi, leader of the Hungarian Arrow Cross, or of Corneliu Zelea Codreanu, 'Captain' of Romania's Iron Guard.

The waters were further muddied by the fatal misinterpretation of fascism on the Left. Some of the first attempts to make sense of fascism, in Italy and

---

[1] Quoted in Payne, S.G., 1995, *A History of Fascism 1914-45*, London, 228.

elsewhere in the early 1920s, were made by its left-wing opponents, who put two and two together and came up with five. What has been called the 'agent theory' of fascism assumed that fascist movements were essentially a spin-off of capitalism, especially capitalism in its late or 'imperialist' phase. Mussolini and Hitler, in this simplistic interpretation, were the creatures or agents of big business, landowners and monopoly capitalism, which 'employed' fascists to smash strikes and left-wing parties and generally oppress the working class. This became the standard explanation of communists in particular for Mussolini's rise to power, and was formally adopted by the Comintern in 1924. It is true that the Italian Fascists' vicious attacks on the Left, which made them notorious from 1919, suited the interests of employers and landowners. It is also true that both Mussolini and Hitler, as they approached and attained power, learned to live with big business, even if many of their rank-and-file members remained suspicious of such links. Both Italian Fascism and Nazism, however, in common with all fascist movements, exhibited from the start a violent animosity towards capitalism, as part of the established power structure exploiting the common people. By misinterpreting fascism in this way, therefore, communists in particular also underestimated fascism's appeal: if fascists were simply the puppets of capitalism, then it was capitalism which remained the enemy, and anyone on the Left, like social democrats, who sought to work within the 'capitalist' system was 'objectively fascist'. This myopia split the Left throughout the interwar period, and cost all enemies of fascism dear.

One of the benefits of studying East European fascisms is that a comparison of these with the better-known Italian Fascism and Nazism yields striking parallels, and in the process the elements of a coherent ideology do emerge. Our understanding of this comparative aspect, and the light it throws on fascism, deepened in the 1960s, when some of the first truly in-depth studies on the subject were published. Ever more information has become available since then on the more obscure and baffling fascist movements, especially the East European ones. Gradually it became clear what fascists were for, as well as what they were vehemently against, and in the last twenty years especially historians have come to a tentative consensus on the matter.

How, then, to define the term? Fascism has been succinctly described by Stanley G. Payne as a form of 'revolutionary ultra-nationalism'.[2] This brings us to the nub of the matter: the core value of all fascisms, past and present, is nationalism, and a nationalism of a particularly virulent and hate-filled form, in which the nation is conceived in racial terms, as an organic whole. As a consequence of this racist mindset, elements seen as 'polluting' the nation's racial purity, whether Jews or national minorities or homosexuals, were treated as a deadly threat which had to be eliminated. So-called racial science was widely

[2] Payne, *A History of Fascism*, 14.

disseminated by the early twentieth century, and recent research on eugenics and racial nationalism shows that 'Interest in race and eugenics was . . . more widespread in Central and Southeast Europe than historians have recognized.'[3]

All of fascism's other distinctive traits flow from this absolute centrality of the nation in fascists' world view. The movements which sprang up in the period following the First World War all shared a sense that the nation was in crisis and in deadly peril, whether from defeat in war, or from the threat of communist revolution, or from internal enemies, or from the exploitative oppression of traditional elites. Central to this sense of peril, of course, was the Russian Revolution and the rise of world communism, an internationalist ideology which negated everything that nationalists held most dear. Fundamental, also, was a burning conviction that the nation had to be reborn, or to find itself anew, what Roger Griffin, one of the leading authorities on fascism, has rather grandly called 'paleogenesis'.[4] The urgency of this national rebirth, moreover, was a principal reason for fascism's contempt for liberal democracy and party politics generally, as a practice which divided, rather than united, the nation in its hour of greatest danger, and which reduced the nation's life to a sordid, corrupt competition for power. Fascists, by contrast, saw themselves as constituting a 'movement', rather than a political party, and one which represented the entire mass of the nation. Transcending the first stage of what Robert O. Paxton has termed the 'five stages of fascism', and making the transition to a political party willing and able to compete for seats in a national assembly was an effort most fascisms were never able to make.[5] For the same reason, the need for unity, the nation required charismatic leadership, from a decisive, commanding Führer or Duce who could intuit the nation's will and its needs without the tiresome distraction of voting. And this same sense of urgency explains fascists' open embrace of violence as a political weapon as well as an end in itself: the enemies of the nation, whether leftists or liberals, had to be physically destroyed or otherwise eliminated.

A final characteristic of all fascisms is their radicalism. Fascists were not conservatives. They saw themselves as revolutionaries, intent on effecting a nationalist revolution, in which every single member of the nation, racially defined, would be raised up and cherished. As a consequence fascists were as much opposed to the traditional elites of their societies – the landowning class, the plutocrats and capitalists, the wealthy middle class – as they were to liberal democrats and to the Left. This is the crucial distinction, already alluded to, between fascists and conservative authoritarians, who after all

---

[3]   Turda, M. and Weindling, P.J., 2007, 'Eugenics, Race and Nation in Central and Southeast Europe 1900-1940: A Historiographical Overview', in M. Turda and P.J. Weindling (eds), *Blood and Homeland: Eugenics and Racial Nationalism in Central and Southeast Europe 1900-1940*, Budapest and New York, 14.
[4]   Griffin, R., 1993, *The Nature of Fascism*, London, 2.
[5]   Paxton, R.O., 1998, 'The Five Stages of Fascism', *Journal of Modern History*, LXX, #1, March, 11.

which one?

wished to conserve the existing order, and despite the capacity of both sides, in certain circumstances, for making common cause against communism or democracy. The goal of fascists' nationalist revolution was a nation without social distinctions or class divisions, what fascists themselves called 'national socialism'. This levelling tendency, sometimes mistaken for socialism itself, put fascists on a potential collision course with traditional elites, even if the priority in the interim was the attack on communism and liberal democracy.

Fascism in Eastern Europe took many forms, but it is important to bear in mind that it was not the dominant political trend in the interwar period. As we have seen, the fear of communism, combined with the inherent weaknesses of liberal democracy in the region, meant that conservative authoritarian regimes multiplied, and in these circumstances fascists were effectively redundant. The support given by Mussolini to some local fascist movements, like the Croatian *Ustaša*, was not sufficient to alter this situation. Hitler's arrival in power in 1933 certainly changed the balance of forces, and throughout the remainder of the 1930s the attractive power of Germany's economic and political resurgence could only increase. Yet right down to late 1940, when the Iron Guard were briefly co-opted into government by Antonescu, Italian Fascism and Nazism remained the only two fascist movements which exercised power at all. In 1941, as a result of the Nazis' conquest and partition of Yugoslavia, the *Ustaše* were installed in power in an enlarged Croatia; and in the winter of 1944–45 a Nazi-controlled Arrow Cross government ruled those parts of Hungary not yet taken over by the Soviet Red Army. And in the notionally independent Slovakia created by Hitler's partition of Czechoslovakia in March 1939, Monsignor Josef Tiso's Slovak People's Party ruled dictatorially with the assistance of native fascists. Everywhere else fascist movements remained on the fringes, an extremist accompaniment to the prevailing conservative authoritarianism. It was only the wartime dominance of the two fascist powers, Italy and above all Germany, that permitted East European fascists even a toehold on power. The very proximity and aggressive agenda of the Axis powers ensured that, for peoples directly victimised by them, like Czechs and Poles, fascism was unlikely to be popular, although Czech and Polish fascists did exist.

Who, then, constituted fascism's constituency in Eastern Europe? As with the mainstream movements, much of the initial impetus behind the formation of East European fascist movements came from the lower middle class, and from the ranks of the officer corps and veterans; both Ferenc Szálasi and his proto-fascist forerunner Gyula Gömbös, for instance, were former officers. Right-wing, nationalist and especially racist-minded intellectuals and members of the professional classes, such as Professor Alexander Cuza, the university lecturer who inspired his student Codreanu, lent their respectability to many fascist movements. Students like Codreanu and jobless graduates reflected the general youthfulness of fascism across Europe, and this intellectual proletariat in turn reinforced fascism's self-image of itself as modern, the force of the future.

Fascism also had working-class support, at least among those segments of the working class who remained non-unionised, unskilled or unemployed, or able only to find menial occupations as concierges, domestics, office messengers and the like. This was a class naturally anti-capitalist but also anti-Semitic, especially if working for Jewish employers, and because of its nationalism disinclined to support a radicalism of the Left. Another distinctive feature of East European fascism was its relatively strong base among the peasantry. In these largely agrarian societies the revolutionary potential of the peasantry was, in Eugen Weber's words, 'a constant reality'.[6] Yet Eastern Europe's peasant masses were not natural recruits for communism, especially as the anti-peasant nature of the Soviet experiment next door became more apparent. Instead many peasants, especially the smallholder class and the landless agricultural labourers, felt let down by the mass-based peasant parties which had either failed to achieve power or had failed to force meaningful land redistribution; and the wretched position of these peasants was rendered infinitely worse by the effects of the Depression. Peasants were also, in many East European societies, peculiarly receptive to anti-Semitism, being accustomed to regard the Jewish shopkeepers and moneylenders in their midst with extreme hostility. Peasants were equally susceptible to fascism's exaltation of them as the core of the nation, racially pure, unpolluted by modern society and mystically in tune with the soil. Finally, one of the distinctive features of East European fascism was the support it received from at least some of the clergy, which in turn reflected the religiosity of fascist movements in the region. This was particularly marked in Romania, where from the start the Iron Guard identified with Romanian Orthodoxy, and where Orthodox priests, especially in rural areas, returned the compliment. Hungarian, Slovakian, Croatian, Serbian and Polish fascists all stressed their religious belief, and in both Catholic and Orthodox societies the Church, if it did not formally endorse fascism, clearly shared its nationalism, its anti-communism, and its anti-Semitism. In most countries the church hierarchy eventually distanced itself from fascism, once it became clear what excesses this led to; but there can be no denying a certain identity of values. Josef Tiso, the Catholic priest who headed the 'independent' Slovak puppet state of 1939–45, typifies this embarrassing convergence.

The phantom fascist regimes of the Second World War, like Tiso's, will be discussed in their place. Here it is fitting to describe the two largest East European fascist movements, the Arrow Cross in Hungary and the Iron Guard in Romania.

Like Germany and Italy, *Hungary* at the close of the First World War provided the perfect matrix for the rise of fascism, even if the exercise of power remained firmly in the hands of Horthy's regency. The initial impetus came

---

[6] Weber, E., 1965, 'Introduction', in H. Rogger and E. Weber (eds), *The European Right: A Historical Profile*, London, 11.

from the outrage Hungary's nationalists felt at the country's partition by the Treaty of Trianon, on top of the brief but profound shock of the Hungarian Soviet Republic in 1919. The rump state was crippled by dire economic dislocation and burdened by the need to absorb thousands of embittered refugees from the successor states, many of whom settled in Budapest and became the ideal fodder for extremism. Radical-right movements like Gömbös's *MOVE* had their origin in this period; between 1918 and 1920 over a hundred such 'patriotic associations' had been founded, often in secret, and whose purpose was to counteract the cronyism of the traditional elite by infiltrating the state bureaucracy and the government-sponsored political machine. Another ingredient was Hungarian racial theory, which stressed the ancient, pagan roots of the Magyars; the Turanian Society, founded before the First World War, affected to trace the Magyars back to the mists of time, worshipped the Hungarian god of war, Hadur, and claimed that Jesus Christ was of Magyar stock. Such Turanian, or 'Hungarist' thinking, which presumed that the Magyars ought by racial right to dominate the entire Danubian basin, fed into post-war frustrations at Hungary's humiliating position, by which point there was no shortage of racial theorists, like the anthropologist Lajos Méhely, for whom 'the race is sacred' and Jews the ultimate racial pollutant.[7] The relative stability of the 1920s, and the conservatism of the Horthy system, kept fascism at bay; but in the 1930s the more 'respectable' right-radicalism of Gömbös started to make headway under the impact of the Depression and the changing international situation. The election of 1935, which returned a parliament more in tune with right-radical ideas, and Hungary's gravitation towards the Axis powers, in the end facilitated the emergence of a genuine fascist movement.

There was a bewildering variety of fascist groups in Hungary, many of which directly aped German fascism by appropriating the label 'national socialist', and all of which were unashamedly racist. In June 1932 two of these groups merged and adopted a green-shirted uniform and the Hungarian double cross of two arrows crossed on a green background, stylised to resemble the Nazi swastika – hence Arrow Cross. The internecine squabbling between these and other groups was only ended when, in October 1937, they coalesced into what was initially called the Hungarian National Socialist Party, under the leadership of Ferenc Szálasi. Repeatedly banned by the government, this movement kept reforming under a different name; it was not until March 1939 that it formally named itself the Arrow Cross Party, the label under which it has subsequently been known. Szálasi, who had founded his own Party of National Will in 1935, was the most successful propagandist of the racist and

[7]   Quoted, Turda, M., 2013, '"If Our Race Did Not Exist, It Would Have to Be Created": Racial Science in Hungary 1940-1944', in A. Weiss-Wendt and R. Yeomans (eds), *Racial Science in Hitler's New Europe 1938-1945*, Lincoln, NE and London, 245.

Hungarist viewpoint, although it should be stressed that at no point did this enigmatic figure evolve any sort of coherent political programme. Szálasi's most accessible publication, *The Way and the Aim* (1936), is a turgid rant, full of deeply confused pronouncements such as: 'Hungarism means socialism, the tuning together of the moral, spiritual and material interests of the I and the Us.'[8] According to Szálasi, the Hungarians were, together with the Germans and the Japanese, one of the three master races on earth. Yet this visionary and impractical racist was at the same time the very type of the charismatic fascist leader, whose messianic appeal and patent sincerity won large numbers of recruits, once conditions were favourable. Though a fervent nationalist who rejected Marxism as a foreign, Jewish-influenced import, Szálasi was a social leveller, advocating land redistribution and support for the workers in a corporatist, nationalised economy.

As a result, in the peculiar circumstances of severe economic distress and international instability, and despite Szálasi's imprisonment on charges of subversion between 1938 and 1940, the Arrow Cross briefly became one of the biggest fascist movements in Eastern Europe. Membership, at its peak, was broad, with peasants constituting some 13 per cent of its support, the middle class 36 per cent, and a sizeable working-class contingent. From a base of 127,000 members in 1937, the Arrow Cross reached 250,000 by 1939, and in the elections of that year it cornered 25 per cent of the vote, harvesting, together with the other Nazi-type parties, 49 seats in parliament and becoming the third biggest party. Simply because the Arrow Cross existed, the Horthy government felt increasingly pressured to anticipate fascist demands. In the course of 1938–39 fresh anti-Semitic legislation was passed, this time with more serious consequences. Jews were effectively excluded from a variety of professions and banned from holding public office; eventually, in 1941, interracial marriages were forbidden. Hungary also, under this pressure from within, aligned itself even more firmly with the Axis powers, joining Hitler's Anti-Comintern Pact in January 1939. Thus, the Arrow Cross exerted an influence on Hungarian public life without even being in power; it helped that its electoral fortunes were lavishly subsidised by Nazi Germany, and that the Horthy regime was well aware of this uncomfortable fact.

In *Romania*, by contrast, native fascism played a much more violent and prominent role from a much earlier point, even if, as in Hungary, fascists remained frozen out of power by the conservative authoritarian establishment throughout the interwar period. And whereas Hungarian nationalists were radicalised by Hungary's losses at the end of the First World War, Romania's nationalists arguably experienced a sort of identity crisis as a result of Romania's gains: not only did this economically backward and politically corrupt state

[8]   Quoted in Weber, E., 1964, *Varieties of Fascism: Doctrines of Revolution in the Twentieth Century*, New York, 157.

suddenly double in size and population in 1918, but ethnic minorities now accounted for 28 per cent of the population, including 1.5 million disaffected Hungarians. The threat of communism, given Romania's proximity to the Soviet Union, was another factor in the emergence of fascism. Of particular concern to Romanian nationalists, however, was the 'Jewish problem': especially in the newly acquired territories, Jews were not only numerous but highly visible, being largely unassimilated and Yiddish-speaking. Although Romania's Jews only accounted for 4.2 per cent of the population as of 1930, in urban areas generally this constituted over 14 per cent, and in some towns of Bessarabia, Bukovina and Moldavia more than half the inhabitants were Jewish. Anti-Semitism had a long pedigree in Romania, and it was anti-Semitism which gave rise to the first stirrings of fascism after 1918.

Alexander Cuza, politician and professor of political economy at the University of Iaşi in Moldavia, was by 1920 preaching what he called 'national Christian socialism' to his students; this entailed land redistribution, political rights for the lower classes, and above all the restriction of Jewish economic activity and Jewish access to education, followed by expulsion of Jews from the country. Cuza was a classic racial nationalist, obsessed with the dangers of racial miscegenation through Romanian females being defiled by sexual contact with Jews. Among Cuza's students was his godson Corneliu Zelea Codreanu, son of a teacher and follower of Cuza, who was inspired to organise attacks on Jewish fellow-students and those who associated with them. Codreanu was if anything even more nationalist, anti-communist and anti-Semitic than Cuza, as well as fervently religious, with a mystic belief in the value of personal sacrifice, even of violence, on behalf of the nation. It was at Codreanu's suggestion that Cuza, in 1923, founded a political party, the League of Christian National Defence (LANC), which continued this emphasis on violence coupled with a messianic concern for the welfare of the common people. As Codreanu wrote in 1920, 'It isn't enough to defeat communism, we must also fight for the right of the workers. They have a right to bread and they have a right to honour.'[9] Even as a student Codreanu was involved in attempts to divert the working class from communism through self-help organisations and a stress on Romanian national identity.

In 1923 Codreanu and his student associates had their first taste of prison, for plotting to murder various political figures who, by supporting the granting of full citizenship to Jews in 1920, explicitly associated themselves with 'Jewish influences.' It was while in prison that Codreanu claimed to have been inspired by an icon of the Archangel Michael to save the nation. Once released, he and his followers established a work camp in rural Moldavia, which was to be a 'Christian cultural home', but as a result of a run-in with the local

---

[9]   Codreanu, C.Z., 'National Christian Socialism', in Weber, *Varieties of Fascism*, 165.

police, in 1924, the young idealists were beaten up and arrested; released on the intervention of Cuza, they were refused legal redress by the police prefect. Codreanu thereupon shot the prefect dead in full public view. His subsequent trial for murder turned Codreanu into a national figure, and demonstrated just how popular defiance of authority could be. In a trial moved to the other end of the country to guard against a sympathetic jury, Codreanu was nevertheless acquitted after five minutes' deliberation, and paraded around the streets like a hero. He was then brought back to Iași after a triumphant round trip of the country which saw thousands turn out to acclaim his passing. Codreanu consolidated his celebrity by marrying the daughter of a humble railway worker in 1925, in a ceremony also attended by thousands.

In 1926, Cuza's LANC won ten seats in the parliamentary election; but this provoked a rift with Codreanu, who in true fascist fashion saw the transition to a mere political party as a betrayal. In reaction, Codreanu in June 1927 founded the Legion of the Archangel Michael, a conspiratorial organisation confined to a select band of like-minded ideologues; the political wing of the Legion, set up in 1930 to lay the foundations for a genuine mass movement, was what was called the Iron Guard, Romania's main fascist movement. Guardism or legionarism remains difficult to analyse, in part because it never produced a coherent political programme, and was not so much a political party as a messianic faith. It was organised on the principle of unconditional obedience to the 'Captain', as Codreanu now styled himself, with legionaries divided up into 'nests' of a dozen or so members. The most that Codreanu produced by way of guidance was his *Nest Leader's Manual* (1933), which exhorted members to pursue 'the ever deeper popular penetration of the new spirit of Work, Honesty, Sacrifice and Justice'. The legionaries proclaimed their belief 'in God, . . . in a new Romania which we shall conquer through Jesus Christ and through integral nationalism, acting through the country's Legions.'[10]

What this meant in practice was a 'back to the land' campaign, intended not to create a political party but to forge a new breed of 'Romanian man' by dint of work and the force of example. Numbers were small to begin with, with some 2,500 subscribers to the Legion's periodical, *Ancestral Land*, but slowly increased over the next two years through a series of propaganda marches around the north Romanian countryside. Public meetings only started in 1929. The Legion retained its heavy religious overtones, as well as an overt anti-Semitism; but it vastly strengthened its populist base by reaching out to the most economically downtrodden, ignorant and credulous element in Romanian society, the peasantry. Codreanu records one such expedition to a remote part of Moldavia in 1930. He and his followers arrived on horseback decked out in feathered hats and white linen smocks with crosses, like crusaders. Of the

[10] Quoted in Weber, *Varieties of Fascism*, 100.

peasants who gathered around them he commented, 'None among them knew who we were and what we wanted, but all of them had the premonition we had come to save them.'[11] The legionaries did not just orate, however, but usually joined in village work, helping to build bridges and dykes, repair roads and gather the harvest; often they stayed for weeks in communities where no urban politician had ever set foot. The Legion's first political successes were in precisely such remote rural constituencies. With the onset of the Depression, however, its appeal broadened geographically and socially; in a context of plummeting agricultural prices, a decline in real wages and where civil servants remained unpaid for months, fascism's potential recruitment base was always likely to expand.

By 1930 the founding of the Iron Guard, the Legion's political wing, reflected Romanian fascism's progression from movement to political party. In the 1931 elections the Iron Guard attracted a mere 34,000 votes, or 1.2 per cent of the total; yet later that year Codreanu and his father were returned to parliament in by-elections, and by the general election of July 1932 the new party had a total of five seats. What limited the Guard's rise as a party, however, even as it raised their newsworthiness to stratospheric heights, was their predilection for violence. Codreanu had already set an example in this regard, and it is estimated that between 1924 and 1939 no fewer than eleven political murders were committed by legionaries. In retaliation, 501 legionaries were killed by the authorities. The movement's frequent changes of name were due to the fact that the government kept dissolving it because of its violent behaviour; it would then re-brand itself under a new name. This happened in 1931, again in 1932, and again in December 1933, during a particularly violent election, which saw the deaths of half a dozen legionaries; at the end of the month, in revenge, three legionaries assassinated Ion Duca, the Liberal prime minister, before surrendering themselves to the police.

The Iron Guard's survival, and their continuing success, depended to some extent on Codreanu's ability to sidestep legal blame for such outrages, despite his obvious complicity. It also depended on the dire economic climate, the unpopularity of the ruling Liberal Party, and on King Carol's willingness to tolerate the Guard, as a sort of counterweight to the liberals. The result was an atmosphere in which support for the Guard spread. In 1936 Codreanu founded a Legionary Workers' Corps to exploit discontent among the industrial working class, which soon had some 6,000 members. The international scene, in particular the growing dominance of the two fascist powers, made its own contribution; and interest in the Iron Guard – now formally renamed All For the Fatherland – was heightened by the deaths of two legionaries, Ion Moța and Vasile Marin, fighting for Franco's nationalists in the Spanish Civil War,

---

[11] Codreanu, C.Z., 1976 [1936], *For My Legionaries (The Iron Guard)*, Madrid, 271.

and which the legionaries portrayed as 'a confrontation between communist atheism and Christianity'.[12] The funeral in Bucharest of these two 'martyrs', in February 1937, turned into a mass demonstration of legionary popularity, which King Carol now saw as a direct threat. The Iron Guard's high point was in the relatively free elections of December 1937, when All For the Fatherland polled 16 per cent of the vote and won 66 parliamentary seats, making it the third largest party in the country.

Yet the essential impracticality as well as uncontrollability of Romanian fascism was revealed in the next three years. Codreanu steadfastly refused to join any coalition government, and the gulf between the Iron Guard and the palace was deepened by their loudly advertised hostility to Carol's Jewish mistress. The breakdown of negotiations was one of the factors influencing the king's proclamation of a royal dictatorship in February 1938; but the open support of the Iron Guard by Nazi Germany meant Carol could hardly rest easy with the Guard's leader at large, and Codreanu was arrested, tried for complicity in previous legionary crimes, convicted and sentenced to ten years' hard labour. In Codreanu's absence, those legionaries who had so far escaped imprisonment, under the interim leadership of Horia Sima, radicalised still further, indulging in a spate of assaults, beatings and shootings. In response, on 29–30 November the government of Armand Călinescu had Codreanu and thirteen other legionaries murdered 'while trying to escape'. Over the following year a state of open warfare between the guardists and the government spiralled out of control. The legionaries were infiltrated by the police, and many of them were tortured, beaten to death or summarily executed. In revenge, the legionaries assassinated Călinescu in September 1939. Across the country, the government ordered local prefects to select and execute three legionaries for every county; their bodies were then strung up in public places in an attempt to intimidate the rest. Dozens of legionaries in government internment were shot.

King Carol's downfall as a result of Romania's forced cession of territories in 1940, and the subsequent dictatorship of General Antonescu, turned the fortunes of the Iron Guard right-side up again. In September 1940 Antonescu, at German urging, declared an amnesty for all legionaries, invited the guard into coalition, and proclaimed a National Legionary State, with Sima as deputy prime minister and five other legionaries in the cabinet. As a party of government, however, Romania's fascists soon proved their unsuitability: they were simply too radical, violent and irresponsible to coexist with Antonescu. In November they unleashed an anti-Jewish pogrom, and started summarily murdering various political enemies, including the historian and former prime minister, Nicolae Iorga, whom they kidnapped and tortured to death.

---

[12] Săndulescu, V., 2007, 'Sacralised Politics in Action: The February 1937 Burial of the Romanian Legionary Leaders Ion Moța and Vasile Marin', *Totalitarian Movements & Political Religions*, VIII, #2, June, 261.

Antonescu, motivated above all by German pressure to keep Romania stable and ensure oil supplies to Hitler in preparation for the coming assault on the Soviet Union, was forced to turn on his supposed partners. In January 1941, in response to an attempted coup by Sima, the Iron Guard was brutally crushed by the Romanian army, with the full support of Hitler, who clearly preferred having a stable Romania under Antonescu to one destabilised by fascists. For four days fighting raged in Bucharest, with a guardist-controlled radio station broadcasting songs glorifying death. The legionaries managed to kill several thousands, including Jews, before succumbing, while their own dead were so numerous that the corpses had to be hung on meathooks in the city's abattoirs. The regime which took Romania into war in June 1941 had therefore come full circle, and conservative authoritarianism proved more than equal to native fascism.

Fascism in Eastern Europe was a complex phenomenon. It could, as in Romania, be initiated and inspired by academics and the educated, or semi-educated; but it was clearly populist both in nature and in its support, appealing to both the rural and urban masses. All the successor states had similar problems: difficulties with economic integration, with minorities, with making pluralist politics work. All suffered under the hammer blow of the Depression, and were victims of the international situation, with most incapable of withstanding the gravitational pull of Nazi Germany in the 1930s. But East European fascism was clearly also an indigenous product: it was not just copied from outside models in Italy and Germany. The most striking features of East European fascism were its abiding radicalism and its inability to overcome the entrenched power of conservative authoritarianism. As we have seen, Eastern Europe had plenty of authoritarians, so fascists were not only redundant, but bound to remain radical and anti-establishment. Because East European societies remained so backward, however, there was still a deep vein of popular dissatisfaction to be worked by fascist movements. In many respects fascists in this period appealed to the same dissatisfactions and needs that, after 1945, gave communism its momentary allure. What made fascism seem the more attractive option, between the wars, was the stigma attached to the Left of being associated with the Soviet Union and – however unjustly – with Jewishness, in other words, with non-national forces. Nationalism, in this period, was inevitably as strong as the popular yearning for social justice. By appealing to both, fascism achieved a temporary success in some quarters, before pulling the house down on itself, and on everyone else.

8

The East European origins of the Second World War

It is worth remembering that the Second World War literally began in Eastern Europe, over an East European dispute, even if there were obviously global issues at stake by September 1939. This means that the East European milestones on the road to war are familiar ones; most students have heard of the *Anschluß*, the Munich crisis, the invasion of Poland. The specific regional quarrels, by contrast, are less familiar, as is Eastern Europe's unenviable position as a bone of contention between the two regional hegemons, Nazi Germany and the Soviet Union. This German-Soviet rivalry was implicit in the entire post-1918 scenario: Eastern Europe between the wars constituted a power vacuum, waiting to be filled. A Western perspective can blind us to the fact that, just as an East European dispute was the trigger for the war, so Eastern Europe was the crucial battlefield of the conflict, especially once the Soviet Union was involved.

After January 1933, when Hitler was appointed German chancellor, the nature and goals of the Nazi dictatorship made some sort of conflict, whether regional or general, seem much more likely. In this threatening situation the governments and peoples of Eastern Europe were on the whole helpless pawns, with only limited ability to shape events; the initial hopes of the Allies at Versailles, that the successor states would act as a brake on a resurgent Germany, and a buffer against Soviet communism, proved to be singularly ill-placed. Instead, the region found itself subjected to external pressures it was poorly equipped to withstand. These pressures were partly economic, rooted in East European societies' vulnerability to German domination, which in turn was facilitated by the Western powers' own disengagement from Eastern Europe, both economically and politically; they were partly strategic, since the region proved the testing ground for a complex clash of competing ideologies, intertwined with related strategic goals. The specifically East European origins of the war are to be sought in this collision of economic and strategic interests.

Economic interests

Specific aspects of Eastern Europe's economic position made it a tempting prospect for Nazi Germany, but also encouraged the gravitation of East European governments towards Germany even before 1933.

Economic protectionism, the tendency to put up trade barriers to shelter manufacturing and agriculture from outside competition, returned as a result of the Depression, and yet in the longer term remained self-defeating. Apart from putting up tariffs, governments resorted to a number of desperate measures to combat the slump. Most of them were forced to abandon the gold standard, in order to hive off their economies from the worst effects of the Depression. There was a region-wide resort to state intervention in the economy: cancellation of debt for agricultural producers, reduction of taxes, subsidisation of farm prices and, most strikingly, the creation of state-owned purchasing bodies for buying up agricultural produce. There was less governments could do for native industries, whose goods simply could not compete abroad; but overall the rise in state intervention, and the sudden enthusiasm for Keynesian 'pump priming', were perhaps factors in disposing public opinion towards an even more drastic form of interventionism, namely communism, after 1945. Despite such measures, however, the economic prospects of the entire region remained grim. As Iván T. Berend has observed, none of these small to medium-sized economies was ever likely to achieve self-sufficiency in this period: 'They could not manage without imports; consequently, they had to export.'[1] And exporting, given the almost total lack of a market for East European goods and produce in Western Europe, not to mention the Soviet Union, meant exporting to Germany.

Even before the Depression, the logic of seeing Eastern Europe as a sort of economic hinterland was apparent to most German statesmen and businessmen, and in this relationship Germany, for all the economic handicaps imposed on it by Versailles and the Depression, was bound to be the dominant partner. As one German diplomat put it in 1928, for the successor states 'the impulse towards the German language, economy and culture bears the character of a geographical-historical necessity.'[2] The establishment of the Nazi dictatorship, itself a product of the economic crash, only served to accentuate and deepen this dependency; indeed, furthering it became one of the principal economic goals of the Nazi regime. East European governments, for their part, were only too glad to grasp this economic lifeline, their readiness spurred by the spectacle of a rapidly industrialising Soviet Union. The transformation of the latter into an economic and military superpower was well under way by the early 1930s; by 1938 the Soviet Union was the third largest economy in the world, after the United States and Germany, and this not unreasonably petrified East European leaders. In the absence of meaningful economic and diplomatic support from

[1]   Berend, I.T., 1998, *Decades of Crisis: Central and Eastern Europe before World War II*, Berkeley, CA, Los Angeles, CA and London, 243.
[2]   Quoted in Okey, R., 1982, *Eastern Europe 1740-1980: Feudalism to Communism*, London, Melbourne, Sydney, Auckland and Johannesburg, 168.

Britain and France the inclination of East European governments to curry favour with Hitler was understandable, if misguided.

In these circumstances the attempts of East European governments to insulate their economies from the worst effects of the Depression could never be enough; they also needed to be part of some larger economic structure, in this case Germany's regional hegemony. The principal instruments of this subordination were so-called clearance agreements between Germany and its East European neighbours, also known as blocked-mark or exchange clearance agreements. An East European exporter wishing to sell on the German market paid into his own country's central bank a sum, in the native currency, equivalent to its value in German Reichsmarks; a German exporter did the same in reverse, paying Reichsmarks into the German central bank. As the exchange system built up, trade deals were effected by each national bank paying its exporter out of the accumulated deposits. These bilateral trade treaties, by which each state undertook to export to its partner in return for importing from it, were effectively a form of barter obviating the need for currency transfers, and preceded the Nazi regime. They had their roots in the weakness of both the German mark and East European currencies, and the consequent need on both sides to hoard reserves of hard currency. Initially suggested by Austria in 1931, the first clearance agreement was concluded between that country and Yugoslavia in January 1932. In the same year Germany signed similar treaties with six different countries in south-eastern Europe, and the Nazi government enthusiastically continued the policy. The Italian government followed suit. The Nazi regime also concluded, in the course of 1934–5, a series of separate trade agreements with Hungary, Yugoslavia, Bulgaria and Romania, which guaranteed the purchase of East European produce through a system of quotas and subsidies, the net effect of which was to lock these countries into even more barter with the Third Reich. The advantages, however, were striking: Hungary's agricultural exports doubled in a single year; Germany's share of Bulgarian exports went from 30 per cent to 43 per cent between 1929 and 1937, of Yugoslavian exports from 9 to 22 per cent; by 1938, 31 per cent of Estonia's imports and 39 per cent of Latvia's were German in origin. Only in the Baltic states, unusually, did Germany face competition, from Britain; but the overall pattern of German economic preponderance was not broken. Apart from Austria and Czechoslovakia, industrialised economies whose trade with Germany declined in the 1930s, East European countries purchased between 25 and 30 per cent of their imports from Germany. This was a powerful incentive to cleave ever closer to the Nazi regime, whatever the political objections. It is estimated that between 1933 and 1939 Germany's share of Eastern Europe's trade increased from one-sixth to a half. Germany suddenly had ready access to vital raw materials and foodstuffs, an assured supply of which was crucial for Hitler's war plans. The East European states gained an essential lifeline to the expanding German economy at a time when markets further afield were closed to them.

Strategic pressures and the clash of rival imperialisms

We still tend to associate the term 'imperialism' with Western domination of non-Europeans. The history of Eastern Europe in the twentieth century, however, serves to remind us that imperialism can also be contiguous, exercising control over peoples in close proximity to the imperialist power. There are three aspects to the role that imperialist visions, and the strategic imperatives accompanying them, played in the origins of the Second World War. Firstly, and most obviously, there are the world view and strategic goals of what has rightly been called Nazi imperialism, and which was firmly focused, not overseas, but on Eastern Europe itself. A subsidiary component of Nazi Germany's imperialism, because allied to it, is the imperialism of Fascist Italy. Secondly, we should not forget what Hugh Seton-Watson called the 'small-power imperialisms' of East European states: one of the factors facilitating Nazi Germany's policy of divide and rule was the rivalry and bad feeling between individual states.[3] Thirdly, only a blinkered apologist for Soviet communism would deny that the Soviet Union had its own imperialist counter-vision, rooted partly in the commitment to defend communism and extend its sway if possible, but partly also in the Soviet conviction that the territories lost after 1918 should be gathered back under Moscow's control. The expansion of this vision to encompass additional parts of Eastern Europe, it should be stressed, developed only in the closing stages of the Second World War and after.

Nazi imperialism

We can hardly understand the war's origins unless we recognise the twin pillars upon which National Socialism, and hence Nazi Germany's foreign policy, were based. Firstly, Nazism was not only ultra-nationalist but racist, in that it assumed the racial superiority of Germans, and the racial inferiority of others. This meant that the Nazi regime considered the German people entitled to dominate Europe, especially Eastern Europe, and that the largely Slavic population of the region should in the longer term be displaced by a 'nucleus of eighty to one hundred million colonizing Germans.'[4] Even before coming to power, Hitler made it clear that this aim of dominating Eastern Europe took priority over any revival of Germany's pre-war colonial empire: in 1932 the Führer envisaged the eventual expulsion of Czechs, Poles and others to Siberia. In the interim, however, Nazi policy towards Eastern Europe was rather more rational, and presupposed the establishment of a *Großraumwirtschaft* or

---

[3]   Seton-Watson, H., 1967 [1962], *Eastern Europe between the Wars 1918-1941*, 3rd edn, revised, New York, Evanston, IL and London, 320.
[4]   Quoted in Kaiser, D.E., 1980, *Economic Diplomacy and the Origins of the Second World War: Germany, Britain, France and Eastern Europe 1930-1939*, Princeton, NJ, 60.

'extra-territorial economy', whereby the German people's well-being would be safeguarded through the secure supply of foodstuffs and raw materials from the lands immediately adjacent to the Reich.

Secondly, coupled with Nazi racism was the belief, building on pre-Nazi attitudes among Germans generally, in the need for *Lebensraum* or 'living space'. The assumption that Germany's burgeoning population could only be accommodated by the acquisition of additional territory for resettlement preceded the First World War. What Woodruff D. Smith calls '*Lebensraum* imperialism' became part of Germany's aims during the war, reaching its fullest realisation in the Treaty of Brest-Litovsk in 1918.[5] Post-war, the Nazis were thus not the only voices inclined to take up this agenda, an inclination reinforced by Germany's wartime experience of blockade and starvation. But the Nazis' racist outlook gave the quest for *Lebensraum* an obsessional urgency, and by contrast to pre-war imperialism, Nazi imperialism concentrated entirely on Eastern Europe. As Hitler put it in *Mein Kampf*, 'such a territorial policy cannot be fulfilled in the Cameroons, but today almost exclusively in Europe.'[6] In his *Secret Book* (1928), Hitler was even more explicit: Germany must acquire 'sufficient living space for the next hundred years', and this 'can only be in the East.'[7]

These underlying preoccupations of racial superiority and demographic displacement only became obvious once the Second World War began; but in the six years previous the Nazis' goal of regional hegemony became ever clearer. The trade agreements with East European states locked them into Germany's orbit, while the Western powers' hesitancy or indifference confirmed the trend. When, in 1938–9, Germany finally embarked on territorial aggrandisement, it encountered minimal resistance from France and Britain, and willing assistance among the successor states.

Fascist imperialism

Mussolini's regime made its own contribution to destabilising Eastern Europe, even if the principal focus of Fascist imperialism was Africa. Since Italy already possessed much of the Adriatic littoral, together with the Dodecanese Islands, it treated the western Balkans as its natural sphere of influence. In addition, Austria was seen as a potential Italian satellite; certainly Mussolini posed as Austria's protector. For most of the interwar period, however, with the exception of the brief occupation of Greek Corfù in 1923, Italian policy in the region

[5] Smith, W.D., 1986, *The Ideological Origins of Nazi Imperialism*, New York and Oxford, 83, 187.
[6] Quoted in Bell, P.M.H., *The Origins of the Second World War in Europe*, London and New York, 80.
[7] Quoted in Bell, *The Origins of the Second World War in Europe*, 80.

was relatively restrained. Mussolini was content to subsidise the Austrian *Heimwehr*, to keep Yugoslavia weak by covert support for Macedonian and Croatian nationalists, to browbeat Greece where he could, and to exercise a preponderant influence in the domestic affairs of Albania. Fascist adventurism was also held in check by the unfavourable international climate of the 1920s.

The rhetoric of the regime was nevertheless bellicose from the start, and by the early 1930s Fascism's inherent propensity for aggression was seeking expression on the international stage. Mussolini lauded war as both noble and natural, 'like eating a plate of macaroni.'[8] Imperialism, the subjugation of other societies by the strong, was 'an eternal and immutable law of life.'[9] In 1934 Mussolini was still capable of posing as defender of the existing order, when he mobilised the Italian army in response to the attempted Nazi coup in Vienna, at which point Hitler hastily backed down. Italy's attack on Ethiopia in 1935, however, was a fateful stage in the breakdown of international order, because by demonstrating the toothlessness of the League of Nations and the passivity of the Western powers, it emboldened Hitler's regime, drove Italy itself towards an alliance with Germany, and reinforced the sense of isolation and helplessness among East European governments, faced with the rise of these two predatory regional hegemons. Italo-German intervention on the nationalist side in the Spanish Civil War completed the discomfiture of the Western democracies and underlined Eastern Europe's vulnerability. Much of the manoeuvring of East European governments from the mid-1930s reflected this uncomfortable reality.

'Small-power imperialisms'

Nationalism, and the burning desire to revise the post-war settlement, were obvious factors in German and Italian policy in Eastern Europe. Equally important were the rivalries and animosities of the East European states. Some were frankly revisionist, with designs on their neighbours' territory, based either on historic claims or the existence of stranded minorities; others, the targets of this revisionism, hoped to maintain the territorial status quo; several were upholders of the status quo in one direction, while entertaining revisionist ambitions in another. It is no exaggeration to say that these divisions rendered any sort of coordinated response to aggression problematical.

In theory the territorial status quo was guaranteed by the so-called Little Entente, a system of alliances concluded in 1920–1 between Czechoslovakia, Yugoslavia and Romania, with the encouragement of France. The Little Entente was designed for common defence against Hungarian revisionism,

---

[8]   Quoted in Bell, *The Origins of the Second World War in Europe*, 61.
[9]   Quoted in Knox, M., 1984, 'Conquest, Foreign and Domestic, in Fascist Italy and Nazi Germany', *Journal of Modern History*, LVI, #1, March, 17.

a need seemingly given point by ex-King Charles of Habsburg's attempts, in 1921, to regain his throne. The treaties establishing the Entente aimed to resist any Habsburg restoration, as well as any changes to the borders agreed by the Treaties of Trianon and Saint-Germain. At the time of the 1925 Locarno Treaty between France, Britain and Germany, whereby the latter reaffirmed acceptance of its post-war Western boundaries, France also concluded military alliances with Poland and Czechoslovakia.

In reality, and despite regular talks on military cooperation after 1929, and the creation of a permanent council and secretariat in 1933, the Little Entente proved hardly worth the paper it was written on. Long before the mid-1930s, when Germany's economic attraction as well as its military recovery became irresistible to East European governments, it was apparent that France's interest in the Little Entente was primarily defensive, and implied no serious commitment of French forces to the region. The building of the Maginot Line along the Franco-German frontier, undertaken between 1929 and 1934, sent out all the wrong signals about French willingness to protect Eastern Europe. Great Britain's disinterest in the region was even clearer. Just as crippling, however, were the divisions between East European states, which can be rehearsed briefly.

Next to the Germans, *Hungarians* were arguably the most obsessively revisionist people in Europe. No Hungarian political group accepted the terms of the Treaty of Trianon, by which historic Hungary had been partitioned. The fact that the territories ceded to Czechoslovakia, Romania and Yugoslavia in 1920 were inhabited by majorities of Slovaks, Romanians and South Slavs respectively, as well as ethnic Magyar minorities, was irrelevant. Coupled to this intransigence was a long-standing imperialist assumption that the Hungarian nation was the natural 'people of culture' in the Danubian basin, entitled to dominate the peoples surrounding them; this was an attitude still being articulated by Hungarian politicians in the 1930s. The treatment of Magyar minorities in neighbouring states was the subject of repeated appeals by the Hungarian government to the League of Nations, even though this treatment varied. Hungarians in Yugoslavia were undoubtedly discriminated against in terms of educational provision, and subjected to expropriation of landed estates; some were even deported following King Alexander's assassination. In Romanian Transylvania many Hungarian nobles were subjected to expropriation, although many were allowed to retain their estates; considerable restrictions were placed on Magyar-language education, and after 1918 positions in state employment became increasingly difficult to attain for minorities. Only in Czechoslovakia did Magyars fare better, profiting from firmer democratic rights, a more relaxed educational policy and even, despite the expropriation of large estates, from land redistribution to Magyar peasants, who also benefited from protective tariffs in 1930. Such relative mildness did not, however, make the Magyar minority much better disposed towards Czechoslovak rule.

Hungary's relations with the successor states thus remained poisonous. A massive propaganda effort was sustained throughout the interwar period, aimed at winning over opinion in the West to the justice of Hungary's cause. An early convert was Mussolini, who connived in the *Ustaša* plot to murder King Alexander in 1934; despite having recently expelled *Ustaša* members, Hungary was accused of complicity in the assassination. Hungary's relationship with Romania, however, was the worst, and as Germany's regional preponderance increased in the 1930s, both states found themselves in an unseemly competition for German favour, on Hungary's side in the hope of securing Hitler's support for revision, on Romania's side in the hope of averting revision. This slavish relationship paid off for Hungary in the short term. By the First Vienna Award of September 1938, Hungary profited in two stages from the partition of Czechoslovakia, receiving the southern, largely Magyar-inhabited slice of Slovakia, and then sub-Carpathian Ruthenia in March 1939. Hungary also won its competition with Romania, following the fall of France in June 1940: by the Second Vienna Award, mediated by Germany, Romania was forced to cede north Transylvania to Hungary in August 1940. Reacquisition of the Bačka region from Yugoslavia followed the German assault on that country in 1941.

Bulgaria posed a lesser threat to the status quo than Hungary, because its potential for doing so was much less. If Bulgarian nationalists had an imperialist goal it was the 'big Bulgaria' denied them in the nineteenth century, and although Bulgaria had gained territory subsequently its defeat in 1918 lost it access to the Aegean, never to be regained, except briefly during the Second World War. Bulgaria's weakness and friendlessness forced it to accept this situation, while at the same time ensuring a murderous relationship with IMRO, the Macedonian revolutionary nationalist movement. Bulgarian foreign policy for much of the period after the toppling of Stamboliski in 1923 was based on cooperation with Mussolini's Italy, which held out hopes of support for revision vis-à-vis Yugoslavia; but relations were worst of all with Greece, which possessed much of Macedonia and most of the Aegean coast. It was not until the mid-1930s that the Zveno regime felt strong enough to challenge IMRO, by reducing its base at Petrich, and cultivating better ties with Yugoslavia. The royal dictatorship of Boris III continued this delicate balancing act, signing a pact of eternal friendship with Yugoslavia in January 1937 and, in July 1938, adhering to the Salonika agreement, whereby the Balkan states undertook never to use force against one another. Following the Munich crisis of 1938, however, Boris' government found it impossible to resist the pressure to side with the Axis powers, especially since this could pay revisionist dividends. In September 1940 Hitler forced Romania to cede the Southern Dobrudja back to Bulgaria; but the quid pro quo was Bulgaria's accession to the Tripartite Pact in March 1941. Further gains at the expense of Yugoslavia followed the latter's invasion by the Axis in April 1941; and the Axis conquest of Greece rewarded

Bulgaria with its lost strip of Aegean coastline. As with Hungary, however, the ultimate price for this was Bulgaria's enforced participation in the Nazi-Soviet war.

Interwar *Poland* was by definition imperialist, however much its patriots might repudiate the suggestion. From its foundation Poland included substantial numbers of ethnic Germans, and in 1919 took over large numbers of Ukrainians, Jews and Belorussians, and some Lithuanians, Czechs and Slovaks. Much of this territory was temporarily lost in the seesaw war with Soviet Russia, but by 1921 Poland's eastern frontier reincorporated Vilnius, a sizeable slice of Belarus minus Minsk, and eastern Galicia. Relations with Lithuania were permanently soured by the re-occupation of Vilnius in October 1920; and the dispute with Czechoslovakia over Teschen was equally bitter. The Czechoslovakian government tried, and failed, to take this largely Polish city by force in January 1919, but was repulsed by the Poles. In July 1920, however, at the low point of the Polish-Soviet War, Poland felt obliged to accept a partition decided by the great powers: Poland retained most of the city, but Czechoslovakia was awarded the coal-rich territory to the south known as Trans-Olja. As a result any sort of Polish-Czechoslovak cooperation was impossible down to Czechoslovakia's partition by Hitler in 1938, when Poland reclaimed the remainder of the Teschen area. The ground had been prepared for this carve-up in January 1938, when Hitler and Colonel Józef Beck, the Polish foreign minister, agreed that 'the whole structure of the Czech state was impossible.'[10] In addition to these regional ambitions, the colonels' regime even entertained delusions of winning a role overseas, bizarrely arguing that Poland should be allotted some of Germany's former African colonies, as an outlet for Poland's surplus peasantry as well as its Jews. This internally riven state, which had every interest in promoting a stable international environment, was itself a potential threat to the status quo. It was hardly surprising that, when Poland's turn on the chopping block arrived in 1939, its neighbours eagerly queued up to profit from its demise.

Expansionist aims were hardly the preserve of large, seemingly powerful states like Poland. *Lithuania*, smarting from its loss of Vilnius in 1920, compensated itself in 1923 by seizing the largely German-inhabited port of Memel (Klaipeda) from Germany; as a result it remained on bad terms with both its huge neighbours. Lithuania was eventually awarded Vilnius in 1939, following the Nazi-Soviet partition of Poland, only to be swallowed up itself by the Soviet Union the next year. *Greece*, despite or perhaps because of its catastrophic expulsion from Asia Minor in 1922, and the collapse of its dreams of a revived Greek empire, harboured pretensions to influence in chaotic Albania, which put it on a collision course with Fascist Italy. *Yugoslavia*, like

---

[10] Quoted in Thorne, C., 1972, *The Approach of War 1938-39*, London, 55.

Poland seen from its inception by many of its constituent peoples as exercising a sort of Serb imperialist dominion over them, played a bullying role against Bulgaria in an attempt to neutralise the terrorist organisation IMRO. This rebounded on King Alexander personally, when IMRO collaborated with the Croatian *Ustaša* in the King's assassination. Yugoslavia's vulnerability to nationalist terror did not hinder the Stojadinović government from concluding that Austria's *Anschluß* with Germany was 'inevitable', and a 'purely domestic question.'[11]

Finally, the *Soviet Union* was also a revisionist power. Clearly, this communist state did not see itself as imperialist; that was the crime of 'capitalist' societies like Britain, France and Germany. Yet Soviet revisionism, aiming to reacquire territories formerly held by the tsars, made its own contribution to the internecine rivalries of East European states, while the mere existence of the Soviet Union on their borders struck fear into the hearts of East European rulers and elites. During the Russian Civil War, with the exceptions of the three Baltic republics and Finland, all of whom concluded peace treaties with the Soviets in 1920, no state even had diplomatic relations with this pariah regime, which preached world revolution; it was only with the signature of peace treaties and the necessary demarcation of borders that some minimal links were established. Borders agreed in this early period, however, were seen as only provisional by the Soviet government. Finland's possession of eastern Karelia, and Romania's of Bessarabia, were disputed by Moscow, as was the entire Polish-Soviet border and the very right to exist of the new Baltic states. Abhorrence of communism did the rest. Greece and Albania only formally recognised the Soviet Union in 1924; Bulgaria established relations only to break them off following the Soviet-inspired uprising of 1923; and some successor states – Czechoslovakia, Yugoslavia, Romania and Hungary – delayed recognition until the 1930s.

The only states to cultivate active ties with the Soviet Union almost from the outset were its two fellow outcasts, Germany and Turkey. In the case of Germany, which declared a policy of benevolent neutrality during the Polish-Soviet War, in the vain hope of border adjustments, the Weimar government soon found Soviet help in circumventing the arms restrictions imposed upon it by Versailles. Almost immediately upon conclusion of a German-Soviet commercial agreement, in May 1921, the German army began secret military collaboration with Moscow, whereby German personnel received training in forbidden weaponry like tanks and aircraft; in return the Soviet Union was advised on its own arms build-up. The Treaty of Rapallo of April 1922, which re-established formal relations between the two countries, while mutually renouncing claims for reparations or territorial compensation, further deepened this relationship, which continued until Hitler's advent to power in 1933. With

---

[11] Quoted in Thorne, *The Approach of War*, 38.

Turkey, too, the Soviet Union shared common enemies in the Western Allies, who were occupying territory in both countries as of 1920. The Soviet-Turkish treaty of March 1921 established diplomatic relations as well as agreeing borders, and subsequently Soviet arms supplies made a material difference to the Turks in their successful war against Greece and its Western backers.

The profound ideological chasm between the Soviet Union and Eastern Europe remained, but long before the end of the 1920s it was apparent that the Soviets were resuming the mantle of a great power, and becoming adept at using the traditional arguments of diplomacy. In 1924 Comintern was still advocating national self-determination for the 'oppressed minorities' of Poland, Czechoslovakia, Romania, Yugoslavia and Greece. By 1929 Stalin's commissar for foreign affairs, Maxim Litvinov, was blithely concluding friendship treaties with some of these same states, in order to loosen their ties with the Western powers and weaken a perceived anti-Soviet coalition. Economically, too, the Soviet role in the region was increasingly felt. When the Depression hit, the Soviets hardly improved the situation in Eastern Europe by dumping their own products on the market, although the initiation of Stalin's first Five Year Plan in theory posited greater commercial cooperation. Even Hitler's accession to power did not immediately send German-Soviet relations into deep freeze. On the contrary, since Comintern's line on fascism was that it was essentially the gravedigger of capitalism, proof of the latter's terminal crisis, Stalin looked on the Nazi dictatorship with remarkable complacency to begin with; only after a couple of years did Moscow start urging European communist parties to form 'popular fronts' in the fight against fascism.

By the time Soviet policy changed direction it was arguably too late to coordinate any credible defence against Nazi imperialism, not least because the Soviet Union's revisionist agenda was still undeniable. The first breach in the network of East European alliances originally set up by France to box Germany in was the friendship pact signed between Germany and Poland on 26 January 1934. Poland's foreign minister Józef Beck was inspired to conclude this deal, logical enough from a Polish perspective, partly through fear of the Soviets, but partly also by his contempt for France and hatred of Czechoslovakia. The response of Czechoslovakia and France to this blow was finally to turn to the Soviets; in the words of French foreign minister Louis Barthou, the USSR was 'the only great counter-weight in the East against Germany'.[12] First, the Soviet Union had to be persuaded to join the League of Nations in 1934. Secondly, a Franco-Soviet pact of mutual assistance was concluded in May 1935, followed two weeks later by a similar pact between the Soviet Union and Czechoslovakia. The only problem with these belated measures was that the security they provided was minimal. Apart from the hostility this supping

[12] Quoted in Macartney, C.A. and Palmer, A.W., 1962, *Independent Eastern Europe: A History*, London, 322–3.

with the Communist devil aroused elsewhere, including in Britain, the Soviet-Czechoslovak treaty only came into force if Czechoslovakia's ally France had already come to Czechoslovakia's aid. In short, the Soviet Union's commitment to 'fighting fascism' remained notional, while the fear it inspired in East European governments bulked as large as ever. The extent to which Stalin's regime had abandoned ideological struggle in favour of great power politics became fully apparent with the signature of the Nazi-Soviet Pact in August 1939.

The road to war 1935–9

Given our Western-oriented notions of chronology, which habitually date the outbreak of the Second World War from September 1939, it is worth noting that Eastern Europe's full involvement in the war was only reached in June 1941, with the Nazi invasion of the Soviet Union. This chapter, however, takes the story down to 1939; the following two years belong properly to the treatment of the war itself.

Nazi Gradualism 1933-36. Unlike the origins of the First World War, which continue to be controversial, there is not much dispute that Nazi Germany is key to explaining the origins of the Second World War. Germany was the principal revisionist power, with multiple grievances rooted in the perceived denial of national self-determination by Versailles: the ban on *Anschluß* with Austria; the stranding of Sudeten Germans in Czechoslovakia; the status of Danzig and the German minority in Poland; the presence of German enclaves across Eastern Europe from the Baltic to Yugoslavia. Nazism as an ideology was pan-German, aiming at the unification of all Germans; and Nazi racism insisted on the German people's right to dominate the continent, and to displace 'inferior' peoples, especially in Eastern Europe. As Germany recovered after 1933, and Germany's natural economic hegemony in Eastern Europe reasserted itself, so too grew the prospect of all these issues being opened up. Nor were the Western powers, Britain and France, anywhere near as engaged, economically and strategically, in Eastern Europe. On the contrary: conscious of their own weakness, divided as to how to respond to the fascist dictatorships, and anxious to buy time, France and Britain each in its own way followed a policy of appeasement after 1935.

Caution guided Hitler's foreign policy during his first three years in power, even though the Nazi regime's immediate withdrawal in 1933 from the League of Nations, and from the World Disarmament Conference, were clear signals that its sympathies did not lie with international cooperation. It was not until 1935, emboldened by Mussolini's invasion of Ethiopia, that Germany announced it would no longer be bound by the Versailles armaments restrictions. German rearmament affected the regional balance of forces at once. The psychological watershed, however, was in March 1936, when Germany marched troops into the Rhineland; the tacit acceptance by Britain and France of this open breach of the Versailles system had a profound effect in Eastern Europe. So too did the involvement of Italy and Germany in the Spanish Civil War, which again was tolerated by the Western powers. This signalled to Hitler that his expansionist agenda in Eastern Europe could proceed, and to East European governments that they were basically on their own, and would have to make their own accommodation with Hitler. Only Czechoslovakia continued to follow a Western-oriented foreign policy, and even that was necessarily counter-balanced by the Soviet alliance of 1935.

The bilateral trade treaties strengthened Germany's economic ties with the region. In secret, however, Hitler was framing plans for territorial expansion by late 1937, and was willing to risk war with the Western powers in pursuit of this. The notorious Hoßbach memorandum of 10 November envisaged a simultaneous attack on both Austria and Czechoslovakia. Ostensibly, and in terms of public preparation for such expansion, the Nazi regime based its claims on the principle of national self-determination, gathering fellow Germans into the Reich. In reality, Hitler's designs were far more about securing resources, industrial capacity and population, as a springboard for yet further expansion eastwards; as Hitler put it to his generals, 'The aim of German policy was to make secure and to preserve the racial community and to enlarge it. It was therefore a question of space.'[13] Hitler was determined 'to solve Germany's problem of space at the latest by 1943–45', by which he clearly meant an attack on the Soviet Union.[14] In preparation for this supreme objective, which would simultaneously smash communism and secure *Lebensraum*, Germany first needed to augment its resources at the expense of Central and Eastern Europe.

Anschluß. The *Anschluß*, or union of Austria and Germany, was in the end carried out bloodlessly, and rather unexpectedly, in March 1938. By this point circumstances were radically different from July 1934, when Italy still posed as Austria's protector and Hitler had hastily to disavow involvement in the Austrian Nazis' attempted coup. Two years on international support for an independent Austria was eroding visibly. By 1936 Hitler and Mussolini were allies, and in November 1937 the latter even declared that 'he was tired of mounting guard over Austrian independence.'[15] In the same month the British government intimated to Hitler that Britain was prepared to countenance 'democratic change' in Austria's status. In 1938, Kurt von Schuschnigg,

---

[13] Hoßbach memorandum, 10 November 1937, in Adamthwaite, A. (ed.), 1980, *The Lost Peace: International Relations in Europe 1918-1939*, London, 189.
[14] Hoßbach memorandum, 10 November 1937, in Adamthwaite (ed.), *The Lost Peace*, 190.
[15] Quoted in Macartney and Palmer, *Independent Eastern Europe*, 334.

Dollfuß' successor as chancellor of the authoritarian *Ständestaat*, effectively provoked *Anschluß* by announcing a plebiscite on 9 March, as to whether Austrians wanted a 'free and German, an independent and social, a Christian and united Austria'.[16] Schuschnigg clearly intended to rig this, but it was a disastrous miscalculation, since Hitler reacted by ordering an immediate mobilisation. On the night of 11–12 March German troops marched into Austria where, rather to Hitler's surprise, they were greeted with near-universal enthusiasm. A subsequent plebiscite on 10 April, while undoubtedly rigged, confirmed the satisfaction or at least acceptance of *Anschluß* by most Austrians. Not all were ecstatic. Communists, social democrats and liberals were among the 70,000 arrested in the wake of the takeover, and Jews were especially vulnerable: hundreds committed suicide, and notoriously some were forced to scrub the pavements of Vienna by local Nazis and jeering onlookers. Indeed, the spontaneity of Austrian anti-Semitism in March 1938 was one factor in the Nazis' subsequent decision to control it, by means of a more systematic expropriation of Jewish property, followed by expulsion of Jews from the Reich. *Anschluß* for the sizeable Jewish community meant the loss of jobs, businesses and other property, prior to forced emigration; by late 1939 over 125,000 Austrian Jews had fled, including the world-famous founder of psychoanalysis, Sigmund Freud.

Munich. Ostensibly the three and a quarter million Sudeten Germans were the reason for the next stage of Nazi aggression, against Czechoslovakia, in September 1938. In reality, national self-determination was of secondary importance to Hitler compared with the accession of territory, resources and industrial capacity which a partition of Czechoslovakia promised. Yet there was no denying that the Czechoslovak state was deeply riven, with the dominant position of the Czechs resented by Slovaks as well as Germans, Magyars and Ruthenes, and that the Sudeten German problem in particular was exacerbated by the world economic crisis, the effects of which had fallen most heavily on these highly industrialised parts of the country.

Ever since Hitler's rise to power in 1933 many Sudeten Germans had been demanding Germany's intervention on their behalf, despite being arguably in a better position than any other minority in Eastern Europe. The 'Activists' among Sudetenlanders, who advocated working within the Czechoslovak system, saw their support fall away dramatically. In these circumstances it was not long before Prague banned the Sudeten German Nazi Party, in October 1933. Into this gap stepped Konrad Henlein's Sudeten German Homeland Front, in 1935 renamed the Sudeten German Party (*SdP*). In the elections of 1935, the *SdP* astonished everyone by winning 63 per cent of the German vote, and forty-four seats in the chamber of deputies, making it the second

---

[16] Quoted in Bell, *The Origins of the Second World War in Europe*, 228.

largest faction in the assembly. In the last local elections of May 1938, the *SdP* overwhelmed the Activist opposition among Sudeten Germans, mopping up 78 per cent of German votes. The *SdP* was not simply a flag of convenience for Nazis; on the contrary, it stood for German autonomy within Czechoslovakia, and did not formally espouse an annexationist stance until 1937, which enabled it to operate legally. Henlein, despite accepting subsidies from Hitler, instead saw his movement as a 'broad church', representing a specifically Sudeten German standpoint.[17] Yet the *SdP* was also undoubtedly represented hardline German nationalism, and in the absence of the banned Nazi Party it effectively became Hitler's stalking horse, the excuse for ratcheting up demands on the Czechoslovak government. The Austrian *Anschluß*, moreover, as a British diplomat reported, unleashed 'an avalanche of national feeling among the Sudeten Germans'; and the British military attaché commented that 'Nothing short of incorporation in the German Reich will [now] satisfy the majority of people.'[18] The *SdP* soon abandoned any pretence of moderation, and while Henlein's renewed demand for autonomy, on 24 April, stopped short of mentioning annexation, he had already agreed with Hitler that 'We must always demand so much that we can never be satisfied.'[19] This increased the incentive for Hitler to see his own demands through.

Until *Anschluß* the Czechoslovakian government was determined not to be intimidated by Nazi Germany, while doing its best not to give offence. Czechoslovakia's armed forces remained formidable by comparison with other East European states, and on paper at least the country had the backing of both France and the Soviet Union. *Anschluß*, however, seriously undermined Czechoslovakia's position, physically by exposing it to attack from the south, and morally by the clear signal it sent of a lack of Western resolve.

One nail in Czechoslovakia's coffin was the fall of the Popular Front government in France, on 10 April, and its succession by a government much more pessimistic about France's ability to resist Nazi aggression, and whose foreign minister already thought Czechoslovakia 'a doomed nation.'[20] To make matters worse, the French general staff was adamant that France was in no position, militarily, to honour its commitment to defend Czechoslovakia.

French defeatism was reinforced by British ambiguity. While British appeasement was rooted in a sense of unpreparedness for conflict, there is no doubt that significant elements of the British establishment were more inclined to sympathise with the alleged injustices done to the Sudeten Germans, and to

[17] Cornwall, M., 2011, 'The Czechoslovak Sphinx: "Moderate and Reasonable" Konrad Henlein', in R. Haynes and M. Rady (eds), *In the Shadow of Hitler: Personalities of the Right in Central and Eastern Europe*, London, 214.
[18] Quoted in Thorne, *The Approach of War*, 56.
[19] Quoted in Bruegel, J.W., 1973, *Czechoslovakia before Munich: The German Minority Problem and British Appeasement Policy*, Cambridge, 173.
[20] Quoted in Thorne, *Approach of War*, 58.

be critical of Czechoslovakia for not accommodating its minorities, not least because they were woefully misinformed; Prime Minister Neville Chamberlain, for instance, was not even aware that, until March 1938, the Czechoslovak cabinet contained three German Activist ministers. In reality neither France nor Britain was willing, at this point, to go to war in defence of Czechoslovakia, especially not if it meant cooperating with the Soviet Union.

The result, in the summer of 1938, was a spiralling crisis in which Hitler's increasingly belligerent demands on behalf of the Sudeten Germans were met with resistance in Prague, but increasingly placatory responses from Britain and France; Anglo-French pressure on Czechoslovakia to make concessions led to a progressive collapse of Czechoslovak resolve. At British and French insistence, President Beneš opened negotiations with Henlein, but these foundered on the latter's patent unwillingness to accept anything short of outright partition. In late July London forced Czechoslovakia to accept mediation; this eventually compelled Beneš's acceptance on 2 September of full autonomy for the Sudetenlanders, only to be rendered irrelevant by Henlein breaking off negotiations and fleeing to Germany, in a climate of rising, planned disorder among the Sudeten Germans. Hitler openly threatened war on 12 September but, to his astonishment, was forestalled by Chamberlain's offer to negotiate a peaceful settlement. In a series of personal summits in the last two weeks of September, and despite repeated war scares brought on by Hitler's bellicose rhetoric, the British and French governments concluded a deal over Czechoslovakia's head: the Sudetenland would be ceded to Germany forthwith and, were Czechoslovakia to refuse, France would consider itself freed of all obligation to its ally. The Four-Power Agreement reached at Munich on 29–30 September, under the notionally neutral chairmanship of Hitler's ally Mussolini, was one Prague was forced to accept, and signalled the first stage in Czechoslovakia's dismemberment. In supplementary agreements Czechoslovakia's other enemies rushed in for their share of the spoils: on 1 October Poland demanded and received some 800 square kilometres of industrial territory around Teschen, while the First Vienna Award of 2 November transferred southern Slovakia and southern Ruthenia to Hungary. Czechoslovakia was stripped of its frontier defences, as well as 11,000 square miles of territory, most of its industrial capacity, and 800,000 Czechs, included in the lost territories.

The Munich settlement remains to this day the most egregious example of democratic principles sacrificed on the altar of *Realpolitik* and perceived strategic necessity. The British and French governments were unready for war, and desperate to buy time; but they were also shamefully unready to support a fellow democracy against naked aggression. Despite strident support for Czechoslovakia in some quarters, Western Europe's relationship with Eastern Europe was summed up all too aptly by Chamberlain's notorious broadcast to the British public on 27 September, in which he expressed horror at the possibility of war 'because of a quarrel in a far away country between people of whom we know nothing.'[21]

Prague. The Munich agreement was represented on both sides as an implementation of the principle of national self-determination. The hollowness of this claim was exposed in March 1939, when Nazi Germany presided over the final partition of Czechoslovakia, incorporating seven and a quarter million Czechs within the Reich.

The rump Czechoslovakia created by Munich was crippled in both its foreign and domestic relations, being too weak to oppose Germany, and forced to concede the maximum demands of Slovaks and Ruthenes. Beneš and his cabinet resigned in October 1938, and under German pressure the new 'Czechoslovak' government of non-party officials banned the Communist Party and forced the merger of other parties into two new but largely meaningless groups. Anti-Semitic legislation was adopted, and Czechoslovakia's foreign policy aligned with that of the Axis, leaving the League of Nations and reducing the armed forces. Autonomous Slovakia, under Monsignor Tiso, became effectively a one-party state, with the Hlinka Guard, the paramilitary wing of the People's Party, responsible for enforcing Tiso's anti-Semitic and anti-Czech agenda.

In the end the tensions between the government in Prague and the autonomous provinces provided Hitler with the excuse for further intervention. When President Emil Hácha dismissed both the Slovak and Ruthene governments early in March 1939, Hitler responded by ordering Tiso to proclaim Slovak independence, or face abandonment to Hungary; at the same time he encouraged Hungary to annex the remainder of Sub-Carpathian Ruthenia. The Czech president and prime minister were summoned to Berlin and, in the small hours of 15 March, were bullied into signing an agreement handing the remainder of the Czech lands over to the 'protection' of Germany. German troops commenced the takeover of the 'Protectorate of Bohemia and Moravia' late the same morning.

For the French and especially the British governments the dissolution of Czechoslovakia came as relief from an obligation they no longer wished to acknowledge; as the British foreign secretary had long since confided to the American ambassador, 'let Hitler go ahead and do what he likes in Central Europe.'[22] Hitler's blatant hypocrisy in taking over rump Czechoslovakia, however, is generally held to have effected a sea change in British public opinion. Gradually, government policy towards Germany also hardened, however reluctantly, and other developments in Eastern Europe that spring reinforced this shift.

---

[21] Quoted in Thorne, *Approach of War*, 80.
[22] Joseph Kennedy to State Department, 12 October 1938; quoted in Thorne, *Approach of War*, 94.

Memel. Hitler was already, in late 1938, eyeing Memel (Klaipėda), the majority-German inhabited port ceded to Allied control by Germany in 1919, and taken over by Lithuania in 1923. Lithuania, under the repressive rule of Antanas Smetona and his Nationalist Party since 1926, was no democracy, although as a result of German protests an uneasy autonomy for the Klaipėda province was restored in 1935, and a new trade treaty signed with Germany in 1936. By the time of the Munich crisis, however, agitation among Memel Germans in favour of annexation by Germany had reached fever pitch, and Nazi organisations operated in the enclave freely. The Prague takeover prompted renewed demonstrations, and on 20 March Lithuania was presented with an ultimatum, to cede the territory to Germany or face the consequences. The treaty transferring Memel to the Reich, including coastline to the south linking it to the East Prussian border, was signed on 23 March.

Tirana. Piqued by Hitler's successes, and anxious not to be outshone, Mussolini took advantage of the general breakdown of international order to occupy Albania in April 1939. This had been planned for some time, and was hastened by the fall of Yugoslavia's fascist-friendly Prime Minister Stojadinović in February, and by the end of the Spanish Civil War on 28 March.

Italy had played the role of regional great power in Albania throughout the interwar period, but its principal instrument in doing so was Ahmed Zogu, who became prime minister for the second time in December 1924. Zogu established something like order in a country riven by tribal conflict, to such an extent that, in 1928, he had himself crowned as King Zog, dispensing with the name 'Ahmed' as insufficiently European. Zog's rule was authoritarian but modernising, introducing a national police force, the beginnings of an education system, abolition of the veil for women, and a well-intentioned if largely ineffective attempt at land reform. By the late 1930s, the king was becoming increasingly impatient of Italian interference, but the effects of the Depression on Albania made him more, rather than less, dependent on Mussolini's support; Zog's marriage in 1938 was a belated, but futile, effort to evade domination by founding a dynasty. When, on 25 March, Italy demanded that Albania accept protectorate status, Zog had no means of resistance. His departure from Tirana, with his wife and newborn son Leka, preceded the landing of Italian forces at Dürres on 7 April by only a few hours.

Danzig and the invasion of Poland. Hitler's attack on Poland, ostensibly over the status of Danzig and the alleged oppression of Germans in Poland itself, was the culminating act of aggression in the name of national self-determination. It also expressed a historic German animus against the Poles; Hitler in particular had a virulent loathing for them, but was hardly alone in this. Beyond the Polish question, however, it is worth stressing that, following Austria and Czechoslovakia, Poland was the final stepping stone to the ultimate goal, an assault on the Soviet Union. Paradoxically, reaching this stage also required Hitler to do a deal with his ideological arch-enemy, Joseph Stalin.

War with Poland was also likely, finally, to involve Germany against France and Britain who, in the wake of the Prague takeover, reluctantly guaranteed Poland's independence, if not its borders. This was no deterrent to Hitler; on the contrary, all the evidence suggests that by early 1939 he regarded his Western opponents with contempt. To confront them over Poland, however, Hitler had to buy off the Soviet Union. The task, however glaring the ideological contradictions of a Nazi-Soviet bargain, was made all the easier by the Soviets' own revisionist agenda, and Western reluctance to envisage an alliance with communism.

The result was the notorious Nazi-Soviet Pact, or 'treaty of non-aggression', of 25 August, a cynical trade-off for both parties, but the indispensable prelude to the Polish campaign. For Hitler, the point of eliminating Poland was to prepare the way for an attack on the USSR, but for the moment he needed Stalin's neutrality while Germany dealt with Anglo-French intervention in the West. For Stalin, there was clearly a desire to buy time, since Nazi Germany was undoubtedly a threat; on the other hand, the terms of the deal suggest that Stalin hoped to buy Hitler off indefinitely. This was a simple non-aggression pact: each side agreed that, if one of the two signatories were involved in a war, the other would remain neutral, regardless of who started the war; this meant Hitler had a green light to attack Poland. In return, Hitler tacitly accepted a Soviet annexation of the eastern half of Poland, territories lost to the Soviets in 1921. A secret protocol assigned Estonia and Latvia as well as Finland to the Soviet Union's sphere of influence, in effect accepting a de facto reacquisition of these territories, or parts of them, by the Soviets; it was understood, too, that the Soviet Union had an 'interest' in the Romanian province of Bessarabia. Just as important were the economic aspects of the Pact: the Soviets promised Germany access to raw materials and foodstuffs which proved invaluable in keeping the Nazi war machine functioning for the next two years. The Soviets also undertook to purchase goods from other countries for onward sale to Germany, such as East Asian rubber. The result was that, when war came, Nazi-Soviet trade freed Germany from the effects of the Allied blockade, and strengthened the German military for its 1940 campaign against the Western powers; it was certainly no thanks to 'Uncle Joe' Stalin that Britain, on its own after the fall of France in June 1940, did not go under in the winter of 1940–1.

As for Poland, that country was the first to be subjected to the full horrors of Nazi blitzkrieg or 'lightning war', after German forces attacked on 1 September. The Anglo-French declaration of war on Germany, on 3 September, did little in practical terms to help the Poles. The *Wehrmacht*'s all-out assault, involving rapid motorised advances and aerial bombardment, was designed to unleash maximum violence, terror and demoralisation. Cities and civilians were deliberately targeted in order to spread terror, as well as clog Poland's infrastructure as the populace fled the German advance. Polish forces resisted stubbornly, inflicting some 50,000 casualties on the Germans while suffering

200,000 casualties themselves. In addition, Poland was invaded from both sides: without warning, Soviet forces entered from the East on 17 September, and by 28 September the country had been partitioned roughly equally along the rivers Narew, Bug and San. After twenty-one years' independence, Poland had once more been expunged from the map; but the suffering of its inhabitants was only just beginning.

As mentioned, the spread of the war in Eastern Europe was not completed until 1941. The region's problems, however, had already dragged France and Britain into the conflict. Especially in Eastern Europe, the widening conflict took on an elemental aspect, because for East Europeans this became literally a war for survival, rendered all the deadlier for its ideological edge.

9

Hell's Kitchen

Eastern Europe in the Second World War

The Second World War was unprecedented in its destructiveness and cost in human life, and Eastern Europe was the principal killing field. The war also served as the antechamber for a political revolution: the decades-long Soviet hegemony established in its wake ushered in the most determined and brutal attempt yet at the modernisation of the region.

These political consequences of the war are described in Chapter 10. This chapter summarises the war in military and political terms. It then analyses why the conflict has been termed 'total war', with its mass involvement, its ideological character and its racial animus. The impact of the Nazi 'New Order', and the appalling suffering inflicted on, and by, East European peoples, made the region ripe for communist takeover.

Course of the war

At the risk of some crudity, the key developments of the entire conflict break down into three main phases.

1. *1939–41*. In the first phase Germany and the Soviet Union, by mutual agreement, extended and consolidated their territorial dominance of the region; this period of uneasy but profitable condominium was brought to an end by the Nazi invasion of the Soviet Union in June 1941.

The four weeks' conquest and partition of Poland by this 'unholy alliance' in September 1939 was the prelude to a long agony for the Polish people. Germany formally annexed west-central Poland. In these territories brought 'home to the Reich' plans were rapidly implemented to expel the Polish population en masse and replace them with German settlers, a policy foreshadowed during the First World War. The south-central wedge of pre-war Poland, by contrast, was renamed the *General-Gouvernement*, under the despotic rule of Dr Hans Frank, and was designated as the dumping ground not only for displaced Poles, including Polish Jews, but also for Jews rounded up from other parts of conquered Europe, while the Nazis decided their fate. In the east, the Soviets took over the former *kresy*, from the Latvian border down to Romania. With total disregard for national self-determination, Stalin awarded the area around Vilnius to Lithuania; the remainder of Soviet-occupied Poland, however, was directly annexed to the Soviet Union.

In both halves of occupied Poland the conquerors set about decapitating Polish society by deliberately targeting the elite. In the territories directly annexed by Germany some two-fifths of the population were arbitrarily reclassified as 'German'; the remainder were stripped of basic rights, making them liable to deportation or forced labour, and their children ineligible for schooling. The Catholic Church was proscribed, its property confiscated, and clergy arrested or deported or shot. In the *General-Gouvernement* most educational institutions of culture were shut down on the ground that the Poles were not a 'people of culture'; this racially based denial of history even extended to public monuments, like the multiple statues of the composer Frédéric Chopin which the Nazi authorities melted down. Thousands of members of the Polish intelligentsia and professional classes were interned in camps, where many perished; 15 per cent of teachers, 45 per cent of doctors, 57 per cent of lawyers died in the course of the German occupation, disproportionately affecting the Jewish community. A total of 2.8 million Poles were deported to Germany as slave labour, where thousands died working on starvation rations. Some 200,000 Polish children, deemed 'racially salvageable', were kidnapped to be raised as 'Aryans' by German foster-parents. And this long list of brutalities does not include the thousands of Poles arbitrarily executed: the 57,000 killings that took place during the invasion, the hundred hostages executed every time a single German soldier was killed by the resistance, the sporadic public hangings and shootings on the street.

In Soviet-occupied Poland conditions were hardly better. For political rather than racial reasons, despite their history of targeting national minorities, the Soviets made a point of arresting as many of the 'ruling classes' as they could, from politicians and army officers, to landowners and bureaucrats, petty officials and trade unionists. For many, this was fatal: in April 1940 over 21,000 were shot, 4,000 alone in the notorious massacre in the Katyń forest outside Smolensk. Of the civilian population, more than 300,000 Poles were deported to concentration camps in Soviet Central Asia and the Arctic, where thousands died, apart from the untold fatalities en route. Back in the occupied territories, the Soviets nationalised industry, took over all organs of government and media, and imposed collectivisation of agriculture. Apart from token gestures to Belorussian and Ukrainian national identity, Soviet control by the end of 1940 was absolute.

In the meantime the Soviet Union pressed ahead with its plans for forcing on Finland a dependency like that intended for the Baltic states. The Finnish government, however, resisted accepting a Soviet naval base at Hankö to close off the Gulf of Finland, or ceding the Karelian isthmus to the Soviets, as well as territory on the Arctic Ocean, all of which Stalin deemed essential for Soviet security. From the Finnish perspective, by contrast, there could be no concessions to communism under any circumstances. Negotiations broke down in mid-November; on 30 November Soviet forces used a border incident as pretext for invasion. A puppet government was set up on 1 December under the Finnish Communist Otto Ville Kaasinen, which promptly signed a treaty with the Soviets on 2 December.

What became known as the Winter War did not, however, go according to plan. Although the Soviets were able to commit 1.2 million men to Finland's 461,000, they were unprepared for winter warfare, and their leadership as a result of Stalin's purges was poor. The Finns, under Marshal Mannerheim, were trained to fight in sub-Arctic conditions, including on skis; and given the intractable Finnish frontier, their defence could be largely concentrated along the so-called Mannerheim Line spanning the Karelian isthmus. Against this stubbornly defended barrier massed Soviet assaults, even when supported by air superiority during the few hours of daylight, broke in vain. By 27 December the Soviets had to suspend operations, having completely failed to make a breakthrough, while sustaining heavy losses. Finland had appealed for assistance to the League of Nations, which duly expelled the USSR from its ranks on 14 December, while calling for member-states to render Finland what help they could; although this did not result in any practical support for the Finns, the fact that France and Britain at least started planning it was a factor inducing Stalin to settle for less than total conquest. Despite momentarily successful Finnish counter-attacks, renewed Soviet offensives in February finally breached the Mannerheim Line, and sheer weight of numbers forced the Finns back to negotiations. By 9 March Mannerheim advised the government to sue for peace.

The Treaty of Moscow of 12 March gave the Soviets most of the territory they demanded, at a cost of 200,000 Soviet and 25,000 Finnish dead. The value of resisting lay in the fact that Stalin, worried about his defences in the Far East, accepted that an independent, democratic Finland would continue to exist, but the price was still high. Finland lost a tenth of its territory; it also had to cope with an influx of 400,000 refugees. As a result Finland proved a ready recruit, in 1941, for Hitler's war against the Soviet Union, in preparation for which Germany re-equipped the Finnish army. The poor Soviet performance in the Finnish war was a factor in reinforcing Nazi perceptions of Soviet weakness.

The Winter War made its own contribution to the intensification of the war in the West, in that Germany's invasion of Norway was a direct result of Allied intervention in Scandinavia. A far greater transformation of the strategic picture followed the rapid Nazi conquests in the spring of 1940. The fall of France in particular, by shifting the balance of power so radically in Germany's favour, prompted Stalin to consolidate his grip on Eastern Europe, in compensation for Nazi gains implicit in the Nazi-Soviet Pact. It also encouraged Mussolini to enter the conflict on Germany's side so that Italy could pursue its expansionist agenda in the Balkans. Hitler, however, strongly discouraged this, as making Soviet intervention more likely.

None of this deterred Stalin from tightening his grip on the Baltic states, since the Allies' rout in the West made his security dilemma acute. On 15 June Soviet forces crossed the Lithuanian border on the trumped-up pretext of 'anti-Soviet activities'. On 17 June Latvia and Estonia were simultaneously presented with ultimata, demanding that they install pro-Soviet governments, overseen by Soviet agents, allegedly to prevent them conspiring against Soviet interests. Military occupation of all three states was complete by 18 June. These puppet governments then held elections in which only a single, pro-Soviet party stood, and in early August the resulting assemblies unanimously passed resolutions demanding incorporation in the USSR. The Baltic states' independence had lasted a mere twenty-one years. Mass arrests proceeded from the moment Soviet forces took over. On 13–14 June 1941, literally overnight, thousands were rounded up and deported to Soviet concentration camps; conservative estimates record 60,000 Estonians, or 4 per cent of the population, 34,000 Latvians (1.5–2 per cent), and 38,000 Lithuanians (1.5–2 per cent). Among the victims were president Konstantin Päts of Estonia, and the former Estonian prime minister Joran Tõnisson, who disappeared without trace.

The day after the Franco-German armistice was signed, on 23 June, Stalin also moved to shore up the Soviet Union's south-western flank, forcing Romania to retrocede Bessarabia and the Bukovina. King Carol had no effective means of resistance, and Soviet occupation followed on 26 June although, in response to German objections, Stalin left the southern, Romanian-inhabited half of the Bukovina in Romanian hands. As with the Baltic states, the annexation of Bessarabia and north Bukovina meant the formal creation of a 'Moldavian Soviet republic' later in the year; it also meant the deportation of several hundred thousand ethnic Romanians to forced labour in Central Asia.

Bessarabia's loss triggered a feeding frenzy among Romania's neighbours. Hungary immediately renewed its claim to Transylvania, as did Bulgaria over south Dobrudja. King Carol threw himself on the mercy of Hitler, whose dilemma was real. At the very time he was drawing up plans to attack the Soviet Union the next year, Hitler was faced with a possible Hungarian-Romanian conflict which might interrupt German access to Romanian oil, and could even provoke Soviet intervention. As a result the Germans exerted serious pressure on Carol to make concessions on both fronts. In the end, Hitler imposed a compromise with the Second Vienna Award of 30 August. This gave Hungary the northern two-fifths of Transylvania, and Romania the southern three-fifths. By the Treaty of Craiova on 7 September, Romania ceded south Dobrudja to Bulgaria; the day before, the discredited Carol II fled the country, being succeeded by the military strongman Antonescu.

The year 1940 closed with Italy's entirely unprovoked invasion of Greece. General Metaxas had pursued a policy of studied neutrality, despite multiple provocations, yet on 28 October Italy abruptly presented an ultimatum to Greece, which was firmly rejected; Italian troops started crossing the border from occupied Albania within hours. So incompetent was the Italian campaign, however, that the Greeks achieved a spectacular reversal, chasing the Italians back into Albania and almost to Vlorë (Valona) before the end of the year. Shortly after, in the first weeks of 1941, Italian forces were also routed by the British in North Africa, compelling Mussolini to turn to Hitler for rescue.

Metaxas nevertheless preferred to exercise caution, turning down a British offer of assistance lest this provoke German intervention. The general, however, died suddenly on 29 January, unaware that Hitler, determined to avert any British involvement that might delay the assault on the Soviet Union, had already resolved to stamp out this Balkan brushfire. The fact that Metaxas' successor, Alexandros Koryzis, immediately accepted British intervention only added urgency to German plans. Throughout the winter Hitler steadily recruited East European allies to the Tripartite Pact, signed by Germany, Italy and Japan in September 1940. Some recruits were more willing than others. Hungary, for instance, positively volunteered to do so in November; jealous of Hungary's sudden rise in status, Romania and Slovakia acceded two days later. Finland had already signed an agreement granting Germany the right to transfer troops through Finnish territory to Norway. By March 1941, by which time preparations for Operation Barbarossa were well advanced, Bulgaria and Yugoslavia were ready to join as well. With German troops stationed in Romania, poised to move south via Bulgaria and Yugoslavia, everything was ready for delivering a hammer blow to the Greeks.

The invasion was momentarily derailed by a Serb-led coup in Yugoslavia on 26–27 March, in protest at the Cvetković government's intended accession to the Pact. Cvetković and the regent, Prince Paul, were shouldered aside by the openly pro-British general Dušan Simović, and the underage Peter II was proclaimed regnant. More significantly, a Yugoslav-Soviet treaty of friendship was signed by the new government on 6 April. It was never put to the test, for on the same day Hitler unleashed the full fury of German blitzkrieg on Yugoslavia, while invading Greece from Bulgaria. Belgrade was bombed savagely, while German, Italian and Hungarian troops attacked from all sides. In Hungary's case this represented a flagrant breach of the Hungaro-Yugoslav friendship treaty signed only two months before, but for the Horthy cabinet compliance with Germany's wishes outweighed such considerations; in despair the Hungarian prime minister, Count Teleki, committed suicide. Yugoslavia, weakened by two decades of internal strife, collapsed within weeks under this concerted attack; on 17 April King Peter and his government fled abroad, and organised resistance was at an end. The only elements of the armed forces to show serious fight were Serb; other ethnicities, who felt that the state lacked legitimacy, put up only a token resistance or surrendered wholesale. The country was swiftly partitioned. Germany incorporated northern Slovenia into the Reich, while Italy took over the southern half and a substantial strip of the Adriatic coast. Hungary recovered the areas north of the Drava River, as well as territory between the Danube and Tisza Rivers. The Croatian *Ustaša*, under Ante Pavelić as *poglavnik* or leader, were permitted to set up an 'Independent State of Croatia' (NDH), in reality a German-controlled puppet state, but including Bosnia-Hercegovina. Montenegro was occupied by Italy, Kosovo and a strip of western Macedonia assigned to Italian-controlled Albania, and most of Macedonia taken over by Bulgaria. A rump Serbia was administered on Germany's behalf by the Serb general Milan Nedić.

Greece's conquest was equally rapid. Despite the landing of British forces at Salonika, neither the Greeks nor their allies could stem the German advance. By 23 April the largest Greek army was obliged to surrender; Athens was taken on 27 April. British troops evacuated to Crete accompanied by the Greek king and government, but were forced out by June. The entire Balkan Peninsula was under Axis domination by the middle of the year. Italy, Germany and Bulgaria jointly occupied Greece. A collaborationist government was installed under General Georgios Tsolakoglou, but this did nothing to shield the Greek people from the consequences of Axis occupation.

2. *1941–43*. In the second phase of the war Eastern Europe became the principal killing field of the entire conflict, its peoples trapped between Nazi Germany and the Soviet Union. This phase started with the launch of Operation Barbarossa, the German-led invasion of the Soviet Union, which achieved stunning initial successes, only to halt in late 1942 after a second major offensive. The Germans' surrender at Stalingrad in January 1943 heralded the beginning of a steady Soviet counter-offensive, and a general turning of the tide for the Allies. In this vast turmoil East Europeans were heavily involved, as both victims and perpetrators. The first meeting of Allied leaders at Tehran in late 1943 marks the close of this second phase. This was when the 'grand alliance' agreed something like a common strategy for victory, and when the fate of Eastern Europe was provisionally settled.

Barbarossa's impact was so devastating in large part because the element of surprise was so complete. Despite the months-long Axis build-up, and plentiful advance warning from his agents, Stalin remained egregiously blind to the imminent onslaught. Yet Stalin had this much excuse: from a rational standpoint it made no sense at all for Hitler to abandon the Nazi-Soviet Pact, when the war with Britain was unfinished, and Germany benefited so obviously from Soviet neutrality. In the year and a half the Pact was in effect, Germany imported via Russia 865,000 tons of oil, 14,000 tons of manganese, 14,000 tons of copper, 15,400 tons of rubber, and 1.5 million tons of grain. The German navy refuelled at Soviet Murmansk during the Norwegian campaign, and the Luftwaffe had the advantage of Soviet weather reports during the Battle of Britain in 1940. Stalin's mistake was to overlook the extent to which Nazi policy was driven by racial hatreds and the obsession with *Lebensraum*. Hitler had always wanted to crush the 'subhuman' Slavs, extirpate communism, and lay the territorial foundations of a thousand-year Reich. The Nazis' assumptions of racial superiority meant they gravely underestimated their opponent.

To begin with, however, such assumptions seemed more than justified. Barbarossa began with the largest force ever assembled in European military history, some 3.6 million men, the majority German, but including substantial contingents of Romanians, Hungarians, Italians, Finns and others. For many East Europeans, the anti-communist nature of the campaign gave it the flavour of a crusade. The main thrust of the German attack was directed against Leningrad and Moscow; as before, Hitler and his generals hoped for a quick, knockout blow through blitzkrieg. Soviet forces, taken completely by surprise, were overwhelmed in a matter of weeks, despite increasingly fierce resistance.

The territorial rearrangements made by the Nazis in conquered Soviet territory showed their intentions to be frankly exploitative. Hitler made this explicit in July 1941, when he warned assembled subordinates that Germany's mission in the East was 'first to rule, secondly to administer and thirdly to exploit.'[1] The entire occupied area was divided up into four *Reichskommissariats*, under the notional overlordship of Alfred Rosenberg. In reality Rosenberg never exercised much control over individual governors, each of whom ruled his particular satrapy as brutally as he saw fit. The real authority in these territories was in fact the SS. Some former Polish territory was annexed directly to the Reich as the 'Warthegau', while Western Galicia was attached to Hans Frank's *General-Gouvernement*. Bessarabia was handed back yet again to Romania, which also occupied the territory east of the Dniester known as Transnistria. The former Baltic states plus Belarus as far east as Minsk became the '*Reichskommissariat Ostland*', under Hinrich Lohse. The '*Reichskommissariat Ukraine*', under Erich Koch, covered a huge area stretching from Brest-Litovsk along the Dnieper to Dnepropetrovsk. The even greater swathe of territory behind the front remained under the jurisdiction of the army. In none of these areas, despite some collaboration, was anything other than a notional 'native' participation involved; Nazi control, and Nazi contempt for the inhabitants, remained total.

Several things stand out about Barbarossa. First was the rapidity of the Axis advance. By the end of September, when the advance finally halted, the whole of European Russia from Lake Ladoga south to the Sea of Azov was in Axis hands. Second was the number of prisoners taken. Although many Soviet units fought hard, others showed less appetite for defending the motherland of socialism, and entire army groups were bypassed and surrounded. By the end of the year, the Germans claimed to have taken nearly four million men prisoner.

[1]   Quoted in Mazower, M., 2008, *Hitler's Empire: Nazi Rule in Occupied Europe*, London, 149.

A third striking aspect of the invasion is the fact that, to begin with, the invaders were welcomed with open arms by many inhabitants of the Western Soviet Union. This was hardly surprising, given that, in the north, these were territories of the former Poland and Baltic states. The *Wehrmacht* arrived in the Baltic territories, for instance, within a couple of weeks of the mass deportations of June. Not only had the population there already been terrorised by the Soviet occupation in 1939–40, with hundreds of thousands murdered or deported to the Soviet gulag, but in the panic following the Nazi invasion Soviet authorities, prior to retreating, executed thousands more political prisoners on suspicion of being collaborators. Equally revealing was the joy of many Belorussians and Ukrainians. As one Ukrainian recalled, 'Everybody was glad the Germans had come'; and numerous photos recorded *Wehrmacht* troops being greeted with the traditional welcome of flowers, bread and salt.[2] The invasion revealed starkly the unpopularity of Soviet rule, even if the celebrants' trust in their Nazi 'liberators' was soon cruelly disappointed.

Obviously, not every Soviet citizen was joyful. On the contrary, the further the invaders went, entering ethnic Russian districts, the more the population was inclined to flee them, quite apart from the Soviets' scorched-earth policy, ordering everyone to destroy resources and shelter before evacuating. Another consequence of Barbarossa was thus a huge increase in the number of displaced people: some 25 million refugees were forced eastwards by the fighting.

A final aspect of Barbarossa was the contemptuous and brutal attitude of the conquerors towards virtually all the peoples they encountered. The Nazis' assumptions of racial superiority affected their relations with allies as much as the reactions of enemies, and this arrogance was entirely self-defeating. In contrast to their attitude towards Western Europe, the Nazis saw the largely Slav inhabitants of Eastern Europe – not to mention Jews and Roma – as subhuman. Their systematic and habitual brutality turned potential collaborators into foes and resisters, and found expression in a number of ways. Even before the invasion provision was made for a war of ideological and racial extermination against Soviet communist officials as well as Jews, with the formation of the so-called *Einsatzgruppen*, or 'action groups'. This was a typical Nazi euphemism for dedicated killing squads. The primary purpose of the *Einsatzgruppen*, each responsible for a designated sector of the front, was summarily to execute all such captives. As the front advanced, thousands of Soviet officials, but increasingly also large numbers of Jews, were rounded up, forced to dig their own mass graves, and shot on the spot. Before the end of 1941 this first overt act in the mass murder of the Jews had accounted for some half a million deaths; by the spring of 1942, long before the creation of purpose-built death camps such as Auschwitz or Sobibór, the figure was

[2] Quoted in Mazower, *Hitler's Empire*, 158.

probably closer to three-quarters of a million. The crucial decisions to embark on what the Nazi leaders referred to, in another chilling euphemism, as the 'final solution', in other words the more systematic and industrially organised mass murder of Europe's Jews, were taken in late 1941 and early 1942. The locus of this genocide, for the most part, was in Nazi-occupied Eastern Europe. But in addition to these atrocities, Nazi policy towards the rest of the population swiftly alienated millions. Foodstuffs and other resources were confiscated, offers of assistance largely rejected, and the population as a whole treated with suspicion.

The role of Germany's East European allies in the Soviet war was a strictly subaltern one, although the contributions of Finland, Hungary and above all Romania were not negligible. The Finns regained the territory ceded to the Soviets in 1940, but thereafter played a purely holding function in the north. Hungary's Mobile Corps reached the Donets in the initial offensive, only to be withdrawn at the insistence of the Hungarian government. In 1942, however, German pressure led to the despatch of a much larger force of about 250,000 to fill a gap in the line around Voronezh. The Romanian contingent was arguably the most significant: not only was Romania entrusted with occupied territory, but it protected the Germans' flanks in the fighting around Stalingrad. Only Bulgaria avoided serious commitment; Boris III never actually declared war on the Soviet Union, on the ground that Bulgarians would not be enthusiastic allies against fellow Slavs, and were too ill-equipped to participate. Bulgaria's principal contribution was to assist in the occupation of Yugoslavia and Greece. Following Boris' death in mysterious circumstances in August 1943, the country's main dilemma was how to extricate itself from the Axis cause while avoiding Soviet invasion.

The Nazis' siege of Leningrad and Moscow in 1941–2, and the fight for Stalingrad, were crucial phases in the Nazi-Soviet war, but peripheral to a history of Eastern Europe. More relevant was the Soviet counter-offensive around Stalingrad in 1942–3. Germany's allies paid bitterly for their involvement. Romania's total losses were 155,010 dead, wounded and missing, a quarter of all Romanian troops on the eastern front. The Hungarian Second Army was overwhelmed within a matter of days in mid-January, at an estimated cost of 190,000 casualties. German counter-attacks took place without much meaningful assistance from their shattered Hungarian and Romanian allies.

The massive clash of armoured units at the battle of Kursk, in July 1943, a 'cauldron of totalitarian violence' in the words of the Soviet journalist Vasily Grossman, also turned much of Belarus and eastern Ukraine into a blasted wasteland.[3] In a series of follow-up offensives Soviet forces reached Kharkov on 28 August, Kiev on 6 November. In the meantime Fascist Italy's

---

[3] Quoted in Ferguson, N., 2006, *The War of the World: Twentieth-Century Conflict and the Descent of the West*, London, 573.

148

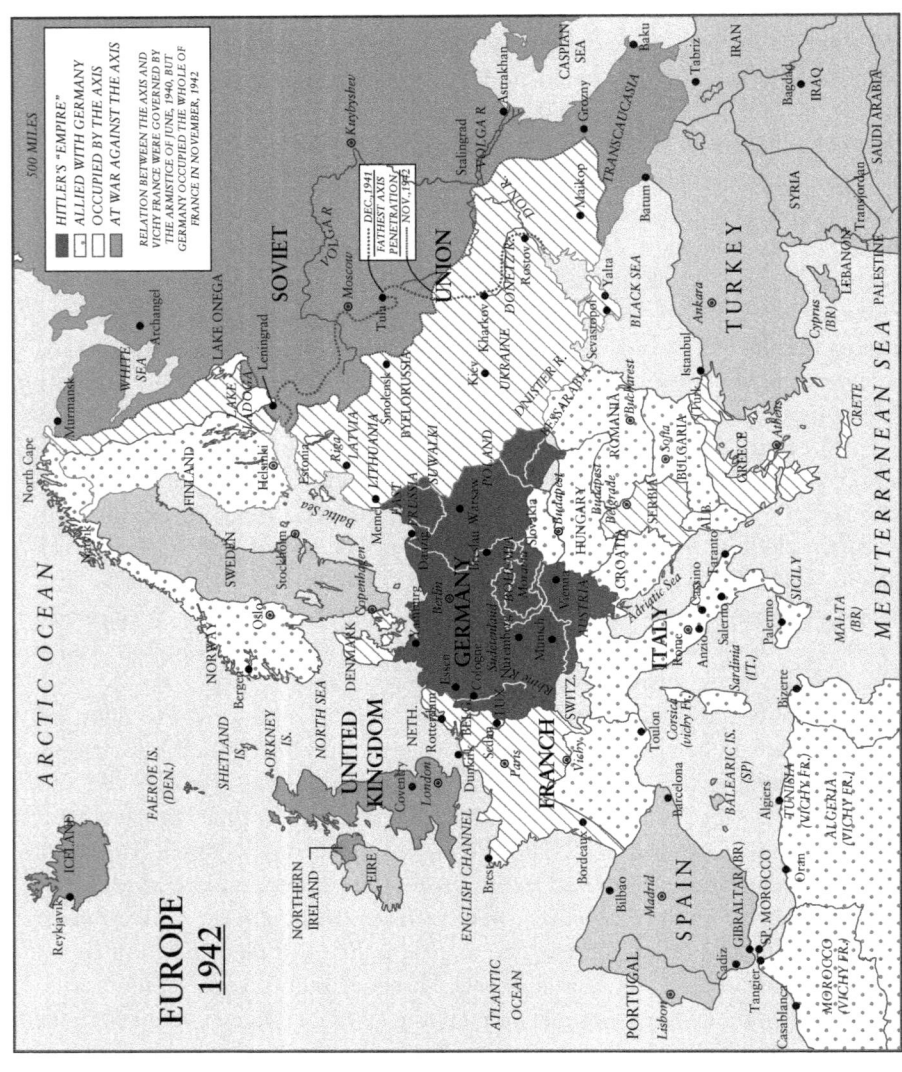

Map 4 Eastern Europe by 1942.

surrender unleashed chaos in occupied Greece, Albania and Yugoslavia, since the Germans had to scramble to take control from Italian forces in the face of ongoing resistance movements. By January 1944 the Red Army had crossed the old Polish border of 1939, but well before then it was apparent that German defeat was finally achievable.

The capstone to this phase of the War was the conference between Stalin, US President Franklin D. Roosevelt and British Prime Minister Winston Churchill at Tehran in November–December 1943. The Allies agreed to fight on until Germany surrendered unconditionally; and although the dismemberment of Germany was not agreed in so many words, it was understood that German power was to be permanently weakened. The American and British leaders tacitly agreed that the Soviet Union would keep the territorial gains it had made in 1939–40; this meant accepting the Baltic states' permanent loss of independence if not formally recognising their 1941 incorporation, as well as accepting the shifting westwards of a restored Poland's eastern border, thus allotting all of Belarus and the Ukraine to the Soviets. The western Allies promised finally to open a second front, which would take the pressure off the Soviets. Already, the de facto abandonment of Eastern Europe to Soviet hegemony was taking shape. Roosevelt and Churchill may have deluded themselves on this score, but Stalin undoubtedly took away from Tehran the conviction that the West's commitment to national self-determination was no more than pious lip service, and that he had carte blanche to establish Soviet-friendly governments in most of Eastern Europe.

3. *1944–45*. In the final phase of the war the logic of Soviet domination gathered pace, but so too did the tempo of death and destruction. Renewed Soviet offensives took the Red Army by mid-June 1944 to the borders of the former Baltic states, in the north, and to north-east Romania and most of the Ukraine in the south. By August the Soviets were approaching Warsaw and Slovakia, entering Hungary, and pushing into the heart of Romania. By October they had reached Belgrade, and by November had invested Budapest, defended bitterly by the Nazis until February 1945. Long before then Soviet troops had relentlessly advanced across former Polish territory and into Germany, taking Berlin in April. Although the war with Germany formally ended on 9 May, fighting continued in Czechoslovakia until the 11th, when the Soviets entered Prague.

As the Red Army advanced, the allegiance of Germany's East European allies weakened, while at the same time resistance by subject peoples strengthened, albeit with often unintended tragic results.

The Finnish government found itself on the losing side by the end of 1943, and tried in vain to negotiate a truce with the Soviets. A Soviet offensive in June 1944 retook virtually all the gains of the Winter War, and by the time an armistice was concluded in September 1944 Finland was lucky to emerge with the borders of 1940, some additional territorial losses and a large indemnity to pay. Finland was, however, the only East European state apart from Greece to retain its independence and a democratic political system intact.

Hungary's Admiral Horthy, one of Hitler's least enthusiastic satraps, was seeking to exit the conflict by early 1944. It was the revelation of Horthy's fruitless peace feelers to the western Allies that prompted Hitler in March to send German troops into Hungary, compel Horthy to appoint as premier the pro-German General Döme Sztójay, and install a German plenipotentiary to keep an eye on things. The Sztójay government strove to keep in step with its Nazi masters, sending a new army to the front, and suppressing anti-Nazi parties. The period between March and July was also when the Hungarian authorities, under SS supervision, deported some 400,000 Hungarian Jews, roughly half the country's Jewish minority, to their deaths at Auschwitz. The realization of what was happening to these people, coupled with Romania's sudden change of sides at the end of August, appears to have led Horthy's regime finally to renege on its Faustian bargain. The deportations of Jews were halted, and a new prime minister was appointed; more significantly, Horthy accepted that peace feelers had to be extended to the Soviets, not the West. The result was disaster: having announced a Hungarian Soviet armistice on 11 October, Horthy was summarily ousted by the Germans and a puppet government installed under Ference Szálasi and the fascist Arrow Cross. Szálasi's writ, however, scarcely ran outside of Budapest and the Nazi-occupied west of Hungary; and while Szálasi occupied himself with grandiose plans for a future fascist society, his followers ran amok in Budapest, massacring opponents and Jews in the interval before the Soviets finally stormed the capital. Hungarian fascism, rabidly radical to the end, died along with the remnants of royal Hungary in the ruins of Budapest.

Romania's Marshal Antonescu also proved himself something less than Hitler's staunchest ally, once the going got tough. Romanian troops shared fully in the disasters of the eastern front. By the spring of 1943 Antonescu, like Horthy, could see that Germany was unlikely to win the war, and tried to initiate peace talks with the western Allies to defend Romania against Soviet communism. Confronted with Allied solidarity, however, Antonescu felt he had no option but to fight on at Hitler's side, since he too saw the war against the USSR as a struggle to preserve civilisation against barbarism. Antonescu was also paralysed by the fear that Hitler might punish any disloyalty by handing the remainder of Transylvania over to Hungary. As a result Romanian troops were trapped defending the Crimea, with only 150,000 out of 230,000 men escaping from Sevastopol in May 1944. With Soviet forces entering Romania, 22-year old King Michael, with the unanimous support of party leaders, summoned up the courage to depose the dictator. On 23 August the king summoned Antonescu to the palace, and locked him and his closest associates up in a large safe containing the royal stamp collection. A provisional government, headed by General Constantin Sănătescu and representing all parties, including the minuscule Romanian Communist Party, immediately broke off relations with Germany, sued for an armistice, and announced that Romania was henceforth fighting on the Allied side. The Romanian switchover had huge strategic consequences. Apart from the loss of Romania's armed forces, it deprived Hitler of his last access to oil reserves apart from Hungary, and opened up Bulgaria to Soviet invasion. Romania also committed its forces to fighting on the Allied side, and made a serious contribution to the offensives in Hungary and Czechoslovakia, during which the Romanian army lost a further 160,000 men.

After the death of Boris III Bulgaria, under the regency of Bogdan Filov, kept itself out of the maelstrom up to this point but, as with Hungary and Romania, its efforts to conclude peace were futilely directed at the western Allies, not the Soviet Union. On 5 September the Soviets formally declared war on Bulgaria; three days later the Bulgarian government, desperate to avoid occupation, declared war on its former ally, Germany, thus bizarrely finding itself at war with both powers. On the night of 8–9 September a coalition of Agrarians, Zveno, social democrats and communists, calling itself the Fatherland Front, seized power in Sofia under Kinon Georgiev as prime minister. Bulgaria's experience of the war had been mercifully brief; its real travail was yet to come.

Finally, the puppet regimes under German occupation, in Slovakia and Croatia, found themselves shunted aside as the Soviets advanced. Although much of Yugoslavia, including Bosnia, had been taken over by Josip Tito's communist-led Partisans by late 1944, most of Croatia was held by German forces until the spring of 1945. In Slovakia Tiso's government, which had contributed 50,000 troops to the eastern front, was threatened by the so-called Slovak National Uprising of August–October 1944, in which rebel units of the Slovakian army joined forces with communists and other political groups and fought German occupation forces. Although some 50,000 participated in the uprising, it proved nevertheless to be premature, and was suppressed with savage reprisals. Soviet forces only liberated Slovakia in March 1945; Tiso and his cabinet fled on 1 April, and the Red Army entered Bratislava on the 4th. The return of former Czechoslovakian president Beneš to the country, on 3 April, signalled most Slovaks' tacit acceptance that reunion with the Czechs was likely to follow.

The nature of the war in Eastern Europe

It seems impossible to do justice to the enormity of the horrors that overtook millions of East Europeans in the Second World War. Nevertheless, some sort of balance sheet, however inadequate, can be drawn up by looking at three aspects of the war's nature. Firstly, this was arguably a 'total war' in a far more literal sense than anywhere else in this global conflict, in that the fighting affected all aspects of the societies involved, sucking everyone and everything into its maw. Secondly, this totality in turn was the direct product of Hitler's 'New Order', an unprecedentedly ruthless attempt to remake the entire region into Nazi Germany's political, economic and demographic hinterland. Thirdly, the sheer cost in human terms, ranging from mass death to displacement, impoverishment and moral degradation, is worth dwelling on for its own sake. When Britons and Americans, in particular, dilate on the sacrifices made by their peoples during the war, they should bear in mind that these sufferings pale almost to insignificance in comparison with those of Eastern Europe.

1. *Total war*. Considerable attention has been devoted in recent years to what constitutes a 'total war', but most scholarly opinion agrees that a 'radicalization of warfare' in the modern era 'reached its climax during the Second World War.'[4] Total war, as defined by Stig Förster, involved total war aims: the unconditional surrender of one's enemies, and their complete subjugation. It required total methods: waging war with maximum ruthlessness and destructive effect, in complete disregard of all norms of international law, in pursuit of victory. It necessitated a total mobilisation of all resources of society, military, economic and social, as well as the brutal exploitation of the conquered. It mandated total control: a dictatorial, centralised organisation in which all aspects of life, for both conquerors and conquered, were controlled for the purposes of warfare. Implicit in these four totalities was 'the erosion of the boundaries between the military and civilians'; civilians on both sides were either a resource or a target, in a conflict in which there could be no bystanders.[5]

What gave this total war its especially hideous edge, in Eastern Europe, was the ideological and racial motivation with which it was waged. It is a truism that, the longer the War went on, the more ruthlessly it was waged by both sides. Yet the Nazis' racial outlook meant that they regarded their West European and American opponents very differently than they looked upon the peoples of Eastern Europe, and their conduct reflected this. In addition to seeing the war in the East as a racial war against subhumans, the Nazis also considered themselves to be conducting a crusade to extirpate communism which was mysteriously conflated with Jewish influence, as Hitler's lifelong obsession with 'Judeo-Bolshevism' attests. In this crusade the conquerors found at least some willing coadjutors among most of the peoples of Eastern Europe. Collaboration, by both official bodies and individuals, was perhaps inevitable in the circumstances, whether it took the form of delivering logistical support, military service, or assisting in the perpetration of atrocities against communists and Jews.

---

[4] Förster, S., 2007, 'Total War and Genocide: Reflections on the Second World War', *Australian Journal of Politics & History*, LIII, #1, March, 68.
[5] Förster, 'Total War and Genocide', 71–2.

The racial and ideological animus with which the war in Eastern Europe was prosecuted thus not only resulted in widespread suffering and mass murder, culminating in genocide; it ended by provoking a furious resistance. Some resistance was nationalist or loyalist, in other words loyal to pre-war regimes or a government-in-exile, and motivated by patriotic opposition to the invaders. Other resistance was communist-led, in most cases only appearing once the Soviet Union was attacked in June 1941, and motivated above all else by the desire to relieve the pressure on the socialist motherland. Still other resistance was a matter of physical survival: confronted with a choice between death or enslavement at the hands of the occupiers, many took to the forests or hills for simple reasons of self-preservation, or to avenge atrocities already committed. Many, if not all, resistance movements transcended not only nationality, but class and gender, making them genuinely transnational; as a Ukrainian cleric reported to the Pope in May 1943, the armed bands in western Ukraine were 'people of all nationalities, Germans, Jews and Ukrainians.'[6] Whatever the motives, resistance deepened the downward spiral, because it was used by the Nazis as an excuse for ever more savage reprisals, in turn sharpening the will to resist and lending it an additional savagery. The abandonment of civilised norms on both sides, in so far as they had existed, rapidly snowballed.

2. *The Nazi 'New Order'*. Essential to understanding the elemental nature of the war in Eastern Europe was the mismatch between the 'New Order' the Nazis envisaged for the region, and what this meant for the inhabitants. This disjunction applied to the whole of occupied Europe, but it was over Eastern Europe that the German grip was tightest. The ground had been prepared by almost a decade of economic and political hegemony, and it was eastwards that the Nazis looked for the resources, manpower and *Lebensraum* to sustain their thousand-year Reich.

Planning the New Order divided into two phases, for in 1939–41 Nazi Germany was an ally of the Soviet Union, obliged to share Eastern Europe with its arch-enemy and future victim. In this first phase, there was much talk of a Nazi-Soviet 'zone of peaceful development' and the relationship in trade terms was a mutually profitable one. Within Germany's sphere of influence Nazi officials touted a 'community of nations' (*Völkergemeinschaft*), and this Nazi vision for a time found a cooperative response among many Europeans, especially those who saw Nazism as a lesser evil than communism. This willingness to collaborate, however, foundered on the Nazis' nationalist supremacism, what Mark Mazower calls 'the Germans' almost total incapacity to respond to the political opportunity that opened up for them.'[7]

---

[6]   Quoted in Drapac, V. and Pritchard, G., 2017, *Resistance and Collaboration in Hitler's Empire*, London, 66.
[7]   Mazower, *Hitler's Empire*, 7.

The second phase, from 1941 on, showed just how incompatible the Nazis' imperialist goals were with the interests of everyone else, and this was nowhere clearer than in Eastern Europe. In purely economic terms, Nazi policy was egregiously exploitative. It was pointed out long ago that the Nazis had two options in occupied Europe: they could either utilise resources and manpower rationally, making it in the interests of occupied populations to cooperate with them, or they could pursue 'a policy of smash-and-grab'.[8] They chose the latter. In occupied territories, they deliberately, with no regard for the consequences, proceeded simply to confiscate foodstuffs and raw materials. As Hitler himself put it, 'The real profiteers of this war are ourselves, and out of it we shall come bursting with fat!'[9] Or in the words of Hermann Goering, responsible for economic policy in the occupied territories, 'I intend to plunder, and plunder copiously.'[10] Referring to the Greeks, Goering continued in August 1943, 'let them perish as long as no German starves.'[11] They did. Erich Koch, in charge of the Ukraine, announced his intention in March 1943 to 'get the last ounce out of this country. I have not come here to spread bliss. I have come here to help the *Führer*.'[12] Even Germany's allies were forced into one-sided trade deals, whereby raw materials, fuel and foodstuffs were handed over on credit, but never paid for. Long before the rollback on the eastern front started, this policy had caused famine and thousands of deaths from starvation.

The Nazis commandeered not just food and raw materials but labour, initially by recruiting paid workers but increasingly, as conquest opened up Eastern Europe, for free. In Hitler's view, 'Russia is our Africa, and the Russians are our negroes' – and so too were millions of Poles, Ukrainians and other Slavs.[13] Of 7 million foreign workers in Germany by 1944, at least 2.8 million came from Eastern Europe, not counting the slave labour camps in Poland like Auschwitz-Birkenau. Conditions in such camps, especially the meagre rations, led to a dire mortality rate; as Nazi officials admitted, this amounted to 'extermination through labour'.[14] As the war intensified, and more German men were drafted into the armed forces, the demand for replacement slave labour soared. By the start of 1943 East Europeans were being literally snatched off the streets in terrifying round-ups, as when 35,000 people were seized over four days in Warsaw in January 1943. Fear of being rounded up in this way was a compelling motivation for thousands of East European men, and women, to join their local resistance movement or partisan unit.

[8]   Wright, G., 1968, *The Ordeal of Total War 1939-1945*, New York, 117.
[9]   Quoted in Wright, *The Ordeal of Total War*, 117.
[10] Quoted in Wright, *The Ordeal of Total War*, 117.
[11] Quoted in Mazower, M., 1993, *Inside Hitler's Greece: The Experience of Occupation 1941-1944*, New Haven, CT and London, 9.
[12] Quoted in Crampton, R.J., 1997, *Eastern Europe in the Twentieth Century – And After*, 2nd edn, London and New York, 182.
[13] Quoted in Craig, G.A., 1980, *Germany 1866-1945*, New York, 745.
[14] Mazower, *Hitler's Empire*, 310.

A final aspect of the New Order that made its imperialist nature explicit was colonisation. Hitler cherished a vision of displacing the 'inferior' peoples of Eastern Europe and resettling the entire region with racially sound Germans, and even before the invasion of the Soviet Union this megalomaniacal dream was taking practical shape. The plan, as Eastern Europe was gradually depopulated, was to replace Poles, Ukrainians, Russians and others with the so-called *Volksdeutsche* or ethnic Germans living in the region. In October 1939, a special '*Reichskommissariat* for the Strengthening of Germandom' was set up within the SS, under Himmler's personal direction, to expropriate and expel non-Germans and resettle Germans, a vast and, as it proved, largely impracticable project. The Nazi regime also, in 1939–40, signed a series of treaties with the Soviet Union and the Baltic states, providing for the 'repatriation' of some 600,000 *Volksdeutsche* from those countries. The Baltic Germans were the first to be offered the prospect of coming '*heim ins Reich*' or home to the Reich; but as Soviet territory also fell under Nazi control other pockets of Germans were included. By mid-1941, 14,000 *Volksdeutsche* had been moved from Estonia, 50,000 from Latvia, 53,000 from Lithuania, 11,000 from the Białystok area, 57,000 from east Galicia, 67,000 from Volhynia, and a staggering 189,000 from Bessarabia and the Bukovina. Of these 475,000 people, some 200,000 were settled in western Poland, while 275,000 had to be kept in resettlement camps pending placement. Failing sufficient numbers of *Volksdeutsche*, the German government also launched a programme encouraging *Reichsdeutsche*, or citizens of Germany itself, to take up this national task of colonising *Lebensraum*, but unsurprisingly the response was a tepid one, given the turmoil on the eastern front. Before the whole experiment collapsed in ruins only about 40,000 *Reichsdeutsche* had committed themselves.

3. *The cost in human terms.* In the meantime millions of non-Germans had also been uprooted, but far more unsympathetically, like the million or so Poles, including Polish Jews, who were driven from their homes in western Poland and dumped in the *General-Gouvernement*, with little thought given to how they might survive, or how the occupation authorities there might cope with such numbers. The fate of the Poles was however replicated many times over across the region for the next six years, and this human cost of the war in Eastern Europe is its grimmest aspect.

The most direct way of conveying this cost is the death toll. Of the 40-odd million Europeans who perished in the Second World War, a figure that includes the 6 million Jews from across the continent, the overwhelming majority were undoubtedly inhabitants of Eastern Europe and the Soviet Union, even if precise figures for the region are hard to come by. The figures for the Soviet Union alone, including its 1939–41 annexations, are almost beyond comprehension, between 23 and 25 million. What is also striking is that the number of civilian deaths far outstripped the number of military personnel who died. This was in part due to aerial bombardment, but it owed far more, in Eastern Europe, to the deliberate targeting of the civilian population, because this was from the Nazis' point of view a racial war. Of the Soviet dead, for instance, 9 million were soldiers, including many women recruited as front-line troops, sharpshooters, partisans, even fighter pilots, and whose testimony has been movingly chronicled by Svetlana Alexievich.[15] 18 million of those Soviet deaths, however, were civilians, either shot, or starved to death, or dead from disease or forced labour. Just as shocking is the proportion of deaths, in some countries, in relation to the total population. In Poland, 22 per cent of the pre-war population, or about 6 million people (including 3 million Polish Jews), died between 1939 and 1945. In Yugoslavia, 10.8 per cent of the population as of 1941, or 1.15 million people, did not survive the four years 1941–45, with the rider that the majority of Yugoslavs died at the hands, not of Germans or Italians or Bulgarians, but of fellow-Yugoslavs. The Belarus Soviet Republic, scene of the most apocalyptic tank clashes of the war, but also of ferocious combat between invaders and partisans, was described by an American journalist as 'the most devastated country in Europe'.[16] German reprisals against partisan attack were ruthless; according to German sources, for every single German soldier killed in Belarus, 73 Belorussians died, thousands literally rounded up as hostages and shot in reprisal, some 345,000 in all. Overall, a quarter of the population of Belarus in its 1939–41 borders, or 2.2 million people, died between 1941 and 1944. A similar hostage policy was practised in Yugoslavia, where Germans and Italians faced not only a loyalist but also a communist-led resistance, and where the rule was a hundred Yugoslav hostages executed for every German soldier killed. A special contribution was made by the racist contempt with which the Germans treated Soviet prisoners of war: of 5 million Soviet soldiers taken prisoner, 3 million died in German concentration camps. Two million of these died before March 1942, penned up with little to no shelter and food throughout the winter, in temperatures of $-40°C$, with well-documented evidence of cannibalism towards the end. Untold thousands of East Europeans died of malnutrition and starvation in Greece, in the Soviet Union, in Yugoslavia, because the conquerors hoovered up whatever foodstuffs they could. The case of the Greek famine is one of the better documented: Red Cross estimates suggest that in 1941–3, 250,000 people died as a direct or indirect result of food shortages.

War has always been accompanied by suffering, but what distinguishes the Second World War is the extent to which killing and mass death were the expressions of racist, nationalist and other ideological convictions. The mass murder of Jews known so inaptly as 'the Holocaust' remains the emblematic

---

[15] Alexievich, S., 2017, *The Unwomanly Face of War*, translated by R. Pevear and L. Volokhonsky, London.
[16] Quoted in Mazower, *Hitler's Empire*, 487.

atrocity of the War, and most of this deliberately planned and executed genocide was carried out in Eastern Europe. The attempted extermination of the Jews should not, however, distract attention from the other mass murders perpetrated. Hitler's infamous 'commissar decree' of 6 June 1941, for instance, singled out captured Soviet officials for summary execution, because the Nazis saw the war as being waged against the cancer of communism as much as on racial grounds. These twin attitudes filtered down to the lowest ranks of the German armed forces, facilitating what Omer Bartov calls the 'demodernization' of warfare on the eastern front, the assumption that, as a result of the 'utmost primitiveness' with which the war was conducted, all restraint could be abandoned in waging a war of 'civilization' against barbarism.[17]

In addition to Jews and communists, the Roma and Sinti were also targeted by the SS, whose special department for the 'fight against the gypsy nuisance' had already interned and forcibly sterilised most of Germany's 30,000 Roma and Sinti as 'asocial' beings before the war, as a racial threat to the *Volk*. Following the invasions of Poland and later the Soviet Union, increasing numbers of Roma and Sinti came under Nazi control, and some 250,000 fell victim to the *Einsatzgruppen*. Abundant documentary evidence uncovered in East European and former Soviet archives since the fall of communism now 'consistently pushes the arrow of the barometer toward genocide.'[18] At Auschwitz a section of the camp was reserved for Roma, who were singled out by German doctors and scientists for bizarre and inhumane experiments, most of which resulted in agonising deaths. Twenty thousand Roma and Sinti perished at Auschwitz alone. Even experts find it hard to agree on firm figures for the overall number of Roma and Sinti dead; in Europe as a whole the numbers range from a minimum of 130,500 to a maximum of 285,650, or as much as 50 per cent. In Eastern Europe, where the process of rounding up, internment or summary execution was especially random, even the maximum figures may well be underestimates: Austria, 8,250; Bohemia and Moravia, 6,500; Germany, 15,000; Estonia, 1,000; Latvia, 2,500; Lithuania, 1,000; Poland, 35,000; Romania, 36,000; Slovakia, 10,000; Yugoslavia, 90,000; Greece, 50; Bulgaria, none.

Other nationalist antagonisms had similarly deadly results. Ante Pavelić's *Ustaša* in Croatia devoted a considerable portion of its energies towards exterminating the ethnic Serb communities within the borders of the NDH. As a Ustaša minister put it in June 1941, the intention was to deport one-third of the Serbs, convert another third, and kill the rest. Separate statistical compilations by a Serbian and a Croatian historian in the 1980s agree that, broadly, probably more than 300,000 Serb men, women and children were

[17] Bartov, O., 1994, *Hitler's Army: Soldiers, Nazis and War in the Third Reich*, Oxford, 12, 17, 28.
[18] Weiss-Wendt, A., 2013, 'Introduction', in A. Weiss-Wendt (ed.), *The Nazi Genocide of the Roma: Reassessment and Commemoration*, New York and Oxford, 7.

murdered by the *Ustaša*, many of them at the death camps at Jasenovac and Slava Gradiska. Recent research also confirms that the *Ustaše* saw deportation of Croatia's Roma to Jasenovac, where between 16,000 and 40,000 of them were literally beaten to death, as a 'social-hygienic act'.[19] On top of this, the NDH regime also sent 26,000 Croatian and Bosnian Jews to their deaths at Auschwitz. The levels of violence employed by the Croatian fascists shocked even German SS officials. In retaliation the Serb-dominated loyalist resistance movement, the *Chetniks*, perpetrated their own atrocities against Croats as well as Bosnian Muslims, who had opted for a policy of passivity under *Ustaša* rule, but whose neutrality was ignored by the aggrieved Serbs. In occupied Serbia, the collaborationist Nedić regime assisted the SS in gassing to death or deporting to Auschwitz 25,000 Jews; by May 1942 the responsible SS representative could report to Berlin that Serbia was the first state in Europe to be entirely 'Jew free'.

In the formerly Polish provinces of eastern Galicia and Volhynia, under Nazi occupation after June 1941, the Organisation of Ukrainian Nationalists (OUN) concluded by 1943 that 'the future Ukraine would best be secured by the ethnic cleansing of Poles.'[20] A Ukrainian Central Committee in Kraków, tolerated by the *General-Gouvernement*, encouraged Ukrainians to join the Nazi *Hilfspolizei* or auxiliary police, and in 1941–2 'about 12,000 Ukrainian policemen assisted about 14,000 German policemen in the murder of about 200,000 Volhynian Jews.'[21] In the spring of 1943, most of these Ukrainian policemen joined the Ukrainian Insurgent Army (UPA), subordinate to Stepan Bandera's wing of the OUN, and it was this far-right movement which undertook to exterminate all Poles in the area. OUN-Bandera carried out the mass killing of some 40–60,000 Poles in Volhynia between March and December 1943, frequently with horrific refinements; they also attacked and murdered rival Ukrainian nationalists, and in the end OUN-Bandera were probably responsible for the deaths of as many Ukrainians as Poles. Polish self-defence units in the area responded by killing Ukrainians, and by mid-1944 a full-scale Polish-Ukrainian civil war was raging in western Ukraine and south-eastern Poland, independent of the larger struggle.

Romania under Antonescu, whose anti-Semitism rivalled Hitler's, made its own voluntary contribution to the death toll. Awarded Transnistria as occupation territory, Antonescu used it as a dumping ground for Romania's minorities; as the Romanian foreign minister suggested in July 1941, this was an opportunity 'for total ethnic liberation . . . for a cleansing of our nation . . . If

---

[19] Korb, A., 2013, 'Ustaša Mass Violence against Gypsies in Croatia 1941-1942', in A. Weiss-Wendt (ed.), *The Nazi Genocide of the Roma: Reassessment and Commemoration*, New York and Oxford, 76.

[20] Snyder, T., 2003, *The Reconstruction of Nations: Poland, Ukraine, Lithuania, Belarus 1569-1999*, New Haven, CT, 155.

[21] Snyder, *The Reconstruction of Nations*, 162.

need be, use machine guns.'[22] Transnistria was plundered by Romanian troops, who also murdered about half the province's 180,000 Jews in the process; the remainder fled eastwards into German-occupied Ukraine, where some were executed by *Einsatzgruppe D*, while others were forced back across the river. In the place of Transnistria's Jews the Romanian government deported some 25,000 Romanian Roma, about half of whom died as a result. Meanwhile most Jews in Bessarabia and the Bukovina suffered a similar fate: of 275,000 Jews in these two territories, 40,000 died and the rest were interned in the Ukraine. The deportation of Jews from Romania was accompanied by horrific cruelties. At Iaşi in Moldavia a pogrom on 28–29 June 1941 killed several thousand of the town's 45,000 Jews; the remainder were loaded onto cattle cars, in which several thousand more died of dehydration while being shunted eastwards across the countryside in mid-summer heat. In all, some 13–15,000 people died in the 'Iaşi action' alone. Odessa, which fell to Romanian troops in October 1941, became the scene of gruesome crimes. In response to a bomb attack by the Soviet resistance, Antonescu ordered the reprisal killing of 18,000 Jews. The Marshal was explicit about his desire to 'get the Yids out of the city immediately', ordering the army to 'Pack them into catacombs; throw them into the Black Sea!'[23] Clusters of bodies were left hanging from Odessa's street lights and tramcar cables in this 'city of hanging corpses'; in the end at least 22,000 died.[24] Altogether Antonescu's regime was responsible for somewhere between 115,000 and 180,000 Jewish deaths in the occupied Ukraine, and some 250,000 to 300,000 Romanian Jewish deaths.

The longer the war lasted the more difficult it becomes to disentangle the mass murder of Jews from that of other groups and nationalities. This imprecision applies in particular to the Roma and Sinti, whose numbers were traditionally conjectural and who were frequently rounded up and executed randomly, together with Jewish victims. There can, however, be no doubt that the incremental decisions to embark on the genocide of Europe's Jews were arrived at precisely because of the 'problem' the Nazi regime had saddled itself with by conquering most of Europe, and in particular so much of Eastern Europe. By taking over so many European countries the regime found itself confronted anew by the dilemma of what to do with large Jewish minorities, some of them swollen by refugees from the Reich. The conquest of Poland, with its 3 million Jews, and of the western Soviet provinces, highlighted the issue.

Something like a consensus has emerged that the Nazi regime did not start the war, let alone come to power in 1933, with the fixed intention of murdering millions of Jews. Of course, Hitler detested the Jews and preached the

---

[22] Quoted in Mazower, *Hitler's Empire*, 376.
[23] Quoted in Mazower, *Hitler's Empire*, 338.
[24] Mazower, *Hitler's Empire*, 338.

establishment of a racially 'pure' nation by excising Jews from German society. Faced with huge numbers of additional Jews in occupied Europe, however, the regime reached for ever more radical counter-measures. To begin with, Jews in occupied Poland were deported to ghettoes, forced to live in cordoned-off suburbs, many of them in the *General-Gouvernement*. Warsaw, Łódż and other cities hosted these ghettoes, where conditions became ever more unhealthy and desperate. The invasion of the Soviet Union represented another radicalisation. The *Einsatzgruppen* and other bodies found themselves murdering far more Jews than Soviet officials, and as the *Wehrmacht* crossed the former Baltic states and the western Soviet Union, Lithuanian, Latvian, Estonian and other nationalists not only welcomed the Germans, but assisted in the rounding-up of local Jews and, in several well-recorded incidents, their brutal murder in public places. At Kaunas, in Lithuania, on 28 June, 'German soldiers merely stood and watched as locals beat Jews to death in the streets'; altogether about 7,000 were murdered in Kaunas alone.[25] In Riga, on 1 July, the Germans were assisted by Latvian auxiliaries in killing some 400 Jews in similar fashion. In Borisov, Belarus, drunken Belorussian policemen, albeit under SS supervision, killed 8,000 Jews; most were shot in the forests outside town, but some escaped and had to be hunted down and killed back in Borisov. In an incident only brought to public notice decades later, virtually all the Jews in the tiny Polish town of Jedwabne – at least 340 out of 2,000 people – were murdered on 10 July 1941 by about forty of their Polish neighbours, with little instigation from the Germans. All over Eastern (and Western) Europe, the mass murder of Jews, though initiated by the Nazis, was very much a pan-European project.

Such brutal methods, however – mass shootings, beating to death or even gassing people in specially constructed trucks – were soon found to exact too high a psychological toll on the perpetrators. By late 1941, the Nazi leadership came to the conclusion that the most practical way to conduct mass murder was to concentrate it in purpose-built death camps. The construction or rather expansion of such camps, finalised at the Wannsee conference in January 1942, and later code-named 'Operation Reinhard' in memory of the assassinated '*Reichsprotektor*' of Bohemia and Moravia, Reinhard Heydrich, who chaired the meeting, marks the final shift towards 'industrialised killing'. All over Europe, Jewish populations not already exterminated were rounded up and deported eastwards to the camps. In this period occurred the carefully coordinated murder of over 1.2 million Polish Jews in the course of 1942, and the expansion of deportations of Jews from across the continent; the mass deportation, between March and June 1943, of the 49,000-strong Jewish community of Salonika in Greece, about a quarter of the city's population; and the extermination at Auschwitz of about half

---

[25] Ferguson, *The War of the World*, 453.

of Hungarian Jews. The Hungarian 'action' of July 1944, however, in some respects marked the apogee of the Auschwitz camp's activity. By mid-1944 a reluctance to cooperate with the genocide was emerging among those East European leaders who still had some agency in the matter, because it was obvious even to the committed that the Nazis were losing the war. By then, too, a realisation of what was happening was beginning to reach the outside world, and while this did not, nor was likely to, lead to concerted attempts at intervention, it contributed to the first stirrings of resistance among Jews themselves, as told in Chapter 10.

The sheer destructiveness of the war, physically and demographically, was a major factor in shaping post-war developments. Vast tracts of Eastern Europe were bereft of infrastructure, housing, industrial capacity, agricultural productivity and population. Urban centres lay in ruins: 90 per cent of Warsaw and Gdańsk were rubble; Budapest's famous bridges destroyed by the retreating Germans. This devastation made the task of post-war reconstruction daunting, but it also made more plausible, at least for a while, the proposition that only a radical transformation of society and state could effect this reconstruction. In short, the groundwork was laid in many East Europeans' minds for the imposition of a communist system, and in many cases its joyful acceptance.

The war toppled regimes and ruling elites across the region. By 1942 there was not a single state of the interwar period in Eastern Europe which had not been conquered and partitioned by the Axis powers, or dragooned into a Nazi-led coalition. Hitler presided over a short-lived but nightmare empire of vassal and puppet states, while enslaving millions of East Europeans in forced labour camps. The predictable result was the emergence of resistance movements, not all of them intent on restoring the pre-war order. On the contrary, communist-led resistance in particular was the harbinger of political revolution either during or after the war; and in the meantime the rivalry of communists and non-communists saw some countries – notably Yugoslavia, Greece and Poland – descend into civil war well before 1945. Not all the bloodletting was political: the war also unleashed nationalist antagonisms which spiralled into mutual slaughter, at least in Yugoslavia, Poland and western Ukraine. In the process the ethnic cleansing which had begun with the First World War was in some areas ratcheted up a notch.

In the meantime the conflict had led to the deaths of millions and traumatised and brutalised the survivors. Entire societies had been socially decapitated, in the sense that thousands of the pre-war elite had been killed, imprisoned or driven into exile. Into the political vacuum thus created stepped Stalin's Red Army. It is this aspect of 'war as revolution' which constitutes the focus of the next chapter.

10

War as revolution

Political consequences of the Second World War

Wars are not just fought militarily; they are also political struggles. Governments go to war for political reasons, and in the course of any conflict their war aims, in other words the political objectives of fighting, expand or contract depending on circumstances. The course of the Second World War in Eastern Europe is a classic example of how war, once begun, can escape the control of its original begetters. What began as a war of territorial expansion and racial aggression by Hitler's Germany ended by destroying the entire interwar order of Eastern Europe. The defeat of Germany and its allies not only obliterated Nazism and the conservative authoritarian regimes, but fatally weakened what little was left of interwar democracy. The Soviet Union's military victory was also a victory for communism, enabling the imposition of a uniform political system. The groundwork for this political revolution was laid during the war itself, in particular by the complex interaction between occupiers, collaborators and resistance movements.

This theme of 'war as revolution' has been most cogently analysed by Jan T. Gross.[1] If one of the principal reasons for the rise of interwar fascism was the gulf between narrow ruling elites and the broad mass of the population, it is also clear that the war widened this gulf, making the extreme solution represented by communism seem, for a while, the only plausible solution to a significant number of people. But it is also obvious that the war created a host of other preconditions for revolutionary change. Paradoxically, while immensely destructive, it stimulated economic development and social change. It discredited old elites, and removed whole classes of society, including inconvenient national minorities, from the equation. It placed an unprecedented amount of private and public property at the disposal of the new rulers, and made their appropriation of these assets seem more acceptable. Above all, the war made increased intervention by the state seem not only necessary but positively desirable.

This chapter examines the dilemma confronting both governments-in-exile and collaborationists: was it more patriotic to accept defeat and collaborate, or to resist, and at what cost? It then describes the two main types of resistance,

[1] Gross, J., 1997, 'War as Revolution', in N. Naimark and L. Gibianskii (eds), *The Establishment of Communist Regimes in Eastern Europe 1944-1949*, Boulder, CO and Oxford, 17–40.

loyalist or restoration resistance, and communist-led resistance, and analyses the strengths and weaknesses of each. It is also worth mentioning what might be called existentialist resisters, those, like the Jews and others, for whom resistance was a choice between potential survival and certain death. Finally, the ingredients of political revolution came together in the closing stages of the war: as the Soviets rolled back Nazism, the often internecine struggle between resistance movements shifted dramatically in favour of those which were communist-led, and non-communist resisters were either sidelined or eliminated altogether. In international terms, the overwhelming military contribution of the Soviets meant that there was little the western Allies could do, apart from rhetoric, to avert communist dominance. As so often, the outcome of the war was radically different from that envisaged by those who began it.

The dilemma of the defeated

The toppling of pre-war political elites and the wholesale partitioning of states that occurred as the war expanded has already been described. Here it is worth noting that the defeated – as opposed to Germany's hapless allies – divided into two broad categories. On one side were those who accepted the reality of defeat and even, to some extent at least, accepted the consequences by collaborating. This category included the *Ustaša*-led 'Independent State of Croatia' (NDH), General Nedić's puppet administration in Serbia, General Tsolatoglou's in Greece, and the Ukrainian OUN. It also subsumed all those East Europeans who, for whatever reasons, actively participated in the war on the side of Nazi Germany, whether by impromptu massacres of Jews, by serving as camp guards, or by enlisting in German-led auxiliary police battalions or units of the Waffen SS. On the other side were those who emphatically did not accept the situation, and attempted to mount some sort of resistance either within occupied territory or from exile.

The motivations of the 'accepters' are perhaps the most challenging to disentangle, since the mere fact of collaboration is often seen as sufficient ground for condemnation. Yet we risk doing collaborators an injustice by simply judging them as morally deficient. Undoubtedly, much collaboration was ideologically motivated, and not that far removed from fascist. It could also, particularly in the territory conquered from the Soviet Union, spring from a sincere, indeed visceral, hatred of communism. This was also a motive for loyalist resisters who, once their country's communist party was involved in resistance too, regarded with horror the prospect of communists becoming the ultimate victors; this was especially the dilemma of loyalists in Yugoslavia and Greece. For some collaborators, however, we have to accept that their motivation was one of patriotism: confronted with foreign invasion and occupation, accompanied by the flight of the former government and the threatened collapse of public order, some collaborators saw it as their duty to step in and, if they could, mediate between their fellow countrymen and the occupiers. That collaboration inevitably involved such individuals in unacceptable moral choices and made them thereby complicit in atrocities and gross human rights abuses was often not appreciated until it was too late.

The motives of resisters, by contrast, seem more straightforward. Both governments-in-exile, and those claiming to represent them on the ground in Nazi-occupied Eastern Europe, were undoubtedly animated by simple patriotism and the desire to liberate their countries from the invaders. One by one, as the Axis tide swept east, governments-in-exile sprang up, most of them based in London. President Edward Beneš claimed to speak for the defunct Czechoslovakian Republic, although it was not until July 1940 that the British government recognised this, and the United States only followed suit in October 1942. General Władysław Sikorski led the free Polish government first from Paris and then London and, after his death in an aircraft accident in July 1943, his place was taken by the Peasant Party leader Stanisław Mikołajczyk. This was not a continuation of the colonels' regime, but a democratic coalition of the four main parties, committed to returning Poland to constitutional, pluralist politics. King Peter II of Yugoslavia presided over a cabinet in London which was in principle multiparty and multinational. King George II of Greece based his government initially in London and then, from March 1943, in British-occupied Egypt. The establishment of an Albanian government-in-exile was initially hindered by the fact that Britain and France had recognised Mussolini's annexation of Albania in March 1939; only once Italy entered the war did the question of who represented Albanian interests on the Allied side arise. Despite King Zog's arrival in London with a hundred sacks of gold abstracted from the Tirana treasury, it was not clear how much allegiance he commanded back home, and the British Foreign Office preferred to keep Zog in 'warm storage' pending clarification.[2] All governments-in-exile, however, faced intractable problems: apart from whether they were even recognised as representing their country, what allegiance did they command in reality, and how could they communicate with what followers they had? The Yugoslav and Greek governments-in-exile, and their monarchs, did not necessarily command universal allegiance, in part because of their poor pre-war record, in part because of their speedy collapse in 1941; this dissatisfaction found expression in the emergence of republican as well as communist alternatives on the ground.

The dilemma of resisters actually in occupied Europe was most acute. Where governments had formally accepted defeat, resistance was an illegal act

---

[2] Fischer, B.J., 1999, *Albania at War 1939-1945*, London, 106, 110.

in defiance of legitimate authority. Where a government had refused to accept defeat by fleeing abroad, as in the case of the Polish or Yugoslav or Greek governments, the choice for its citizens left under enemy occupation was still almost impossible. Open resistance by uniformed military personnel was out of the question, and in any case such personnel, as in Poland, were quickly disarmed and disbanded, where they were not interned or murdered en masse, as happened to thousands of Polish officers on both sides of the Nazi-Soviet divide. Those spared faced the subsequent dilemma of whether to resist at all, and if so, on what basis, with what means, and with whom. For some, like the Polish regular army officer Józef Garliński, wounded at the front in 1939 and then demobilised, joining the underground resistance was a near-automatic choice, which nevertheless bespoke considerable courage; captured by the Gestapo in 1943, Garliński was lucky to survive internment in Auschwitz and Neuengamme. For others, like the non-Serb population of Yugoslavia, loyalty to the ostensibly multi-ethnic, but in reality still Serb-dominated royal government-in-exile was hardly automatic. For still others, like the Serbs at risk of extermination at the hands of the *Ustaša*, or the Belorussians, including Jews, forced to flee Nazi atrocities and seek refuge with Soviet partisan units in the forests, or the Jews of the Warsaw ghetto who finally rose up against the Nazis in April to May 1943, or the thousands who sought to avoid conscription as forced labour by joining whatever local resistance movement was on offer, resistance was not a choice but an existential necessity. For non-communists, resistance was a patriotic duty, if only to forestall the threat of communist takeover at war's end; but this could be complicated if, as in Yugoslavia, the communist-led resistance increasingly looked like the only one delivering results.

The strength of Tito's Partisans in Yugoslavia took some time to become apparent, however, and was very much the exception to the rule, since elsewhere, with the exception of Czechoslovakia, communists were thin on the ground, and in any case did not stir a muscle until the Soviet Union was invaded. In the meantime the three main non-communist resistance movements were the Home Army (*Armia Krajowa* or AK) in Poland, the Chetniks in Yugoslavia, and the National Republican Greek League (EDES) in northwestern Greece. The latter, as the name implies, did not even favour the restoration of the Greek monarchy. The AK was firmly loyal to the government-in-exile. The Chetniks, under Colonel Draža Mihailović, were the official resistance of the royal Yugoslav government-in-exile, and in recognition of this Mihailović was promoted to general and appointed war minister. In reality, because of the physical obstacles to regular communication Mihailović was only intermittently in touch with London. He failed to win many adherents among non-Serbs, and his strategy of lying low until Allied help was imminent meant that the Chetniks made little impression on the Axis occupation. Worse, the Chetniks' anti-communism led them into some disastrous decisions, notably agreeing to a live-and-let-live arrangement with the Germans in return for the freedom to attack Tito's Partisans.

Communist resistance belongs in a class of its own, not least because the motives of communists for resisting were so clearly aimed at a political revolution at war's end if not before. Yet prior to 22 June 1941, when the Soviet Union was invaded, East European communists as elsewhere took no part in resistance. According to the terms of the Nazi-Soviet Pact, Germany was the Soviet Union's ally, and although the Comintern condemned fascism, it also saw the Axis powers were as mere variants of the same 'capitalist' enemy. Only when, to Stalin's bewilderment, Hitler betrayed him in favour of all-out war did Moscow call on communist parties everywhere to resist. In most countries, whatever post-war communist propaganda maintained, the response was pretty feeble, given the paucity of numbers; only in Yugoslavia and Greece did communist-led resistance gather genuine force, and then only because the Partisans' appeal was deliberately couched in patriotic terms, enabling non-communists to contemplate throwing in their lot with the communists.

Jewish resistance was unique, in that Jews everywhere in occupied Eastern Europe had the most elemental reasons for resisting, while at the same time had so few practical means of doing so. Jewish communities, even where not already ghettoised and deprived of almost all agency, were hampered by an understandable if fatal reluctance to imagine the worst, a lack of access to any arms, and a fear of making things worse by resisting. In this spirit many Jewish leaders reluctantly cooperated with the Nazis in regulating the wretched conditions in the ghettoes and even assisting in the selection of thousands for the death camps. Only rarely did outright resistance, at any cost, come to be seen as a rational option by Jews, and even then the opportunities for meaningful resistance were agonisingly few. Armed resistance was mounted only in exceptional circumstances, most famously in the Warsaw ghetto uprising of April to May 1943, but also in the ghettoes of Częstochowa in June 1943, Białystok in August 1943 and Vilnius in September 1943. At Białystok several hundred denizens rose up with only a few arms; most were killed, but some escaped to join the local Home Army partisans and survived. The Częstochowa uprising lasted five days, at the end of which 1,500 Jews were killed, some by their own hand; a further 500 burned to death in the ghetto's ruins. The Warsaw ghetto's first armed resistance was in January 1943, as a result of which deportations to the death camps were temporarily suspended. In the following three months the ghetto's inhabitants prepared for a last-ditch fight, and when German forces again entered the ghetto, on 19 April, they were met with stubborn, building-by-building opposition. In the course of nearly a month's fighting some 13,000 Jews died, many burned alive as the Germans systematically torched each block, at a cost of possibly 300 German soldiers and policemen. Equally remarkable acts of resistance occurred in the death camps. A prisoners' uprising at Treblinka in August 1943 resulted in several guards being killed, and although 1,500 prisoners were mown down in retaliation seventy escaped, and the gassing of Jews was halted for a month. At Sobibór, in October 1943, the prisoners managed covertly to kill eleven of their SS guards before the alarm was given; several hundred prisoners then escaped, and although most were tracked down and killed the camp was shut down in the aftermath. Elsewhere, especially in the occupied Soviet Union, Jews joined partisan units where they could; as a German official commented in late 1942, 'it is well known that many Jews are fleeing to the bandits [partisans]. They recognize that they are going to be eliminated sooner or later, so they choose the lesser evil.'[3] Some Jews even managed to escape the fighting almost completely, like the 1,236 led by the Bielski brothers, who survived in the woods near Nawahrudak (Nowogródek) in western Belarus.

War as resistance: Loyalist or restoration resistances

How do the two main types of resistance movement, loyalist and communist-led, compare in terms of what they achieved? In Eastern Europe the results were inevitably skewed in favour of the communists by the larger geopolitical outcome of the war, the fact that communism's heartland, the Soviet Union, emerged by late 1944 as the unchallengeable regional hegemon. Yet given the strength of loyalist resistance in some countries, and Stalin's need to tread carefully in his relations with his western allies, the outcome might not have been uniformly in favour of communism, had the latter's followers not behaved with such cunning and ruthlessness.

The objective of loyalist resisters was a restoration of the pre-war regime, albeit in some cases on condition of substantial reform. In this regard, the Polish Home Army (AK) was the largest and most cohesive resistance in all of occupied Eastern Europe. It also tragically illustrates the inherent weaknesses of loyalist resistance, given the larger context.

The Polish government-in-exile, recognised by Britain and France, was led by General Władysław Sikorski as both prime minister and commander-in-chief. Sikorski had been a persistent critic of the colonels' regime, and part of his coalition's appeal was that it stood for a more democratic post-war Poland. Being based abroad, Sikorski's principal task was to organise the tens of thousands of Polish refugees and service personnel who had fled the country, and to try to coordinate resistance in Poland itself from a distance, hampered by communications difficulties.

[3] Quoted in Nolte, H.-H., 2005, 'Partisan War in Belorussia 1941-1944', in R. Chickering, S. Förster and B. Greiner (eds), *A World at Total War: Global Conflict and the Politics of Destruction 1937-1945*, Washington, DC and Cambridge, 264.

Resistance in Poland in fact sprang up spontaneously even before conquest was completed. The Warsaw city authorities commissioned General Marian Tokarzewski to organise a resistance movement; units of the armed forces took to the forests where they could, and a partisan war of sorts was mounted in 1939–40. Any coordinated resistance faced enormous problems due to the confusion caused by the joint Nazi-Soviet invasion, mass displacement of population, and above all by the Nazis' ferocious reprisals against any, or no, sign of opposition, coupled with the mass round-up and extermination of the Polish elite by both Nazis and Soviets. Remarkably, a parallel underground government was established under the noses of the German occupiers. The government delegate in Warsaw, Professor Jan Piekałkiewicz, set up four departments: a political council, an administrative structure, the military force known as the Home Army, and a 'directorate of underground struggle', which oversaw a rudimentary but extensive network of welfare relief, including educational services. In a situation where Polish-language education was banned by the Germans, the underground organised classes for up to a million primary school pupils; it also ran secondary school classes, and the four main universities of Warsaw, Kraków, Lwów and Wilno all ran underground courses. Newspapers were published at great risk, including an English-language one for escaped British POWs; an underground theatre flourished. Most impressive was the Home Army, which in August 1944 numbered some 380,000 men, women and children. The AK was hampered by its lack of arms, and its strategy was to reserve an all-out uprising for the moment liberating forces reached Polish soil; but despite this it mounted an ongoing resistance. This included administrative sabotage; the targeted assassination of SS officials and policemen; intelligence work, including the smuggling to the British of a complete set of parts for the Germans' V2 rocket; aiding escaped Allied POWs to evade recapture; and disruption of the railways. An estimated one out of every eight German trains bound for the eastern front was either delayed or damaged by the AK, which also accounted for some 150,000 German lives in the end.

Unfortunately for the AK the logic of its situation worked against it. Britain and France made no serious effort to assist Poland in 1939–40, and after mid-1940 Britain was itself beleaguered, and too far away for logistical support by way of air-drops. Until June 1941 the Soviet Union was an enemy occupier. Even after the commencement of Barbarossa, and Stalin's discovery that he needed the Poles as allies, Soviet assistance to Poland's loyalist resistance was a double-edged sword. At Churchill's urging, the Soviets and Poles re-established relations, and concluded an agreement in July 1941, whereby the hundreds of thousands of Polish internees in the Soviet gulag were released, in order to form a loyalist army on Soviet soil under General Władysław Anders. By March 1942, with little Soviet help, Anders had collected 70,000 men and their families, many seriously undernourished following their ordeal, and few of whom relished the prospect of fighting alongside their former Soviet oppressors. Requests from Anders for these Poles to be shipped west to fight on the western Allies' side were initially resisted by Sikorski, and greeted with charges of 'cowardice' by Stalin, but in the end Stalin accepted that such unwilling allies would be better off out of his way, and the loyalist forces, by August 1942 some 115,000 soldiers and civilians, were transported to the West via Iran. As a result Poles fought and died on the Italian front, in France and the Netherlands despite the fact that many of them came from territories already abandoned to Soviet takeover by the Tehran agreement. Meanwhile the Soviets allowed a Polish communist, Wanda Wasilewska, to found the Union of Polish Patriots (ZPP), tasked with creating a Polish unit for the Red Army, the Tadeusz Kościuszko Division, under the command of Colonel Zygmunt Berling.

Relations between the Polish government-in-exile and Moscow worsened in 1943, as it became apparent that the Soviets were intent on retaking the territories seized from Poland in 1939; they reached rock bottom in April, when the Nazi regime announced to the world its discovery of the mass graves of Polish officers murdered by the NKVD in 1940. Despite Soviet denials, only definitively proven to be false on the opening up of the Soviet archives in 1990, Sikorski demanded an independent enquiry by the Red Cross, at which point Stalin suspended relations. The Poles' bargaining position was not improved by Sikorski's death in July 1943; and in December, the western Allies accepted Stalin's position on Poland's post-war boundaries.

The AK faced an excruciating dilemma in the summer of 1944, as the Red Army approached Warsaw. For largely political reasons the AK's commander General Tadeusz Bór-Komorowski, in agreement with the London government, decided it was imperative to launch a general uprising against the Germans, coinciding with the Soviets' arrival but also establishing control of the capital by the AK, rather than the few Polish communists fighting with the Red Army. The result was a two-month agony culminating in disaster: despite initial successes against the Germans the insurgents were ill-armed and outnumbered and, crucially, reports of Soviet tanks outside Warsaw were inaccurate. The Soviets were indeed within striking distance, but their high command was currently distracted by Romania's changing of sides, which opened up new opportunities in the Balkans. On the other hand, it was undoubtedly in Stalin's interests to allow the Germans to crush the AK uprising, which he termed 'a mindless brawl mounted by adventurers'.[4] Nor did the Soviets make any serious attempt to air-drop help to the Poles, or facilitate western air-drops from Soviet airfields. For 63 days Poles and Germans waged a bitter struggle for Warsaw, with the insurgents initially driving the Germans out, and then defending the ground taken, block by block, against a ruthless counter-attack. As the Germans retook each district they systematically massacred insurgents

---

[4]   Quoted in Ascherson, N., 1987, *The Struggles for Poland*, London, 127.

and civilians alike, then set fire to the buildings. By the fighting's end, on 2 October, some 200,000 Poles had died, and 93 per cent of left-bank Warsaw was smouldering rubble. The outcome of the uprising literally reduced the number of Poles willing and able to oppose communist takeover in the remaining months of the war.

The other major loyalist resistance movement was Mihailović's Chetniks in partitioned Yugoslavia. In 1941 the Germans failed to disarm all the royal Yugoslav army, and some units accordingly took to the hills, in the time-honoured Balkan tradition of the *četa* or armed band. The term *četnik* (member of a *četa*) is itself ambiguous: some *četnici* served Nedić's puppet regime, thinking that the patriotic course was to act as a buffer between the Nazis and the Serb population. Others remained loyal to the government-in-exile, and these coalesced around Mihailović in western Serbia. Mihailović's early operations against the Germans attracted the notice of Britain's Special Operations Executive (SOE), charged with supporting resistance movements; and Mihailović was eventually promoted to general and appointed war minister.

The important thing about the Chetniks, however, and the principal factor limiting their efficacy as a resistance, was that they remained based almost exclusively on the Serb population, whether in Serbia, Bosnia, Croatia or Montenegro. As a result, their main energies were focused on resisting atrocities against Serbs in the *Ustaša*-controlled NDH, which governed both Croatia and Bosnia. Many Chetniks, moreover, were hardly concerned with restoring the old Yugoslavia; rather, they aimed for a more explicitly Serb-dominated state. It did not help that the government-in-exile, though composed of Serbs, Croats and Slovenes, was hopelessly split and gave Mihailović no clear lead, while communications between London and the Chetniks remained poor. Mihailović was not even in control of all Chetniks, especially those units in the NDH and Montenegro, who conducted their own savage struggle against both Croats and Muslims.

A final characteristic of the Chetniks posed them with a fatal dilemma: not only were Mihailović and his supporters Serb nationalists, which limited their appeal to non-Serbs, but they were royalists, loyal to King Peter. As such, they could hardly envisage active cooperation with a rival resistance movement dominated by the Yugoslav Communist Party. Despite talks between Mihailović and the Partisan leader Tito in 1941, therefore, the Chetniks increasingly saw the Partisans as, if anything, a greater danger to Yugoslavia's future than the Axis occupiers. Mihailović's long-term strategy involved lying low to avoid reprisals against the civilian population, and awaiting the arrival of liberating outside forces before rising up. This led Mihailović gradually into a policy of live-and-let-live towards the German and Italian occupying forces, alternating with joint operations against the Partisans, who by contrast positively courted reprisals as a means of drumming up support. The ambiguity of Chetnik policy, seen from outside, led to charges of active collaboration; and while this was undoubtedly never Mihailović's intention it was sufficient, by the end of 1943, for the British to transfer support from the Chetniks to the Partisans, on the assumption that it was the Partisans who were killing most Germans. In comparison with Tito, who had a clear strategy appealing to most Yugoslavs, Mihailović was politically inept. A Chetnik congress of delegates from across the country, convened in January 1944 to drum up political support, was attended mainly by Serbs, and suggested that the Chetniks could not imagine a post-war Yugoslavia not dominated by Serbs. By June 1944 Mihailović had been dropped as war minister, and in September King Peter formally called on his subjects to rally behind the Partisans. Mihailović ended the war a fugitive from Tito's newly established regime, and in 1946 was tried and executed for 'collaboration'.

Loyalist resistance in *Greece* operated in many respects under even greater difficulties. King George's government-in-exile seemed discredited by its association with the Metaxas dictatorship, followed by its defeat and flight to London. What non-communist resistance manifested itself was initially overshadowed by the communist-led resistance which sprang up after Hitler's invasion of the Soviet Union. Although the Greek Communist Party was tiny, the broadly based National Liberation Front (EAM) created in September 1941 proved popular, appealing especially to the young and to women, for whom its message was unusually emancipatory. The armed wing of EAM, the National People's Liberation Army (ELAS), rapidly became 'much the largest of the resistance movements in occupied Greece', partly because of its readiness to court reprisals by aggressive attacks on Axis forces.[5] At its height in 1944 ELAS numbered 60,000 fighters, many of them women.

Non-communist resistance in Greece was for the most part vehemently anti-monarchist, like the National Republican Greek League (EDES), which emerged in the north-west under the leadership of General Napoleon Zervas, an opportunist who did not believe in fighting the occupiers more than he had to.[6] Reversing this situation resulted from consistent British support for the Greek monarchy, and the fact that republican resisters like Zervas were more anti-communist than they were anti-monarchist. British attempts to encourage cooperation between ELAS and EDES had some successes, such as the joint destruction of the Gorgopotamus railway viaduct in November 1942; but for the most part the two movements remained hostile to one another. Neither could agree on power-sharing, with EAM/ELAS demanding key ministries and a post-war referendum on whether to retain the monarchy. In October 1943 ELAS, bolstered by arms seized from the surrendered Italians, began to attack EDES, claiming that the latter was collaborating; EDES fought back, and other

[5] Clogg, R., 1992, *A Concise History of Greece*, Cambridge and New York, 128.
[6] Mazower, M., 1993, *Inside Hitler's Greece: The Experience of Occupation 1941-1944*, New Haven, CT and London, 140.

anti-communist groups joined 'security battalions' organised by Tsolakoglou's puppet regime, in a vicious circle of atrocity and counter-atrocity. When EAM established a Political Committee for National Liberation in March 1944, and Greek troops stationed in Egypt mutinied in support of EAM's programme, Churchill induced the King to appoint as prime minister Georgios Papandreou, a Venezelist who, it was hoped, had sufficient authority to appeal to both sides.

In April 1944 Papandreou reached an agreement with EAM, whereby the latter accepted subordinate roles in the cabinet. This arguably decisive concession was only possible because of shifts in the grand alliance: Stalin effectively was willing to abandon Greece, and with it the Greek communists, to predominantly British influence, in return for firmer Soviet control in the rest of Eastern Europe. The Papandreou government's arrival in Athens on 18 October thus coincided with the reversal of EAM's fortunes, and the bad feeling led to a renewal of civil war in December. Greece's royal government thereafter profited from the country's accessibility to Britain's armed support, an advantage available to no other country in Eastern Europe.

In *Albania*, it remained hard to determine what constituted loyalist resistance, given King Zog's questionable status and the difficulty of estimating how many supporters he had on the ground. Resistance to the Italian occupation was initially low-level, fed by the Italians' tactlessness, corruption and mismanagement of the economy. Serious armed resistance only really began in the spring of 1940, and was confined largely to the mountainous north, led by traditional tribal leaders whose allegiance to the distant Zog was notional.[7] The picture changed in June 1940, when Italy declared war against Britain; after this Britain provided considerable material support for Albanian resistance. The Italian invasion of Greece in October intensified this trend: Britain now used Zog as a figurehead, and British operatives encouraged Zogists in Albania to prepare for an uprising. By the end of 1941 Italian control barely ran beyond the major towns and communication routes.

Two developments in 1941 complicated the dilemma of loyalist resisters. The first was Yugoslavia's partition in April, when the province of Kosovo was added to occupied Albania. Overnight, nationalist dreams of a Greater Albania were realised, albeit at the hands of Nazis and Italians. Secondly, the invasion of the Soviet Union led to the revival of Albanian communism. At the urging of Yugoslavia's communists, the Albanian Party was formally refounded; and in September 1942 its 33-year-old leader, Enver Hoxha, secured the support of the northern Zogists for a National Liberation Movement (NLM). In response, an assortment of liberal nationalists and republicans formed the anti-communist and anti-Zogist National Front (*Balli Kombëtar* or BK) in November, under the rather ineffectual leadership of a former diplomat. The BK stood for a

---

[7] Fischer, *Albania at War*, 130.

'free, ethnic and democratic Albania', code for their desire to retain Kosovo following liberation.[8] Their strategy towards the occupation, however, was essentially passive, so as it became apparent that the most active resistance was the NLM, British support shifted, as in Yugoslavia, to the communist-led resistance. The NLM's edge over BK increased when, in September 1943, Fascist Italy collapsed. Although the Germans rushed to establish a firm grip over Albania, they could not prevent a substantial number of weapons falling to the NLM. This provided a crucial boost to communist-led resistance.

By contrast non-communist resistance in Albania looked supine if not actively collaborationist. In October 1943 Zogists formed the Legality Movement in an attempt to make common cause with the BK and other nationalist resisters. Liberal nationalists and monarchists were increasingly bedevilled, however, by the unexpectedly tactful nature of the German occupation: unlike the Italians, the Germans respected Albanian sensitivities, formally recognised Albania's 'relative' sovereignty, and appointed the moderate liberal Mehdi Frashëri, 'one of the most respected living Albanians', as regent.[9] Frashëri was committed to a non-communist Greater Albania, but also, as he proclaimed in January 1944, to an uncensored press, social reform and 'democratic principles that eliminate all dictatorships'.[10] The irony was that this genuinely liberal government depended on the protection of Nazi Germany, which made it easy for Hoxha's NLM to portray Frashëri as collaborationist and fascist. By November 1944, when the Germans were finally forced to withdraw from Albania, non-communist resistance was comprehensively discredited.

Resistance in the German-occupied *Protectorate of Bohemia and Moravia*, and in Tiso's 'independent' *Slovakia*, started with certain built-in disadvantages. The dismantling of Czechoslovakia meant that potential leaders were either exiled, imprisoned or under Gestapo surveillance, while the armed forces were disbanded. Slovakia's separate status after March 1939 rendered doubtful whether a united Czechoslovakia could ever be restored, and while the Nazi-Soviet Pact lasted neither Czech nor Slovak communists showed any interest in resistance. Communists apart, various groups started organising even before the outbreak of the war in the west, all of them committed to 'the vision of a free, socially just, and democratic Czechoslovakia', but the country was out of reach of Allied aircraft in the early years of the war.[11] Perhaps the greatest disincentive to resistance was a general sense of betrayal, which left a legacy of demoralisation and bitterness towards the western Allies if not the Soviet Union. Certainly there was a disinclination to risk too much, especially since

---

[8]   Quoted in Fischer, *Albania at War*, 133.
[9]   Fischer, *Albania at War*, 172.
[10]   Quoted in Fischer, *Albania at War*, 174.
[11]   Luža, R., 1973, 'The Czech Resistance Movement', in V.S. Mamatey and R. Luža (eds), *A History of the Czechoslovak Republic 1918-1948*, Princeton, NJ, 344.

even mild acts of resistance, such as demonstrations, were met with ferocious Nazi repression.

Nevertheless, elements loyal to the exiled ex-president Beneš worked from 1938 to undermine the German occupation. By 1940, a Central Committee for Home Resistance (ÚVOD) was established in the Protectorate and in tenuous contact with London. As elsewhere the strategy was to create a network of resisters in preparation for an uprising at the right moment. For much of the war ÚVOD's principal contribution was in the realm of intelligence. The Czechs had a centrally placed informant (codename A-54), in the Germans' Prague military intelligence service, until his arrest and execution in 1942. As a result, Czechoslovak intelligence, and hence the Western powers, knew of the planned attack on Poland three months in advance, and of the 1940 attack in the west three weeks in advance; in 1941 A-54 was one of the sources, ignored by Stalin, warning of Operation Barbarossa.

The invasion of the Soviet Union changed the dynamics of resistance, in that it immediately drew the hitherto quiescent Communist Party of Czechoslovakia (CPCS) into the fray. The CPCS was under instructions from Moscow to make common cause with ÚVOD, but it also had fewer qualms about committing overt acts of resistance, and there was consequently a sharp rise in sabotage. In London Beneš, fearful that ÚVOD's comparative inactivity would lead to a loss of Western support, concluded that the non-communist resistance should also strike a significant blow, and that the newly appointed *Reichsprotektor*, Reinhard Heydrich, would make a suitably prominent target. It was a disastrous decision. In May 1942 two ÚVOD agents, one Czech and one Slovak, parachuted into the Protectorate and succeeded in mortally wounding Heydrich. The Nazi response was a terrifying wave of arrests and executions. Most notoriously, two villages randomly selected, Lidice and Ležáky, were razed to the ground, and all the male inhabitants of Lidice and everyone in Ležáky were shot. Meaningful Czech resistance all but ceased, after a total of 23,000 individuals had been executed.

In Slovakia there was also a non-communist resistance, and a communist resistance which started organising only after the Soviets were attacked. Despite its enforced independence, and the economic boom brought by participation in the war, Slovakia's alliance with Nazi Germany was never popular. Some Slovak soldiers refused to join in the assault on Poland in 1939, and those sent to assist in Operation Barbarossa were so disturbed by Nazi atrocities that Tiso's government felt obliged to suspend its deportations of Jews. Even more unpopular was Slovakia's declaration of war in December 1941 on the United States, home to large numbers of Slovak émigrés. In the Christmas Agreement of 1943 both democratic and communist resistance leaders formed a Slovak National Council (SNC), which affirmed its loyalty to the Czechoslovak state, the equality of Czechs and Slovaks, and its commitment to staging an uprising in cooperation with Beneš' government-in-exile, once the Red Army reached

Slovakia's borders. Such plans were encouraged by the fact that the Slovakian army was 'honeycombed with disaffected officers and men', most of whom were willing to join the uprising.[12]

Tragically, the SNC got the timing disastrously wrong. Uninformed of a change in Soviet strategy, whereby the Red Army advanced through Romania rather than into Slovakia, an inadequately prepared SNC was tipped into acting by a partisan ambush of German forces on 27 August, prompting a full-scale German occupation. Mountainous central Slovakia was turned into a killing ground, the insurgents outnumbered and outgunned. Stalin refused to allow western Allied air-drops to the Slovaks, although he did authorise participation by Czechoslovakian units. The uprising was crushed by 29 October, at a cost of 10,000 army and partisan dead, 3,723 civilians murdered in reprisals, and 30,000 people deported to concentration camps. The future leader of the CPCS, Alexander Dubček, was severely wounded in the fighting, and his brother killed.

The Slovak National Uprising, though a failure, was nevertheless a genuine cross-party resistance. Although the communists claimed all the credit, in the high Stalinist period those communists who led it found themselves tainted with the charge of collusion with 'bourgeois' parties.

War as revolution: Communist-led resistance

Communist-led resistance in individual countries was inextricably linked to the fortunes of loyalist resistance movements, from whose setbacks and internal contradictions communism in most instances profited. The purpose of this section is mainly to stress the broad commonalities of communist resistance. In the end the principal reasons for communism's success in Eastern Europe were the patronage and armed might of the Soviet Union; but there is no denying that, by the war's end, communism in certain countries had built up a considerable mass membership, and acquired unexpected patriotic credentials.

There were several reasons for communism's transformed prospects. In contrast to their loyalist rivals communists espoused a coherent ideology, which they professed with all the fervour of fanatics trained for years in argument and logic-chopping. Communists were also graduates in the school of hard knocks. Not only had many of them survived decades of underground existence, banned, imprisoned and sometimes tortured in their native lands; some had survived exile in the Soviet Union, where Stalin had purged East European communists as readily as Soviet ones. As a result East European

[12] Josko, A., 1973, 'The Slovak Resistance Movement', in V.S. Mamatey and R. Luža (eds), *A History of the Czechoslovak Republic 1918-1948*, Princeton, NJ, 372.

communists exhibited a discipline and a cold-blooded dedication that their rivals could rarely match. The economic stimulus provided by the war itself had, by expanding the number of people employed in industrial enterprises, also expanded the number of potential communists. Finally, wartime resistance gave communists everywhere – once they put the dark confusion of the Nazi-Soviet pact behind them – the chance to pose as defenders of their countries' national independence; resistance proved, or seemed to prove, that communists too could be patriotic.

It is thus unsurprising that, where a communist-led resistance got seriously under way, the potential for civil war between communists and non-communists was very real. Other resisters, whether royalist, conservative authoritarian, liberal democratic, republican, nationalist or agrarian, were bound to regard communists with suspicion if not outright loathing. Only social democrats shared ideological ground with communists, and were hence in theory allies, but after years of social democrats being castigated by the Comintern as 'objectively fascist', there was too much bad blood between these two left-wing groups for cooperation to come naturally. It was also difficult for non-communists to ignore the extent to which East European communists were simply the instruments of Soviet control.

Communists did sometimes find they could make common cause with non-communists, as long as the latter accepted the Party's leading role. In such cases there was usually a sense, on the part of non-communists, that the communist-led resistance was in fact the most effective means of opposing occupation. As a result, Tito's Partisans in Yugoslavia, Enver Hoxha's in Albania, and the Slovak National Uprising were able to command genuine cross-party support, and attracted volunteers from across the spectrum while the war lasted. Where this was not the case, as in Poland, a clash was all but inevitable.

By virtue of their success as mass-based resistances the Yugoslav and Albanian communists deserve to be considered first. In *Yugoslavia* Josip Broz, nicknamed Tito, became a communist as a prisoner of war in revolutionary Russia. Tito spent another five years in Yugoslav prisons for left-wing activity, and another two in Moscow working for Comintern, before becoming leader of the Yugoslav Communist Party (YCP) in 1937, leaving the Soviet Union just in time to avoid possible liquidation in Stalin's purges. Despite Tito's awareness of Soviet communism's darker side, he was a loyal Stalinist. Certainly the Yugoslav communists made no move against the Axis occupation until the Soviet Union itself had been invaded; thereafter Tito strained every nerve to support the Soviet cause.

The YCP had the advantage over the Chetniks, and every other political group, that it was unambiguously Yugoslav, unidentified with any nationality, committed to Soviet-style national self-determination, and hence to a resurrected but federal state. Tito himself, the son of a Croat and Slovene, was literally Yugoslav, and under his leadership the YCP, which deliberately styled its fighters Partisans to emphasise this supranational character, attracted all nationalities and parties to its ranks. Partisan strategy accepted, indeed welcomed, Axis reprisals, on the assumption that the populace would be driven to join the resistance out of sheer desperation. This only widened the rift between Partisans and Chetniks, whose goal was to lie low and minimise the cost to civilians. Thanks to their attacks on occupation forces the Partisans, in contrast to the Chetniks, had to be highly mobile, abandoning towns for the countryside, especially the inhospitable mountains of Bosnia, moving constantly to evade a succession of Axis offensives designed to exterminate them. Despite this peripatetic and dangerous existence, the Partisans simply by surviving increasingly seemed the more effective resistance, even though Tito, like Mihailović, was driven early in 1943 to offer a truce to the Germans, on condition that his forces be allowed to concentrate their fire on the Chetniks instead – precisely the collaborationist charge that, after the war, was brought against Mihailović. Tito made little secret of the fact that his ultimate goal was the seizure of power, but there is no denying the broad support his movement attracted from all classes and nationalities.

This clear objective emerged early when, in November 1942, the Partisans convened a multiparty conference of delegates at Bihać in northern Bosnia, and formed an Anti-Fascist Council of National Liberation of Yugoslavia (AVNOJ), effectively a communist-led provisional government. This was partly in response to reproofs from Stalin, who worried that Tito's open avowal of seeking a takeover might alienate the western Allies, and urged a popular front resistance, if only for form's sake. Stalin also found Tito's independence of mind irritating, and indeed the roots of the later Tito-Stalin split of 1948 are to be found in their wartime relationship. AVNOJ challenged the authority of not only the NDH and the Nazis, but the royal government-in-exile as well. Despite near-annihilation in early 1943, by the middle of that year the Partisans nevertheless controlled much of central Bosnia, and Italy's surrender in September resulted in large amounts of weaponry falling into Partisan hands. In November 1943 Tito held a second AVNOJ conference at Jajce, which announced that a restored Yugoslavia would be federal in structure; at the same time Partisan successes induced Britain to switch support from the Chetniks to Tito. In the end the Partisans received more practical support from the western Allies than from the Soviets. In May 1944 King Peter, under British pressure, dropped Mihailović as war minister; in June the new prime minister of the government-in-exile, the Croatian Peasant Party leader Ivan Šubašić, was tasked with forming a coalition with the Partisans. On 1 October Red Army units entered north-east Yugoslavia; Tito, with Soviet help, took Belgrade shortly after, and although Šubašić, on his return, nominally headed the administration, everyone knew it was the Communist Party that ruled the country. Most important, Yugoslavia's communists had achieved liberation largely on their own.

In *Albania*, as in Yugoslavia, the communist-led NLM not only posed as, but to a large extent was, a broadly based coalition of communists and non-communists. The NLM also received a significant arms boost following the Italian surrender in September 1943. As in Yugoslavia, too, the principal non-communist resistance, BK, was compromised as collaborationist by its tacit acceptance of the regency installed by the Germans. The Albanian Communist Party's dependence on the Yugoslavs for tutelage and logistical support meant that Enver Hoxha accepted that Kosovo would be restored to Yugoslavia once the war was over, a stance that led the Zogists to break ranks with the NLM in November 1943. Nevertheless the overall situation favoured the NLM: Germany was clearly losing the war by 1944, and the NLM had a decisive edge over their disunited rivals. Hoxha, like Tito, won psychological ground by proclaiming the NLM to be Albania's provisional government at a congress in Përmet on 24–28 May. As German forces prepared to withdraw in the summer of 1944 the NLM, now 40,000-strong, became bolder. The climactic battle for Tirana, launched in late October, and undertaken consciously for its propaganda value, was nonetheless a hard-fought business that took three weeks. Significantly, even before the fighting ended Albanian communists were dividing between those who, like Hoxha, maintained their loyalty to Stalin and downplayed the help received from Tito, and those who, like the Party's chief organiser Koçi Xoxe, accepted Yugoslav tutelage, which put them in a perilous position after the war.

In partitioned *Czechoslovakia* the Communist Party's position was a paradoxical one. Although the CPCS was one of the only mass-based communist parties in Eastern Europe during the interwar period, its subordination to Moscow cost it popularity and members, and by the time of Munich it numbered only around 30,000. After partition communists were a threatened species, but in any case it was only after the invasion of the Soviet Union that either Czech or Slovak communists showed serious interest in resistance. In the Protectorate the reign of terror following the assassination of Heydrich made any resistance extremely perilous: 3,649 CPCS members were executed in retaliation, and another 5,687 died in concentration camps. Only in May 1945, with the Germans on the point of surrender and the Red Army fighting its way through Slovakia, did it make sense to stage an uprising, and at that point spontaneous risings occurred across the Protectorate, culminating in an insurrection in Prague on 5 May, four days before Soviet armoured units entered the capital. It is difficult to determine whether these uprisings were led by the CPCS, or represented a determined effort by non-communists to show that the Czechoslovak government-in-exile still commanded some loyalty. The Czech National Council formed in Prague claimed to act on behalf of the government-in-exile, but although its nominal leader was an aged non-communist, its deputy leader was the communist Josef Smrkovský. The picture is complicated by the fact that, as of 5 May, American forces were sixty miles from Prague, whereas the Red Army was 120 miles away. The evidence suggests that many insurgents hoped for liberation by the western Allies rather than the Soviets. They were to be cruelly disappointed.

Geopolitical reality gave the CPCS an unfair but decisive advantage. Since Tehran a degree of Soviet influence in Czechoslovakia was tacitly accepted by the western Allies, and Beneš himself saw Stalin's goodwill as essential for Czechoslovakia's post-war security. Accordingly, Beneš had already agreed that all right-wing parties should be banned from politics after liberation. By implication Beneš accepted that power would be shared between four Czech and two Slovak parties: on the Czech side, the national socialists, People's Party, the CPCS and the social democrats; on the Slovak side, the SCP and the democrats. When Beneš returned in the wake of the Red Army in April 1945, he announced a provisional government in which the communist party, though numerically outnumbered, enjoyed an obvious preponderance. Klement Gottwald, CPCS leader, became deputy prime minister, and the key ministries of the interior, agriculture and labour were allocated to communists. In addition, as the Soviets crossed the country, communist-controlled councils were set up, all of which followed Moscow's line rather than Beneš's instructions. Thus, communist predominance was a reality even before the Prague uprising, and even members of Beneš's entourage, after years in exile, found themselves under arrest on trumped-up charge of wartime collaboration, or otherwise intimidated.

In Slovakia, the Slovak National Uprising was a genuinely cross-party effort, albeit unsuccessful. Despite their losses, Slovak communists were in a better position than their democratic allies, not least for having so clearly identified themselves with the cause of the nation. As the Soviets arrived, therefore, there was far more active cooperation with them. Slovakia was also the first part of Czechoslovakia to be liberated, with the Red Army reaching Bratislava by 4 April. In the National Front government formed by Beneš that month, the Slovak communist Viliam Široký was appointed one of two vice-premiers.

In *Greece*, the communist-led EAM/ELAS was by far the largest and most active resistance movement in the country; but despite this numerical strength, its position was weakened from the start by Britain's heavy involvement on behalf of the royalists. Apart from the provocation offered by loyalist groups, it is hard not to conclude that ELAS's reluctance to cooperate with such groups, and the ease with which relations with them degenerated into open conflict in the winter of 1943–44, were the products of frustration at this imbalance. EAM/ELAS was also out-manoeuvred by prime minister Papandreou into accepting minor cabinet positions in April 1944. Papandreou showed political acumen by distancing himself from the pre-war dictatorship, and promising democratisation and social welfare, which undercut communism's potential appeal. The decisive blow to EAM/ELAS, however, was delivered by Stalin, who warned the Greek communists against confrontation with Papandreou and the British. In the meantime, ELAS carried on with a low-level but vicious campaign against right-wing groups, conducting a series of assassinations right up to the point of German withdrawal. ELAS's strength was such that, all across Greece, it was first to move into the subsequent vacuum, proceeding 'to destroy what vestiges remained of the traditional state.'[13] By the time Papandreou and his cabinet arrived at Athens in October, the forces of communists and nationalists were fairly evenly balanced, and the bad feeling between them intense.

Elsewhere in the Balkans, communists either took over countries directly, as in Yugoslavia and Albania, or acquired a predominant role backed by Soviet troops, as in Romania and Bulgaria. In Greece, 'the obvious course for the communist leaders was to consolidate their power.'[14] Accordingly, while Papandreou with British backing secured Athens, the situation in the provinces was controlled by ELAS, and fighting there continued while the Germans retreated, leaving the population thoroughly polarised between communists and their opponents. The stage was set for a civil war which, starting in late 1944, raged on and off for the next three years. Arguably, however, the communist cause was lost at the outset when, in December 1944 to January 1945, government forces backed by British troops succeeded in wresting control of Athens from ELAS; the crushing of his fellow communists was tacitly accepted by Stalin, who kept other Balkan communists from intervening. Several thousand ELAS fighters died in bitter street battles. Despite holding most of Greece, therefore, EAM/ELAS felt driven to sign a truce in January. This put them at a serious disadvantage when the government started rooting out communists, and tensions continued to worsen.

A similar process, but in reverse, governed the fortunes of the Communist Party in *Poland*. Here, despite the size and legitimacy of the loyalist Home Army, Soviet backing was decisive in turning the tables in favour of the communists. By mid-summer 1942, when General Anders' army departed to fight on the side of the western Allies, Stalin knew he needed to fashion pro-Soviet instruments to control post-war Poland. Stalin had already sanctioned the revival of the Polish Communist Party as the patriotic-sounding Polish Workers' Party (PWP). In February 1943 he authorised formation under Soviet command of Berling's Kościuszko Division, which attracted not only communists but also those for whom service with Berling offered their only chance of reaching home. The Kościuszko Division expanded into the I and II Polish Armies under Soviet command, while the People's Guard was renamed as the People's Army (AL), and once the Nazis had crushed the loyalist Warsaw uprising, it was this communist-organised force which then established control over 'liberated' Poland, and entered Warsaw in January 1945. The AL's role consisted mainly of interning and in some cases summarily executing not only anyone who could plausibly be accused of collaboration, but also members of the loyalist Home Army. This included sixteen AK leaders, arrested, tried and

[13] Close, D.H., 1995, *The Origins of the Greek Civil War*, London and New York, 116.
[14] Close, *The Origins of the Greek Civil War*, 117.

convicted in Moscow in June for belonging to 'illegal' organisations. In short, Polish communists played no role in resistance; their main function was to act as enablers of Soviet power.

Of communist resistance in Hitler's satellite states there is little to be said, despite its post-war mythologising by communist regimes, for the simple reason that there were so few communists, with so few opportunities for mounting meaningful resistance. In *Hungary* by 1942 there were only about twenty members of the Communist Party not in Horthyist prisons, and although the communists were 'known to be the bravest' in the Hungarian underground, this movement remained minuscule.[15] Most of the party leadership that survived the Stalinist purges, like Mátyás Rákosi, remained safely in Moscow for the duration of the war. Even after 1941 there was little the resistance, communist or otherwise, could do against the Horthy regime. Nor did the resistance 'lift a finger' against the Nazi takeover in October 1944.[16] Even with deliverance around the corner, a leading Hungarian communist estimated that, as of December 1944, party membership was a mere 3,058. Only after Hungary's surrender, and the establishment of a coalition government including the Hungarian Communist Party, did membership soar to half a million by October 1945, in what looks like an access of pure opportunism. Hungary was 'liberated', not by insurgent native comrades, but by the Soviets.

Communists in *Bulgaria* fared little better until 1944, even if, despite the party's decimation in the 1920s, there were more of them on the ground. Some communists had been parachuted back into the country by Stalin after 1941, in the hope of destabilising one of Hitler's potential allies. The only result was heightened vigilance by the Bulgarian authorities, who in 1942–4 rounded up 15,000 people, including many communists; the majority were interned in concentration camps. Those communists still at large engaged in partisan activity, including some high-level assassinations early in 1943, and at its height this resistance numbered perhaps 18,000; but Bulgaria never experienced anything like the communist-led resistance seen in Yugoslavia or Greece. The communists also had to cope with other political parties' reluctance to join them in any sort of popular front. Eventually a loose coalition of communists, Zvenists, Agrarians and Social Democrats came into being in February 1942 as the Fatherland Front, under the Agrarian Nikola Petkov; after the summer of 1943 this started to attract members, but by August 1944 this still only numbered 3,600. The government's watchfulness was not affected by Boris III's death in August 1943; Filov as regent for the six-year-old Tsar Simeon simply carried on as before. Communist prospects only changed in 1944, when

---

[15] Deák, I., 2000, 'A Fatal Compromise? The Debate over Collaboration and Resistance in Hungary', in I. Deák, J.T. Gross and T. Judt (eds), *The Politics of Retribution in Europe: World War II and its Aftermath*, Princeton, NJ, 39.

[16] Deák, 'A Fatal Compromise?', 55.

Bulgaria's delicately balanced policy of neutrality broke down. Allied bombing raids, coupled with rising food shortages and inflation, created conditions favourable to resistance. Most important was the sudden approach of the Red Army following Romania's switching sides in August. Following the Soviet Union's declaration of war on Bulgaria, partisan activity increased, so that when the Fatherland Front staged a very traditional type of coup on 9 September, it was with the help of partisan forces in Sofia. The new government was a coalition led by the Zvenist leader Colonel Kimon Georgiev, and included only four communists out of fifteen ministers; but in the shadow of the Red Army there was little doubt which party wielded the greatest influence.

There is least of all to note about communist resistance in *Romania*. Antonescu's regime from 1941 paid particular attention to the possibility of communist subversion, hunting down most of the 'native' or ethnic Romanian Party members; a small minority, many Jewish, spent the war in the Soviet Union. By the time of King Michael's coup in August 1944, and Romania's cross-over to the Allied side, the number of communists in the country probably did not exceed a thousand, most in prison. General Sănătescu's government of national unity included only one communist. The subsequent expansion of communist influence in Romania, as elsewhere, owed far more to Soviet hegemony than to communism's numerical strength.

The closing months of the Second World War in Eastern Europe saw the foundations for a political revolution laid in most countries; in some the revolution was effectively completed. The Baltic states, devoured by the Soviets in 1940 and then overrun by Germany, were reincorporated into the USSR, although not without serious resistance, especially in Estonia and Latvia. In Yugoslavia and Albania the Communist Party was in control by the end of the fighting. Germany, including Austria, was under Allied military occupation or 'four-power control'. Poland, Bulgaria and Romania were formally independent and governed by multiparty coalitions; in reality the deciding influence in each country was Soviet power, exercised through the local Communist Party. Czechoslovakia and Hungary, for the moment, were governed by genuinely multiparty coalitions, in which communist influence was not yet dominant. These two states apart, only Finland and Greece emerged from the war as truly independent, with the rudiments of a pluralist political system in place. Finland, despite its assistance to Nazi Germany against the Soviets, was lucky to escape the fate of its East European neighbours, in part because Stalin hesitated to risk confrontation with the West on this issue, and also because of the Finns' acceptance of a special strategic and economic relationship with the USSR. Greece owed its escape to the accident of its geography, which facilitated British support for a non-communist government, and to the cynical trade-off whereby Stalin effectively abandoned the country to the western Allies' sphere of influence. The northern and southern extremities of Eastern Europe were thus exempt from the fate that overtook the rest of the region in the next few years.

PART III

Saddling cows

11

Great leap backwards

The imposition of communism 1944–8

Stalin is reported to have said that introducing communism to Poland was like trying to saddle a cow; in short, he perceived the problematical nature of the exercise. For Poland, read the whole of Eastern Europe. The imposition on the region of Soviet-style, one-party dictatorships, together with command economies based on heavy industrialisation and the collectivisation of agriculture, transformed these largely agrarian societies beyond recognition. Yet the human cost of this giant experiment in forced modernisation was high. Having survived the horrors of the Second World War, East Europeans found themselves deprived of any effective say in their lot, subjected to the terrors of a police state and, after an initial period of phenomenal economic growth, condemned to a steadily declining standard of living, which remained a depressing feature of Eastern Europe for the next forty years.

This communisation of the region had global ramifications, for it was both a cause and a product of the ideological division and superpower confrontation known as the Cold War. Many of the Cold War's causes were East European ones, forcing Eastern Europe into the Soviet camp. This made the region's political liberalisation, and hence its economic rejuvenation, next to impossible, although the essential diversity of East European societies kept breaking through the hard crust of political conformity imposed on them collectively.

This chapter first details how the realities of the 'grand alliance', in the closing stages of the war, settled most of Eastern Europe's fate. It then charts the stages by which the region was brought, piecemeal, under Soviet control, for this was not a foreordained process: Stalin's intentions shifted depending on circumstances, and the communist parties of individual countries did not always act according to plan. The chapter also considers the novel ways in which local communist parties extended their influence. The tactics and determination varied from country to country, but what all these stories had in common was the conscious stealth and dissimulation with which communists established control.

The breakdown of the 'grand alliance'

If Eastern Europe became a power vacuum at the close of the First World War, the vacuum was well and truly filled at the end of the Second. After 1918

Map 5 Eastern Europe by 1945.

neither Germany nor the Soviet Union was in a position to claim undisputed hegemony; by 1945, the Soviet Union's physical presence in the region was the undeniable consequence of the contribution Soviet arms made to victory over Nazism. In the East European context the Soviet Union was the only power capable of defeating Germany, and this translated into a recognition by the western Allies that there was not a great deal they could do to avert Soviet domination of the area.

The first signpost on the road to Soviet hegemony was the Tehran conference in late 1943, where Roosevelt and Churchill conceded that the Soviet Union be allowed to reclaim the territory gained in 1939–40; this involved abandoning the Baltic peoples and Bessarabia to inclusion in the Soviet Union itself, and accepting that, in compensation for its losses to the east, Poland's borders would be shifted westwards at the expense of Germany. The Polish government-in-exile only learned of this stitch-up by the great powers after the fact. In December, a Czechoslovak-Soviet alliance ceded the largely Ukrainian-inhabited sub-Carpathian Ruthenia to the USSR; the Soviets thereby not only gathered in most Ukrainian speakers, but secured a common border with Hungary.

The next significant meeting of the great powers was between Churchill and Stalin (Roosevelt was ill) at Moscow in October 1944, the notorious 'percentages agreement' on south-eastern Europe. According to this, Soviet influence in Romania, for example, would be 90 per cent, while that of the Western powers would be 10 per cent. In Greece, by contrast, Western influence would be 90 per cent, and Soviet 10 per cent. In Bulgaria the Soviets would have 75 per cent, in both Yugoslavia and Hungary the split would be 50–50.[1] At no stage was there any precise definition of what such percentages meant. The significance is rather what the percentages stood for. Churchill and Stalin were practising 'a curious diplomacy, resorting to arithmetic in the quest for an influence that neither wanted to define precisely.'[2] Stalin was determined to exercise predominant, if not maximum control, in most of south-eastern Europe, whereas Churchill's hope of an equal division of influence was a pipe dream. It was the Soviet Union which had boots on the ground in Eastern Europe, and Stalin was the final arbiter of how much predominance the Soviet Union required. Stalin 'thought in theological terms about his new possessions: to ensure the victory of the true religion, the new communist faith, he would have to ensure absolute sovereignty over his new realm.'[3]

In the historiography of Cold War origins it is now generally agreed that neither the western powers nor the Soviets were intent on confrontation to

---

[1] Churchill, W.S., 1954, *The Second World War*, vol. 6: *Triumph and Tragedy*, London, 226–8.
[2] Mastný, V., 1979, *Russia's Road to the Cold War: Diplomacy, Warfare, and the Politics of Communism 1941-1945*, New York, 211.
[3] Plokhy, S., 2010, *Yalta: The Price of Peace*, New York, 357.

begin with, not least because, until May 1945, fighting Nazism was the priority. Stalin, despite his mistrust of the 'capitalist' powers, did not set out to extend communist rule over the whole of Eastern Europe; instead, his main concern was Soviet security. Accordingly Stalin regarded as essential a neutralisation of German power for the foreseeable future, and more or less complete control over three countries on the USSR's borders: Poland, Romania and Bulgaria. In Hungary and Czechoslovakia, by contrast, Stalin was initially content to tolerate genuine coalition governments in which communists played a role, but not necessarily a decisive one. Greece was effectively written off. Nor was the Sovietisation of Finland considered to be vital; rather, subject to Finnish reparations and a foreswearing of anti-Soviet foreign policy, Stalin decided he could afford to avoid conflict over that country. While the war was still in progress, Stalin was anxious not to provoke his western allies, but the bottom line in all these calculations was Soviet security. In a famous remark, made in April 1945 to Tito and his fellow Yugoslav communists in Moscow, Stalin claimed that 'This war is not as in the past; whoever occupies a territory also imposes on it his own social system. Everyone imposes his own system as far as his army has power to do so. It cannot be otherwise.'[4]

In the western camp Churchill was the more suspicious of Soviet intentions, but equally aware of the need for Soviet cooperation against Hitler, and of Britain's relative powerlessness to influence developments in Eastern Europe. Roosevelt was just as conscious of the dangers of communism but, until his death in April 1945, remained convinced that, if Stalin's security concerns could be met, he would have less incentive to extend communist influence. Roosevelt, moreover, like Wilson in 1919, had his eye on a bigger prize: the projected United Nations Organisation, to improve on the record of the League of Nations, would only work if both the United States and the USSR were fully committed to upholding it. Roosevelt has ever since been accused of a certain naïvety in this regard. The reality in 1945 was that, with every month that passed, the tendency of local communists in Eastern Europe to concentrate ever more power in their hands became more obvious. Stalin, for his part, was bound to be suspicious of a United States which, he already knew, was about to demonstrate its nuclear capability against imperial Japan.

In February 1945 Stalin and Churchill had their last summit with Roosevelt at Yalta in the Crimea. By this stage, much of Eastern Europe's fate was decided, with communist governments in Yugoslavia and Albania, and communist-dominated ones in Poland, Romania and Bulgaria. In territorial terms Yalta simply confirmed the Soviet Union's gains at the expense, not only of Poland and Germany – the northern half of East Prussia, centred on Königsberg, later renamed Kaliningrad, was assigned to the Soviets – but of Romania

---

[4] Quoted in Djilas, M., *Conversations with Stalin*, translated by Michael B. Petrovich, Harmondsworth, 90.

and Czechoslovakia. Germany would be subject once defeated to military occupation and four-power control; the Allied Control Commission included France as one of the occupying powers. The so-called Oder-Neisse Line became the new German-Polish border, handing Pomerania east of the Oder River and the whole of Silesia to Poland. Bizarrely, the Soviet Republics of Ukraine and Belarus were accorded membership of the United Nations, to accommodate Stalin's fears that the Soviet Union would be otherwise permanently outvoted by the United States and its allies. Deserters or traitors, wherever they might be on the cessation of hostilities, were to be handed over to their country of origin; this provision had dire consequences for the thousands of Soviet Cossacks, Ukrainians and others who had served with the *Waffen SS*, as well as Yugoslav nationals caught fighting on the Axis side. While the fate of these 'victims of Yalta' was not always as deadly as depicted, the fact remains that it was fatal for many, and many innocents were caught up in this tragedy.

The seeds of subsequent Cold War were planted with two seemingly innocuous documents issued on 10 February, the Declaration on Liberated Europe and the Declaration on Poland. The former asserted the great powers' determination to assist the peoples of liberated countries 'to solve by democratic means their pressing political and economic problems.' This meant that interim governments should be 'broadly representative of all democratic elements in the population and pledged to the earliest possible establishment through free elections of governments responsive to the will of the people.'[5] The Declaration on Poland agreed the same, but with the explicit proviso that Poland's provisional government would be 'reorganized' to include elements from the Polish government-in-exile; it also reiterated the commitment to 'free and unfettered elections as soon as possible on the basis of universal suffrage and secret ballot.'[6] The devil behind these fine words, however, lurked in the detail, and both sides knew it. When Western leaders accepted that Poland's government would merely be 'reorganized' they implicitly acknowledged that the Soviet-controlled government was in charge; any inclusion of non-communists would be pure window-dressing. And promising 'free and unfettered elections' was valueless, as Roosevelt and Churchill knew well, without Western observers present. When one of Roosevelt's delegation pointed out the elasticity of the Yalta declarations, the president agreed, protesting that 'it's the best I can do for Poland at this time.'[7] For this reason, to patriotic Poles, the word 'Yalta' has remained synonymous with betrayal ever since.

What followed was a gradual breakdown of trust on both sides, which reminds us that 'the war had been won by a coalition whose principal members

---

[5] 'The Declaration on Liberated Europe', in McCauley, M. 1995, *The Origins of the Cold War*, 2nd edn, London and New York, doc. 10, 122.
[6] 'Poland at Yalta', in McCauley, *The Origins of the Cold War*, document 9, 121.
[7] Quoted in Plokhy, *Yalta*, 251.

were already at war – ideologically and geopolitically if not militarily – with one another.'[8] In the spring of 1945 Stalin 'had not yet developed a clear idea of what to do with his Eastern European conquests.' It was still conceivable that local communist parties 'could coexist with other left-leaning parties in a so-called people's democracy.'[9] But at the same time the Soviet crackdown on potential opponents in Poland was becoming known in the West. As early as February the NKVD was deporting thousands of Poles eastwards for interrogation, especially if they were members of the Home Army, and in some cases simply liquidating them. Most notoriously, the AK's commander-in-chief, General Leopold Okulicki, who had just ordered the AK's dissolution to avoid conflict with the Soviets, was arrested with fifteen other underground leaders. These men were put on trial in Moscow in July, and sentenced to ten years' imprisonment for allegedly conspiring with Nazi Germany against the Soviets; Okulicki was murdered in late 1946.

Long before Stalin, Roosevelt's successor Harry S. Truman and Churchill assembled at Potsdam, in July 1945, it was obvious that Stalin regarded himself as having a free hand in Eastern Europe. Truman had already shown a new brusqueness and belligerence in his dealings with the Soviets, accusing them in April of not carrying out agreements entered into at Yalta. In response, Stalin informed Truman and Churchill that 'the Soviet Union cannot agree to the existence in Poland of a government hostile to it', and that the West was making no effort 'to consider the interests of the Soviet Union in terms of security.'[10] He also reminded the western Allies that he had left them a free hand in Greece. Churchill pointed out how little the Soviets were adhering to the 'percentages agreement', accused Tito of becoming 'a complete dictator', and denied any comparability with Greece, since the object of British intervention there was to facilitate genuinely free elections.[11] In advance of Potsdam, the Polish provisional government was finally 'reorganised' to include six democratic politicians, in a cabinet of twenty dominated by communists. Stanisław Mikołajczk's position as deputy prime minister, and the popular acclaim which greeted him on arrival in Warsaw, could not disguise the stranglehold exerted by Władysław Gomułka's PWP. In tacit acceptance of this fact, the American and British governments recognised this as the Polish provisional government on 5 July.

Much of Potsdam was concerned with agreeing the Soviet Union's entry into the war in the Far East. Truman's tough line towards the Soviets was undoubtedly due to the Americans' successful testing of the first atomic bomb on 16 July, while Stalin's foreknowledge of this spurred him on to stake out as

[8]   Gaddis, J.L., 2005, *The Cold War: A New History*, London, 6.
[9]   Plokhy, *Yalta*, 379.
[10] Quoted in Plokhy, *Yalta*, 379.
[11] Plokhy, *Yalta*, 380.

much influence as possible while he still could. With regard to Eastern Europe, the ongoing argument over communist influence in Poland, and by extension in other countries of the region, was one of two issues embittering the atmosphere at Potsdam. The other was what to do about Germany and the Germans.

The striking thing about the German question is that the Big Three never resolved the most important issue, what sort of political system should be implemented in Germany. The Western powers were convinced that the only safeguard against the revival of Nazism was a democratic system, and by implication a free market economy. Stalin was intent on keeping Germany as weak as possible. The problem for both sides was that, at the end of hostilities, Germany was physically divided by the facts of Western and Soviet military occupation.

By 1945 the Allies had abandoned earlier ideas of dismembering Germany; it was accepted that it would remain united, albeit shorn of an Austria restored to full independence to diminish Germany's potential power. An Allied Control Commission would administer occupied Germany; the same four-power control applied to Austria. In both Germany and Austria the three Western powers occupied three separate zones, while the easternmost zone fell to the Soviets; and although both Berlin and Vienna were deep inside the Soviet zones, each capital was also subject to four-power control. The Western powers agreed on the principle of reparations, and that most of the sums collected would go to the Soviet Union. These reparations could be made in kind, with the result that, in the Soviet zone, a wholesale dismantling of German industry, and the shipping of industrial plant and equipment to Russia, took place, making any sort of economic reconstruction problematical in both East Germany and the new Poland. Finally, formal sanction was given for the mass expulsion of ethnic Germans from Eastern Europe, where this had not already begun. German communities, scattered across Eastern Europe for centuries, had been a source of constant friction with Germany's neighbours. Now, the Nazis' loss of the war set in motion what might ironically be called the 'final solution' of the German question, 'the destruction of German life outside Germany.'[12]

Millions of Europeans were displaced by 1945, among them the 7 million forced labourers stranded in Germany; 2.8 million of these were from Eastern Europe or the Soviet Union. Sheltering, feeding and controlling these victims of Nazism, as well as enabling them to return to their homelands if they wished, was a major headache for the occupying forces. Now fresh floodgates of misery were opened as ethnic Germans either fled westward to escape the Soviets, or were forcibly expelled by the governments of liberated Eastern Europe, in what was arguably 'the largest single refugee movement in European history.'[13]

[12] Mazower, M., 1998, *Dark Continent: Europe's Twentieth Century*, London, 219.
[13] Mazower, *Dark Continent*, 220.

The exodus of Germans was triggered by the Red Army's advance into German territory, accompanied by looting, random massacres and mass rapes, in a grim payback for German atrocities in the Soviet Union. Germans and others were also motivated by a simple fear of living under communist rule. Altogether it is estimated that 5 million Germans fled eastern Germany in the winter of 1944–5, in atrocious conditions ensuring that thousands succumbed to starvation, hypothermia or violence; in one of the most horrifying incidents, 7,000 drowned when a Soviet submarine torpedoed the liner *Wilhelm Gustloff*, crammed with refugees and service personnel, in January 1945. The westward shifting of Poland's borders gave a further impetus, in that the Polish government was now authorised to expel not only *Volksdeutsche* but former citizens of the Reich, hitherto living in territories assigned to Poland. The mass expulsion of the three million Sudeten Germans of Czechoslovakia was also sanctioned by the Big Three as the only practical solution to the problem they had posed. Even in advance of formal authorisation, Czechoslovak local authorities were already physically forcing Germans to leave, like the 25,000 citizens of Brno simply escorted to the Austrian border. Similar 'ethnic cleansing' was carried out by the Yugoslav, Hungarian and Romanian governments, expelling 300,000, 213,000 and 250,000 Germans respectively. A rough total of 12.3 million ethnic Germans were expelled from Eastern Europe between 1944 and 1948. Untold numbers, possibly as many as two million, died of exposure or hunger en route, or after their arrival, destitute and homeless, in Germany or Austria. The element of 'rough justice' meant that this brutal treatment of millions, many innocent of any wrongdoing, was shrouded in silence on both sides for decades; but to this day the issue of compensation has complicated relations between the Germans and their neighbours. In the shorter term, the expulsion of so many people meant that post-war communist regimes had vast quantities of confiscated land and property to dispose of, which gave them great leeway in terms of dispensing favours and facilitating nationalisation.

The stages and process of communist takeovers 1944–8

Some of the preliminary stages of communist takeovers have already been described, for the process in some cases was under way before the war's end. Yugoslavia and Albania were effectively under communist rule by late 1944, whereas the governments of Bulgaria, Romania and Poland were communist-dominated by mid-1945. Until relations between the Soviets and the West broke down in 1947–8, Hungary and Czechoslovakia were able to exist in a sort of political halfway-house. Greece and Finland escaped Sovietisation entirely. Germany and Austria, under joint military occupation, posed a peculiar problem, in that installing any sort of unitary government required both sides to agree on the political system to be implemented; in Austria's case this was eventually settled, but in Germany's it never happened. Indeed, it was the failure to agree on a common policy towards Germany which led to the final confrontation in 1947–48.

One of the first scholarly attempts to analyse communist takeovers in Eastern Europe divided the process into three main stages. The first was a period of *genuine coalition*, where power was, at least initially, truly shared, with all parties agreed on a programme for short-term change, such as prosecution of wartime collaborators, land reform or social welfare measures; here communists were usually in a strong position thanks to either Soviet power or a genuinely popular base, but were not yet dominant. In the second stage, *bogus coalitions* were created, in a deliberate effort to give the appearance of multiparty rule, but where the communists always exercised effective control; the partners in such sham coalitions were sometimes 'shell' parties, ostensibly separate but in reality controlled by communists, or they were non-communist ministers who were no longer really independent, in other words chosen by their own parties. In the third stage, monolithic *one-party control* was imposed, even if the regime nominally styled itself a form of popular front; all opposition was banned, and political opponents were jailed, exiled or executed.[14]

This model is least relevant in the cases of Yugoslavia and Albania, monolithic communist regimes from the start. It helps explain the situation in Poland once we grasp that the coalition formed there in June 1945 was always bogus; even if, for form's sake, Stalin tolerated the presence in government of non-communists like Mikołajczyk, the latter soon realised their powerlessness. The model remains most useful for understanding the uneven rate at which four countries in particular – Romania, Bulgaria, Hungary and Czechoslovakia – were communised. Their fate reflects the Soviet Union's changing strategic needs: whereas Stalin considered control of Romania, Bulgaria and Poland vital for Soviet security, it was only once relations with the West were breaking down that Hungary and Czechoslovakia became essential buffers against the outside world. On the other hand, there is no doubt that the manner in which communists extended control over one country after another contributed to the onset of the Cold War, because in most cases it was rightly assumed, in the West, that nothing East European communists did happened without Stalin's authorisation.

In the general process of communist takeovers, what was new was the reliance on stealth and false appearances. This reflected lessons learned from the period after 1917, when East European communists had made a number of overt but clumsy attempts to seize power. In 1944–45 simply trying to annex countries like Poland and Romania would have been too risky.

---

[14] Seton-Watson, H., 1956, *The East European Revolution*, 3rd edn, London, 163–71.

Instead, the message impressed on all communists, where there was still a substantial opposition, was to share power, or at least convey the appearance of doing so. Where possible, as in Poland, Romania and Bulgaria, this was quickly translated into real power; but elsewhere the appearance of coalition government was maintained. Stalin was content to leave things this way until 1947–8, when the degeneration of relations with the West induced him to batten down the hatches. In 1944–5, by contrast, he found the openness with which Tito and Hoxha seized power in Yugoslavia and Albania positively alarming, an impression heightened by Tito's tense stand-off with the western Allies over control of Trieste in mid-1945. Much of Stalin's animus against the Yugoslav communists was rooted in a fear that they were getting out of control, and risking a break with the Western powers. Elsewhere, therefore, the emphasis was on 'gradualism and camouflage'.[15] While there was no 'blueprint' for imposing communism across the region, the 'striking similarities in the tactics used' suggests that 'Stalin expected each Communist leader to adapt and modify to suit local conditions.'[16]

These tactics included, firstly, the avoidance where possible of armed force. With the obvious exceptions of Yugoslavia and Albania, where communists literally fought their way to power, communist influence depended on the pretence that there was popular support for communism. In reality, communist parties would not have been able to take over were it not for the presence of the Red Army, but this was in general played down.

Secondly, communists relied on deliberate subterfuge to maintain this illusion of popular support and cooperation with other political parties for as long as possible. As the German communist Walter Ulbricht told a young follower returning to Berlin in May 1945, 'it's got to look democratic, but we must have everything in our control.'[17] To this end communist terminology and nomenclature were expressly avoided. Communists ostentatiously formed 'popular fronts', designed to give the impression of a patriotic, multiparty coalition, with reassuringly inclusive names such as Fatherland Front, or National Liberation Front. Such coalitions could be real enough, in that they purposely co-opted members of other left-wing and 'bourgeois' parties, and otherwise respectable figures like nobles, priests and professionals. Popular leaders like King Michael of Romania, or President Beneš of Czechoslovakia, were initially retained. Stalin personally urged Tito to bring King Peter back to Yugoslavia, on the understanding that this was purely tactical: 'Take him back temporarily, and then you can slip a knife into his back at a suitable

[15] Hammond, T.T., 1975, 'The History of Communist Takeovers', in T.T. Hammond and R. Farrell (eds), *The Anatomy of Communist Takeovers*, New Haven, CT and London, 22.
[16] Hammond, 'The History of Communist Takeovers', 21.
[17] Quoted in Leonhard, W., 1957, *Child of the Revolution*, translated by C.M. Woodhouse, London, 303.

moment.'[18] Communists also mouthed the language of political pluralism, talking up democracy and the will of the people, and promising elections and constitutions. The more the appearance of legality, democratic legitimacy and popular support was maintained, it was reasoned, the less likelihood of opposition or outside intervention.

Camouflage took on a more literal meaning when communists infiltrated other parties, joining them formally as members in order covertly to shape their internal debate, while in reality working towards communist goals, ideally by arguing for a merger of the host party with the communists. This 'entryism' was a tactic especially favoured with regard to left-wing parties, as well as with trade unions and professional bodies. In Hungary, for instance, the social democrat Erik Molnár had been a secret communist since the 1930s, overseeing communist infiltration ever since. When the National Peasant Party won 32 seats in the Hungarian election of 1945, fifteen of these were secret communists. Something similar went on in Bulgaria with the social democrats and the agrarians, and in Romania with the Ploughman's Front. In some cases, such as that of the Union of Patriots in Romania, communists practised the ultimate deception, founding completely bogus parties, which then argued for coalition with the communists to further the illusion of cross-party support.

Thirdly, communists demonstrated that they had a clearly thought-out strategy for achieving dominance by the single-mindedness with which they focused on key positions and other means of control. With few exceptions, communists demanded, and got, appointment as ministers of the interior, of justice, of information and sometimes of agriculture. The interior ministry gave them control of the police force and hence public order, including the ability to harass, prosecute, imprison and otherwise eliminate political opponents, often by the simple expedient of smearing them with the charge of being fascists or wartime collaborators. The justice ministry controlled judicial appointments and hence the court system, which could be similarly perverted. Control of the ministry of information gave communists access to radio, the most powerful contemporary medium, as well as the means of interfering with opponents' publicity, including opposition newspapers, often by denying them printing paper, a resource in short supply immediately after the war. It also gave communists control of press accreditation, another potent tool. Agriculture, if in communist hands, became the means of controlling land redistribution, the key to winning the allegiance of peasants, especially since communists to begin with were careful not to hint at their ultimate goal of collectivisation. These posts gave communists control over both information and scarce post-war resources, as well as the ability physically or politically to eliminate their rivals. To begin with, it was the parties on the right which bore the brunt of

---

[18] Quoted in Hammond, 'History of Communist Takeovers', 22.

communists' attention, many of them being persecuted or banned outright. Liberals, social democrats and agrarians were accepted in some countries as acceptable candidates for cooperation; indeed, in some cases they were given no choice. Gradually, however, the ability of non-communists to influence events or to exercise power at all was systematically whittled away. In the phrase made famous by the Hungarian communist Mátyás Rákosi, they succumbed to the communists' 'salami tactics': slice by slice, 'like pieces of salami', non-communists were swept from the board.[19]

Poland was first exposed to the east wind of communist takeover, even if the stages of its subversion were among the most protracted. The Soviet-sponsored Lublin Committee's provisional government had the advantages of being first to arrive in the territory liberated by the Soviets, of having its own forces on the ground to do its bidding (not to mention the NKVD), and of knowing that much of the Home Army had already been eliminated by the Nazis. It was this government which the Soviet Union recognised, and which took over Warsaw in January 1945. The question facing them was whether they accepted elements of the Polish government-in-exile into their ranks. This was the subject of fraught negotiations at Yalta and Potsdam; the result was the formation in June 1945 of a coalition including eight ministers (out of twenty-six) from the Peasant Party, the Polish Socialist Party (PSP), the Democratic Party and the Labour Party. The dominant party in this coalition, however, was the communist-led Polish Workers' Party (PWP), which rapidly overawed its coalition partners. A majority of the PSP's leaders were still in exile, and those in Poland were intimidated by communist accusations of being too right-wing, where they were not forced out of politics altogether. The only serious rival to the PWP was the Peasant Party, but when its leader Mikołajczyk returned to Poland he and his party were subjected to constant harassment. At first this took the form of trying to take over the PP by entryism, but Mikołajczyk frustrated this by refounding it with stricter entrance requirements, and by January 1946 this new Polish Peasant Party (PPP) had 600,000 members, making it the largest political grouping in the country. Polish peasants were not impressed by the new government's offer of land redistribution, which was a clear attempt to bypass the PPP, and despite the un-communist concession that most land would be distributed in small plots of 2–3 hectares.

By mid-1946 battle lines were clearly drawn, with the PPP insisting loudly on the 'free and unfettered elections' promised in the Yalta Declaration. When Mikołajczyk refused a pact with the PWP and opposed them in a June 1946 referendum over creating a senate, the PWP, which controlled the interior

---

[19] Ignotus, P., 1975, 'The First Two Communist Takeovers of Hungary: 1919 and 1948', in T.T. Hammond and R. Farrell (eds), *The Anatomy of Communist Takeovers*, New Haven, CT and London, 394.

ministry and hence the police force, unleashed a barrage of intimidation tactics. The PPP were refused newsprint for publicity, a thousand members were arrested, branch offices closed down, and voting urns confiscated by the police before votes could be checked, thus ensuring victory for the PWP. The national elections of 19 January 1947, however, were the point at which the extent of communist subversion became obvious outside Poland too. Again, intimidation was rife, including the arrest of 100,000 PPP members, the detention of 142 PPP candidates, their arbitrary disqualification in ten out of 52 electoral districts and, to cap it all, open voting in some districts, with public intimidation of voters. The predictable result was the first of many blatantly rigged elections: independents received 9.6 per cent of the vote, and the million-strong PPP a derisory 10.3 per cent, while the communist-led Democratic Bloc received an improbable 80.1 per cent. Thereafter the communists swiftly completed their takeover of the state. To preserve the appearance of multiparty democracy the malleable leader of the former Socialists, Józef Cyrankiewicz, was appointed president, and a new constitution modelled on that of the Soviet Union was passed on 19 February. Mikołajczyk, fearing for his life, fled abroad in the autumn of 1947, after which organised opposition to the regime ceased. Finally, in December 1948 Poland's remaining parties merged with the PWP to form the Polish United Workers' Party (PUWP). The one-party state had arrived.

Romania was the first country after Poland to be exposed to direct Soviet influence. Stalin originally intended a takeover by the team of Romanian communists he had held in readiness throughout the war, and although King Michael's August 1944 coup and declaration of war on Germany saved Romania from Soviet occupation, it was clearly deemed by Stalin to lie within the Soviet sphere of influence. For the moment Stalin was content to leave Michael in place: the Romanian army made useful cannon fodder, but in addition the Romanian Communist Party (RCP) was tiny. The communists hastened to set up a variety of front organisations designed to sound innocuously patriotic but non-communist: the Society for Friendship with the Soviet Union; the Union of Patriots; Patriotic Defence; and – to appeal to peasants – the Ploughman's Front. These four bodies joined forces with the RCP and the trades unions in October 1944 to form the National Democratic Front (NDF), a typical communist-led omnium gatherum. In the meantime the government of General Sănătescu continued the war on the Soviet side. In December 1944, under Soviet pressure, Sănătescu was replaced by General Nicolae Rădescu.

Under the Rădescu government communist influence in Romania was suddenly ratcheted up. By early 1945 the RCP leadership visited Moscow, and on their return started to organise industrial unrest, accusing the government of being anti-worker and anti-communist. Rădescu himself was the target of many protests, and at one such meeting violence was used against the demonstrators; Rădescu then played straight into the RCP's hands by denouncing communists generally as 'foreigners without God or a nation.'[20] The Soviets peremptorily demanded Rădescu's dismissal, and on 6 March he was succeeded by Petru Groza, leader of the Ploughman's Front, at the head of an NDF coalition including the communists. Groza was a figurehead, the non-communists in his cabinet all susceptible to communist pressure and, most importantly, communists now controlled the ministries of the interior, justice and the national economy, while Soviet officials in effect ran Romania's oil, timber and shipping industries, as well as its ports. The NDF government was further bound to the Soviets by the forced retrocession by Hungary to Romania of North Transylvania; it was then encouraged to recoup its popularity by confiscating the property of ethnic Germans, collaborators, Hungarian landowners, the Orthodox Church and others, giving it enviable patronage resources. In this period, too, Marshal Antonescu and his associates were tried and executed, in the spring of 1945, to identify the country with the fight against fascism.

In May 1946 elections were held, but only after a law had been passed making registration by non-members of the NDF next to impossible. The poll, unsurprisingly, returned 348 NDF deputies, as opposed to 29 for the Hungarian People's Union, a communist shell-party, while the once mighty National Peasant Party won a meagre 33. The polls were undoubtedly rigged even if, ironically, the NDF by this stage had some genuinely popular support. In the next year, however, as the communists systematically rooted opponents out of the state apparatus, this favourable opinion dissipated, and when the Cold War clampdown started in the summer of 1947, increasing numbers of the opposition were arrested and tried for imaginary offences. Non-communist parties were banned, and social democrats forced into merger with the RCP as the Romanian Workers' Party. A symbolic capstone was set on communist control when, in December 1947, the now dispensable King Michael was forced into abdication and exile.

Bulgaria underwent one of the quickest and most brutal takeovers. The communist-led Fatherland Front was effectively in charge from September 1944; but the problem was more one of eliminating, not only the wartime elite, but also a courageous democratic opposition. The tactic of smearing individuals or groups as 'fascist' was used to particular effect; while some targeted in this fashion were accurately identified, the majority were victims whose only fault was to be in the communists' way. Within months of taking over the Fatherland Front government killed off tens of thousands of potential opponents in this way. Indeed, this very ferocity was one reason why opposition to the Communist Party stiffened in Bulgaria, requiring a renewed onslaught on civil liberties. Formally, Bulgaria remained a monarchy; the fact that it was also subjected to four-power Allied control may, tragically, have been a factor

[20] Quoted in Crampton, R.J., *Eastern Europe in the Twentieth Century – And After*, 2nd edn, London and New York, 229.

encouraging the opposition's temerity. In reality the Soviets regarded this Allied Control Council (ACC) as a formality which in no way impeded them.

As elsewhere, the trick was in controlling the machinery of state violence. Communists from the start held the ministries of the interior and justice, and hence the police and judiciary. A communist was one of the three-man regency governing on behalf of Tsar Simeon. A new police force was loyal to the Communist Party. The army was more of a problem: with the exception of the Zvenists, most of the officers were royalists and hardly natural recruits to communism. The biggest obstacle, however, was the bureaucracy, and here the communists simply resorted to force. Thousands of state employees, possibly in excess of 50,000, were summarily executed as 'war criminals': 'In the country which had seen the fewest war crimes in Eastern Europe there were more alleged war criminals than anywhere else.'[21] In the spring of 1946 the regime turned its attention to the wartime political class: three regents, 160 parliamentary deputies and many others were tried and convicted of crimes against the people; a hundred were executed immediately.

Having eliminated the right wing, the Fatherland Front now confronted its opponents on the centre-left, in particular the mass-based agrarian party, BANU. Early in 1945 the communists had succeeded in intimidating BANU's leader, G.M. Dimitrov, into fleeing the country; his successor, Nikola Petkov, however, was of tougher fibre. In July Petkov and the social democratic leader, Kosta Lulchev, resigned their ministries in the Fatherland Front government, in protest at the smear tactics and intimidation being used against their followers. Both took false comfort from a decision to postpone a general election, as a result of their protests, backed up by Western representatives on the ACC. The postponement merely gave the communists more time to identify and target their opponents, and when the poll was held in November, the Fatherland Front won an improbable 86 per cent of the vote, and no opposition parties were represented in the national assembly at all. For the next year an uneasy stalemate reigned: the regime completed its takeover of the army; a referendum was held in September 1946, abolishing the monarchy; and in October a second general election was held for a grand national assembly, empowered to write a new constitution. In these blatantly rigged elections the Fatherland Front coalition won 78 per cent of the vote and 364 seats, versus 101 oppositionists. Stalin's longtime henchman as head of Comintern, Georgi Dimitrov, took over as prime minister.

In June 1947, despite repeated representations by Petkov to the ACC about the communists' overt abuse of power, the United States Senate voted to ratify a peace treaty with Bulgaria, thus winding up the ACC. Petkov, who represented a groundswell of peasant resistance to collectivisation, posed a genuine threat

---

[21] Crampton, *Eastern Europe in the Twentieth Century*, 225–6.

to communist control. He was arrested ahead of the US Senate vote, and put on trial in August, accused of a variety of crimes bizarre even by the standards of Stalinist purges, such as plotting to overthrow the government in collaboration with Greek monarcho-fascists. Following his inevitable conviction, Petkov was executed three days after the peace treaty with the Allies came into effect in September. The social democrats avoided decimation by voting for merger with the communists; their former leader Lulchev was sentenced to fifteen years in prison for daring to vote against government legislation. A Stalinist-type constitution was passed into law in December 1947. Bulgaria's takeover was completed.

The Soviet zone of occupied Germany, which only in 1949 took formal shape as the German Democratic Republic (GDR), or *East Germany*, was subjected to communist takeover in some respects due to circumstances created by the end of the war. Four-power occupation did not mean that permanent division was intended; on the contrary, both the Soviets and the Western powers assumed that Germany would remain united, Austria apart. The problem was that neither side could agree on what sort of Germany that should be; nor could they agree on how to administer their different zones, either economically or politically. As a British official put it, 'It is inconceivable that a Germany which is not treated as an economic unit could very long be treated as a political unit.'[22] Yet no peace treaty could be signed with Germany, as of 1945, because there was no German government to sign it with, and in the meantime the differences between the Soviets and the West made agreement less and less likely. With time, each side was forced to implement measures for regulating economic life, simply in order to feed, house and employ millions of people in a shattered land, in some parts of which it was estimated up to half the population were refugees. In the end, some form of political administration had to be implemented, and in this respect the Soviets were far readier to start the process and impose it from above than the West, where there was more concern to build democratic institutions from the bottom up.

In the Soviet zone, the desire of the Soviets to control the political process was obvious from the start, despite attempts to camouflage it. A group of Moscow-trained German communists led by Walter Ulbricht was flown into Berlin as soon as the capital was taken in April 1945, and one of the first measures taken was to authorise formation of political parties. The German Communist Party (KPD) rapidly took over most local administration, under Soviet supervision, but always, where possible, with compliant non-communists installed in figurehead positions. To foster the illusion of plural participation other parties were permitted; but from the first the KPD was the dominant element. Translating this Soviet-backed dominance into electoral gains, however, was a

---

[22] Quoted in Fulbrook, M., 1991, *The Fontana History of Germany 1918-1990: The Divided Nation*, London, 132–3.

different matter. By late 1945, once local elections were held in the Soviet zone, as well as in neighbouring Austria, it became clear that the KPD was unlikely to win mass electoral support as long as its principal rival for the working class vote, the Social Democratic Party (SPD), was still able to compete freely. The SPD, Germany's oldest political party, was too strongly entrenched, even when deprived by the Soviet authorities of basic political tools like newsprint, office space, even electricity. In addition, the KPD was by now indelibly associated in most Germans' minds with the Soviets and the excesses of the Red Army. In April 1946, therefore, facilitated by the flight westwards of thousands of SPD activists, a forced merger of the KPD and the SPD was effected as the Socialist Unity Party of Germany (SED). In the western zones, by contrast, the SPD remained a vocal and extremely anti-communist voice.

This shotgun wedding on the left was one of a series of developments in the Soviet zone which widened the gulf with the West. Reparations, agreed at Yalta, proved especially vexatious. The Soviets were all in favour of punitive reparations both in cash and in kind, and were not too concerned about how a country largely in ruins coped with this. Soviet depredations reduced the industrial capacity of their zone by 26 per cent, and by 1948 some 1900 factories had been dismantled and shipped eastwards – one indication that the Soviets 'had no firm intention to remain on German soil in the long term.'[23] By contrast the Americans and British, in charge of the more industrialised west, were anxious to see their sectors become self-sufficient, if only to reduce the crippling cost of occupation. In frustration, the Americans and British finally joined their two zones as 'Bizonia' in January 1947. The Soviet policy of stripping Germany of its productive capacity was seen as unsustainable by the Western powers; yet Western reluctance to continue dismantling plant in western Germany for shipment eastwards was taken ill by the Soviets, leading them to slow down transfer of much-needed foodstuffs from the Soviet zone to the western zones. In the meantime the Soviets and the SED pressed ahead with other changes. A land reform of September 1945 effectively eliminated the Junker landowner class by confiscating some 7,000 large estates, or 30 per cent of arable land in the Soviet zone; cunningly, smallholders' plots were for the moment left untouched. The bureaucracy, the teaching profession, the universities and the judiciary were thoroughly purged; and while this was a necessary weeding out of Nazis, such dismissals were almost uniformly replaced with SED trusties. In short, German communists were following the sort of 'salami tactics' that, replicated across the region, convinced Western leaders they were witnessing systematic subversion.

By the time President Truman came before Congress in March 1947 to announce the so-called Truman Doctrine, whereby the United States pledged

---

[23] Fulbrook, *The Fontana History of Germany*, 154.

to fund anti-communist campaigns in Greece and Turkey but also, in a clear challenge to the Soviets, to 'contain' communism by defending the rights of people everywhere freely to choose their own form of government, the rift over Germany already seemed unbridgeable. The details of the European Recovery Program (Marshall Aid), unveiled in June 1947, merely heightened Stalin's paranoia about a capitalist assault on Soviet security, prompting the formation of the Communist Information Bureau, or Cominform, in September, and the final crackdown on non-communists in Eastern Europe.

In Germany the breaking-point came with the Anglo-American decision to set up an autonomous administration for Bizonia, creating the rudiments of a West German state. Even more decisive was the introduction of a currency for the western zones, regarded as essential for kick-starting economic revival by tapping into the energies currently trapped in the black market. The introduction of the Deutschmark in the west in June 1948, however, was taken by the Soviets as the final straw. Four days later, the Soviets imposed a total blockade of the western sectors of Berlin, deep in the Soviet zone but, as Germany's capital, still under four-power control. This final gamble by Stalin to force western withdrawal from Berlin was famously circumvented by airlifting vital supplies to West Berlin, a massive operation continued until, in May 1949, Stalin conceded failure. By that point, the need to accept the division of Germany into two states, one democratic, the other communist, was apparent to both sides. After elections in the western zones and the drafting of a constitution, the latter was approved by the Western powers and came into force in May 1949, creating the Federal Republic of Germany. In the East a German Economic Commission took over control of the economy in March 1948, but only in October 1949 was the German Democratic Republic founded. The name, as with so much else in the Soviet system, was deeply inaccurate. The prime minister was the former social democrat Otto Grotewohl, but everyone knew that the real power was wielded by Ulbricht, secretary-general of the SED. Under Ulbricht's rule East Germany became one of the most stifling regimes of the Soviet bloc.

Austria deserves mention in conjunction with East Germany, because its fate was so different. This had to do with the decision reached by the Allies in November 1943, rooted in the desire to reduce German power, to treat Austria as Hitler's 'first victim'. Austria, according to this logic, had been forcibly annexed in 1938 and thus should be restored to an independent existence. As a result, as with Germany, a four-power occupation was agreed on, with Vienna, like Berlin within the Soviet zone, also subjected to four-power control; and in the final days of the war Anglo-American forces entered the country from the west, while the Soviets took over the east. Yet in December 1944, representatives of Austria's pre-*Anschluß* parties formed a provisional National Committee, to coordinate armed resistance as well as a political response. In April 1945 this group stepped forward and formed a provisional administration for Vienna, with a social democrat as mayor; a provisional government for the entire country, carefully composed to include all the pre-war parties save the Nazis, was agreed on 27 April, and the democratic constitution of 1920 was proclaimed as provisionally valid. At the same time the 75-year-old social democrat Karl Renner, first chancellor of the interwar republic, offered himself to the Soviet authorities as an interim leader. To begin with, the western Allies regarded Renner's government as a Soviet puppet, but in November this suspicion lifted, when the provisional government held the first free elections since 1930. These produced a shock for all, not least the over-confident Communist Party: the conservative Austrian People's Party (ÖVP) took over 50 per cent of the vote and 85 seats; the Social Democratic Party of Austria (SPÖ) 44 per cent and 76 seats; and the Communist Party a derisory 5 per cent and four seats.

Despite the ÖVP's clear victory all parties continued in a grand coalition to facilitate cooperation with the occupying powers, and Renner was elected president in December 1945. Austria was thus differently situated than Germany, in that from the end of 1945 it had a popularly elected, democratic, unitary government, which all four occupying powers accepted, and the fact of coalition, not to mention its meagre electoral base, meant that the Communist Party was never able to achieve the sort of dominance possible in other countries. The fact that, after November 1945, the ministry of the interior, and hence the police force, was run by a social democrat made a difference too. The Soviets' control of much of the Austrian economy, under the justification of collecting reparations, worked to the disadvantage of the Austrian communists in subsequent elections, since they were not unnaturally associated with Soviet rapaciousness, and never won above 5 per cent of the vote. The widening rift between the Soviets and the West also benefited Austria: the country received much-needed foreign aid, first from the UN Relief and Rehabilitation Administration, and then, in 1948, from the Marshall Aid programme. The Tito-Stalin split of 1948 resulted in the Soviets dropping their support for Yugoslavia's territorial claims against Austria, enabling the latter to arrange its own terms with Tito. A peace treaty between Austria and the four powers nevertheless took until May 1955 to be realised; in the end Austria bought an end to occupation by accepting international neutrality, whereby it undertook never to join a military alliance such as NATO, or to allow foreign military bases on its territory, or to seek *Anschluß* with Germany. On these terms, Soviet acquiescence was finally secured.

Hungary was the classic example of 'salami tactics', including the subversion of entire parties to act as fronts for communist control. Yet initially the imposition of one-party rule in Hungary formed no part of Stalin's plans. The four-party coalition government formed in December 1944 was a genuine one, and although a quarter of the provisional national assembly convened by it was communist, it governed in a relatively consensual fashion for the next year. This included a land redistribution programme which, by redistributing 33 per cent of arable land among small farmers, proved wildly popular. In November 1945 genuinely free elections were held, which accurately reflected the balance of social and political forces elsewhere in Eastern Europe: the Smallholders' Party (SHP) received 57 per cent of the vote, with the Social Democratic Party (SDP) and Hungarian Communist Party (HCP) tying well behind for second place with 17 per cent each, and the Hungarian Peasant Party (HPP) coming last with 8 per cent. Both the president, Zoltán Tildy, and the prime minister, Ferenc Nagy, were Smallholders; but in view of the country's continuing occupation by the Red Army, and pending conclusion of a peace treaty, the coalition was continued. Now, however, the HCP insisted on installing one of their own, László Rajk, as minister of the interior.

It was a fateful change. Communist infiltration of key security bodies was purposeful and increasingly effective; in particular the Department for the Defence of the State (AVO), later the dreaded State Security Department (AVH), functioned as a 'private army of the communists'.[24] The HCP had numerous moles in other parties. Increasing pressure was placed on the communists' main rival, the SHP for its allegedly chauvinist views. Both the SHP and the Catholic Church were ceaselessly denounced as anti-Russian, with some justice, and as anti-Semitic, with rather less. In the course of 1946 Rajk suppressed a thousand Catholic youth organisations, and blocked the formation of SHP-affiliated trades unions. In 1947 Church control of the school system was abolished. After conclusion in February 1947 of a peace treaty, which sanctioned the permanent stationing of Soviet troops on Hungarian soil, the pressure intensified, at a time when East-West relations were becoming increasingly tense. Béla Kovács, the SHP's general secretary, was arrested in March; prime minister Nagy, while abroad, was blackmailed into resigning in May by threats to his baby son. Nagy's replacement was 'a communist stooge'.[25] Tildy was forced to step down as president in July, and a new electoral law empowered Rajk to disqualify opposition candidates at whim. The elections of August 1947 saw the HCP-led list of parties win 45 per cent of the vote, but even in adverse conditions opposition parties combined still took 50 per cent of the poll. With Stalin demanding a complete crackdown on opposition across the region, dissident voices were progressively silenced. The HCP and SDP merged in June 1948 to form the Hungarian Workers' Party (HWP), the army was sovietised, and the outspoken cardinal-primate, József Mindszenty, was put under house arrest in December 1948. In April 1949 fresh elections ensured an HCP triumph by forbidding any opposition candidates at all, and a Soviet-style constitution was enacted shortly after. Hungary had made the transition to a one-party, Stalinist dictatorship under one of the most notorious of the 'little Stalins', Mátyás Rákosi.

---

[24] Crampton, *Eastern Europe in the Twentieth Century*, 223.
[25] Crampton, *Eastern Europe in the Twentieth Century*, 224.

Czechoslovakia was the last state to succumb to communist takeover, but there was nothing inevitable about this. The most democratic and economically developed country in the region between the wars, in 1945 Czechoslovakia was not treated as a defeated state, but deemed as being on the winning side. The Czech-Slovak condominium was restored, with a guarantee of Slovak autonomy if not federalism; the German and Hungarian minorities were forcibly expelled. In contrast to the situation elsewhere, the Communist Party of Czechoslovakia (CPCS) was genuinely popular and mass-based, especially in the more industrialised Czech lands. President Beneš was accepted as the country's legitimate leader, even if his post-war position owed much to his generally pro-Soviet policy since the 1930s. The National Front coalition government agreed in 1945 was, on the face of it, a genuine one. The social democrat Zdeněk Fierlinger became prime minister, and communists held seven out of twenty-five ministries. The programme agreed in April 1945 promised full civil liberties while aiming at extensive nationalisation of industry and the economy, together with a land reform based on property expropriated from the minorities.

The devil was in the detail. Apart from the fact that it had been the Red Army, not the Americans, who liberated Czechoslovakia, and that the presence of so many communists in government was a direct result of Soviet pressure, the posts held by the CPCS were all crucial: the interior, defence, agriculture, education and information. Fierlinger was known to be subservient to Soviet interests, and the minister of defence, General Ludvík Svoboda, was a crypto-communist. From this beachhead communist influence could easily be rolled out if required. Three considerations stayed the CPCS's hand in 1945–46. One was the international situation, which made Stalin still willing to tolerate coalition government in Czechoslovakia. Another was the fear of moving too fast, and prompting a more coordinated fightback by non-communists. Thirdly, the CPCS was confident that its mass base would translate into electoral victory when the time came.

The first post-war elections in May 1946, which by all accounts were conducted freely and fairly, showed that the communists did indeed command respectable support, when they won 38 per cent of the vote; 40 per cent in the Czech lands, 30 per cent in Slovakia. Party membership in March 1946 was over a million. Yet this was far from overwhelming, and the other parties together totalled 61 per cent: Czech National Socialists, 18 per cent; People's Party, 16 per cent; SDP, 13 per cent; and the Slovak Democrats, 14 per cent. For the next year, therefore, an increasingly uneasy coalition governed, now with Gottwald as prime minister; formally the democratic parties held fifteen ministries to the communists' nine, but two of the social democrats and General Svoboda leaned towards the communists. The police force, bureaucracy, local government bodies, trades unions and army were increasingly populated with communist adherents. Political debate remained open, but behind the scenes non-communist broadcasting and newspapers struggled for resources, which were allocated by the communist-controlled information ministry, and the commanding heights of the economy were gradually being nationalised. The extent and determination of communist subversion did not go unnoticed, with communist control of the police arousing especial alarm; by mid-1947 polls suggested popular support for the CPCS was sinking. By January 1948 it reached 25 per cent.

In the context of the Cold War, however, Czechoslovakia's chances of avoiding takeover were much reduced. Stalin's intervention, in July 1947, brusquely forbidding the Czechoslovak government from applying for Marshall Aid, came like a bolt from the blue, and profoundly demoralised the democratic parties. The CPCS started more actively infiltrating other parties, while mounting a concerted campaign of vilification against the Slovak Democrats in particular; in response, the democratic parties showed a growing awareness of the need to counter-organise. By February 1948 an open rift had developed between communist and non-communists in the cabinet. The latter demanded an end to communist infiltration of the police; in reply the CPCS mobilised the trades unions to form 'action committees' at local level, and Václav Nosek, communist minister of the interior, ominously announced the formation of a 15,000-strong, armed people's militia. In protest, and in an attempt to force President Beneš to come down on their side, the non-communist ministers resigned on 20 February, a move which backfired disastrously. The elderly and ailing Beneš, reluctant to offend the Soviets, dithered; in the meantime the trades unions organised mass demonstrations in support of the CPCS. Decisively, the Soviet Union assured Gottwald of its support, assembling troops on the Czechoslovak frontier. On 25 February Beneš gave way, and approved the formation of a cabinet, half of whom were communists, the remainder pliable fellow-travellers, with the exception of Jan Masaryk, kept on as foreign minister at Beneš's insistence. Shortly after, in an incident never satisfactorily explained either as suicide or murder, Masaryk's body was found beneath an upper-storey window of the foreign ministry. In the following months, non-communist parties were either taken over or shut down completely, and in May new elections created a suitably subservient national assembly, which voted in a suitably Soviet-style constitution. Beneš resigned in June, and Gottwald assumed the presidency, with Antonín Zapotocký as prime minister. The last outpost of democracy in Eastern Europe outside of Finland, Austria and Greece had fallen.

12

National communism vs Stalinism

A special episode in the story of Eastern Europe's communisation concerns the famous breach between Tito's Yugoslavia and the rest of the Soviet bloc in 1948, which demonstrated that Soviet control was not total, and that it was possible to be that seemingly contradictory thing, a 'national communist'. This chapter describes that rupture, and the way in which it forced the Yugoslav Party, which still considered itself communist, to evolve a different way of 'building socialism'. In the short term this enabled Yugoslavia to pose as a maverick but relatively benign socialist state; in the longer term 'Titoism' had grave implications for the cohesion of Yugoslavia itself. The Tito-Stalin split, however, had consequences far beyond Yugoslavia. It intensified Stalin's security concerns in the rest of Eastern Europe, leading him to insist on an ever greater ideological conformity. The chapter accordingly considers the appalling human cost of Stalinism, for it is no exaggeration to say that the imposition of communism, in so short a time span, traumatised entire societies, and in the longer term made some sort of revolt against the system all the likelier.

The Tito-Stalin split of 1948

The Prague coup was followed shortly after by an event that took observers in both the communist and the non-communist world completely by surprise: an open rift between Tito's Yugoslav Communist Party (YCP) and the Soviet Union. With hindsight this quarrel was always likely, despite the fact that, in ideological terms, there was nothing to distinguish Tito from Stalin. Both were ruthless believers in the communist vision; Tito and his closest associates, indeed, prided themselves on being loyal Stalinists. Yet it was increasingly obvious, in the aftermath of the war, that Stalin had a problem with the Yugoslav communists. The Yugoslavs, in turn, felt that they constituted a special case, and resented Stalin's insistence on total conformity. In the end the Yugoslav-Soviet break was about control; it had nothing to do with doctrine.

One reason for the split was the YCP's war record, and the fact that Yugoslavia counted as one of the victors at the end of the war. The Yugoslav communists were tremendously proud of this, and it did not matter that, in the larger picture, the decisive factor in the defeat of Nazi Germany and the withdrawal of its forces from Yugoslavia, as elsewhere, was the Red Army.

Although the latter helped liberate Belgrade and northeastern Yugoslavia, the Partisans nevertheless considered themselves to have liberated most of the country, albeit with 'fraternal socialist assistance'. Moreover, the Yugoslav communists were very conscious of the fact that, in terms of material aid, they owed far more to the Western powers than to Stalin, who was free with advice but little else. They were also shocked at the brutality, including multiple rapes, with which Soviet troops behaved during their brief transit across Yugoslav soil in 1944, and the cynicism with which Stalin shrugged off Yugoslav protests. Stalin, for his part, had his share of headaches from the Yugoslavs. During the war he feared that Tito's open ambition to take power in Yugoslavia might unduly alarm the western Allies, especially the British, who after all committed forces of their own to prevent just such an eventuality in Greece. Stalin was also convinced that Tito's political strategy was wrong, and that by recruiting non-communists into the Partisans Tito risked the Party's core being overwhelmed by peasants and petty bourgeois. In fact, although this genuinely broad base of the Yugoslav Party probably explains its unity in the face of Stalin's later attacks, Tito's control over his party was just as unbending as Stalin's.

Certainly the regime which took power in October 1944 was a consciously Stalinist one. Tito's boast was that the Yugoslav communists were not only Stalin's most loyal disciples, but his most valuable ones, because of their successful wartime resistance. In the post-war period, Yugoslavia deliberately modelled itself on that other multinational, but communist, state, the Soviet Union. The constitution adopted in January 1946 copied the Soviet one of 1936, and proclaimed a Federal People's Republic of Yugoslavia, composed of six 'socialist republics'. In part, this involved restoring some of the constituents of the interwar kingdom: Serbia, Croatia, Bosnia-Hercegovina and Montenegro. This restoration of historic national identities, as in the USSR, was important, because it sent a signal that national identity was recognised. Equally important, however, were the newcomers: the creation of Slovenian and Macedonian republics was the first time these nationalities had been recognised as administrative units. Most interesting of all, within the Serbian republic two areas of high interethnic mixture, Vojvodina and Kosovo, were created as 'autonomous regions' (later provinces), a recognition that such intermixture required special administrative consideration to safeguard the rights of the Hungarian and Albanian minorities there. In representative terms, in addition to a constituency-based Federal Council, or lower chamber, there was provision for a second chamber, the Council of Nationalities, comprising twenty-five representatives from each republic, plus fifteen each from the two autonomous regions. Of course, as with the Soviet Union, this federal structure was to begin with a sham. The greatest equality shared by the republics was that they were all equally powerless, since real authority, according to the constitution, rested with the Communist Party. Only much later did the federal system come to mean anything and, as with the Soviet Union, in the end it was a recipe for dissension and conflict. But for the moment Tito's Yugoslavia was a carbon copy of the Soviet Union, even down to the brutal repression of dissent, and the liquidation of 'fascist' opponents, whether Croat or Serb.

After the war economic and political relations with the Soviet Union continued to cause friction. The Soviets assumed, as they did in the rest of Eastern Europe, that they could impose a trade treaty on Yugoslavia which grossly favoured the Soviet side. They also demanded, and got, the setting up of joint-stock companies, for shipping and air transport, which were a rather elaborate way of milking the Yugoslav economy. In view of this patronising attitude, Tito's assumption that he had a genuinely independent role to play in the communist world was bound to lead to trouble. Yugoslav waywardness, as Stalin saw it, led to real crises in international relations. Whether it was Tito's aggressive advance on Trieste in 1945, or the shooting down in 1946 of American spy planes, or obstinately continuing to support the communist side in the Greek civil war, Tito's confrontational attitude towards the West created the impression that it was Stalin who was seeking conflict, since all communists were assumed to be Stalin's puppets.

Given the tensions with the West by mid-1947, Stalin's move against Tito was part of a wider attempt to consolidate communist control of Eastern Europe, but also to enforce total conformity, in which case Tito's independence was intolerable. Stalin accordingly tried to pull rank, insisting that Yugoslavia cease its assistance to the Greek communists, as well as interfering in Tito's plans for a Balkan confederation. This last was Tito's imaginative, if impractical, way of circumventing Bulgaria's pretension to Macedonia, by including all South Slavs within the same state framework. Never likely to be implemented, its promotion irritated Stalin, while Tito's grandiose habit of advising other communist parties in the region was equally unforgivable.

It is clear now that, in preparation for some form of anti-Tito coup, individuals willing to work as Soviet agents were recruited from within the Yugoslav Communist Party, the discovery of which profoundly shocked most Yugoslavs. The first indication of a break came in March 1948, when the Soviets abruptly withdrew all their advisers from Yugoslavia, claiming that they were 'surrounded by hostility'.[1] This was followed, after a ritual denunciation of Tito's 'deviationism' – code for not doing what Stalin wanted – by the Yugoslav Party's formal expulsion from Cominform in June. In the letter of 27 March the Soviet Party accused the Yugoslavs of being hostile to the USSR and guilty of all manner of deviations from orthodox Marxism-Leninism, comparing them to the arch-enemy, Leon Trotsky, and virtually calling on Party members to take matters into their own hands and oust Tito and his associates. In a famous

[1] Soviet Party to Tito, 27 March 1948; quoted in Stokes, G. (ed.), 1991, *From Stalinism to Pluralism: A Documentary History of Eastern Europe since 1945*, New York and Oxford, 58, note 1.

reply on 13 April, the Yugoslavs denied all the charges, and claimed to be true communists loyal to Stalin, but made the remarkable assertion that 'No matter how much each of us loves the land of socialism, the USSR, he can, in no case, love his own country less.'[2] It was an epochal moment because, even more unforgivably in Stalin's eyes, Tito was implicitly asserting that this 'national communism' had just as much validity for other communist parties. In the short term, at any rate, such protestations were in vain, because for Stalin this was not about ideological purity but about control.

Stalin, however, miscalculated badly. He assumed there were enough Moscow-loyal Yugoslav communists to effect regime-change; as he claimed, he had only to wag his little finger, and 'no more Tito.'[3] In reality the 470,000-strong Yugoslav Party proved, on the whole, more loyal to Tito than to Stalin, and in the aftermath of the split Tito's regime moved swiftly against anyone suspected of being fifth columnists; in the end some 12,000 Yugoslav communists suffered internment on inhospitable Adriatic islands for being Stalinists, rather than Titoists. Within Yugoslavia the split had two momentous consequences. Firstly, it made it imperative for the YCP to evolve a genuinely 'separate path' to socialism since, like all Marxists, they had to justify their break with Stalin on ideological grounds. This eventually led to the concept of 'workers' self-management', a more decentralised form of communism which, the Yugoslavs argued, was more in line with Marxist teaching, and which became a potential separate model for communists. Secondly, the split forced Yugoslavia to turn outwards: bereft overnight of Soviet aid, the regime put out feelers to the West and, by 1949, was in receipt of both financial and military aid. This golden bridge with time made Yugoslavia, which remained communist but never rejoined the Soviet bloc, one of the few relatively open and liberal societies of the communist world. In the rest of the Soviet bloc, however, the consequences of the Tito-Stalin split were altogether grimmer.

The Stalinisation of Eastern Europe 1947–53

The process whereby the rest of Eastern Europe was subjected to the full rigours of Stalinist-type communism was already under way by the time of the Tito-Stalin split, but the latter became an additional justification for Stalinisation. The very existence of an apostate communist regime on Stalin's doorstep became all the more reason for a clampdown elsewhere, as 'Titoism' joined the other, innumerable threats to the communist experiment. Millions paid

[2] Yugoslav Response, 13 April 1948; quoted in Stokes, *From Stalinism to Pluralism*, doc. 9.II, 60.
[3] Quoted in Rothschild, J., 1989, *Return to Diversity: A Political History of East Central Europe since World War II*, New York and Oxford, 132.

with their lives or their freedom for Stalin's pursuit of monolithic, crushing conformity.

What has been termed 'mature Stalinism', as a variant of communism, has been memorably defined by Joseph Rothschild as

> the enforced imitation of Soviet political, administrative, and cultural institutions; absolute obedience to Soviet directives and even hints; administrative supervision by Soviet personnel; bureaucratic arbitrariness; police terror uncontrolled even by the local party; economic deprivation while pursuing overambitious industrial investment programs and undercapitalized agricultural collectivization drives ("lunar economics"); colonial-like foreign-trade dependence on the Soviet Union; isolation from the non-communist world and to some extent even from other people's democracies; synthetic Russomania; a mindless cult of Stalin adulation; and resultant widespread social anomie, intellectual stagnation, and ideological sterility.[4]

Lapidary though it is, Rothschild's summary hardly conveys just how traumatic the imposition of the Stalinist system on Eastern Europe, in so short a period, must have been. In the process the economies and social structure of these societies were radically transformed forever, and it would be fair to say that, as a result, the standard of living of millions was indeed raised, and social equality was in the end greater. Such claims, however, ignore the human cost. Having been first stripped of political rights and civil liberties by one-party dictatorships, people were dispossessed, driven into exile, imprisoned, tortured and murdered in the inflexible pursuit of what was claimed to be socialism. Moreover, the fantastic economic growth initially generated by the process itself eventually petered out, to be succeeded by economic stagnation and a steady degeneration of living standards. It has to be questioned whether this omelette was worth the breaking of so many eggs.

The Cold War context which provided the excuse for Stalinisation has been touched on in passing. Here it is sufficient to reiterate that the creeping Sovietisation of individual countries by early 1947 was accelerated in response to western moves like the announcement of the Truman Doctrine, the withdrawal from coalition agreements with communists in West European countries, and Marshall Aid, and culminating in Stalin's creation of the Communist Information Bureau, or Cominform. This, like Comintern before it, was an umbrella organisation for ensuring uniformity and obedience among communist movements everywhere, and had its first formal gathering at Sklarska Poręba in Poland in September 1947. It was at this point that Stalin instructed those communist parties still in coalition with non-communists to abandon their power-sharing and simply seize power. This process was completed with the Prague coup of February 1948, with the exception of East

---

[4] Rothschild, *Return to Diversity*, 145.

Germany, where the final breakdown of East-West cooperation, leading to the Berlin blockade and the formation of the GDR, played out over 1948–49.

In terms of political institutions Stalinisation necessitated the adoption of a Soviet-style constitution, which enshrined the leading role of the Communist Party in implementing 'democratic centralism' – an expression in which 'centralism' was the operative word, 'democratic' merely a veneer, just as the self-designation of these communist dictatorships as 'people's democracies' was a bitter sham. What all such constitutions had in common was a structure in which the Party dominated the state apparatus, as well as permeating organisations at every level of society, such as trades unions, youth organisations and professional bodies. In this system the central committee of the Party, and in particular the political bureau or politburo of top Party leaders, were the driving forces of government, the real decision-makers. Within the politburo the most important and powerful position was that of secretary-general (or sometimes first secretary). This was Stalin's position within the Soviet Party, the base from which he had consolidated his power; in Eastern Europe a similar personality cult was built up around leaders like Rákosi, Todor Zhivkov and Tito. Beneath the politburo the cabinet of prime minister and ministers was very much a secondary, subordinate organ of government, the executive arm as it were of the Party itself.

Not only was the Communist Party the most important organisation in the state, it would be no exaggeration to say that the party was the state. This was an elite group, never allowed to reach more than around 10 per cent of the population. In line with Leninist principles membership was restricted, obtainable only after probation and rigorous examination of one's grasp of doctrine. Membership could also be revoked in periodic purges, in theory to guard against opportunists joining. Within the membership as a whole a system soon developed, as in the Soviet Union, whereby an inner group was nominated as especially trustworthy; belonging to this list of the *nomenklatura* was essential for appointment to any position of power or influence, from politburo member to officer's rank in the armed forces, to factory manager, to newspaper editor or school headteacher. This brought tangible rewards as well as responsibilities. Party members were entitled to better rations in the hard post-war years, and even after the economy recovered they continued to have access to special shops open only to them, selling foodstuffs and goods unavailable to ordinary citizens. Party members, especially the *nomenklatura*, benefited from better housing, health care and holidays, not to mention consumer goods and other privileges, such as an official car. With time, as the communist system became entrenched, opportunities for self-enrichment became irresistible to many party members. As early as the mid-1950s, Tito's former lieutenant Milovan Djilas denounced the way in which the Party, in Yugoslavia as elsewhere, had become a 'new class' of privileged beings, remote from the hardships of the masses in whose name they wielded power.

The representative institutions that, in a real democracy, are supposed to exercise some form of restraint over government, because composed of political parties freely competing for power in fair elections, were in this Stalinist system mere rubber stamps. The outward appearance of pluralism was maintained by the name of the ruling party – Hungarian Workers' Party, Socialist Unity Party, Polish Workers' Party and so on – and by the regular charade of elections in which there were usually multiple parties to choose from, but where the alternatives were hollow fronts, and the ruling party always secured an overwhelming majority of the popular vote. In societies where control of the media and all expression of opinion were monopolised by the party-state, it goes without saying that none of the electoral results produced by such a system could be regarded as remotely credible. The press, radio and the new medium of television were all state-controlled and reflected only the party line, ensuring that no news unfavourable to the regime reached the public legally. Education systems were entirely taken over by the state, and the curriculum reorganised along Marxist-Leninist lines. As in the Soviet Union, there was an increasingly rigid invigilation of cultural output of all sorts, whether literary, scholarly or artistic.

In economic terms Stalinism in Eastern Europe, as in the interwar Soviet Union, meant a break-neck modernisation through policies of central planning, nationalisation of private property, heavy industrialisation and the collectivisation of agriculture. The forcible implementation of this programme in the Soviet Union had caused turmoil enough in the interwar period, including the deliberate starvation of millions; in Eastern Europe it was imposed more quickly, with predictably traumatic effect. At the core of mature Stalinism was rigid state planning of all economic activity. Industrial firms were nationalised, starting with the biggest, but even small businesses like private shops and restaurants were gradually made impossible by the requirements of centrally coordinated production targets, as well as by the progressive elimination of any sort of free market in goods and services. Five-year plans laid down production norms (usually entirely unrealistic), allocated resources and regulated prices and wages, without however much thought given to whether, or where, there was a market for the goods being produced. The emphasis from the start was on heavy rather than light industry, so all the Soviet bloc countries invested in giant steel mills and other metallurgical plant, in cement works, extraction industries and the construction of infrastructure projects like roads, dams and apartment blocks for the new class of industrial workers. Heavy industry proliferated across the region, even in tiny Albania, and regardless of whether the raw materials were readily to hand. None of these schemes, considering the times, showed any regard for the possible environmental degradation involved, with consequences that by the late communist period were becoming literally life-threatening in some countries. The focus on heavy industry meant that production of consumer goods was always competing for scarce resources and lagging behind, if not non-existent, and what little was produced was invariably of poor quality. Central planning also meant, ironically, that societies touted as 'dictatorships of the proletariat', specifically created to raise up the working class, became increasingly exploitative and oppressive towards the workers. Production targets required long hours and constant exhortation to 'fulfil the plan', and in a system where trades unions were controlled by the Party and any form of collective bargaining, let alone strike action, was strictly forbidden, workers had no effective means of protesting. Most astonishing was the progressive introduction, from as early as the late 1940s, of piece-work, the nineteenth-century practice denounced by Marx himself as the acme of capitalist exploitation, whereby workers were paid according to how many units of production they made within the allotted time. Always highly unpopular, these 'work norms' were producing serious unrest by the early 1950s. Such a system of rigidly controlled production was also spectacularly wasteful and inefficient and, because not subject to any sort of independent invigilation, became an invitation to corruption and a flourishing black market, which served as a sort of alternative economy, completely untaxed by the party-state.

Crucial to the whole industrialisation agenda was the collectivisation of agriculture. Following the Soviet example, most East European governments in the transition period of 1944–8 started by redistributing land among the peasantry, which had the twin advantages of eliminating the old landowning nobility, while simultaneously pacifying the peasants. The ultimate objective of collectivisation was only introduced once the communists were firmly in control, and in some countries, for instance Hungary, was not determinedly implemented until the late 1950s. In most of the region, however, land was gradually appropriated to form large collective farms, permitting greater mechanisation of farming, and a concomitant reduction in the number of labourers required. The surplus population was directed towards industrial jobs in the rapidly expanding cities. This process alone acted as a vast engine of social change and dislocation. Displaced agricultural workers, often housed in hastily built, sub-standard tenement blocks with little in the way of local infrastructure or amenities, became a large class of the alienated. Collectivisation nevertheless inevitably transformed agrarian societies into industrial ones. In several countries collectivisation was actively resisted, or shrunk back after being chaotically attempted. In Poland and Yugoslavia, in particular, opposition was so entrenched that the Party soon abandoned collective farms as impractical, and within a few years of this relaxation most land was again being farmed privately, although state farms survived in the territories taken over from Germany. In most of the region, however, the change was permanent.

To cap it all, Stalinisation meant the subordination of East European countries' economies to that of the Soviet Union. Bilateral trade treaties were signed between the Soviets and individual countries, whereby trade flowed back and forth with the Soviet 'centre', but not laterally between the East bloc countries, in a system which has been compared to the spokes of a wheel, all connected to the hub but with no contact with one another. Clearly intended to reinforce each country's dependence on the Soviet Union, this arrangement exercised a profoundly distorting effect on the entire region, denying natural economic exchange and diversification in favour of rigid control and uniformity.

Finally, Stalinisation rested on, and was fundamentally dependent on, a system of political terror common to all the Soviet bloc states. As in the Soviet Union, it soon became apparent that a system so economically irrational, and accompanied by the systematic elimination of all opposition, had to be enforced, and seen to be enforced; indeed, manufacturing enemies to persecute, and traitors to be exposed and vilified, became part of the *raison d'être* of the party-state. In countries like Poland, Bulgaria or Yugoslavia, the physical elimination of opponents was going on even as the Party took control, and in response to such political murders many other potential opponents fled abroad if they could. The principal instrument of consolidating communist power further was the police, and in all East bloc countries there was a feared distinction between the regular police force and the political or secret police: the State Security Policy (*Stasi*) in East Germany, the Romanian *Securitate*, the AVH in Hungary, Tito's UDBa and the rest. This was the executive organ of state terror, responsible for arresting, interrogating, torturing and, if required, executing those accused of crimes against the people's democracies. The political police and the state's judiciary, especially after the full clampdown and the Tito-Stalin split, orchestrated a series of bizarre, Soviet-style party purges, complete with extravagant accusations of espionage, terrorism and betrayal of the people, forced confessions and hysterical public show trials of these alleged traitors to the communist cause.

It must be stressed that the Stalinist show trials of the late 1940s and early 1950s were ritual purges of the Communist Party membership, rather than the wider public. In the paranoid atmosphere of the Cold War it was deemed essential, just as Stalin had done in the 1930s, to rally the party and the general population by conjuring up internal enemies to be flushed out and exterminated. We now know that the top leadership, at least those who commissioned these spectacles, were perfectly well aware that the accused, themselves party members, including senior figures, were wholly innocent. Below that level, however, everyone unquestioningly accepted the alleged guilt of the accused, however absurd the charges. What is more, the accused often voluntarily confessed to offences they had not committed, either from fear of torture, or in the (usually misplaced) hope of protecting their families, or because they genuinely believed in the need for the party to offer up such scapegoats for the cause of solidarity.

One of the earliest purges, in Hungary, involved the former minister of the interior László Rajk, a ruthless ideologue, veteran of the Spanish Civil War and wartime resistance in Hungary, who had coordinated the 'salami tactics' whereby the Party's opponents were methodically eliminated between 1945 and 1948. Yet in May 1949 Rajk was arrested, accused of betraying his comrades in Spain, acting as an informer for the Horthy regime, and finally of spying for Tito, the French and the Americans. Rajk nevertheless publicly confessed to all these crimes, and with two other 'accomplices' was duly convicted and executed in October. His successor as interior minister from 1948 to 1950, János Kádár, who persuaded Rajk to confess for the good of the party, was himself then charged with being both a Horthyist hireling and an agent of Western imperialism. His torturers beat him, painted him in mercury to impede his breathing, and urinated in his mouth; Kádár was lucky to escape with three years in prison. His successor, Sándor Zöld, on being warned he was about to be arrested, promptly shot his entire family before turning the pistol on himself.

Similar purges were replicated across the region. The Bulgarian deputy prime minister, Traicho Kostov, was charged in the spring of 1949 with a dizzying array of offences: Trotskyism, Titoism, collaborating with fascists and spying for the West. Unusually, despite initially confessing to all this, Kostov in December 1949 retracted his confession in the court room; the public broadcast had to be halted, and Kostov was hastily executed a few days later. Władysław Gomułka, a staunch communist leader in 1945, but also one who did not disguise his belief that Polish communists should be flexible in how they exercised power, by for instance approaching collectivisation gradually, or trying to reach an accommodation with the Catholic Church, was sacked as Party boss in September 1948 for exhibiting national communism and 'right-wing deviationism'. Expelled from the Party and imprisoned in 1951, Gomułka nevertheless survived, despite Soviet pressure for a show trial, possibly because his successor Bolesław Bierut also resented Soviet domination, and hesitated to sanction too harsh a punishment against fellow Poles. The smaller fry of the Party, especially those who had fought in Spain or the wartime resistance, were not so fortunate: many were regularly tortured, and many sentenced to death.

One of the most shocking show trials was that of the former Czechoslovak secretary-general, Rudolf Slánský, and thirteen other prominent Party officials in November 1952. Almost all the defendants, charged with the usual improbable offences, happened to be Jewish, a fact that reflected Stalin's increasing anti-Semitic paranoia in his final years. Slánský, like Rajk, was another ruthless, dedicated communist who had been central to implementing the takeover of 1947–8; others, like the deputy trade minister Rudolf Margolius, were starry-eyed idealists who sincerely believed they were building socialism. Neither loyalty nor idealism nor their forced confessions saved the Slánský group from ritual public humiliation, followed by execution; in a macabre final twist, the agents transporting their ashes for disposal wound up scattering them under the tyres of their car to gain traction on an icy winter road. Margolius' widow, like her husband a survivor of Auschwitz, described the equally shocking way in which the general public, and even the victims' families, heaped obloquy on them; one defendant's wife and teenage son publicly denounced him as a traitor and rejoiced in his death sentence. Heda Margolius and her son endured years of hardship and discrimination for their connection to the 'traitor' Margolius.

The cumulative impact of these purges is impossible to overestimate, but they clearly achieved their intended effect of salutary terror. The figures are startling. It has been estimated that, in Hungary alone, a total of 700,000 people were prosecuted between 1948 and 1953, out of a population of ten million; 400,000 were actually sentenced, and 5,000 were executed. The Polish Party membership declined by about a quarter in the same period; the Bulgarian, by about 40 per cent between 1948 and 1951; the Czechoslovak by 30 per cent between 1948 and 1954. It should be stressed that these figures do not represent deaths, but rather the number of persons purged, that is, expelled from the Party. In all countries the psychological effect of such turmoil was, firstly, to alienate those who were not Party members; the fact that the purges were known to be orchestrated by Soviet representatives in each country, with Soviet officials frequently present at interrogations and torture sessions, simply reinforced this reaction. Secondly, the effect on Party members was twofold. Most believers in the ideology initially accepted the truth of the charges, and were duly convinced that the people's democracies were beset by spies and traitors. In the longer term, however, especially when those who survived the purges returned from the camps in the period of 'de-Stalinisation', the effect on communists themselves was profoundly demoralising. The excesses of the Stalinist period in Eastern Europe set the scene for a tremendous revulsion of feeling in the mid-1950s.

13

The perils of de-Stalinisation
Poland and Hungary in 1956

Stalin died in March 1953. It says something for how little Russia has progressed politically, since then, that a 2017 comic film on the subject was banned from screening by Vladimir Putin's government for being insufficiently respectful.

East Europeans had little enough to laugh about by the early 1950s, but it is a measure of the importance of individuals in history that Stalin's death made a difference. His Kremlin successors relaxed their grip in a process that came to be known as 'de-Stalinisation'. This involved, in the Soviet Union, an initial period of collective leadership, the renunciation of the leadership cult, an attempt to de-emphasise heavy industry and produce more consumer goods, and above all a scaling back of state terror and mass incarceration. In Eastern Europe, paradoxically, de-Stalinisation, like Stalinism, had to be imposed by Soviet fiat, because the 'little Stalins' were unsurprisingly reluctant to implement it. For the results resembled lifting a pressure-cooker lid: as soon as the lid is raised, escaping steam threatens to scald the cook. De-Stalinisation in Eastern Europe released a series of pent-up explosions, as the grievances of workers, farmers, nationalists and, above all, of purged members of the region's communist parties came rushing out, demanding change. Eastern Europe's irrepressible diversity broke through yet again.

This chapter charts the mixed fortunes of de-Stalinisation in Eastern Europe. It summarises what de-Stalinisation was supposed to mean, and surveys the conditions obtaining by 1953, particularly in economic terms, and how this affected the general population. It then describes the political implications of de-Stalinisation. Between 1953 and 1956 the danger of de-Stalinising became increasingly plain to Eastern Europe's Communist leaders and their Soviet overlords, yet the pressure from below to reform remained hard to ignore. Strikingly, the greatest impatience with the results of Stalinism was expressed earliest, and most forcibly, by the supposed principal beneficiaries of a socialist system, the industrial working class. The attempted implementation of the 'new course' decreed by the Soviets produced varying results. Some regimes were more willing to change than others, but the mere suggestion that improvements might be possible served to galvanise the citizenry. Most unsettling of all was the effect on society of gradually releasing political prisoners, those immured in the camp system and horribly abused as a result of the Stalinist purges. Finally, an unquantifiable but profound shift in attitudes towards the 'little Stalins' was caused by the Soviet Union's unexpected reconciliation with Tito's Yugoslavia in 1955. This suggested that Stalin's expulsion of the Yugoslavs owed more to caprice than doctrinal differences, and that all those loyal East European communists hounded to their deaths as 'Titoists' had been innocent all along.

By 1955 the pressure-cooker was about to blow, as leaders struggled to contain demands for greater openness, accountability and a change in economic policy. In Poland and Hungary, in particular, this pressure culminated in revolutions, of a sort. Emboldened by Nikita Khrushchev's famous 'secret speech' of February 1956, acknowledging the innocence of Stalin's victims, would-be reformers were levered into power by popular demand in Poland and Hungary. But whereas the advocates of a 'national communism' in Poland were, after a tense stand-off, permitted to remain in place, in Hungary the reform movement rapidly escalated into something more like a nationalist revolt against Soviet domination. The result was the crushing of the Hungarian revolution by Soviet armour, followed by a brutal crackdown.

De-Stalinisation and its discontents

The 'new course' announced by the Soviet leaders in early 1953 was to some extent a function of the jockeying for primacy within the Soviet politburo, a contest eventually won by Khrushchev in 1957, but it nonetheless signalled a willingness to ease the strain of mature Stalinism. The Soviet leaders themselves, however, were divided on the issue: some favoured economic reform and limited political liberalisation; some were averse to change; others approved of de-Stalinisation, as long as the party did not surrender its leading role. Because they were only familiar with their own system, the Soviets decreed a sort of one-size-fits-all de-Stalinisation for Eastern Europe that hardly took account of the fact that all the East bloc economies were at different stages. Because the Soviets had adopted a collective leadership, they exhorted East European parties to do the same. They recommended a shift from capital-intensive heavy industry to light industry and more production of consumer goods, regardless of the fact that such transformations take time and are inherently wasteful. Their call for greater investment in agriculture took no account of the chaos that had overtaken most East European farming since the imposition of Stalinism. Above all they reckoned without the likely consequences of relaxing the Stalinist terror in societies which had been subjected to a brutal and alien domination in the course of a mere five years.

The problem was in the implementation. The very call for a new course implied there was something wrong with the old one, yet this in itself was problematical for most communists, accustomed as they were to accepting the party's word as gospel.

The prospect of change also suggested that some sort of debate about the change needed was possible, indeed desirable. Debate, however, carried the possibility of disagreement, of different points of view. How far could this go? It soon became apparent that no one knew, least of all the Soviet collective leadership, who rapidly fell out with one another over this very issue. In the meantime, however, the sense that there might be a genuine debate was sufficient to trigger one within East European communist parties, as well as spontaneous unrest among the working class. The Soviets' instinctive reaction to this was to effect a change of personnel in East European parties, rather than consider whether the system they had imposed was flawed to start with. It was left to reform-minded East European communists to come up with alternative ways of 'building socialism'.

The reformers, however, had first to get past their own Stalinists, because almost everywhere the reaction of party leaders to de-Stalinisation was one of horror. After years of terrorising their respective populations, it was not only humiliating but possibly dangerous for Rákosi in Hungary, or Ulbricht in East Germany, or Hoxha in Albania, to relax that terror. These 'little Stalins' had been willing executors of Stalin's will and were personally responsible for the deaths or suffering of their compatriots. The survival of a clearly Stalinist faction in the Soviet leadership gave out conflicting signals: how long would de-Stalinisation remain Soviet policy?

No such qualms held back the industrial workers in 1953, whose dissatisfaction with Stalinism boiled over at the slightest suggestion it might be ameliorated. In most cases unrest was the consequence of the local party leadership not only failing to respond to the signals coming out of Moscow, but pressing ahead with an intensification of industrialisation. First in line were the tobacco workers of Plovdiv in Bulgaria, who in May came out in a spontaneous strike against new 'work norms' which prescribed longer hours for less pay. Bulgaria under Dimitrov's successor Vulko Chervenkov had undergone a crash course in heavy industrialisation, with little regard for the social disruption and genuine hardship involved. Firmly repressed by Chervenkov, these unorganised protests nevertheless induced the Bulgarian leader to announce his own 'new course' later in the year. In Czechoslovakia there were similar demonstrations and strikes at the end of May, in protest at the regime's announcement that it was devaluing the currency to counter the inflation caused by overheating the economy, thus inflicting considerable financial loss on the population. The most serious unrest involved some 20,000 workers at the former Škoda factories in Plžen; here workers defaced portraits of Stalin and the recently deceased Klement Gottwald, tore down the Soviet flag and, most alarmingly, demanded free elections. Only by mobilising thousands of tame trade unionists and party members, while denouncing the workers as 'bourgeois and social-democratic provocateurs', was the new collective leadership of Czechoslovakia able to regain control. In Hungary there was similar unrest in Budapest and other industrial centres.

Most serious of all was the violence in East Germany, where Ulbricht's regime was determined to press ahead with Stalinist policies, in defiance of economic reality. From 1952 the regime launched an all-out programme of nationalisation; in the cities artisans and small tradesmen were forced out of business, while in the countryside the first wave of collectivisation started. The result was a slump in agricultural production, food shortages and the introduction of rationing in the spring of 1953. This crash course in Sovietisation failed to take into account the fact that, uniquely in Eastern Europe, East Germans still had the option, if they were brave or desperate enough, of fleeing to West Berlin. Between 1949 and 1953 the number of East Germans who decided on flight rose from 60,000 to 297,000 per year, which represented a serious drain of manpower and skills, as well as a poor advertisement for communism. Some 50 per cent of these refugees were skilled workers, and 14 per cent were farmers.

Ulbricht in desperation turned to the Soviets in April 1953, only to be advised to adopt his own 'new course', reduce the pace of industrialisation, and relax the pressure on the population. Within the SED, too, a de-Stalinising faction soon emerged, but Ulbricht, inflexible by temperament, doubled down on 28 May and appealed for a 10 per cent raising of industrial output. Despite being promptly rebuked by the Soviets, Ulbricht insisted on abiding by the 10 per cent increase in 'work norms' originally announced.

The result was an explosion. On 16 June construction workers in East Berlin came out on strike against the increase in production quotas, which meant a decrease in real wages. More and more workers joined the demonstration, and before the day was out their demands became political, calling for the government's resignation and free elections. By 17 June the strike was general, paralysing not just the capital but Leipzig, Dresden and other cities; in part this was because East Germans could listen to radio broadcasts from West Germany, reporting on the East Berlin disturbances. There were attempts to occupy government buildings, and the red flag was torn down from the Brandenburg Gate. At this point, after forty-eight hours of escalating chaos, the Soviet military commander in East Berlin proclaimed martial law and called out Soviet tanks to take back control of the streets; the Soviets had to act themselves because, as of 1953, there was still no East German army. Precisely because the 'uprising' had been spontaneous it was relatively easily put down, even if we now know that it was also 'the product of a much broader level of popular dissatisfaction with the SED regime.'[1] Officially twenty-one demonstrators died in the fighting; unofficial estimates of the number killed were as high as three thousand. Forty-two people were executed; over 20,000 were arrested.

[1] Stibbe, M., 2006, 'The SED, German Communism and the June 1953 Uprising: New Trends and New Research', in K. McDermott and M. Stibbe (eds), *Revolution and Resistance in Eastern Europe: Challenges to Communist Rule*, Oxford and New York, 38.

The East German uprisings shook all the Communist regimes, not least because the spectacle of a 'people's democracy' brutally suppressing protests by its working class was such a disastrous one. Stalinists immediately argued that de-Stalinisation had been taken too far, and proponents of the 'new course' were weakened in the short term. Nowhere was this more striking than in the Soviet Union, where the disturbances of 1953 led to the fall of Lavrenti Beria, formerly Stalin's most feared henchman but ironically one of the principal advocates of de-Stalinisation. Beria's politburo colleagues used the uprisings as a pretext for arresting and executing him. In East Germany Ulbricht used Beria's fall to purge his own de-Stalinising rivals; the East German regime also benefited, in that the Soviets agreed to cancel reparation payments and lower the costs of Soviet occupation. The regime also determined never to allow living standards to drop too low, and henceforth subsidised everything; the result was that the price of a bread roll or a tram ticket was the same in East Germany in 1989 as it had been in 1953. The immediate outcome of the 1953 uprising was therefore repression: Stasi surveillance was increased to the point that, notoriously, there was one police informer for every sixty-six citizens. Yet precisely because dissatisfaction with the Stalinist command economy was so undeniable by 1953, advocates of de-Stalinisation could not be ignored in the longer term.

It remains to offer a brief overview of the conditions to which East European societies had been reduced by the mid-1950s.

In economic terms there is no denying there had been extremely rapid growth across the region as a result of industrialisation. This was to some extent because all the East bloc countries save Czechoslovakia and East Germany were largely agrarian societies and thus starting from a low base. In what economists call the 'extensive strategy', growth can be stimulated by adding things to the economy, such as the extraction of raw materials, construction and, above all, extra supplies of labour. In Eastern Europe the stimulus came from the mere act of creating industrial plant on a huge scale, the expansion of mining and especially collectivisation, which released millions of 'underemployed' peasants and women into the urban workforce. This extensive strategy delivered remarkable growth in Eastern Europe throughout the 1950s; but once the surplus labour derived from collectivisation had been soaked up, this closed system, relying almost entirely on the state for stimulus, began gradually to run out of steam, and the rate of growth started steadily falling. At this point, by the beginning of the 1960s, it would have made sense, in a rationally organised economy, to resort to the 'intensive strategy': import new technology to keep industrial production modern and competitive, while exporting as much as possible in order to pay for the technological imports. This, however, required access to the world market, at world market prices. By the mid-1960s even Marxist-trained Soviet and East European economists were reaching this conclusion. The communist command economy, however, did not permit re-entry into a global market; its entire premise was that socialism could be built without capitalism.

Later this premise was comprehensively abandoned, when East European communist regimes, bizarrely, started borrowing heavily from Western banks to finance their failing system. In the early 1950s, however, this larger systemic failure was unanticipated. For ordinary East Europeans there were more obvious and immediate problems.

The most visible sign of change was the phenomenal growth of industrial cities, many of them entirely new, built pell-mell around giant steel mills, mines or factory complexes. Nowa Huta in Poland, founded in 1949, grew from 18,000 inhabitants in 1950, to 101,900 by 1960, to 250,000 at its peak. Hungary's Sztálinváros (Stalintown, in the post-Stalin period Dunaújváros) was in 1950 a collection of tents and barracks housing the male and female workers shipped in to build it; a year later it contained 14,708 people. East Germany's Stalinstadt (later Eisenhüttenstadt) mushroomed from 2,400 to 15,130 inhabitants between 1952 and 1955. Nowa Huta was deliberately sited next to Kraków, in order to overwhelm this ancient city with class-conscious proletarians. Sztálinváros, built on unsuitably sandy soil that necessitated constant rebuilding, was a prestige steel mill erected in a country without iron and coal, which had to be imported from fellow-socialist states. Stalinstadt was situated in the extreme east of the GDR, ostensibly for its proximity to Ukrainian and Polish raw materials, but in reality to keep it as far as possible from potential western air raids.

Despite the grandiose designs for modern accommodation, complete with shops, restaurants, theatres and all the appurtenances of socialist culture, living conditions in these new towns lagged far behind the industry that engendered them. The hordes of transplanted peasants who manned the steel mills and factories, housed in bleak tenement blocks with little to do other than go to work, turned to drink, pub fights and prostitution; as one disillusioned Polish youth official rather priggishly described the workers of Nowa Huta, they 'had no cultural standards at all. No education, no need for higher things. They were constantly drunk, they entertained themselves by fighting.'[2] In the suburbs of Sztálinváros, thrown up without indoor plumbing, rubbish collection or paving, thousands lived in overcrowded slum conditions worthy of nineteenth-century Manchester, keeping their own livestock in unfinished buildings. Chronic food shortages were compounded by demanding hours and inadequate pay. In Gale Stokes's words, 'No democracy could have created such havoc in such a short time.'[3] The alienation and disillusionment was well

---

[2] Quoted in Applebaum, A., 2013, *Iron Curtain: The Crushing of Eastern Europe 1944-1956*, New York and London, 377.

[3] Stokes, G., 2012, *The Walls Came Tumbling Down: Collapse and Rebirth in Eastern Europe*, 2nd edn, New York and Oxford, 6.

expressed by Adam Wajyk's 'Poem for Adults' (1953), describing Nowa Huta: 'The large mob, push suddenly/Out of medieval darkness: an inhuman Poland,/ Howling with boredom on December nights.'[4] Throughout the communist period this city, created to showcase socialism, became instead 'a flashpoint of overt struggle and dissent.'[5]

Parallel with hypertrophied urban growth was the depopulation and industrialisation of the countryside. This vast experiment in social engineering was only partly successful, in that collectivisation was in some countries frustrated or even reversed with time. Initially, however, collectivisation was railroaded through, producing huge social strains. The Yugoslav communists launched one of the earliest collectivisation drives, in the teeth of stubborn peasant resistance, and Yugoslavia's expulsion from the Soviet fold in 1948 only caused Tito to intensify collectivisation, to demonstrate his communist credentials; by 1950 more land had been collectivised in Yugoslavia than anywhere else in Eastern Europe. Only after 1953, as the pressure on Yugoslavia eased, did the urgency go out of collectivisation; peasants were allowed to withdraw from the collectives, and as early as 1954 over 80 per cent of land was back in private hands. Poland was another early collectiviser, although Gomułka recognised the hostility of Polish farmers to the idea; as he confessed in April 1945, 'At this stage there isn't any sense in even thinking about Polish collective farms.'[6] Once Gomułka had fallen, in part because of his foot-dragging over collectivisation, Bierut stepped up the pace; but even this most Stalinist of regimes had collectivised only 9.2 per cent of arable land by 1955, despite brutal persecution of farmers, and the forced requisition of grain and meat. Farmers responded by not sowing crops, and the number of livestock plummeted, as farmers simply consumed their animals rather than hand them over. By 1956 the countryside was in turmoil, a contributory cause of the political upheaval that year.

In Bulgaria, another society where peasants traditionally followed their own agrarian party, the new regime proceeded at first with caution, forming voluntary cooperatives rather than collective farms. Even so, very few peasants joined these. Only with the first five-year plan, in 1949, was forcible collectivisation attempted. There was intense peasant resistance, comparable to the disastrous implementation of Soviet collectivisation in the 1920s: peasants burnt their crops, hid what they did harvest, and slaughtered their animals rather than surrender them, resulting in poor harvests and mounting food shortages. Under Chervenkov some half-million smallholdings were collectivised in 1950–1, but the cost was a rolling chaos in the countryside. Hungary saw a popular

[4] Quoted in Applebaum, *Iron Curtain*, 384.
[5] Lebow, K., 2013, *Unfinished Utopia: Nowa Huta, Stalinism and Polish Society 1949-56*, Ithaca, NY, 5.
[6] Quoted in Applebaum, *Iron Curtain*, 226.

land redistribution immediately after the war but, as in Bulgaria and Poland, the peasants' attachment to the land they acquired ensured that the period of aggressive collectivisation, in 1950–3, was accompanied by comparable mayhem and suffering. As in Poland, peasant discontent was a powerful catalyst for revolution in 1956. Romania experienced similar difficulties; it was not until the 1960s that most land was collectivised.

Most paradoxical of all was the situation in Czechoslovakia, which in the 1930s had an intensive and productive agricultural sector, 'at a much higher level of development than Soviet farming', but which, after several years of Stalinism was dragged backwards.[7] Collectivisation from 1949 produced chaos, as urban party workers sent out to enforce the process were met with indifference and hostility; some were even murdered. Collectivisation reached its peak in 1952; by 1953, 43 per cent of peasant farms had been taken over. There was a big drop in agricultural production, especially of livestock, and even party leaders concluded that the policy was a failure. A move to allow peasants to leave collective farms, however, was vetoed by hardliners, with the result that Czechoslovakia was in effect brought down to the level of its East European neighbours.

Industrialisation and collectivisation were the most important engines of change; but factories and farms were not the only objects of nationalisation. The communist vision also demanded that all private enterprise, however small, be squeezed out of the economy. What one Polish minister termed the 'war over trade' was waged with single-minded intensity by all the communist regimes. Private businesses, family shops, restaurants, even cafés were seen as inherently capitalist, and therefore inimical to socialism, and were progressively driven out of existence by price regulation, taxation, denial of supplies and raw materials, restrictions on the number of employees permitted, a blizzard of other regulations, and legal penalties for non-compliance with such rules. The result was the elimination of the private sector, with a concomitant deterioration in the quality and range of consumer goods and services, their availability, and the flavour of life generally. In some cases proprietors of firms successfully applied to become managers in their newly nationalised premises; in most cases they were simply driven out of business. Within a few years a remarkable levelling down had been effected, in that the entrepreneurial middle class had been effectively eliminated. Enterprises and the state bureaucracy were increasingly managed by ideologically approved working-class party members, many of them seriously underqualified for such roles. Huge numbers of women joined the workforce as manual labourers, technicians or professionals, but for the most part this simply meant they were exploited equally with men.

---

[7] Myant, M., 1989, *The Czechoslovak Economy 1948-1988: The Battle for Economic Reform*, Cambridge and New York, 45.

Communism achieved an unprecedented social mobility of a sort, in that education was now free for all, and as a result millions of Eastern Europe's poorest classes were lifted out of poverty and illiteracy; there was, however, an element of snakes-and-ladders involved, in that upper and middle-class people went downwards. In secondary and tertiary education there was positive discrimination in favour of children from peasant and proletarian backgrounds, whereas those from 'bourgeois' or 'reactionary' families were often denied such access; Václav Havel, Czechoslovakia's leading dissident in the late communist period, was blocked from higher education precisely because he was the son of a wealthy businessman whose firm was nationalised in 1948. In the same fashion, high culture was now something everyone could enjoy, sometimes given ostentatious reality by piano concerts in steel mills; on the other hand, the party-state strictly controlled what was permitted, whether in the theatre, literature, or art.

Most deadening of all was the moral impact of Stalinism. Strict conformity, reinforced by police terror, made for the stultification of imagination and individual initiative. For those citizens who were not Communist Party members this merely resulted in a general fatalism and a corrosive cynicism about the new rulers. Among party members it spelt ideological rigidity and timidity, as well as an excruciating sycophancy towards one's superiors. Long before the communist system collapsed in 1989, it had suffered a sort of intellectual brain death. In *The Captive Mind* (1953), a famous analysis of the communist ideology, the Polish poet and former communist Czesław Miłosz remarked on how party members resorted to '*ketman*' (a term from the Muslim world), a sort of doublethink or acting needed to disguise one's true thoughts in a hostile environment. Such pretence was both soul-destroying and hard to maintain; sooner or later the 'captive mind' had to revolt. Stalinist communism, moreover, with its conviction that it understood the 'laws of history', that 'everything is understandable and explained', nevertheless had a blind spot: 'Stalinists have no knowledge of the conditions human plants need in order to thrive.'[8] The 'new faith', as Miłosz dubbed communism, purported to perform miracles of materialist achievement: 'It shows the doubters new buildings and new tanks. But what would happen if these miracles suddenly stopped?'[9] This was the situation which threatened to develop within a few years of the grand design being imposed.

Mention of faith is an appropriate point at which to discuss Stalinism's other weak spot, in addition to its failure to deliver an earthly utopia. There was little doubt that as of 1945 religion still held a prominent place in most East Europeans' minds. This was most noticeable in strongly Catholic countries like Poland and Hungary; in Orthodox societies the church, because

[8]   Miłosz, C., 1985 [1953], *The Captive Mind*, translated by Jane Zielonko, Harmondsworth, 200.
[9]   Miłosz, *The Captive Mind*, 221.

historically so associated with the old order, possibly commanded less devotion. Nevertheless religion remains to this day one of the few domains where secular, totalitarian regimes intrude at their peril. Religious conscience was a force that even communists recognised as intractable, and which they hesitated to attack. Attack, however, the communist regimes did. Officially atheist, they progressively reduced the role of the churches in society, and harried religious leaders and personnel, a hostility reciprocated by Pope Pius XII, who formally excommunicated members of communist parties everywhere. In Poland the Catholic primate, Archbishop Stefan Wyszyński advised his clergy to swear an oath of loyalty to the communist state, but himself refused to do so; he was indefinitely detained, and large numbers of clergy experienced a similar fate. Hungary's primate, Cardinal József Mindszenty, was arrested, tortured and subjected to a show trial in 1949, at the end of which he was sentenced to life imprisonment; he remained in prison until the revolution of October 1956. The communist regimes might confiscate church property and persecute the clergy, but such policies rebounded on them in terms of public opinion. Such persecution even seems to have made religion popular again, after a long period of increasingly secular attitudes in the first half of the century. Because religion stood for a set of values outside the communist system, churches despite their fundamental conservatism came to be seen as defenders of human rights. The treatment of religion was a principal cause of communism's waxing unpopularity.

The fumbling and often half-hearted efforts of individual regimes to plot a 'new course' thus risked exacerbating already existing discontents, as shown by the disturbances of 1953. Two external factors added to the unstable mix of regime indecision and popular dissatisfaction. One was the Soviets' formal reconciliation with Tito in 1955. The other was the bombshell lobbed into loyal communists' minds by Khrushchev's 'secret speech' of February 1956.

It is worth analysing the impact produced in the rest of Eastern Europe by the Soviets' admission that 'Titoism' was no longer the devil with horns, and that what came to be called 'socialist polycentrism', or the forging of different paths to the same goal, was permissible.

At Stalin's death the rift between the Yugoslavs and the rest of the communist world seemed unbridgeable. Tito's government was aware that neighbouring communist countries at Soviet urging had drawn up plans for an invasion of Yugoslavia, which had only been averted by the greater distraction of the Korean War in 1950. East European regimes had spent years drumming up hysteria about infiltration by Titoist agents, the purges of 1949–52 had been designed to root out alleged Titoists like Rajk and Slánský, and Yugoslavia was generally depicted as a cat's paw of Western imperialism. The lead in mending bridges was undertaken by Khrushchev, who early in 1954 felt confident enough of his position to suggest that the break with Tito had been a 'mistake' on Stalin's part. More important, Khrushchev was convinced that reconciliation would send out a global signal that the new Soviet leaders were less confrontational; it was also desirable, on security grounds, to entice Yugoslavia back into the Soviet fold if possible. Khrushchev had to contend with the opposition of Stalinist hardliners, with whom it was an article of faith that 'Tito was and remains anti-Soviet'.[10]

By 1955, however, Khrushchev was sufficiently in the ascendant to ignore these objections, and in May he and other top Soviets flew to Belgrade. Khrushchev blamed the decision to break with Yugoslavia on Beria, rather than Stalin, and made the crucial concession that he still regarded the Yugoslav communists as Marxist-Leninists. In response, the Yugoslavs made it clear they agreed, but retained the right to be Marxist-Leninist in their own way. Despite their gratification at being vindicated of deviationism, the Yugoslavs also stuck to their claim to be more in line with orthodox Marxist-Leninism than the overtly centralised Stalinist model. According to the Yugoslavs, Yugoslavia's communism was based on 'direct democracy, guaranteeing the maximum amount of democratic workers' self-government through managerial bodies.'[11] In practice, the Yugoslav model was still a top-down command economy, in which the leading role of the party was never yielded; and the much-vaunted independence of workers was less real than advertised. Obstreperous dissidents like Milovan Djilas paid for their temerity in pointing this out with expulsion from the party and years in prison. On the other hand, the Yugoslav Party itself was progressively decentralised, passing more decision-making to the parties of individual republics. There was greater liberty to engage in private enterprise; collectivisation of agriculture was steadily reversed; and Yugoslavia's openness to world trade, including Western tourism, did gradually make the country unique in the communist world, not least because Yugoslavia never did join the Soviet-dominated Warsaw Pact, founded in 1955.

Just as important was the effect of Soviet-Yugoslav reconciliation in Eastern Europe. This was implicit in the declaration issued at the end of Khrushchev's visit, which effectively endorsed the right of all the 'people's democracies' to follow their own path to socialism. Both sides celebrated 'Faithfulness to the principles of mutual respect and non-intervention in internal affairs for whatever reason, economic, political or ideological, because matters of internal organisation, of different social systems, and different forms of socialist development remain solely the concern of each country individually.'[12] This promising assumption was to be tested to destruction within the next year and a half. In the meantime, however, Tito openly suggested that East bloc leaders who had committed Stalinist excesses had some questions to answer, in

---

[10] Quoted in Fejtö, F., 1974, *A History of the People's Democracies: Eastern Europe since Stalin*, translated from the French by D. Weissbrot, Harmondsworth, 55.
[11] Quoted in Fejtö, *A History of the People's Democracies*, 55.
[12] Quoted in Fejtö, *A History of the People's Democracies*, 55, 58.

particular those who, in the Rajk and Slánský show trials, 'had shed the blood of innocent communists.'[13] It soon became apparent that quite a few people in neighbouring countries agreed with Tito.

Finally, Khrushchev himself lifted the lid of Pandora's box with his 'secret speech'. Made to a closed session of the Soviet Communist Party's twentieth congress in February 1956, but at which leaders from the East European parties were also present, this was the most forthright acknowledgement to date that Stalin – Khrushchev was careful not to implicate himself and his colleagues – had unjustly condemned untold thousands of fellow communists and other unfortunates to death or imprisonment. Stalin was thus made the scapegoat for all the evils of the communist system. Khrushchev charged Stalin with responsibility for the mass arrests, deportations, executions and show trials, and for the ostracism of Tito's Yugoslavia which had divided the communist world. Stalin, in short, had brought the entire ideology into discredit; it was up to committed communists to rescue the project.

The secret speech did not remain secret for long. In April the Polish Party leadership, now led by Edvard Ochab following Bierut's death in March, decided to brief party members; at one meeting four members fainted in horror at the revelations. By this point leaked copies of the transcript were circulating, and by June the US State Department was able to publish the text. For the benefit of anyone who had not yet heard of it, the speech was then broadcast in multiple languages by Radio Free Europe and other Western media. Not all communist regimes thought it wise to communicate anything but a watered-down version to their publics since, with good reason, they feared the consequences; but the damage was already done. For, whereas in the Soviet Union communism had been the established system for two generations, in Eastern Europe it had been imposed only a short time, and popular revulsion at the revelations of the secret speech was all the stronger.

The Polish challenge 1953–6

Poland, as even Stalin acknowledged, was a special case. There was much bad blood in Russo-Polish relations, and the events of the war had done nothing to improve matters. Even Polish communists, who owed their accession to power to the Soviets, had reason to fear and resent them: those, like Gomułka, who survived the war by not being in the Soviet Union knew perfectly well that numerous comrades had perished in Stalin's purges, and many of them then endured all the suffering of the period 1948–53. Yet there was no escaping the

---

[13] Quoted in Fejtö, *A History of the People's Democracies*, 59.

bear's embrace. Control of Poland was deemed essential for Soviet security, and as a result Soviet officials played a prominent role in Communist Poland from the start. The Polish minister of defence and commander-in-chief of the armed forces, notoriously, was the Soviet Marshal Konstanty Rokossovsky, who insisted on seeding the officer corps with strategically placed Russians. As in East Germany, Soviet 'advisers' sat in on decision-making at every level of the Polish Party-state, and the defence offered by Polish communists for this state of affairs was always that any attempt to dispute this would have been fruitless. The Polish Party, it was argued, acted as an indispensable intermediary between Soviet power and the Polish people.

Despite these constraints, Poland was ripe for de-Stalinisation. Collectivisation was a disaster, alienating millions of peasant farmers; the persecution of the Catholic Church outraged even greater numbers in what was still a deeply religious society; and above all Poland's demonstrable vassalage offended Poles' well-developed sense of nationhood. These grievances, moreover, were shared by a significant number of party members, some of whom, like Gomułka, had already expressed reservations about the nature and pace of Stalinism, and had paid for this personally. The party was thus split between a blindly obedient Stalinist wing, and a pragmatic faction increasingly convinced that communism would only work in Poland if the Polish Party were truly in charge of things. In short, this was an argument for a form of 'national communism'.

Signs of a thaw in the regime started after Stalin's death with a (non-lethal) purge of the UB, Poland's secret police. In December 1953 a top security official, Colonel Józef Swiatło, defected to the West; the following year he started broadcasting his memoirs from Munich into Poland, and horrified the Polish public by detailing widespread abuses of power, including torture and blackmail, and the extent to which the Soviets effectively supervised the Polish security service. In particular, Swiatło highlighted the injustice done to loyal, patriotic party members like Gomułka. By the end of 1954 Bierut decided to transfer the notorious public security minister, Władysław Radkiewicz, to another post; at the same time Gomułka was quietly released from house arrest.

Over the next year a combination of increased relaxation of control by the regime, a greater boldness on the part of party members and intellectuals in demanding change, and a certain intangible but unmistakable pressure from below produced a snowball effect. In January 1955 the party formally acknowledged the unjust and repressive nature of the Stalinist period, and condemned its own record. Crucial was the leadership's decision to relax censorship. Younger party members started criticising the leadership openly in the weekly *Po prostu* (Straight Talk), and discussion groups like the popular *Krzywe Koło* (Crooked Circle) sprang up across the country. Taking advantage of the regime's greater tolerance, a breakaway Union of Communist Youth was formed, and university campuses became hotbeds of increasingly frank debate. The summer of 1955 saw Warsaw host the World Youth Festival, in accordance with an international commitment the regime soon wished it had not undertaken. Over several weeks an influx of foreigners, including left-wing students, musicians and artists, wearing Western or exotic ethnic clothes, listening to and playing Western music like jazz, hitherto frowned upon in the Soviet bloc as 'decadent', and with an altogether more liberated attitude towards discussion as well as personal relationships, 'broke a permanent hole in Poland's isolation', and made the younger generation's appetite for change all the stronger.[14] Exposure to outside contacts also showed up the falsity of communist propaganda; as one young musician recalled, 'Young people from the capitalist world were healthy and well-dressed, even though we'd been told that everything there is bad.'[15] Pressure for more such contacts with the wider world induced the regime to permit the first international festival for 'new music' at Warsaw in October 1956, which happened to coincide exactly with the political convulsion of that month. The successful outcome of the 'Polish October' resulted in a continuation of the festival over the next decade, multiplying connections between not just Polish but Soviet and East bloc musicians and what a recent study calls the 'transnational new-music community.'[16]

The stage was therefore set for even greater ferment in 1956, following the revelations of Khrushchev's secret speech, whose repercussions were particularly strong in Poland. Bierut died in Moscow shortly after the speech, his demise possibly hastened by dread of its implications; the new first secretary, Ochab, was a moderate anxious to de-Stalinise. As in Hungary, however, pressure for change from below threatened to outstrip anything the party was willing to contemplate. Most alarming was a recurrence of activism among the working class. In April workers at the Żerań motor works in Warsaw demanded, to the horror of visiting politburo members, more democratic government, greater press freedom, and a more equal relationship with the Soviet Union.

Ochab nevertheless took a step potentially creating far greater ferment, when his government started releasing political prisoners. In the spring of 1956 between 30,000 and 40,000 victims of the Stalinist purges, as well as former Home Army members, gradually reappeared in Polish society. The effect of this, as elsewhere, is hard to exaggerate. Loyal communists who had escaped the purges learned for the first time that party comrades had been arrested, tortured and subjected to extreme suffering and humiliation, all for nothing. Ordinary citizens were even more inclined to see these revelations as confirming all their objections to Soviet-imposed communism. Party members, for the most part, still wanted to believe that communism could be made to

---

[14] Ascherson, N., 1987, *The Struggles for Poland*, London, 152.
[15] Quoted in Applebaum, *Iron Curtain*, 447.
[16] Jakelski, L., 2013, *Making New Music in Cold War Poland: The Warsaw Autumn Festival 1956-1968*, Berkeley, CA, 136.

work; but the trajectory that later led to full rejection of the ideology really started at this point.

On 28 June came an explosion: outraged by yet another attempt to raise production schedules, and after a failed effort to negotiate a better deal with the government, workers in Poznań took to the streets, demanding 'bread and freedom' – a significant pairing – as well as 'Russians out!' and 'Down with the Muscovites!' They also waved the national flag, sang hymns, denounced the Soviet Union and, fatally, attacked UB headquarters and local party offices. Weapons were seized and in the mayhem shots were fired. This was enough for the government to order in the army and security forces. At the end of this day-long rebellion, there were an estimated fifty-four dead, 300 wounded and several hundred arrested.

Poznań was a wake-up call for the PUWP, even if it showed that, for any repressive regime, reacting swiftly and brutally to such demonstrations is probably the surest way to contain them; the pressure-cooker lid can, at least temporarily, be screwed firmly shut. Some Polish communists, however, took the hint that the answer to discontent was to continue with de-Stalinisation. As the prime minister, Józef Cyrankiewicz, admitted, 'Our chief concern is to raise the standard of living of the working population as quickly as possible.'[17] There was an enquiry into the Poznań disturbances, which dismissed the suggestion that they were the result of Western incitement, and concluded that 'the workers' demands were justified in the main.'[18] Not everyone agreed with this dispassionate analysis, however, and as the summer progressed a split developed between de-Stalinisers and hardliners, who supported the Soviet line that the unrest was indeed the result of western subversion. In this face-off the de-Stalinisers increasingly turned towards Gomułka who, although no longer a member, was one of the few leading communists with the prestige and the popular support to implement change without abandoning the party's leading role. Ochab appointed more moderates to the politburo, and Gomułka was finally readmitted to the party early in August; the Soviets' well-known suspicion of him as a 'national deviationist' froze matters there. In the meantime the pressure from below did not abate. There was a million-strong festival of the Virgin at Częstochowa in August, which showed the undimmed popularity of the church. Those arrested at Poznań were tried in September, in a process remarkably open by Soviet bloc standards, and were given remarkably lenient sentences. Unrest and outspoken hostility to Soviet influence continued to roil the factories, and Gomułka consolidated his popular appeal by demanding his reinstatement as party leader, as well as the recall of Rokossovsky to Moscow.

The struggle between hardliners and moderates peaked in October with an attempt by the former to engineer an internal coup. Ochab at this point

---

[17] Quoted in Fejtö, *A History of the People's Democracies*, 97.
[18] Quoted in Fejtö, *A History of the People's Democracies*, 97.

threw in his lot with the moderates, and recommended adoption of Gomułka's agenda; a central committee meeting was called for 19 October to debate this. In support of both Gomułka and Ochab, workers' committees, party intellectuals and even elements of the secret policy and army mobilised to face down the hardliners.

The Soviet reaction was a dramatic one. On 19 October Khrushchev himself, accompanied by politburo members, the commander of Warsaw Pact forces and eleven Soviet generals, flew uninvited into Warsaw to attend the Polish Party's Eighth Plenum in person. Simultaneously Soviet forces assembled on Poland's borders, east and west, and armoured units in Poland were ordered up to the capital. In response, Ochab and the central committee dug in their heels, co-opting Gomułka and three other reformers onto the committee and accepting Gomułka's candidacy to become party leader, in Ochab's place; only then did the Polish Politburo meet with their unexpected Soviet guests.

Khrushchev, famous for his crudity and bluster, started by flatly accusing Gomułka of being a closet nationalist, intent on abandoning socialism and taking Poland out of the Warsaw Pact. In an eyeball-to-eyeball confrontation stretching into the early hours of the 20th, the Polish Politburo, Gomułka included, finally convinced the Soviet leader that his fears were misplaced. Gomułka, like Tito before him, stressed that he considered himself no less committed a communist than Khrushchev, but that the Poles, like the Yugoslavs, simply had to run their own show. Symbolically, it was agreed that Rokossovsky would return to the Soviet Union, and that the Soviet presence within the Polish party-state would be much less visible in future. In return, Gomułka undertook to suppress expressions of anti-Soviet sentiment, and to accept the continuing presence of Soviet troops on Polish soil as a vital link in Warsaw Pact defences. On this understanding, the Soviets backed down, and once Khrushchev had departed, Gomułka was able to speak as leader of the party to the crowd waiting outside. For the first time in Poland a communist leader's address was greeted with rapturous applause, as Gomułka promised that collectivisation would not only stop but would be reversed; that the Poznań workers had been legitimately protesting; and, crucially, that 'There can be different types of socialism.'[19] A formal Polish-Soviet treaty confirmed these points on 14 November.

The Polish revolution of 1956, if that is the right term, was a victory for autonomy within the communist system, rather than a defeat for communism. For the first time, an East European party won recognition of the right to do things differently, according to what it deemed necessary, and as long as Soviet security concerns and the carapace of ideological conformity were maintained. In the longer term Gomułka's rule proved to be as autocratic and unimaginative

---

[19] Quoted in Bethell, N., 1972, *Gomułka: His Poland and His Communism*, Harmondsworth, 215.

as all the other communist regimes, with the result that by the end of the 1960s a whole new set of discontents had bubbled to the surface over the regime's abysmal economic record. In 1956 Poland effected a personnel change, rather than systemic change, but in so doing it avoided the fate that overtook Hungary a few weeks later.

The Hungarian revolution 1953–6

Poland and Hungary offer parallel cases of an attempt to de-Stalinise in the face of hardline, Stalinist resistance. But whereas the Polish communists were able to get away with a self-managed transition to 'national communism', in Hungary events rapidly escalated into a full-blown nationalist revolt against Soviet domination, with tragic results. Each case raised the recurring question of whether the communist system was reformable at all.

By 1953 there was no shortage of Hungarian communists convinced that a more humane, consensual way of 'doing' communism was possible, and who wanted to respond to the Soviets' call for de-Stalinisation. Charting a 'new course', however, was arguably even more problematic for the Hungarian Communist Party, because of the ferocity of the purges conducted under Mátyás Rákosi. Rákosi, a textbook specimen of the lifelong, fanatical communist, had served Béla Kun's Soviet Republic, spent seventeen years in the Horthy regime's prisons and survived Stalin's purges, and his paranoia rivalled Stalin's own. Rákosi's ruthlessness in pushing through a programme of extreme Sovietisation, and eliminating rivals like Rajk, made it difficult for him to contemplate any form of relaxation, and he waged a bitter rearguard campaign against the advocates of change. Even the Soviets found Rákosi difficult to budge. In June 1953 they literally ordered him to initiate de-Stalinisation by scaling back his cult of personality; one way of signalling a new course, they suggested, was to separate the offices of party leader and prime minister, both occupied by Rákosi. As someone recalled, Rákosi 'had objections to everyone whose name was mentioned; he had something against everyone. Everyone was suspect, except him alone.'[20] Nevertheless, even Rákosi could hardly withstand Soviet pressure, and he reluctantly accepted the Soviets' suggestion of Imre Nagy as prime minister, while retaining the party leadership.

Nagy, like Rákosi, was another lifelong communist and 'Muscovite' who returned from exile in the Soviet Union, but who had emerged with clean hands from the Stalinist period. When, as prime minister, he duly announced a new course, it turned out he meant it. Sensationally, Nagy made this announcement

[20] Quoted in Gati, C., 1986, *Hungary and the Soviet Bloc*, Durham, NC, 131.

publicly on 4 July 1953, before the Hungarian parliament, rather than to the party central committee behind closed doors. There was to be an immediate relaxation of collectivisation: peasants were given the option of leaving the hated collective farms, with the result that some 500 closed within the year. Nagy also reduced investment in heavy industry, and stressed the need for improving the supply of consumer goods; in the course of his first year in office living standards went up 15 per cent. Most daringly, Nagy released most of the 150,000 surviving victims of Rákosi's purges, and closed labour camps; coupled with this came the admission that 'rehabilitation' – in the macabre jargon of communism – was due the victims, both living and dead. Nagy even had Gábor Péter, the former secret police chief, arrested for 'trespassing against socialist legality'; Péter was given a life sentence in April 1954, with Rákosi characteristically blaming everything on him.[21]

What Nagy meant by his version of the 'new course' has since been sifted out of his speeches, together with a short book he wrote while out of office in 1955–6, subsequently published abroad as *On Communism* (1957), and the lengthy reflections he produced while awaiting trial and eventual execution in 1956–8. These sources suggest that Nagy was one of the few prominent communists left by the early 1950s who genuinely believed in what a later reformer, Alexander Dubček, called 'socialism with a human face'. Nagy was convinced that a humane, workable socialism was only possible with popular participation in the political process, even by non-communists. Stalinism had, in Nagy's opinion, turned socialism upside-down, and by its totalitarian methods risked alienating everyone. As he put it, 'Power is increasingly being torn away from the people and turned sharply against them.'[22] Strikingly, Nagy appeared willing to return to the coalition politics of 1944–7, in other words to a multiparty system. He specifically proposed, on attaining power in 1953, a 'popular people's front' of this type. Later, he claimed to rediscover in Marx an emphasis on morality and justice. True socialism, for Nagy, must defend 'the most simple basic laws of morals and justice, which must rule the relations between private individuals, and must also be the chief laws governing the contacts between nations.'[23] Clearly, Nagy was something of an idealist, a theoretician in politics; it seems strange that such a personality should have survived the Rákosi era at all. Nevertheless, the tinge of otherworldliness and sincerity in this bespectacled and decidedly uncharismatic communist endowed Nagy with an undoubted moral authority and prestige.

Nagy did not have an easy ride, despite owing his elevation to the Soviets; on the contrary, Rákosi and his fellow Stalinists did what they could to obstruct

---

[21] Quoted in Litván, G. (ed.), 1996, *The Hungarian Revolution of 1956: Reform, Revolt and Repression 1953-1963*, London and New York, 207.
[22] Quoted in Swain, G. and Swain, N., 2003, *Eastern Europe since 1945*, 3rd edn, Basingstoke and New York, 85.
[23] Quoted in Swain and Swain, *Eastern Europe since 1945*, 85.

the new course, emboldened by the power struggle going on in the Kremlin at the same time. Rákosi's position as party leader enabled him to delay and even sabotage Nagy's economic policy, and he instilled a hesitancy regarding the new policies among local party officials, who were uncertain whom to obey and, like Rákosi, fearful of relinquishing control. In October 1954 Nagy appealed to the central committee, which endorsed his reforms by a substantial majority; by March 1955, however, Nagy's position was undermined by events in the Soviet Union, where the politburo were experiencing doubts about slowing down industrialisation. Rákosi seized this opportunity to mount a full-scale attack on Nagy for his alleged 'rightist deviation', his talk of a multiparty system and his poor economic management – itself the result of Rákosi's obstructive tactics. Sensing a change in the wind blowing from Moscow, the central committee agreed to sack Nagy as prime minister, and expelled him from the party in April. A further seeming discouragement to reform came with the formation, in May 1955, of the Warsaw Pact. From the Soviet viewpoint, this was a defensive reaction to the West's NATO; but the treaty establishing the pact specifically provided for 'mutual fraternal aid' between the countries of Eastern Europe, a principle which made nonsense of the agreement they stitched up with Tito that year, but which was evoked by the Soviets in both 1956 and 1968.

Rákosi's victory, however, was a pyrrhic one, since it was becoming increasingly clear that he was not in a position to reimpose full-blown Stalinism. Shortly after Nagy's dismissal the Soviets yet again changed tack by reconciling with Tito, thereby reaffirming their tolerance of 'separate paths to socialism'. This had a wide-ranging effect throughout Eastern Europe, because of its implicit condemnation of Stalinist conformity, and of those, like Rákosi, who had so brutally enforced it. Nor did the Soviets hide their opinion that Rákosi should step down, since it was obvious he had little remaining support within the party. In Hungary, as in Poland, the cumulative effect of Nagy's two-year premiership, the release of political prisoners and the confusing signals coming from Moscow was that pressure for change, and above all for a free discussion of what change was needed, was mounting. The role of the Hungarian Party's press was crucial here, as was the example of intellectuals who, in characteristically East European fashion, saw themselves as standard-bearers. In October 1955, for example, the Writers' Association, naturally a party-dominated body, demanded the lifting of censorship, and Rákosi reluctantly agreed. A discussion group, the Petőfi Circle, named after the nineteenth-century poet (and nationalist icon) Sándor Petőfi, was founded in March 1956; after a few private meetings to test the waters its organisers held their first public discussion, an event attracting thousands. By the summer the Petőfi Circle meetings had become mass events, increasingly critical of the party leadership.

Something like a revolution in public and party sentiment was set in motion when, in March, the government announced the 'rehabilitation' of László

Rajk, the senior communist executed in 1949. Many party members, who had believed the charges against Rajk, felt betrayed by the admission of party error; worse, they felt shamed by their own approval of Rajk's liquidation at the time. Two days after the announcement, the writer Sándor Lukácsi openly accused Rákosi at a party meeting of being 'a Judas whose hands are red with Rajk's blood.'[24] People started referring to Rákosi as 'the bald murderer'. By this point, too, copies of Khrushchev's 'secret speech' were beginning to circulate in Hungarian translation, despite Rákosi's attempts to suppress it. The effect was particularly strong in Hungary because the speech specifically acknowledged the murder of Béla Kun and other Hungarian communists in the 1930s.

Rákosi's fall was finally triggered by the Poznań riots in Poland at the end of June, an event Rákosi took as justification for a purge of Nagy and his supporters. The Soviet leadership, however, got wind of Rákosi's plans and stepped in again, bluntly ordering him to resign. On 18 July Rákosi complied, opting for retirement in the Soviet Union, rather than risk it in Hungary. The Soviets clearly intended to dump Rákosi, but they hesitated to reinstate a thoroughgoing reformer like Nagy. As a result, Rákosi's successor was Ernő Gerő, basically a Stalinist from Rákosi's stable, but whose presence at the top, the Soviets hoped, would be balanced by the appointment to the politburo of János Kádár, a survivor of Rákosi's purges and an avowed de-Staliniser.

As with Gomułka in Poland, the fact that Nagy remained frozen out of party counsels only increased the discontent; the pressure for more meaningful change was now intense. On 6 October, the funeral of the 'rehabilitated' Rajk became the occasion for a massive, but peaceful, demonstration of between 250,000 and 300,000 people in Budapest, with Nagy heading the procession. Like any other movement for change, the sheer number of people who turned out for Rajk's obsequies was a powerful catalyst for change, because it showed the strength of popular feeling. Gerő, conscious of the fragility of his position, responded by readmitting Nagy to the Communist Party on 13 October. On the 16th students at the University of Szeged, in southern Hungary, organised their own, non-party union, and called on students elsewhere to affiliate with them. On 20 October came news of the confrontation in Warsaw between Gomułka and the Soviets, the result of which was so obviously a defeat for the latter that it produced an immediate effect in Hungary too. The students of Budapest University now joined the Szeged non-Party union, and on 22 October issued a sixteen-point agenda calling for Nagy's reappointment as prime minister, multiparty elections, and the withdrawal of Soviet troops from Hungary.

What was striking about the students' resolution, which quickly attracted mass support, was the strongly nationalist tone, for instance the demand that

---

[24] Quoted in Fejtö, *A History of the People's Democracies*, 82.

the Soviet red star be replaced by the coat of arms associated with Hungary's leader in 1848–9, Lajos Kossuth. The resolution also proposed, for 23 October, a march to the statue of József Bem, a Polish general who fought on Hungary's side in 1848, a deliberate gesture of solidarity with the Poles. The huge crowd which turned out on the afternoon of the 23rd, swelled by non-students of all kinds, remained in place throughout the day, and got progressively more vocal. Their most insistent demands were for the students' resolution to be broadcast on state radio, and for Nagy to be appointed prime minister. Instead, at 8 pm they got a radio broadcast by Gerő, denouncing their 'nationalistic demonstration' as 'counter-revolutionary'. At 9 pm, Nagy finally addressed the crowd, and quickly found he had to abandon the usual communist greeting of 'comrades' in order to be heard at all. To everyone's disappointment, Nagy urged people to disperse; but the mood was by now too volatile. Shortly after, some demonstrators committed the first overtly revolutionary act, which was to tear down the huge post-war statue of Stalin on Heroes' Square; the photographs taken the next day by foreign journalists, showing fragments of Stalin's head being abused by passers-by, broadcast to the world a clear demonstration of how bitterly Soviet domination was resented. Another crowd besieged the central radio station, demanding that the students' resolution be broadcast in response to Gerő's. The AVH forces guarding the building fired into the demonstrators; the latter, supplied with arms by sympathetic regular police and troops from nearby barracks, stormed the station. Gerő, hearing of this first armed confrontation, appealed to the Soviets for back-up, and by midnight Soviet tanks were appearing on the streets of Budapest. Confused fighting continued through the night between the demonstrators on one side, and the AVH and the Soviets on the other.

It was clear even to the Soviets, monitoring the situation closely, that Gerő had lost control of events, and with Soviet approval Nagy was reappointed premier, with Kádár as party first secretary. The reasoning in Moscow was evidently that only moderates like Nagy and Kádár could control matters. In the meantime, however, heavy fighting continued for the next five days in Budapest and elsewhere between the Soviets and the supporters of change. The initial fighters, taking on Soviet tanks with 'Molotov cocktails' and what arms they had seized from the AVH, were soon joined by much of the regular Hungarian army, from 28 October under the leadership of Colonel Pál Maléter. Certainly the popular perception of the Soviets as foreign oppressors was coming more to the foreground, rendering the position of the new administration an extremely difficult one.

There has been debate ever since as to the nature of events in Hungary in 1956. Was it, as many immediately assumed in the West, a national, anti-communist uprising? Or was it something more complicated, a movement in favour of reforming, but not abolishing, the communist system, which then got hijacked by what the Soviets and party hardliners subsequently insisted were 'bourgeois counter-revolutionaries'?

In truth there was much of both. Nagy and his supporters within the HWP undoubtedly hoped to save communism by somehow making it more humane and democratic. In addition, some contemporary observers saw the emergence across the country of workers' committees as evidence of a genuine social revolution. The British left-wing journalist Peter Fryer claimed – to the consternation of the British Communist Party – that there was a real 'people's revolution' going on, and that everyone he spoke to was adamant they did not want to dismantle socialism.[25] However, the evidence collected from eyewitness afterwards points to something more than mere social protest. According to Bill Lomax, another contemporary observer, the ubiquitous revolutionary councils were for the most part explicitly anti-Soviet; more significantly, the demands they relayed to the new government in Budapest consistently listed the need for multiparty elections by secret ballot, the release of Cardinal Mindszenty, the withdrawal of Soviet troops and Hungary's secession from the Warsaw Pact. The mood on the street was both anti-Russian and anti-communist. In the words of one student, 'We spoke less about political subjects, but if we did, we were cursing the Russians.' Another remembered, 'There was a wild anti-communist spirit rampant.'[26] Working-class insurgents were among the most outspoken: 'The workers didn't believe in anything the communists promised them.'[27] Even Nagy, despite his prestige, began to lose support as long as he remained unclear as to whether he would place himself at the head of this groundswell; he was trapped between the pressure of popular support and the fear of Soviet reaction.

The dilemma was real, and it was not long before events spiralled out of control. No sooner had Nagy, on 27 October, announced the formation of a Patriotic People's Front government, than it became apparent the HWP was disintegrating. Real control outside Budapest was exercised by the revolutionary councils, and all their demands pointed towards radicalisation. On 28 October Nagy entered into negotiations with the insurgents, largely to ensure public order, while at the same time the Soviets agreed to withdraw their forces; on the 29th Nagy abolished the hated AVH. On the 30th the councils rejected the PPF cabinet, demanding a coalition based on a multiparty system. Nagy conceded this and recognised the councils as 'democratic organs of local autonomy', on which the government would rely for support.[28] The former parties of the pre-communist period rapidly reconstituted themselves. Cardinal

---

[25] Fryer, P., 1957, *Hungarian Tragedy*, London, 52–3.
[26] Quoted in Lomax, B., 1976, *Hungary 1956*, London, 155.
[27] Lomax, *Hungary 1956*, 156.
[28] Quoted in Crampton, R.J., 1997, *Eastern Europe in the Twentieth Century – And After*, 2nd edn, London, 298.

Mindszenty was released from house arrest. Twenty-five new, non-communist newspapers started publication.

It could not last. The official Soviet reaction, on 30 October, was to sanction a coalition government, as long as the socialist economic model was not abandoned, and Hungary remained part of the Warsaw Pact. Behind the scenes, however, the Soviet leadership was coming to the conclusion that matters had gone too far. Their decision on the 31st to intervene militarily was strengthened by the Suez crisis in the Middle East; with the United States at odds with Britain and France over this issue, the possibility of any concerted western response to a Soviet invasion of Hungary, already remote, was made even less likely.

On 1 November, as it became obvious that Soviet units were massing on Hungary's borders, a desperate Nagy announced that Hungary was leaving the Warsaw Pact, and henceforth considered itself a neutral state, like Austria; coupled with this was an appeal to the United Nations for assistance. No such assistance, in the context of the Cold War, was ever likely: apart from the distraction of Suez, the American government, however much it might denounce the Soviet intervention, had no intention of disturbing the status quo in Europe, which included Soviet hegemony in Eastern Europe. The full Soviet invasion commenced on 4 November, and once again Hungarian freedom fighters disputed the streets of Budapest and elsewhere with Soviet armour, an unequal struggle which was over by the 14th, at a cost of 2,500 Hungarian and 700 Soviet dead, 20,000 Hungarian and 1,500 Soviet wounded. Kádár, who remained a member of Nagy's government until 1 November, disappeared for the next week, only to resurface on the 7th in the wake of the Soviet forces, having volunteered to re-establish communist, and Soviet, control. Kádár's subsequent crackdown was brutal. Some 20,000 people were imprisoned; 341 were executed. An estimated 200,000 fled to the West. Nagy, who had sought refuge in the Yugoslav embassy, was eventually lured out by a promise of safe conduct abroad, and promptly arrested. Together with Maléter and the journalist Miklós Gimes, he was executed in June 1958.

Conclusion

The Kádár regime in Hungary lasted until the late 1980s, and from the 1960s became one of the most liberal of the East European Communist dictatorships. In Eastern Europe the effect of the Soviet invasion was to reaffirm communist rule, and with it Soviet hegemony. In the longer term, the suppression of the Hungarian revolt had a profoundly demoralising effect not just in Hungary, but in the rest of the Soviet bloc and among communists around the world. The events of 1956 prompted many individuals to abandon their belief in communism for good.

This progressive hollowing-out of East European communism as a belief system was the paradoxical result of 1956: while communist dictatorship was outwardly entrenched, internally any claim it might ever have had to legitimacy was destroyed. A system which could only be maintained by force was not one likely to command allegiance. What remained was a pretence. Poland in 1956 shook off day-to-day Soviet control, but remained locked into a command economy which proved increasingly inefficient and sclerotic; by the late 1960s the inadequacies of this system threatened new eruptions of popular discontent. In Hungary outward conformity was achieved, at the price of inward distaste and cynicism. In the rest of the Soviet bloc the party-state was reinforced, but regimes were on the whole more reluctant than ever to countenance change or experimentation. Quite apart from the question of whether the system was reformable, there was little enthusiasm for finding out. Only in Yugoslavia, which remained a maverick regime, was there a continuing tinkering with the mechanics of communism; and in Albania, for reasons to be explained, a completely different turn was taken in the 1960s, towards a model emulating Communist China.

In the final analysis both Poland and Hungary, for different reasons, could be said to have got Stalinism out of their systems after 1956. What remained was still communism, but both regimes evolved their own way of being communist. In the rest of the region there was less incentive to change.

14

Last chance saloon? The Prague Spring of 1968

The spectacle of Soviet control reimposed on Hungary through the barrels of tanks, in 1956, was a terrible own goal for communism as an economic and political system. It suggested that only force would keep Eastern Europe communist and that the natural desire of East European peoples for independence was bound to break through again.

In 1968 there was another attempt, not to overthrow the communist system, but to reform it from within. What was dubbed the 'Prague Spring' was an experiment in controlled change which attracted genuinely popular support in Czechoslovakia; but this perhaps inevitably pushed things beyond the bounds of the permissible in Soviet eyes. It transpired that the margins of Soviet tolerance for experimentation were very narrow indeed.

This chapter first examines the basic problem confronting all the communist regimes in Eastern Europe by the 1960s. An ideology committed to achieving a classless, equal society by nationalising the means of production, while at the same time suppressing all non-communist political activity, had produced a series of identikit tyrannies without delivering sustainable economic growth. By 1960 economic stagnation was becoming undeniable to all but the most ideologically blinkered, and economists were beginning to wrestle with the problem. They came to the same conclusion: growth could only be restored by injecting new stimuli into the economy, principally some elements of a free market. The question was how to achieve this. It was on this question of economic rejuvenation that the theorists bumped into a sort of glass ceiling: any truly fruitful discussion of economic measures logically implied a loosening of political constraints, to enable genuine debate. Yet political liberalisation in turn implied questioning the leading role of the Communist Party. It was this glass ceiling that the reformers of the Prague Spring ran up against.

The chapter also provides a general survey of the East European landscape between 1956 and 1968. After the 1956 upheavals there was little appetite for tinkering; for the most part the communist regimes remained stuck in neo-Stalinist stasis. Only in Hungary, paradoxically, did the Kádár regime begin to achieve a more liberal form of communism, while Yugoslavia continued to forge a unique path of its own. In the three democratic exceptions, Finland, Austria and Greece, quite different traditions prevailed.

The chapter finishes with an account of Dubček's brave but possibly naïve attempt at 'socialism with a human face', terminated dramatically by the Soviet invasion of August 1968. The result was to choke off any residual belief in communism's reformability.

The basic problem

We cannot understand 1968 without appreciating that, by the 1960s, there was a growing realisation even among communists that the Soviet-style command economy was not working.

This awareness was shared by Soviet as well as East European observers, at least the more economically literate among them. The Soviet economist Abel Aganbegyan, in June 1965, submitted a secret report to the Politburo which concluded that the Soviet Union's growth rate, in marked contrast to that of the United States, was slowing down, and that this was primarily due to the high level of Soviet defence spending, and the centralisation and lack of accountability in economic matters. This shocked the Soviet leaders, most of whom took the economic growth of the past for granted, and indeed assumed that communism itself was the only guarantee of rising living standards. In response the regime of Leonid Brezhnev, Khrushchev's successor since 1964, attempted a variety of minor reforms designed to give managers greater freedom, but without the crucial freedom to set their own prices, and dismiss surplus workers, these had little effect. Nor was the Soviet system terribly good at introducing new technology, despite Soviet successes in the space race.

These signs of the Soviet model's limitations were hardly confined to the Soviet Union. By the early 1960s the story across communist Eastern Europe was one of slowing growth, even stagnation. Czechoslovakia's economic growth peaked in 1960 at 11.7 per cent, but was down to 6.2 per cent in 1962, and stopped completely the next year. Poland's economy, always sluggish despite the virtual abandonment of collectivisation and a partial legalisation of private enterprise, remained hamstrung by Gomułka's insistence on central control; the country had a permanent trade deficit, because it had little to sell besides agricultural produce and coal, and the standard of living remained poor. Bulgaria, despite the beginnings of a tourist industry relying on holidaymakers from the Soviet bloc, continued to be dependent on the Soviets for aid into the 1960s. East Germany, the only regime apart from Czechoslovakia to have started with an established industrial base, nevertheless saw a decline in industrial growth from 12.4 per cent in 1959 to 6.2 per cent by 1961, its economic viability not enhanced by the steady haemorrhaging of population to West Germany. Only Romania, thanks to abundant natural resources and late industrialisation, broke the trend with growth rates of 9.5 per cent in 1958,

11.1 per cent in 1959, and a startling increase in steel production of 52 per cent; this was due to the construction of a single huge steelworks at Galați, and the expansion of the chemicals industry and shipbuilding.

In the same year as Aganbegyan's report, 1965, the Czech economist Ota Šik alerted his country's leaders to similar problems. Šik also blamed the command economy: the rigid control of all aspects of economic life from the centre, he argued, inevitably impeded growth. Economic recovery, by implication, was only attainable by decentralising, and by readmitting at least some elements of a market economy. Such criticisms were hardly unique to Czechoslovakia. In Hungary too reformers were arguing for market-oriented reform and less centralisation as early as the mid-1950s.

Romania excepted, the problems faced by all the East European communist regimes were basically variants of the Soviet problem. Most of the resources funnelled into their economies in order to kick-start industrialisation – the so-called extensive strategy – had been exhausted by this point, and there was nothing left to put in. The ability to invest further dropped, and with the drop in investment came a tailing off in the provision of consumer goods, in so far as this had ever been addressed. Consequently, growth slowed. And, as the economists realised, an economy which had already nationalised the means of production and banned private enterprise was unable to provide additional stimulus. Since capitalism was identified as inimical to social equality, with no regard to what the future source of wealth might be, the Soviet bloc states remained trapped in an economic cul-de-sac. The disadvantages of following the Soviet model were most apparent in a formerly advanced society like Czechoslovakia. Zdeněk Mlynář, a young Czech sent to Moscow in 1950 to study law, and who returned in 1955, was shocked to realise that the backward conditions of the Soviet Union 'had since been successfully imported into Czechoslovakia.'[1] The problem was arguably even more deep-rooted in the hitherto agrarian societies of the rest of Eastern Europe. As a result, East European societies were ill-equipped to keep up with the modernisation distinguishing the developed world by the mid-twentieth century.

In any honest comparison of the communist system with western societies, the former was bound to come off worse. By the 1960s those few Soviet bloc citizens who could be trusted to travel abroad without defecting knew perfectly well that communist propaganda about the horrors of the capitalist West were, at best, quarter-truths. Free market economies did indeed harbour troubling inequalities of income and opportunity. When it came to the range and quality of consumer goods, however, or the fact that westerners did not queue for goods in short supply, communism's track record was undeniably less impressive. This was vividly illustrated by the so-called kitchen debate

---

[1] Mlynář, Z., 1980, *Night Frost in Prague: The End of Humane Socialism*, translated by Paul Wilson, London, 28.

of July 1959 between Khrushchev and US vice-president Richard Nixon, held at an American exhibition in Moscow on household appliances within the purchasing power of the average American worker. The contrast was most striking for East Germans, some of whom at least were in a position to compare West Germany's post-war 'economic miracle' with their own existence. Equally revealing is the outburst of the Bulgarian Party boss, Todor Zhivkov: 'Ah, what were we playing at when we destroyed private property? What have we put in its place? We can't find a substitute for it.'[2]

Beyond this economic conundrum there loomed the even more intractable problem of the political 'glass ceiling'. Whenever clear-sighted reformers argued for economic rationality, they ran up against the logic of the one-party state, built on the premise that there was no objective truth outside of Marxism-Leninism. No alternative political ideology or movement was permissible, yet the need for fresh thinking was so obvious that communist leaders kept returning to the question of how to foster it. The dilemma was that communists, even the most reform-minded, 'wanted to open up the system while retaining full control over it.'[3]

The events of 1956 only reinforced this nervousness about losing control, and the period after was one of neo-Stalinist backlash. In this context it is worth considering the international dimensions of this debate among communists as to the right strategy. Apart from the maverick Yugoslav regime, there were by the mid-1950s three additional communist states: China, North Korea and North Vietnam. The debate in Eastern Europe was increasingly affected by the views of Mao Tse-tung's Chinese Communist Party, views which led in 1960–1 to an open rift between the Soviets and Red China. This Sino-Soviet breach in turn reflected the shifting constraints of the Cold War as much as doctrinal differences.

One of the central aspects of de-Stalinisation, promoted by Khrushchev after 1953, was the concept of 'peaceful coexistence': although the communist system would inevitably, in Khrushchev's view, overtake the capitalist West, in the meantime the danger of nuclear war made a lessening of international tensions desirable. This was very much a legacy of the Korean War (1950–3), which had scared everyone. In this spirit, too, Khrushchev had promoted reconciliation with Tito in 1955. Mao, by contrast, saw himself as a better Marxist-Leninist than the Soviets and favoured a more confrontational approach to 'western imperialism'. Although Mao's brand of communism was arguably closer to Tito's or Gomułka's 'national communism', Mao was shocked by the Hungarian revolt of 1956, and from the late 1950s criticised Yugoslavia's 'modern revisionism' as weakening socialist solidarity.

---

[2] Quoted in Crampton, R.J., 1997, *Eastern Europe in the Twentieth Century – And After,* 2nd edn, London, 242.
[3] Schöpflin, G., 1993, *Politics in Eastern Europe 1945-1992*, Oxford and Cambridge, MA, 132.

Khrushchev, to preserve a common front with Mao, responded by adopting a markedly cooler tone towards Tito. In November 1957, the Moscow conference of the world's communist parties adopted a resolution crafted largely by Mao which, while reaffirming the Soviet Party's leadership of the global movement, also emphasised the need for the closest cooperation between communist parties, in view of the continuing threat from imperialism. By implication Yugoslavia's 'revisionism', and its flirtation with the West, were incompatible with this. By the spring of 1958 the unrepentant Yugoslavs were being denounced by both Moscow and Beijing for 'national communism'; the Chinese even accused the Yugoslavs of engaging in subversion of East European communist parties on behalf of the United States.

By the end of the decade the Soviet and Chinese leaderships were increasingly at odds, the Soviets adopting a defensive attitude, the Chinese challenging the global status quo. In many respects both states were practising traditional great power politics, each fearful of the other. These differences finally became undeniable in June 1960, at the Romanian Party Congress: in response to Khrushchev's stress on the need for 'peaceful coexistence', the Chinese reiterated the need for constant vigilance against the evils of imperialism, and openly accused the Soviets of 'revisionism'. In November, at the world communist gathering in Moscow, the Chinese with Albanian backing denounced their hosts for betraying the cause of world revolution. China increasingly took over patronage of Albania; the Soviet response of cutting Albanian aid merely drove the latter into China's arms. The world communist movement was split.

Undeterred, Khrushchev launched the 'second de-Stalinisation' in November–December 1961, intensifying his criticisms of Stalin and once again attempting to liberalise party policy without, at the same time, relinquishing one-party control. Khrushchev proclaimed the abandonment of the 'monolithic concept of power'; in other words he was prepared to accept differences of opinion within the confines of communist rule.[4] This was an attempt to square the circle, and yet again the ambiguity of Soviet policy led to confusion as to just what the Soviets were willing to tolerate; 'the distinction between 'reform', the improvement of the existing system, and 'democratisation', the genuine redistribution of power, was never made clear.'[5] Arguably this confusion was at the root of the Prague Spring; arguably, too, it was recognised by the Chinese Party as confirmation that Soviet communism was losing the plot. Certainly Mao took Khrushchev's humiliating retreat before the United States over the Cuban missile crisis of October 1962 as proof that Khrushchev's dream of peaceful coexistence was a waste of time. Long before Khrushchev was toppled by Brezhnev in October 1964, the Sino-Soviet rift was a matter of public knowledge; indeed, it was Khrushchev's failure to preserve unity in

[4]　Schöpflin, *Politics in Eastern Europe*, 128–9.
[5]　Schöpflin, *Politics in Eastern Europe*, 130.

the communist world, or even in the Soviet Union's backyard, that prompted Brezhnev's coup against him. By the mid-1960s the communist dilemma had come full circle: all efforts to rejuvenate the economy seemed doomed to failure by political inflexibility.

Regional developments 1956–68

The East European communist regimes had, on the face of it, more to gain by sticking with the status quo. They were dependent on the Soviet Union for aid and military protection, and feared any threat to this state of affairs. On the other hand, the instinctive Stalinists among them – Antonín Novotný in Czechoslovakia, Ulbricht in East Germany, Gheorghe Gheorghiu-Dej in Romania, Todor Zhivkov in Bulgaria, Enver Hoxha in Albania – had never really approved of the 'new course', or the rehabilitation of Tito, and consequently welcomed Chinese opposition to 'revisionism'. They also welcomed China's criticism of the one-sided economic relationship between the Soviet Union and its East European satellites: a proper 'fraternal' policy, the Chinese pointed out, should be based on 'the principles of complete equality and reciprocal advantages'.[6] In the end, however, even the most unreconstructed of them recognised the need for some change, and thanks to China's role, the Soviet leadership was more mindful of the need to allow them some leeway.

Two countries took advantage of the Chinese factor to disengage from Soviet tutelage. In *Albania* Enver Hoxha was one of the most resistant to de-Stalinise, since this involved admitting to the judicial murder of Xoxe and other 'Titoists'; and Hoxha remained bitterly opposed to Khrushchev's reconciliation with Tito. In May 1956 Hoxha narrowly survived an attempt to topple him by Tito, who sought to profit from the current thaw in Soviet-Yugoslav relations. Two Politburo members caught trying to flee to Yugoslavia were promptly shot as Titoist agents. Hoxha increasingly aligned himself with China, a persistent critic of the Yugoslav regime. At the same time, he was anxious not to break openly with the Soviets, not least because Albania was heavily dependent on Soviet aid, and from 1958 had the additional advantage of Chinese aid. As a result, the 'golden years' of the late 1950s saw Albania finally achieve record economic growth and a general improvement in health, educational levels, literacy and living standards, even if the concomitant collectivisation of agriculture completely disrupted domestic food production and made the country even more dependent on 'fraternal' aid.

---

[6] Fejtö, F., 1974, *A History of the People's Democracies: Eastern Europe since Stalin*, translated from the French by D. Weissbrot, Harmondsworth, 150.

Nevertheless, the paternalistic relationship with the Soviets was not a happy one. In 1959 Soviet aid was increased, although Hoxha was convinced this was only because Khrushchev needed Albania as a missile base against the West. In addition Khrushchev now perversely advised Albania against industrialisation; according to Hoxha the Soviet leader 'wanted Albania to be turned into a fruit-growing colony which would serve the revisionist Soviet Union, just as the banana republics in Latin America serve the United States of America.'[7] By 1960 relations worsened when Hoxha publicly sided with the Chinese. In an attempt to strong-arm Hoxha, Khrushchev halted grain shipments to Albania, threatening outright famine; the Chinese stepped into the gap, immediately buying grain on the western markets and shipping it to Albania. At the Moscow summit in November 1960, Khrushchev denounced the Albanians as 'provocateurs'; Hoxha's speech to the congress, in response, sensationally commented that 'Soviet rats have food, but Albanians are dying of starvation.'[8] The Albanians ostentatiously withdrew from the congress the next day; all Soviet aid was cut off in April 1961, and later the Soviets took the unprecedented step of breaking off diplomatic relations with this fellow-communist regime. Chinese aid, both financial and material, replaced Soviet and, until China too proved insufficiently Stalinist for Hoxha, Albania remained a Chinese satellite on the south-eastern flank of the Soviet bloc.

Romania also exploited Sino-Soviet differences to adopt a more independent stance. As with Albania, the Romanians' divergence was rooted in their resentment of Soviet domination, particularly the Soviets' growing insistence on integrating all East bloc economies into a single Soviet master-plan. This took organisational shape in 1961 with the Council for Mutual Economic Assistance (Comecon), which aimed to do for Eastern Europe what the European Economic Community (EEC), founded in 1957, looked set to do for Western Europe. In the case of Romania, however, the Soviets found that Stalinist industrialisation had been all too successful: once Romania's industrialisation was running full throttle, its leaders proved reluctant to scale it back. The Polish and Bulgarian regimes were in a similar position. Unlike Czechoslovakia and East Germany, Romania, Poland and Bulgaria were starting from much further back, and Comecon seemed designed to keep them all in a state of dependency. In March 1963, sensationally, the Romanian Communist Party declared that Romania's cooperation with other socialist countries would be based 'on the principles of national sovereignty and independence, equality of rights, fraternal aid and mutual interest'.[9] By lending reality to guidelines the Soviets assumed were for show, agreed largely to placate Mao's China, the Romanians signalled unmistakably their determination to implement a 'national communism'. In

[7] Halliday, J., 1986, *The Artful Albanian: The Memoirs of Enver Hoxha*, London, 219.
[8] Quoted in Fejtö, *A History of the People's Democracies*, 153.
[9] Quoted in Fejtö, *A History of the People's Democracies*, 160.

July, Gheorghiu-Dej threatened to veto Soviet plans for further integration, and Khrushchev, weakened by his humiliation over Cuba in 1962 and the ongoing rift with China, was forced to abandon them. Henceforth increasing economic variegation, within the parameters of communist control, was an ever more obvious feature of communist Eastern Europe.

Thereafter Romania followed an increasingly independent foreign policy too. It resumed diplomatic relations with Albania, ostracised since the breach with the Soviets. Despite the deep freeze in Sino-Soviet relations, Romanian trade with China continued to grow. This visibly independent stance consolidated Gheorghiu-Dej's position within the Romanian Party and, in so far as this could be estimated in a dictatorship, with the Romanian people. The removal of Russian-language classes as a compulsory subject in Romanian schools was undoubtedly popular. Under Nicolae Ceauşescu, who took over on Gheorghiu-Dej's death in 1965, the habit of not so subtly distancing Romania from the Soviets continued. Ceauşescu not only cultivated ostentatiously warm relations with Tito and China's Chou En-lai, but established diplomatic relations with West Germany, and fully supported the latter's *Ostpolitik* of rapprochement with East Germany. The habit changed to open defiance when, in response to the Soviet invasion of Czechoslovakia in 1968, Ceauşescu's regime, alone among the Warsaw Pact states, not only refused to contribute troops, but furiously denounced it in public. Overnight Ceauşescu's popularity in Romania soared, as did his reputation in western capitals. 'National communism' clearly had benefits.

As suggested, Poland and Bulgaria found themselves in a similar position to Romania, in that their economies remained largely agrarian while undergoing substantial industrialisation; unlike Romania, however, neither showed much inclination to kick against Soviet direction of their economic strategy. Each managed to find a market for its agricultural produce in fellow-communist countries and, increasingly, the wider world. Politically, each remained subservient to Soviet interests despite the accumulating costs of living with a Soviet-style command economy.

Poland's stagnation seems the more remarkable, since 1956 gave Gomułka more leeway to implement a form of communism that suited Poland. Yet the general consensus is that Gomułka had little appetite for experimenting, beyond sticking with the virtual abandonment of collective agriculture which was already a reality by 1956. And while Gomułka was no Stalinist he was undoubtedly authoritarian, committed to the unimaginative implementation of Marxism-Leninism. In the bitter climate of the Sino-Soviet altercation the Polish Party sided instinctively with the Soviets, while maintaining good relations with both Albania and Yugoslavia.

The regime in 1956 made a timid start with decentralising the economy, but since this was only half-heartedly implemented the results were predictably meagre, and by 1959 Gomułka swung back in favour of even greater control.

By the early 1960s the amount invested had the effect of triggering inflation and a further drop in living standards, forcing government to opt for austerity and price increases instead. The only bright aspect was rising agricultural productivity, thanks to decollectivisation; and the one thing Gomułka got right was to lift restrictions on the founding of small businesses, which permitted a mini-boom in private enterprise. Politically, however, the regime's dismal record meant increasing repression, and the so-called 'Partisan' faction, led by General Mieczysław Moczar, came to prominence. The views of the Partisans were a blend of Stalinist authoritarianism and anti-Semitism, which Moczar seemed instinctively to reach for as a means of distracting people from the government's record. Coupled with this was a renewed crackdown on freedom of expression. On the extreme left, a minority of hardline Stalinists dared, in 1964, to circulate a pamphlet denouncing Gomułka for being too lax; this group was expelled from the party, its leader fleeing to Albania. On the other wing, voices calling for liberalisation got equally short shrift. The *Krzywe Koło* discussion group, so influential in 1956, was shut down in 1962. Thirty-four intellectuals and artists who addressed an open letter to Polish premier Cyrankiewicz in 1964, protesting at restrictions on freedom of expression, were accused of treason by the party press, although in the end only one of the signatories was jailed. Perhaps most symptomatic of the unease among party members was the 'Open Letter to the Party' by two young graduate students, Jacek Kuroń and Karol Modzelewski, in 1965. As Marxists Kuroń and Modzelewski made it clear they rejected parliamentary democracy, but argued that the party had become a stultifying elite; they advocated an 'anti-bureaucratic revolution' of workers' councils, whose control would be safeguarded by 'trades unions absolutely independent of the state with the right to organize economic and political strikes.'[10] This radical idea, foreshadowing the Solidarity movement of 1980–1, which Kuroń and Modzelewski helped shape, earned its authors prison sentences in 1965. Gomułka seemed to have no other strategy, for dealing with rising popular discontent than to let the Partisan faction indulge their anti-Semitism. In response to Israel's victory in the Six Days' War of 1967, bizarrely, the Polish government launched an 'anti-Zionist' drive, expelling Jews from the party, and in many cases forcing them to emigrate.

Conditions in *Bulgaria* reflected to some extent the confused lead given by the Soviet leadership, but on the whole Bulgarian communists inclined towards unreconstructed Stalinism. In the wake of Khrushchev's 'secret speech' the party strongman, Chervenkov, was briefly demoted by his colleagues, but by 1957 Chervenkov was again the dominant figure, firmly repressing any tendencies towards fresh thinking. So 'anti-revisionist' was Chervenkov that

---

[10] 'The Kuroń-Modzelewski Open Letter to the Party' (early 1965), in Stokes, G. (ed.), 1991, *From Stalinism to Pluralism: A Documentary History of Eastern Europe since 1945*, New York and Oxford, 114.

he even followed Mao's lead for some years, launching his own 'great leap forward' along Chinese lines in 1958, with the aim of trebling agricultural production. Like the Chinese original, this was a miserable failure, raising productivity by only 18 per cent; unlike China, Bulgaria was fortunate enough to escape famine. In 1961 the central committee finally toppled Chervenkov, and his successor Todor Zhivkov adopted a policy of more overt compliance with Moscow, not least because Bulgaria remained completely dependent on Soviet aid. Although a Bulgarian tourist industry developed in the 1960s, the 1965 Soviet loan of 530 million roubles symbolised the country's continuing dependency.

Hungary under Kádár, after a period of repression, took full advantage of the 'second de-Stalinisation'. Free of the threat of a neo-Stalinist backlash within his own party, Kádár felt secure enough to engage in a certain amount of economic experimentation and a gradual political liberalisation. Increased Soviet aid enabled Kádár to reduce spending on armaments and raise the standard of living by investing more in consumer goods. Agricultural productivity was improved by admitting former smallholders to the new collective farms. Small-scale private enterprises such as restaurants were permitted. Elements of central planning were abandoned when, in 1964, price controls were relaxed and a limited amount of profit allowed. An important signal was sent out to Hungary's alienated intellectuals by Kádár's statement in 1961 that 'He who is not against us is for us.'[11] In other words, as long as Hungarians did not question one-party rule much else would be tolerated. An amnesty was declared for those imprisoned after 1956, and censorship was relaxed. Foreign travel became easier, tourism was actively promoted, and translations of western works became more common. A new pragmatism distinguished Hungary in the 1960s. Children of formerly middle-class parents were finally admitted into higher education, and the state started employing non-party members in the bureaucracy, the economy and cultural life. In return, intellectuals learned to accept that, in the words of one émigré writer, they had 'many freedoms, if not freedom itself.'[12] Ordinary Hungarians benefited from a higher standard of living under '*gulyás* communism'. By the late 1960s Hungary counted as one of the most liberal as well as prosperous of the East bloc countries. At the very point that the Prague Spring got under way in Czechoslovakia, Kádár introduced his 'New Economic Mechanism', designed to widen marketisation. The Soviet invasion of Czechoslovakia, however, forced Kádár to put these innovations on hold.

The German Democratic Republic, or *East Germany*, existed in a sort of international limbo throughout the 1950s, because no international treaty regulating its status had been concluded, and formally no state outside the

---

[11] Quoted in Fejtö, *A History of the People's Democracies*, 167.
[12] Quoted in Fejtö, *A History of the People's Democracies*, 169.

Soviet bloc recognised its existence. This did not hinder Ulbricht's SED from consolidating power; but the regime faced an ongoing crisis because of the porous nature of its border with West Germany. By the early 1960s nearly three million people had fled from East to West Germany; this was not only a political embarrassment but constituted a serious drain on the economy. In August 1961, therefore, Khrushchev finally gave Ulbricht the go-ahead to construct a wall between the Soviet sector of occupied Berlin and the western sectors, always the easiest escape route for Easterners. Construction started literally overnight and was a traumatic experience for ordinary Berliners; family members were arbitrarily separated from one another and, famously, one East German border guard leapt to freedom at the last moment before one section of the wall was put in place. The Berlin Wall, with elaborate security features including watch-towers whose guards were authorised to shoot would-be escapees, but also extended along the whole frontier with West Germany, remained in place until its fall in 1989, the most vivid symbol of the Cold War, but also of communism's failure as an ideology. Justified by the regime as a defence against infiltration by western spies, it was in reality a means of imprisoning the entire East German population. Thereafter the economy stabilised, since the workforce no longer had the option of escape; but since a free, prosperous West Germany remained both audible and visible to most East Germans, thanks to radio and television, Ulbricht's regime continued to be one of the most repressive in the East bloc. Dissident intellectuals were silenced and forced into exile; others were denied any platform at all. As Ulbricht, with unselfconscious irony, intoned, 'We shall not permit false, dangerous and pernicious ideas to be imposed on the people.'[13] The economy by contrast improved, to some extent helped by increased trade with Red China.

The 'Soviet Socialist Republics' of Estonia, Latvia and Lithuania, Belarus and the Ukraine had all been forcibly incorporated into the Soviet Union, in the case of the Baltic states as recently as 1940; but it would be fair to say that their inhabitants, with the exception of the committed communists and ethnic Russians living among them, were anything but voluntary. Yet throughout the communist period the Soviet authorities persisted, all evidence to the contrary, in regarding the Baltic peoples, the Belorussians and the Ukrainians as integral parts of Soviet society.

The story of the *Estonians*, *Latvians* and *Lithuanians* after 1945 is particularly grim. A Soviet-era riddle, with characteristic black humour, asked 'What is the biggest country in the world? The answer, 'Estonia', was because 'its shores are on the Baltic, its capital's in Moscow, and its population's in Siberia.'[14] To be sure, not all the population of the three Baltic states suffered this fate, but the reality was bad enough. The mass deportations of 1941

---

[13] Quoted in Fejtö, *A History of the People's Democracies*, 186.
[14] BBB World Service broadcast heard in Hungary, June 1987 (personal recollection).

decapitated entire societies, targeting the political, economic and intellectual elites of each country and their families – anyone, in short, who might offer coordinated opposition to Soviet rule. Armed resistance to Soviet rule in some areas was maintained for years: the 'Forest Brothers', as Baltic resisters in all three republics were called, were not finally extirpated until 1952, in part because of a mistaken, if not irrational, hope that the Cold War might turn hot and bring western intervention. At their peak the Forest Brothers numbered between 0.5 and 1 per cent of the population; the strength of individual resistances fluctuated depending on the injustices perpetrated by Soviet rule. One particularly obdurate Estonian, August Sabe, was not cornered by the KGB until 1978, at the age of seventy, and drowned trying to escape capture. Soviet reconquest in 1944 added those accused of collaboration or resistance to the tally of the displaced and murdered. As Soviet rule tightened tens of thousands were deported to Siberia, from captured partisans to 'bourgeois nationalists' to Jews to Jehovah's Witnesses. The biggest deportations came with collectivisation: in one mass expulsion alone, 'Operation Priboi' of March 1949, over 90,000 Baltic citizens, 28 per cent of them children, were declared 'enemies of the people' and forcibly transported to Siberia. As a Lithuanian daughter of 'kulaks' recalled, 'We thought then that the whole Lithuanian nation had been deported.'[15] In the place of the native inhabitants thousands of ethnic Russians were imported into the republics, changing their ethnographic balance for generations to come. In the meantime the Sovietisation of Baltic societies proceeded apace: industry and commercial businesses were nationalised; agriculture was collectivised; the media, education and religion were subjected to communist control, reinforced by the full apparatus of the Stalinist police-state. All the evidence suggests that native Baltic communists, supervised by their Soviet masters, were anxious to demonstrate their loyalty to Stalin; as one Latvian poet toe-curlingly apostrophised the Soviet leader, 'Your name glows for us like the flaming sun,/Like an eternal flame that calls to battle.'[16] For most inhabitants of the Baltic republics, however, the Stalinist period was one of chronic fear and insecurity, if not worse.

In these circumstances there is not a lot to say about Baltic societies, even under the relatively more relaxed conditions of the post-Stalinist period. Soviet policy did not deny the existence of national identities and cultures, but it undoubtedly assumed a gradual process of 'Sovietisation': in 'building socialism' the national character of the Baltic peoples would be subsumed within a new, 'Soviet' identity. There is little evidence, however, that this worked for more than a tiny minority. On the contrary, as in the rest of Eastern Europe,

---

[15] Quoted in Lieven, A., 1993, *The Baltic Revolution: Estonia, Latvia, Lithuania and the Path to Independence*, New Haven and London, 91.
[16] Quoted in Misiunas, R. and Taagepera, R., 1993, *The Baltic States: Years of Dependence 1940-1990*, expanded and updated edn, London, 117.

de-Stalinisation permitted a tentative resurfacing of Baltic national culture, albeit under a carapace of communist ideology. The federal structure of the Soviet Union positively facilitated this: as in Yugoslavia, the very existence of an Estonian, Latvian and Lithuanian Communist Party meant that these bodies insensibly started to practise a form of 'national communism'. One sign of this was the cautious 'nativisation' of the party apparatus after 1953: the replacement of ethnic Russians with native Baltic Party members. Another was the return of those deported to the Gulag, especially after Khrushchev's 'secret speech'. Yet the 1956 upheavals in Poland and Hungary made both Soviet and Baltic communists nervous about letting 'nativisation' get out of hand; as a Latvian party newspaper opined in 1957, 'National communism is nothing but sophisticated bourgeois nationalism.'[17] That same year Khrushchev effectively halted the Baltic republics' national revival by purging all three parties' membership; at the same time, the Soviets tried to engineer a numerical balance between native Balts and ethnic Russians which would defuse discontent.

In the 1950s and 1960s the irrepressible diversity of the Baltic peoples' culture gradually manifested itself again in literature and the arts; an early harbinger of this revival was the Estonian poet, novelist and later Nobel Prize winner Jaan Kross, whose collection of poems about his period of forced labour in Soviet mines, *The Coal Concentrator*, was published in 1958. Despite a Soviet campaign against nationalism, it was abundantly clear by 1968 that Baltic national consciousness could not be kept down. Yet paradoxically, as industrialisation in the three republics intensified, their relative prosperity attracted a second influx of both Russians and non-Russians from across the Soviet Union. By the mid-1960s there were more than a million Russophones in the Baltic Republics, a trend that ensured ethnic tensions would continue to simmer.

Belarus exhibited in many respects the least developed sense of national consciousness of all East European peoples, even after decades of existence as a Soviet Socialist Republic. This owed much to the ruthless action Stalin took in the 1930s to extirpate any sign of independence in the republic, despite its theoretical autonomy. The presence of the Orthodox Church in Belarus was systematically eliminated, and a purge of the Belorussian Party was implemented in 1933 by the Soviet central committee, replacing most of the leading officials of the Republic with Russians; in addition, an estimated 90 per cent of the literary intelligentsia were either shot or exiled to the Gulag. There was little possibility of change until after Stalin's death, but even after 1953 Belarus remained firmly under Russian control; only in the 1960s did a new generation of Belorussian leaders emerge. The Republic's importance as a major producer of dairy products, and its locus as the centre of the Soviet electronics industry,

---

[17] Quoted in Misiunas and Taagepera, *The Baltic States*, 137.

made Belarus relatively prosperous. Unlike the Ukrainians, Belorussians in this period exhibited few signs of restlessness, nor was there much of a Belorussian émigré community to keep grievances alive.

Matters were decidedly different in the *Ukraine*. There, the Stalinist period, in particular collectivisation in the early 1930s, was implemented with such brutality, and so little regard for the famine that attended it in 1932–3, as to create the understandable conviction among Ukrainians that they were the target of a deliberate genocide, what Ukrainians refer to as the *Holodomor* or great hunger. Only properly researched since the 1980s, the *Holodomor* is conservatively estimated to have caused between 4.5 and 5 million deaths in 1933 alone, and perhaps as many as 10 million deaths in the rest of the decade. Reliable figures are impossible to come by, not least because, as Nikita Khrushchev admitted in his memoirs, 'No one was keeping count.'[18] Robert Conquest, in a trail-blazing study in 1986, concluded not only that 5 million died in the Ukraine and 2 million elsewhere, but that the process of 'de-kulakisation' preceding the famine, whereby entire villages were deported to the Gulag, accounted for another 6.5 million deaths, most of them in the camps. A party official described the 'unearthly quiet' of a village devastated by famine: 'I saw people dying in solitude by slow degrees, dying hideously, without the excuse of sacrifice for a cause. . . . The most terrifying sights were the little children, with skeleton limbs dangling from balloon-like abdomens. . . . Everywhere we found men and women lying prone, their faces and bellies bloated, their eyes utterly expressionless.'[19] Cannibalism was common.

To argue, however, that the *Holodomor* represented a systematic effort to exterminate the Ukrainian people, ignores the fact that non-Ukrainian Soviet citizens also died in their millions as a result of collectivisation. Furthermore, in the wealth of documentation available since the collapse of the Soviet Union no single source has been found showing that Stalin ordered an attack on Ukrainians as such. Rather, Stalin saw himself as conducting a war against obstructive peasants of all nationalities, and whose elimination by starvation he considered an acceptable, indeed desirable, side-effect of collectivisation. The preponderance of Ukrainians among the dead reflects the fact that the overwhelming majority of Soviet grain producers lived in the Ukraine; and the high proportion of smallholders relative to the peasant population as a whole meant resistance to collectivisation was correspondingly stronger. Whatever the explanation, however, Ukrainians' sense of grievance over the *Holodomor* remains both real and justified to this day.

Ukrainians' suffering did not end there. Apart from the horrors of the war, armed resistance by the nationalist UPA to the reimposition of Soviet control continued in western Ukraine into the early 1950s, much of it in protest against

---

[18] Quoted in Reid, A., 1998, *Borderland: A Journey through the History of Ukraine*, London, 116.
[19] Quoted in Reid, *Borderland*, 118.

the forcible resettlement of Ukrainians across the new Polish-Soviet border. Because Ukrainian opposition to Soviet rule was also rooted in religious differences, the Greek Catholic Church in western Ukraine was an especial target, and after the war most of the Church leadership was forced into exile; a minority accepted the authority of the Russian Orthodox Church. A second famine followed prolonged drought in the late 1940s, compounded by Stalin's refusal to relax grain requisitions. When Khrushchev, concerned at reports of cannibalism, attempted to reason with Stalin, he was fiercely rebuked: 'You're being soft-bellied! They're deceiving you! They're counting on being able to appeal to your sentimentality when they report things like that!'[20] Finally, nearly half a million Ukrainians had been deported to Siberia and Central Asia by the time Stalin died.

Only after that point did things improve for Ukrainians. Post-war reconstruction, despite chronic food shortages, was aided by massive capital investment, and the industrial base destroyed during the war was largely rebuilt by 1950. Although most of this was old-fashioned heavy industry, Ukraine rapidly regained its position as the highest per capita producer of pig iron, sugar and steel-smelting. Equally important was a sustained Ukrainian cultural revival, a development only made possible by de-Stalinisation, and which reflected the ambiguity of the Russo-Ukrainian relationship and Ukrainian national identity. In February 1954 the Crimea was formally transferred from the Russian Socialist Republic to the Ukrainian, despite having a population 71 per cent Russian and only 22 per cent Ukrainian; according to the official Soviet explanation at the time, this was 'yet another affirmation of the great fraternal love and trust of the Russian people for Ukraine', even if the real decision was made by Khrushchev rather than the Russian people.[21] Ethnic Ukrainian membership of the Ukrainian Party crept upward, after decades of Russian preponderance. Ukrainian literature started to exhibit a more overtly national consciousness, exemplified by Oles' Honchar's novel *The Cathedral* (1968), deploring the Stalinist-era destruction of cultural monuments like churches. A Ukrainian historical journal was launched in 1957, Ukrainian encyclopaedias proliferated, and a multi-volume dictionary of the Ukrainian language came out in 1970–80.

By the late 1970s too much had happened in the Ukrainian cultural sphere for Brezhnev's regime to suppress it entirely. Brezhnev, himself an ethnic Russian from the Ukraine, instinctively favoured repressing freedom of expression; in his opinion Khrushchev had let things get out of hand. From the early 1960s, new restrictions were imposed on writers and artists deemed guilty of 'bourgeois nationalism', and arrests and trials of dissident intellectuals took

---

[20] Khrushchev, N., 1971, *Khrushchev Remembers*, translated by Strobe Talbot, with an introduction, commentary and notes by Edward Crankshaw, London, 206.
[21] Quoted in Magocsi, P.R., 1996, *A History of Ukraine*, Toronto, Buffalo, NY and London, 653.

place in 1965–66. Brezhnev was particularly alarmed by Ukrainian dissidents publishing their works in Czechoslovakia during the Prague Spring, and the invasion of 1968 was in part prompted by this fear of contagion spreading. The crackdown on Ukrainian 'local nationalism' culminated in the removal, in May 1972, of Petro Skelest as first secretary of the Ukrainian Communist Party; Skelest had not only promoted greater use of the Ukrainian language but had proved too tolerant of dissidents generally. In the longer term, however, and despite Russians' dismissive attitude towards Ukrainian national identity, industrialisation itself ensured that the existence of the Ukrainian nation could no longer be denied. In particular the urbanisation of the Ukraine, the fact that by 1979, 53 per cent of the population lived in towns, meant that 'the Soviet system had produced a highly educated and nationally conscious Ukrainian stratum of the population.'[22] The Ukraine remained divided between ethnic Russians and Ukrainians, but as long as it was still in the Soviet Union this seemed to pose no problem; Ukrainian nationalism, however, was more obvious than ever before.

Tito's *Yugoslavia* was a maverick communist regime which, until the late 1960s, seemed to enjoy the best of both worlds. The breach with the Soviets left Yugoslavia outside the Warsaw Pact, forever apprehensive of Soviet interference; in compensation western material and moral support was important in enabling Tito's regime to survive. Given the constraints of Soviet threat and western links, Yugoslavia evolved a hybrid brand of communism which, while inherently inefficient, nevertheless decentralised sufficiently to raise standards of living, while giving the six Yugoslav republics an increasingly real autonomy. The result was a relatively open society which seemed to offer an example, at least to western sympathisers, of a communist regime that 'worked'.

Tito contributed to this illusion by helping found the 'non-aligned movement' with countries like India, which insisted that they were in neither the Soviet nor the western capitalist camp. In domestic policy, 'Titoism' became associated with 'workers' self-management', a system of participatory workers' councils; the idea was that such councils would take over the functions of state bureaucracy, eliminating the need for central planning. It is not obvious, however, that self-management meant all that much in practice, or made things more efficient; what did happen is that control of the economy was increasingly a republican responsibility, meaning it was the communist party at republic level making crucial economic decisions such as setting prices. The six republics increasingly acted as economic units, trading with one another. Nevertheless there is no denying that Yugoslavia became something of a success story under Tito, and one of the highest growth rates in the world in the 1950s. This was

---

[22] Magocsi, *A History of Ukraine*, 663.

partly due to Yugoslavia's crash course in industrialisation; but it was also due to Titoist decentralisation, creating an impetus towards marketisation, if not a completely free internal market. A new constitution in 1963 incorporated economic interests by creating special regional chambers to manage the local economy. In 1965, the regime eased currency convertibility; arguably this was the crucial step in aligning Yugoslavia with the outside world market. At the same time, there was a significant relaxation of border controls and restrictions on people's freedom to travel, both into and out of the country. Not only were Yugoslavs free to seek work abroad, especially in West Germany, where by 1970 some 400,000 Yugoslav *Gastarbeiter* or guest workers were employed, sending valuable western currency back to relatives at home. It was now also much easier for foreign tourists to visit Yugoslavia, which in the 1960s became the first communist country to attract large-scale tourism, providing the regime with a huge economic boost. Yugoslavia's openness to western influences, coupled with Tito's opulent lifestyle, prompted grumbling among purists; but in 1966 this led to the fall of the principal hardliner, Aleksandr Ranković, who was discovered to have tapped Tito's telephone lines. Ranković's fall signalled an even greater relaxation of control, particularly with regard to Yugoslavia's multiple nationalities; but it was precisely this greater prominence of nationality issues which spelt trouble for the future.

The Prague Spring

The lack of economic growth across communist Eastern Europe was just as obvious in Czechoslovakia; indeed, the decline in living standards and general backwardness were if anything more acutely felt in a country which was the most economically advanced in the region before the imposition of communism. Czechs and Slovaks were also aware that theirs had been the last genuine democracy in Eastern Europe down to 1938. These memories of economic and political modernity undoubtedly contributed to the reform movement known as the Prague Spring. At the same time, Alexander Dubček and his supporters were adamant that they wished to reform, not abolish, communism. In the wake of their failure, the conviction spread across the entire Soviet bloc that, if reform could not be achieved in Czechoslovakia, it could be achieved nowhere.

The premises for any reform in Czechoslovakia, prior to January 1968, when Dubček became leader of the Czechoslovak Party, seem questionable. Under Dubček's predecessor Novotný, leader since 1953, Czechoslovakia remained essentially Stalinist throughout the 1950s and 1960s. Novotný, a lifelong communist of the technocratic type, was described by one of Dubček's later aides as 'this primitive, essentially authoritarian person', 'an uneducated man who, as compensation, possessed a wide range of practical knowledge.'[23] Put more brutally, Novotný presided over 'a personality cult without the personality.'[24] Like Hungary's Rákosi, Novotný was implicated up to his neck in the purges of the Stalinist period, but after Stalin's death managed to retain the personal confidence of Khrushchev; his grip was therefore all the stronger after 1956. The events of that year confirmed all Novotný's suspicions that de-Stalinisation had been a dangerous mistake.

Real pressure for reform did not build up until the early 1960s, and took two forms. One was the pressure of economic reality described above: the gradual realisation, among the more economically literate party members, that the Soviet command economy was simply no longer working. The economist Šik's conclusion was that rigid control from the centre actively impeded growth, especially once all the capital derived from confiscating property and nationalising industry had been used up. The only feasible way of stimulating fresh growth and capital accumulation, according to Šik, was to decentralise, and readmit some elements of a market into the economy.

The other pressure was political, a gathering momentum within the party for a genuine de-Stalinisation. In particular there was pressure to set the record straight about the purges of 1949–54. To some extent this was due to the force of example since 1956: everyone knew, for instance, that Hungary's purge victims had been 'rehabilitated' that year. To some extent it was generational: younger members of the party, like Dubček and Zdeněk Mlynář, simply could not help questioning what had happened, because they honestly did not know. The cumulative effect of Khrushchev's denunciations of Stalin was to redouble these members' questions, especially over the role of the leadership. Novotný was reluctant to agree to any sort of enquiry; but Khrushchev's renewed criticism of Stalin in 1961 pushed him into a corner. Thus, in 1962, a Commission of Rehabilitation was set up. Its first result was to clear Slovak communists like Gustáv Husák of the charge of 'bourgeois nationalism' for participating in the Slovak National Uprising of 1944. Those implicated in the Slánský trial of 1952 had to wait several years more before being completely rehabilitated, although the Commission did come to the conclusion that they had not been guilty as charged. It was enough: not only was the partial admission of party error sufficient to make some clearing out of Stalinists essential, but the mood within the party shifted towards a greater openness. An early sign of this thaw was the fact that in 1963 Václav Havel, a self-taught dramatist hitherto held back by his bourgeois background, was able to stage his play *The Garden Party*, a coded satire on a society in thrall to a feared bigwig. Novotný, characteristically, salvaged his position by offering up various subordinates as scapegoats, and as a consequence found himself

---

[23] Mlynář, *Night Frost in Prague*, 68, 72.
[24] Quoted in Crampton, *Eastern Europe in the Twentieth Century*, 319.

surrounded by more and more reformers. The most important of these, as it turned out, was Dubček, whom Novotný was forced to accept as first secretary of the Slovak Party in April 1963.

Dubček was in many respects typical of a new generation in his inclination towards greater openness, and his belief that a more humane version of communism was possible. His credentials were impeccable. Born in 1921, he had grown up in the Soviet Union, after his idealistic parents moved there in 1925 to help 'build socialism'. After helping found a town in Kirghizstan, the family moved to central Russia before returning to Czechoslovakia in 1938. Dubček's memoirs provide a fascinating account of growing up in Stalinist Russia, which convinced him that the Soviet model ought not to be slavishly copied. Dubček recalls seeing corpses in the street during the famine of 1932–3. He describes being required, in 1937, to tear out of his school textbook a picture of Marshal Tukhachevsky, recently executed in the purges and now an 'unperson'. In wartime Slovakia the Dubček family was caught up in resistance. The two sons fought in the 1944 uprising, with only Alexander surviving. Their father Stefan was interned in Mauthausen concentration camp along with fellow communists Novotný and Viliam Široký; Novotný, however, acted as a *capo* or camp trusty, and was thus always well-fed while others starved; Široký betrayed Stefan Dubček's plans for escape, and then used the same plans to escape himself. The Dubčeks therefore had personal reasons for thinking poorly of later party superiors, but also for perceiving a gap between theory and practice.

After the war Dubček climbed the party ladder rapidly, but none of his posts involved him in the dirty work; this was one of the qualities which appealed by the 1960s. Dubček was also remarkable for his honesty even when this was perilous. When one of his fellow wartime partisans died in 1952, the year of the Slánský trial, having been expelled from the party for 'bourgeois nationalism', Dubček was one of only three party members to attend the funeral, and made a tearful graveside speech, praising his friend as a 'true revolutionary'. As a journalist privately noted, Dubček stood out for such 'innocent honesty. He may well reach the top of the Party – but he is much more likely to find himself in prison.'[25]

From the moment Dubček became Slovak Party leader he was involved in an increasingly open struggle with Novotný. He refused to discipline the Slovak Party organ for its identification of Široký, now Czechoslovakian prime minister, as heavily implicated in the 1952 purges; Široký, humiliated by the bad publicity, felt obliged to step down. Dubček created a loyal power base in Slovakia precisely because of this openness. The Slovak Party press, at least, became genuinely controversial, discussing not only Stalinist criminality but

---

[25] Quoted in Shawcross, W., 1990, *Dubcek: Dubcek and Czechoslovakia 1918-1990*, London, 61.

also economic reform. What proved popular in Slovakia caught on in the Czech Party as well. Restrictions on the exercise of religion were eased, and for the first time since the Stalinist period foreign travel became possible, at least for some. The one tactical error committed by Dubček, characteristically, was not to weed out the Slovak Party's own Stalinists; the result was that enough hardliners remained, by 1968, to mount a reaction.

What brought Novotný's reign to an end, however, was the stuttering economy. Novotný felt obliged to clear Šik's 'New Economic Model' for implementation in early 1967; this involved less control and subsidy from the centre; allowing enterprises to keep most of their profit, either for increased wages or reinvestment; a limited amount of private enterprise, mainly in services; and greater flexibility with regard to prices. From the start, however, the NEM was probably doomed to failure, and not just because it represented only a tinkering with the command economy; its provisions were also actively sabotaged by Novotný and his allies, as well as thousands of rank-and-file members who felt threatened by its provisions. Reformers like Šik and Dubček complained about such foot-dragging. By late 1967 the divisions were undeniable, and Novotný's position was weakened by two additional factors. As a Czech, he had persistently alienated the Slovak Party. More fatally, Novotný lost the support of the Soviets under Brezhnev. Not for the first time, a Soviet signal of indifference touched off a serious attempt at reform, which then turned out to be too serious for the Soviets to permit. The visiting Brezhnev, asked who should lead the Party, replied 'That's your affair.' This forced Novotný's resignation in January 1968; the party central committee immediately appointed Dubček in his place.

From the start Dubček's leadership promised a breath of fresh air. As he informed members in February, in words remarkable from a lifelong communist, 'The party exists for the working people; it must be neither above, nor outside society, but an integral part of it. Democracy is not simply possession of the right and means of free expression of opinion, but also the government's attention to the opinion so expressed, and the genuine participation of everyone in the process of decision-making.'[26] It should be emphasised that Dubček and his supporters were anxious not to risk confrontation with the Soviets. However, the very opening up of the system, and especially Dubček's call for popular participation, generated such a wave of discussion and freethinking that, almost from the beginning, Moscow began to get nervous. George Schöpflin comments that the sheer rapidity with which events spun out of control suggests the impossibility of reforming communism: the least debate implied criticism of what had gone before, and communism was simply not structured to tolerate criticism. There was also a real contradiction between reforming a system in

---

[26] Quoted in Fejtö, *A History of the People's Democracies*, 220.

which the party retained overall control, and democratisation which, if taken in the proper sense, implied a genuine multiparty system with genuinely free elections, which the party might well lose.[27] It now seems clear that Dubček and his associates did not see this antithesis, and therefore honestly did not expect to encounter Soviet opposition.

In April the reformers brought out their Action Programme, announcing the party's renunciation, not of its leading role, but of its aspiration to control society totally: 'The Party cannot enforce its authority. Authority must be won again and again by Party activity.'[28] This stopped short of promising multiparty elections, but acknowledged the right of non-communist parties to exist and express their views. Mlynář, closely involved in drafting the Action Programme, confirms that the party was intended to act as a sort of political referee, and for this purpose the programme revived the concept of a 'national front', an umbrella organisation acting as a genuine consultative body. The Action Programme also confirmed the lifting of the censorship, which had already come into effect within weeks of Dubček taking over. As Dubček later admitted, 'I knew that I needed a free press to help me open the way to basic reforms, political as well as economic.'[29] The programme proposed extending the right to foreign travel, compensating victims of the purges and their families, adopting Šik's reforms in their entirety, harmonising relations with the churches, and implementing autonomy for Slovakia.

The implications of the Action Programme were even more radical than its contents. Quite apart from the unresolved choice between mere 'reform' and democratisation, there was also the programme's effect on public opinion. Not only was there an immediate and ever-swelling upsurge of public discussion, but non-communist organisations quickly sprang into life, and what polls were conducted (another novelty) indicated strong support for a return to a multiparty system. More ominously, some of the debate quickly took on a more nationalist and, by implication, anti-Soviet tone. The famous article '2000 Words', for example, by the novelist Ludvík Vaculík, in June 1968, not only criticised the party as 'the new aristocracy', but warned of the danger of outside intervention, and suggested that Czechs and Slovaks had a duty to resist such interference.[30] The more open such comment, the more likely a Soviet reaction; yet having set the ball of reform rolling, it is difficult to see how Dubček could halt such talk, short of abandoning the whole project.

In reality, the room for manoeuvre with regard to the Soviets was small to non-existent. Brezhnev's politburo made clear their alarm even before the

---

[27] Schöpflin, *Politics in Eastern Europe*, 130.
[28] Text in Dubček, A., 1993, *Hope Dies Last: The Autobiography of Alexander Dubcek*, London, 297.
[29] Dubček, *Hope Dies Last*, 132.
[30] Vaculík, L., 'Two Thousand Words to Workers, Farmers, Scientists, Artists and Everyone', 29 June 1968, in Stokes (ed.), *From Stalinism to Pluralism*, 126, 127.

Action Programme was published. At a summit in Dresden in March, Brezhnev openly accused Dubček of losing control and inviting external threats to the socialist camp. Dubček's strategy throughout, however, was to let facts speak for themselves; if the 'dinosaurs', as he later described the Soviet leadership, could see the Czechoslovak government had no intention of turning against the Soviet Union, all would be well. As spring passed into summer, Dubček found himself caught between a vocal domestic pressure to continue, and external pressure from the Soviet and other East bloc regimes to reimpose control. In mid-July the Soviets and Warsaw Pact states, minus Romania, addressed an open letter to the Czechoslovak central committee, demanding an immediate abandonment of the reform programme, the suppression of 'anti-socialist' organisations, and the resumption of censorship. In reply Dubček, after clearing his response with the central committee and explaining his position, unprecedentedly, in a televised address to the country, refused to accept that his course was anti-socialist, while reiterating his commitment to the cause of democratisation. In an atmosphere of rising tension Dubček was invited to come to Moscow and refused, insisting any discussions take place on Czechoslovak territory.

The final, decisive confrontations were a succession of Soviet-Czechoslovak meetings at Čierná-nad-Tisou, on the Soviet border, from 29 July to 1 August, and then at Bratislava on 3 August. At the former, Brezhnev insisted on crossing the border every day in an armoured train, alleging fear of 'anti-socialist' attacks, before returning to the safety of Soviet soil for the night. At both meetings, the Czechoslovaks protested in vain their loyalty to communism and the Soviet Union but, in Dubček's words, 'What we were trying to do was beyond their comprehension.'[31] Soviet fears were not in themselves incomprehensible. Brezhnev may genuinely have feared the emergence of a dissident communist bloc composed of Yugoslavia, Romania and now Czechoslovakia. Even more important was the Soviet perception of what Dubček seemed to overlook: the Czechoslovak reforms could lead to real democratisation and the probable loss of Czechoslovakia to communism. For Brezhnev this threatened the entire system of Soviet security achieved at the end of the Second World War, a charge he levelled explicitly at Dubček. As János Kádár bluntly asked Dubček three days before the Soviet invasion, 'Do you really not know the kind of people you are dealing with?'[32]

After the Bratislava summit, it is clear, the Soviets decided on intervention, and on the night of 20–21 August Warsaw Pact forces, again without Romanian participation, entered Czechoslovakia from East German, Polish, Soviet and Hungarian territory. Simultaneously Dubček and the rest of the party leadership were taken captive by Soviet commandos and secretly flown to Moscow.

[31] Dubček, *Hope Dies Last*, 165.
[32] Quoted in Mlynář, *Night Frost in Prague*, 157.

Unlike Hungarians in 1956, ordinary Czechs and Slovaks chose not to resist by force. There were isolated clashes and, overall, between 80 and 200 people were killed in the course of this 'fraternal socialist assistance'. The populace confined its resistance to changing or removing road signs to confuse the invaders, refusing to provide them with food or drink, and haranguing tank crews to return whence they came. Much of this was captured by the multitude of foreign and Czechoslovak journalists and television camera crews still free to roam the streets. The invasion was timed to forestall the convening of the Czechoslovak Party congress. In the absence of the Party leadership, however, the rank-and-file clandestinely held their congress in a Prague factory, where some 12,000 delegates roundly condemned the invasion and elected another, equally reformist, central committee. A last opinion poll conducted on 14–16 September suggested that 94 per cent of the populace still supported Dubček and reform.

Ultimately none of this could stand against Soviet power, but it did mean the Soviets had to 'negotiate' with Dubček, after a fashion. With the country occupied, and open resistance driven underground, the Soviets concentrated on breaking Dubček's will, so that they could maintain some semblance, however unconvincing, of Czechoslovak compliance. After several days of browbeating, a dejected Dubček finally signed the Moscow Protocols of 26 August, which represented a complete abandonment of the Prague Spring. The protocols required a clampdown on 'counter-revolutionary forces', the reimposition of censorship, the prohibition of non-communist organisations, a purge of ministers not approved by the Soviets, and the acceptance of indefinite occupation by Warsaw Pact forces. On this basis, a demoralised Dubček, still Party leader, was allowed to go home. Those party members who had never agreed with reform or, like Dubček's fellow-countryman Husák, concluded that accommodation with the Soviets was essential, gradually came to the fore.

In the context of the Cold War, and American entanglement in Vietnam, there was never any likelihood that the West would come to the assistance of Dubček's reform movement, any more than there had been in 1956. Implicitly, the West accepted that Eastern Europe lay within the Soviet Union's sphere of influence; suggesting otherwise risked nuclear confrontation. The stage was therefore set for a reaffirmation of Soviet hegemony. In October Brezhnev announced what was soon termed the 'Brezhnev Doctrine'. On the one hand, the Soviet leader hypocritically proclaimed, 'We resolutely oppose interference in the affairs of any states.' On the other hand, 'an action such as military assistance to a fraternal country to end a threat to the socialist system' was fully justified.[33] The Brezhnev Doctrine set Soviet control of Eastern Europe in stone for another generation.

---

[33] Text in Stokes (ed.), *From Stalinism to Pluralism*, 133.

Husák took over from Dubček as party leader in April 1969; the latter was eventually expelled from the Party in 1970. To the end of his life Dubček never got over the shock of the Soviet invasion: 'That they should have done this to me, after I have dedicated my whole life to cooperation with the Soviet Union, is the great tragedy of my life.'[34] In the meantime Husák, like Kádár in Hungary, presided over an attempt at 'Kádárisation': the stern repression of dissent, coupled with a determined effort at improving living standards, while affirming total allegiance to the Soviet Union. Economically, Husák could claim some limited success, in that discontent was kept within acceptable limits. Politically, Husák implemented 'normalization', in other words a return to the conformist obedience of the past, involving a massive purge of the party membership, weeding out some 600,000 members by 1970. This wholesale shedding of active members, however, accelerated the brain death of Czechoslovak communism: bereft of all the reform-minded individuals who had powered the Prague Spring, many of whom either escaped abroad or retreated into internal exile, the party simply no longer had the imagination or the daring to attempt meaningful change. Instead, the absence of discussion within the party meant that what real intellectual life there was in Czechoslovakia necessarily took place outside the party, among the ranks of the disillusioned and the dissident.

[34] Quoted in Shawcross, *Dubcek*, vi.

15

Absurdistan, or 'real existing socialism' 1968–80s

This chapter describes the final, stagnant years of communism in Eastern Europe, following the 1968 invasion of Czechoslovakia. Outwardly Soviet hegemony seemed set in stone; inwardly, the entire edifice was rotting. We could date the beginning of the end from November 1982, when Leonid Brezhnev, living symbol of this stagnation, died, and it became apparent that even members of the Soviet Politburo recognised the need for reform. Nevertheless it took another three years of gerontocracy before Mikhail Gorbachev initiated meaningful change. Up to the mid-1980s, the insistence of the East European communist regimes, following the Soviet lead, was that they represented a sort of nirvana, that, all evidence to the contrary, they had achieved what Brezhnev called 'real existing socialism'.

This gap between pretence and reality, which for most East Europeans was all too obvious, meant that political life became increasingly absurd: the party mouthed its slogans, while everybody, including party members, got on with the problems of everyday existence. The situation was described as 'breathing under water' by the Polish dissident Stanisław Barańczak, citing a science fiction story by Stanisław Lem about a distant planet whose inhabitants had to spend all their lives under water.[1] The theme endured down to 1989: *Absurdistan* was the apt title of a British television documentary on late-communist Czechoslovakia.

Several things flowed from 1968. Firstly, Soviet power continued to set strict limits to how far individual regimes could amend 'real existing socialism'. Secondly, it was increasingly clear that fewer and fewer East Europeans, including party members, wholeheartedly believed in communist ideology. Thirdly, the economic decline of communism was, paradoxically, only mitigated by an increasing turn towards western capital as well as technology: by the 1980s most East European regimes were heavily indebted to western banks and partially dependent on imported goods. Finally, in reaction to the impracticality and injustices of communist rule, there emerged, in some East European societies, an alternative set of values, a minute body of dissident opinion focused on the recreation of what has been called 'civil society', a

---

[1] Barańczak, S., 1990, *Breathing under Water and Other East European Essays*, Cambridge, MA and London, 2.

private space where individuals could live a life separate from, or parallel to, the all-pervasive party-state. Some East Europeans, in other words, bravely set the example of breathing above water, even if the majority continued to obey the party-state.

The economic but also geopolitical aspects of communist Eastern Europe's final two decades will be dealt with first. Then four case studies will be made of late communism. Czechoslovakia represented a hardline regime struggling to maintain the official ideology. Hungary was a halfway house, where a freer economic and cultural atmosphere prevailed. Romania offered a unique blend of neo-Stalinist repression and megalomaniacal personality cult, with horrific consequences for its inhabitants. Yugoslavia illustrated the insoluble challenge posed to communist regimes by long-repressed but also artificially whipped up nationalisms.

Jurassic Park: General problems of late communism

Alexander Dubček describes his fruitless debate with the Soviets in the summer of 1968 as 'Talking to the Dinosaurs', and this saurian metaphor seems an apt one for the late communist regimes. Not only were individual leaders visibly geriatric, but their approach to the problems confronting them was outdated and unimaginative.

No one typified this more than Brezhnev: in his final years, Brezhnev was clearly ailing, and functioned only with the assistance of plentiful medication and alcohol. His two immediate successors, Yuri Andropov (died February 1984) and Konstantin Chernenko (died March 1985), were equally frail. When the fifty-four year old Gorbachev took over in 1985, he prompted a Moscow joke: 'Who supports Gorbachev in the Politburo? Nobody – he can walk all by himself.'[2] East European communist leaders were just as grey and uninspiring.

Ageing leaders tend to be conservative in temperament, instinctively opting for the status quo and as little experimentation as possible. This was the lesson learned from 1956 and 1968. As far as ideology went, Zdeněk Zeman makes the point that, for men like Brezhnev, the intellectual refinements of communism were of relatively little interest. Stalin had after all been 'not an intellectual . . . not born in a city, he had no university education and he was not well travelled.' And in his long dominance Stalin created a generation of party apparatchiks rather like himself: 'It became honourable for his associates to regard themselves as mechanics of power, for whom politics became reduced

[2] Doder, D., 1986, *Shadows and Whispers: Power Politics inside the Kremlin from Brezhnev to Gorbachev*, London, 268.

to problems of technical manipulation'.[3] This applied to men like Novotný or Husák, Ulbricht or Erich Honecker, Ceauşescu or Hoxha. They had little of the questing intellectual curiosity of a Lenin; instead, the ideology was a given, not to be questioned. Society was seen in mechanistic terms, like so many components to be pulled apart and put back together again, like an engine. Given the dire economic condition of the Soviet Union and its satellites by the 1970s, this mental conservatism constituted a failure of leadership.

Communism's economic failure was strikingly obvious by the 1970s, manifesting itself in multiple ways. The inefficiency of the command economy, with its centralised control of production and its lack of incentives, was reflected in 'an extraordinary slowdown in economic growth' across the region.[4] From 1975 to 1980 the average growth rate per capita for Eastern Europe as a whole, excluding the Soviet Union, was 1.4 per cent, which was down steeply from 'a healthy 4.2 per cent' in 1970–5; for the period 1980–5 the growth rate was 1.0 per cent, and in 1985 there was no growth at all. After 1985 individual economies, even relatively successful ones like Hungary's, were actually recording negative growth.

Another index of economic failure was the standard of living. Although communist Eastern Europe's standard of living in the 1980s was reckoned to be 'probably a third higher' than that of the Soviet Union, this was poor consolation compared to the West.[5] Even official statistics noted a decline in the per capita rate of growth of living standards: from 2.5 to 1.4 in Czechoslovakia, from 3.6 to 2.0 in Bulgaria, from 4.0 to 1.2 per cent in Romania, and so on. This was despite rising levels of indebtedness to western banks, of which more shortly, an indebtedness incurred precisely in order to shore up standards of living. Those living under communist regimes may have had only the foggiest notion of the gap between their quality of life and that of the increasingly successful European Economic Community, but they would have been shocked by the facts. By 1980, despite the jolt of the 1973 oil crisis, the average gross national product of West European member-states of NATO was $7,000; the average per capita GNP in Soviet-controlled Eastern Europe was $4,000.

In part the poor economic performance was due to the distorted priorities of communist regimes. Not only had they, in true Stalinist fashion, concentrated on investing in heavy industry while neglecting light industry and the production of consumer goods, but the Cold War meant their defence budgets were wildly inflated, given the size of their economies. Military expenditure by Warsaw Pact countries was always shrouded in secrecy, but everyone knew that, while the Soviet Union felt its satellites did not contribute enough to defence, the satellites

[3] Zeman, Z.A.B., 1991, *The Making and Breaking of Communist Europe*, Oxford and Cambridge, MA, 252.
[4] Gati, C., 1990, *The Bloc That Failed: Soviet-East European Relations in Transition*, London, 107–8.
[5] Gati, *The Bloc That Failed*, 107.

felt they paid far too much. Even the official statistics ranged from between 2 and 6 per cent of GNP, but the real figures were probably much higher. In 1988 the economic historian Iván T. Berend, a member of the Hungarian Party's central committee, created a sensation by complaining publicly that Hungary's military budget was greater than its spending on health, education and research combined. In addition, at the behest of the Soviets, East bloc regimes were locked into a supportive role aiding left-wing insurgencies and movements around the globe, part of the Cold War competition with the West.

The Soviet-style command economy, despite some striking successes, also failed to develop new technology. This failure was most apparent in computer technology. Acknowledging the West's superiority in this regard, the Soviets took advantage of a period of detente in the mid-1960s to start importing computers and, more importantly, the sophisticated components of computers such as microchips. Production of such goods was eventually copied in the communist world, and by the 1980s some countries, like Bulgaria, became suppliers to the rest of the Soviet bloc. Even then, such dependency on western imports made the Soviets and their satellites vulnerable to any sudden downturn in East-West relations, as happened after the Soviet invasion of Afghanistan in 1979, when the United States retaliated by blocking the sale of computer parts. And even when trading conditions were stable the inefficiencies of central planning meant that much of what was imported, at considerable cost in hard currency, was wasted. The Hungarian government, for instance, imported large numbers of computers in the 1970s, for which the office blocks in which they were to be used were not yet built; stored in open sheds over the winter, the delicate internal components of the equipment were found to be useless by the spring. In Poland, during the year-long existence of the independent trade union Solidarity, a dossier was compiled of wastage at the Ursus tractor factory: piles of equipment 'rusting in the snow. Brand-new Rolls-Royce spare parts were found on a scrap-heap'.[6]

After initially decrying 'bourgeois consumption' in the Stalinist period, the post-Stalinist regimes accepted the need to become more consumer-oriented. Despite the fact that cheap food, housing, education and health care became universal features of East European societies under communism, there was no denying these were also 'shortage economies.'[7] East bloc economies by the 1970s were notorious for their chronic shortages of consumer goods, as well as the generally poor quality of what goods were on offer. The type of goods produced for the domestic market was always behind demand, leading to a dearth of everything from clothing to household appliances to washing

---

[6] Garton Ash, T., 1983, *The Polish Revolution: Solidarity 1980-82*, London, 107.
[7] Bren, P. and Neuburger, M., 2012, 'Introduction', in P. Bren and M. Neuburger (eds.), *Communism Unwrapped: Consumption in Cold War Eastern Europe*, Oxford and New York, 7.

powder and toilet paper. Queuing for goods in short supply became a way of life throughout the Soviet bloc, with people spending hours waiting in line for scarce commodities. Timothy Garton Ash described the situation in Poland by the start of the 1980s: 'One had to queue for so much now, not merely for meat, but for butter, sugar, potatoes, rice, fruit, not to mention soap or washing powder, starting at five in the morning, and then again after working an eight-hour day, for another three or four hours until supper, the women's pale exhausted faces closed against the icy drizzle'.[8] Consumers got used to organising their own queue committees to minimise frayed tempers, and for much sought-after goods, such as furniture, places in the queue would sometimes be allocated months before. There were no private enterprises engaged in importing foreign goods, nor was the state in a position to pay for such imports. Yet western goods remained the standard of comparison, and in this competition the communist command economies were bound to lose.

Clumsy attempts were made at imitating western products such as blue jeans, but the results were unsatisfactory, nor could Soviet bloc manufactured goods ever find much of a market in the developed West. By the 1960s some regimes were negotiating deals with western manufacturers, allowing the latter to set up production plants in Eastern Europe; in one of the first of these deals, the Italian firm Fiat won a contract to produce cars in Poland in 1966, at a price within the means of Poles, and the 'Polski Fiat' became a ubiquitous phenomenon. Such deals, however, were the exception to the rule; overall the East European states traded largely with the Soviet Union, and where they could with one another and other communist states like China, as well as selected countries in the 'Third World'.

The most astonishing sign of communism's economic failure was that societies which still had a huge agricultural sector were compelled to import food. This was an indictment of central planning which, in the absence of a market system, could not guarantee efficient planting, harvesting, storage or distribution. Notoriously, the Soviet Union was reduced to purchasing grain from Canada, the United States and Australia at intervals from the 1960s, primarily in years when the harvest was poor. As an energy-rich economy the Soviet Union earned the hard currency for such purchases, where it could not simply trade in kind, through the sale of oil and natural gas abroad. Such a strategy, however, depended on the price of energy remaining high, and made the Soviets vulnerable to global market fluctuations beyond their control; it also made them vulnerable to any deterioration in East-West relations. The East European regimes did not have the option of selling raw materials on the open market. They remained dependent on the Soviets for much of their energy needs, and what they could not produce in foodstuffs they either imported

---

[8]   Garton Ash, *The Polish Revolution*, 106.

from abroad, or did without. A popular song in Hungary, by 1980, depicted the exchange between a restaurant waiter and a customer, who orders one dish after another, only to be told it is not available. The story of the East German who, confronted for the first time with a banana, tried to eat it unpeeled, may be apocryphal, but typifies the low consumer expectations of the late communist period. In Poland, despite its large number of livestock producers (mainly independent farmers), meat shortages were among the principal causes of worker unrest by the 1970s, and led directly to the formation of Solidarity in 1980; as it was, food prices in Poland, as everywhere else, were heavily subsidised by the state.

Shortages of consumer goods and foodstuffs resulted early on in a flourishing black market, a 'secondary economy' operating independently of the party-state's authority.[9] Those workers or state employees with access to consumer goods or services were in a position to steal them and sell them privately, usually but not invariably well above the official cost, and in much less time than it took to purchase legally. The penalties for such black market activity were severe, but the rewards if undetected were worth it, and it soon became apparent that a corrupt officialdom could be bribed to turn a blind eye or, even better, co-opted into the transaction. Official corruption indeed was endemic from an early stage, with some of the most compromised being party members, even at the highest levels. The fact that so many party officials were experienced black marketeers was one of the reasons why, after the fall of communism, former communists emerged as the region's most effective and ruthless private entrepreneurs: they had both the experience and the unscrupulousness to succeed in business, as well as enough illegally accumulated wealth to give them a head start in the new capitalist world.

What is striking about such black market activity is that, depending on the regime, much of it was initially tolerated by the party-state, as an unofficial but tacit correction to the 'shortcomings of the socialist sector'.[10] Farmers who sold off part of their produce on the open market, or individuals who set up small catering businesses or repair shops or other services for their own profit, were supplying something that the command economy could not. With time, such private enterprise expanded to the point it became difficult for the authorities to shut it down, assuming party officials themselves were not engaged in such activity. Such black market work tended to produce several distorting effects. Firstly, people tended to work far harder for their own profit than they did for state enterprises, whose inefficiency was proverbial precisely because their workers spent so much of their spare time moonlighting. Secondly, the secondary economy, by providing at least some outlet for individuals' economic energies while partially satisfying consumer demand, arguably 'promoted political

---

[9] Schöpflin, G., 1993, *Politics in Eastern Europe 1945-1992*, Oxford and Cambridge, MA, 176.
[10] Schöpflin, *Politics in Eastern Europe*, 176.

stability.'[11] Thirdly, such black market activity was, by its nature, conducted out of sight of the authorities and was hence completely untaxed. It is anyone's guess how much wealth the secondary economy siphoned off from the primary economy, but the cost was undoubtedly enormous.

A practical illustration of the absurdities of the black market economy was provided by a Hungarian dissident, János Kenedi, whose *Do It Yourself: Hungary's Hidden Economy* was published in the West in the early 1980s. Kenedi set out to build his own house, and soon found that every step of its construction, from securing the empty plot, to receiving planning permission, to finding contractors and materials, was only possible by resorting to the black market. Shortages and bureaucratic delay were facts of life, but for the right price and with the right contacts – many of them party officials by day – everything could be negotiated. In Kádár's Hungary, this intricate network of illicit market economy became tacitly accepted by the regime as a necessary safety valve; other communist regimes were less tolerant, and their economies were correspondingly more sclerotic as a result.

Another bizarre example of openly practised black market activity was the street trade in coupons required to purchase goods in Tuzex, Czechoslovakia's chain of state-run hard-currency shops. Originally restricted to westerners in search of scarce commodities, these shops, like similar outlets elsewhere in the East bloc, rapidly became a magnet for hustlers who bought up the coupons and sold them on illegally to East European consumers. The hustlers effectively acted as capitalist middlemen, brazenly making in half an hour what a factory worker earned in a month; but in the process 'Tuzex were said to generate twice the hard currency earned through tourism', and more than the entire Czechoslovak glass industry.[12]

The ultimate indictment of the East European command economies was the fact that, in the end, they all wound up borrowing money from the capitalist West. Yugoslavia was the first communist regime to turn to the West for aid, although initially this was only because Stalin drummed it out of the Soviet bloc; between 1949 and the early 1960s the United States government provided several hundred million dollars in aid to Yugoslavia. Tito availed himself regularly of this financial crutch, and in the 1970s Yugoslavia took out a series of foreign loans; it has been estimated that between 1960 and 1990 Yugoslavia amassed some $4 billion in World Bank-authorised loans. Servicing the interest alone on this debt was crippling, and was a significant factor in the country's descent into political chaos after Tito's death in 1980.

Where the Yugoslavs led, the Soviet Union and its Warsaw Pact satellites eventually followed. The USSR's intermittently high grain imports were

---

[11] Schöpflin, *Politics in Eastern Europe*, 177.

[12] Bren, P., 2012, 'Tuzex and the Hustler: Living It Up in Czechoslovakia', in Bren and Neuburger (eds), *Communism Unwrapped*, 34.

where possible paid for in kind, but when this was not an option there was no alternative to taking out foreign loans. By 1981 $31 billion were owed by the Soviets to a variety of western creditors. Communist Eastern Europe minus the USSR also went on a borrowing spree: by 1970 the Warsaw Pact countries collectively had a foreign debt of $4 billion, rising to $26 billion in 1976 and $60.7 billion in 1981. Bulgaria by 1980 spent 40 per cent of its hard currency earnings simply on servicing its foreign debt, although after that point it managed to reduce its indebtedness by half, to a mere $1.8 billion, thanks to its development of a successful computer industry. Hungary's debt rose between 1970 and 1979 from $1 billion to $9.1 billion; ten years later it had reached $20 billion. Poland was the most spendthrift and consequently the most compromised of the lot: it already owed $20 billion by 1979, but by 1981 this had risen to $25 billion, of which $6 billion went on food imports. By the time the regime finally collapsed in August 1989 the total debt was $40 billion. Romania, an oil producer, was hit hard by the 1973 OPEC crisis, and by 1981 its foreign debt was $10.2 billion; Ceauşescu then decided to pay it all off, and by 1987 the debt had been reduced to under $5 billion; the resulting austerity, however, had calamitous results for Romanians' standard of living, contributing significantly to the violent end of the regime in 1989. Only Czechoslovakia showed caution in borrowing from the West, and by 1980 its indebtedness was the lowest per capita in the region. East Germany was a peculiar exception: the Basic Treaty of 1972 with West Germany provided Honecker's regime with direct monetary payments from the Federal Republic, and by the late 1970s East Germany was being subsidised by West Germany to the tune of about DM600 million a year. A decade later the figure was DM6 billion a year, some 15 per cent of national income.

Just as important as communism's economic failure, if harder to quantify, was its political, or what should perhaps be called its moral, failure. This had two aspects. One was the brain death of the movement ostensibly still responsible for 'building socialism'. Not only were party leaders bereft of ideas for solving the problems confronting them; the membership was equally clueless, and cynical about the prospects for meaningful change, where it was not complicit in corruption and black market activity. Those few members who still professed a sincere faith in the principles of Marxism-Leninism did so in the face of the reality all around them. A significant index of communism's cumulative demoralisation in this period was the decline in membership. While membership remained an important consideration for those seeking advantages, access to goods and services, or just social status, and even in the 1980s 8.1 per cent of the population across the region were still party members, this still represented a steady decline. Communism moreover decreasingly appealed to the young: in Poland in 1970, about a quarter of the Party's membership was under thirty, by 1985 less than 7 per cent. In Hungary, only 7.5 per cent of members were under thirty by this point. The most striking illustration of communism's irrelevance was in Poland in 1980–1, when the Polish United Workers' Party (the communists) lost 216,000 members within the first six months of the new, non-communist union Solidarity's existence; many of these absconding members appear to have joined Solidarity instead. Solidarity's eventual suppression in December 1981 reinforced the conviction, not just in Poland but across the Soviet bloc, that communism no longer had credible solutions to the problems besetting these societies.

The second aspect of communism's political failure was the emergence, not so much of a coherent political alternative, which was impossible in a one-party system, but of what can only be described as a moral fightback. What has variously been termed 'dissidence' or 'anti-politics' or 'civil society' manifested itself at first tentatively and to some extent in coded form, since the penalties for open defiance of the regime were severe. Not much in the way of dissidence or opposition was possible under regimes as repressive as Romania or East Germany, although it was not unknown. It was most practicable where a relatively liberal regime was prepared to tolerate it, as in Hungary or Poland or Yugoslavia, or where a sufficiently brave and tactically skilful group of individuals was willing to risk it, as was the case in Czechoslovakia.

The vast majority of people did not, for obvious reasons, engage in open dissent. Popular discontent was instead expressed obliquely through jokes, the black humour of which was a universal feature of East European societies under communism. As the Soviet political instructor is said to have asked the worker, 'What is the basis of the Soviet economic system?' Answer: 'You pretend to pay us, and we pretend to work.'[13] There were jokes about shortages, as in the Polish story about the customer in a butcher's shop who asks for one type of meat after another, only to be told it is unavailable; what impresses the butcher, however, is that the customer remembers the names of the meats. There were jokes brilliantly summarising the entire communist experience, as in 'The Seven Wonders of Czechoslovakia' (1989):

> Everybody has a job.
> Although everybody has a job, nobody works.
> Although nobody works, the Plan is fulfilled by 105 percent.
> Although the Plan is fulfilled by 105 percent, there's nothing in the shops.
> Although there's nothing in the shops, we've got enough of everything.
> Although we've got enough of everything, everybody steals.
> Although everybody steals, nothing ever goes missing anywhere.
> And the Eighth Wonder of the World is that it has been working
>   for forty-one years.[14]

[13] Hosking, G., 1992, *A History of the Soviet Union 1917-1991*, final edn, London, 386.
[14] Graffito in Brno, November 1989, in Wheaton, B. and Kavan, Z., *The Velvet Revolution: Czechoslovakia 1988-1991*, Boulder, CO, 10.

Such humour, despite its underlying bitterness, deflected people's frustration over conditions they could do little to change.

Another area where the younger generation especially expressed their sense of alienation was in their response to popular music. The persecution and attempted suppression of certain types of music went back decades, since the Soviets and their satellites viewed such western cultural imports as inherently degenerate and dangerous. There was good reason for such apprehension. Any music seen as subversive of socialist values, from jazz in the 1950s to rock'n'roll to heavy metal to punk, constituted a counter-culture in a sense quite inapplicable in the West. The 'overt rebelliousness' of rock'n'roll in particular, not to mention its stress on individualism and sexual freedom, was viewed with consternation, and for a while governments tried to ban outright the music of groups like the Beatles and the Rolling Stones. As Sabrina Petra Ramet puts it, for communists 'Western rock seemed to encourage the withdrawal from social engagement to a focus on personal feelings; the glorification of the West; the infiltration of political skepticism, if not outright dissidence; the introduction of cultural standards, fashions, and behavioral syndromes independent of party control; and a general numbness thought to foster political indifference and passivity.'[15]

Yet it was impossible indefinitely to ban such cultural products, in a world where western music could be occasionally heard on external radio and television broadcasts, or smuggled in on tapes or records. To placate young people, some regimes eventually allowed western bands to tour, but the predictable result was chaos: on the first occasion the Rolling Stones were invited to appear in Eastern Europe, at Warsaw in April 1967, the concert ended with a riot when police tried to curb audience enthusiasm. Thereafter visits by western bands were a rarity, but indigenous groups started to appear. By the 1970s and increasingly the 1980s there arose a lively pop music scene, much of it unashamedly imitative of western models, yet wildly popular with the young, precisely because seen as subversive of the grey communist order. An early rock group in Czechoslovakia, the Plastic People of the Universe, became the trigger for a more wide-ranging dissident movement when they were prosecuted, in 1976, for alleged 'counter-revolutionary' and 'degenerate' activity. The punk music scene elsewhere in Eastern Europe was particularly outrageous. In Yugoslavia groups like the Bastards and Laibach went out of their way to mock the wartime Partisan generation, with their use of Nazi imagery and uniforms. Polish bands, especially after the suppression of Solidarity, took provocative names such as Delirium Tremens, Shortage, Paralysis and – again, flirting with taboo allusions – Goering's Underpants. Numerous groups were banned for subversive songs or generally offensive antics, such as Hungary's

[15] Ramet, S.P., 1995, *Social Currents in Eastern Europe: The Sources and Consequences of the Great Transformation*, 2nd edn, Durham, NC, 237–8.

Coitus Punk Group, who made a habit of tearing live chickens apart on stage and slashing themselves with razors. Some, ominously, expressed unmistakably nationalist or racist sentiments, like the Hungarian group Mosoly's call for a 'Gypsy-free zone'.[16] East bloc regimes remained uncertain how to deal with the pop music scene. It is hard not to conclude that the persistence of openly subversive music made its own, unquantifiable contribution to the accelerating rot of communism in the 1980s.

Those expressing dissident political opinions, by contrast, were taking primarily moral stances, which in turn had political implications, since they constituted a challenge to the party-state in the name of fundamental human rights. Some of the earliest dissidents were members of the party, whose run-ins with the system's intolerance of criticism often earned them expulsion and imprisonment if not worse. Milovan Djilas was one of the earliest critics of Tito's authoritarianism and the corruption of the party elite in Yugoslavia. Jacek Kuroń and Karol Modzelewski, whose open letter to their fellow Polish communists got them jailed in 1965, emerged in the 1970s as leading proponents of an alliance between intellectuals and the working class. So did the historian Adam Michnik, jailed following the student protests of 1968, later reduced to working as a labourer before being allowed to emigrate in the mid-1970s. Michnik nevertheless returned in 1977 and threw himself into the ferment of activism leading to the formation of Solidarity; his *Letters from Prison* (1985), published clandestinely in the aftermath of Solidarity's suppression, became one of the emblematic documents of East European dissidence. In Hungary, where debate was increasingly tolerated, dissident Party members like the novelist György Konrád and the sociologist Iván Szelényi reflected the increasing impatience of intelligent citizens with the sheer inefficiency of 'real existing socialism'. Something had to give, but in most countries the party simply was not listening. In the words of the émigré Polish philosopher Leszek Kołakowski in 1971, 'the dead and by now also grotesque creature called Marxism-Leninism still hangs at the necks of the rulers like a hopeless tumor.'[17]

It was in this context that critics of communism came up with the twin concepts of 'anti-politics' and 'civil society' as mechanisms for coping with life in such a political dead-end. 'Anti-politics' was the title of a book published, again only in the West, by Konrád in 1984. The premise of anti-politics was that, in a situation where active opposition to the party-state was not only difficult but dangerous, the individual's only option was to turn inwards, and live according to the dictates of his own conscience rather than the party's precepts. Such a stance was anti-political in the sense that those who adopted it were determined, not only to disengage from the regime, but not to impose

---

[16] Ramet, *Social Currents in Eastern Europe*, 258.
[17] Quoted in Stokes, G., 2012, *The Walls Came Tumbling Down: Collapse and Rebirth in Eastern Europe*, 2nd edn, New York and Oxford, 23.

their views on others. What the Czech playwright Václav Havel called 'living in truth', rejecting the lies of the regime and acting according to an inner system of morality, was the only course for those who wanted to respect themselves. As Michnik put it in 1979, 'Our freedom begins with ourselves.'[18]

The problem with anti-politics was that even such quiescence constituted a challenge to communist rule. Those who, following the example of Ludvík Vaculík in 1967, insisted on 'making speeches as if we were grown up and legally independent' were, rightly, recognised by the party-state as a threat.[19] The mere act of circulating one's thoughts privately in self-published or *samizdat* form was taken as a breach of 'socialist legality' and earned Michnik, Havel and many others prison sentences. Out of this came the dissidents' additional preoccupation with 'civil society', the assertion that citizens were entitled to live their own lives as private individuals, and did so involuntarily simply by having thoughts of their own, such as religious beliefs, or a disbelief in party propaganda. It was Havel who articulated this sense of civil society most trenchantly. His famous letter to Gustáv Husák, the Party leader, circulated in *samizdat* in 1985, pointed out that most people only accepted the party's rule out of fear, and inveighed against the 'gradual erosion of all moral standards, the breakdown of all criteria of decency, and the widespread destruction of confidence in the meaning of any such values as truth, adherence to principles, sincerity, altruism, dignity and honour.'[20] In and out of prison throughout the late 1970s and the 1980s for his involvement with the dissident movement, Havel acquired a moral stature that made Husák's regime fear him all the more, not least because it also attracted attention from abroad. Havel's 1988 essay on 'The Power of the Powerless' remains the classic assertion of the value of civil society: 'Under the orderly surface of the life of lies . . . there slumbers the hidden sphere of life in its real aims, of its hidden openness to truth.'[21] Eventually, Havel implied, the futility of the communist regimes' position would become undeniable. That point was approaching faster than even he appreciated.

A final element of the moral fightback was religious. Religious sensibilities were something that communist regimes had always been reluctant to tread on too heavily, for all the harassment of church leaders, confiscation of church property and general discouragement of religious belief. In this sense the core of a faith-based opposition to the party-state had never gone away, even if by the 1960s most of the main religions had come to an uneasy detente with communism. In the 1970s, however, it became harder to ignore the fact that

[18] Quoted in Stokes, G., 1993, *The Walls Came Tumbling Down: The Collapse of Communism in Eastern Europe*, New York and Oxford, 22.
[19] Quoted in Stokes, *Walls Came Tumbling Down*, 2nd edn, 25.
[20] 'Open Letter to Dr. Gustáv Husák', in Havel, V., 1987, *Living in Truth*, edited by Jan Vladislav, London and Boston, MA, 15.
[21] "The Power of the Powerless", in Havel, *Living in Truth*, 57.

for millions of East Europeans religion was still the most important factor in their lives. This was most obvious in Catholic societies like Poland and Hungary, where the election in 1978 of the Polish cardinal Karol Wojtyła as Pope John Paul II prompted extraordinary mass demonstrations of religious fervour. The new pontiff, like many clergymen, already had a record as a critic of the party; indeed, Wojtyła was part of a trend whereby, for perhaps the first time in its history, Catholicism in Eastern Europe became identified with the defence of basic human rights and democratic values. This common ground between the church and political dissent became obvious with the foundation of Solidarity in 1980, much to the bafflement of western left-wingers, who marvelled that a genuine workers' movement could be so ostentatiously tied to religiosity. In Orthodox countries the link between religion and dissent was less clear, not least because of Orthodoxy's long-standing subservience to state authority. In East Germany, by contrast, and to a limited extent in Romanian Transylvania, Lutheranism and Calvinism also became vehicles for dissent. In East Germany becoming a pastor was one of the few careers open to anyone from a 'bourgeois' background, or who had fallen foul of the regime. Lutheran churches thus became the focus of what dissent there was in the GDR.

Finally, we cannot grasp the extent of communism's failure in Eastern Europe without considering the wider Cold War context. The Soviet Union's ability to impose its will on Eastern Europe was increasingly impaired by the competition with the United States and the West. This had much to do with the commitment to a global arms race, which placed increasing strains on the inefficient Soviet system. The Soviet Union and its East European satellites were also committed to subsidising left-wing governments and insurgencies around the world, from Vietnam to Angola to Latin America. Occasional bouts of detente in the 1960s and 1970s offered some respite from these burdens, but made the Soviet bloc as a whole vulnerable to a sudden freezing of the international temperature, especially the one that set in after the Soviet invasion of Afghanistan in 1979. President Ronald Reagan from 1981 initiated a massive American arms build-up, and in this final round of the competition the Soviets found themselves inexorably outspent. Arguably the straw that broke the Soviet camel's back was the Americans' announcement of the Strategic Defense Initiative, otherwise known as 'Star Wars', in March 1983. This planned investment in satellite-guided missile defence, although pie-in-the-sky given the limited state of technology at the time, prompted a near-panic in the Soviet military establishment. How was a credible response to be mounted? Where was the money to come from?

One last product of Cold War politics, or rather of an outbreak of detente, had a direct impact on the stability of East European regimes. As a consequence of West German chancellor Willy Brandt's *Ostpolitik* of building normal relations with East Germany, formal peace treaties were signed in 1970–1 between the USSR and Poland, on the one side, and West Germany on the other. These finally guaranteed the western borders of both the Soviet Union and Poland, a fact of huge psychological significance to the Soviets, and which prompted them to call for an international conference to confirm it. In August 1975, the Helsinki agreements on European security were signed between the Soviet Union and its Warsaw Pact allies and the NATO states. This Helsinki Final Act agreed on international recognition of East Germany. In return, the Soviets and their allies signed what they assumed was an anodyne undertaking by all signatory states to respect 'civil, economic, social, cultural, and other rights and freedoms'.[22] American administrations after this regularly cited the Final Act in their dealings with the Soviets, which the latter just as regularly ignored. More importantly, the fact that East European communist regimes had signed the Final Act gave their dissidents a stick with which to beat their governments over human rights issues. For the first time, dissidents like Havel could argue, perfectly correctly, that the denial of basic civil and other rights, as defined at Helsinki, was an act of illegality. The lengths to which this argument could be taken were shown most famously in Czechoslovakia, by the (non-) organisation known as Charter 77.

Four case studies in late communism

Czechoslovakia after August 1968 underwent a process known, with unselfconscious irony, as 'normalisation'. Dubček was initially kept on, as a screen for the gradual purging of the party, and was only replaced by Husák in April 1969. The Soviets' purpose in this subterfuge was to provide apparent legitimation for the scrapping of the Prague Spring reforms and the expulsion of reformers. The purge – though not the execution – of members was well under way by 1969; as one leading member put it, 'It will not hurt the Party to lose two or three hundred thousand members.'[23] In the event the numbers were much higher, by some accounts up to 600,000, or 28 per cent of the membership. This included 2,000 journalists or half of those in the country; 900 university professors and 1,200 other academics. Between 130,000 and 170,000 Czechs and Slovaks fled the country while they still could.

'Normalisation' represented a serious brain drain for both party and country. Party membership had always been high in Czechoslovakia, and the dropping out of so many of the educated elite posed an obstacle to any sort of intelligent debate about the economy, or anything else. In the past, between 70

---

[22] 'The Helsinki Accords, August 1 1975', doc. 26 in Stokes, G., 1996, *From Stalinism to Pluralism: A Documentary History of Eastern Europe since 1945*, 2nd edn, New York, 161.
[23] Quoted in Fejtö, F., 1974, *A History of the People's Democracies: Eastern Europe since Stalin*, translated from the French by D. Weissbrot, Harmondsworth, 471.

and 80 per cent of managers, 70 per cent of cultural workers, 60 per cent of university teachers, had been party members. The vitiation of intellectual life was increased by the dissolution of artists' associations and other professional organisations. To get published, under 'normalisation', any writer was required to sign a declaration disavowing the aims of the 1968 reforms, which were explicitly condemned as 'counter-revolutionary'. Those who refused were blacklisted, could not publish, and saw their existing works removed from circulation. They were also unable to get any sort of professional employment, and so wound up as window-cleaners, janitors, furnace-stokers and so on. The novelist and playwright Ivan Klíma describes this shadow existence in *My Golden Trades* (1992). Václav Havel for a while survived as a brewery labourer. The director of an art publishing house was replaced by an ex-waiter. Even among the non-intellectual membership genuine involvement in party work virtually ceased after 1968: a report of 1982 found that up to a third of members were completely inactive.

Not all creativity was stifled by normalisation; on the contrary, for many cultural workers making their peace with the regime was essential if they hoped to work at all. Recent research shows how the regime exploited this human desire for a quiet life through the new medium of television. Party leaders had been shocked at the speed with which, thanks to media coverage, events had spun out of control in 1968; so in the 1970s the regime consciously used TV to promote the public's acceptance of normalisation. Skilfully written serial dramas offered viewers a form of escapism through 'contemporary plot lines and familiar, every day conundrums', and in the process 'transformed the political into the non-political', since the majority of citizens had no desire to challenge the regime.[24]

Economically Czechoslovakia remained a halfway house, condemned to repeat the mistakes of the past while unable to experiment much. Prices were again strictly controlled, and the law permitting limited free enterprise was dropped. There was a return to central planning, especially in agriculture, where Husák's regime actually expanded collective farming; and in industry, where it continued to invest in polluting heavy industry. By the early 1980s Czechoslovakia's growth rate had become a shrinkage rate: in 1981 it was –0.1 per cent, in 1982 –0.2 per cent. GNP per capita was 60 per cent of that of neighbouring Austria, whereas in 1960 it had been 90 per cent. Husák did manage to reorder the economy in favour of greater provision of consumer goods, and in the period 1970–78 private consumption rose by 36 per cent. This was paid for in part by reducing investment and spending on armaments and 'fraternal' foreign aid. It was also paid for directly, in that consumer goods were increasingly imported, incurring a balance of trade deficit. As with the

[24] Bren, P., 2010, *The Greengrocer and His TV: The Culture of Communism after the 1968 Prague Spring*, Ithaca, NY, 125, 148–9.

rest of the Soviet bloc, this made Czechoslovakia vulnerable to downturns in the economic health of the West, as well as the vagaries of the Cold War; after the Soviet invasion of Afghanistan, western credits for trade and technology dried up.

Against this dreary backdrop Czechoslovakia, rather against the odds, became one of the first serious focal points for dissent. After 1968 some party members tried to form opposition groups, but the leaders were swiftly jailed. Effective opposition, or rather dissidence, started as a series of isolated, uncoordinated individual acts in the period 1972–75, and to begin with critics of the regime were careful to stress that they were not challenging the party, and were not even a political movement. Prominent writers like Havel and Vaculík, their works banned, could only publish illegally in *samizdat*; some, like the novelist Milan Kundera, considered this futile and emigrated if they could. For a tiny minority unable or unwilling to leave, however, the urge to express themselves freely was so fundamental they were bound to keep falling foul of the authorities.

What gave dissidence a new stubbornness was the Helsinki Final Act. The Czechoslovakian government signed up to Helsinki under the impression that this formal commitment to respect basic rights, like the right to freedom of expression, could be safely ignored in practice. They were consequently quite unprepared for the way in which the prosecution in 1976 of a little-known Czech rock group, the Plastic People of the Universe, served as a focus for principled dissent. The Plastic People and other groups were put on trial for 'degenerate' activity, as evidenced by their lyrics and performances, but put up a spirited defence: accused of vulgarity, they read out in court Lenin's claim that 'bureaucracy is shit'.[25] Four of the twenty-two defendants received sentences of eight to eighteen months for 'disrespect for society'. It was at this point, in September 1976, that Havel and others intervened, publicising the injustice with a letter to the German Nobel Prize winner Heinrich Böll. This in turn led, on 1 January 1977, to a declaration known as Charter 77. In this Havel and 240 other signatories, many former party members like Zdeněk Mlynář, demanded that Czechoslovakia honour its international commitment on human rights, and promised that they would continue to point out when they thought the government was falling down in this regard. They denied being a political organisation: Charter 77, they claimed, 'has no rules, permanent bodies or formal membership . . . It does not form the basis for any oppositional political activity.'[26]

Needless to say, the Husák regime disagreed. In 1977–80 some sixty Chartists were jailed, the most celebrated being Havel, whose *Letters to Olga*, his wife,

[25] Ryback, T.W., 1990, *Rock Around the Bloc: A History of Rock Music in Eastern Europe and the Soviet Union*, New York, 141–8.
[26] Quoted in Stokes, *The Walls Came Tumbling Down*, 27.

belong to the great literature of dissent. After serving four years of a lengthy sentence, most of them performing hard labour, Havel was only released when he contracted pneumonia. Other Chartists were forced out of the country. Ordinary citizens may have been unmoved by the dissidents' activities, may even have regarded them as foolish cranks; but year by year the profile at home and abroad of figures like Havel grew, and with it their moral stature. In the absence of any formal opposition, and given the underlying unpopularity of the regime, the Chartists amounted to something like a moral opposition, if not a practical political one. As a consequence, when in the course of 1988–89 the bankruptcy of the regime became undeniable, it was the Chartists who stepped forward as the natural spokesmen and leaders of the first genuine, organised protest. Husák stepped down in December 1987, and was succeeded by Miloš Jakeš, but the latter displayed no greater understanding of how to regenerate the ailing economy, even with the example of the Soviet Union's Mikhail Gorbachev before him.

Hungary under János Kádár became, by contrast, the most liberal of the East bloc regimes – Yugoslavia excepted – as its pursuit of economic prosperity increasingly departed from strict Marxist-Leninist principles. There were clear limits to how far '*gulyás* communism' could go, but Kádár as a former victim and then enforcer of Stalinism was uniquely placed to sense these limits. The key to Kádár's success in deconstructing communism from within always depended on this survivor's instinct, and maintaining the totemic institutions of the one-party state. In the economic sphere, whatever its fundamental unsoundness, Kádár's New Economic Mechanism, begun in 1966, did bring Hungary the greatest material prosperity of all the East bloc states.

Not only was much central planning abandoned, but managers of enterprises positively had to make a profit, both to reduce the need for state subsidy and to reinvest in the enterprise. Farmers on collective farms were offered incentives, such as fewer compulsory crop deliveries, payment in cash, and retaining some produce for private gain. With time, this mix of collective and private market economics became more profitable, simply because it was more efficient. The state still retained responsibility for long-term planning, but day-to-day production and marketing were effectively decentralised, introducing a rationality hitherto sorely lacking. Some Hungarian produce and goods even became valued by the non-communist world, and famous Hungarian brands like Tokaj wine started to earn hard currency. Hungary became one of the only East bloc countries where shortages, especially of foodstuffs, were rare. In the 1970s national income went up by an average of 6 per cent per annum, and real consumption by 4 per cent. After 1968, to be sure, Kádár applied the brakes somewhat: the original intention of setting up a stock exchange of sorts, exposing Hungary even more to market forces, was shelved, and for much of the 1970s economic liberalisation froze. Only in the 1980s did decentralisation resume, and for the first time enterprises could issue bonds, the beginnings at least of a capital market. By the mid-1980s the private sector totalled some 50,000 businesses. A small entrepreneurial class had re-emerged, and a significant minority of workers became accustomed to doing the same sort of work they did in their official jobs, but for a profit in the free market. This boosted productivity, but mainly in this private sector. In effect, a communist regime had created its own 'secondary economy'.

Despite Hungary's economic record, problems remained. Not only were the remnants of the old centrally planned economy hopelessly inefficient, but Hungary was vulnerable to outside pressures. The oil embargo of 1973 in particular forced Hungary to turn to the USSR for its relatively cheap energy. In return, however, Hungary had to invest in Soviet energy projects, with a consequent drain on manpower building them. More telling, Hungarian exports, though saleable in the non-communist world, were simply not competitive enough. The regime was still subsidising too many inefficient companies. The result was a rise in the foreign trade deficit, which went from $1 billion in 1970 to $9 billion in 1979. This imbalance led Hungary, in 1982, to apply for membership of the International Monetary Fund and the World Bank. Membership gave Hungary access to outside loans, but at the price of conforming to IMF and World Bank lending conditions. This membership drove the resumption of decentralisation, and economic decentralisation also implied some sort of political liberalisation.

Hungary was thus well placed to take advantage of the reforming lead given by Gorbachev after 1985. Many of the ingredients of a pluralist society were already there, including a private sector and significant intellectual autonomy. Kádár's government since the 1960s had relaxed censorship, permitted foreign travel, and welcomed not only tourism but foreign investment, represented by landmarks such as the Budapest Hilton Hotel, completed in the 1970s, or by the scholarship funding provided from the early 1980s by George Sörös, the émigré hedge-fund tycoon. Hungary remained a communist system, but an increasingly open one, where the circulation and debate of ideas was possible; and it was the younger generation of communists who took the lead in initiating meaningful change. In the era of Gorbachevian *perestroika* and *glasnost*, then, Hungary was undoubtedly best placed to evolve an alternative system without violence. Whether that alternative was quite what party leaders had in mind remained to be seen.

Romania presented a stark contrast. Despite a superficial show of populism in the 1960s, and a decided turn towards 'national communism', the dead hand of Stalinism remained firmly in place. By the end of the 1980s only Albania, frozen in its own little time warp since the early 1960s, had a worse record for economic backwardness and abuse of human rights than Romania.

Even under Gheorghiu-Dej, Romania's leader until 1965, Romanian communists displayed a marked tendency to play the nationalist card as a means of consolidating their power. Ceauşescu simply intensified this, most famously when he refused to participate in the invasion of Czechoslovakia in 1968. National communism was aimed outwardly, as when Ceaușescu dared publicly to affirm Romania's historical claims to parts of the Soviet Moldavian Republic, or when the regime trumpeted Romania's 'Dacian' past as a former Roman colony, thus proving the Romanian presence in the area long before Slavs or Hungarians. Just as important, it was aimed inwardly at Romania's Hungarian minority, a policy which increasingly poisoned relations with Hungary. Matters came to a head when Ceaușescu reacted with fury to the publication in Hungary of an impeccably academic history of Transylvania; the Romanian government took out a full-page advertisement in the London *Times*, in April 1987, accusing the Hungarians of being 'Obsessed by the wish to contest the Romanian character of Transylvania'.[27] It was the regime's persecution of the Hungarian Calvinist pastor László Tőkés, in 1989, which triggered the protests and fighting that led to Ceaușescu's downfall.

National communism worked in the short term, in that Ceaușescu for a while seemed to enjoy a genuine domestic popularity. Less understandable is the lionising which Ceaușescu's stand against the Soviets earned him in the West: he was praised for his alleged understanding of global problems by American presidents from Nixon to Carter, and in 1978 was accorded a state visit by the British government, including an honorary knighthood from Queen Elizabeth II – which did not deter Ceaușescu from bringing his own food-taster to dinner at Buckingham Palace. Such attention was of course strategic: the enemy of the West's enemy was seen as its friend, and in addition the British hoped to sell Romania jet engines. Yet Ceaușescu's vaunted independence was always a pose, designed to reinforce his position in Romania itself.

Ceaușescu was a good example of the 'mechanic of power': an uneducated man whose Marxism was of the simplest kind, and who accepted as an unalterable truth that heavy industry, collectivisation and rigid one-party control were essential for the building of socialism. His policies were a chilling illustration of the exaggerated rationalism of communism as a political philosophy, the belief that mankind and even the natural world were perfectible, to be engineered this way and that to achieve the desired result. The problem was that what Ceaușescu, with characteristic grandiosity, referred to in 1969 as a 'multilaterally developed socialist society' did not work any better than elsewhere.[28] Romania's inefficient industries did not produce much worth exporting, and thus did nothing to earn hard currency. Much industrialisation, especially in the 1970s, was financed by borrowing, and by the end of the decade Romania's foreign debt totalled over $10 billion; servicing this debt

---

[27] Advertisement, 'A Conscious Forgery of History under the Aegis of the Hungarian Academy of Sciences', *The Times*, 7 April 1987.

[28] Quoted in Tismaneanu, V., 2003, *Stalinism for All Seasons: A Political History of Romanian Communism*, Berkeley, CA, 206.

alone spiralled. In 1981, therefore, Ceauşescu threw the machine into reverse: Romania, he proclaimed, would pay off its entire debt by 1990. This meant exporting virtually everything that could be exported, which in Romania's case meant foodstuffs and natural energy resources, as well as banning imports. The result was the steady immiseration of the Romanian people. Romania, still a major agricultural producer, became a country suffering chronic food shortages, with malnutrition common, and reported cases of death from starvation. An important oil producer, it was a country whose citizens were limited to the use of one 40-watt light bulb per room and where, in a bad winter, there was an increasing incidence of deaths from hypothermia, due to lack of domestic fuel. By the mid-1980s, to conserve energy, 'the state reduced the temperature in factories, offices, schools, and even hospitals to 57 degrees Fahrenheit'.[29] In such circumstances repression was all the more essential, and what limited freedom of expression existed became a thing of the past. Imprisonment of suspected oppositionists was commonplace, accompanied by allegations of torture at the hands of the *Securitate*, Romania's feared secret police. One popular writer of children's books had her works banned, because the drawing of a cat in one allegedly bore a resemblance to Ceauşescu.

To shut out the reality, the Ceauşescu regime developed a personality cult verging on the demented, and making Stalin's look modest by comparison. Ceauşescu's inclinations in this direction were prompted by his visit to China and North Korea in 1971, which impressed upon him the desirability of mass indoctrination, reinforced by veneration of the all-powerful leader. Ceauşescu was regularly hailed as the 'Great Leader', the 'Enlightened One', the 'Supreme Personality' and the 'Danube of Thought'. Coupled with this was an equally bizarre elevation of Ceauşescu's wife and family which has been called 'dynastic communism'.[30] Elena Ceauşescu, the wife, was the linchpin of this nepotism, sitting on the Politburo and acting as vice-premier; her son Nicu rose rapidly also. Elena, compared with whom, one foreign diplomat observed, 'Nicolae is a teddy-bear', claimed on obscure grounds a qualification in engineering, collected honorary degrees like posies, and prided herself on her self-awarded membership of the Academy of Sciences. More seriously, Elena with her husband's full support launched a drive to increase Romania's birth rate by banning not only abortions but contraceptives of all sorts; the results, in a country on the verge of famine, were a shocking spike in the number of deaths from illegal terminations, and an abundance of abandoned children in Romania's run-down orphanages.

Ceauşescu indulged in Ozymandias-like building projects, like the monstrous 'Palace of the People' in Bucharest, which involved razing much

---

[29] Massino, J., 2012, 'From Black Caviar to Blackouts: Gender, Consumption and Lifestyle in Ceauşescu's Romania', in Bren and Neuburger (eds), *Communism Unwrapped*, 243.
[30] Tismaneanu, *Stalinism for All Seasons*, 225.

of the historic centre of the city to build it. In the countryside, the regime in the 1980s embarked on a policy of 'systematisation', obliterating villages and concentrating the population in new towns and suburbs; this had the added advantage of targeting the ethnic Hungarian minority in particular.

The greatest tragedy of the Ceauşescu dictatorship was that, for all its absurdity, this crude conflation of Marxism and a frothing Romanian nationalism worked. Opposition within the party and the wider populace was limited, and even those who dared to voice criticism of the regime tended to share its nationalist agenda. One reason for this, it has been suggested, is that the Romanian Communist Party never produced any major theorists. In other East bloc countries the existence of such thinkers, most of them alienated from the party by the mid-1980s, furnished a base for either reform communism or dissidence. Romania had no such luck, with the result that the revolt, when it came, was more elemental and violent.

Yugoslavia in the post-Tito period provides an example of how repressed nationalism could bubble to the surface, especially in a multinational state like Yugoslavia – or the Soviet Union.

It is worth stressing that, for all Tito's success at steering a course between the Soviets and the West, while maintaining a communist system with relative prosperity and fewer restrictions on personal freedom, all was not well even before Tito's death in 1980. On the contrary: it was clear that economic growth was not guaranteed even under this maverick form of communism. In particular the genie of nationalism could not so easily be stuffed back into its bottle.

An early harbinger of trouble was the demonstrations that convulsed Priština, capital of the supposedly autonomous province of Kosovo, in 1968. These had their origins in the grievances of Kosovo's Albanian majority, still denied meaningful self-rule by the Serb-dominated local party. In reality Kosovo had been tightly controlled from Belgrade ever since the imposition of communism, and Albanians remained disadvantaged: in the 1960s illiteracy was still around 50 per cent in Kosovo, unemployment 20 per cent, and most professional and official jobs were filled by Serbs. Albanians in 1968 demanded a genuine, as opposed to nominal, autonomy, and although their demonstrations were firmly repressed Tito started making significant concessions in response. An Albanian-language university was created, a major economic advance for Albanians. More significantly, Tito recognised Kosovo as yet another argument for further decentralisation. In 1969, the party adopted a measure designed specifically to address the sensibilities of Yugoslavia's peoples. This 'ethnic key' applied to the composition of the party's central committee; henceforward, each republic, including the two autonomous provinces, Vojvodina and Kosovo, was to have equal representation on the committee and its sub-committees. In short, the party was deliberately Balkanised, turning it into a patchwork quilt of nationalities in all its working bodies. In theory the party remained committed to a supranational image, because it was communist; in practice, the representatives of individual republics increasingly saw themselves, and each other, as representing separate national interests.

Where all this might lead was soon apparent: the revival of nationalism. The Tito regime's attitude towards nationalism, in its first two decades in power, was that modernisation and socialism would kill it off. After Tito, it is more accurate to say that the inadequacy of economic development helped exacerbate nationalism, but the nationalism had clearly been there all along. It also became clear that efforts to foster a specifically Yugoslav patriotism had, at best, only limited appeal: Yugoslavs seemed to rally around Tito against Stalin, and again in 1968; but these were the high points. In the relative absence of outside pressures after 1968, the Yugoslav republics' tendency to squabble with one another resumed. Increasingly they argued about how to divide the economic cake, and the communist parties at republican level increasingly saw themselves as representing republican, rather than Yugoslav, interests.

The initial focus of reviving nationalism was, unsurprisingly, Croatia in the 'Croatian Spring' of 1970–1. By the 1960s there was an increasingly vocal nationalist revival in Croatia, led by the cultural organisation *Matica Hrvatska* (literally Croatian Queen Bee), dating from the nineteenth century and refounded in 1967. *Matica Hrvatska*'s publications, especially the periodical *Kritika*, openly discussed the supposedly disadvantageous plight of Croats in Bosnia-Hercegovina. Croatian intellectuals, partly in reaction to Serb insensitivity, started disputing the unity of the Serbo-Croat language. Most controversially, Franjo Tuđman, an ex-Partisan general turned historian, began questioning the number of Serbs murdered by Croatia's wartime *Ustaša* regime, in effect downplaying fascist atrocities. These overt displays of nationalism clearly alarmed Croatia's Serb minority and split the Croatian party down the middle, but those articulating such sentiments found there was considerable popularity to be had by standing up to Belgrade.

Tito's initial response, while denouncing extreme nationalists like Tuđman, was to continue decentralising, amending the constitution in 1971 to ensure that any decisions by the federal government must be agreed by consensus among the republics. In the end, however, the Croatian party's inability to control its nationalists resulted in a crackdown. Tito was concerned about the danger of a Serb reaction; as he warned in July 1971, 'In some villages the Serbs out of nervousness are drilling and arming themselves. . . . Do we want to have 1941 again?'[31] In November 1971 students at Zagreb University demanded greater autonomy; provocatively, they also demanded a separate seat for Croatia at the United Nations general assembly. In response, Tito sent troops into Zagreb, arrested student leaders, banned *Matica Hrvatska*, and purged the Croatian

---

[31] Quoted in Lampe, J.R., 1996, *Yugoslavia as History: Twice There Was a Country*, Cambridge, 204.

party. To demonstrate even-handedness, he also purged the Serbian party, thus eliminating an entire generation of party stalwarts and facilitating the rise of apparatchiks like the future Serbian party leader Slobodan Milošević. But for the foreseeable future the snake of Croatian nationalism was seemingly scotched.

Tito's final response to the Croatian Spring had more fateful consequences. The process of decentralisation was significantly furthered by Yugoslavia's fourth constitution of 1974. This most complex of constitutions was intended to reassert the central, controlling role of the Yugoslav Communist Party; such was the purpose of the bewildering tiered voting for republican and federal assemblies, which gave the appearance of mass participation while leaving selection of candidates with the party leadership. On the other hand, the power of the republican parties, to veto federal action was left in place and, although Tito remained president for life, on his death in 1980 the presidency was to rotate, yearly, from republic to republic. This was a recipe for paralysis in the face of any really serious crisis over the economy, let alone issues of nationality.

From 1981 it was precisely such a crisis which overwhelmed communism in Yugoslavia. As a result of the constitutional changes the Kosovo Albanians, some 90 per cent of the province's population, for the first time had something like real autonomy, and dominated the provincial party, although not necessarily the security services, where the Serbian party retained a presence. Priština University now produced an Albanian educated class, and more funds were channelled into Albanian-language schools. Self-rule, however, could only advance Albanians' prosperity so far. Because of Yugoslavia's deteriorating economy, the increasing numbers of degree-holders were largely unemployed, and Albanian-speakers, unlike Kosovo's Serbs, could not so easily relocate to other parts of Yugoslavia in search of work. This was the root of the unrest in March 1981, when Albanian students started protesting at their living conditions and lack of career prospects. The reaction of the police was to disperse the students by force, which meant the protests spread to the general populace. The provincial party appealed to Belgrade; martial law was proclaimed and the Yugoslav National Army deployed. Officially, twelve people were killed in the riots; unofficially the figures were probably higher.

The bloodshed polarised the two ethnic communities of Kosovo, Muslim Albanians and Christian Orthodox Serbs, beyond possibility of reconciliation. Albanians were convinced the only solution was republic status for Kosovo, so they could fully take control. For Serbs, the idea of an Albanian-dominated Kosovo was already anathema; republic status would leave the Serb minority at the mercy of the Albanians, without any means of protection by the Serbian republican government in Belgrade. To forestall further intervention by the Yugoslav party, the Albanian-led provincial party ruled with a heavy hand: according to Amnesty International, in 1981–5 some 3,000 Albanians were arrested, and 100 killed, for 'nationalistic' offences. The Albanian response was a mounting harassment of Serbs, which fuelled Serb emigration to Serbia and Montenegro, and a wave of Serb nationalist hysteria, not just in Kosovo, but among Serbs across the federation.

As far as can be ascertained, the majority of those who died in Kosovo as a result of interethnic violence were Albanians. This did not, however, register with most Serbs, wherever they lived; and as the 1980s progressed it became apparent that a huge nationalist backlash was building up among Serbs over the Kosovo situation. To fathom how this could happen in a communist-led state, officially committed to the discouragement of nationalism, we must understand that Yugoslavia was the victim of its own relative liberalism. By communist standards the degree of freedom allowed the media and intellectual life in Yugoslavia was exceptional, and nowhere was more so than in Serbia. Gradually a stream of alarmist and openly nationalist literature about the 'Kosovo question' sprang up, which Tito probably would not have tolerated. Lurid, though usually unsubstantiated reports of Albanian 'atrocities' against Serbs found their way into print, and were given airtime by the Serbian media. Books and pamphlets purporting to chronicle the 'Golgotha' of the Serbs in Kosovo found a ready market. Poets, artists, novelists, journalists and historians all contributed to the hysteria, which culminated in a notorious memorandum published in September 1986 by members of the Serbian Academy of Arts and Sciences. The SANU memorandum hit public opinion in Serbia like a bombshell. For the first time since the war, respected intellectual figures were being allowed to speak out on a nationalist issue. Explosively, the memorandum claimed that Serbs had been failed by Yugoslavia; a minority everywhere except Serbia and Montenegro, they were denied the influence their numbers entitled them to. Worst of all, the memorandum offered the inflammatory opinion that 'The physical, political, legal and cultural genocide of the Serbian population of Kosovo . . . is a worse historical defeat than any experienced in the liberation wars waged by Serbia from the First Serbian Uprising in 1804 to the uprising of 1941'.[32]

The SANU memorandum was a watershed in the history of communist Yugoslavia. The fact that cultural and intellectual leaders could strike such an envenomed tone, and could write, uncritically, of 'genocide' was an indication of just how far public opinion in Serbia had gone. It also, understandably, sent out shock waves across Yugoslavia, among non-Serbs everywhere. If Serbia, the largest and most populous of the republics, was succumbing to such nationalist hatreds, where would this lead? The stage was set, in Serbia itself, for the rise to power of someone who knew how to channel these nationalist emotions for his own ends.

---

[32] Quoted in Judah, T., 2000, *The Serbs: History, Myth and the Destruction of Yugoslavia*, 2nd edn, New Haven, CT, 49.

16

The Solidarity phenomenon
in Poland 1980–9

Solidarity, the independent Polish trade union which sprang up, seemingly out of nowhere, in August 1980 and lasted until December 1981, was a phenomenon for several reasons. Firstly, this was the first non-communist mass organisation to appear in the Soviet bloc since the imposition of the one-party dictatorships; that it existed at all, let alone was uneasily tolerated by the Polish government and the Soviets for more than a year, spoke volumes for the fundamental weakness and paralysis of will that had overtaken most communist regimes by this point. Secondly, Solidarity was a genuinely mass movement, a demonstration of working-class autonomy whose mere appearance issued a blistering rebuke to a regime claiming to speak on behalf of the proletariat. But Solidarity was also more than just a workers' movement: for the first time, working-class protest was joined and advised by dissident intellectuals, many of them former party members. This coalition of workers and intellectuals was new, and gave Solidarity a coherence and purposefulness hitherto lacking in any East European society. Finally, if 1968 can be seen as communism's last chance to reform, then the meteoric trajectory of Solidarity, despite its seeming extinction, suggested that communism in Eastern Europe really was on its last legs. It still took the initiation of change in the Soviet Union itself, after 1985, to push the whole rickety structure over; but the Solidarity episode, with hindsight, really was the beginning of the end.

This chapter focuses on events in Poland, although these should be seen against the backdrop of economic and institutional atrophy evident everywhere in communist Eastern Europe. As with all historical events, Solidarity did not appear out of thin air, and the first section deals with its 'prehistory' going back to the late Gomułka era. What is striking about the period after 1970 is how a pattern was repeated: in an attempt to dig itself out of its economic problems, the Polish regime resolved to raise revenue by increasing prices, only to run into a storm of often violent working-class protest, and then backed down. The pattern displayed itself in 1970, and then again in 1976 and 1980; and it was in the interval between the latter two confrontations that the alliance of workers and intellectuals was forged. Solidarity's astonishing emergence and even more astonishing success in mobilising support, while forcing the Polish Party onto the back foot, is the focus of the middle section. Finally, despite Solidarity's suppression and the internment of many of its leaders, it soon became apparent that the organisation had merely gone underground: it survived in shadowy parallel to the regime until the pressing economic situation of the late 1980s, and the presence of a reformer in the Kremlin, forced the party to accept Solidarity as the only feasible support for the economic reforms deemed necessary. The chapter takes the story up to the start of the 'Round Table' talks of 1989, which presaged the holding of partially free elections and the unexpected collapse of the party-state.

The prehistory of Solidarity 1968–80

Poland was always one of the less promising candidates for communisation, and Stalin himself considered the Poles too nationalist and individualist to accept communism readily. It was Poland's misfortune, however, to form an essential component of the Soviets' post-1945 security system; and Gomułka, for all his 'national communism', was committed to keeping the country within the Soviet bloc.

By the late 1960s, however, Gomułka's sclerotic regime was increasingly unpopular. The anti-Semitic campaign unleashed by the party in 1967 disgusted many members, large numbers of whom resigned. Parallel with the Prague Spring of 1968 Poland underwent its own crisis. In January 1968 the government shut down a production of the nineteenth-century play *Forefathers' Eve*, by Poland's national bard Adam Mickiewicz, about the Polish uprising of 1830, because its most famous line, 'Moscow sends only rogues to Poland,' was greeted with thunderous applause. In protest against the closure Warsaw students staged a three-months' strike; when the students were finally clubbed into submission by the security police there was further popular revulsion. One of the student leaders, Adam Michnik, later emerged as Poland's most prominent dissident. The striking feature about Poland's 1968, however, was the non-involvement of the working class, for whom this confrontation had little relevance.

In 1970 the shoe was on the other foot, when the workers were targeted by the regime. Two weeks before Christmas, the government announced hefty price rises, with sugar up 14 per cent, flour 16 per cent and meat 17 per cent. This was a consequence of Gomułka's attempts at economic rationalisation, similar to that begun in Hungary, and which involved concentrating investment in certain key industrial sectors, such as electrical appliances, chemicals and precision tools, in the hope of increasing Poland's export potential. Such concentration, however, necessarily diverted funds from other areas like housing and health care; it also, crucially, meant cutting back employment, a freeze on wages, and a reduction in subsidies for food. The price hikes of December 1970 thus came on top of a noticeable deterioration in living standards that were already dire, and they were greeted with an immediate, spontaneous explosion of worker protest, especially in the Baltic ports, where a communist party office was ransacked and set on fire. The regime reacted with comparable savagery, crushing the rioting workers with both security police and the army; several scores of people were killed and over a thousand wounded. Unrest did not stop there: the workers staged sit-in strikes in the shipyards, elected strike committees, and demanded the right to organise free, independent trade unions. By January 1971 the strike action had spread from Gdańsk and Gdynia to Szczecin in the west.

The spectacle of Poles killing Poles profoundly shocked everyone, and was followed by something unprecedented: the party central committee sacked Gomułka and replaced him with the more emollient Edward Gierek. Gierek made a great show of appearing in person at the shipyards, with his new prime minister in tow, and pleading with the strikers for trust and reconciliation. In effect Gierek backed down. He not only rescinded the December price rises, but raised wages all round. It was a significant moment: for the first time, concerted popular action had toppled a communist leader, and forced the party into a U-turn.

Gierek's solution to the problems besetting Poland was to placate the workers at the expense of economic rationality; as someone crudely put it, this amounted to stuffing their mouths with sausage. It was ultimately, however, a self-defeating strategy. The government embarked on a huge and extraordinarily costly drive to increase meat production, largely through upping the subsidy for this; in addition, incentives were offered to farmers, such as granting them legal ownership of their land. This massive expansion of investment had to be paid for, and the Gierek regime did so by borrowing: in the 1970s $20 billion of state debt was racked up, $6 billion of which went on food imports, including feed for livestock. Ironically, this did not solve the problem of supply, since the regime had simultaneously given everyone a wage increase, so whatever meat and other foodstuffs there were almost immediately sold out. Shortages, queues and frustration remained permanent and seemingly ineradicable features of Polish life. Worse, the drive for foreign investment as well as foreign loans, coupled with the wage increases, led to inflation, thus eroding any progress made in fiscal terms. The increased availability of foreign capital failed to achieve a genuine technological modernisation, and instead went to line the pockets of the corrupt party elite. Despite rocketing levels of debt, Poland's economy therefore remained unproductive, and the chances of paying off the debt receded ever further into the future.

In June 1976, the spending spree came to a halt, when Gierek's government was forced to admit that the policy of unlimited subsidy was a failure. Having tried, just as before, to limit expenditure by cutbacks and a wage freeze, they reached yet again for the risky remedy of price rises, and touched off yet another explosion. This time, however, the move had been planned. When the predictable wave of strikes and demonstrations broke out, the security forces were ready for them. Protests were met with carefully measured force; there were fewer casualties, despite mass beatings, arrests and imprisonment.

The biggest difference between the disturbances of 1970 and those of 1976, however, was the extent to which the workers' cause in 1976 was now supported by the intelligentsia. This was in turn the fruit in Poland of what we have already referred to as 'anti-politics', the gradual evolution across Eastern Europe of a consensus among dissidents, former party members and non-communists alike, that since the communist system was unchallengeable but also unreformable, the only option for the powerless majority was not to fight it, but rather to ignore it and construct an alternative existence. This did not, however, mean retreating into an inward-looking passivity; on the contrary, if a thinking citizen were to live ethically, then it was morally imperative to help one's fellow victims of state oppression. In practical terms, this led to the formation of Solidarity's forerunner, the Committee for the Defence of the Workers (*Komitet Obrony Robotników* or KOR).

KOR was started in the wake of the 1976 unrest, to organise legal advice for workers caught up in the disturbances, as well as help for their families; prominent members included Jacek Kuroń, Jan Józef Lipski, Michnik and others. From the start KOR was intended to be non-political, precisely because of the need to avoid outright confrontation with the authorities, if such action was to be of any help. According to Lipski, who later wrote a highly readable history of KOR, it was meant to 'appeal to ethical values . . . rather than political attitudes.'[1] However, the mere existence of such an organisation was oppositional, and by implication political. KOR was not, for example, an underground movement, since it existed to act with the authorities on behalf of the imprisoned workers and their families. As the range of its activities widened, however, and as the government turned its attention to those activities, confrontation was inevitable, and KOR found itself forced to operate to some extent clandestinely. From its original remit, KOR increasingly worked, to quote Lipski again, 'to stimulate new centres of autonomous activity in a variety of areas.'[2] In other words, KOR's activists saw themselves as recreating the rudiments of civil society, independently of the party-state.

KOR's activities included publishing, with complete illegality, on a hitherto unprecedented scale: its newspaper *Robotnik* (*The Worker*), after one year, was selling 20,000 copies every two weeks, and by 1979, 50,000 copies. *Robotnik* was not KOR's only publication; it gradually expanded to produce other newspapers and journals. So popular was the demand for this form of uncensored medium that an Independent Publishing House, NOWA, was set

---

[1]   Quoted in Stokes, G., 2012, *The Walls Came Tumbling Down: Collapse and Rebirth in Eastern Europe*, 2nd edn, New York and Oxford, 29.
[2]   Quoted in Stokes, *Walls Came Tumbling Down*, 29.

up in 1977, which published books by Polish authors banned by the regime, such as Czesław Miłosz's *The Captive Mind*, as well as foreign works in translation like George Orwell's *Nineteen Eighty-Four*. KOR also branched out into education: rather like the wartime resistance, from 1977 it organised a 'flying university', which held lectures by dissident intellectuals like Michnik. Attendance at such events was high, despite the risk of arrest and imprisonment for doing so. Another important result of KOR's work was the beginning of independent, if illegal, trade union activity. The first secret committees were started in 1978, in response to an obvious demand for this among the Baltic shipyard workers in particular. Among the workers who first involved themselves was a Gdańsk shipyard electrician, Lech Wałęsa, one of a number of workers who wanted to commemorate those killed in the disputes of 1970. Such proto-trade union activity became an integral part of KOR's programme, which after all was founded on a belief in workers' self-help, especially their right to organise themselves, regardless of the party's ban on any activity not authorised by itself.

Two years after KOR's inception an event occurred which few Poles can have anticipated, whichever side of the political divide they were on, but which the communist regime could have done nothing to prevent. In October 1978 the archbishop of Kraków, Karol Wojtyła, was elected Pope John Paul II. The Catholic Church in Poland had long since achieved an uneasy accommodation with the communist party in that, in return for Catholics being allowed to practise their religion without serious hindrance, the church on the whole refrained from vocal criticism of the regime. At the same time, the rank-and-file of the clergy were strongly identified with the people, a community of interest made easier by the fact that confiscation of church lands in the Stalinist period erased the church's former role as a social oppressor. In fact, precisely because the church was obviously of the people, and had also been persecuted, it had a relatively liberal image in terms of human rights. John Paul II exemplified this image. Active in the wartime underground theatre before his ordination as a priest, the new pope had been an outspoken defender of moral values throughout the communist period. The emotional effect of his election among Poles both in and out of Poland was tremendous, and paradoxically was not confined to non-communists or even non-Catholics. One Polish-American recalls being telephoned in New York by a Jewish fellow émigré, exclaiming excitedly that 'We have our own Pope! Our own Pope!'[3] Even Gierek felt he had no option but to congratulate 'a son of the Polish nation' upon his elevation.[4]

John Paul had no sooner gone to Rome than the dilemma arose for the Polish Party of how to respond to his request to visit his native land as pontiff. Both Gierek and Brezhnev in Moscow dreaded the inevitable excitation of

[3]   Quoted in Ascherson, N., 1987, *The Struggles for Poland*, London, 191.
[4]   Quoted in Ascherson, *The Struggles for Poland*, 191.

public feeling, knowing full well the intimate connection between Catholicism and nationalism in Poland. Yet the Pope was in terms of international law an independent sovereign. An outright refusal to let him visit risked vehement protests, which would in turn necessitate repression, possible Soviet intervention, and unforeseeable diplomatic ructions. In the end the paralysed Polish government accepted a nine-day papal visit in June 1979, which was another big moral turning point. The regime discretely faded into the background, while Catholic volunteers across the country organised the tour as if the party-state did not exist. The ecstatic but orderly mass turnout for John Paul staggered the regime, but it also staggered the people themselves. The sheer number of people who flocked to see the Pope, wherever he went, showed in unmistakable fashion the existence of that alternative society, many of whom were of course lifelong believers; but even those who did not believe could respond to the pontiff's carefully worded, but nevertheless explicit emphasis on the importance of moral values, basic rights and human dignity. Possibly a quarter of the population of Poland turned out simply to see the Pope. His tour concluded with the last of a series of vast, open-air masses in his former episcopal see of Kraków, where people wept in the streets at John Paul's assurance that 'every stone and every brick is dear to me.'[5] In the wake of this mass happening, the communist party looked shrunken and somehow irrelevant.

Solidarity 1980–1

The impetus for the formation of Solidarity was, yet again, provided by the familiar pattern of attempted price rises by a bankrupt and economically desperate regime. The rises were announced in August 1980, and once again provoked spontaneous strikes across the country, starting at Gdańsk on the 14th. This time, however, it was the workers rather than the regime which was the organised side. Thanks to KOR's nation-wide information network, especially organs like *Robotnik*, news of other strikes soon became a matter of general knowledge, and each cluster of striking workers knew they were not alone. Hence the strike, initially confined to the Baltic shipyards, extended like wildfire; eventually it became so widespread that an inter-factory strike committee had to be set up, and it was this overarching body which came to be known as Solidarity.

Another benefit of the worker-intelligentsia connection was the determined self-discipline and emphasis on non-violence of the strikes. This was

---

[5]   Quoted in Ascherson, *The Struggles for Poland*, 191–2.

acknowledged by the strikers themselves: Lech Wałęsa, who became one of the principal leaders of the shipyard strikes and their most visible spokesman, admitted in December 1980 that 'KOR taught us this job.'[6] Anna Walentynowicz, the crane operator at the heart of the first sit-in strike in Gdańsk, was equally clear that 'It was owing to these groups [the KOR activists] the strikes took a peaceful course.'[7] Before, what Michnik calls the 'psychology of captivity' had given the 1970 and 1976 upheavals the character almost of 'slave revolts', violent but ultimately futile, despite the concessions wrung each time out of the terrified party-state. Now, the workers had their own newspapers, their own information network, their own cadre of organisers, in a neat reversal of the classic communist takeovers of the 1940s. Wałęsa, who famously clambered over a wall to join the Gdańsk strike and dominated it from the beginning, was one of those who had come to prominence through the KOR network. He was also a born leader, with finely tuned political antennae. So despite the fact that – as before – the authorities almost immediately conceded a wage increase to palliate the impact of the price hikes, Wałęsa instinctively sensed that this time the strikers wanted more. They wanted not just more money, or even more sausage, but more autonomy, the real freedom to organise and express their demands without constant fear of victimisation and repression.

The inter-factory strike committee on 17 August issued Twenty-One Demands, which included the right to form free trade unions; the right to strike at all; publication of the Demands in the mass media; and the right to 'full public information on the socio-economic situation' of the country, coupled with the right for 'all social groups and strata' to participate in future discussions of reform.[8] KOR's intellectuals, several of whom were involved in the drafting of the Demands, worried about the one for independent trade unions. Michnik remarked afterwards that a non-communist union was 'impossible in a communist system, but the workers didn't know this.'[9] Other KOR activists, however, followed Wałęsa's instincts and backed the crucial demand for precisely this reason: achievement of a non-party trade union would shatter the party's claim to speak for the workers. In the end, the series of agreements reached between the various strike centres and the government, at Szczecin on 30 August and Gdańsk on 31 August, and collectively known as the Social Accords, conceded this central demand, and Solidarity was officially born. In return, Solidarity acknowledged the party's leading role 'in the state' – a deliberately ambiguous formulation which both sides agreed on.[10] The government also conceded the right to strike, the lifting of censorship

[6]   Quoted in Bernhard, M.H., 1993, *The Origins of Democratization in Poland: Workers, Intellectuals and Oppositional Politics 1976-1980*, New York, 202.
[7]   Quoted in Bernhard, *The Origins of Democratization in Poland*, 202.
[8]   Quoted in Garton Ash, T., 1983, *The Polish Revolution: Solidarity 1980-82*, London, 43.
[9]   Quoted in Stokes, *The Walls Came Tumbling Down*, 39.
[10] Quoted in Garton Ash, *The Polish Revolution*, 69.

and, significantly, the broadcasting of Sunday mass on state radio. In tacit recognition of the real setback sustained by the regime, Gierek was shortly after dumped by his party comrades for Stanisław Kania as first secretary.

The news of the Social Accords, once broadcast nationally, prompted a wave of free local unions in other sectors of the economy, all of them anxious to affiliate with Solidarity. Thus in the course of the next few months Solidarity's growth in membership was startling. By the point at which, on 3 October, the new union felt obliged to flex its muscles with a token one-hour work stoppage, it could already bring 3 million members out on the streets. At its peak in 1981, Solidarity numbered some 10 million Poles, or one-half of the adult population. The despised party-controlled unions withered on the vine, while the government looked increasingly incapable of arresting the phenomenon. The lifting of censorship meant that events in Poland attracted world media attention, intensifying the regime's embarrassment. What could no longer be ignored was that Solidarity was a truly mass, working-class movement, what Timothy Garton Ash, with pardonable exaggeration, called 'the first genuine workers' revolution in history'.[11] It was not, of course, a movement controlled by the communist party, which from the very start posed a paradox: while Solidarity spoke for millions, and commanded their enthusiastic allegiance, it could not hope to control the state itself. Kania's regime continued, despite the Social Accords, to treat Solidarity as a non-partner, a somehow illegitimate challenger to 'socialist legality'. Moreover, behind the Polish Party everyone was well aware that the Soviet Union was distinctly alarmed by the situation. In the Solidarity camp Wałęsa, too, had problems riding this tiger of long-repressed expectations, and as the year progressed the outright confrontation inherent in the situation edged ever nearer. In March 1981 a serious contest of wills developed over whether there would be a Rural Solidarity of agricultural workers. The government vetoed this, as something not included in the original Accords; in response, the union called a four-hour national strike, the near-total success of which forced Kania to climb down. The difficulty experienced in extracting such concessions, however, began to convince activists below Wałęsa that more radical action was now required. It was the old dilemma of 1956 and 1968: however successful Solidarity proved to be as a mechanism for wringing tactical concessions out of the regime, only political reform could deliver real economic improvement, and for that the party had to relax its grip on the state.

The latter scenario, of the party relaxing control, was hardly imaginable as of 1981. On the contrary, everyone knew from the start how improbable this was, because the threat of Soviet invasion seemed very real. According to documents that became public in 1988, Brezhnev apparently contemplated intervention as

[11] Garton Ash, *The Polish Revolution*, 311.

early as December 1980, but was privately warned off it by the outgoing Carter administration. From January 1981 the Soviets had to reckon with the possible reaction of Ronald Reagan, whose consistently bellicose, anti-Soviet rhetoric had the Soviets convinced for most of his first term that they were dealing with a warmonger. How long fear of Western involvement would have staved off Soviet intervention must remain conjectural, although we know the Soviet politburo opposed intervening as late as December 1981; what we do know is that from February 1981 the Polish Party was already making its own plans for resolving the Solidarity problem. It was in this month that Kania brought in as defence minister General Wojciech Jaruzelski, who started planning the imposition of martial law. Mindful of avoiding the near-fatal confrontation of 1956, the party leadership was determined to keep control of events, rather than accept the humiliation of seeing it done by the Soviets. Another reason for mastering the situation was the very real danger of the communist party itself disintegrating. Just as in the Czechoslovak Party in 1968, some members were calling openly for a democratisation of the party, and there was an increased traffic in reform plans between regional party organs, or what party jargon termed 'horizontalism'. Most party members, however, simply bailed out. The party continued to lose members, and by the fall of 1981 membership was down to three million, about one million of whom also joined Solidarity.

On Solidarity's side, too, the logic of the situation drove the union inexorably towards confrontation. Its advocacy of workers' interests increasingly assumed political dimensions, because only politically could the economic problems it existed to rectify be addressed. Solidarity's October programme of 1981 effectively breached the no-go zone of the party-state, calling for the lifting of all remaining restrictions on private ownership of business, and crucially for free local elections. As the programme put it, 'Pluralism of views . . . should be the foundation of democracy.'[12] Modest though these demands were, they nevertheless formally challenged the one-party system, and provided the final excuse for a crackdown. That same month Jaruzelski took over from Kania as party leader, another clear signal to Moscow that the Polish comrades were ready to act and could be trusted to do so.

The imposition of martial law on the morning of 13 December, therefore, should not have come as a surprise to anyone, but Solidarity's leadership was caught completely unawares. Jaruzelski had organised everything with a soldier's attention to detail: army units were deployed at key points across the country, in order to ensure the maintenance of essential services; a curfew was imposed; all media were placed under military supervision; a blanket state censorship was resumed; and most of Solidarity's leaders were interned following raids on their homes in advance of the proclamation of martial

---

[12] Quoted in Stokes, *The Walls Came Tumbling Down*, 44.

law. Jaruzelski himself made the proclamation on national television at six in the morning, and in a clear allusion to the Soviets he informed Poles that 'Our country stands at the edge of an abyss.'[13] The takeover was not without bloodshed: some ninety persons are estimated to have been killed resisting martial law. But with Wałęsa and most of the leadership out of circulation the great experiment appeared to be over.

Solidarity underground 1981–9

In reality Solidarity, like Poland, was not yet dead. On the contrary, the period following the proclamation of martial law saw the coming into its own of that alternative, civil society which Solidarity, and KOR before it, had helped to create. Martial law proved in the end to be an own-goal for Jaruzelski's regime for, once proscribed, Solidarity simply went underground. Wałęsa and the other main leadership figures remained in custody until the lifting of martial law in July 1983, and although individuals were released the regime did not relax its overall control or permit a revival of the trade union. Some prominent Solidarity members, however, managed to escape internment, notably Zbigniew Bujak; and these activists simply carried on, despite the obvious perils of defying the regime. They formed, in April 1982, a Temporary Coordinating Commission (*Tymczasowa Komisja Koordinacyjna* or TKK); as with KOR in the 1970s, this involved mutual aid, the dissemination of news, and some educational activity. Bujak was an activist much influenced by the example of Václav Havel in Czechoslovakia. Like Havel, he had his sights set on the creation of 'a system of social structures independent of the state.' In the end, Bujak hoped, 'the government will control empty shops but not the market, employment but not the means to livelihood, the state press but not the flow of information, printing presses but not the publishing movement, telephones and the postal service but not communication, schools but not education.'[14]

This was nothing if not ambitious, and there was a practical limit to such underground activity, just as there was only a limited number of Poles willing to risk prison for such goals. Moreover, from an underground position the TKK found it much more difficult to remain attuned to the mood of ordinary Poles; it repeatedly under- or over-estimated the numbers willing to turn out for strikes or demonstrations. To some extent, too, the underground Solidarity was able to persist because, within certain limits, the government was willing to let it: Jaruzelski, with some shrewdness, was not intent on a rigid enforcement of public conformity like Husák's Czechoslovakia. Rather,

---

[13] Quoted in Stokes, *The Walls Came Tumbling Down*, 46.
[14] Quoted in Stokes, *The Walls Came Tumbling Down*, 126.

Jaruzelski's strategy was to spike Solidarity's guns by selective concessions, all of which stopped short of giving up the party's leading role. Hence, for instance, the permission given in 1982 to form 'self-governing' unions: these formally had the right to strike, but not for political reasons. Despite the stigma attached to these organisations some 2.5 million people joined them within a year, presumably in the belief that it was better to be a member of some union than not at all.

Another canny move by Jaruzelski was the decision publicly to prosecute the security police officers who, in October 1984, were revealed to have murdered a popular priest, Father Jerzy Popiełuszko. That these rogue state officials were prosecuted at all, and that their trial was televised, was a revealing public relations gesture. Rather like Gorbachev after 1985, whom Jaruzelski was quick to imitate with a relaxation of the censorship and a general amnesty for Solidarity activists in 1986, the general hoped to liberalise the system without surrendering overall control. Jaruzelski also aimed to avoid giving the slightest pretext for Soviet intervention, which he suggested was his principal motivation in 1981. It may be that it was precisely Jaruzelski's own experience of deportation in 1940–1 – the dark glasses he habitually wore were the result of snow blindness incurred in the Russian winter – that made him so determined to forestall Soviet action. After 1985, however, it became increasingly apparent that this was less likely. Over the next few years, therefore, a curious shadow play was enacted, a competition for hearts and minds. It was evident to everyone that Solidarity still existed, like ectoplasm; on the other hand, the party itself was edging cautiously towards some form of reform initiative.

In this changed atmosphere, Solidarity had a clear moral edge, and continued to command the allegiance of many in a way the party no longer could. Wałęsa and other released activists continued to contribute, anonymously, to TKK's underground weekly *Tygodnik Mazowsze* (Masovian Weekly). In 1983 Wałęsa was awarded the Nobel Peace Prize; the regime was mightily embarrassed when it transpired that Wałęsa refused to collect the prize in person, for fear that he would be barred from returning to Poland. Wałęsa's wife Danuta, sent to collect the prize in his place, was then humiliatingly strip-searched at the airport on her return. When the government issued its general amnesty in 1986, Solidarity was quick to re-establish its presence in any legal or even semi-legal way it could, and the government undeniably tolerated this. Public alienation manifested itself in seemingly absurd or petty ways: for instance, the inhabitants of one town took to going out for a stroll, en masse, as soon as the government-controlled evening news came on. The local authorities imposed a curfew to prevent this, so everyone instead went for their stroll during the afternoon broadcast. This stalemate, with Solidarity handicapped by its illegality, and the party still insisting on its primacy, persisted into the late 1980s.

Ultimately, it was the government's clear economic failure, coupled with the crucial developments in the Soviet Union, which tipped the balance in Poland toward cooperation rather than confrontation. Even a regime led by the astute Jaruzelski had no clear solution to the economic nightmare of low productivity, massive debt and inflation. Under martial law rationing was brought in, but even after the lifting of martial law Poles continued to suffer from shortages of milk, meat and sugar, and the median income fell by some 10 per cent. Between 1981 and 1989 some 300,000 people left the country. Early in 1987, the leadership finally accepted the advice of its economic experts that Poland must start a serious drive to increase exports to the outside world, rather than to its fellow East bloc regimes and the Soviet Union. To do this, moreover, the government was advised to sanction the creation of private enterprises, a move which also presupposed the acceptance of something like a free market. In November 1987 Jaruzelski held a referendum on two questions. Firstly, would the population accept the need for economic reform, with the clear implication that this would entail price rises and an at least temporary decline in the standard of living? Secondly, would Poles accept the party's version of 'democratisation', which amounted to saying that the party was contemplating 'sharing' power, while nevertheless retaining overall control? This was referred to as 'pluralism in a socialist context.'[15]

This was a characteristically subtle attempt by Jaruzelski to gain public compliance with party policy: if people voted 'no' then they would appear to be rejecting economic reform. What still defies analysis, however, is that the government, having actually won a 'yes' to both questions, then announced that it had in fact lost, since the total number of votes cast did not constitute a majority of the electorate. No one was quite sure what to make of this; but the practical result was to convince the Solidarity leadership that the opportunity to open up some sort of dialogue with the government was too good to miss. Solidarity, in short, was prepared to support Jaruzelski's economic reforms, in return for its re-legalisation, in precise terms 'the right to express and represent social interests.'[16] It should be noted that, by this point, Wałęsa and other Solidarity leaders were beginning to fear irrelevance, because of the proliferation of strike movements not even controlled by them. It was a sign that a genuine pluralisation of Polish society was taking place, beyond the control even of Solidarity, let alone the party.

It took all of 1988 for the two sides to agree on the format for negotiations, despite the fact that Jaruzelski clearly had the green light from Moscow for some sort of reform, and that Solidarity was cautiously willing to cooperate. In August 1988 the government formally offered re-legalisation of Solidarity, if the union would engage to control any wildcat strikes that might result

---

[15] Quoted in Stokes, *The Walls Came Tumbling Down*, 141.
[16] Quoted in Stokes, *The Walls Came Tumbling Down*, 141.

from the agreed price increases. The seemingly interminable delays in agreeing anything except talks about talks only served to heighten the volatility of public opinion, and the latter half of the year was disturbed by a series of strikes over which Solidarity had very little control; it was this very instability which ultimately drove the party to the negotiating table. The latter, in famous imitation of the secret Paris negotiations of 1973 finalising US withdrawal from Vietnam, was literally a round table, to emphasise that both sides had a common goal. The talks started on 6 February 1989, were co-chaired by Wałęsa and Jaruzelski's interior minister, Czesław Kiszczak, and concluded on 5 April, against a background of increasing hopes for change elsewhere in Eastern Europe.

The Round-Table Agreement of 7 April was a complex would-be trade-off, which made two main provisions. Firstly, Solidarity was re-legalised as a trade union. Secondly, and just as path-breaking, it was agreed that a general election would be held in June 1989, the only just description of which is 'semi-pluralist', or partially free. For a new, two-chamber parliament the communist party, together with its allied 'front' parties, would be guaranteed 65 per cent of the seats in the *Sejm*, or more powerful lower house; the remaining 35 per cent, 161 seats, would be completely open for all parties to compete for, including the communists and their allies. For the weaker senate, or upper house, by contrast, there was to be a completely free election; the senate was expected to act as a constitutional brake on the communist-dominated *Sejm*. The Round-Table Agreement also provided for a new president who, while exercising wide powers, would be elected by both houses of parliament; this, in turn, was designed to ensure that the communist party had the last say. The elections themselves were to be held with complete freedom of association, and even some media access for opposition groups.

The Round-Table Agreements, remarkable though they were, were not intended to be revolutionary, in other words to result in a complete overthrow of Poland's communist regime. On the contrary, not only did the party confidently assume that it would thereby retain its leading role, in return for these generous concessions to Solidarity and other non-communists; but Solidarity was implicitly accepting the party's leading role, in return for the indispensable boon of legality and an agreed, if probably limited, political role. Both sides were undoubtedly influenced by a sense of what they assumed was politically possible and what was not: in the Soviet Union in March and April 1989, Gorbachev's own regime was also holding similarly managed elections to a new Congress of People's Deputies, for which, again, a proportion of seats were reserved for the (still ruling) communist party, and a proportion for a medley of opposition groups. Where the Soviet Union led, everyone nervously agreed they could probably safely follow.

The results of the elections duly held in June 1989 will be described in the chapter on the revolutions of that year in Eastern Europe. Suffice it to say here that these results were nothing that either side expected. On the contrary, the Polish elections fully deserve the epithet revolutionary, because they demonstrated conclusively the communist party's utter lack of democratic legitimacy. To that demonstration the Solidarity phenomenon had made an indispensable contribution.

PART IV
All change?

17

The bear vanishes

Gorbachev and the roots of revolution 1985–9

Enough has been said to illustrate the systemic failure and unreformability of communism in Eastern Europe by the 1980s. It was also apparent that significant numbers of East Europeans, including communists, knew that something was wrong. As long as the dead hand of Soviet hegemony rested on the region, however, the likelihood of change seemed remote.

The period after March 1985, when Mikhail Gorbachev became leader of the Soviet Communist Party, constitutes a reminder of the importance of individuals in history. For although East European communism's problems cried out for action, it was not until Gorbachev initiated reform in the Soviet Union itself, accompanied by Soviet disengagement from Eastern Europe, that the circumstances working against the communist system came into their own. Gorbachev as Soviet leader was the essential precondition for East European revolution. As Mark Kramer puts it, 'What changed in 1989, compared to earlier crises in Eastern Europe, was not the depth of popular opposition to the Soviet-backed regimes. Instead, what changed was the whole thrust of Soviet policy in the region.'[1]

This chapter first explains how Gorbachev became possible, in a Soviet system that had become a byword for immobilism and lack of imagination. While our preoccupation is with Eastern Europe, rather than Russia and the Soviet Union, this 'Gorbachev factor' is an indispensable part of understanding the revolutions of 1989, just as the present-day policies of Putin's Russia continue to affect the region. Gorbachev's attempted reforms, moreover, arguably played a major role in causing the later break-up of the Soviet Union itself, and the achievement or regaining of independence by additional East European peoples, hitherto involuntary Soviet citizens. It is also important to understand not only Gorbachev's agenda and original goals, but how these changed. Between his accession to power and about mid-1988, the Soviet leader was on a sort of learning curve: only past a certain point did his regime initiate changes that had truly revolutionary implications. And although it is clear that Gorbachev did not intend to dismantle Soviet hegemony, when it became apparent that pressure was mounting in Eastern Europe for genuine

---

[1] Kramer, M., 2011, 'The Demise of the Soviet Bloc', *Journal of Modern History*, LXXXIII, #4, December, 788.

revolution he did nothing to avert it. East European regimes and East European dissident movements were already reacting to signals emitted by Gorbachev well before 1988; but the decisive impetus for revolution was the radically altered international landscape created by Gorbachev's foreign policy.

The making of a Soviet reformer

The stagnation of the command economy by the time of 'real existing socialism' affected the Soviet Union as well as its East European satellites. By the 1980s the increasingly common perception within the Soviet party was that there was a problem with declining growth; the dilemma was what to do about it. Here the party's gerontocratic leadership was a serious impediment to any fresh approach. The ailing Brezhnev was temperamentally averse to change; worse, by the time of his demise he had staffed the upper echelons of the party with officials of similar age and outlook: 'Top officials acquired lifetime job security under Brezhnev, and this meant almost automatic security for countless officials in the middle and lower levels of the party and government bureaucracy.'[2] The 49-year-old Gorbachev on his appointment to the politburo was remarkable for being on average twenty years younger than his colleagues. The one exception, significantly, was the man responsible for bringing Gorbachev forward, the 66-year old KGB chief Yuri Andropov. Equally important, it was Andropov, rather than the presumed heir apparent Konstantin Chernenko, who emerged as the obvious candidate for the post of general secretary when Brezhnev died. Yet Andropov too was ailing, a victim of kidney disease. His succession in February 1984 by the visibly doddering Chernenko seemed to symbolise the general debility of the Soviet system. Even when Gorbachev took over in March 1985, the average age of the politburo was still a ripe 67.

Brezhnev's regime showed little sign of knowing how to grapple with the Soviet Union's multiple problems. Declining growth rates were compounded by low productivity, rising energy costs despite the country's abundance of oil and gas, a succession of bad harvests leading to a tenfold increase in food imports between 1970 and 1980, and labour shortages. The sheer inefficiency of the command economy was startling. Even after decades of collectivisation much of the Soviet Union's food harvest was wasted due to negligence and poor storage: in an average year a fifth of the grain harvest and up to a third of potato crops were simply left to rot. Industrial inefficiency was due in part to the state's failure to invest in or procure new technology; but it was also due to widespread corruption, including the theft of materials and services

---

[2]   Doder, D., 1988, *Shadows and Whispers: Power Politic Inside the Kremlin from Brezhnev to Gorbachev*, Harmondsworth, 46.

from the workplace to meet the needs of the black market, and rampant alcoholism.

The Soviet Union's multiple commitments in the Cold War were an additional source of weakness. For decades the Soviets had borne the principal burden of propping up the communist East European regimes: up to the late 1980s there were thirty Soviet divisions, or 565,000 troops, stationed in East Germany, Czechoslovakia, Poland and Hungary, and a further seventy divisions, or 1,400,000 men, in the western Soviet republics. The Soviets contributed nearly two million of the Warsaw Pact's three million-strong establishment. If we add to this the military hardware required the total cost was enormous. Beyond Eastern Europe the Soviets for years had funded, armed and trained communist parties and insurgencies and regimes from Central and South America to Africa to the Far East. Since 1979 the most expensive and politically damaging commitment of all, supporting a left-leaning regime in Afghanistan against a western-supported Islamist resistance, had turned into the Soviets' very own Vietnam, exacting a steady toll in Soviet conscripts' lives and resulting in a corrosive alienation of ordinary families from the regime, but from which, for prestige reasons, the Soviets found it difficult to extricate themselves. On top of all this the global arms race with the United States was entering a new and dangerous phase. The Reagan government's massive arms build-up, especially 'star wars', threatened the Soviets with an open-ended defence expenditure commitment in which, given the technology involved, the Soviet side seemed in real danger of being left behind.

In these circumstances, even before Brezhnev's passing, there was a gathering power struggle going on within the Soviet Party between immobilists and reformers. Andropov, despite the brevity of his tenure, provided an indispensable prelude to the more far-reaching reforms implemented by Gorbachev. He understood that the party's only hope of reversing decline was to jump to a younger generation, which had the education and breadth of mind to confront the problems of the computer age. Andropov also recognised that corruption in the party reached into the highest levels, and stamping it out would be key to achieving change. Andropov's background in the KGB also gave him a realistic understanding of the Soviet Union's economic and military weaknesses. Once in charge, he set about changing personnel, and it was this wholesale weeding out of the inefficient and the corrupt which cleared the way for Gorbachev. Andropov above all grasped that an understanding of science and technology, and an ability to think outside the box, would be crucial in making the Soviet Union competitive again. He proved unable to dictate the terms of his succession, however, and with Chernenko's elevation in February 1984 the immobilists appeared to have regained control. Even when Chernenko himself died in March 1985, Gorbachev's selection was by no means assured. Despite his demonstrable energy and intelligence it was only his endorsement at the eleventh hour by certain key figures in the gerontocracy that clinched it for him.

Gorbachev, born in 1931, was the first Soviet leader who was entirely a product of the Soviet system, and this perhaps gave him unprecedented insight into its weaknesses. The son of peasants, he was shaped by his own family's experience of Stalinism: both grandfathers had been denounced as 'enemies of the people', one experiencing exile in Siberia, the other suffering arrest, interrogation and torture for 'crimes' he had not committed. During the war the young Gorbachev worked in the field with his mother like everyone else, since his father was at the front. After the war, Gorbachev made it to law school in Moscow partly due to his obvious academic ability, but also because of his unusual, medal-winning record as a farm worker and tractor mechanic. Gorbachev was the first Soviet leader actually to have a serious higher education. Zdeněk Mlynář, Dubček's aide in 1968, was Gorbachev's university contemporary in the 1950s, and testified to Gorbachev's questing intelligence and ability to think independently. According to Mlynář, one of Gorbachev's favourite expressions was a line from Hegel: 'Truth is always concrete'; but in Gorbachev's usage this meant that general principles did not always square with reality.[3] As a young official, Gorbachev was known for actually studying the works of Marx and Lenin, rather than simply parroting quotations from them. In short, 'He thought of himself as a Marxist . . . but his Marxism was flexible and undogmatic.'[4] Here was a pragmatist who could change course, if he thought it necessary.

Gorbachev's learning curve 1985–8

All the evidence suggests that until mid-1988 Gorbachev sincerely believed that he could make communism work. The parallel with Dubček's experiment in 1968 is striking. One of Gorbachev's closest advisers, Alexander Yakovlev, revealed in the 1990s that the new government to begin with saw fixing the Soviet system as comparable to repairing a car's engine: with a few worn-out parts replaced and the tightening of a few bolts the machine would function flawlessly again. It was only after a couple of years that Gorbachev's team were forced to conclude that they needed to replace the engine entirely, that they needed a different system.

In the beginning, however, the intention was reform, not revolution. Here the personal impression Gorbachev made from the moment he took office played an important role. In a refreshing contrast with his predecessors, he was a fluent, natural speaker with a friendly and even witty manner, arguably

---

[3] Brown, A., 1997, *The Gorbachev Factor*, Oxford and New York, 31.
[4] Brown, *The Gorbachev Factor*, 32.

'the first Soviet leader to be an instant television personality.'[5] Gorbachev astonished party colleagues and Soviet citizens with his frank admission that things needed fixing, his refusal to employ the tired jargon of party duckspeak, and his appeal to the public for their support. Within weeks of taking over he instilled a renewed sense of purpose in the party and raised hopes of improvement among the general populace, even if there was also widespread resistance to his agenda among party hardliners and the *nomenklatura*.

At the root of Gorbachev's agenda was the 'new thinking' on foreign policy, the insight that the global competition of the Cold War, particularly the nuclear arms race, posed an existential threat to the survival of socialism and the Soviet Union itself. In a much-discussed article in May 1984, the political scientist Georgi Shakhnazarov claimed that 'In the nuclear age war can no longer be considered as a means for achieving political objectives.' Instead, both sides in the Cold War needed to engage in serious arms control, since for both 'only collective security is possible'.[6] Shakhnazarov, later one of Gorbachev's more influential advisers, even tentatively suggested that the potential for mutual annihilation rendered the traditional Marxist-Leninist emphasis on class struggle anachronistic; rather, both sides had to adopt a 'planetary' approach to foreign policy, to strive for cooperation, not dominance, in the interests of human survival. Fundamental to the 'new thinking', too, was the perception that the repressive nature of the Soviet regime, in particular its persecution of dissidents, had a consistently bad effect on relations with the West; and the huge military expenditure required to maintain parity with the Americans not only contributed to international tension but made serious domestic reform almost impossible.

That such ideas were being floated at all says something for the readiness of the Party's more reform-minded members to entertain them. Gorbachev soon made it obvious that he shared such concerns by surrounding himself with advisers like Shakhnazarov, and by putting out feelers almost at once to the Americans for arms limitation talks. To this end, in June 1985, he appointed as foreign minister the Georgian Eduard Shevardnadze who, despite his lack of experience, saw eye to eye with Gorbachev on the need for radical initiatives in foreign relations. Gorbachev was also much influenced by Yakovlev, who by 1987 was one of the most important figures in the Party hierarchy. As early as November 1985 the 'new thinking' was already bearing fruit, when Gorbachev met and charmed President Reagan at Geneva, where the two superpowers agreed in principle to a 50 per cent reduction in strategic nuclear weapons. Settling the details would take time, but an important psychological barrier had been surmounted.

---

[5] Doder, *Shadows and Whispers*, 271.
[6] Quoted in Doder, *Shadows and Whispers*, 224–5.

On the domestic front Gorbachev's leadership was associated with two buzzwords that entered common parlance around the globe, *perestroika* and *glasnost*. *Perestroika* (restructuring, reconstruction) was a fairly woolly term for what turned out to be not just economic but also, in the end, political reform. *Glasnost* (openness, transparency) signified a willingness to lift restrictions on freedom of expression and be honest with the Soviet public, on the assumption that only by getting the people on board could their support be won for the reforms needed.

Perestroika was conceived initially in largely economic terms. Gorbachev seems to have intended 'accelerating' the economy by permitting 'a very partial marketisation', rather like '*gulyás* communism' in Hungary, allowing greater autonomy for enterprises and some individual profit-making, while retaining most elements of central planning.[7] The Soviet-style command economy, however, was essentially incompatible with a market economy, and the regime's definition of *perestroika* mutated as this realisation sank in. 'Acceleration' in this initial period involved three strategies: setting higher production targets, inherently unrealistic in view of the underlying inefficiency of the system; 'streamlining' production by introducing an extra tier of bureaucratic overseers, which simply led to greater confusion and costs; and rejecting shoddy goods while penalising enterprises and workers for producing them. This resulted in a slump in production and increased shortages, together with a drop in earnings due to the denial of productivity bonuses, which fuelled a growing anger among the workforce. The public mood was made worse by Gorbachev's anti-alcoholism campaign, which aimed to boost productivity by restricting the sale of alcohol. This simply drove alcohol production into the black market, with a catastrophic effect on both public health and state tax revenue, 12 per cent of which derived from alcohol sales. By mid-1986 'acceleration' was proving a complete failure, and Gorbachev was beginning to envisage political as well as economic change.

As Mark Galeotti reminds us, the paradox of these attempts to reform the Soviet system is that members of the party elite, Gorbachev included, 'knew very little about economics' because, as Marxists, they had never been taught basic supply-and-demand.[8] In specific terms economic *perestroika* was implemented through three laws, which created such turmoil that, by 1988, Gorbachev came to the conclusion that a political *perestroika* was unavoidable. This political *perestroika*, in effect an attempt to democratise the system, ultimately led to the break-up of the Soviet Union in 1991.

This economic unravelling began with the Law on Individual Labour Activity, passed in November 1986. This freed from state control and legalised small private enterprises, run by the self-employed or employing only a handful of

---

[7]   Brown, *The Gorbachev Factor*, 131.
[8]   Galeotti, M., 1997, *Gorbachev and His Revolution*, New York, 55.

people, which had already sprung up on the black market. Such activity was still only supposed to be part-time, and by 1989 the number of individuals involved was still small, hardly the flourishing private sector needed to invigorate a stagnating economy. The Law on State Enterprises, of June 1987, gave greater autonomy to managers, while encouraging workers to elect their managers; in particular it loosened restrictions on production targets, wages and above all the prices enterprises could set. In theory, this should have given managers and workers greater incentives to make enterprises competitive and profitable. In practice it led simply to workers awarding themselves higher bonuses, and businesses charging higher prices without a corresponding improvement in quality, which in the process fuelled inflation. In Archie Brown's view it 'did much more harm than good.'[9] Finally, the Law on Cooperatives, in May 1988, sanctioned the creation of what were in effect private businesses, as long as they took the form of cooperatives belonging to a minimum of three members. By the end of the year cooperatives numbered some three quarters of a million members, mainly in the service sector. None of this peripheral activity, however, was enough to turn the economy around, and a majority of state enterprises operated at a loss. There was still no real free market in labour or raw materials, nor were there any private banks to fund investment. Economic *perestroika* threatened to make an inefficient system even more inefficient.

Parallel with economic *perestroika* was the growing momentum for greater *glasnost* or openness. Again, to begin with it was not clear that Gorbachev interpreted *glasnost* as involving much more than a greater frankness of discussion among the elite, and a greater willingness to listen to popular grievances. Gorbachev undoubtedly hoped that, by involving the public, he would acquire greater leverage for getting reforms past the party elite. Just as with previous attempts at opening up debate in Eastern Europe, however, once the floodgates were down it would prove difficult to haul them up again. The remarkable thing about Gorbachev was that, on this subject, he was capable of changing his views in response to changing events. The more obstruction he encountered from the party, the more he leaned toward ever greater *glasnost* to overcome this. In the process Gorbachev not only realised that the party was part of the problem, he became in effect a convert to social democracy.

In the meantime Gorbachev's initial strategy was eye-opening enough. He gave frank interviews to the state media which, at his insistence, were reported on accurately, and by the fall of 1985 he was talking openly to western media. In February 1986 the Soviet government agreed to let the Jewish dissident Anatoly Shcharansky emigrate to Israel. Party organs, long notorious for their dullness, started to follow Gorbachev's lead and became sources of genuine and increasingly open debate.

[9] Brown, *The Gorbachev Factor*, 147.

Glasnost underwent its greatest test when, in April 1986, one of the nuclear reactors at Chernobyl in northern Ukraine exploded, spewing untold quantities of radioactivity into the earth's atmosphere and requiring a massive operation lasting weeks simply to contain the fire. To begin with the state, Gorbachev included, responded with traditional secretiveness, refusing to divulge any details, and even ordering Kiev's May Day parade to go ahead; but with radiation being detected as far away as Scandinavia within days this was not something that could be covered up. Only then did the authorities finally make a public announcement of the disaster and start an emergency evacuation of the nearby town of Pripyat. Public panic at the lack of information on the health hazards being posed increased disillusionment with the regime, and with time led to the formation of the first ecological movements in both the Soviet Union and Eastern Europe. To this day the number of deaths clearly attributable to radiation poisoning remains heavily disputed. By 1989 the government admitted that some 20 per cent of Belarus was contaminated, as was a large part of northern Ukraine, eastern Poland and western Russia. Nearly two million acres of agricultural land had to be taken out of use, if only temporarily, and Pripyat remains a ghost town at the centre of a nineteen-mile exclusion zone; the total bill for the clean-up was $2.7 billion.

In Gorbachev's own words, Chernobyl was 'a turning point', in that it provided a stark illustration of the Soviet command economy's literally life-threatening failings.[10] Emerging details of poor construction and maintenance standards, overly secretive safety precautions and even siting decisions constituted an indictment of central planning, but also of state secrecy. Gorbachev, shocked at his own instinct to cover everything up, concluded that the only answer to problems like Chernobyl was ever greater *glasnost*. Given the absence of any opposition in a one-party system, he reasoned, it was all the more important to encourage debate and for the media to hold those in power to account. In addition to gradually appointing like-minded allies, Gorbachev therefore told a delegation of writers in June 1986 that they had a key role to play in challenging the 'managerial stratum' within the party who were resisting change.[11] Thus emboldened, the Union of Writers elected a new board of *glasnost* advocates, who attacked the censorship over precisely such issues as Chernobyl and environmental pollution. Ukrainian and Belorussian writers in particular were quick to voice resentment that their peoples bore the brunt of Chernobyl. As Oles Honchar, one of Ukraine's most famous writers, asked, 'why should the Ukrainian land fall victim? Why should Ukrainian children suffer these satanic doses?'[12] In December 1986 Gorbachev caused an international sensation by releasing the dissident scientist Andrei Sakharov

---

[10] Quoted in Brown, *The Gorbachev Factor*, 163.
[11] Hosking, G., 1992, *A History of the Soviet Union 1917-1991*, final edn, London, 418.
[12] Quoted in Plokhy, S., 2018, *Chernobyl: History of a Tragedy*, London, 289.

from internal exile; returning to Moscow under a glare of media coverage, Sakharov promptly criticised Gorbachev for not going far enough.

Glasnost snowballed in 1987, which saw 'a veritable festival of banned literature' like Evgeny Zamyatin's *We* and Boris Pasternak's *Doctor Zhivago* appearing or reappearing on Soviet bookshelves.[13] Film and television documentaries became noticeably more critical and daring. There was intense interest in lifting the veil on the crimes of Stalinism, and in November 1987 Gorbachev furthered this process by creating a commission for the rehabilitation of Stalin's victims. For the first time it became possible for people to discover the true fate of parents and grandparents who had disappeared in the purges.

The further this process went, however, the more obvious it was that not everyone was happy with *glasnost*, let alone *perestroika*. On the contrary, the conservative wing of the party concluded that Gorbachev had opened Pandora's box. In March 1988 the journal *Sovietskaya Rossiya* published an open letter, inspired by Gorbachev's rivals in the politburo, attacking *perestroika*. Some of the opposition was from those who saw their privileged position endangered. Some was from reform-minded members who saw, quite correctly, that *glasnost* and *perestroika* undermined the party's leading role, and that Gorbachev had simply gone too far; worse, his foreign policy stance implied the end of Soviet hegemony in Eastern Europe and imperilled the security of the Soviet Union itself. Such criticisms were given added point by the fact that, the longer Gorbachev was in power, the louder the popular clamour for change. Some of this pressure came from within the party, as exemplified by Boris Yeltsin, brought in by Gorbachev as a reformer in December 1985, but who by November 1987 was such a vocal critic of Gorbachev's timidity that the latter felt obliged to sack him.

The growing signs of a backlash, by the spring of 1988, convinced Gorbachev that the one-party state itself needed refashioning. Only by democratising the decision-making process within the party, it was reasoned, could further progress be made. The real start of the 'Gorbachev revolution' came at the 19th Party Congress in June 1988. It was agreed that party officials would henceforth be elected by secret ballot, ideally with multiple candidates. In addition, the decision was taken to hold partially free elections early in 1989 for a new supreme representative assembly, the Congress of People's Deputies. Just as was shortly after agreed for Poland with the Round-Table Talks, this 2,250-member body would have a proportion of seats reserved for the communist party, while others would be open to contestation by communists and non-communists alike. Voting would be by secret ballot, with some members representing territorial constituencies, some nationalities, and some public organisations like the party, occupational and professional bodies, and the like. The congress

---

[13] Hosking, *A History of the Soviet Union*, 418.

would then elect a new president of the Soviet Union who, it was assumed, would be the leader of the Communist Party. The congress also had the final task of electing a legislature of 450 members, the Supreme Soviet.

To the wonderment of the world, elections to the Congress of People's Deputies duly took place in March 1989. With the emergence of this semi-democratic body, Gorbachev set in motion events over which he ultimately had no control. Divided within itself, the Soviet Communist Party could no longer agree on a common destination, while the economic situation continued to deteriorate. In the absence of any firm control by the party-state the peoples of the Soviet Union, especially those in the East European soviet republics, increasingly took control themselves, or tried to. This was a recipe for conflict and the dissolution of the Soviet state; but it was also a unique opportunity for the country's constituent peoples to determine their own fate.

The Gorbachev revolution and Eastern Europe 1985–9

In the meantime *glasnost* was having an equally astonishing impact on international affairs, in that by the end of 1986 it was clear a big shift was taking place in attitudes on both sides of the Cold War. This had a profound effect on Eastern Europe.

It took some time for Gorbachev to convince that inveterate cold warrior Ronald Reagan that he meant business. The Soviet-American summit at Reykjavik in October 1986, though it led to no immediate agreement, was crucial in that at this point the two men developed a truly cordial personal rapport. Gorbachev's release of Sakharov in December, followed by the release in February 1987 of 140 political prisoners, offered additional proof that he was serious about domestic reforms, and helped consolidate the favourable mind-set in the western camp. In April 1987 Secretary of State George Schultz arrived in Moscow to negotiate a substantive agreement on arms limitation. By September Schultz and Shevardnadze had agreed in principle to eliminate so-called intermediate-range nuclear forces, or INFs. The final result was the signature of the INF Treaty at Washington in December 1987, the first-ever reduction in the number of nuclear weapons since the start of the Cold War and only recently, in October 2018, pronounced no longer workable by President Donald Trump.

Coupled with the solid achievement of the INF Treaty, Gorbachev also effected another significant reduction in global tension by announcing, in February 1988, that the Soviets would commence a phased withdrawal of their forces from Afghanistan, finishing by February 1989. Motivated as much by domestic considerations as strategic ones, the Soviet disengagement from Afghanistan had a deep significance for communist Eastern Europe. Given that the reason for going into Afghanistan – to prop up a pro-Soviet regime – had been precisely that used to justify 1956 and 1968, the implication was that Gorbachev no longer saw military intervention in Eastern Europe as defensible or practicable. And so it proved.

The road to Soviet disengagement from Eastern Europe was not a straightforward one. We now know that Gorbachev initially had no desire to abandon Soviet hegemony in Eastern Europe; on the contrary, he undoubtedly hoped that the communist parties of the region would remain in power and continue in alliance with the Soviet Union. Shortly before becoming general secretary, at a meeting with East European leaders in March 1985, he stipulated in orthodox terms that the entire Warsaw Pact must 'defend socialist gains.'[14] As late as January 1988, Gorbachev was still insisting to the new leader of the Czechoslovak Party, Miloš Jakeš, that the Soviets had been justified in invading in 1968, and that Soviet *perestroika* was 'within the framework of socialism.'[15] By this point, however, the Soviet leader had come to the conclusion that, just as the Soviets had to cut their losses in the arms race and Afghanistan, so the unswerving maintenance of hegemony in Eastern Europe might no longer be justifiable. The East European regimes, in varying degrees, seemed increasingly unsustainable as well as unreformable; nor was it necessarily any longer in the Soviet Union's interests to support them – at least not by force. For much of 1987 Gorbachev seemed to be of two minds. In February at a Warsaw Pact summit he informed the officials present that the Soviet Union 'will not impose its own policy on anyone and will not call on you to act like us. We will, however, hope for solidarity and understanding.'[16] Yet in November, on the occasion of the seventieth anniversary of the Bolshevik Revolution, Gorbachev was capable of saying in one and the same speech that the East European parties were 'fully and irreversibly independent', but their relations with the Soviets must be based on 'the principle of socialist internationalism.'[17] The most significant passage, however, was the remark that there was 'no model of socialism to be imitated by all.'[18]

If Gorbachev seemed unable to make up his mind it is not surprising that East European leaders were not sure which way to jump. Long before the end of 1987 it was obvious that Moscow's 'line' had changed and, just as in the 1950s, this posed a dilemma for the Warsaw Pact regimes. Reactions to Gorbachev took three forms. In Hungary and Poland the leadership welcomed the new course and sought to take advantage of it. In Czechoslovakia, East Germany,

[14] Quoted in Kramer, 'The Demise of the Soviet Bloc', 791.
[15] Quoted in Svetlana Saranskaya, S. et al., 2010, 'Chronology of Events', in S. Savranskaya, T. Blanton and V. Zubok (eds), *Masterpieces of History: The Peaceful End of the Cold War in Europe*, Budapest, xxxii.
[16] Quoted in Kramer, 'The Demise of the Soviet Bloc', 798.
[17] Quoted in Kramer, 'The Demise of the Soviet Bloc', 800.
[18] Quoted in Crampton, R.J., 1997, *Eastern Europe in the Twentieth Century – And After*, 2nd edn, London, 408.

Romania and Bulgaria, by contrast, the reaction was one of consternation; these neo-Stalinist regimes clearly hoped that Gorbachev would fail or be ousted by the conservatives in the CPSU, and hunkered down to ride out the storm. At the popular level, however, the reaction to Gorbachev was on the whole one of unbridled enthusiasm mixed with incredulity. An early sign of the mood on the street was Gorbachev's visit to Prague in April 1987 when, to the astonishment of the Husák regime, the Soviet leader was greeted with applause and cries of 'Gorby! Gorby!' as his limousine sped into town.

In practical terms Gorbachev's initial policy towards Eastern Europe consisted of exhortations in favour of economic reform and greater openness. This was the theme of his meetings with Warsaw Pact leaders in January and November 1986. Where regimes were already experimenting with a relaxation of the command economy, as in Hungary and, to some extent, in Poland, this was encouraged. Jaruzelski's edging toward talks with Solidarity from 1986 on was in large part made possible by the different tone emanating from the Kremlin. These reforming regimes also benefited from the improvement in East-West relations brought about by Gorbachev, as for instance when the American government decided in February 1987 to lift the economic sanctions imposed on Poland after Solidarity's suppression in 1981. By June 1987 Reagan was positively pushing at this open door, recommending to Congress that 'most favoured nation' trade status be accorded both Poland and Hungary.

As far as the hardline regimes were concerned, it was apparent by mid-1987 that Gorbachev's words were falling on deaf ears. In April Erich Honecker publicly rejected the suggestion that East Germany should embrace either *perestroika* or *glasnost*, and the East German regime's paranoia was hardly lessened when, in June, Reagan made his famous appeal in front of the Berlin Wall, 'Mr. Gorbachev, tear down this wall!'[19] When the Soviet leader visited Bucharest in May, he was greeted with open disdain by Ceauşescu, whom he infuriated by referring pointedly in a public speech to Romania's dire economic conditions, and reminding the 'Danube of Thought' of Lenin's dictum that 'socialism is not created on orders from above.'[20] In July Bulgaria's Zhivkov suggested the party should play a reduced role in government and the economy, but given Zhivkov's autocratic record it was not clear what this might mean in practice, and Gorbachev in fact accused the Bulgarian leader of merely paying lip service.

Just as in global relations, 1988 was pivotal for Eastern Europe's fortunes. The two reformist regimes, especially Hungary's, continued to follow Gorbachev's lead. In May, following the start of Soviet withdrawal from Afghanistan, the Hungarian Party replaced the aged Kádár with the pragmatist Károly Grosz who, while adamant that the one-party state be retained, nevertheless signalled

[19] Quoted in Gaddis, J.L., 2005, *The Cold War: A New History*, London, 235.
[20] Almond, M., 1992, *The Rise and Fall of Nicolae and Elena Ceauşescu*, London, 214.

his desire for 'a Hungary that is open, integrated into the world.'[21] Imre Pozsgay, the politburo member responsible for the media, presided over an increasing liberalisation, and in July the most significant step of all was taken when Grosz permitted the formation of non-communist organisations. Within months a slew of non-communist political groupings had been founded: the Hungarian Democratic Forum (MDF), the Alliance of Free Democrats (SzDSz), and the Alliance of Young Democrats (Fidesz). An early sign in September 1988 of just how tolerant the regime had become was the mass demonstration of environmentalists against the building of a hydro-electric dam on the Danube at Gabčikovo-Nagymaros between Hungary and Czechoslovakia.

In July 1988 the Soviet leader broached his vision of a 'common European home' before the Polish Communist Party. In September, a senior foreign policy adviser informed the international press that 'We have given up the Brezhnev principle of limited sovereignty.'[22] On 7 December, before the UN General Assembly, Gorbachev informed the world that the Soviet government intended unilaterally to reduce its armed forces by half a million men; that Soviet foreign policy was now aimed at furthering 'the common interests of mankind'; and that henceforth the East European member-states of the Warsaw Pact should be able to evolve 'without Soviet interference.'[23] In effect the Brezhnev Doctrine, whereby the Soviet Union claimed the right to intervene in Eastern Europe in the name of preserving socialism, had been abandoned, even if Gorbachev did not explicitly say so at the time. When western journalists asked Gorbachev's urbane press spokesman what the difference was between Gorbachev's policy and Dubček's Prague Spring, he merely quipped, 'Twenty years'.[24] Much later, in September 1989, a foreign ministry spokesman joked that the Brezhnev Doctrine had been supplanted by the 'Sinatra Doctrine', a reference to the singer's hit tune 'I did it my way'.[25] East European regimes, on this reading, were literally free to find their own way to socialism – or some other destination.

There is little doubt that Gorbachev did not, with these sensational pronouncements, expect the entire edifice of East European communism, and the Soviet hegemony that underpinned it, to disintegrate. Yet the question inevitably arose: what if the peoples of Eastern Europe wanted to abandon the communist experiment entirely? What if they came out in favour of multiparty elections and some form of pluralist system, including a non-communist one? Nobody, as of December 1988, was quite sure what the reaction of Gorbachev or the Soviet Communist Party would be if matters were put to the test.

---

[21] Quoted in Stokes, G., 2012, *The Walls Came Tumbling Down: Collapse and Rebirth in Eastern Europe*, 2nd edn, New York and Oxford, 113.

[22] Quoted in Crampton, *Eastern Europe in the Twentieth Century – And After*, 408.

[23] 'Address by Mikhail Gorbachev at the UN General Assembly Session (Excerpts)', 7 December 1988, Wilson Center Digital Archive. http://digitalarchive.wilsoncenter.org/document/116224

[24] 'Address by Mikhail Gorbachev ...', 7 December 1988.

[25] Quoted in Brown, J.F., 1991, *Surge to Freedom: The End of Communist Rule in Eastern Europe*, Twickenham, 62.

18

The power of the powerless
The velvet revolutions of 1989

The communist regimes of Eastern Europe, Yugoslavia and Albania excepted, collapsed in 1989 and, to the surprise of both participants and onlookers, this change was mostly bloodless. These were genuine revolutions: within a few months – days in some cases – a political system that had seemed permanent and unassailable crumpled and disappeared, ceding power to unlikely coalitions of democrats committed to holding free, multiparty elections, most of which duly took place the following year. At the same time these newly democratic polities abandoned the Soviet-style command economy and exposed themselves to the uncertainties of the world market economy. Even if, more than thirty years later, a certain disillusionment with liberal democracy has set in, there can be no denying the revolutionary nature of this upheaval.

There was nothing inevitable about the revolutions of 1989. On the contrary, the 'Gorbachev revolution' in the Soviet Union was the essential precondition for regime change in Eastern Europe, even if that was not what Gorbachev intended. The overarching context of the winding down of the Cold War was crucial. Nevertheless, there were also multiple indigenous reasons for revolutionary change. The revolutions also differed in terms of typology: some were led from above, others depended on mass but peaceful mobilisation at street level, and one – Romania's – was a palace coup relying on violent popular revolt.

This chapter first examines these three main types of revolution: regime-initiated, mass mobilising, and internal coup-cum-revolt. It summarises the indigenous factors which, apart from the international context, made it possible for East Europeans to effect change. The chapter then describes the revolutions in turn, illustrating the considerable overlap between developments in each country, since it is clear there was a certain 'copy-cat' effect as news of revolution elsewhere spread. As so often in revolutionary situations, there came a moment when those desirous of change realised they were not alone, and masses of individuals became emboldened. A final section deals with the messy aftermath of revolution: the finalisation of free elections spilling over into 1990, and developments which, like the re-unification of the two Germanies and the collapse of Albanian communism, played out over a longer period. The tragic disintegration of Yugoslavia, arguably accelerated by the end of the Cold War and the 1989 revolutions, is reserved for the following chapter.

Typology and preconditions of revolution

The first type of revolution, seen in Poland, Hungary and, to some extent, Bulgaria, was regime-led. Change was initiated by the ruling party which hoped thereby to remain in power. In Poland and Hungary, however, the process thus begun, once popular pressure started to mount, morphed into revolution, sweeping the regime away. Only in Bulgaria did a reformed Communist Party remain in office.

These top-down revolutions owed much to the example set by Gorbachev's Soviet Union, as well as the fact that Soviet troop withdrawals began in the spring of 1989. Indeed, at crucial points Gorbachev gave developments a decisive prod. The final result, at least in Poland and Hungary, was far more radical than Gorbachev had intended, but it must always remain to the Soviet leader's credit that he was willing to accept this outcome. The bellwethers in this type of revolution were undoubtedly the Poles, whose transition from round-table talks to partially free, multiparty elections by June 1989 incentivised the Hungarian and Bulgarian parties to continue with reforms. The formation of the first non-communist government in Poland, at the end of August, was epochal, and the Soviet acceptance of this encouraged the opposition in neighbouring countries to hope they too might seize the opportunity offered. Hungary played an equally important role in 1989 by opening its borders to the West, a decision with an especially destabilising effect on East Germany and Czechoslovakia. By late 1989, the Hungarian and Bulgarian regimes felt impelled to respond to events in East Germany and Czechoslovakia with yet further liberalisation; crucially neither party by this point, and in the light of events elsewhere, felt able to insist on the sort of semi-free elections already held in Poland, and instead offered genuinely free, fully contestable elections in 1990.

The second category of revolution was more complicated, but can be described as 'popular'. In East Germany and Czechoslovakia seemingly entrenched, hardline regimes suddenly crumpled in the face of mass, peaceful demonstrations, in a literal illustration of 'people power'. Although revolutionary change, when it came, happened with startling rapidity, it was also the culmination of a general inner weakness which had been months, even years in the making. There was the increasingly insistent message from Gorbachev that these regimes needed to adapt or die, reinforced by the absence of any backlash against Gorbachev within his own party. There was the spectacle of the Polish party negotiating with Solidarity, being humiliated by them at the polls, and voluntarily ceding power to them in August. There was above all the lifting of Cold War barriers by Hungary, beginning in May 1989, which triggered a mass exodus of East Germans to the West, and encouraged those left behind to take to the streets. In neither East Germany nor Czechoslovakia, crucially, did the leadership have the nerve to do what the Chinese party did in Beijing's Tiananmen Square in June 1989, on the very same day that Poland held its elections, and use tanks to crush a democratic demonstration in blood. When the hardliners in East Berlin and Prague even suggested such a course, they were promptly sidelined, not least because Gorbachev made it clear the Soviets would not back this 'Tiananmen option'.

Two things stand out about these popular revolutions. The first is the speed with which the ruling party folded and ceded control of events; this was the fruit of that decades-long intellectual and moral degeneration noted in previous chapters. The second is the lack of organisation on the side of the demonstrators. As Stephen Kotkin reminds us, revolution was not the triumph of a newly emerged 'civil society', which scarcely existed as of late 1989, apart from a handful of principled activists like Havel. Rather, revolution was the product of a spontaneous, 'unorganized mobilization' of mass dissatisfaction, a sort of 'bank run' on the party-state's credibility.[1] Once people had turned out in sufficient numbers, and could see they were not alone, they were encouraged to continue doing so; conversely, the regimes, confronted with this unmistakable evidence of popular will, and conscious of their lack of external support, collapsed in a funk.

The third type of revolution was unique to Romania. An attempt by the regime violently to repress protest in the provincial town of Timişoara backfired when elements of the army appear to have sided with the protesters. This pattern was repeated in the capital, when a mass rally staged to show 'support' for the regime went badly wrong. Amidst bloody clashes between the *Securitate* on one side and the crowd and the army on the other, during which Ceauşescu fled the capital, long-sidelined members of the party elite seized the opportunity offered to depose and then execute the leader and his wife. Despite the cathartic bloodshed, however, what was effected in Romania was revolutionary, but it was an unfinished revolution, a palace coup taking advantage of a genuinely popular revolt.

Apart from their differences of type, none of these revolutionary events could have unfolded without certain preconditions. The most essential, as noted, was the readiness of the Soviet Union under Gorbachev to accept wide-ranging change. This in turn was conditioned by the global context, in which connection it is important to stress that the 1989 revolutions received little direct encouragement from the West. On the contrary, western governments, the US administration of George H.W. Bush to the fore, were reluctant to be seen involving themselves in East European affairs, lest this be taken by the Soviets as interference in their sphere of influence. As in 1956 and 1968, the danger of a sudden Soviet intervention was taken seriously, despite Gorbachev's track record by 1989. In addition, even as events in Eastern Europe unfolded,

---

[1] Kotkin, S., 2009, *Uncivil Society: 1989 and the Implosion of the Communist Establishment*, with a contribution by Jan T. Gross, New York, 6, 7.

there was a sharp reminder of the potential alternative in China's Tiananmen Square massacre. Many in the West found it hard to believe the Soviets might not suddenly reverse course; it was even harder for most East Europeans.

Beyond this international context several other preconditions peculiar to Eastern Europe facilitated revolution. First was the groundwork laid by advocates of 'civil society' in determining how revolution was achieved, and what was being sought. Bearing in mind Kotkin's caveat that the number of open advocates of civil society, with the unique exception of Solidarity in Poland, was tiny, we should not exaggerate the extent to which they can be said to have initiated or even led revolution. As of January 1989, for instance, the number of active dissidents in Czechoslovakia was estimated by the security services to be about 500 individuals, of whom only sixty could be said to play any sort of leadership role. Yet dissidents there nevertheless were, and at the crucial moment in 1989 they not so much started revolution as put themselves at the head of something already under way. Dissidents also played a role in articulating 'powerful humanist critiques of the state-socialist regimes', and thereby kept in the back of people's minds a yearning for certain fundamental freedoms denied by the communist system: freedom from fear of arbitrary arrest and imprisonment; freedom of movement; freedom of association; freedom of conscience and expression; freedom to engage in private economic activity.[2] At the same time dissidents like Havel and Michnik, not to mention the millions-strong Solidarity movement, repeatedly advocated these freedoms non-violently. The disciplined peacefulness – Romania excepted – of the mass demonstrations of 1989 was an implicit rebuke to the violence not only threatened but, at points, exercised by the party-state. So too was the spectacle of thousands chanting, as during the East German revolution, 'We are the people.'

Beyond this hankering after basic rights, East Europeans were undoubtedly motivated by a cumulative economic desperation. Despite nearly full employment, and universal health care and education, years of shortages, poor quality goods and a general decline in living standards had taken their toll. The underlying inefficiencies of the command economy, even where mitigated by a limited admixture of private enterprise, were only temporarily disguised by the communist regimes' profligate borrowing, and by the late 1980s this avenue of relief was closing down. Conditions were direst of all in Romania, and help to explain the violence of the revolution there; but just as eloquent a testimony to communism's failure was the mass exodus of East Germans in 1989, once the opportunity arose, and which contributed to the entire system's destabilisation.

Another precondition was mounting environmental concern. The Chernobyl disaster was not confined to the western Soviet Union, but threatened the whole of Eastern Europe with radiation poisoning. Yet Chernobyl was only the most

[2] Kenney, P., 2002, *A Carnival of Revolution: Central Europe 1989*, Princeton, NJ, 9.

alarming example of how communism had degraded the environment. By 1989 children in northern Czechoslovakia were going to school wearing face masks to guard against atmospheric pollution. The first-ever non-communist organisation in Bulgaria, *Ecoglasnost*, was formed in April 1989 in protest against the toxicity emitted by Romanian and Bulgarian steel mills along the Danube. Public opinion in Hungary was by 1988 openly mobilising, in defiance of the authorities, against a joint Czechoslovak-Hungarian dam project on the Danube.

It is difficult to gauge the role played by nationalism in 1989, especially since overt displays of national feeling tended to be sternly repressed after 1956. Yet apart from the embrace of 'national communism' by individual regimes from Tito onward, the popular resentment of Soviet domination had never really gone away, and was clearly not far from the surface in Poland, Hungary and Czechoslovakia especially. The same applied to many of the republics of the Soviet Union, and the constituent nations of Yugoslavia. Nationalist sentiment should be seen rather as something that rose to the surface unbidden, once revolution was under way or achieved; and this was nowhere more obvious than in East Germany, where the possibility of reunification with West Germany was raised within weeks of the fall of the Berlin Wall. The 'strong presence of nationalism in 1989' also, as Paul Betts reminds us, explains the ease with which xenophobia and resentment of western tutelage surfaces to this day: 'today's potent brew of nationalism, religious conservatism and racism in eastern Europe is hardly just a reaction to 1990s neo-liberalism, but found overt expression in 1989 as well.'[3]

A final precondition of revolution was the youthfulness of so many participants. Many demonstrators in 1989 belonged to a generation wholly grown up under the communist system, yet had also escaped the terror of Stalinism. This made young people less afraid of the regimes, and more disposed to stick their necks out by demonstrating. This was also, thanks to universal education and mass media, a better educated and informed generation than any before it. The young were arguably more environmentally aware than their elders. They had also been affected by what contact they had with western 'counterculture', in particular music, with its exaltation of individualism, personal freedom and hedonism.

The revolutions of 1989

While some revolutions in 1989, such as Poland's, had a longer incubation period than others, the majority came to a head between June and the end of

[3]   Betts, P., 2019, '1989 at Thirty: A Recast Legacy', *Past and Present*, 244, #1, August, 271–305.

the year. It helps to consider them according to the typology outlined above, but it is also worth noting that there was a decided 'knock-on' effect: each revolution was in various ways affected by developments elsewhere.

1. *Regime-led revolutions*. The Round-Table Agreement of April 1989 in *Poland* provided for semi-free elections, held on 4 June. As agreed with Solidarity, the Polish United Workers' Party (the communists) and its puppet 'coalition' partners, the United Peasant Party and the Democratic Party, were guaranteed 65 per cent (264) of the seats in the *Sejm* or lower house; 35 per cent (161) *Sejm* seats and all 1,000 Senate seats were open to all contestants. Election to the contested *Sejm* seats and the Senate seats was on a winner-take-all basis, although the leading candidate also had to win 50 per cent plus one of the votes cast; where no clear winner emerged, run-off elections were to be held on 18 June, with all candidates below the 50 per cent threshold excluded. In addition, 35 *Sejm* seats were reserved for the so-called national list of prominent communists such as Prime Minister Mieczysław Rakowski and other ministers, but again with the proviso that the winners had to gain 50 per cent plus one of the votes. This complex arrangement was designed to ensure that the Communist Party continued to exercise the 'leading role'. Both communists and Solidarity assumed the party would remain in power, with Solidarity acting as an official opposition.

The results of the first round – held on the same day as the Tiananmen crackdown in China – dumbfounded both sides. In virtually all seats where there was a contested election, Solidarity simply swept the board. It took 160 free *Sejm* seats, and picked up the last remaining one in the run-offs; in the Senate, designed to exercise a brake on the *Sejm*, it took 92 seats in the first round, before hoovering up another seven in the second. Just as startling was the comprehensive humiliation of the party: since voters had the option of crossing out candidates' names, in seat after seat the communists and their allies did not even approach the 50 per cent threshold and were thus eliminated. Worse, the communists failed to reach the threshold in 32 of the 35 uncontested seats reserved for the leadership, with the result that the prime minister and most of the cabinet did not win seats at all. Formally the party still held a majority in the *Sejm*, if not the Senate; but morally the elections were a resounding victory for Solidarity, and a demoralising body blow for the party.

The next three months saw an historic unravelling of communist power. Two crucial psychological humps had to be crossed in the process. Firstly, and most remarkably, the Communist Party accepted it had lost the election, and convincingly so; and while it took longer to relinquish the levers of power there was no attempt to falsify the poll. Secondly, Solidarity had to be persuaded that, since the communists were bereft of all legitimacy, it was the trade union's responsibility to step in and take power themselves. The enormity of such a step, as well as fear that Solidarity was being inveigled into some trap by the communists, made acceptance of power too much to contemplate for some members. General Jaruzelski initially proposed that Solidarity form a coalition with the communists, a suggestion Wałęsa refused. In the interim Jaruzelski was only elected to the new presidency, on 19 July, with the votes of Solidarity, a further demonstration of communist weakness. In the end Wałęsa managed to persuade his colleagues that government tumbling was the only responsible option, and support for a Solidarity-led coalition was ensured on 7 August, when the communists' former puppet parties, the United Peasants and the Democrats, unexpectedly broke free and promised their backing to Solidarity. Jaruzelski again invited Solidarity to form a government, and when Communist Party leader Rakowski telephoned Gorbachev for instructions, he was unmistakably nudged towards the exit when the Soviet leader advised him to accept the loss of power, since the Polish party was 'crap'.[4] The first non-communist government in Eastern Europe since the late 1940s was duly sworn in on 24 August, albeit with some key ministries still in communist hands; the new prime minister, Tadeusz Mazowiecki, was so nervous that he fainted during the proceedings.

Hungary by the start of 1989 was already well advanced on the road to a multiparty system, even if the Communist Party clearly expected to retain its leading role. For much of the year, in what has been called the 'negotiated revolution', it was the communists, rather than their still feeble opponents, who set the agenda, in the hope of maintaining control.[5] As events elsewhere unfolded, however, the dynamics changed and the party found itself losing control, as pressure mounted to be more accommodating than originally intended.

On 11 January Hungary's parliament voted to allow freedom of assembly and association, thereby tacitly legitimising the non-communist organisations already formed; the party's central committee formally endorsed a multiparty system the following month. Before that, on 28 January, politburo member Imre Pozsgay, who saw himself as Hungary's Gorbachev, caused a sensation by demanding a reappraisal of what he deliberately called the 'popular uprising' of 1956; by implication this was an admission that suppressing the uprising had been wrong, and that the party's justification for holding power ever since was illegitimate.[6] Significantly, no rebuke came from the Kremlin. The party and its opponents, moreover, were encouraged to go further by other Soviet moves, not just the election in March of the Congress of People's Deputies, but even more the historic beginning of Soviet troop withdrawals in April; the moral impact of this latter development in particular is hard to exaggerate. In the meantime

[4] Quoted in Stokes, G., 2012, *The Walls Came Tumbling Down: Collapse and Rebirth in Eastern Europe*, 2nd edn, New York and Oxford, 150.
[5] Brust, L. and Stark, D., 1992, 'Remaking the Political Field in Hungary: From the Politics of Confrontation to the Politics of Competition', in I. Banac (ed.), *Eastern Europe in Revolution*, Ithaca, NY and London, 28.
[6] Crampton, R.J., 1997, *Eastern Europe in the Twentieth Century – And After*, 2nd edn, London, 393.

the Polish Round-Table Talks had agreed on June elections. Further emboldened, reformers in the Hungarian party pressured the rest of the leadership to initiate Hungary's own round-table negotiations, initially scheduled to begin on 8 April. The hardliners within the party still saw this as a way of dictating terms to the opposition groups; but this approach was thwarted when the opposition refused, demanding that the regime negotiate with them as a united group, the 'Opposition Round Table'. In a significant concession, the government agreed, and the talks duly started on 13 June. Another moral corner was turned on 16 June, when an estimated 350,000 people attended the reburial of Imre Nagy, the executed leader of 1956, in a televised ceremony that lasted eight hours. Desperate to identify with this moment of national reaffirmation, Pozsgay, prime minister Miklós Németh and the speaker of parliament were allowed to attend and lay wreaths.

Even before the Polish elections and Hungary's own round-table talks, the Hungarian regime made a distinctive contribution to the year of revolution when it announced it was dismantling the barbed wire along Hungary's frontier with Austria. In a famous photo opportunity on 2 May, Hungarian foreign minister Gyula Horn posed for the world's media as he and his Austrian counterpart symbolically cut a section of the border fence. This signal to the West that Hungary was opening itself up triggered a swelling exodus of East Germans that summer, contributing to the destabilisation of both the GDR and Czechoslovakia.

Hungary's 'negotiated revolution' gradually turned into a cave-in. The round-table talks finished in September with an agreement to hold genuinely free, multiparty elections early in 1990; unlike the Polish agreement, the party did not even try to negotiate a reserved number of seats for itself in the planned parliament. In October the Hungarian Socialist Workers' Party (the communists) split between reformers and hardliners, and then formally dissolved itself; the reformers promptly set up a Hungarian Socialist Party (HSP), committed to social democracy, the first former Communist Party to do so. On 23 October a new, democratic constitution was published, ditching the 'people's republic' in the country's title and renaming it the Republic of Hungary. The final sign that the old regime was finished was the forcing of a referendum on the question of the presidency. The September agreement provided for a strong president, elected by popular vote in advance of the general election. Fearing that a reformed communist like Pozsgay might take advantage of this, the Alliance of Free Democrats and Fidesz campaigned for a weak presidency, elected by parliament after the national elections. The clear if narrow majority for the latter option, when the referendum took place on 26 November, effectively destroyed Pozsgay's chance of attaining the presidency. When elections were held in March 1990, not only did non-communist parties, led by the Hungarian Democratic Forum, take the overwhelming majority of the votes, leading to a coalition of non-communists under József Antall, but the reformed communists received only 8 per cent of the seats in parliament, freezing the HSP out of power.

Bulgaria provides the peculiar example of a revolution initiated by the regime, albeit in response to popular pressure and developments elsewhere, but at the end of which a reformed Communist Party remained in power through democratic means. This was as much a tribute to the communist leopard's ability to change its spots and take advantage of its dominant position, as it was proof of the weakness of Bulgarian civil society.

Early in 1989 Todor Zhivkov, in power since 1961, seemed as unassailable as ever. Despite token statements of support for Gorbachev-style reform, Zhivkov instead preferred playing the nationalist card and continued his campaign against Bulgaria's ethnic Turkish minority. By mid-year, however, this transparent distraction tactic showed signs of backfiring. In May the army was deployed to suppress ethnic Turkish protests against the policy of forcible assimilation, organised by the newly emerged Democratic League for the Defence of Human Rights; in the ensuing violence some hundred people were reported killed. Zhivkov's reaction was draconic, decreeing a rolling deportation of ethnic Turks to the Turkish border which, by July, had affected 300,000 people, caused a labour shortage and aroused international condemnation, not least from Turkey. At the same time opposition groups among the majority Bulgarian-speaking population continued to emerge: in addition to the environmental movement *Ecoglasnost* an independent trade union, *Podkrepa* (Support) was founded in February 1989, and by July human rights groups were denouncing the deportation of ethnic Turks as 'contrary to our national character'.[7]

The real impetus towards regime change, however, came from within the party. Zhivkov's politburo colleagues concluded that his policies were wreaking havoc on the economy as well as ethnic relations, and that the party must embrace reform or perish. At a summit in early July, a group led by foreign minister Petŭr Mladenov intimated to Gorbachev that they were anxious to 'carry out change', to which the Soviet leader merely replied, 'We sympathize with you, but it's your business.'[8] This was enough of a green light, but Zhivkov's grip was not finally loosened until 8 November, when the turmoil elsewhere in Eastern Europe encouraged the politburo plotters to demand his resignation; Zhivkov complied two days later, seemingly uninfluenced by the fall of the Berlin Wall the night before. Mladenov took over as party leader.

Zhivkov's fall was greeted with popular jubilation, but what followed exceeded all expectations. Mladenov, a lifelong communist in office since 1971, announced that Bulgaria under his direction must become a modern, democratic society. The party's leading role was renounced and, most startling of all, multiparty elections were promised in 1990, as well as round-table talks

---

[7] Quoted in Stokes, *The Walls Came Tumbling Down*, 172.
[8] Quoted in Stokes, *The Walls Came Tumbling Down*, 173.

with opposition groups to agree on electoral procedure. In response to these announcements a number of groups coalesced on 8 December to form the Union of Democratic Forces (UDF), and demonstrations started to exert real pressure on Mladenov to go further. On 14 December, for instance, some 20,000 protesters surrounded the Bulgarian parliament demanding the abolition of the party's monopoly on power, which duly followed. Behind Mladenov's somersaults, however, was the calculation that the reformed Communist Party was well placed to win a free election. It held significant advantages in terms of experienced personnel, organisation and resources, not to mention still being the government, whereas the disparate opposition groups, only recently formed, lacked all these things. In addition to its inexperience the UDF was still largely urban and intellectual.

Round-table discussions began in January 1990, and agreement was reached in March for elections in June. Before this the Communist Party renamed itself the Bulgarian Socialist Party (BSP). The result of the June elections was a convincing win for the BSP, which won the popular vote and gained a clear majority of the seats in the new, democratically elected national assembly. Mladenov did not last long as prime minister, being toppled the next month as a result of emerging scandal over his willingness to use force against protesters early in 1989. Despite this, and rather to everyone's astonishment, pluralist politics in Bulgaria was there to stay.

2. *Popular revolutions. East Germany* was one of the most obdurately change-resistant regimes in the east bloc. The Socialist Unity Party, through its 90,000-strong security police, the *Stasi*, kept a close watch over the GDR's seventeen million inhabitants; it has been estimated that in the late communist period up to 180,000 individuals were employed by the *Stasi* to act as informants on their fellow citizens. Over the lifetime of the GDR half a million people, or one in thirty citizens, spied on their neighbours, a social outrage depicted in Florian Henckel von Donnersmarck's 2006 film, *The Lives of Others*. As a result there was little overt dissidence, outside of the Lutheran Church, right down to 1989. Honecker's disagreement with Gorbachev's advice that the east bloc regimes should emulate Soviet *glasnost* was patent, as was his hope that Gorbachev would soon be toppled. The East German regime was horrified by Poland's June elections, just as it tacitly applauded China's brutal suppression of the Tiananmen Square demonstrators.

Yet this seemingly monolithic regime was brought down by a series of popular protests. The first form these protests took was a mass exodus. The second involved thousands of East Germans peacefully demonstrating on the streets of the GDR's major cities.

The process began in March 1989 when, to curry favour with the West, Hungary announced that it intended acceding to the 1951 UN Convention on Refugees. On 2 May Hungary demilitarised its border with Austria; on 27 June it ostentatiously started dismantling the barbed-wire fencing between the two countries. Since the West German government had for decades offered automatic citizenship to any East Germans who wished to claim it, in the course of the next four months thousands of East Germans started going 'on holiday' to Hungary via Czechoslovakia, and then promptly fleeing to West Germany via Austria. Starting as an imperceptible trickle, with first individuals and then entire families abandoning their vehicles near the border and unobtrusively crossing it, by late summer this exodus was nearing biblical proportions, especially after the Hungarian government announced on 3 August, to Honecker's fury, that it would treat East Germans as asylum seekers. On 11 September alone 11,000 people crossed into Austria, while additional numbers, temporarily blocked by Czechoslovakia from crossing its territory, crowded into West German embassies in Prague and even Warsaw, seeking West German passports. The East German regime, in desperation, scored a public relations disaster by agreeing to convey all those camped out in the grounds of the West German embassy in Prague to West Germany via the GDR, but in sealed trains to avoid the possibility of contact with other East Germans. As news of the trains leaked out, they were mobbed at Dresden station by thousands more people trying to board them. The population drain threatened to rival that last seen in 1961, when the Berlin Wall was erected.

In response to the obstacles the regime continued to place in the way of those fleeing, those left behind started to demonstrate. Since 1982 the Sankt Nikolai church in Leipzig had been the scene of weekly vigils for peace, an objective officially in line with regime propaganda and, as such, tolerated. In the spring of 1989 these vigils started to attract up to a thousand participants; one in March had to be dispersed by force. Now, starting on 4 September, the Leipzig vigil became the focus for those demanding reform: 1,200 to begin with, several thousand at the next two vigils. This was East Germany's 'head above the parapet' moment: there were no easily identifiable leaders, but the more people turned up, the more wanted to attend too. On 25 September 8,000 did so, chanting 'We're staying!' and, in a pointed comment on a regime claiming to represent the working class, 'We are the people!' By 2 October there were an estimated 10,000.

The Leipzig demonstrations gathered pace, ironically, just as the GDR prepared to celebrate its fortieth anniversary on 7 October. Gorbachev and other east bloc leaders arrived for the festivities in the wake of several demonstrations dispersed with violence by the *Stasi*, and with Honecker planning a Tiananmen-style crackdown; the latter course was not taken only thanks to Gorbachev's clear intimation that, in the event of an uprising, the Soviets would not intervene. The crunch point came on Monday, 9 October: with the security forces under instructions to respond to the slightest provocation with all-out repression, violence was only averted by the intervention of Kurt Masur, director of Leipzig's orchestra who, backed by a handful of local dignitaries and party officials, broadcast an appeal to the demonstrators to be completely peaceful.

The *Stasi*, confronted, in the words of one officer, with some 50,000 'entirely normal people shouting "Wir sind das Volk!"', did not open fire.[9]

Thereafter the weekly demonstrations not only got bigger, but spread to other towns and cities. When it became clear that Honecker, nothing daunted, intended crushing the next demonstrations, his less bloodthirsty comrades finally forced his resignation on 18 October, replacing him with the more emollient Egon Krenz. Krenz presided over the party-state's accelerating collapse, purging hardliners and opening the borders with Czechoslovakia. In the meantime the demonstrations were assuming monstrous proportions. By 23 October more than 200,000 people marched through Leipzig; on 4 November possibly one million demonstrated in East Berlin, demanding such unheard-of extravagances as an end to the party's monopoly and free elections. Faced with this unnerving proof of their unpopularity, the politburo appointed a reformist prime minister, Hans Modrow, and resolved to introduce new visa regulations. At the 7 pm press conference scheduled on 9 November to announce this, however, the politburo member deputed to do so incautiously informed the world's press that the lifting of travel restrictions would come into effect immediately. The effect was electrifying, as thousands of Berliners massed at the checkpoints to see if they could cross the Wall. In the absence of clear instructions to the contrary the border guards started letting people through holus-bolus. By midnight hordes of people were pouring through in both directions, as well as dancing and celebrating on the Wall itself, the defining image of East European communism's collapse.

The collapse of East German communism took some weeks more. On 17 November Modrow disbanded the hated *Stasi*. On 23 November the government initiated round-table talks with the recently formed opposition group New Forum; on 1 December the party's special status was abolished; on 3 December the entire politburo and cabinet resigned, but with Krenz and Modrow kept on as caretakers; on 7 December the East German parliament announced multiparty elections for March 1990; and on 8 December the SED, now under Gregor Gysi, renamed itself the Party of Democratic Socialism (PDS). An unshackled press started investigating communist corruption and *Stasi* abuses of power. East Germans generally seemed torn between renouncing the effectively defunct regime and all its works, and trying to salvage some form of socialist system from the wreckage. The GDR, however, was about to be overtaken by much broader developments: on 28 November West German chancellor Helmut Kohl for the first time raised the possibility of effecting the reunification of the two Germanies. It was the really big question which had been waiting in the wings all this time, and which would dominate the following year.

---

[9] Quoted in Kotkin, *Uncivil Society*, 59.

Czechoslovakia's 'velvet revolution' took shape in a similarly unexpected and pell-mell fashion, and again with virtually no bloodshed. This was yet another revolution coming seemingly out of nowhere, toppling a regime which right up to November 1989 gave all the appearance of being rock solid. As Tony Judt writes, 'Nowhere else was so much achieved so quickly, at so little human cost and with so strong a chance of success.'[10]

Throughout the year the hardline regime of Miloš Jakeš looked on in consternation as the pace of change accelerated in Poland, Hungary and then East Germany, assisted by the occasional nudge from Gorbachev's Kremlin. Yet the Czechoslovak Party's position was a strong one, dissidents were few in number and most of the population unwilling to stick their necks out. In January 1989, for instance, a demonstration commemorating the death of Jan Palach, the student who burned himself to death in 1969 in protest at the Soviet invasion, attracted 4,000 protesters, including Václav Havel; but over the next few days they were forcibly dispersed and many of them, Havel included, were arrested. May Day saw sporadic protests on behalf of human rights, again easily dealt with. Havel, sentenced to eight months in prison in February, was quietly released in May, another sign of regime confidence. In the wake of China's Tiananmen massacre, the chief organ of the Czechoslovak Party expressed its full approval. Even on the anniversary of the 1968 invasion, with Solidarity about to take office in Poland and thousands of East Germans fleeing westwards, the government felt secure enough to tolerate the demonstrations of a few thousand.

Beneath the surface there was undoubtedly rising excitement over the events in surrounding countries. One indication of this was the fact that a statement issued in late June by Havel and others, calling for freedom of speech and association, attracted the unprecedentedly high number of 20,000 signatures. Research based on the oral testimony of participants suggests that this sort of response did not come out of nowhere, but reflected 'long months, even years, of slow mobilization.'[11] By the fall this collective anticipation was palpable: on 28 October, the anniversary of Czechoslovakian independence in 1918, and with mass protests occurring in the GDR, upwards of 10,000 collected in Wenceslas Square in Prague; and in the most serious clash yet, riot police waded into the crowd when the participants refused to disperse, arresting over 300.

The dam of popular feeling only burst on 17 November, eight days after the fall of the Berlin Wall, with the East German regime in full meltdown. An official commemoration of a Czech student's murder by the Nazis, in 1939, turned into an impromptu demonstration against the regime. Several thousand

[10] Judt, T., 1992, 'Metamorphosis: The Democratic Revolution in Czechoslovakia', in I. Banac (ed.), *Eastern Europe in Revolution*, Ithaca, NY and London, 115.
[11] Kenney, *A Carnival of Revolution*, 297.

of the 30,000 mostly student participants insisted on marching to Wenceslas Square, demanding the resignation of the regime and free elections. They were met by the riot police, and in the mayhem several students were badly beaten; a false rumour spread that one of them had been killed. It seems clear that the police were under orders to overreact, but to what purpose remains obscure to this day: was the violence to be used as pretext for even worse repression, or did elements within the party hope the outcry would lead to Jakeš's downfall?

This was the spark triggering Czechoslovakia's 'unorganized mobilization'. The next day, the 18th, thousands of students defied the authorities on the streets yet again. The same day Havel and others stepped forward to form an action group, Civic Forum, to coordinate protests. The next day a similar group was launched in Bratislava called Public Against Violence (PAV). Havel's contribution here was crucial, since he alone seemed to appreciate the opportunity opening up for radical change. Havel stressed the absolute need for the demonstrators, as in East Germany, 'to avoid violence and above all to prevent further polarization.'[12] Moral pressure was to be exerted against the regime by continuing to demonstrate, while making clear the demonstrators were open to dialogue.

In response to Civic Forum's emergence the number of demonstrators rocketed, with 200,000 turning out on the 19th, and for the next week and beyond both Prague and Bratislava were paralysed by monster crowds, demonstrating peacefully for change. Demonstrations were held after working hours so as not to disrupt production. Specifically, Civic Forum and PAV demanded the resignation of those responsible for the 1968 invasion; the resignation of those responsible for suppressing previous demonstrations; a special commission to investigate police brutality; and the release of all political prisoners. Hundreds of thousands gathered on the 20th, chanting 'Freedom!', 'Resign!', 'This is it!' and 'Now is the time!' In a play on the literal meaning of Jakeš (bell), people jingled their house or car keys, to signal that time was up for the party chairman in particular. Havel and Civic Forum took over the Magic Lantern Theatre for a sort of continuous committee meeting, coordinating the protests and drafting a programme for democratic reform. On the 21st the first breakthrough was achieved when prime minister Ladislav Adamec met with Civic Forum, implicitly accepting the group's legitimacy. At that evening's demonstration Havel addressed the crowd for the first time, informing it of Adamec' promise not to introduce martial law, and to investigate police brutality. On the 23rd the Bratislava crowd erupted with jubilation at the first public appearance since 1969 of Alexander Dubček. The following day Dubček arrived in Prague, and at the evening demonstration appeared on a balcony in Wenceslas Square with Havel, looking 'as if he has stepped straight out of a

---

[12] Judt, 'Metamorphosis', 114.

black-and-white photograph from 1968.'[13] In the wake of thunderous applause for the pair news arrived that Jakeš, the politburo and the central committee had resigned. Karel Urbánek took over as general secretary, with Adamec as caretaker prime minister; but the party's malign hold on public affairs was broken.

On 28 November Adamec pledged that the party would abandon its leading role and two days later, symbolically resuming sovereignty, the Czechoslovak national assembly voted to remove the clause in the constitution enshrining the communist monopoly. From this point on events moved with bewildering rapidity, especially after a two-hour general strike, held with impressive solidarity during the lunch break, demonstrated the revolution's popular support. Talks between the government and Civic Forum/PAV quickly agreed to form a coalition cabinet, although Adamec' initial proposal for a communist-dominated government was roundly rejected. By 7 December agreement was reached on a cabinet composed mostly of non-communists, under the Slovak communist Marian Čalfa. On the 9th Gustáv Husák resigned the presidency, and the call immediately went up for either Dubček or Havel to be elected in Husák's place. In a final amicable compromise, Dubček was voted in as speaker of the national assembly on the 28th, while Havel was wafted to the presidency on the 29th, with multiparty elections scheduled for the coming year. The new president addressed the country on New Year's Day with the evocative words, 'People, your government has returned to you.'[14]

3. *Revolution as popular revolt/internal coup.* Romania's revolution was the only one in 1989 which saw serious bloodshed, and to this day its circumstances remain murky. Starting with spontaneous popular revolt and bloody repression, revolutionary change was only possible because elements of the army changed sides, at which point an alternative leadership emerged from the ranks of the party. The Ceauşescu regime was violently terminated, but that which succeeded it, while it ushered in multiparty elections, was initially also authoritarian.

It is hard not to conclude that both the violence and the speed of the Romanian upheaval owed much to the fact that, of all the east bloc regimes, Ceauşescu's was the most repressive. The *Securitate* ruled through victimisation and fear, and the population was ground down by the decade-long drive to eliminate Romania's foreign debt; even after the entire hard-currency debt was declared paid off, in March 1989, the regime continued to ration food and energy. A bitter contemporary joke asked, 'What's small, dark, and knocking at the door?' Answer: 'The future.'[15] Yet as winter closed in, despite revolutionary events

---

[13] Garton Ash, T., 1990, *We the People: The Revolution of '89 Witnessed in Warsaw, Budapest, Berlin & Prague*, London, 94.
[14] Quoted in Garton Ash, *We the People*, 7.
[15] Quoted in Kotkin, *Uncivil Society*, 70.

elsewhere, the regime still seemed impregnable. At the 14th Party Congress, on 24 November, the 71-year-old Ceauşescu was reconfirmed as leader to chants of 'Ceauşescu and the people', and bored his well-trained audience with the ritual, hours-long speech, punctuated by 67 standing ovations.

Yet on 15 December an explosion was touched off in the western city of Timişoara (Temesvár), where the popular Calvinist pastor and dissident László Tőkés was about to be transferred to another parish. Tőkés, a Transylvanian Hungarian, had a lengthy history of speaking out against the regime's mistreatment of Hungarians and his clerical superiors' subservience. His posting to Timişoara was punishment for this outspokenness; but there too his denunciation of policies like the 'systematization' of villages got him into trouble, while earning the devotion of his parishioners. When Tőkés appealed to his flock to witness his eviction, forty elderly parishioners formed a human chain around his residence, defying the *Securitate*. Additional townspeople, apprised of the stand-off, joined in, and by the 16th a considerable crowd had assembled. By evening, when Tőkés, to avert bloodshed, implored his supporters to disperse, a popular mood of defiance had taken over; the crowd flooded into the town centre, smashing windows under cover of darkness and shouting imprecations against the regime. The authorities' attempt to disperse the demonstrators with water cannon only infuriated them, and by the 17th Timişoara was in uproar, which culminated in the sacking of party headquarters and the seizure of several tanks.

In response to this open defiance Ceauşescu predictably chose the 'Tiananmen option', ordering the *Securitate* and army to crush the demonstrators with force: 'if they don't submit, they'll have to be shot.'[16] Security forces duly opened fire on the crowd, and in the course of 17–18 December dozens of people were killed and hundreds wounded; the rumour mill vastly exaggerated the number of dead. With supreme complacency, Ceauşescu on the 18th departed for a two-day state visit to Iran. In his absence, the military commander in Timişoara committed the tactical error of holding workplace meetings in the city's factories, at which for the first time the widespread shooting of 'fascist' demonstrators was admitted. The result was rapidly spreading outrage and wildcat strikes, at which point the local commander backed down, ordering troops to be withdrawn from the city centre. Within hours 40,000 people had massed in the main square, and a 'Romanian Democratic Front' was proclaimed. Timişoara was out of control, and strikes and demonstrations broke out in other urban centres.

Back in Bucharest by 20 December, Ceauşescu still did not grasp the seriousness of the situation, or rather he remained convinced he had only to decree order for it to prevail. A mass rally was convened in front of party headquarters

---

[16] Quoted in Kotkin, *Uncivil Society*, 84.

on 21 December, at which point the regime's hollowness was revealed for all
to see. When Ceauşescu addressed the crowd, live on national television, he
was suddenly interrupted by angry cries of 'Ceauşescu dictator!' For three
excruciating minutes, before transmission was cut, millions of Romanians
watched the *Conducător* stutter and stop, flailing his arms in a vain attempt to
command silence. It was the signal for spontaneous combustion. Hundreds of
thousands turned out to join the demonstration, refusing to disperse even when
fired on overnight by the *Securitate*. An attempt by Ceauşescu the next day to
make a second public address was greeted with open derision by the crowd,
who attacked party headquarters and stormed the building. Nicolae and Elena
Ceauşescu only just managed to escape from the roof by helicopter, hoping to
rally support in the provinces.

This was the end. Crucially, the popular uprising which broke out on the
21st was facilitated by the defection of top army commanders and possibly
even *Securitate* officers, whose abandonment of Ceauşescu's regime was in
turn communicated to units on the streets, many of whom openly joined the
people. The details of this volte-face remain obscure. The generals' defection
may have been prompted by the mysterious death on the night of 21–22
December of defence minister General Vasile Milea who, the regime claimed,
committed suicide for his 'treason' in not implementing Ceauşescu's orders to
fire on the demonstrators. Whether suicide or execution, Milea's death seems
to have effected a revulsion of feeling within the officer corps. In the meantime
former high-ranking members of the party, led by Ion Iliescu, together
with dissident intellectuals, stepped forward and announced formation
of a National Salvation Front (NSF). It was this small circle who, with the
army's backing, took over the main media outlets and government buildings,
coordinated the several days' street fighting against holdout *Securitate* units,
and proclaimed a new government. It was the NSF which declared Ceauşescu
deposed and which, having tracked the Ceauşescus down to the provincial
town of Tirgovişte, arranged for their hasty, kangaroo-court 'trial' and
immediate execution by firing squad on 25 December. This was a judicial
murder, justified by the NSF on the ground that, as long as the dictator and
his equally ferocious wife were at large, there was every possibility they might
stage a comeback.

Deep-laid plot or inspired opportunism? Even specialists remain uncertain.
Protesters, army defectors and putschists within the party appear to have acted
spontaneously; indeed, the degree to which Ceauşescu's regime had controlled
society, up to the very point of explosion, would have made any attempt at a
plot or prior coordination of protest suicidal. What is clearer is that the Iliescu
regime which took over, while nowhere near as horrifying as Ceauşescu's, was
essentially authoritarian. Multiparty elections were eventually held in May
1990, but were not so subtly manipulated to deliver victory for the NSF; and
subsequent protest demonstrations were dealt with by mobilising Romania's

miners to terrorise the urban population. Only later in the 1990s would this successor regime dare to hold anything like free elections.

Aftermath 1990–91

With the exception of Poland, which had led the way in 1989, all those countries which experienced revolutions in 1989 held multiparty elections in the course of 1990, all of which, apart from Romania's, were fairly conducted and confirmed in power governments with a genuine popular mandate. Even Bulgaria, where the reformed communists clung to office, was a functioning pluralist polity. The economic transformation of East European societies was a far more painful and long-drawn-out process; but in a political sense these were genuine revolutions, in that communist dictatorships were replaced by more or less viable democracies. A similar process was under way by 1990 in Yugoslavia's constituent republics, and in the Soviet Union, although the outcome was far less positive. It remains to account for the belated revolution in Albania, and the complex series of events which led to one of 1989's least expected outcomes, the reunification of Germany.

1. *Albania catches up 1990–92.* Enver Hoxha, Albania's 'artful dictator', died in office in April 1985, having preserved his country in a Stalinist time warp since his seizure of power in 1944. Hoxha's puritanical brand of Marxist-Leninism had caused him to break with the 'revisionist' Soviet Union in the 1960s; and by 1978 he had broken off relations with his next patron, Red China, following the latter's rapprochement with the USA in 1972, and especially its embrace of economic liberalisation in the late 1970s. The ending of Chinese aid and the consequent need for total self-sufficiency made communist Albania one of the most isolated as well as impoverished societies in the world, its people forbidden all contact with foreigners. Hoxha's last potential rival, prime minister Mehmet Shehu, mysteriously 'committed suicide' in 1981.

Hoxha's successor, Ramiz Alia, tried to maintain this arm's-length policy toward the outside world, but even this regime could not remain unaffected by the events of 1989. The downfall of east bloc regimes, and in particular the bullet-riddled fate of Romania's Ceaușescu, suggested that survival depended on ending Albania's isolation and showing some willingness to reform.

As so often with rigid tyrannies, however, even the slightest concessions generated a hunger for more. An amnesty for political prisoners, in November 1989, was followed by a rash of strikes and demonstrations in the spring of 1990. In May some elements of economic decentralisation were introduced, foreign investment was legalised, the penal code relaxed and, for the first time since 1967, the practice of religious belief was permitted. The regime sought to mend fences abroad, restoring relations with the Soviets in July 1990; the

US government, however, made relations dependent on the implementation of free elections. By the summer economic conditions were deteriorating, and increasing numbers of Albanians were attempting to flee the country; in October the regime received a blow when the country's most renowned writer, Jamail Kadare, sought asylum in France, declaring 'The promises of democracy are dead.'[17] In December university students in Tirana staged a two-day demonstration demanding not only better living conditions but multiparty elections, and as this attracted ever greater support the party's central committee finally agreed to legalise independent political parties. In response the first non-communist party since the 1930s, the Democratic Party of Albania (DPA) was founded on 12 December, led by the economist Gramoz Pashko and the cardiologist Sali Berisha. By March 1991, when multiparty elections were indeed held, the DPA had a membership of 60,000 and fronted the first opposition newspaper, *Democratic Revival*.

The elections accelerated the snowballing effect. Although the Communist Party won 60 per cent of the votes, violent protests resulted in four people being killed, and in the face of mounting unrest the government consented to revise the constitution, so that Albania was no longer a socialist republic. In June 1991 a government of national unity was formed, including opposition parties, but conditions continued to worsen, with serious food shortages triggering mass flight, this time by sea to Italy. In desperation, the communist-led government scheduled fresh elections for the spring, but before they could be held the cabinet fell apart; a caretaker government under Vilson Ahmeti took over in December. The elections of March 1992 completed Albania's political revolution: the DPA won a convincing victory, and formed a cabinet under Aleksander Meksi, with Sali Berisha elected president. Democratic transformation, however, by no means solved Albania's economic problems, and in the mid-1990s Albania descended into chaos.

2. German reunification 1989–90. The question of German reunification was raised at the end of November 1989, when chancellor Kohl published a ten-point programme for achieving this. Reunification was not, however, the automatic goal of all East Germany's democratic revolutionaries. On the contrary, some of the most prominent dissidents, in particular the members of New Forum, hoped to preserve the GDR and with it some form of German socialism, on the ground that, after forty years' separate existence, an attachment to socialist values was something distinguishing East Germans from their co-nationals in the 'capitalist' Federal Republic. New Forum warned compatriots not to become 'rent-slaves of Western capitalism.'[18] Behind this putative East German sense of identity, in addition, there lurked an entirely rational apprehension that, even under Gorbachev, the Soviet Union, which

---

[17] Quoted in Vickers, M., 1995, *The Albanians: A Modern History*, London and New York, 216.
[18] Quoted in Kotkin, *Uncivil Society*, 63.

had endured so many sacrifices to defeat Nazism and impose its system on East Germany, would never countenance a reunited Germany. This assumption was shared by western leaders, many of whom thought it inadvisable to push Soviet tolerance too far. President Bush stressed he had no desire to 'dance on the [Berlin] wall'; while British prime minister Margaret Thatcher was positively hostile to reunification, on the ground that it risked a revival of aggressive German nationalism.[19]

Rather to everyone's surprise, however, the geopolitical situation was favourable to a resolution of the German question. Crucially, Gorbachev was amenable to discussing it, and proposed a four-power summit to do so; as his adviser put it the day after the Berlin Wall was opened, 'This is the end of Yalta.'[20] In a climate of practical nuclear disarmament and general detente, Gorbachev was anxious to eliminate anything that might imperil smooth East-West relations, not least because the Soviet government was actively considering applying to the West for financial assistance. With one East European satellite after another rushing to adopt multiparty systems, it was clear that the old Soviet hegemony in the region would have to be renegotiated, in the interest of reinforcing what the Soviet leader referred to as the 'common European home'.[21] As long as Soviet security concerns were adequately addressed, Gorbachev was prepared to be accommodating. There were also the issues of what the future of the Warsaw Pact would be, what status a reunited Germany would have, and what to do with the 380,000 Soviet troops stationed in the GDR.

Then there was the undeniable fact of German national sentiment in both East and West. The eagerness of West German conservatives like Kohl and his Christian Democratic Union (CDU) for reunification was a matter of record; and both the Social Democratic and Free Democratic Parties, in the West, were in favour of reunification, even if the SPD argued for delaying it. And in East Germany, as it turned out, attachment to the principle of socialism and a separate East German identity ran a poor second to nationalism, not least because reunification, in many people's minds, appeared to offer the quickest route to West German levels of material prosperity. Already in early November, in the mass demonstrations being held night after night in East German cities, the initial cry of 'We are the people' had changed to 'We are one people'.[22] It was a striking indicator of the public mood, suggesting the GDR was doomed.

Before the end of December 1989, with the blessing of the great powers, Kohl and Modrow, the GDR's caretaker prime minister, met to discuss reunification. On 1 February 1990 Modrow proposed a united state, federal in structure

---

[19] Quoted in Stokes, *The Walls Came Tumbling Down*, 245.
[20] Quoted in Stokes, *The Walls Came Tumbling Down*, 245.
[21] Gorbachev, M., 1988, *Perestroika: New Thinking for Our Country and the World*, new updated edn, London, 195.
[22] Stokes, *The Walls Came Tumbling Down*, 166.

but neutral in international law, in other words tied to neither of the rival alliances, Warsaw Pact or NATO. Kohl, however, held out against this and instead proposed, as a preliminary to any political resolution, the unification of German currencies, by extending the mighty Deutschmark to East Germany. This, whatever headaches it posed the FRG in the longer term, was a brilliant psychological ploy, at a stroke signalling to East Germans that they were on the brink of being absorbed into West Germany's legendarily robust economy. It was increasingly apparent that the West German government held the strongest cards, and the weak, interim administration in East Berlin could only helplessly follow Kohl's lead.

As a result, in mid-February, even before elections were held in East Germany, the two German governments and the four occupying powers still responsible for the German states' fate agreed to talks on the basis of two-plus-four, that is, the two Germanies would negotiate the terms of re-unification before this was ratified by the USSR, the USA, Britain and France. At the international level, the key to reunification at this point was the close relationship between Gorbachev on one side and Bush and Kohl on the other. Both the latter were anxious to reassure Gorbachev and avoid endangering his position by being seen to inflict any sort of policy defeat on the Soviets. Gorbachev in turn was increasingly preoccupied with domestic affairs, especially spiralling nationality problems and a deteriorating economy. The crucial question was Germany's position between the two superpower blocs.

US secretary of state James Baker resolved this question in February 1990 by convincing Gorbachev that a reunited Germany outside NATO would be a loose cannon and hence a potential threat to the USSR, whereas within NATO it could be controlled by the US and its allies. In addition, it was understood that a re-united Germany would never be allowed to acquire nuclear weapons. In an exchange that has fuelled huge, if exaggerated, controversy ever since, President Bush promised Gorbachev that NATO had no intention of expanding eastward beyond the reunited Germany. This made sense at the time, since no one in February 1990 imagined that the Soviet Union itself might break up; there was thus no question at this point of newly democratic countries like Poland needing to join NATO for their own security, and 'NATO governments tried their best to discourage East European leaders from even broaching the topic.'[23] A final inducement to the Soviets was the proposal of West German financial assistance. Kohl shrewdly committed his government to pay $7.6 billion towards the cost of relocating Soviet troops stationed in East Germany, on top of a $1.9 billion loan to the USSR, interest-free. On this basis, Gorbachev undertook to withdraw Soviet forces from East Germany by 1994.

---

[23] Kramer, M., 2009, 'The Myth of a No-NATO Enlargement Pledge to Russia', *The Washington Quarterly*, XXXII, #2, April, 43.

The 18 March elections in the GDR were thus held in an atmosphere of fevered excitement, and constituted a virtual 'referendum on unification.'[24] By this point some twenty new parties had been formed, apart from the PDS; but the principal contenders were clones of the two main parties in West Germany, the right-wing CDU and the left-wing SPD. A CDU-led coalition, the Alliance for Germany, won convincingly with 48 per cent of the vote; the SPD trailed with 22 per cent and the PDS with 16 per cent, while New Forum, the advocates of an independent, social democratic East Germany, were nowhere. In the wake of this clear vote for reunification, a coalition including the SPD was formed under the latter's leader, Lothar de Mazière.

The new government immediately entered into negotiations with West Germany, on the basis of the latter's founding law, the *Grundgesetz*, which provided for the accession of new provinces to the existing FRG. In the interval, by prior agreement, the currency union took place on 1 July. East Germans queued to exchange their nearly worthless East Marks for Deutschmarks, on a one-to-one basis. This extraordinarily favourable rate was at Kohl's insistence, and for purely political reasons, so as not to leave East Germans feeling humiliated and panic-stricken at the collapse of their currency. The immediate effect of the currency union, however, was to create economic union well ahead of political union. The East German economy entered a steep decline, and in the course of 1990–1 industrial productivity in the East went down by 60 per cent. After reunification, the new federal government had to set up a special agency, the *Treuhandanstalt*, for privatising and selling off East German state enterprises and other assets. This was paid for through a German Unity Fund, set up on the assumption that $70 billion would cover it; in reality the truer cost, down to 2019, was nearer $2 trillion.

The final treaty between the two Germanies adopted the FRG's electoral law as well as its federal structure: GDR-era *Bezirke* (districts) were abolished and replaced with pre-1945 *Länder* (provinces) to facilitate this. Poland's borders were guaranteed in advance by both German parliaments. As a result the two-plus-four treaty was signed in Moscow on 12 September 1990 by all six parties, with formal reunification taking place on 3 October. Germany was reunited for the first time since 1945. In the first federal elections of the reunited state, in December that year, Kohl's CDU took the predictable award of 55 per cent of the vote.

---

[24] Stokes, *The Walls Came Tumbling Down*, 248.

19

The wages of nationalism

Yugoslav, Soviet and Czechoslovak break-up

Yugoslavia, the Soviet Union and Czechoslovakia were all multinational states, and their fate at the end of the communist period cannot be understood without taking this into account. All three disintegrated between 1991 and 1995, but the roots of their demise go back much further. This is not to say that break-up was inevitable; on the contrary, the record of some multinational states suggests that, if the institutional mix is right, polities embracing more than one ethnic group can be viable. In the case of our three states the problem had much to do with the fact that all were communist dictatorships. Communism in these states simultaneously repressed and, paradoxically, encouraged the nationalism of their constituent peoples, a problem exacerbated by economic decline. In Yugoslavia and, to a lesser extent, the Soviet Union break-up was both caused and accelerated by nationalism, and in both cases, in varying degrees, the results were war, ethnic cleansing and displacement, and the creation of new states. Only Czechoslovakia effected a 'velvet divorce' without loss of life.

Yugoslav break-up

1. Incubation period. The peculiar mix of nationality problems and economic decline which plagued late-communist Yugoslavia has been outlined above. These problems reached crisis proportions in the late 1980s, independent of events elsewhere in Eastern Europe; but the lessening of Cold War tensions as a result of the 'Gorbachev revolution', followed by democratic revolutions in 1989, had an unquantifiable effect on Yugoslavia. Unlike these other revolutions, however, the upheavals in Yugoslavia were not about liberation from Soviet hegemony. In Mark Thompson's words, Yugoslavs 'had no outer wall to demolish; their demons lay all within.'[1]

Of all Yugoslavia's nationality problems the most poisonous by the 1980s was the Serb-Albanian antagonism over Kosovo (Kosova in Albanian), seen

---

[1] Thompson, M., 1992, *A Paper House: The Ending of Yugoslavia*, London, 7.

by Serbs as one of the cradles of their nation, but where since Ottoman times Albanians constituted the overwhelming majority. The welling-up of Serb nationalist anxiety over Kosovo coincided with Slobodan Milošević's rise to leadership of the Serbian Communist Party, a classic example of the party apparatchik who learned to play the nationalist card as a sure-fire route to popularity.

Until April 1987 there is not much evidence that Milošević was particularly nationalistic; but when he was sent to Priština by Serbian president Ivan Stambolić to hear the grievances of Kosovar Serbs, he transformed the political atmosphere across Yugoslavia by openly taking their side. Confronted with the spectacle of Kosovo's Albanian police beating back Serbs clamouring to be heard by him, Milošević declaimed before television cameras that 'No one should beat you!', and that 'You should stay here. This is your land.'[2] Replayed on news broadcasts repeatedly over the following days and weeks by Milošević's cronies in the media, this seemingly unscripted intervention had a profound impact: here, it seemed to Serbs everywhere, was someone who would stand up for them. On his return to Belgrade Milošević, according to one witness, 'was like a heated stove. He was full of emotions. He could not control his feelings. He could not calm down.'[3] Small wonder, for posing as protector of the Serbs was Milošević's route, as he saw it, to supreme power as a second Tito.

Milošević's first move in this direction, in September 1987, was to oust his mentor, Stambolić, by portraying him as too moderate, and assume the presidency himself. He then packed the party apparatus with his supporters and proceeded to storm the country, holding a series of monster rallies across Serbia, in the two autonomous provinces of Vojvodina and Kosovo, and in neighbouring Montenegro. The strident nationalist tone of these rallies attracted tens of thousands, and an estimated one million turned out to hear Milošević in Belgrade. The purpose was to drum up support for a revision of Serbia's constitution, abolishing the autonomy of Vojvodina and Kosovo. As a result of this 'street democracy', Milošević succeeded in intimidating the Party leadership in all these territories into stepping down, to be replaced by his allies. This gave Milošević control of four out of eight votes in Yugoslavia's federal council, enabling him to bully the remaining four republics into amending the 1974 constitution. The two provinces' autonomy was formally abolished in March 1989, while Albanian protests were put down with violence.

There is considerable irony in the fact that, just as 'people power' was achieving democratic change in the rest of Eastern Europe, Milošević was using it to whip up nationalist frenzies. Milošević's initial purpose, supported

---

[2]   Quoted in Silber, L. and Little, A., 1995, *The Death of Yugoslavia*, London, 37.
[3]   Quoted in Stokes, G., 2012, *The Walls Came Tumbling Down: Collapse and Rebirth in Eastern Europe*, 2nd edn, New York and Oxford, 218.

wholeheartedly by many Serbs, was to take control of the federal system and recentralise Yugoslavia, on the ground that Serbs were at risk of victimisation in every republic save Serbia and Montenegro. The only problem with this strategy was that it petrified non-Serbs. The spectacle of Milošević riding to supreme power on a wave of Serb nationalism understandably alarmed the other republics, especially those containing Serb minorities – Croatia, Bosnia-Hercegovina and Macedonia. By 1989 forces were already at work in favour of political pluralism, just as elsewhere in Eastern Europe. In part a consequence of Yugoslavia's decentralisation since the 1950s, in part a popular response to the other 1989 revolutions, this potential democratic revolution ran headlong into Milošević and his nationalist supporters. The party leadership in each republic was already conscious of the need to legitimise itself via free, multiparty elections; the threat of a Serb-led recentralisation gave this trend added urgency.

The tendency towards pluralism was most pronounced in Slovenia and Croatia, for different reasons. Slovenia was economically the most advanced of the republics and the most 'central European' culturally, and Slovenes were proud of the fact that, with only 8 per cent of the population, they were responsible for 20 per cent of GNP and 25 per cent of hard-currency exports. Croatia too was economically more advanced than the southern republics, if politically less open since suppression of the 'Croatian Spring'; but in the Croats' case a nationalist resentment of their enforced inclusion in Yugoslavia had never really gone away. Both republics resented being net contributors to the federal budget, which they saw as subsidising the poorer, less efficient south.

While the republics squabbled, the unwieldy, collective federal government seemed powerless to control the crisis. In March 1989 the rotating presidency appointed Ante Marković federal prime minister, with the specific brief of implementing economic reforms which, had they been followed up, might have stabilised the situation. Marković's undoubted successes in reducing inflation and introducing additional elements of marketisation, however, were immediately frustrated by the republics' own economic policies. Yugoslavia's decentralisation had gone too far, with the result that Marković had no way of enforcing his reforms. The federal government's economic weakness was brutally demonstrated when, in December 1990, Milošević's Serbia simply raided the federal bank to the tune of $1.8 billion in order to subsidise wage increases and other electoral sweeteners.

In reaction to Milošević's rise, as well as the 1989 revolutions, both Slovenia and Croatia legalised non-communist political activity and promised multiparty elections for 1990. In the meantime the principal bond holding Yugoslavia together, the Communist Party, disintegrated. In January 1990 the Slovene Party seceded from the all-Yugoslav party over precisely the issue of whether Yugoslavia should be democratised. When the republics controlled by

Milošević made clear their preference for neo-Stalinist recentralisation, and the avoidance if possible of free elections, the Slovene delegation literally walked out, followed by the Croatians. The federal party could no longer claim to speak on behalf of all Yugoslavs, and with the party crippled the federal government wielded even less authority. The rotating presidency was inherently weak, and the sole instrument of power left it was the Yugoslav National Army (JNA) which, because its officer corps was overwhelmingly Serb, tended to gravitate towards Serbia as its natural master. As Yugoslavia's crisis deepened the JNA's non-Serb conscripts returned to their home republics, while its Serb-dominated rump sided with Milošević.

Multiparty elections duly went ahead in Slovenia in April, and in Croatia in April to May. In Slovenia a coalition of non-communists, DEMOS, swept the board in the elections for the national assembly. The presidency, however, was won by Milan Kučan, leader of the reformed Slovenian communists, largely on the basis of his record in standing up for Slovenia's interests against the federal government. This was not a vote for outright independence, but it did indicate support for a looser confederation, as well as closer ties with the European Community. As one DEMOS member put it, 'Yugoslavia as a concept is exhausted. Slovenia simply wants to join Europe and is not willing to wait for the rest of Yugoslavia to catch up with it.'[4] It was therefore logical for Slovenia, in July 1990, to proclaim itself a sovereign republic, entitled to secede from Yugoslavia if it wished.

In Croatia the results were more complicated and altogether more ominous. The newly formed Croatian Democratic Union (HDZ), led by the arch-nationalist Franjo Tuđman, won both parliament and the presidency, with the Communist Party a poor second. Won under a first-past-the-post system with 41.8 per cent of the vote, this was undoubtedly a democratic result, but it also starkly exposed Croatia's ethnic divisions. The vote of the half-million Serb minority (12 per cent of the population), most of whom lived in Zagreb and were still committed to a multi-ethnic state, split between the reformed Communist Party, which gained a respectable 34.5 per cent, and the ethnic-based Serbian Democratic Party which won only one seat. The divisiveness came largely from the Croat side. Tuđman's language during the election created a climate of fear among Serbs which could not be dispelled thereafter. He stressed Croatia's historic identity as a state, talked pointedly of its 'different culture', and displayed a not-so-covert anti-Semitism.[5] Worst of all he praised the genocidal *Ustaša* regime of the Second World War which, according to Tuđman, 'also stood for the historic aspiration of the Croatian people for an

---

[4]   Quoted in Cohen, L.J., 1993, *Broken Bonds: The Disintegration of Yugoslavia*, Boulder, CO, San Francisco, CA and Oxford, 90.
[5]   Quoted in Cohen, *Broken Bonds*, 211.

independent state.'[6] The response among Croatia's rural Serbs, in the so-called Krajina, was one of deep hostility. Pluralist politics had already produced an interethnic face-off.

Where Slovenia and Croatia led, the other republics followed, since free, multiparty elections were now seen as the key to political legitimacy. In November to December all four republics held polls, and even in Serbia's case there can be little doubt that the results reflected popular opinion. In Serbia Milošević's rebranded communists, the Socialist Party of Serbia, took 77 per cent of the vote, and Milošević was easily elected president. A similar result was achieved in Montenegro, where Milošević's ally Momir Bulatović won 66 per cent of the vote. In Macedonia and Bosnia-Hercegovina outcomes mirrored the ethnic composition of the population. There was no overall winner in Macedonia: the nationalist Democratic Party for Macedonian Unity/IMRO took the largest share of the vote (31.7 per cent) with 38 seats in the 120-seat legislature; the reformed communists 25.8 per cent and 31 seats; while the Party of Democratic Prosperity, representing most of Macedonia's Albanian minority, came third with 9.2 per cent and 11 seats. This forced a compromise: the reformed communist Kiro Gligorov was elected president, and in March 1991 a non-party cabinet of technocrats took office.

In Bosnia-Hercegovina the consequence of free elections was a division along nationalist, or rather communal, lines. Alija Izetbegović's Party for Democratic Action, representing Bosnia's 43.7 per cent of Muslims, won 32 per cent of the assembly seats; the Serbian Democratic Party, under the ultra-nationalist Radovan Karadžić, won 26 per cent of the seats on behalf of the Serb population of 31.4 per cent; and the Bosnian branch of Tuđman's HDZ won 15 per cent for the republic's 17.3 per cent of Croats.

Democratic elections thus had the effect of reinforcing divisions between republics and ethnicities, and made secession and war more likely, not least because Milošević's position was enhanced and consequently even more alarming to non-Serbs. Confrontation seemed likeliest to occur soonest in Croatia, where the Krajina Serbs busily armed themselves and blockaded roads leading to their settlements. In August 1990, despite the questionable nature of the exercise, the Krajina Serbs held their own referendum on secession, which according to them showed overwhelming support for autonomy; they followed up in February 1991 by declaring an Independent Republic of Krajina and expressing their desire, impracticably, to unite with Serbia. Tuđman, accustomed to dealing with more emollient urban Serbs, underestimated the stubbornness and paranoia of the Krajina Serbs, and throughout the winter of 1990–1 made a number of ineffectual attempts to assert the Croatian government's authority over them. The first deaths occurred on 31 March 1991, at Plitvice,

---

[6]   Quoted in Silber and Little, *The Death of Yugoslavia*, 91.

when Serbs fired on a Croatian police detachment; over the next few months this inter-communal conflict in Krajina and Slavonia widened, as paramilitaries on both sides involved themselves, and JNA units stationed locally increasingly intervened on the Serb side. The problem for the Croatian government, apart from the challenge to its territorial integrity, was that the country's southern borderlands were anything but ethnically homogeneous: Serbs and Croats had lived there intermixed for centuries, a fact wilfully ignored by the Serbs, who insisted they were defending 'Serbian lands' against 'Croatian fascists'.

2. *Independence and war.* Long before the killing began, the logic of the situation increasingly led toward secession if not war. *Slovenia*'s 1990 declaration of sovereignty laid the legal foundation for eventual independence. For the moment the Slovenians continued to advocate a looser, confederate restructuring of Yugoslavia; but in case this could not be agreed, preparations were quietly made for issuing executive orders and a currency, taking over border posts and above all assuming control of arms depots and raising a national army. In December 1990, following Milošević's electoral victory in Serbia, the Slovenes held a referendum on independence: should it happen if no progress were made towards confederation in the next six months? Following the overwhelmingly affirmative response, a formal date was set for 26 June 1991.

The Slovenes' resolve was only strengthened when, in March 1991, Milošević himself repudiated the federal government's authority, as insufficient to protect the interests of Serbs. In the spring a series of summits were held at republican level, completely bypassing the federal authorities, but coming no closer to any agreement; and Serbo-Croat relations were further worsened when Croatia held its own referendum on independence in May. The results were deeply alarming, in that most Croats voted for, while Croatian Serbs almost universally boycotted the poll. The Slovenian government then brought forward its declaration of independence by one day to 25 June, taking federal officials and the JNA by surprise.

A confused, ten-day conflict followed, in which Slovenia's fledgling but much better prepared army faced down conscript JNA units led by conflicted commanders, reluctant to wage an all-out war on behalf of a Yugoslav unity in which nobody any longer seemed to believe. From the viewpoint of Serb nationalists in the JNA, moreover, Slovenia was simply not worth fighting over, since it possessed no Serb minority. After a ceasefire was arranged, JNA units accordingly pulled out of Slovenia on 19 July. Forty-nine people had been killed and 307 wounded on both sides. At this point Milošević seems to have concluded that recentralising Yugoslavia was a hopeless cause; and by transferring JNA units to Croatia, superior firepower could be assembled there for defending Serb interests.

Croatia's secession was more problematic in that, unlike Slovenia, it harboured a sizeable and hostile Serb minority, and the JNA had no sooner withdrawn from Slovenia than full-scale slaughter broke out in the republic's southern and eastern borderlands. The war that raged until January 1992 was distinguished by its brutality and the deliberate targeting of civilians. The population on both sides had been conditioned by tightly controlled media to see their neighbours in terms of Second World War stereotypes, Serbs as '*Četniks*' and Croats as '*Ustaše*'. Croatian and Serbian television had for months been screening endlessly repeated images, often without commentary, of wartime atrocities. The Croatian declaration of independence, which quickly followed Slovenia's, could not conceal the near-total lack of preparation for war on the Croatian side, whereas the Croatian Serbs had been arming for months, and were now reinforced by the JNA. It was the latter which made the war so lopsided, as the army passed from ostensible mediators to open participants; and this imbalance of firepower was worsened, in September 1991, by an ill-considered UN arms embargo on all parties, which seriously disadvantaged the Croats, as it later did the Bosnian government in its war. The concentration of firepower on the Serb side meant that the bulk of the atrocities, at least to begin with, were committed by Serb combatants. Much of the fighting and most of the atrocities were committed by freelance paramilitaries, often descending on the countryside from Zagreb or Belgrade for the weekend, and motivated as much by the chance of plunder as by nationalism. The fighting from the start was aimed, not at big victories over the other side's forces, but at displacing civilians and thus changing the demographic balance in this village or that. Indeed, the ferocity of the conflict can only be understood by grasping that this 'ethnic cleansing', as it was labelled, was the whole point.

The other aspect of the Croatian war which explains its almost desultory course is that Serb goals were strictly limited. Once the Croat population had been chased out, and the frontiers of Serb-inhabited areas rounded out, then a ceasefire made sense. Other aspects of the conflict, for instance the bombardment of Dubrovnik and devastation of the Croatian coast by Montenegrin forces, made little sense other than as a demonstration of having the upper hand, and as a sort of cultural vandalism. At any rate, once the Serbs' basic goals were achieved, hostilities could be ended. A truce was negotiated by former US secretary of state Cyrus Vance on 3 January 1992, although due to the continuing volatility of the front line it was not until March that a UN Protection Force (UNPROFOR) was positioned to keep the two sides apart. This meant accepting the de facto partition of Croatia for the foreseeable future. The truce owed little to the hapless mediation of the European Community, nor was it influenced by, let alone conditional upon, international recognition of Slovenian and Croatian independence on 15 January.

The Serbo-Croat quarrel remained a 'frozen conflict' for the next three years, until the even more savage war in Bosnia reached its climax in the summer of 1995. Taking advantage of extensive military preparation and rearmament, covertly connived at from 1994 by Bill Clinton's administration in the US, Croatia profited from NATO's gradually escalating intervention in Bosnia, first, suddenly to overrun the Serb-held parts of eastern Slavonia in May 1995, bypassing UNPROFOR; and second, to move in force against the Krajina Serbs in August. Since Bosnia's Serbs by this point were under threat of NATO attack, which deterred Yugoslavia from active intervention, Croatia's 'Operation Storm' was a swift success, retaking all Croatia's territory, and in the process 'ethnically cleansing' the area of its 500,000 Serbs, who fled to Bosnia or Serbia. A centuries-old ethnic intermixture had been erased, seemingly forever.

The three-year war in *Bosnia* was even grimmer than Croatia's. An uneasy coalition representing all three nationalist parties was formed after the 1990 elections, with Izetbegović as president, a Croat as prime minister, and government posts distributed to reflect the republic's communal divisions. Despite being tarred from the start as an Islamic fundamentalist by Serbs and Croats, Izetbegović insisted his government had no option but to govern in the name of a multicultural, supranational Bosnian identity: 'Bosnia is impossible to divide, because it is such a mixture of nationalities.'[7] The Serbs were the principal obstacle to this project; their leader Karadžić was one of the first to deploy the fundamentalist slander, essential for demonising the Muslims and justifying any excess against them. As in Croatia, fear of the 'other' spawned local militias, and the poisonous atmosphere was worsened in 1991–2 by the fighting next door in Croatia. In Bosnia's case, however, unlike those of Slovenia and Croatia, outside action unintentionally supplied the spark leading to armed conflict: the EC made diplomatic recognition of Bosnia conditional on a referendum showing the agreement of all three national communities.

This put Izetbegović in a quandary. Remaining in Yugoslavia risked domination by Milošević and the republics he controlled, since Macedonia had also declared its independence, uncontested, on 21 November 1991. Yet there was little doubt Bosnian Serbs feared independence would cut them off from their fellow Serbs and render them permanently powerless. In the referendum at the end of February, Muslims and Croats voted overwhelmingly for independence, but most Serbs boycotted the exercise. On 1 March, in response to violence at a wedding, Serbs started raising barricades in Sarajevo, and urban fighting spread. The formal recognition of Bosnian independence by the EC and the United States, on 6 April, made in the hope that it would calm the situation, instead proved the catalyst for all-out war. Karadžić's Serbs, backed by the JNA, retreated to the mountains overlooking Sarajevo and subjected it to sporadic bombardment, pitiless sniper fire and a siege that lasted for the next three years. In the rest of the republic, especially the east and northwest, a rapidly formed Republican Serb Army under General Ratko

---

[7]   Quoted in Cohen, *Broken Bonds*, 146.

Mladić, assisted by paramilitaries from Serbia, immediately started 'ethnic cleansing' of both Muslims and Croats. All too often, this meant slaughtering the men of a community in gratuitously barbarous fashion, systematically raping the women, looting and torching homes, and generally terrorising the non-Serb population into flight. A depressing aspect of the Bosnian war was what can only be termed 'cultural genocide': the determination of the Serbs, in particular, to erase any trace of their enemies' cultural monuments, as if to deny that they had ever existed. A large number of historic mosques, many dating from the early Ottoman period, were deliberately dynamited and razed to the ground. By the end of 1992 the Bosnian Serbs' self-styled '*Republika Srpska*' (Serbian Republic) controlled some 70 per cent of Bosnian territory.

In Hercegovina, home to the largest concentration of Croats, supported by Tudman's government in Croatia, the fragile coalition with local Muslims broke down in 1993 and fighting raged between the two communities. Entire villages were put to the flames and their inhabitants either massacred or driven out. The town of Mostar was ravaged during this Croat-Muslim sideshow and its historic Ottoman bridge was destroyed by Croat shelling.

Some general points about the Bosnian war are in order. Firstly, the agenda of the Bosnian government was not, as claimed by Serb and Croat nationalists, the creation of a fundamentalist Islamic State; on the contrary, Izetbegović remained committed to a multinational Bosnia, and his government and armed forces continued to include Serbs as well as Croats. Secondly, the aim of Serbs and Croats by contrast was very obviously to carve out ethnically homogeneous mini-states, which could then, it was hoped, be attached to their respective 'mother' countries. Thirdly, the ability of the Serbs and, to a more limited extent, the Croats to implement this agenda was directly related to their greater access to weaponry denied the Bosnian government as a result of the international arms embargo. Finally, the conflict was prolonged by the ambivalent attitude of the outside world towards it. It is not obvious that outside intervention by, say, the UN in the early stages of the war would have been effective; what is clear is that no consensus existed, until very late, as to what should be done, because most governments took the attitude that the three parties to the conflict were all somehow equally to blame, and that the war was the product of inextinguishable, 'ancient' hatreds. Instead, the EC (the European Union as it became in 1993) and UN made the fatal error of trying to mediate impartially, expanding UNPROFOR's presence in Bosnia while maintaining the arms embargo. This empowered the stronger side further, while disadvantaging the weaker side. In the meantime the international community arguably prolonged Bosnia's agony by designating certain towns, like Srebrenica in eastern Bosnia, as 'safe havens' for Muslim refugees, and ferrying humanitarian aid to their inhabitants and to besieged Sarajevo. This policy seemed like fattening victims for the slaughter, since it did little to impede either side from continuing with hostilities.

By the end of 1993 the combatants had reached military as well as political stalemate, but it took another year and a half for outside intervention to assume any coherent purpose. A 'Contact Group' consisting of the US, Russia, Britain, France and Germany was formed in April 1994, but could not agree how to stop the fighting, or what shape intervention should take, if any. The role of the British and French governments in delaying meaningful action seems especially shameful. Change only came once, by the spring of 1995, the military balance had subtly shifted. Croatia's armed forces had been covertly built up with American assistance. The Bosnian army, despite the arms embargo, was finally making advances at the expense of the Serbs; and Milošević, despite supporting the Bosnian Serbs, was anxious to escape the economic sanctions imposed on rump Yugoslavia by the UN. Most decisively, the Clinton administration, mindful of intensifying public outrage at the situation, and increasingly impatient of British and French obstruction, signalled its willingness to impose a settlement by the threat or use of force, under UN auspices. In May 1995 a European Rapid Reaction Force (RRF) was formed, essentially from British and French troops, to supplement UNPROFOR with combat-ready units, and on 16 June the UN Security Council authorised its deployment. At the same time the US, via NATO, conducted air strikes against Bosnian Serb ammunition dumps surrounding Sarajevo. The Serbs responded by taking several hundred UN personnel hostage, and for the next few weeks there was stalemate.

On 10–13 July, however, Mladić's Bosnian Serb army overreached itself when it overran the safe haven of Srebrenica, where thousands of Muslims were holed up under the ostensible protection of a Dutch battalion of UN peacekeepers. Without clear authority from the UN to resist, the peacekeepers were intimidated into withdrawing. Following Mladić's assurances of safe passage, some 8,000 men and boys were separated from their families, taken to a separate location, and on 14 July systematically massacred, in the worst single atrocity of the war. Although details only emerged later, the unaccounted disappearance of so many individuals gave the game away. This affront to international law, coupled with uproar in the world's media, and capped on 28 August by an equally notorious mortar-bombing of Sarajevo's marketplace, finally impelled western governments to act. NATO air cover for the remaining peacekeepers was stepped up, while the RRF opened up a secure corridor to Sarajevo, and the Bosnian Serbs were for the first time subjected to concentrated air strikes. By this point Croatia was bringing 'Operation Storm' to a victorious conclusion in neighbouring Krajina. Together with Bosnian government advances, by November the Serbs' share of Bosnia's territory had been reduced to under 50 per cent.

The international community's intervention forced all sides – Yugoslavia, Bosnia and Croatia, with Milošević acting for the Bosnian Serbs – into peace negotiations in November, overseen by the Americans at Dayton, Ohio. The Dayton Agreement, formally signed at Paris on 14 December, froze the

Bosnian conflict in a form that has been problematical ever since. Bosnia emerged as a unique state, nominally governed by a central administration in Sarajevo, but in reality containing two separate 'entities', the Federation of Bosnia-Hercegovina, comprising the Muslim, Croat and some of the Serb population; and the *Republika Srpska*, a sprawling archipelago of Serb-inhabited territory extending around Bosnia's northern and eastern rims, and over which the Sarajevo government had little practical control. A NATO-supplied Implementation Force (IFOR) was responsible for keeping the peace, and an EU-appointed 'high representative' was charged with overseeing the implementation of the peace agreement, with wide-ranging powers, including the dismissal of elected officials if necessary. Bosnia and Hercegovina, to give it its formal title, has since remained a weak state, heavily dependent on EU subsidies and other forms of international aid, with a limping economy, high levels of unemployment and, worst of all, little achieved in the way of inter-communal reconciliation and reintegration. Those 'ethnically cleansed' have not been able to return to their homes, and the Serbs, in particular, who continue to vote for hardline nationalists, show few signs of recognising the evil done in the name of their nation.

The resolution of the *Kosovo* question forms a belated coda to the tragedy of Yugoslavia's break-up. Yugoslavia's crisis originated in the Serbo-Albanian antagonism over Kosovo, but the tensions there remained on the back-burner until the late 1990s. During the Slovenian, Croatian and Bosnian wars Kosovo was quiet, in part because Milošević kept a tight lid on any sign of Albanian unrest, but also because the Albanians, under the leadership of Ibrahim Rugova and his Democratic League, pursued a strategy of passive resistance. Rather like the East European dissidents of the 1970s and 1980s, Kosovan Albanians constructed a sort of alternative society, providing themselves many of the educational and health services denied them by the Serb-controlled state, and with financial aid from the Kosovar émigré community. By 1998, however, patience with this situation among the younger generation of Kosovar nationalists was wearing thin, and from March of that year armed attacks on Yugoslav security forces by the Kosova Liberation Army (KLA) signalled a new, more confrontational phase of the Serb-Albanian relationship.

Milošević's reaction to the KLA was to crack down hard, mounting a campaign to eradicate them; by September Yugoslav operations had killed 700 and rendered a quarter of a million homeless. The availability of arms following the collapse of public order in neighbouring Albania, however, made it difficult for Milošević to maintain control, and fighting intensified throughout the winter of 1998–9. This in turn brought Kosovo to the attention of the international community. The Clinton administration wanted to avoid a repeat of the Bosnian tragedy, and there was greater willingness in other capitals too to contemplate intervention on behalf of some restored form of autonomy for Kosovo. In February 1999 the Contact Group convened both sides at Rambouillet, in France, specifically to discuss autonomy as the only practical solution. Milošević rejected this; nor would he accept the proposal to station NATO troops in Kosovo, despite an unambiguous threat from NATO that it would start bombing Yugoslavia if he did not comply. Convinced he could crush the KLA and that the Contact Group's threat was an empty one, Milošević continued with the offensive, and NATO launched its bombing campaign on 24 March, targeting Yugoslav forces in Kosovo, but also military installations and other infrastructure in Belgrade and elsewhere.

In response, Milošević played what he thought was his trump card, the wholesale expulsion of Albanians from Kosovo, which he hoped would force NATO to back down. This time the Yugoslav authorities seemed determined to effect a complete 'ethnic cleansing' of the province: in the last week of March hundreds of thousands of Albanians were rounded up at short notice and, in an action reminiscent of the Second World War, transported by rail or bus to the frontiers of Albania and Macedonia and ordered to leave. Thousands fled voluntarily, fearing summary execution. Milošević, however, miscalculated: despite differences of opinion within its ranks NATO held firm, and after seventy-eight days of aerial bombardment Milošević was forced to throw in the towel, by which point some 5,000 Kosovars had died and as many as 850,000 had been turned into refugees. On the Yugoslav side a third of military capacity was destroyed, large parts of the country were left without electricity and water, and several hundred Serbs had been killed.

Yugoslavia conceded defeat on 10 June 1999. By the agreement signed at Kumanovo Yugoslav forces withdrew entirely from Kosovo, to be replaced by KFOR, an international peacekeeping force; displaced Kosovars were free to return home, and an autonomous Kosovan government under UN supervision was formed. In revenge, returning Albanians conducted their own form of 'ethnic cleansing' against the Serbs, some of whom were murdered and many of whom fled; it was only thanks to the protection provided by KFOR that a Serb enclave in the north survived. Kosovo's separate status remained contested by Belgrade, but this has not impeded its government in the end from proclaiming formal independence, as Kosova, in 2008.

Soviet break-up 1990–1

1. Incubation 1985–90. Compared to Yugoslavia's bloody demise the break-up of the Soviet Union is not only easier to explain, but was relatively bloodless; it was also one of the most profound developments in recent world history. From the perspective of Eastern Europe the significance of Soviet break-up was the sudden emergence or re-emergence of six independent states: Estonia, Latvia, Lithuania, Belarus, Ukraine and Moldova. The larger story of Soviet break-up, involving a total of fifteen new states, need not concern us here. Suffice it to mention, however, that one of the nationalities to secede from the Soviet Union was Russia itself, a fact essential to understanding the last quarter-century of Eastern Europe's history.

It has been remarked that the one factor that Gorbachev left out of account in his drive to reform Soviet communism was the persistence and strength of nationalism. Yet the Soviet Union, like the Russian Empire before it, was demonstrably a multinational state; indeed, the federal structure adopted in the 1920s was designed (as in Yugoslavia in 1945) to accommodate the fact of nationality, while drawing its fangs by building a socialist society. This project failed. The longer the Soviet Union existed, the stronger the nationalism of its constituent peoples, in some cases where it had not existed before. Then, in the 1980s, Gorbachev's policies of *glasnost* and political liberalisation revealed what David Marples calls the 'submerged dilemma' of all multinational states: if the nationalities of such a state are conscious of their separate identity and unhappy with their lot, then nothing short of unremitting tyranny can repress their yearning for national self-determination.[8]

In addition to the corrosive effect of nationalism, it is also worth noting what Mark Kramer calls the 'spillover' effect on the Soviet Union of Eastern Europe's democratic revolutions.[9] The mere fact that revolutions were possible, and indeed expressly tolerated, in what Soviet citizens had long regarded as a legitimate Soviet sphere of influence, had an inevitable impact on the Soviet Union itself. There was the implication, first, that such change could be replicated in the Soviet Union. There was active encouragement of such change by the pressure groups, political parties and leaders of newly independent East European states. There was the demonstrable discrediting of Marxist-Leninist ideology through the collapse of regimes built on its premises, which potentially included the Soviet Union. There was the lessening fear of the party-state made possible by *glasnost* and the visible power of non-violent resistance, once organised. Finally there was, in reaction, the undoubted alarm and anger felt by hardliners in the Soviet Communist Party, and in the Soviet military, at the 'loss' of Soviet hegemony in Eastern Europe. This was perceived by many in the party as a blow to Soviet prestige, an undermining of Soviet socialism, and above all a threat to Soviet security. Furthermore, the more the non-Russian nationalities of the Soviet Union clamoured for autonomy or even independence, the greater the disquiet of the hardliners. This made for a volatile situation.

The 'Gorbachev revolution' truly opened the floodgates in 1989, when partially free elections were held for the Congress of People's Deputies. As

---

[8] Marples, D.R., 2004, *The Collapse of the Soviet Union 1985-1991*, Harlow, 48.
[9] Kramer, M., 2003, 'The Collapse of East European Communism and the Repercussions within the Soviet Union (Part I)', *Journal of Cold War Studies*, V, #4, Fall, 179–80.

in Yugoslavia, democratic politics, even semi-democratic politics, meant nationalist politics. Even before 1989, as a result of ever more open debate, nationalist antagonisms resurfaced elsewhere in the Soviet Union, for instance between Armenians and Azerbaijanis over Nagorno-Karabakh in 1988, and in April 1989, when Soviet troops fired on Georgian nationalists in Tbilisi, killing twenty.

In Eastern Europe, the *Baltic* peoples led the way. Estonia, Latvia and Lithuania were among the most modern and socially advanced of the Soviet republics. More important, all three experienced twenty-two years of independent statehood in the interwar period, and the extinction of that independence, and the suffering inflicted by Stalinism, were within living memory. Unsurprisingly the Baltic peoples were among the first, as Gorbachev's reforms took hold, to demand the safeguarding of basic rights, up to and including the right to national self-determination.

Helsinki-86, one of the first dissident movements to appear in the Soviet Union, was founded in Latvia in 1986 to monitor Soviet violations of the Helsinki Final Act. Many of the first stirrings of non-communist political activism, as in Eastern Europe, revolved around environmental concerns but these quickly took on nationalist overtones. There was a distinct 'copy-cat' effect across the Baltic region. In 1988 'popular fronts', forerunners of nationalist parties, sprang up in all three republics: the Popular Front of Estonia, in April; the Lithuanian Reconstruction Movement, otherwise known as *Sajūdis*, in June; and the Popular Front of Latvia the same month. Indicative of the underlying strength of Baltic nationalisms was the fact that the communist parties of the three republics were quick to second the popular fronts' calls for greater autonomy, and tried to put themselves at the head of these movements. Communists and non-communists alike were emboldened by the reformist regimes in Hungary and Poland; all were further encouraged by Gorbachevian *glasnost*. The year 1988–9 was one of frequent demonstrations, many on environmental issues, but many also commemorating milestones in Baltic national histories. There were demonstrations on the anniversary of each country's independence in 1918; on the anniversary of deportations to the Gulag in 1940; most famously, on the fiftieth anniversary of the Nazi-Soviet Pact which sealed the interwar republics' fates, on 23 August 1989, two million Balts from all three republics formed a human chain stretching 650 kilometres from Tallinn via Riga to Vilnius, an event widely covered by the world's media. The formation of the Solidarity government in Poland meant that Lithuanian nationalists in particular started receiving direct encouragement and support from this direction.

The more the political process in the Baltic republics opened up, the more obvious it was that the majority of the population favoured independence; but Baltic nationalists faced several dilemmas en route. Firstly, the sizeable minorities of ethnic Russians and other Soviet loyalists in each republic strongly opposed independence, and from 1989 started protesting at the mere idea. Secondly, demands for recognition of the illegal nature of Soviet rule since 1940 were unacceptable even to Gorbachev, since they threatened the territorial integrity of the state. Thirdly, the emergence of popular fronts and reform communists had been made possible by Gorbachev; but a push to achieve independence could lead to his fall, and the very real possibility of a crackdown. Finally, hundreds of thousands of Soviet troops and sailors were stationed in the Baltic republics, so any strategy for independence would have to deal with this awkward fact.

Initially the running was made by the republics' reform-minded national communists, notably Lithuania's Algirdas Brazauskas and Estonia's Vaino Valjas. Symbolically, all three republics renamed their Supreme Soviets Supreme Councils. Then, in November 1988, the Estonian government declared Estonia's sovereignty, in short its right to decide its own fate; from January 1989 Estonian was made the official language, prompting ethnic Russian protests. In the course of 1989 Baltic-Russian relations worsened. In March Soviet loyalists formed an 'Interfront' to coordinate ethnic Russian pushback across all three republics. This did not deter Lithuania from proclaiming its sovereignty in May, followed by Latvia that summer. In November Estonia's Supreme Council declared the 1940 occupation illegal, while Brazauskas led the Lithuanian Communist Party out of the CPSU. The popular fronts were at first content to back the communists in this confrontation with the centre; but in the spring of 1990 they were offered the opportunity to take control themselves, when free multiparty elections were held in all three republics. In March *Sajūdis*, led by Vytautas Landsbergis, took office in Lithuania, and promptly proclaimed the restoration of Lithuania's full independence, while Edgar Savisaar's Popular Front assumed power in Estonia; that of Latvia's Ivars Godmanis followed suit in May. The Estonian and Latvian governments, more circumspect than Lithuania's, declined to press for independence, a caution seemingly warranted by the crisis over Lithuania. Gorbachev flatly condemned Lithuania's declaration of independence as illegal and, when Landsbergis refused to back down, subjected the republic to an oil blockade in April. Only in June, when Landsbergis agreed to put independence on hold, was the embargo lifted, but matters remained stalemated, in an atmosphere of rising tension among ethnic Russians. Certainly the threat of Baltic secession, at a time when a similar outcome loomed in Yugoslavia, was a factor in Gorbachev's waning popular support, and made a hardline reaction against him likelier.

In the *Ukraine* under Volodymyr Shcherbytskyi, party boss since 1972, communist rule seemed firmly entrenched until Gorbachev came to power, and manifestations of nationalism were largely confined to the Ukrainian émigré community. Yet discontent with Soviet – for which read Russian – domination was nevertheless not far beneath the surface, and was encouraged by the events of 1989. A Ukrainian Helsinki Union, with the encouragement of Solidarity in

Poland, was formed in the late 1980s. Late in 1988 an association of nationalist dissidents published a programme in the Writers' Union newspaper, calling for 'genuine sovereignty for Ukraine', the full panoply of rights, a market economy and recognition of Ukrainian as the republic's official language.[10] Once in power, Polish Solidarity actively promoted the foundation of the Popular Movement of Ukraine for Perestroika (*Rukh*) in September 1989, whose membership within weeks soared to 280,000. Adam Michnik and other Solidarity luminaries attended *Rukh*'s founding congress at Kiev, openly hailing Ukraine's 'national rebirth',[11] while the extensive coverage of the congress in Poland's free media 'exposed the Ukrainian public to sensitive issues that were previously taboo.'[12] In Lviv, heartland of Ukrainian nationalism, a crowd of 150,000 assembled in September 1989 to commemorate the fiftieth anniversary of western Ukraine's annexation by the Soviet Union. All of a sudden Shcherbytskyi seemed to have lost control of events, a development which provided Gorbachev with an excuse to replace him with the more reform-minded Leonid Kravchuk.

Kravchuk was not reform-minded enough, however, to approve of *Rukh*, and prevented it registering for the March 1990 elections to the Ukrainian Supreme Soviet. Instead, the more innocuous-sounding Democratic Bloc served as the umbrella organisation for non-communists, both in Ukraine and Belarus, and this bloc won most of the seats it was allowed to contest in the Ukrainian election, as well as the town councils of Kiev and Lviv. The result was that, as in the Baltics, reform communists under Kravchuk found it politic to make common cause with non-communists, while hardliners continued to profess loyalty to the Soviet Union. As in the Baltics, the loyalist faction was the natural refuge of Ukraine's large ethnic Russian minority, even though a substantial number of Ukrainian communists from the start professed a willingness to side with an independent Ukraine, if it came to that. The upshot was that the Ukrainian Supreme Soviet, on 16 July 1990, unanimously passed a declaration of sovereignty, in effect challenging the legitimacy of the Soviet state. Support for *Rukh* never seems to have spread much beyond western Ukraine and the big urban centres, but there can be little doubt that, by 1991, millions of Ukrainians, whether ethnic Ukrainian or Russian, were beginning to imagine the unimaginable.

Belarus lagged significantly behind events elsewhere, but even here there was evidence of a shift in opinion when in October 1988 Martyrology, a group set up to commemorate victims of Stalin, had to be dispersed by riot police in Minsk. In June 1989, with help from Lithuania, a Belorussian popular front, Renewal, held its first congress in Vilnius. Renewal's first demonstrations in Minsk, in February 1990, attracted 100,000 people, and it provided most of

---

[10] Hosking, G., 1992, *A History of the Soviet Union 1917-1991*, final edn, London, 481.
[11] Quoted in Kramer, 'The Collapse of East European Communism (Part 1)', 218.
[12] Kramer, 'The Collapse of East European Communism (Part 1)', 200.

the Belorussian wing of the Democratic Bloc in the elections to the Supreme Soviet in March, winning 20 per cent of the seats. The copy-cat effect was striking in Belarus: in July the Belorussian government issued a declaration of sovereignty. Nevertheless Belarus remained under Communist Party control throughout 1990–1, and was firmly controlled by the Soviet Party and Gorbachev. Thus, 'The Belarusian national movement was not in 1990 in any position to influence Belarusian or Soviet policy.'[13] Most unrest in this period was industrial: from April 1991 there was a wave of strikes, demanding a rescinding of price hikes, but also genuine multiparty elections. Not until the August 1991 coup attempt in Moscow did the Belorussian government show much sign of independent will; its subsequent actions were taken almost entirely for fear of being left behind by Ukraine.

Finally, by early 1989 there was widespread unrest in *Moldova* (in Soviet terminology the Moldavian Socialist Soviet Republic). Moldova was unique: it was the only Soviet republic whose principal ethnic group was not self-contained within the Soviet Union. Its Romanian-speakers shared their nationality with neighbouring Romania, although the republic also contained ethnic Russians in the Transnistrian region, and a tiny minority of Christian Turkic Gagauz in the south. As the revolutions in Eastern Europe unfolded, excitement among Moldovans mounted. The republic's ethnic mixture had dictated a contradictory policy since Stalin's time. Moldova could not be admitted to share nationality with Romania, so the Soviet regime inculcated a bogus Moldovan language, insisted it be spelt with a Cyrillic rather than a Latin alphabet, and promoted the concept of a separate Moldovan nation. However, the regime could not allow Romanian-speaking Moldovans to exert meaningful control over this separate 'national' identity. The cultural elite was dominated by Russians and Ukrainians, and the local party under Simeon Grossu remained subservient to Moscow.

Gorbachev's encouragement of dialogue with the local population was therefore regarded by the Moldovan party with consternation. The opposition groups emerging by 1988, however, focused on three nationalist demands: Romanian should be recognised as the official language of the republic; it should be written in the Latin alphabet; and the Romanian and 'Moldovan' languages should be acknowledged to be identical. In May 1989, with back-up from Poland's Solidarity, a Popular Front of Moldova (PFM) was formed; at a rally in Chişinău, one speaker gleefully announced 'We have finally awakened thanks to the inspiration of Poland.'[14] The PFM promptly demanded that restrictions on the import of literature from Romania be lifted; when the government refused, Moldovans published material independently. In June 1989 a

---

[13] Snyder, T., 2003, *The Reconstruction of Nations: Poland, Ukraine, Lithuania, Belarus 1569-1999*, New Haven, CT and London, 248.
[14] Quoted in Kramer, 'The Collapse of East European Communism (Part 1)', 216.

dissident Association of Historians started demanding an honest investigation into the Soviet occupation in 1939–40. Clamour rose for adoption of the Romanian national flag, and despite government refusal people started displaying it everywhere. In August the Supreme Soviet made 'Moldovan', that is, Romanian, the republic's official language, in place of Russian. Tensions among the Russian and Gagauz minorities mounted, with each declaring their enclaves autonomous. By November 1989 economic disruption, coupled with widespread rioting when the regime attempted to celebrate the 1917 Revolution as normal, thoroughly discredited Grossu, who was replaced by the equally unimaginative Petru Lucinschi.

The fall of Romania's Ceauşescu completely transformed the political mood in Moldova, by raising the real possibility of reunification, and the suddenly free Romanian media took a keen interest in Moldovan affairs. In March 1990 the PFM convincingly won the first free elections to the Supreme Soviet, formed its own administration under Mircea Drus, and stepped up Romanianisation. One highly symbolic manifestation of this was the republic's formal renaming as 'Moldova', to emphasise its historic identification with Romania. By the autumn, however, this policy, and the active hostility shown by many Moldovan nationalists towards minorities, was stirring up an ethnic Russian reaction. On 2 September the Transnistrian Russians, although only a quarter of the region's population, proclaimed a Pridniestrovian Moldavian Soviet Socialist Republic, and in a March 1991 referendum 93 per cent of voters in Transnistria opted to remain in the Soviet Union. Unlike the Baltic republics, Moldova promised full citizenship to its minorities, but the mistrust on the Russian side was by now too great. When, following the coup attempt against Gorbachev, Moldova hastily proclaimed its independence on 27 August, it was already clear that the Transnistrian Russians, backed by Russia's 14th Army, vehemently objected. After a brief outbreak of fighting in the spring of 1992, when it became obvious that the Russian secessionists had overwhelming force backing them, Russia and Moldova signed an agreement whereby Transnistria was free to govern itself. The region remains unrecognised internationally to this day, locked in an economic and political limbo. As for Moldova, pressure for reunification with Romania waned after 1991: Romania seemed less attractive, politically and economically, and the high cost of reunification convinced most Moldovans they were better off on their own.

2. *Worsening interethnic relations and coup attempt 1990–91.* Gorbachev's reforms, however well-meaning, uncorked a bottleful of nationalist genies, and it was this upsurge of nationality problems which intensified hardline opposition to him within the CPSU. The hardliners feared, with reason, that nationalism would tear the Soviet Union apart. In response to the nationality problems, and aware of mounting party unease, Gorbachev for some months in 1990–1 tacked to the right, hoping to get a handle on both problems. In the end, however, Gorbachev proved unwilling to use repressive force against

the Soviet Union's captive peoples. It was this perceived weakness which prompted the attempted coup against him, the failure of which brought the whole structure crashing down.

Lithuania's declaration of independence in March 1990, though later put on hold, raised the stakes immeasurably, for here was a direct threat to Soviet territorial integrity, involving the loss of strategic bases on the Baltic. It also raised, as did the Estonian and Latvian declarations of sovereignty, uncomfortable questions about the rights of ethnic Russians settled in these republics under Stalin; nor were Baltic Russians slow to express their alarm at the prospect of independence. By May 1990 pro-Soviet demonstrations in all three Baltic republics were turning violent. The Baltic republics' collective obduracy, moreover, had potential international ramifications, since the United States had never formally recognised their takeover by the Soviet Union. Yet the problem posed by the Baltics was not confined to them. March 1990 saw Supreme Soviet elections in all the other republics of the union, and in each the result was similar: popular fronts emerged reflective of a stirring of national consciousness even in hitherto quiet quarters like Belarus and Central Asia.

Gorbachev's instinctive reaction was to resist the push towards independence, yet this flew in the face of his own repeated commitment to openness and democratic renewal. Gorbachev was also in a weaker position by early 1990, and despite his election by the Congress of People's Deputies, in March 1990, as president of the Soviet Union, a political title which in theory gave him a role independent of the CPSU. By this point the economic disruption caused by Gorbachev's reforms was delivering, not increased prosperity, but rising prices and an accelerated decline in living standards, and for the first time Gorbachev experienced serious unpopularity: at the May Day parade he was greeted with jeers and cries of 'Resign!'[15] Party hardliners on the right were increasingly critical, but so too were radicals like Boris Yeltsin who attacked Gorbachev for being too timid. The pressure from the nationalities for independence showed no sign of abating; on the contrary, this pressure was coming from an entirely unexpected quarter, from Russia. Yeltsin, elected chairman of the Russian Federation's Supreme Soviet in May 1990, represented a novel Russian self-assertiveness and desire for autonomy, and Yeltsin increased the sense of casting loose when, in July, he dramatically quit the CPSU. If, in addition to all the other sources of nationalist discontent Russian nationalism should find a voice, then this would constitute an alternative centre of power to that of the CPSU and the Soviet government.

Confronted with these challenges, Gorbachev between October 1990 and March 1991 seemed to entertain second thoughts, and in what has been called the 'winter alliance' with the Party hardliners he made a half-hearted effort to

---

[15] Galeotti, M., 1997, *Gorbachev and His Revolution*, New York, 106–7.

re-establish central control. Various hardliners were appointed to key positions, notably Boris Pugo as interior minister, with whose help Vladimir Kriuchkov, head of the KGB, and defence minister Dmitri Yazov started drawing up plans for imposing martial law, in order to crack down on nationalist movements. This led to the formation in December 1990, with KGB encouragement, of 'national salvation fronts' of ethnic Russians and other loyalists in the Baltic republics, the purpose of which was to assist in the restoration of order.

On 11–13 January 1991 matters came to a head, when a bloody attempt was made by troops of the ministry of the interior (OMON) in Vilnius, acting for the 'national salvation front', to take over key government offices, media centres and the legislature; a similar effort was mounted in Riga the next week. In both capitals tens of thousands turned out to defend these sites. Fourteen were killed in Vilnius, including one woman crushed under a tank. In Riga five died during the storming of media centres. With the world's media watching, the crowds stayed in place for days, effectively obstructing both coup attempts. Over the next few months, OMON troops continued to rampage in all three Baltic states, attacking republican officials at border posts.

Gorbachev, unwilling to incur further bloodshed, backed off, disavowing any involvement. In response, the Lithuanian government on 9 February held a referendum on independence, followed by Latvia and Estonia on 3 March; the results, though boycotted by most Baltic Russians, were overwhelmingly in favour of independence. In Moscow, Yeltsin called for Gorbachev's resignation, and a demonstration there protesting against the use of force in the Baltics attracted an estimated 500,000, though banned by the Soviet authorities.

Caught between the hardliners, radicals like Yeltsin and the increasingly vocal nationalities, Gorbachev on 17 March held a Union-wide referendum on whether the USSR should be preserved 'as a renewed federation of equal sovereign republics in which the human rights and freedom of any nationality will be fully guaranteed.'[16] It was a sign of how far things had gone that six republics – Lithuania, Latvia, Estonia, Armenia, Moldova and Georgia – refused to participate; Georgia instead held a separate referendum on independence, which recorded a 99 per cent vote in favour. In Russia, Belarus, Ukraine and the six Central Asian republics, turnout was 80 per cent, with 76.4 per cent responding 'yes'. As a result Gorbachev turned his energies to fashioning a treaty establishing a 'Union of Soviet Sovereign Republics', effectively a confederal decentralisation. Membership would be voluntary; all republics would possess full sovereignty; taxation would be largely devolved to republic level; and the central government's powers remained ill-defined.

This proposed union treaty satisfied nobody and alarmed many, especially hardliners and the military, who saw the drastic shrinkage of Soviet powers

---

[16] Quoted in Galeotti, *Gorbachev and His Revolution*, 113.

as a threat to their positions. A draft text was approved for signature by the Supreme Soviet of the USSR on 12 July, with the final draft published on 14 August; it was now that hardliner discontent crystallised into a decision to topple Gorbachev. In the meantime, however, Russia was confirmed as a rival power centre, when Yeltsin on 12 June was elected president of the Russian Federation. Overnight this reversed the roles of both Yeltsin and Gorbachev: as the democratically elected head of the largest and most populous Soviet republic, Yeltsin automatically acquired a legitimacy Gorbachev never had.

Before this rivalry between the Soviet centre and Russia came into play, the hardliners made their inept attempt at a coup. Interning Gorbachev on 18 August when he went on holiday in the Crimea, Pugo, Yazov, Kriuchkov and others announced a 'state committee for the state of emergency'. The putschists were defeated by Gorbachev's refusal to sign a declaration of martial law, Yeltsin's bold denunciation of the coup and successful appeal for popular support, huge crowds turning out in response to protect the seat of Russian government, the refusal of most of the armed forces to obey orders and, finally, the conspirators' own irresolution and lack of preparation. For a couple of tense days matters hung in the balance, but by 21 August, after some serious street fighting and remarkably few deaths, the coup crumbled: Pugo committed suicide, the other leaders were arrested and Gorbachev was brought back in triumph to Moscow.

The August coup attempt was the beginning of the end for the Soviet Union, for it gave the signal for a general bailing out of subject nationalities. On 20 August, as soon as news of Gorbachev's internment reached their capitals, all three Baltic republics unilaterally renewed their independence, and on the 24th Yeltsin's Russia recognised them as independent states. Ukraine declared independence on the same day, subject to a referendum to be held on 1 December, followed on the 25th by Belarus, and Moldova on the 27th. What remained of the Soviet Union's hold on Eastern Europe would seem to have vanished within a matter of days. But it was even clearer that an additional reason for this general bailing out was 'fear of coming under the control of the emerging new Russia.'[17]

3. *Disintegration*. Formally, Gorbachev was restored to power, although the state of which he was president was disintegrating beneath him. Yet it was one thing for republics to declare independence; it was another to give practical expression to that independence in view of the tangle of shared assets and network of Soviet bases on East European territory, not to mention the delicate issue of ethnic Russians stranded in the seceding states. The even more fraught question of what happened to Soviet nuclear weapons stationed in the Ukraine was an issue of international concern. Working out an amicable divorce was

---

[17] Marples, *The Collapse of the Soviet Union*, 89.

therefore a challenge for all parties; that it was resolved so rapidly and without bloodshed was remarkable.

Break-up was further facilitated by the fact that the Russian Federation was also, effectively, declaring independence. In the days following the coup's failure it was Yeltsin who dominated the situation and dictated events, empowered by public support and his position as leader of the most populous republic. It was Yeltsin who decided to recognise Baltic independence. It was Yeltsin who banned the Communist Party within Russia, and then pressured Gorbachev, on 29 August, to ban it throughout the Soviet Union, thus removing at a blow the greatest single bond between the Soviet republics. On 1 September the Soviet government and the republics signed the new Union Treaty, but it was a moot point how much practical force this would have.

Over the next four months Gorbachev's powerlessness became ever more apparent as the republics, Russia in the lead, exercised greater sovereignty. Armenia seceded at the end of September; Georgia had gone its separate way long ago. The decisive blow to Soviet cohesion, however, was delivered by Kravchuk's Ukraine, which held its referendum as scheduled on 1 December. Against everyone's expectations this was a death blow, whose details are worth bearing in mind in view of events in 2014. Turnout was 84 per cent, and 90.2 per cent of the votes cast favoured independence. Support was strong even in the largely ethnic Russian eastern regions: in Odessa *oblast*, 85 per cent; Luhansk, 83 per cent; Donetsk, 77 per cent. Even overwhelmingly Russian Crimea voted 54 per cent for independence. Yeltsin, who would have preferred to maintain a Union including Russia, Ukraine and Belarus, deferred to such a clear expression of democratic will, which meant Gorbachev's Union Treaty was dead in the water.

On 8 December the presidents of Russia, Ukraine and Belarus met secretly at a hunting lodge in Belarus' Belavezha Forest; significantly, Yeltsin made it a condition of his attendance that Gorbachev was not invited. Here Kravchuk impressed the logic of the situation on Yeltsin and Stanislaŭ Shushkevich: in effect the Soviet Union was no more, and all republics were free to establish independent states. Indeed, from Russia's point of view it was not enough simply to leave the Soviet Union; the latter had to be dissolved, otherwise the Russian government's authority would be continually disputed by the remnants of the Soviet state. The three republics agreed to form a Commonwealth of Independent States (CIS), to which other republics could adhere if they chose. This purely voluntary association, however, would have no effective power over its sovereign, independent member-states.

The Belavezha Agreement was approved by the three parliaments on 11 December; on the 13th the Central Asian republics agreed to join the CIS, on the understanding that their existing borders remained unchanged. This was considered an essential safeguard against future Russian interference on behalf of ethnic Russian minorities. The main purpose of creating the CIS, however, was 'to destroy the Soviet Union, and remove Gorbachev from office.'[18] It succeeded. By the 17th Gorbachev had conceded that the Soviet Union would cease to exist by the end of the year. By mutual agreement Russia took control of the Soviet military, including its nuclear arsenal, on 25 December; this included a special arrangement regarding naval units and bases in what was now independent Ukraine. Russia also took over all Soviet embassies and consulates, now repurposed to represent the Russian Federation abroad. The Soviet Union officially passed into history on 31 December. Its East European successor states faced an uncertain future.

Czechoslovak break-up

The relatively amicable divorce of Czechs and Slovaks in 1993 constitutes our third example of multinational break-up. Although Czechoslovakia's end was not actively sought by most people in either half of the country, and was pushed through by strong leaders claiming to speak on behalf of their respective nations, it is also clear that there was not enough fellow feeling to preserve the bond. Break-up was also achieved without the bloodletting seen in Yugoslavia, or the acrimony bequeathed by the Soviet collapse.

The post-communist government headed by Václav Havel, philosopher-president, was 'a mixed group of dissidents' drawn from Civic Forum in the Czech lands and Public Against Violence (PAV) in Slovakia, and with 'no political experience and no practical agenda.'[19] This caretaker regime nevertheless enacted significant change in advance of free national and republican elections in June 1990. Apart from granting immediate amnesty to 16,000 political prisoners and disbanding the secret police, its most important act in March 1990 was to make Czechs and Slovaks constitutionally equal, renaming the state as the Czech and Slovak Federative Republic. As in the communist period after 1968, the country remained a 'unique, two-member federation', with a federal government and bicameral legislature, and separate governments and legislatures for the Czech and Slovak republics.[20]

Yet despite formal equality Czech and Slovak perspectives on the communist past and the post-communist future were very different. Slovaks in contrast to Czechs were inclined to see the communist period as one of modernisation and progress, to regard the retention of the socialist welfare state as desirable, and to be less supportive of a move to the free market economy and privatisation.

---

[18] Marples, *The Collapse of the Soviet Union*, 96.
[19] Stokes, *The Walls Came Tumbling Down*, 278.
[20] Žák, V., 1995, 'The Velvet Divorce: Institutional Foundations', in J. Musil (ed.), *The End of Czechoslovakia*, Budapest, London and New York, 245.

They were also rather more responsive to nationalist appeals. The Czechs, who after all saw themselves as the leaders of Czechoslovakia's interwar democracy, tended with hindsight to see everything associated with Sovietisation as retrograde, culminating in the national humiliation of the 1968 invasion.

These perspectives were reflected in the 1990 elections. At the federal level and in the Czech lands, the largest party was Civic Forum, which quickly became dominated by a 'neo-liberal' or market fundamentalist wing under Václav Klaus, committed to a thoroughgoing marketisation and privatisation of the economy. The federal government enacted a wide variety of liberalising measures, but was held back from radical 'shock therapy' by Havel and party moderates. In Slovakia PAV initially formed the government, and was soon dominated by a charismatic opportunist, Vladimír Mečiar. A former communist who only joined PAV in 1989, Mečiar like others before him found stirring nationalist resentments a surer path to popularity: as early as 1990 he realised that defending the Slovak armaments industry against federal plans to wind it down was key to the premiership. When PAV repudiated and deposed Mečiar in 1991, he founded his own Movement for a Democratic Slovakia and returned to power in June 1992 on an explicitly populist, xenophobic platform, opposing the dismantling of the socialist economy and demonising Hungarian and Roma minorities. In the same elections Klaus, leading a new Civic Democratic Party in the Czech lands, was confirmed in office in coalition with the conservative Christian Democrats.

In these circumstances, with the Czech half of the country under Klaus's neo-liberals and Slovakia in thrall to Mečiar's nationalists, the two federated governments agreed to part company. This was despite the transfer to the republics, in July 1990, of substantial powers over their respective economies. Neither ruling group represented a majority of the electorate in either republic, but each was firmly in power; the fact that, according to polls, a majority of voters probably did not want a split was ignored, nor was a referendum on the issue held, in part because the federal parliament could not agree on what question should be put to the voters. The total stalemate on whether, and how, to amend the country's constitution led both governments to decide in favour of a 'velvet divorce'. By mutual agreement, a federal 'liquidation' government was formed in June 1992. The decisive impetus, however, was delivered when Mečiar's government insisted on blocking Havel's re-election as president, a move which convinced both sides it made more sense to part. In July 1992 the Slovak national assembly passed a formal declaration of sovereignty; it then ratified a separate constitution on 1 September. On 25 November the federal assembly, having passed laws on the end of the federation, the formal division of property and the rights of the successor states, also passed an act finalising break-up, to come into effect on 1 January 1993.

Czechoslovakia's demise came as a surprise to many outside observers, but with hindsight it is hard not to conclude it was likely as soon as communist rule ended. As with Yugoslavia and the Soviet Union, the Communist Party had bound the country's constituent peoples artificially together, prolonging an association which had been problematical since the formation of Czechoslovakia in 1918. As with the other two multinational states, the nationalism of Czechoslovakia's two main partners proved stronger than whatever tied them together in the past. Unlike the Yugoslavs, and to some extent the Soviet republics, Czechs and Slovaks at least managed to separate without bloodshed and have remained on friendly terms, even at football matches.

20

Eastern Europe in the twenty-first century

Post-communist modernisation

Eastern Europe has seen bewildering changes in the three decades since the collapse of communism, to the point where summarising that change coherently in two chapters seems a foolhardy enterprise. Without descending into excessive detail, however, it is possible to detect a number of broad trends in the post-communist period.

Perhaps the simplest way of understanding developments since the early 1990s is to see them as part of the 'reunification' of Europe as a whole. Freed from the stifling mantle of dictatorship and the command economy, much of Eastern Europe has become more like Western Europe politically and economically. Yet the incompleteness of this process is also undeniable. Standards of living in much of the region remain well below West European norms, while politically certain societies have been latecomers to political pluralism, and in some cases have not yet arrived. In the past decade, however, it has become increasingly obvious that Eastern and Western Europe have more in common than complacent westerners have liked to imagine, not least a vulnerability to both world recession and a disturbing resurgence of nationalism and right-wing populism. Certain East European societies could even be said to be setting a trend towards a new nationalist authoritarianism.

This chapter considers the issue of modernisation, both political and economic, in the most recent history of Eastern Europe. Since Eastern Europe's perceived backwardness has been its most distinguishing characteristic throughout this study, it makes sense to consider to what extent East European societies have 'caught up' in this period.

Political modernisation

It remains a premise of this study that modernisation has remained an issue in Eastern Europe. On this score, a recent history notes that the economic and political disparities between the region and Western Europe, while lessened since 1989, 'remain deep.'[1]

---

[1] Ther, P., 2018, *Europe since 1989: A History*, with a new preface by the author; translated by Charlotte Hughes-Kreuzmüller, Princeton, NJ and Oxford, x.

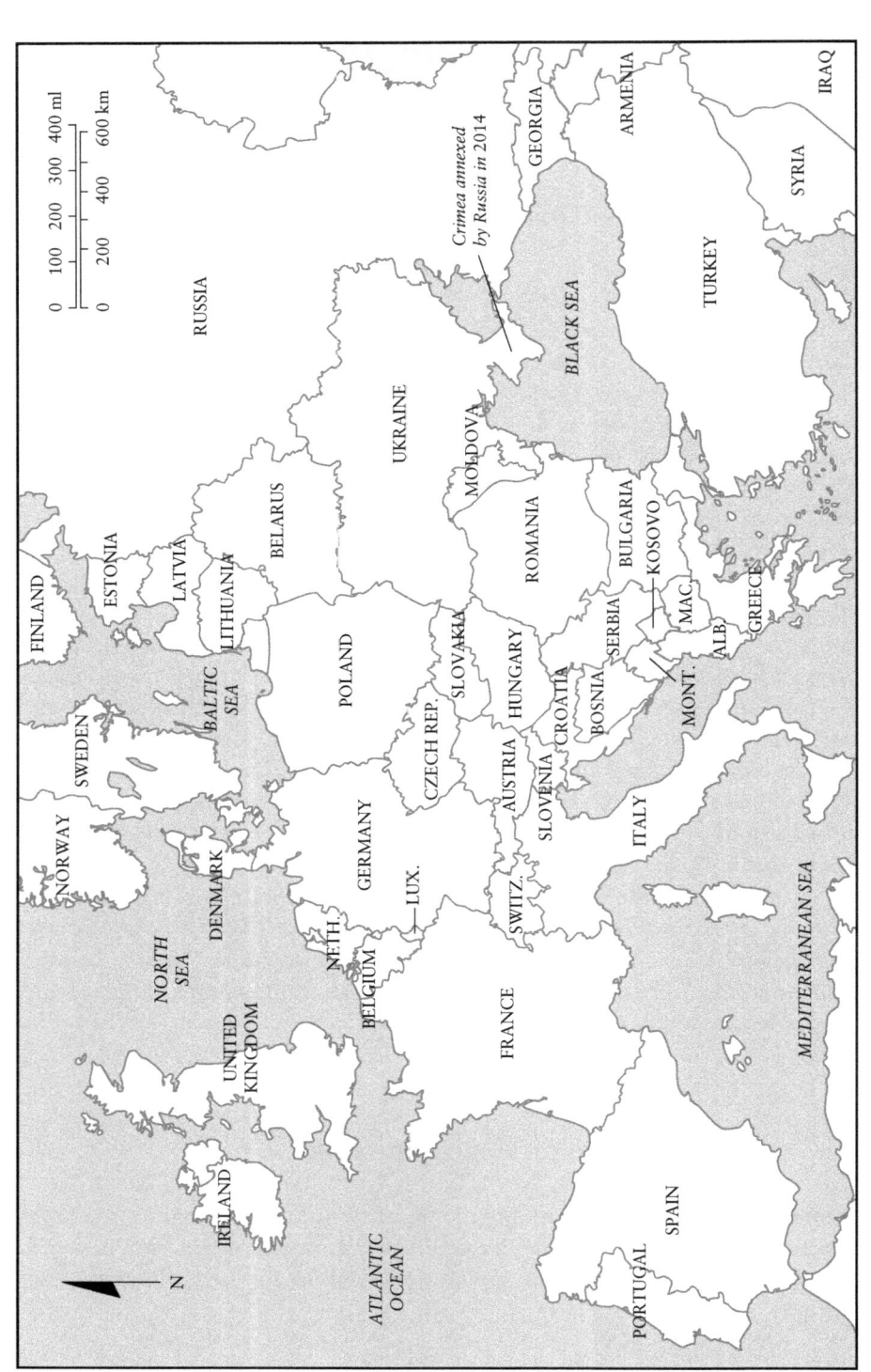

Map 6 Changes in Eastern Europe 1991–2020.

The biggest single aspect of East European societies' political modernisation since 1989 has been their transition from one-party dictatorships to pluralist polities, otherwise known as democracies, characterised by free elections, the rule of law and protection of human rights. This was not perfectly achieved everywhere: not only did authoritarian rule survive in Belarus and Ukraine after the break-up of the Soviet Union, and initially in Romania, rump Yugoslavia and Croatia, but in the last decade a trend towards 'illiberal democracy' has manifested itself in a handful of countries. In Hungary and Poland democratically elected but ultra-nationalist, authoritarian leaders, to some extent profiting from the example set in Russia, have learned how to hollow out democratic polities from within.

We will return to this; but on the whole the shift to pluralism since the early 1990s has proved a permanent one. Most formerly communist-ruled societies have seen an entrenchment of democratic norms, the most striking proof of which has been the fact that reformed communist parties, now committed to accepting the voters' verdict, have shown themselves capable of not only regaining power democratically, but surrendering it again if defeated at the next poll. In such cases the success of reformed communists owed much to popular disillusionment with the transition to a market economy. Four years after the formation of the first non-communist government in Hungary since the 1940s, for instance, the reformed communist Hungarian Socialist Party under Gyula Horn topped the polls in May 1994 and formed a coalition with the Alliance of Free Democrats, remaining in power until 1998, when the increasingly right-wing Fidesz under Viktor Orbán took over. This right-left alternation continued into the next century: the HSP led another government from 2002 to 2010, before Orbán returned to office. In Poland, Solidarity's path-breaking government of 1989–93 paid an electoral penalty for subjecting the country to economic 'shock therapy', as well as fragmenting into factions and running through five prime ministers in four years, and was succeeded by a coalition of the reformed communists, rebranded as the Democratic Left Alliance (DLA), and the agrarian Polish People's Party. Even more strikingly, the DLA's Aleksander Kwaśniewski beat Solidarity legend Lech Wałęsa for the presidency in 1995, and remained in post for the next decade. Poland, like Hungary, saw regular swings between coalitions of left and right, and emerging centrist parties like Civic Platform (2007–15). Only since 2015 has the right-wing Law and Justice Party (*PiS*) shown the same authoritarian tendencies as Fidesz in Hungary. Due to the proportional system of representation, however, coalition pacts between competing parties have become a regular feature of most East European polities.

By any standards this alternation of parties in power, not to mention the celerity with which parties have accustomed themselves to parliamentary deal-making in order to share power, is a remarkable outcome, arguably the single most important aspect of Eastern Europe's political modernisation. Most countries have seen the emergence of a full spectrum of parties, representing opinions from left to right as well as sectional and ethnic interests. One of the first parties to reappear in Hungary, for instance, was the old Smallholders' Party, whose gnarled peasant members were televised as early as 1988 staking out claims to their former farmsteads, collectivised decades early under communism. In Macedonia, rather against expectations, a regular partner in coalitions since 1992 has been the Party of Democratic Prosperity and its successors, representing the country's sizeable Albanian minority. Other sectional interests were merely eccentric, such as the Friends of Beer Party in Czechoslovakia, formed in 1990 in protest at the sheer number of parties competing for voters' attention. Among the early consequences of the plethora of political flavours on offer, as well as the difficulties of forming and maintaining governments, have been a gradual onset of voter apathy and a decline in participation; but this is a malady that Eastern Europe shares with most other democratic societies.

Elections have been conducted for the most part freely, accompanied by a cacophony of media; only in the recent past have governments such as Orbán's in Hungary started systematically seeking control of the media. In most countries democratic constitutions have been agreed on, enshrining fundamental rights, an independent judiciary and the rule of law, even if in individual countries the rights of national minorities have from the start not always been adequately safeguarded; the position of ethnic Russians in Estonia and Latvia, for instance, and of Roma in the Czech Republic and elsewhere, stands out as problematic.

The issues post-communist polities had to wrestle with were inextricably bound up with the legacies of communism itself. There was the prickly question of what was termed 'lustration': literally, how much light these newly liberated societies wanted or needed to shine on the misdeeds of the defunct communist regimes. What crimes had been committed against basic rights in the name of the party-state? Who should be held responsible, and with what consequences? There was the very practical difficulty of deciding whether, and how, private property nationalised under communism, from farms and aristocratic estates to factories and small businesses, should be restored to the original owners or their heirs, and on what terms. There was the related but distinct issue of what to do with the hugely inefficient, loss-making state enterprises with which East European societies were littered, but which still employed a substantial portion of the workforce. How would these fragile economies cope with the mass unemployment bound to result from closing such industry down? There was the problem of rolling back the state's role in subsidising everyday life, from housing to fuel costs to health care, education and much else: how to scale this back without risking destabilising political repercussions, given that the people now had the final say? There were the twin problems, inherited from the old command economy but likely to be exacerbated by any large-scale liberalisation, of corruption and clientelism, problems which some societies like Romania have not surmounted to this day. Finally there was the issue of minority rights, largely hidden from view in the communist period but given unaccustomed prominence in the new democracies, where the airing of grievances was now legitimate, but where the majority's tolerance of such expression clearly had limits.

On lustration the record is patchy, reflecting the differing appetite in each society for confronting the past instead of focusing on the future. In Poland the first non-communist government, obliged initially to share power with president Jaruzelski and with the Soviet Union still a neighbour, preferred to draw a 'thick line' under what the communist regime had done.[2] This owed something to prime minister Mazowiecki's Catholic belief in reconciliation; it owed just as much to the spirit of the Round-Table Talks. As one of the participants recalled, what was important in 1989 'was the principle of not discussing symbolic problems. We were to solve the future, and avoid arguing about the past.'[3] Characteristic of this broadminded approach was the unlikely friendship between Jaruzelski and the former dissident Adam Michnik, two lifelong antagonists who nevertheless learned to respect each other's principles. Other Poles, by contrast, yearned for retribution and prosecutions. By 1992 Jaruzelski was being threatened with prosecution for proclaiming martial law in 1981. By 1998 concerns in Poland over so-called wild lustration – the use of leaked documents or partial evidence to assert collaboration with the communist regime – led to the founding of the Institute of National Remembrance, dedicated to collecting and curating all documentation on 'crimes against the Polish Nation', whether under tsarist, Nazi or communist rule. Set up to ensure a balanced debate about lustration, in the hands of right-wing governments like that of Law and Justice, the Institute has become an instrument for pursuing what nationalists insist is an 'unfinished revolution'. The first *PiS* government of 2005–07, dominated by Lech and Jarosław Kaczyński, tried to prosecute Jaruzelski, but the case never came to court due to the general's declining health. The entire platform of *PiS* since its inception in 2001, however, has been based on a belief that the 1989 revolution was 'unfinished' precisely because anti-communist figures like Michnik and Wałęsa had compromised unnecessarily, even treasonably, with the communists. Although none of the charges levelled by *PiS* in this respect have stuck, their paranoid conviction that the nation is constantly undermined by conspiracy has continued to flavour their approach since returning to power in 2015.

In East Germany, by contrast, a more direct and thorough lustration was forced on the first post-revolutionary government even before reunification.

---

[2] Quoted in Mark, J., 2010, *The Unfinished Revolution: Making Sense of the Communist Past in Central-Eastern Europe*, New Haven, CT and London, 4.
[3] Quoted in Mark, *The Unfinished Revolution*, 231, note 18.

Within weeks of the Wall's opening, the lifting of censorship allowed the media to draw attention to the party elite's privileged life, forcing many officials to resign. Erich Honecker, former party boss, was indicted for the shoot-to-kill policy used for years against would-be escapees to West Germany, although on health grounds he was never brought to trial. Hardest to resist was public pressure to investigate the dreaded state police, the *Stasi*, who started energetically shredding and then burning their secret files as soon as the Wall fell. Enraged, East Berlin crowds stormed *Stasi* headquarters in January 1990 and threw millions of documents into the street. The job of safeguarding such documentation – including painstakingly reassembling shredded documents – was eventually turned over to a federal institution, the *Stasi* Records Agency, in October 1990. On the basis of this archival material, Germany 'engaged in the earliest and deepest confrontation with its past.'[4] It purged some 50,000 former communist officials, conducted enquiries into the communist regime's record, and brought to trial those who could be prosecuted, for instance the border guards who shot those trying to cross the Wall. The most high-profile case was that of Erich Mielke, *Stasi* chief from 1957 to 1989, who was charged with responsibility for the shoot-to-kill policy, a left-wing bombing campaign in West Germany in 1981, and serially surveilling citizens over decades. Mielke was convicted in 1993 for two Weimar-era murders, and sentenced to six years' imprisonment; advancing senility, however, meant he was deemed unfit for further trials and released in 1995. Reunited Germany nevertheless provided other former communist societies with a template for how to approach the communist legacy on human rights violations.

Just how much light to shine in upon these matters, however, has depended ever since on the political chemistry in each country. Czechoslovakia in October 1991 passed a Lustration Law in response to rumours that the State Security Office was destroying records. The idea behind this was that those who had collaborated with the communist regime could be identified and excluded from public office; unfortunately the law made no provision for prosecuting officials who might actually have committed offences against human rights. All the law did was to encourage mutual denunciation, party political score settling and general ill feeling.

In Bulgaria the fact that reformed communists formed the first post-revolutionary government militated against any serious investigation of the *ancien régime*. Once the nationalist and explicitly anti-communist Union of Democratic Forces came to power in October 1999, however, this changed. The new premier, Filip Dimitrov, was determined to decommunise Bulgarian society, and his government was the first in Eastern Europe to prosecute former leaders like Todor Zhivkov and others. The initial charges, however, were either for

---

[4]   Mark, *The Unfinished Revolution*, xvi.

minor pecuniary offences or for 'errors in policy', a vague formulation which made the subsequent trials seem merely vindictive. Zhivkov's trial in 1991–2, memorably fictionalised in *The Porcupine* by Julian Barnes (1992), ended with his conviction for embezzlement and a sentence of seven years' imprisonment, which on health grounds Zhivkov served under house arrest. The overturning of this conviction on appeal in 1997, and abandonment of other charges, was hardly a convincing advertisement for lustration. The very real crimes of the Zhivkov regime, such as the treatment of inmates in the nearly one hundred concentration camps maintained between 1944 and 1989, could only await the attention of historians.

The question of property restitution, or compensation for its loss, was equally difficult, but at least offered some solutions. In many cases real estate such as houses or factories no longer existed, or had been completely transformed: country mansions torn down or turned into schools, convents repurposed as barracks and so on. In such cases restitution could only be made in monetary terms, although instances were reported of urban flat dwellers being awarded cattle in restitution. Some restitution of property was relatively straightforward, and in both Catholic and Orthodox societies the church was one of the biggest beneficiaries. Arable land, too, was easy to restore as long as it had not been built on since nationalisation, and assuming the original owners or their heirs came forward, as many did in countries where the old smallholder class was substantial. Some aristocratic estates also found their way back into private hands. In the Czech Republic the Schwarzenberg family had eight of their estates restored in 1992, although the current prince, a former aide to president Havel and leader of a centre-right party until 2015, was content to leave dozens of other castles, many of them lucrative tourist attractions, in state hands. By 1993 some hundred thousand properties nationalised after 1948 had been returned to the owners. A particular problem was posed by property confiscated from national minorities, especially Germans expelled after 1945. In Czechoslovakia, for instance, restitution was enacted for all property seized after the communist takeover of 1948; this conveniently sidestepped the politically charged issue of whether Sudeten Germans should be compensated. It also elided the question of Jewish property confiscated under the Nazis, although in this case a compromise was eventually reached with Jewish property owners. By and large those countries, like Czechoslovakia and Hungary, which passed comprehensive restitution laws quickly, have managed the settlement of claims more easily. Countries which have not done so, like Poland, have endured decades of wrangling over who owns what. The city of Warsaw, reduced to rubble in 1945 and much of which was rebuilt by private means before the communist regime nationalised everything, is still wracked by bitter disputes over reprivatisation, affecting thousands of blameless tenants threatened with eviction.

Political modernisation, in the sense of transitioning to a reasonably functional pluralism, came late for some countries. The most obvious hold-outs were the successors to the former Yugoslavia. The problematic development of Bosnia-Hercegovina and Kosova, whose emergence as independent states was at the heart of the Yugoslav wars, remains a current problem. Serbia and Croatia, the principal antagonists in that drama, remained until the turn of the century in thrall to nationalist regimes which, if no longer communist, freely relied on the *ancien régime*'s authoritarian traditions.

Milošević's *Serbia* was technically democratic, in that after 1990 parties could legally compete for votes. Two factors, however, made this a pretence. Firstly, Milošević and his Socialist Party of Serbia (SPS) had so effectively taken ownership of the Serb national cause that the SPS clearly enjoyed overwhelming support, especially once the Yugoslav wars were under way. Secondly, Milošević so controlled the media and the security forces in Serbia that the opposition parties, divided among themselves, simply made no headway throughout the 1990s. Until 1995, arguably, Milošević's popularity was genuine; after the expulsion of Serbs from Croatia, and the unsatisfactory conclusion of the Bosnian war, discontent grew over Serbia's pariah status, its economic isolation and the rampant gangsterism fostered by the wars, and control could only be maintained by harsher methods. Montenegro, still joined with Serbia in the Federal Republic of Yugoslavia, was also showing an inclination towards secession after 1996, when Milo Đukanović became its leader. Milošević, president of Yugoslavia from 1997, continued to draw nationalist support from his attempts to repress the armed Albanian resistance in Kosovo; but the 1999 NATO bombing campaign against Yugoslavia, which ended in withdrawal of Yugoslav forces from Kosovo, comprehensively discredited his regime. Despite ongoing repression, including the abduction and murder in August 2000 of Ivan Stambolić, his predecessor as party boss and a potential rival, Milošević's failure to achieve the nationalist agenda, coupled with years of economic deprivation and international sanctions, led to his defeat in presidential elections that September by Vojislav Koštunica, leader of the nationalist but unambiguously Democratic Party of Serbia (DSS). The victory of the DSS and other moderate parties in parliamentary elections in December 2000, despite a sizeable share of the vote going to hardline nationalists, suggested that Serbia had finally turned a corner.

After Milošević's fall Serbia gradually edged towards a less fractious relationship with its neighbours and the European Union, a progress beset with very real dangers for its leaders. Zoran Đinđić, Koštunica's prime minister from January 2001, was committed to economic liberalisation and eventual membership of the EU; but he also understood that a precondition for achieving these goals was demonstrating Serbia's willingness to make amends for the aggression of the 1990s. It was the extradition of Milošević to The Hague to stand trial for war crimes, in June 2001, that led to Đinđić's assassination in March 2003 by outraged nationalists in the secret services. It also led to a nationalist backlash at the polls in late 2003: the extreme Serbian Radical Party won a plurality of the votes and emerged as the largest party in parliament, although not big enough to form a government. Milošević, unrepentant, used his trial to pose as the doughty defender of the Serbs against their enemies; he died of natural causes in 2006, while still in custody.

Thereafter Serbia's leaders had constantly to balance their nationalist emotions with their desire to normalise relations with the outside world. Koštunica, prime minister from 2004 to 2008, accepted Montenegro's decision for full independence in 2006, but he bitterly denounced the widespread if not universal international recognition of Kosovo's declaration of independence, as Kosova, in 2008, and his party renounced the goal of accession to the EU. Under the pro-western, liberal Boris Tadić as president from 2008, however, Serbia started actively cooperating with the Hague tribunal, extraditing a succession of senior figures accused of war crimes. Radovan Karadžić, discovered in hiding in 2008, was convicted of genocide and crimes against humanity in 2016. Ratko Mladić, after sixteen years on the run, was finally arrested and put on trial in 2012, and convicted of war crimes in 2017. Aleksander Vučić, prime minister from 2014 and president since 2017, has played a complex game of seeking rapprochement with Europe and, ostensibly, better relations with Bosnia and even Kosova, while at the same time ostentatiously cultivating closer economic and political ties with Putin's Russia as well as China, as if to demonstrate Serbia's capacity for facing either way. A former outspoken nationalist who claims to see the error of his ways, Vučić has also shown increasing signs of a creeping authoritarianism towards domestic opposition.

Croatia under Franjo Tuđman, like Serbia, spent the 1990s as something of an outcast state, despite the military assistance provided by the West in 1995. This was largely down to Tuđman's unsavoury record as an extreme nationalist, but also his authoritarian and corrupt governing style, complete with Titoesque white uniforms and personality cult. Re-elected in 1997 amidst allegations of vote rigging, Tuđman regularly attacked what little independent media Croatia had, honoured the *Ustaša* regime of the Second World War, rejected calls by the international community to deliver Croats accused of war crimes to the Hague tribunal, and ruled his Croatian Democratic Union (HDZ) with an iron hand.

Only on Tuđman's death in December 1999 could his successors seriously address the issue of reintegrating Croatia with the rest of democratic Europe. The new president, Štipe Mesić, had broken with the HDZ over its interference in Bosnia during the war, and took a less nationalistic and more pro-European line. Mesić was reinforced by the surprise election in 2000 of a centre-left coalition under Ivica Račan, which not only helped Mesić pass legislation limiting his own presidential powers, but signalled readiness to cooperate with the Hague tribunal. The government was assisted by a swing in public opinion: once Serbia extradited Milošević to The Hague in 2001, polls indicated that roughly half of Croats accepted the need to hand suspects over, if this was the price for EU accession. The first indictments against leading suspects, hitherto lauded by the HDZ as national heroes, were delivered in 2001, and although bringing individuals to The Hague took most of the next decade, progress was sufficient, by 2005, for the EU to open accession negotiations. In 2009 a further link with Europe was forged when Croatia was admitted into NATO. Much of Croatian politics since the turn of the century has been dominated by the struggle against corruption, stipulated by the EU as a precondition for accession. The problem was highlighted by the case of Ivo Sanader, HDZ prime minister from 2003, and whose government did most to move Croatia towards both EU and NATO membership. Sanader abruptly resigned in 2009, and in 2010 fled the country, pursued by massive corruption charges; brought to trial in 2011, he was convicted and served five years in prison. Sanader's fall coincided with the conclusion of EU accession talks, and after a referendum in 2012, Croatia formally joined the EU in January 2013.

Another outsider state ever since the fall of communism is *Belarus*. In fact, a case can be made for claiming that communist-style political control has never been relaxed in what has been called 'Europe's last dictatorship', an epithet that does considerable injustice to Putin's Russia. The government of Stanislaŭ Shushkevich was quite unprepared for independence, however advisable it seemed in the wake of the August 1991 coup attempt. Nor did much change for the first two years of independence. Shushkevich and his prime minister, Viacheslaŭ Kebich, were reluctant to dismantle the command economy in the reckless fashion embraced by Yeltsin in Russia. In late 1993 the only member of the Supreme Soviet to vote against independence, Alexander Lukashenko, accused Shushkevich and Kebich of corruption, leading Shushkevich to resign in January 1994. The following July, as a result of legislation passed at Lukashenko's suggestion, direct presidential elections were held, and to most Belorussians' surprise Lukashenko won overwhelmingly, with 45 per cent of the vote; Kebich, hitherto seen as heir apparent, came a miserable second with 17 per cent.

Lukashenko has ruled Belarus with a firm hand ever since, on the basis of an implicit social contract: as long as Belorussians have jobs and relative prosperity, most appear willing to accept their lack of political freedom. The state continues to own most key industries, opposes economic liberalisation, strictly controls the media and brutally restricts any opposition activity. Since 1994 Lukashenko has been re-elected five times, on each occasion by a huge majority, routinely condemned by external observers like the OSCE as 'flawed'. In 2004 a referendum overwhelmingly approved the abolition of presidential term limits. Despite frosty relations with the EU and the United States, including on-off sanctions for human rights abuses, and Lukashenko's strident anti-western rhetoric, nothing seems likely to loosen Lukashenko's hold on power. The key to his political longevity, apart from his own determination, has been his generally amicable relationship with Russia. A 'Union of Russia and Belarus' created in 1999, though in reality notional, was originally proposed by Lukashenko. Apart from a temporary downturn in the Russian link between 2007 and 2010, when Lukashenko appeared to be tacking to the West by tolerating greater dissent, the regime has been propped up by plentiful supplies of cheap Russian oil and gas, which enables Lukashenko to subsidise his country's economy. In short, political modernisation in Belarus has never got off the ground.

Slovakia and Romania are two latecomers which have achieved a more genuine political pluralism since the late 1990s, despite ongoing problems with corruption and occasional abuses of power. *Slovakia*'s first five years as an independent state were dominated by Vlamimír Mečiar's peculiar brand of authoritarianism or 'political primitivism'.[5] Apart from the tasks attendant upon independence, like creating essential institutions and appointing personnel, Mečiar quickly revealed a temperament disinclined to consensual politics and all too ready to deploy strong-arm tactics, such as having the son of president Michal Kovac, one of his fiercest critics, abducted and abandoned in Austria. Mečiar was intolerant of opposition, resisted any privatisation that would be open to public scrutiny, and passed legislation discriminating against Slovakia's national minorities. These populist policies ensured Mečiar's party a plurality of the votes in the 1994 elections, but once it became apparent that 'Mečiarism' was responsible for Slovakia being excluded from NATO and the EU, the public mood shifted, and Mečiar was voted out in 1998. Thereafter Slovakia effected its 'return to Europe' in record time: economic modernisation and a more pluralist political atmosphere resulted in admission to both NATO and the EU in 2004.

The post-revolutionary government of Ion Iliescu in *Romania* exhibited a similar authoritarianism which was hardly surprising, given Iliescu's record as a loyal party member until the 1970s. Iliescu too was intolerant of dissent, and repeatedly mobilised Romania's miners to beat up urban opposition demonstrations; one of these government-directed rampages resulted in six deaths and hundreds of injured. Iliescu also put off hard decisions about dismantling the command economy, while pandering to Romanians' nationalism by vilifying the Hungarian minority. He was not so authoritarian, however, as to cling to power when, in 1996, the voters opted for the more liberal Emil Constantinescu, and for four years a reforming government started a hesitant liberalisation, removing price controls while cutting subsidies for fuel, public transport and over services. This proved too much for the electorate, and in the presidential election of 2000 Iliescu was returned to power. The most alarming aspect of the 2000 election was that Corneliu Vadim Tudor, leader of the

---

[5]   Brown, J.F., 1994, *Hopes and Shadows: Eastern Europe after Communism*, Harlow, 34.

extreme nationalist and explicitly anti-Semitic Greater Romania Party, came second in the first round with 28 per cent of the vote to Iliescu's 36 per cent.

The 2000 election was a wake-up call for Romanians anxious to modernise, as was Romania's failure, in 1997, even to be considered for candidacy to join either the EU or NATO. Probably more decisive in shifting Romania toward Europe, however, was the change in western attitudes following NATO's Kosovo campaign in 1999, which the Constantinescu government vocally supported. A western desire not to contribute to further instability in Eastern Europe made the EU more willing to entertain applications from both Romania and Bulgaria, despite ongoing problems with corruption in both countries. Romania was thus admitted to accession talks in 2000, and in 2004, rather against the evidence, was declared to be both politically and economically ready to join the EU, which it formally did, with Bulgaria, on 1 January 2007.

Ukraine is perhaps the most complex and conflicted latecomer of all. Since independence in 1991 it has experienced two revolutions, innumerable changes of government, the forcible takeover of the Crimea by Russia, and the bloodiest conflict since the Yugoslav wars. Home to a large proportion of ethnic Russians, it has been Ukraine's tragedy to be too close to Russia to be left alone, while not close enough to Western Europe to be meaningfully helped towards genuine pluralism. Yet despite obvious divisions within Ukrainian society and the foibles of its political elite, the country's path to modernisation and Europe has remained blocked largely by the malign role played in its affairs by Russia.

Under the government of Leonid Kravchuk (1991–4), despite the formal trappings of democracy, too much power remained in the hands of the centralised bureaucracy inherited from the Soviet era. Kravchuk avoided embracing a true market economy, retaining trade and price controls, with the result that the economy, rather as in Russia under Yeltsin, rapidly fell into the hands of a 'red director' elite, former party apparatchiks who amassed vast personal wealth by simply expropriating former state-controlled enterprises. This imperfectly reformed economy was stuttering by 1994, when Kravchuk was forced into an early election by the 'red directors', who encouraged anti-government strikes in the industrialised east. Interestingly, Kravchuk's 45 per cent of the vote came from the predominantly Ukrainian-speaking centre-west of the country, while the 52 per cent support for his rival, Leonid Kuchma, was concentrated in the more Russian-speaking southeast.

For a decade Kuchma presided over a spectacularly corrupt regime, pushing through a new constitution in 1996 which 'greatly expanded presidential power, at the expense of transparency and accountability.'[6] Kuchma placated the increasingly vocal Ukrainian nationalists with symbolic gestures, such as making Ukrainian the state language, but did little to restrain the oligarchs

---

[6]   Wilson, A., 2014, *Ukraine Crisis: What It Means for the West*, New Haven, CT and London, 42.

dominating the economy. Elections were essentially bought, and efforts by concerned opponents to throw light on corrupt practices could be literally life-threatening, as illustrated by the fate of Heorhy Gongadze, a journalist whose abduction and decapitation in September 2000 was directly attributed to complaints about him by Kuchma himself.

Such was Ukraine's economic dysfunction by 1999 that Kuchma was compelled to appoint the reformist governor of the national bank, Viktor Yushchenko, as prime minister. The efforts of Yushchenko and his deputy Yulia Tymoshenko to reform the economy ran aground on the oligarchs' resistance, and by 2001 both had been forced out. Each founded a party for the elections of 2002, Yushchenko's Our Ukraine and the 'Tymoshenko Bloc'; but although these parties together won a plurality of seats they could not prevent a new government being formed by Kuchma's preferred candidate, Viktor Yanukovich, whose Party of the Regions drew most of its support from the largely Russian-speaking southeast. When Yanukovich and Yushchenko faced one another in the next presidential election, in 2004, things got particularly nasty. Apart from the routine denial of media coverage to the opposition, in September Yushchenko was found to have been poisoned by a dioxin which nearly killed him, leaving him permanently disfigured. After a virtual tie in the first round, Yanukovich was declared the winner of the run-off on 31 October, despite widespread reports of irregularities. This prompted two weeks of mass protest by opposition supporters, sporting Our Ukraine's orange colours. The supreme court then ordered a re-run of the second round on 26 December, which Yushchenko won convincingly, if narrowly.

This 'Orange revolution', however, quickly ran into the sand, reflecting the extent to which even Yushchenko and his chosen prime minister, Tymoshenko, were simply variants of Ukraine's oligarchical elite. Yushchenko from the start was bound by concessions made to oligarchs, and his promise of an amnesty for Kuchma over the Gongadze case. This led to an early falling out with Tymoshenko, sacked in September 2005. Corruption remained endemic and was actively encouraged from outside by Putin, who regarded the Orange revolution as a western-inspired plot to undermine Russia's influence in its 'near abroad'. One of Yushchenko's few achievements was a constitutional amendment ruling that parliamentary deputies must remain with the parties under which they were elected, a change considered necessarily to prevent deputies being bribed to change allegiance.

Yushchenko's weakness was made clear when, in August 2006, the parliamentary arithmetic compelled him to appoint his rival Yanukovich prime minister. This backfired predictably when Yanukovich challenged the president's power in the constitutional court, resulting in a bizarre competition between president and premier to bribe the judges. Yushchenko was only saved by parliamentary elections in September 2007 which returned the Tymoshenko Bloc as the largest party, and in the circumstances Yushchenko was glad to reappoint Timoshenko as prime minister. Yet the three years of Yushchenko-Tymoshenko government achieved little, in part because the two principals could agree on little and avoided difficult choices, in part because of the world recession's disastrous impact after 2008. In 2010 presidential elections that were at least fairly conducted, Tymoshenko, defending a dismal economic record, lost narrowly to Yanukovich.

It is impossible to understand how Yanukovich went from legitimate election in 2010 to being toppled in Ukraine's second, 'Euromaidan revolution' in February 2014, without appreciating that his victory signalled a return to open kleptocracy and, above all, a win for Russian influence. The Party of the Regions represented first and foremost the interests of Ukraine's Russian-speaking southeast; Yanukovich had no electoral base in the centre-west, heartland of Ukrainian nationalism. Worse, his instincts in government were unabashedly authoritarian as well as venal. Ruling through a mix of electoral corruption, favours to the oligarchs and his extended Donbass family, Yanukovich rapidly fell out with Tymoshenko as prime minister, whose carefully cultivated image as a Ukrainian cultural icon was central to her electoral success. Yanukovich cut the ground from beneath Timoshenko's feet by illegally bribing the deputies of her party to change sides, ousting her in March 2010. Tymoshenko was then charged with negotiating an energy deal with Russia contrary to the national interest and jailed, a blatantly political persecution which became yet another reason for the EU's reluctance to continue with accession talks. Brussels and leading EU states made Tymoshenko's release a condition for resuming negotiations. Yanukovich in response demanded greater financial incentives for complying. In November 2013, yielding to open Russian pressure to opt for membership of Putin's 'Eurasian Union' instead, the Ukrainian government abruptly pulled out of EU accession negotiations entirely.

There can be little doubt that the popular response to this turning away from Europe was both spontaneous and deeply felt. For over two decades Ukrainians had borne the consequences of corrupt and inefficient government, backed by unsubtle Russian pressure in support of an oligarchical elite. EU membership for many Ukrainians, of either Ukrainian or Russian background, meant convergence with European standards both politically and economically. The demonstrations that started on 21 November on the Maidan, Kiev's main square, calling 'For a European Ukraine', rapidly grew until, when the authorities first resorted to police violence in attempts to disperse them, they totalled several hundred thousand. Violence failed to deter further demonstrations, and by early December the Maidan was permanently occupied by a mixture of monster demonstration and street party, conducted in general with good humour, sophisticated organisation and remarkable persistence in sub-zero temperatures. Much has been made of the involvement of Ukrainian ultra-nationalist groups like the Freedom Party and Right Sector; but these were never the guiding influences in what remained a remarkable illustration of 'people power'. Demonstrators included many young people, old age pensioners, well-off middle-class professionals and a significant number of ethnic Russians, like the novelist Andrey Kurkov, whose *Ukraine Diaries* constitutes a vivid record of the 'Euromaidan revolution'.[7]

The Maidan demonstrations remained almost entirely peaceful until, on 18 February 2014, Yanukovich attempted finally to clear the square. He preceded action by passing a series of 'dictatorship laws', designed to criminalise hitherto non-violent protests. A pretext was offered when the demonstrators organised a march on parliament, which was met by militia and rapidly degenerated into a running street battle. An assault on the barricades was launched in the evening, in which six demonstrators were killed, but which failed to dislodge the protesters. The struggle for control of the streets resumed on 20 February, and this time snipers opened fire on demonstrators from government buildings. Documents captured after the revolution revealed that the snipers were under the command of the interior ministry and *Berkut*, the special forces; according to other sources these Ukrainian forces were reinforced by FSB agents from Russia, who supplied additional weapons and planning. Some seventy people were killed but, when the crowd fought back, Yanukovich concluded his time was up. By the time parliament voted, unanimously, to restore the 'Orange' constitution of 2004, suspend the interior minister and release Tymoshenko, Yanukovich was already packing his vast personal wealth, shipping an estimated $32 billion to Russia in trucks, and fleeing on the 22nd. On the same day parliament voted by 328 out of 450 deputies to remove him from office, without the constitutionally required three-quarters, a fact that Russia later claimed made the change of government illegal. To Putin's evident annoyance, Yanukovich fled the country on 25 February. Oleksandr Turchynov, a member of the Tymshenko Bloc, was voted in by parliament as interim president, presiding over a multiparty provisional government. In May 2014 Petro Poroshenko, a pro-western billionaire chocolate manufacturer and oligarch, convincingly won new presidential elections by 54.7 per cent, with Tymoshenko coming a distant second.

Russian claims that the Euromaidan revolution was a 'fascist coup' were wide of the mark. This was a genuine popular uprising, at the end of months of peaceful demonstrations, against a regime widely perceived as corrupt, manipulated by Russia and committed to an anti-European course opposed by most Ukrainians, including many of the Russian-speaking minority. At no stage of the Ukrainian revolution were the ultra-nationalists among the demonstrators in charge or, even more improbably, responsible for firing on their fellow demonstrators. Yet the revolution also confirmed Putin in his determination to seize the Crimea the following month, on the pretext that ethnic Russians

---

[7] Kurkov, A., 2014, *Ukraine Diaries: Dispatches from Kiev*, London.

there were threatened by Ukrainian 'fascism', and to incite a brutal separatist war in eastern Ukraine, in which to date over 14,000 people have died. What is clear is that, by seeking to prop up what was increasingly seen as a puppet regime, in order to keep Ukraine within Russia's sphere of influence, Putin achieved the exact opposite. Ukrainian public opinion, including among Russian speakers in the east of the country, swung decisively against any closer association with Russia and towards the West. Tragically, the 'frozen conflict' in eastern Ukraine renders any speedy accession to the EU unlikely.

A final, crucial aspect of Eastern Europe's political modernisation has been the lure of joining NATO and the EU.

While the question of NATO enlargement has had wider geopolitical ramifications, its role in encouraging political modernisation in East European countries has been equally important. Immediately after 1989 and the collapse of the Soviet Union, there seemed little appetite in western capitals, especially Washington, to expand NATO eastward. This had less to do with any desire to honour Bush's promise to Gorbachev not to do so, than with a general disinclination to undertake fresh commitments and expense once the Cold War ended. By contrast the perspective of East European governments, newly freed from Soviet hegemony but still living in Russia's shadow, was very different: for such countries inclusion in NATO offered the ultimate guarantee against a return to enslavement, and as early as 1991 the so-called Višegrád alliance of Poland, Hungary and what was still Czechoslovakia indicated they would welcome accession. The Yugoslav wars altered western views, precisely because they demonstrated how potentially unstable and vulnerable East European countries were in terms of general security. Václav Havel was an especially eloquent proponent of the view that West European and American governments had a moral obligation to underwrite East European freedoms.

In September 1995, therefore, NATO concluded a study on enlargement, setting forth criteria for membership. Candidate states should have democratic institutions and practise democratic values; they should cultivate habits of cooperation; and they should enjoy good neighbourly relations with one another. Paragraph 6 of the study was aimed squarely at Hungary, stipulating that candidate states 'which have ethnic disputes or external territorial disputes . . . must settle these disputes by peaceful means.'[8] This led directly to treaties between Hungary on the one hand, and Slovakia and Romania on the other, whereby Hungary explicitly renounced any revisionist claims on its neighbours' territory. The study also assumed that, as democratic states, candidates had full civilian control over their military establishments. This had an impact in Poland, where president Wałęsa, until his departure from

---

[8] NATO, Study on NATO Enlargement, 3 September 1995; quoted in Stokes, G., 2012, *The Walls Came Tumbling Down: Collapse and Rebirth in Eastern Europe*, 2nd edn, New York and Oxford, 289.

office in 1995, steadfastly defended the military's independence of civilian oversight; his successor Kwaśniewski successfully subordinated the military by 1997. As a result, the Višegrád countries were all formally invited to join that year, becoming full members in 1999. In 2004 NATO admitted the three Baltic states, Slovakia, Romania, Bulgaria and Slovenia. Croatia and Albania joined in 2009, Montenegro in 2017. It is worth noting that Montenegro's accession was preceded by determined Russian attempts to avert it, including a rumoured coup attempt in 2016.

While the attractions of 'returning to Europe' (however inaccurate the phrase) through membership in the European Union may have waned somewhat in the last decade, for both economic and political reasons, there is nevertheless no denying the magnetic pull for post-communist societies of joining this increasingly prosperous bloc of countries. Even in the early 1990s, before Austria, Finland and Sweden joined, the twelve states of the EU were perceived as enjoying a higher standard of living, and evolved political criteria for membership that had already shaped the domestic politics of former dictatorships like Greece, Spain and Portugal. In short, EU membership was only possible for societies where representative democracy, basic human rights, the rule of law and security of individual property rights were securely enshrined. On these criteria the communist dictatorships of Eastern Europe were automatically barred from membership, even had their governments wished to apply.

The revolutions of 1989 and after transformed the prospects of East European countries. Overnight they could at least aspire to membership, and although the EU was clearly in no rush to welcome these fledgling democracies, with their artificially enfeebled economies, the conditional offer was a powerful incentive to conform to EU standards. These were obviously primarily economic criteria, to be considered below. In a political sense, however, the desire to be considered for accession increasingly spurred East European parties and governments to enshrine basic rights in transparent institutions, to ensure free and fair elections, including a free media, to create an independent judiciary, and at least to attempt to eradicate or control political corruption and cronyism. As we have seen, this conditionality exercised its transformative power on Slovakian politics, leading to Mečiar's eclipse at the polls in 1998. It exerted a powerful if belated influence on the stance of political parties, even ultra-nationalist ones, in Serbia and Croatia: the leader of the Serbian Radical Party, Vojislav Šešelj, voluntarily surrendered himself to the Hague tribunal in 2003, in order to demonstrate, even if for largely cosmetic reasons, his party's commitment to 'European values'. Ukrainians turned out in their hundreds of thousands, in 2013–14, to demonstrate their frustration at Yanukovich's abandonment under Russian pressure of Ukraine's candidacy for EU membership. Clearly not all East Europeans shared this idealised vision of what 'Europe' is supposed to mean; equally clearly, the vision played a role for the last quarter-century in encouraging democratic habits. Only in the last decade have democratic norms in some countries been positively eroded under the twin impact of economic recession and populist nationalism, to the point where, in 2019, a survey revealed that up to 60 per cent of East Europeans felt democracy was under threat. Even then, the same survey recorded a generally high awareness of civil society and a greater readiness to challenge authority than in the past.

Economic modernisation

Post-communist Eastern Europe's economic modernisation was a necessary consequence of the 1989 revolutions, a principal cause of which was the economic backwardness imposed on the region by communism. Modernising consequently meant dismantling the old command economy, removing state-imposed price controls, opening up to the vagaries of the free market, and accepting the necessity of privatisation and free enterprise. That there was bound to be a downside to this modernisation, in the form of unemployment and the shrinkage of the state welfare system, was obvious to some but not all East Europeans. After forty-odd years of Soviet-style drabness many East Europeans believed western levels of affluence and abundance were just around the corner. There was also a sizeable number – those willing to vote for reformed communist parties – who thought some elements of socialism at least should be retained.

In the immediate post-revolutionary period two approaches to the issue of economic modernisation emerged. The first argued for so-called shock therapy: a ruthless abolition of state controls and a submission to the logic of the market, regardless of the short-term economic pain, in the belief that only in this way could societies unleash the wealth-creating energies of individuals. 'Shock therapy' was urged on East European governments by proponents of what is misleadingly called 'neo-liberalism', an unsatisfactory term for unrestrained economic liberalism or what is also called 'market fundamentalism', but which has achieved regrettable currency, to the point that a recent account calls it 'the guiding ideology of this epoch.'[9] Typified by western economists like Jeffrey Sachs and John Williamson, this 'Washington consensus' already had East European acolytes like the Polish finance minister Leszek Balcerowicz and the Czech Václav Klaus. The basic assumption was that East European governments were best advised to get over difficult ground as fast as possible, at whatever cost, before their newly empowered electorates developed second thoughts.

---

[9] Ther, *Europe since 1989*, 18, 32.

The second approach preferred 'gradualism', a retention of state controls, especially employment levels, for as long as possible, in order to cushion entry into the world market. Many leaders across the region, from liberals like Havel in Czechoslovakia to Iliescu and other reformed communists left in power, argued for this softer course; but the reality was that these already bankrupted and debt-laden post-communist governments had few attractive choices. The state industries on which so many depended for jobs were inefficient as well as environmentally disastrous, the external market for what East European factories produced was shrinking or non-existent, and without admitting a greater role for capital investment, indigenous or foreign, the status quo was unlikely to generate economic growth.

With hindsight it is clear neither 'shock therapy' nor 'gradualism' were ideal options for the fragile economies of the former Soviet bloc. It is instructive to highlight some examples of how each worked out in practice.

Poland remains a famous illustration of how 'shock therapy' could work, albeit at a cost. When Solidarity took over in August 1989 the economy was a shambles, with inflation running at 3,000 per cent, a ballooning trade deficit, and so much foreign debt that the government had stopped paying interest on it. In January 1990 Balcerowicz, with Sachs as adviser, 'freed prices, froze wages, permitted companies to import and export goods without special permission, lowered tariffs, cut subsidies to households and businesses, and made the devalued *złoty* convertible to Western currency.'[10] He also negotiated a huge reduction in the debt to be repaid. Prices did indeed go sky-high temporarily, as did unemployment: by 1992, 2.3 million people, or 13.5 per cent of the workforce, were unemployed. On the other hand, goods hitherto unavailable, including foodstuffs, started appearing on the shelves, even if for a while many could not afford them. Businesses sprang up overnight. Even Balcerowicz, however, shrank from immediately privatising state industries, with the thousands of redundancies this implied. The result was that this aspect of modernisation took much longer, and in the meantime the political cost of 'shock therapy' was that Poland's reformed communists actually returned to power in 1993. In the course of establishing normal alternations between left- and right-wing governments, however, economic growth resumed as early as 1992, and a denser, more variegated economy started to emerge, with private enterprise gradually taking the place of the communist-era dinosaurs. Poland's extensive pre-1989 black market economy also came into its own in a genuinely free market: many Poles, after all, were already adept at playing by capitalist rules.

Czechoslovakia, and then the Czech Republic, under Václav Klaus's management was an example of 'shock therapy' gone wrong. Klaus was decidedly 'neo-liberal', and 'rejected government regulation on principle.'[11]

---

[10] Stokes, *The Walls Came Tumbling Down*, 270.
[11] Stokes, *The Walls Came Tumbling Down*, 284.

Introduced in January 1991, Czechoslovakia's shock therapy was tempered by the gradualism favoured by president Havel and others: price controls were lifted, and the currency made convertible, but state industries were kept going, and social welfare spending maintained. Where Klaus excelled, however, was in privatisation, which was done via a voucher scheme: each citizen received a set number of vouchers for the purchase of shares in state enterprises, and which could be retained or sold on. The idea was that private enterprises would spring up with the public as shareholders or through the capital supplied by secondary purchasers, and for the next few years this seemed to work: growth was high with low unemployment into the late 1990s. It turned out, however, that many of the voucher privatisations had fallen victim to corruption, with private citizens cheated out of their vouchers by scammers. Most citizens simply sold their vouchers to banks or investment firms, so that little solidly based private enterprise emerged out of the whole saga. Much industry remained stubbornly unmodernised; firms like the automobile manufacturer Škoda, made profitable by outside, mainly German investment, proved the exception rather than the rule. A sociological study completed in 2012 found that, where mass privatisation was introduced too suddenly or with insufficient preparation, this 'immediately reduced that state's financial capacity, due to high budgetary dependence on the earnings of state-owned firms.'[12] Worse, economic failure where privatisation occurred too rapidly, coupled with the transfer of so much wealth to private hands, often led to increased corruption, which in turn undermined people's faith in democracy. The fact that former communist apparatchiks were well placed to benefit from privatisations added to public dissatisfaction.

Hungary was an example of gradualism, even though it had already become one of the more economically liberal communist regimes. By 1989 Hungary already had a fledgling entrepreneurial class, the rudiments of a banking system and even a stock market. The first non-communist government had little in the way of a coherent economic programme, and shrank from embracing shock therapy. Instead it confined itself to restoring land to smallholders and, in the case of state industries, selling these off. This was a convenient way of attracting foreign investment, and provided government with some ready cash; in addition the newly privatised firms were forced to act responsibly by the existence of a regulatory system. Despite a jump in unemployment in the first few years, and the unhelpful attitude of western banks and the EU to Hungary's foreign debt, privatisation was more or less complete by the late 1990s, and the country was recording modest economic growth.

Exposure to outside economic influences produced, overall, mixed results. Poland, Hungary, the Czech Republic, the Baltic states and Slovenia all were relatively quick in adapting to market conditions, whereas those countries

---

[12] Hamm, P., King, L.P. and Stuckler, D., 2012, 'Mass Privatization, State Capacity and Economic Growth', *American Sociological Review*, LXXVII, #2, April, 301–2.

which delayed this vital transition, like Slovakia, Ukraine, Albania, Romania, Bulgaria and most of the ex-Yugoslav states paid the price in continuing economic inefficiency, without necessarily staving off rising unemployment. The downside of marketisation, however, was vulnerability to predatory foreign capital, and also any global economic downturn, like the recession that started in 2008 – a recession that only Poland succeeded in avoiding.

A key factor in Eastern Europe's economic modernisation was of course its relationship to the EU, whose economic influence was even greater than its political attraction. This, despite the fact that East European countries were on the whole neglected, and even exploited, by Brussels in the immediate post-1989 period. With the exception of East Germany, which had the good fortune to be swallowed up by the EU's most prosperous member-state, the former east bloc countries were not automatic candidates for EU funding; certainly Brussels 'failed miserably' to come up with some sort of 'new Marshall Plan for the Eastern neighbors knocking at its door.'[13] Nor was the EU eager to start accession talks. The EU even maintained tariffs against East European exports, while seeking markets in Eastern Europe for its own goods.

Nevertheless, EU governments eventually accepted that enlargement to include Eastern Europe was inevitable, since the whole idea of the European Community was founded on inclusiveness. For East Europeans, 'membership in the EU was a badge of honor, a stamp of political approval, and a path to prosperity.'[14] Furthermore, the longer accession talks were delayed, the greater the risk that elements in East European societies would conclude membership was not worth the effort.

By the mid-1990s a programme for accession was finally being drafted, designed to prepare candidate countries for staged entry into the union. In addition to political requirements, all candidate states were expected to have a functioning market economy, and to apply EU rules on food standards, environmental protection and so on. The preliminary shortlist of countries up for consideration, issued in 1997, included five states: Poland, the Czech Republic, Hungary, Slovenia and Estonia. This played a role in accelerating compliance by states left off the list, like Latvia, Lithuania, Slovakia and Romania; as a result the first three of these were deemed worthy of formal admission in 2004. Political calculations also played a role: for instance, two of the Baltic states were initially excluded from accession talks to avoid alarming Russia, at a time when NATO was also set to expand eastward; and Romania and Bulgaria were set on a fast-track, after 1999, to avert instability, despite their patent unreadiness in terms of corruption. Despite a certain 'enlargement fatigue', the impact of the 2008 recession, and the ongoing immigration crisis since 2015, EU membership is still sought by the Balkan states, at least

---

[13] Ther, *Europe since 1989*, xv.
[14] Dinan, D., 2004, *Europe Recast: A History of the European Union*, Basingstoke, 268.

formally. Albania and Macedonia are official candidates, the latter impeded up to 2019 by its outstanding dispute with Greece over whether it is entitled to call itself 'Macedonia'. Montenegro and Serbia have been in negotiations since 2008 and 2009 respectively; Bosnia-Hercegovina and Kosova, both trapped in threatening internal or external disputes, remain in a limbo, unlikely to qualify for inclusion any time soon.

In terms of overall results Eastern Europe's economic modernisation has been mixed. There has been a clear rise in standards of living, even if the differential between former east bloc countries and Western Europe remains obvious. GDP in East European countries between 1997 and 2008 doubled, while in Slovakia it tripled. Some states, like Slovenia and Estonia, stand out for their western-level wealth and the thoroughness with which they have carved out niches for themselves in the world economy; Estonia in particular has for some time led the world in cyber and internet technology.

Apart from Eastern Europe's continuing extra vulnerability to the vagaries of the world economy, one proof of the differential with Western Europe has been the level of emigration, which remains high. Simply because, after 1989 and especially after accession to the EU, East Europeans were free to move, there has been a decades-long outflow of talent and manpower. Since 1989 an estimated 2.5 million Poles have emigrated, 3.5 million Romanians, and 100,000 Lithuanians, out of a population of 3.5 million; 10 per cent of Bulgarians live outside of their country. This population drain, often consisting of the young and well-educated, has had a dampening effect both economically and politically. It has also created an entire generation of 'Euro-orphans': East Europeans who spent their childhoods living with one parent while the other was working as a migrant in the EU, or with grandparents because both parents were working abroad. It has fuelled a backlash in Western Europe against the so-called 'Polish plumber' phenomenon, and is undoubtedly in part responsible for the rise of national populism and hostility to the EU from Britain to Italy. This has not gone unnoticed in East European societies, where adherence to 'European values' is already undergoing new strains.

For all the problems, there is another, more positive side to migration, usually unacknowledged by xenophobes in both Western and Eastern Europe. Migration is reversible and is assuaged by instant communications and cheap air fares, rather than being a permanent separation, as in the nineteenth century. Migration also allows for the acquisition of skills and rising expectations from bureaucracies back home. There has also been substantial migration of Ukrainians, Moldovans and others into other East European countries, filling the gaps in the labour market left by emigrants to Western Europe. Before the Covid-19 pandemic, a fifth of the population of Wrocław in Poland was Ukrainian. This has created surprisingly few problems, although as is often the case more could and should have been done to facilitate, rather than impede, integration.

2 1

Eastern Europe in the twenty-first century

Nationalism and geopolitics

Intimately interwoven with the theme of modernisation discussed above is the persistence of nationalism, and the problems arising from this. Despite, or perhaps because of, over six decades of European economic integration, nationalist tensions and conflicts, some of them going back generations, continue to be a continent-wide issue, but in the last three decades it is mainly in Eastern Europe that such problems have provided the tinder for war and atrocity. In addition, and by way of conclusion, Eastern Europe's geopolitical situation deserves separate consideration. Since the turn of the century the malign influence of Putin's Russia has reasserted itself, capitalising on and worsening existing sources of tension within the region. In a curious way Eastern Europe's interwar predicament as 'pig in the middle' is being replayed, with the twin issues of NATO and EU enlargement taking the place of Germany, at least in the minds of Russian strategists. The potential for a renewed East-West confrontation, with Eastern Europe as the contested ground, constitutes the greatest single threat to the region's future.

The persistence of nationalism

Nationalism in Eastern Europe is intimately bound up with both aspects of modernisation considered above, but is still worth a separate section. Certainly nationalism in this region has proved a more powerful and deeply rooted sentiment than adherence to socialism.

The nationalisms of East Europeans, some of them long established, some of more recent inception, were only driven underground by communist rule; in the case of multinational, federated states like Yugoslavia and the Soviet Union, communism can even be said to have unwittingly encouraged the growth of nationalism. In the post-communist period, the fundamental truth was that political pluralism, or democratic politics, automatically meant nationalist politics. Just as nationalism festered and nursed its grievances under communism, so it was a factor in many of the 1989 revolutions and in the collapse of the Soviet Union. It emerged in 1989 fully relegitimised and empowered, and in many countries it had great potential for motivating patriotic citizens to work for the common good. The bloody break-up of Yugoslavia and the Soviet Union, no less than the desire in so many states to break free of Russian domination, and the movement to reunify Germany, were all tribute to the strength of nationalism. An appeal to nationalism had long been a trick up the sleeve of communist leaders, going back to the time of Gomułka and Tito, but proved for many in the 1980s and 1990s a reliable means of recovering or acquiring popularity, as demonstrated by Milošević and Tuđman, Lukashenko and Putin.

In the post-communist period nationalism has had an obvious impact on both domestic politics and on the relations of individual societies with one another. In the domestic sphere, from the moment multiple political parties were legalised, there was no shortage of movements whose principal platform was an appeal to national identity, from Mečiar's HZDS in Slovakia to Tuđman's HDZ to Tudor's Greater Romania Party. In some countries the nationalism shaded all too readily into the sort of racist extremism that fully merits the epithet neo-fascist, as for instance with Greater Romania, *Jobbik* in Hungary, and the Our Slovakia Party of Marian Kotleba. Orbán's Fidesz, with its open anti-Semitism and virulent hostility to immigrants and especially Muslims, skirts this territory, as does the recent phenomenon of the *Alternative für Deutschland (AfD)*, which draws most of its electoral support from the former East Germany. Much nationalist self-expression was unobjectionable, even understandable. There was a wholesale renaming of public thoroughfares and spaces, even cities, often restoring names recalling past national greatness; thus, Budapest's Red Army Street became once again Andrássy Street, while in East Germany Karl-Marx-Stadt reverted to Chemnitz. Governments hastened to scrap school history texts lauding the working class struggle to achieve socialism, and celebrated instead national heroes, saints and even dynasties – although this never translated into any significant support for the restoration of King Michael of Romania or Leka of Albania.

The virulence of nationalism has to a large extent depended on the prevailing economic climate, and in this respect Eastern Europe is no different from Western Europe, as the recent electoral successes of extreme nationalist parties like France's National Front or Italy's Northern League show. Due to the economic tailspin threatened by de-communisation, and the uncertainty surrounding applications for membership of the EU, Eastern Europe's ultra-nationalist 'scene' has always been far livelier, and recently has taken renewed sustenance from the migration crisis since 2015. The economic insecurity and uncertainties engendered by the 'neo-liberal' solutions adopted in many countries risked voters turning back to reformed communist parties, as happened in Poland, Hungary and elsewhere in the 1990s; it also risked a turn towards the ultra-nationalist right by those whose innate tendency was to blame others for economic woes.

One early index of this tendency was the open hostility voiced against immigrants of colour, originally welcomed by communist regimes from left-wing or fellow-socialist countries in the 'Third World' during the Cold War, such as Vietnam, Ethiopia or Angola, and stranded in Eastern Europe following the collapse of communism. As a writer to one Hungarian newspaper frankly opined in March 1992 of African students still in Budapest, 'The Magyar people must be allowed to cleanse themselves from within and rid themselves of the various parasites that have infested their country.'[1] In the former GDR, openly racist antagonism towards non-European guest workers manifested itself soon after reunification, starting in September 1991 with a full-scale pogrom against a guest workers' tenement building at Hoyeswerda in Saxony, which lasted five days and which was then replicated in cities and small towns across the former GDR that autumn. In 1992 the number of right-wing attacks on foreigners doubled over that of 1991, beginning at Rostock in August and, again, spreading across the country until three people died in an arson attack at Mölln. Most of this violence was committed by youth and skinheads with demonstrable neo-Nazi sympathies, but it was clear that many local residents looked on with indifference or even approval, that the local police were reluctant to intervene or were positively complicit, and that much of the hostility, while clearly racist, was also rooted in economic uncertainty and impending factory lay-offs. Nor has this problem gone away: three decades after reunification, the former GDR, especially Saxony, is now the principal bastion of the *AdD*, as evidenced by the federal election results in 2017, and the anti-immigrant demonstrations which really took off in Chemnitz in August 2018.

The most obvious expression of nationalism was in attitudes towards ethnic minorities. After years of communist propaganda downplaying national differences and, as in Yugoslavia, promoting 'brotherhood and unity', it was now acceptable, and could even be politically advantageous, to single out minorities for hostile attention. At the same time, responsible political actors were well aware of the negative image such hostility could attract abroad, and sought to marginalise the more extreme expressions of xenophobia. As the prospect of EU accession neared, toning down deep-rooted nationalist antagonisms and resolving their causes became a matter of practical political necessity. To this day, however, such antagonisms remain.

In Slovakia, part of Mečiar's electoral appeal was his hostility towards the country's 600,000 Hungarians. Iliescu in Romania also found it convenient to feed his compatriots' suspicions about the Transylvanian Hungarians, but government hostility was far surpassed by more extreme nationalists like Gheorghe Funar, mayor of Cluj from 1992 and leader of the Party of Romanian National Unity, who described Hungarians as a 'barbarian migratory people

---

[1] Quoted in Hockenos, P., 1993, *Free to Hate: The Rise of the Right in Post-Communist Eastern Europe*, New York and London, 151.

who still have barbarian genes.'[2] Funar's party was the political wing of a much larger organisation, *Vatra Româneăscu* (Romanian Cradle), which claimed six million members and existed mainly to oppose any minority rights for Hungarians. This is turn was trumped by the racist Greater Romania Party, which harked back to the Iron Guard of the interwar period. Serbia under Milošević, in addition to its role in Yugoslavia on behalf of Serb minorities in Croatia and Bosnia, and intimidating its Hungarian minority in Vojvodina, was eventually undone by its mishandling of the Kosovan Albanians. With Kosova's de facto independence since 1999, the situation is reversed, and relations with Serbia remain stymied over the status of Kosova's Serb minority in the Kosovo Mitrovica enclave. Since 2018 the Serbian and Kosovan governments have been alarming their neighbours by discussing openly the possibility of an exchange of territory as a means of resolving the dispute. Croatia, by contrast, solved its Serb minority problem by brutally driving them all out in 1995, and shows no inclination to let them return.

Some countries, rather against expectations, have managed their minority problems better. Macedonia, home to sizeable Serb and Albanian minorities and some 100,000 ethnic Turks, has demonstrated a capacity for compromise, even co-opting the Albanian Party into government at intervals. Macedonia's greatest problem was its non-recognition by Greece because of the alleged expansionist pretensions of the state's name, which because of its historic resonances Greek governments since 1990 insist can only be used by Greece. The latter used Macedonia's refusal to agree a name change as ground for vetoing its admission to the EU and NATO, with a catastrophic effect on Macedonia's economic and security prospects. Only in the course of 2018–19 was a compromise finally agreed, whereby Macedonia renamed itself 'North Macedonia', and Greece lifted its veto on accession. Yet ratification of this deal was fiercely opposed in both countries by demonstrations and parliamentary obstruction. In 2020 argument was still raging in North Macedonia over whether to remove a giant statue of Alexander the Great, erected in central Skopje by a nationalist government to give gratuitous offence to Greeks.

Bulgaria, from attempting an 'ethnic cleansing' of its Turkish minority in the late communist period, has welcomed significant numbers of them back. The first post-revolutionary government actually apologised to the Turkish community for past actions, and the legislation forcing name changes on Turks and restricting the use of Turkish was repealed. Such reconciliation was expedited rather than impeded by the formation of the Turkish-based Movement for Rights and Freedoms (MRF) in 1990, which succeeded in winning twenty-three parliamentary seats in the elections of October 1992, and has held the balance of power on and off ever since. Despite the persistence

---

[2]   Quoted in Brown, J.F., 1994, *Hopes and Shadows: Eastern Europe after Communism*, Harlow, 198.

of ultra-nationalist factions in Bulgarian politics, the MRF has safeguarded Turkish minority interests reasonably well, and the improvement of Bulgaria's relationship with Turkey following induction into NATO in 2004 has facilitated the MRF's task.

So too, paradoxically, has the establishment of normal relations between Bulgaria and neighbouring Macedonia, which Bulgarian nationalists throughout the twentieth century assumed should be part of the Bulgarian state. In 1991, however, Bulgaria was one of the first countries to recognise Macedonian independence; and Macedonians for their part have come to see themselves as distinct from Bulgarians. The acceptance of this on both sides took much of the international tension out of the 'Macedonian question', which henceforth centred on the absurd dispute with Greece over the country's name.

Poland, which harbours a small German minority of about 300,000, mainly in Silesia, initially regarded these '*Volkswagendeutsche*' with extreme suspicion, at least until the Polish-German treaty of 1991 settled the issue of Poland's western border. The treaty recognised minority rights on both sides, albeit unequally, but equally important was the organising ability of Polish Germans, whose party won seven seats in the parliamentary elections of 1991. Since the 1990s Polish-German relations, inevitably cool to start with, steadily improved, helped by good economic ties, especially tourism; since 2015, however, the approach of Poland's Law and Justice government has been altogether more confrontational.

Apart from the disputes left over from Yugoslavia's break-up, only two minority questions, realistically, have shown serious potential for disrupting international relations. One is the position of Hungarian minorities in Slovakia, Romania and Serbia – or rather, Hungary's policy toward these minorities. Historically, this was an issue which complicated Hungary's relations with the successor states since 1918 and produced tensions even in the late communist period. In the post-1989 age of democratic politics there seemed initial cause for concern on the Hungarian side, in that all three successor states were dominated by demagogues – Milošević, Iliescu and Mečiar – not averse to victimising minorities. Matters were not helped, however, by the clumsy tone adopted by Hungary's new MDF government. József Antall described himself as 'in spirit' prime minister of fifteen million Hungarians, implying some sort of jurisdiction over the five million who lived in surrounding states. Until it lost office in 1994 the MDF appeared to imagine that border adjustments might be possible to rectify the injustices of the Trianon Treaty. Their left-wing and centrist successors took a less inflammatory line, and as negotiations for EU accession began the irredentist noises coming from Hungarian nationalists seemed anachronistic, not least because neighbouring states became more genuinely democratic. Under pressure from the EU and NATO, Hungary signed bilateral treaties with Slovakia in 1995 and Romania in 1996, promising to respect borders in return for basic guarantees of Hungarians' rights. Orbán's

Fidesz government, however, especially during its second spell in office since 2010, has indulged the old nationalist phantasy again. Orbán also fondly refers to the 'fifteen million', and in 2010 Hungary enacted legislation facilitating naturalisation for Hungarian residents outside Hungary; to date over half a million have taken up the offer, over protests from their countries of residence.

The issue of Russian minorities in the three Baltic states is of much greater concern, since their status and rights have been used by Russian governments ever since 1991 as a stick with which to beat their host countries. On the Baltics' side the mere presence of Russian minorities is a constant reminder of Soviet-era domination and population displacement. As of 1989 there were 905,000 Russians in Latvia, or 34 per cent of the population; 475,000 or 30 per cent in Estonia; and 344,000 or 9.4 per cent in Lithuania. Most of these ethnic Russians and other Russian speakers from elsewhere in the USSR had been bussed in under Stalin to take the place of deported Balts and to alter the demographic balance; it is estimated that the number of Russians in Latvia alone quadrupled after 1940. The Soviet government's concern over the fate of these Russian minorities was one of the reasons for opposing independence in 1990–1, and helped trigger the abortive coup of August 1991.

Since independence all three Baltic states had to confront the fact that Russian minorities cannot simply be expelled, and must somehow be accommodated to deny Russia any excuse for meddling. At the same time, the aggrieved nationalism of ethnic Russians has made such accommodation difficult, and since 1999 the attitude of Putin's administration has increasingly leaned towards exploitation of this. Some Russians, mainly those employed directly by the former Soviet state, left after 1991, but not enough to eliminate the problem: as of 2018, the percentage of Russians in Estonia was down 4 per cent to 26 per cent, in Latvia down 9 per cent to 25.3 per cent, and in Lithuania, whose share was always least, down 5 per cent to 4.8 per cent.

Several issues complicate Baltic-Russian relations. Firstly, after independence the Estonian and Latvian governments and their largely non-Russian electorates showed a marked reluctance to accept that ethnic Russians should be entitled to citizenship, and in 1991 Estonia and Latvia both passed laws restricting citizenship to those who held it before 1940 and their descendants. This contrasts with popular front rhetoric in all three Soviet republics in the run-up to independence, which stressed that all ethnic groups would be guaranteed equal rights. It also contrasts with Lithuania's citizenship law, which is 'extremely liberal', doubtless because Lithuania's Russian minority is smaller and hence less of a threat.[3] The shift from transnational accommodation to hostility may be attributable to Russia's attitude, in particular uncertainty over the withdrawal of Russian troops from the Baltics, which was largely

[3]   Lieven, A., 1993, *The Baltic Revolution: Estonia, Latvia, Lithuania and the Path to Independence*, New Haven, CT and London, 310.

completed by the end of 1994; yet Estonian and Latvian leaders seemed to have forgotten Boris Yeltsin's open support for their independence in 1991. Instead, the assumption was that, with the collapse of the Soviet Union, the wishes of ethnic Russians could now be discounted. Estonians and Latvians increasingly referred to Russians as 'illegal immigrants', 'colonists' and 'aliens', even though many Russians had been born in the Baltic states. Gradually the mood among Russians on both sides of the borders soured. Particular irritation was caused by requirements for citizenship, which specified proficiency in the state language that Russians above a certain age were unlikely to acquire. With citizenship also went eligibility for public sector jobs. Gratuitously offensive, too, was the removal of street signs in Russian, given that 63 per cent of the population of Riga, Latvia's capital, were Russian speakers. Despite protest by international organisations like Helsinki Watch, the Estonian and Latvian laws remained in force. In the end it was only the prospect of EU membership which forced Estonia and Latvia, in 1995 and 1998 respectively, to scrap these discriminatory laws, since they flouted basic human rights standards. By the 2010s most Russians resident in the Baltic states had acquired citizenship, even if for many non-citizenship allows free travel into the EU as well as the Russian Federation. Yet considerable damage was done to harmonious relations, and in the hostile atmosphere that has grown up between Russia and the West since 1999, and especially since 2014, the fact that Russians are still influenced by Russian state media continues to haunt the Baltic peoples.

Two final examples of the persistence of nationalism in its most extreme, racist form in domestic politics are anti-Semitism and the continuing discrimination against the Roma.

Despite the fact that most Jewish communities in the region were exterminated or driven out during the Second World War, some East European societies have nevertheless become known for exhibiting 'anti-Semitism without Jews', a phenomenon remarked on in the communist period.[4] One of the first countries where anti-Jewish prejudice resurfaced unmistakably after 1989 was Hungary. It became apparent that the Hungarian Democratic Forum, which formed the first non-communist government, harboured an 'oblique anti-Semitism', with its self-portrayal as 'the nation's single true representative of Hungarian culture', and its distinction between 'real' Hungarians and others.[5] The most prominent exemplar of this was István Csurka, whose election pamphlet in October 1990, entitled 'Wake Up Hungarians!', denounced the 'pursuit of self-interest' by a 'dwarfish minority', standard code for 'Jewish influence'.[6] By September 1991, Csurka was inveighing in the party newspaper against 'the eternal alien-like elite' misleading the Hungarian people; during negotiations for a loan from

---

[4] Lendvai, P., 1971, *Anti-Semitism in Eastern Europe*, London, 21.
[5] Hockenos, *Free to Hate*, 111.
[6] Quoted in Hockenos, *Free to Hate*, 111.

the IMF, Csurka referred to it as 'the strike force of world Jewry'.[7] In August 1992, now a parliamentary deputy and MDF vice-president, Csurka achieved international notoriety with an article claiming that Hungary 'was still ruled by a communist-Jewish-liberal clique', and that 'underprivileged strata and groups' – code for Roma – 'have been living among us for far too long.'[8] It was only when Csurka challenged prime minister Antall for the leadership that the latter summoned up the nerve to expel him from the party. Csurka went on to found his own Hungarian Justice and Life Party and remained an active voice for racist views until his death in 2012.

Nor was Csurka an isolated phenomenon. Ten years after his eclipse, the Movement for a Better Hungary (*Jobbik Magyarországért Mozgalom*, or *Jobbik*) was founded in 2003, describing itself as a 'radically patriotic Christian party', aiming to protect 'Hungarian values and interests'. What this meant in reality was an ultra-nationalist and frankly racist attitude towards minorities, especially Jews and Roma. Since its first participation in elections in 2006 *Jobbik*'s share of the popular vote has climbed from 2.2 per cent to 19 per cent in 2018, and it is currently the second largest parliamentary group with twenty-six deputies. Since 2014 *Jobbik*'s leaders have adopted a more moderate, conservative tone, but it is clear that, whatever the truth of this, the existence of such an extreme competitor has been a factor in the rightward trajectory of Orbán's ruling Fidesz.

Orbán's transformation from the ardent democrat of 1989 to a proponent of what he calls 'illiberal democracy', and his open calls for a Europe of Christian nation-states firmly excluding alien elements, especially Muslims, has been one of the more alarming developments in contemporary Eastern Europe, meriting him the epithet of 'most dangerous man in the EU'.[9] Anti-Semitism has proved an important element in Orbán's world view: he has repeatedly denounced the philanthropic works of the émigré Hungarian Jewish billionaire George Sörös as part of a conspiracy to undermine Hungarian culture, effectively driving out of the country in 2018 the Sörös Foundation-funded Central European University, and passing a 'Stop Sörös' law the same year, intended to prevent non-governmental organisations assisting refugees in making asylum claims. In his election campaign of March 2018, using classic anti-Semitic tropes, Orbán attacked Sörös as part of a collective enemy which was 'not national but international; does not believe in working but speculates with money; does not have its own homeland but feels it owns the whole world.'[10] More recently

---

[7]   Quoted in Stokes, G., 2012, *The Walls Came Tumbling Down: Collapse and Rebirth in Eastern Europe*, 2nd edn, New York and Oxford, 276.
[8]   Quoted in Brown, *Hopes and Shadows*, 38.
[9]   Quoted in Lendvai, P., 2018, *Orbán: Hungary's Strongman*, Oxford and New York, 201.
[10] Quoted in Walker, S., 2018, 'Hungarian Leader Says Europe Is Now "Under Invasion" by Migrants', *The Guardian*, 15 March.

Orbán has accused Sörös of being behind the EU's protests at Hungary's increasingly illiberal policies.

It would be misleading to single out Hungarian anti-Semitism as exceptional, for this is a prejudice found not only in Eastern Europe but resurgent in Western Europe too. What is remarkable is the speed with which anti-Jewish sentiment re-emerged after 1989. In Croatia president Tuđman openly boasted that his wife was neither a Serb nor a Jew, and his HDZ party was awash with anti-Semites, although not so obviously as the even more right-wing Party of Historic Rights. In Poland's presidential election of 1990 Lech Wałęsa was not above pandering to anti-Semitism; certainly he did little to defend former Solidarity colleagues opposing him, like Adam Michnik, from anti-Semitic attacks. Since then, it is true, there has been much progress in Polish attitudes towards the Holocaust, and even the current *PiS* leadership is very nervous about being labelled anti-Semitic. A Czech newspaper published a list of alleged Jews in public life, including Václav Havel, who was not Jewish. In Romania anti-Semitism is an integral bonding element on the ultra-nationalist right, continuing a long-standing tradition in Romanian politics. Overall, anti-Semitism has remained indirect, usually expressed in a code generally understood, and tends to resurface most acutely in times of economic uncertainty. To some extent, in the wake of the Bosnian war and the Kosovo crisis, and in an age of Islamic State terrorism, mass refugees and economic migrants, Muslims have taken the place of Jews as the new bugbear.

Prejudice against Eastern Europe's Roma population has also resurfaced since 1989. The vast majority of Europe's six million Roma still live in Eastern Europe, and in the communist period they officially enjoyed equal status and were entitled to the same housing and education as everyone else. In practice discrimination persisted even in a supposedly socialist environment. Most Roma remained uneducated and as a result had few skills to offer beyond traditional, pre-industrial ones and trading. In some countries, like Hungary, they were forced into urban housing which became de facto ghettoes, shunned by their neighbours; in other countries they remained largely rural. What is remarkable is the speed with which anti-Roma violence erupted after 1989, as if people were venting all the frustrations of communism on this visible minority. In Romania, home to the largest single concentration of Roma, 2.5 million or 10 per cent of the population, the first pogrom took place in the village of Turu Lung as early as January 1990; not only did the local police stand by while the Roma quarter was set alight, but most of the arrests they made were of Roma. In Czechoslovakia North Bohemian skinheads linked to Miroslav Sládek's far-right Republican Party attacked Roma communities in April and May 1990. Violence continued for the next two years; in Prague in November 1991 skinheads attacked Roma with chants of 'Gypsies to the gas chambers!' Hungary saw similar outbreaks, again by skinheads, in Eger and

Miskolc in September 1990; as we have seen, leading political figures publicly referred to Roma as parasites.

To be fair, not only have Roma since 1989 been free to form their own organisations, like the Roma Civic Initiative in Czechoslovakia and a Roma parliament in Hungary, but mainstream parties and organisations have vocally denounced anti-Roma violence and prejudice. In addition, scrutiny from the EU and the United Nations has had some effect in ensuring that East European governments make at least some attempt to protect Roma rights. This has not, however, prevented systematic local discrimination. Municipal authorities in particular have been reluctant to house Roma families, or protect them from arbitrary eviction; as a result far too many Roma continue to live in squalor, suffer random or even orchestrated attack, and face persistent discrimination in the labour market. Before the end of the 1990s conditions in the Czech Republic were so dire that Roma families felt forced to apply for asylum in western countries like Britain and Canada. As recently as 2015 attacks on Roma in Bulgaria, despite generous allocation of EU funds for a 'Roma integration strategy', were so widespread that the European Court of Human Rights formally called on the government to stop local communities demolishing Roma accommodation without providing alternatives. The EU Agency for Fundamental Rights reported, in 2016, that in nine East European states, on average, 80 per cent of Roma still lived below the poverty line, 'a third have no running water, and one in ten have no electricity.' Unemployment rates remained high, and few Roma children attended or remained in school for long. Worse, popular attitudes toward Roma remain stubbornly hostile: most East Europeans believe integration is impossible.[11]

Finally, any consideration of nationalism's enduring hold on East European societies must examine the rise or reappearance, in the last decade or so, of a particular form of xenophobic, even paranoid, nationalism. The bellwether here has, again, been Orbán's Hungary, especially since Fidesz' return to power in 2010; but in many respects the original model for such a world view has been Vladimir Putin. This brooding, beleaguered nationalism has in some cases also fed off the alleged plight of national minorities marooned in neighbouring countries, in particular Hungarians in Slovakia, Romania and Serbia, and Russians in the three Baltic states and, latterly, Ukraine. It has also, however, been directed outwards, fuelling bitter disputes over who authentically represents the nation. It exhibits an especial rancour over how the nation's history should be commemorated, and the question of the 'unfinished' revolutions of 1989. This national populism, which is by no means confined to Eastern Europe, has shown new life recently; whether it becomes the dominant voice of nationalism in the region remains to be seen.

---

[11] As summarised in Krastev, I., 2017, *After Europe*, Philadelphia, PA, 53–5.

Since 2010, when Orbán won a 'super-majority' in the Hungarian parliament, entitling him to amend the constitution, Hungary has served as a role model for authoritarianism, mirroring Putin's 'managed democracy'. Even before a new fundamental law was approved in April 2011, in the face of mass protests, the government had already passed some 350 laws, extending control over the media and politicising the audit office, the prosecutor's office and the judiciary. The new constitution's preamble stressed Hungary's history as a Christian nation defending Europe against the Muslim Ottomans, and its 'national conservative values.' More importantly, it removed or weakened many checks on government, especially the powers of the constitutional court, making it almost impossible to amend the constitution, while Orbán continued to fill the judiciary and other bodies with Fidesz loyalists. In the words of László Sólyom, a former president of the court, this amounted to 'an unconstitutional coup . . . [under] the cover of constitutionality, with constitutional means.'[12] In late 2011 journalists in the state broadcaster struck in protest against government interference; a new law gave the government power over the central bank, prompting protests from the IMF and the EU. Early in 2012, against a background of mass demonstrations, the EU started legal action against Hungary over these constitutional and legal changes, especially the forced retirement of judges over 62 years of age, the centralisation of economic assets, rewriting of the labour code and fundamental democratic norms. In response, Orbán simply denounced the EU's interference, comparing it to the Soviet Union, and declaring that 'Hungarians will not live as foreigners dictate.'[13] By 2019 Freedom House, an organisation which monitors democratic performance, reclassified Hungary as 'partly free', the first time a member-state of the EU has been so designated. In 2020 Orbán utilised the coronavirus pandemic to justify ruling by decree.

There can be little doubt that Orbán's peculiar variety of conservative, xenophobic nationalism strikes a chord with many Hungarians: Fidesz has subsequently won two more national elections, in 2014 and 2018, by a landslide. The ongoing confrontation with the EU has if anything been a source of strength; but just as important have been Orbán's control of the media and his use of scare tactics. In this regard the 2015 refugee crisis was a godsend for Orbán; ever since he has lost no opportunity to bang an anti-immigrant, anti-Muslim and anti-Semitic drum, ostentatiously constructing a border fence with Serbia, railing against the nefarious influence of Sörös, and claiming, in the 2018 election, that 'Africa wants to kick down our door, and Brussels is not defending us.'[14] At the heart of Orbán's vision is a belief that nations, not

[12] Quoted in Lendvai, *Orbán*, 110.
[13] Quoted in Traynor, I., 2012, 'Hungary Prime Minister Hits Out at EU Interference in National Day Speech', *The Guardian*, 15 Mar.
[14] Quoted in Walker, 'Hungarian Leader Says Europe Is Now "Under Invasion" by Migrants'.

supranational organisations, are the natural units of humankind; as he put it in 2012, 'Europe can only be made great again with the help of strong nations.'[15] There is also an avowed authoritarian agenda with Orbán: he has been open in his view that the Hungarian nation is weakened by liberalism, and that what it needs is 'illiberal democracy', the outward form of elections and constitutional government, without the tiresome danger of choosing the 'wrong' party. In his nationalism and authoritarianism Orbán is at one with the likes of Putin and Trump, and has been frank in identifying with their world view.

Orbán's illiberal nationalism as well as his methods were openly admired by Jarosław Kaczyński, leader of Poland's Law and Justice Party, and since returning to power in 2015 *PiS* has implemented its own version of 'illiberal democracy'. Kaczyński and his twin brother Lech originally came to prominence as Solidarity activists, but from the fiercely Catholic and socially conservative wing of the movement, and by 2001, when they founded *PiS*, they were clearly identified with the nationalist right. As mayor of Warsaw in 2002–5 Lech Kaczyński gained notoriety for banning gay pride marches. The Kaczyńskis subscribed to the 'unfinished revolution' thesis, according to which 'it was Solidarity, rather than its communist opponents, that had been defeated in 1989.'[16] Liberals in the post-1989 era were seen as effectively collaborating with reformed communists to create a political order that 'diminished the role of nationalism, the Catholic Church and traditional Polish culture.'[17] In 2005 *PiS* achieved their breakthrough: Lech won the presidential election, while the party became the largest in parliament and formed a coalition with other right-wingers. Their major achievement before losing office in 2007 was a draconic Lustration Law which dramatically expanded the vetting process for weeding former communists out of public life, although this was subsequently watered down by Poland's constitutional court.

Lech Kaczyński continued as president, obliged to cooperate with Donald Tusk's liberal Civic Platform-led government, and in this role he showed a commendable willingness to improve relations with the Ukraine and Lithuania, as well as demonstratively supporting Georgia against Russian invasion in 2008. In April 2010, however, the president and his entourage died when their aircraft crashed near Smolensk, en route to a joint Russian-Polish ceremony commemorating the Katyń forest massacre of Poles by the Soviets in 1940. Although the subsequent official enquiries by both governments concluded that the disaster was a genuine accident, the effect on *PiS* under Jarosław Kaczyński's leadership was transformative. Kaczyński and those around him convinced themselves that the crash was an assassination, engineered by Putin's

---

[15] Quoted in Traynor, 'Hungary Prime Minister Hits Out at EU Interference in National Day Speech'.
[16] Mark, J., 2010, *The Unfinished Revolution: Making Sense of the Communist Past in Central-Eastern Europe*, New Haven, CT and London, 13.
[17] Mark, *The Unfinished Revolution*, 14.

Russia, and that Tusk's government was complicit in both the plot and the cover-up. This conspiracy theory, despite the lack of credible evidence, became central to the *PiS* strategy, to the point that, as of 2017, one in three Poles accepted that Russia was responsible for president Kaczyński's death. In the 2015 elections, for the first time in post-1989 Poland's history, *PiS* won an outright majority, putting it in a position to implement an agenda not that different to that of Orbán in Hungary.

PiS, like Orbán, has moved to control and intimidate the media, and to hobble the judiciary, especially the constitutional court. As early as December 2015 a full-blown constitutional crisis was provoked when the government illegally blocked incoming judges and swore in its own appointees. This triggered, for the first time, the threat of EU sanctions under Article 7 of the accession treaty, for breaching democratic norms, although to date little has come of this, since formal suspension of Poland's voting rights depends on unanimous agreement from other member-states, and Hungary's agreement under Orbán is unlikely. Re-elected in 2019, *PiS* continues to govern in an increasingly authoritarian manner, adopting a left-wing approach to economic issues, but a decidedly right-wing one in cultural matters. Like Fidesz, *PiS* claims to be pro-market but is also interventionist and protectionist, pro-family, anti-abortion, and increasingly hostile to the EU, especially on the question of immigration and asylum seekers. It has also, to be fair, done much to alleviate poverty by its policy of universal child benefit.

This trend towards right-wing authoritarianism is not confined to Hungary and Poland, although the record in other societies is variable. Croatia has swung from right to left and back to right again, with the HDZ once more in power, but with a social democrat, Zoran Milanović, elected president in January 2020. President Vučić of Serbia exhibits ever more authoritarian traits. In Slovakia *Smer* (Direction), the dominant party after 2006, though ostensibly social democratic, habitually governed in coalition with the ultra-nationalist Slovak National Party, well-known for its inflammatory rhetoric against Hungarians and Roma, and its campaign to rehabilitate Jozef Tiso, leader of the wartime fascist regime. *Smer* never convincingly distanced itself from the Slovak Nationals' stance vis-à-vis minorities, and its principal leader, Robert Fico, prime minister until 2018, had a long record of abusing the media, refused point-blank to accept Muslim refugees and cultivated closer ties to Russia. When the journalist Jan Kuciak and his *fiancée* were murdered in March 2018, Fico was accused of indirect responsibility and forced to resign following massive demonstrations in defence of press freedoms and against organised crime. In March 2019 an anti-corruption, socially liberal and pro-EU novice, Zuzana Čaputová, won the presidency convincingly against *Smer*'s candidate. Only in March 2020 did the popular mood swing decisively against *Smer*, when a coalition headed by the explicitly anti-corruption Ordinary People and Independent Personalities Party (*OLaNO*), under Igor Matovic, took office. Miloš Zeman, the social democratic former prime minister and current president of the Czech Republic, has made himself notorious for his anti-Muslim views and readiness to fan hostility to refugees of all sorts. The current Czech prime minister, Andrej Babiš, not only shares Zeman's views, but as a billionaire media mogul, was able to fund his own political party, ANO – for Action of Dissatisfied Citizens – on a largely anti-immigrant platform. The governments of both Romania and Bulgaria remain mired in corruption scandals. The centre-right Bulgarian government of Bojko Borisov, in office almost continuously since 2009, has been repeatedly criticised for its heavy-handedness towards the media and its racist attitude towards minorities. Romania, with hundreds of registered parties and twenty-five prime ministers since 1989, only a handful of whom have served more than two years, has been most distinguished for the sheer instability of its politics. Despite recurrent crusades by various parties to curb corruption, often accompanied by mass public demonstrations, politics remains a battlefield of competing claims. In 2002 a powerful Anti-Corruption Directorate (DNA) was created, which began bringing multiple charges; but the social democratic government in power since 2007 then brought in legislation decriminalising certain corruption offences, on the ground that the DNA itself was illegally colluding with the intelligence service in order to secure evidence. In short, Romanian politicians as a class seem incapable of shaking off authoritarian habits. Only the Baltic states have held out against this creeping tide of national populism.

It may be, as Ivan Krastev has suggested, that the whole process of Europeanisation and democratisation set in motion after 1989 in Eastern Europe has encouraged the trend towards 'illiberal democracy'. Prior to 1989 nationalism and liberalism were plausible allies against communist rule. The Yugoslav wars then gave nationalism a bad name: confronted with the misdeeds of a Milošević or a Tuđman, and anxious to win entry to the EU, many East Europeans felt obliged to downplay their nationalist inclinations. Accession to the EU, however, has brought nationalism out in the open again, because the EU's stress on open borders, freedom of movement and multiculturalism has sharpened the fears of nationalists, not just in Eastern Europe but in Western Europe as well. The rise to prominence of figures like Orbán and Kaczyński is the fruit of this interaction, because East European nationalisms, for better or worse, have remained stubbornly focused on ethnicity and history. In Krastev's words, liberal democracy 'defends not only property rights and the right of the political majority to govern but also the rights of minorities', and this sticks in the craw of ethnic nationalists, who see themselves and their nations as a 'threatened majority', done down by an enforced tolerance of the 'other'.[18] Finally, the refugee crisis of 2015 has had a huge impact on the public mood

[18] Krastev, *After Europe*, 74, 76.

across the continent, but perhaps nowhere more so than in Eastern Europe; the longer-term political consequences of this can only be guessed at, but are unlikely to be positive. The naked populism, xenophobia and disdain for international cooperation displayed by the Trump administration since 2017 have, if anything, reinforced this trend.

Geopolitical trends and the Russian threat

This book is a history of Eastern Europe, not of Russia; but the history of the one is inextricably bound up with the history of the other. It is impossible to close this survey of developments since 1989 without noting Russia's geopolitical impact, especially since its annexation of the Crimea in 2014. After a period of partial eclipse in the 1990s following the collapse of the Soviet Union, since the turn of the century Russia under Putin has rebounded as a major regional power, its influence on the whole not a happy one. Russia is not so much the elephant in the living room as the megalosaur bestriding the back-garden wall.

For much of the 1990s, while East European societies, including newly independent former Soviet republics, struggled to deal with pluralist politics, exposure to the world market and a host of other issues, and while the bloody break-up of Yugoslavia played out, the Russian Federation – itself a newly independent former Soviet republic – went into an economic and social tailspin of its own. This had much to do with the brutal rapidity with which the Yeltsin government chose to dismantle the command economy, thus exposing Russians to the full force of the market without much in the way of a safety net. Matters were made worse by the sheer lawlessness unleashed by the party-state's collapse: much of the privatisation of enterprises was undertaken by former party officials who simply appropriated state assets, and within a short period post-communist Russia became a notorious kleptocracy, in Yeltsin's own words a 'superpower of crime', where the ruthless and corrupt made millions while ordinary citizens were reduced to penury.[19] At the same time attempts by Russia's fledgling parliamentary parties to dispute government policy led to an authoritarian crackdown, and in 1993 the world was treated to the spectacle of Russian tanks bombarding the Russian parliament at the president's behest. Yeltsin's entourage, a clique more in control of affairs than the ill and often drunk Yeltsin, then manipulated the 1996 presidential election to keep Yeltsin in place, and rewarded the emergent class of oligarchs with further handouts of state assets. Putin was very much the product of this system rather than its creator. Despite such strong-arm tactics, the Yeltsin government proved incapable of suppressing

---

[19] Quoted in Galeotti, M., 2018, *The Vory: Russia's Super Mafia*, New Haven, CT and London, 111.

revolt in the Caucasian province of Chechnya, and in 1995 Russian troops were forced to withdraw from the area. The former superpower, it seemed, could not even maintain authority in its own sovereign territory.

With Russia so diminished, the United States was for most of the decade the sole global superpower to turn to when it came to conflict resolution in Eastern Europe; by comparison the EU, despite its economic clout, was powerless. The forcible, US-led settlement of first the Bosnian war in 1995, and then the Kosovo crisis in 1999, was proof that intervention by at least one hegemon was essential, and that hegemon was not Russia; the latter's last-minute, surprise despatch of peacekeeping forces to Kosovo, at the conclusion of NATO's campaign, was more a psychological compensation exercise by the Kremlin than a practical contribution to peace. The EU's power was 'soft': the lure of admission to it was a big incentive to East European governments to effect democratic and economic reform and pursue good relations with one another. In terms of power political realities, however, the club whose membership mattered most to East European governments was NATO. The queue for admission was forming as early as 1991, and the reason for this, even then, was fear of Russia.

This should not be surprising, given Eastern Europe's historic relationship with Russia. Even the much-reduced Russian Federation was still a formidable, nuclear-armed power, its troops still stationed in some East European states until the mid-1990s. Nor does the argument hold water that, because the Bush administration in 1990 promised the leader of the then Soviet Union that NATO would never expand eastward, it was somehow impermissible, in a post-Soviet universe, to offer East Europeans the collective security of membership in NATO. NATO is, and has always been, a defensive alliance; whatever the Putin regime claims to think, NATO harbours no ambition to attack Russia. By contrast Russia is naturally seen as a potential threat by East Europeans. For Poles, or Estonians, or Romanians to take advantage of the window of opportunity to join NATO seemed entirely logical. It also seemed incumbent on western powers, especially the United States, to offer this protection.

With hindsight it is clear that the whole trend of events in Eastern Europe since the collapse of communism has been felt in Russia as a humiliation and that the expansion of NATO, in particular, has been taken by many Russians, rightly or wrongly, as an act of aggression directed against Russia. Judging by his actions since 1999, this is certainly the interpretation placed on events by Vladimir Putin.

Handpicked by the Yeltsin team as prime minister and succeeding Yeltsin as president at the end of 1999, Putin proved far more ruthless than anyone could have imagined, and has since presided over what Grigory Yavlinsky, a liberal from the Gorbachev era, describes as 'peripheral authoritarianism'.[20] Russia

---

[20] Yavlinsky, G., 2019, *The Putin System: An Opposing View*, New York, 16.

remains on the periphery of the global economy because it has never completely modernised, yet it projects power through its sale of mineral wealth to the global 'centre'. In domestic affairs Putin has clung to power via sham elections, a near-total control of the media, and the intimidation or even murder of potential rivals; the law and judiciary are tools for maintaining control, rather than holding power to account, and in 2020 the constitution was amended, enabling Putin to remain in office indefinitely. Intolerant of challenges from within Russia, Putin naturally fears the power of example, the possibility that Russians might effect their own revolution, like the peoples of Eastern Europe. Hence too Putin's need to demonstrate the hollowness of democratic process in the western world, as evidenced by his meddling in the US presidential election and in Britain's Brexit referendum in 2016.

Putin's world view has undoubtedly been shaped by the fact that he grew up in the Soviet Union, the citizen of a feared global power which also dominated, where it did not directly possess, Eastern Europe. Putin was a KGB officer stationed in East Germany when the Berlin Wall came down. He recorded his conviction, in 2005, that the collapse of the Soviet Union was 'the largest geopolitical catastrophe of the twentieth century.'[21] Just as revealing was a speech Putin made after the rigged referendum in Crimea on joining the Russian Federation (97 per cent for), in March 2014: after ridiculing the 'sovereignty parade' of Soviet republics proclaiming independence in 1991, Putin reflected sourly how 'Millions of people went to bed in one country and awoke in different ones', and that as a result the Russian people were now 'divided by borders'.[22] The reference to ethnic Russian minorities in the Baltic states, Ukraine and elsewhere could hardly be more pointed; but as he made clear a few months later, Putin's definition of the 'Russian world' is also highly elastic, and includes anyone 'not necessarily of Russian ethnicity, but everyone who feels to be a Russian person.'[23] For those paying attention, Putin's public utterances since 1999 reveal a conviction that Russia's interests demand unfettered hegemony in Eastern Europe, especially in the former Soviet republics. Western opposition to this hegemony is perceived as part of a general conspiracy to do Russia down, and CIA influence is seen behind every attempt by East European countries like Ukraine to modernise and improve democratic accountability. Such paranoia also serves to reinforce Putin's authority at home; according to the journalist Lilia Shevtsova, 'anti-Westernism is the new national idea.'[24] Certainly since the US invasion of Iraq in 2003 Putin has

---

[21] Quoted in Ther, P., 2018, *Europe since 1989: A History*, with a new preface by the author; translated by Charlotte Hughes-Kreuzmüller, Princeton, NJ and Oxford, 51.

[22] Quoted in Kirchick, J., 2018, *The End of Europe: Dictators, Demagogues and the Coming Dark Age*, New Haven, CT and London, 13.

[23] Quoted in Kirchick, *The End of Europe*, 13.

[24] Quoted in Lucas, E., 2009, *The New Cold War: Putin's Russia and the Threat to the West*, fully revised and updated, New York, 116–17.

habitually referred to the United States, as he did in 2006, as 'Comrade Wolf', who 'knows whom to eat.'[25] In this scenario East European nations are simply so many stalking-horses for Russia's enemies.

It is against this background that Russia's reactions to developments in Eastern Europe for the past decade and more must be understood. Putin's regime displays a neuralgic sensitivity to any manifestation of anti-Russian sentiment in Eastern European politics. It regarded the 'colour revolutions', like Georgia's 'Rose revolution' of 2003 and especially the 'Orange revolution' of 2004 in Ukraine as practice-runs for fomenting unrest in Russia itself. Above all any suggestion that either NATO or the EU might be extended further eastward has been met with extreme hostility.

An early example of Russian heavy-handedness was the cyber attack on Estonia in the spring of 2007, the first-ever instance of such aggression. This had its origins in the Estonian government's decision to relocate a memorial to Soviet war dead from the centre of Tallinn. A monument that, to Russians, symbolised Estonia's 'liberation' from fascism in 1945 was, for most Estonians, also a reminder of their forcible reincorporation into the Soviet Union, as well as the country's annexation by Stalin in 1940. Yet the relocation was immediately denounced by the Russian government as an intolerable affront, ethnic Russians in Tallinn rioted for two days, and the Estonian embassy in Moscow was besieged by government-sponsored youth organisations. On the day rioting in Tallinn began, moreover, Estonian government websites and those of banks, media outlets and other important institutions were disabled by a wave of coordinated denial-of-service attacks. For 'one of the most wired societies on earth', which since independence has pioneered internet facilities, this was a temporarily crippling blow, and despite Russian denials there was never much doubt as to who was responsible.[26]

Another early warning of the lengths to which Russia will go to reassert its regional power was its brief but bloody war with Georgia in the summer of 2008. This lies outside the scope of our study; but the Georgian war was a clear signal that Russia would not tolerate Georgia's moves to join NATO. Just as worryingly for East European governments, Russia's blatant aggression was studiously passed over by the incoming administration of Barack Obama, anxious to 're-set' relations. In July 2009, thirty-two prominent East European leaders, including Václav Havel and Lech Wałęsa, addressed an open letter to Obama, warning that 'Russia is back as a revisionist power pursuing a 19th-century agenda with 21st-century tactics and methods.' The letter was dismissed by one of Obama's advisers as 'Russophobia'.[27]

[25] Quoted in Lucas, *The New Cold War*, 117.
[26] Kirchick, *The End of Europe*, 14.
[27] Quoted in Kirchick, *The End of Europe*, 24–5.

The final evidence of Russia's destructive potential in Eastern Europe, still being played out, was its invasion and annexation of the Crimea in March 2014, and the subsequent war in eastern Ukraine in support of Russian separatists there. This, the first military violation of internationally agreed borders by a major power in Europe since 1945, was Putin's reaction to the 'loss' of Ukraine represented by the 'Euromaidan' revolution in February, and the toppling of president Yanukovich. The revolution followed months of protest at Yanukovich's withdrawal from EU accession talks, which most Ukrainians hoped would finally orient their country westward, rather than subordinating it indefinitely to Russia.

Russia's takeover of the Crimea, and its fomenting of ethnic Russian separatists in eastern Ukraine, in particular the regions of Donetsk and Luhansk, followed a familiar pattern of barefaced denial of involvement, accompanied by covert deployment of Russian technical advisers, the donation of military hardware including sophisticated surface-to-air missiles and, in the end, regular Russian army units. The halting attempts of the new Poroshenko government to regain control of eastern Ukraine were finally thwarted by direct Russian military intervention in September 2014, although not before pro-Russian separatists armed with guided missiles had mistakenly shot down a Malaysian Airlines commercial aircraft in July, killing all 300 people on board and provoking an international outcry. A bitter, seesaw struggle for control of territory was brought to a tentative close, after joint Franco-German mediation overseen by the OSCE, at Minsk in February 2015. According to the Minsk Agreement, Ukraine will be entitled to take back control of its own borders once a new, decentralised constitution has been enacted, and after elections have been held in Donetsk and Luhansk to determine the popular will. Neither of these pious provisions was likely to be met, and to date neither has been met. The Ukrainian conflict, like that in Transnistria, remains 'frozen', even though sporadic shelling by both sides remains a daily fact of life for denizens of the front line. What is clear is that Ukraine's prospects of setting its house in order and joining the EU have been effectively stymied for the foreseeable future.

The record of Poroshenko's government (2014–19) reflects this state of political limbo. Despite consolidating his hold on power in the parliamentary elections of October 2014, which saw a majority of votes go to pro-western parties, Poroshenko could neither implement Minsk and regain control of the rebel eastern provinces, nor, it seemed, get a handle on endemic corruption. Moves that proved popular with Ukrainian voters, like reinforcing Ukrainian language content in the media, and negotiating autocephaly or independence from the Moscow patriarchate for the Ukrainian Orthodox Church in 2018, risked alienating Russian-speaking voters.

So little seemed to have been achieved that, in May 2019, Poroshenko was swept from power by the comedian and actor Volodymyr Zelensky, who capitalised on his celebrity as the star of a television series, *Servant of the*

People, about a fictional Ukrainian president campaigning against corruption. Zelensky won the run-off election by a massive 73.2 per cent to Poroshenko's 24.5 per cent. Once inaugurated, he called new parliamentary elections in which his Servant of the People Party took 43 per cent of the vote, and 254 out of 424 seats. In office, however, Zelensky has struggled to implement his anti-corruption agenda, despite a lowering of tensions with Russia symbolised by an exchange of prisoners in late 2019. Zelensky instead achieved a less welcome celebrity when it transpired that President Trump, in a July 2019 telephone call, sought to trade the resumption of military aid to Ukraine in return for an investigation into the Ukrainian business dealings of the son of Joe Biden, one of Trump's potential rivals in the 2020 American presidential election.

At the same time international condemnation and limited sanctions have been visited upon Russia, but Putin clearly can live with this, while working ceaselessly to undermine western solidarity on the issue. While winding down active Russian involvement in eastern Ukraine after September 2015, in favour of intervention in Syria's civil war, Putin has nevertheless kept the Ukrainian separatist issue on the back-burner, capable of reheating at short notice. The result is a highly volatile situation on the EU's borders, made even more dangerous since 2016 by the perceived disunity of NATO, following the election of the nativist, isolationist President Trump. The latter's open hostility to the EU, distrust of multilateral associations and lukewarm attitude towards Article 5 of the NATO treaty, providing for mutual aid in the event of an attack on any NATO member-state, call the entire post-1989 security set-up in Eastern Europe into question. Comparisons with the breakdown of international order in the 1930s no longer seem exaggerated, and once again Eastern Europe is caught in the uncomfortable space between rival power blocs.

Conclusion

Retirement of a concept?

The introduction to this book laid out the rationale for treating Eastern Europe as a separate region in the course of the 'long' twentieth century. Throughout this period, East European societies have struggled with both economic and political backwardness; the region has been the seat of nationality problems arguably more numerous and complex than in Western Europe; and it has been the plaything of regional or external hegemons, in ways that Western Europe has not. It is hard not to conclude, two decades into the twenty-first century, that all three of these distinguishing characteristics still apply.

Part I of this book explained something of the complexity of Eastern Europe, its 'prehistory' and its making in the cauldron of the First World War. Part II treated the region largely as a test-tube for competing ideological experiments: liberal democracy, conservative authoritarianism, fascism and communism all vied for allegiance in this period, but the region's fate was ultimately determined by its unfortunate position between two fearsome regional powers, Nazi Germany and the Soviet Union, and at the end of unimaginable human suffering in the Second World War it was the latter of these two hegemons that dominated. Part III dealt with the grim consequences: the imposition of communism transformed Eastern Europe, but this came at a cost both to the economy and to the fundamental freedoms of the region's peoples. The whole exercise was only possible *via* dictatorship, and the paradoxical result was that this would-be modernising ideology left the region more backward, in comparative terms. Part IV examined the unique combination of factors leading to revolution in 1989: change in the Soviet Union, coupled with indigenous pressures, enabled most East Europeans to reclaim control of their own destiny. The collapse of communism has been politically liberating, but at the cost of painful economic adjustments, while democratic politics had an explosive effect on multinational states like Yugoslavia and the Soviet Union. Despite the undoubted boon, for many East European societies, of accession to the European Union, most are still coping with the legacies of the communist period, and recently there has been a worrying return to authoritarianism, not to mention the malign influence of a resurgent Russia.

Should the concept of Eastern Europe as a separate region be retired? The short answer has to be 'no', despite the undeniable convergence between Eastern and Western Europe since 1989 in economic conditions and political culture. No one travelling in much of Eastern Europe today, especially in urban centres, can fail to remark on how much more they now resemble western societies. Yet the differences persist. Not only are parts of Eastern Europe, those countries which have not managed the transition to EU membership or even to a fully functioning market economy or political pluralism, trapped in economic and political limbo, but this position leaves them exposed to pressure to throw in their lot with Russia, or to accept investment from Turkey (in the case of Muslim-dominated societies like Bosnia and Kosova) or even China. Given the recent abdication of leadership by the United States, China is in fact becoming increasingly visible in Eastern Europe, both as a market for raw materials and as an investor. The vulnerability and instability of those states excluded from the western 'clubs' of the EU and NATO leaves the rest of the region exposed as well: the Baltic states, Poland and Romania are inescapably concerned at the situation in Belarus and Ukraine; and the whole of the western Balkans is affected by the indeterminate condition of Bosnia, Kosova and, to some extent, Macedonia. As a result Eastern Europe remains 'in between' more powerful economic and political blocs.

There are three aspects to judging Eastern Europe's future direction. One is the extent to which economic prosperity can be more effectually ensured, a question with implications for political stability. A second is the role of ideology, in particular the enduring strength of nationalism in the region. A third is the continuing influence of external hegemons, especially Russia.

As we have seen, Eastern Europe's return, or exposure, to the world market in the past thirty years has been fraught with problems and social strain, despite the immense overall benefits. Where the transition was effected rapidly enough to force adaptation, yet with due care as to the effect on employment, as for instance in Poland, this has on the whole paid off; it is perhaps significant that Poland was one of the few European economies to weather the 2008 recession relatively unscathed. Those countries which opted for a gradual approach to marketisation have, predictably, spent longer coping with the negative legacies of communism. Nevertheless exposure to world economic forces has been risky even for the more advanced East European economies: the effect on these still fragile societies of the 2008 recession, and of the 2010 Eurozone crisis, has been severe, and has yet again tested their electorates' commitment to liberal democracy and their vulnerability to the consolations of nationalism. The effects of the coronavirus pandemic of 2020 are as yet impossible to evaluate, but are bound to be immense.

No one can study Eastern Europe's history in the period we have covered without acknowledging the role political ideologies have played in shaping East Europeans' fate. Millions of East Europeans have been active participants in these experiments. Whether a belief in liberal democracy, or nationalism and its Frankenstein monster fascism, or variants more or less benign or malign of socialism, or a reverence for authoritarian governance, Eastern Europe has seen them all. Nor should we ignore the genuine conviction with which so many

East Europeans subscribed to their chosen creed. Communists in the Stalinist period sincerely held that lies, torture and tyranny were essential ingredients in 'building socialism'. Western critics of East European nationalism in the present day overlook its importance in binding such societies together at their peril. Solidarity activists and dissidents like Václav Havel displayed a courage in defence of free speech and basic rights that most westerners have never needed to muster. Even the fanatics of Romania's Iron Guard acted out of a terrible idealism.

Yet the greatest of these ideologies remains nationalism. Since 1989, commitment to anything like the communism of the Soviet era appears a rarity; that experiment is thoroughly discredited, even if reformed communist parties have retained a following. Commitment to liberal democracy, by contrast, seemed until fairly recently to be holding up well. The attachment of East Europeans to an ethnic conception of the nation, however, remains on the whole greater than that of West Europeans, and has proved a powerful tool in the hands of an Orbán or a Kaczyński, not to mention Putin. And in the past decade and more nationalism's capacity for weakening the attractions of democracy is already again on display. This has to be one of the more worrying question-marks hanging over the region.

Finally, the role of outside powers is still an issue, mainly because of Russia's revived influence in the region. Both the EU and NATO, the latter backed by the indispensable clout of the United States, have acted as external hegemons since the fall of communism, and until recently their influence on Eastern Europe has on the whole been benign. Since the 2008 recession and especially the Eurozone crisis, however, the appeal of the EU is not what it was; and there can be no denying that Brussels' advocacy of a relatively liberal approach to asylum seekers and economic migrants has, since the crisis of 2015, not been received positively in most East European societies. NATO, too, has possibly been fatally undermined from the direction least expected, Washington, where the election in 2016 of a national populist and isolationist president, temperamentally averse to alliances and multilateral action, as well as disturbingly drawn to the Putins of this world, has already shaken confidence in NATO's cohesion. In this scenario, Eastern Europe once again looks vulnerable, at a time when it still needs a helping hand from the West.

Bibliography

I. General

General histories of Europe

Dinan, D., Nugent, N. and Paterson, W.E. (eds), 2017, *The European Union in Crisis*, London.

Eatwell, R. and Goodwin, M., 2018, *National Populism: The Revolt against Liberal Democracy*, London.

Ferguson, N., 2006, *The War of the World: Twentieth-Century Conflict and the Descent of the West*, London.

Halecki, O., 1962, *The Limits and Divisions of European History*, Notre Dame, IN.

Judt, T., 2001, *Postwar: A History of Europe since 1945*, New York.

Kirchick, J., 2018, *The End of Europe: Dictators, Demagogues and the Coming Dark Age*, New Haven, CT and London.

Krastev, I., 2017, *After Europe*, Philadelphia, PA.

Krastev, I. and Holmes, S., 2019, *The Light That Failed: A Reckoning*, London.

Marrus, M.R., 1985, *The Unwanted: European Refugees in the Twentieth Century*, New York.

Mazower, M., 1998, *Dark Continent: Europe's Twentieth Century*, London.

Mudde, C., 2016, *On Extremism and Democracy in Europe*, London and New York.

Müller, J.-W., 2016, *What Is Populism?*, Philadelphia, PA.

Panayi, P., 1999, *Outsiders: A History of European Minorities*, London and Rio Grande, OH.

Ther, P., 2018, *Europe after 1989: A History*, with a new preface by the author; translated by C. Hughes-Kreuzmüller, Princeton, NJ and Oxford.

Histories of eastern Europe

Barańczak, S., 1990, *Breathing under Water and Other East European Essays*, Cambridge, MA and London.

Bideleux, R. and Jeffries, I., 1998, *A History of Eastern Europe: Crisis and Change*, London and New York.

Chirot, D. (ed.), 1989, *The Origins of Backwardness in Eastern Europe: Economics and Politics from the Middle Ages until the Early Twentieth Century*, Berkeley, CA.

Crampton, R.J., 1997, *Eastern Europe in the Twentieth Century - And After*, 2nd edn, London and New York.

Crampton, R.J. and Crampton, B., 1996, *Atlas of Eastern Europe in the Twentieth Century*, London and New York.

Jelavich, B., 1983, *History of the Balkans*, vol. II: *Twentieth Century*, Cambridge and New York.

Longworth, P., 1997, *The Making of Eastern Europe: From Prehistory to Postcommunism*, 2nd edn, New York.

Mazower, M., 2000, *The Balkans: A Short History*, London.

Okey, R., 1986, *Eastern Europe 1740–1985: Feudalism to Communism*, Minneapolis, MN.

Okey, R., 1992, 'Central Europe/Eastern Europe: Behind the Definitions', *Past & Present*, 137 (November), 102–33.

Pavlowitch, S.K., 1999, *A History of the Balkans 1804–1945*, London and New York.

Pearson, R., 1983, *National Minorities of Eastern Europe 1848–1945*, London.

Pittaway, M., 2004, *Eastern Europe 1939–2000*, London and New York.

Snyder, T., 2003, *The Reconstruction of Nations: Poland, Ukraine, Lithuania, Belarus 1569–1999*, New Haven, CT and London.

Stokes, G., 1997, *Three Eras of Change in Eastern Europe*, Oxford.

Sugar, P.F. and Lederer, I.J. (eds), 1994, *Nationalism in Eastern Europe*, 2nd edn, Seattle, WA.

Prusin, A.V., 2010, *The Lands Between: Conflict in the East European Borderlands 1870–1992*, Oxford and New York.

Pre-1918 Origins of Eastern Europe

Armour, I.D., 2012, *A History of Eastern Europe 1740–1918: Empires, Nations and Modernisation*, 2nd edn, London.

Cornwall, M., 2002, 'Disintegration and Defeat: The Austro-Hungarian Revolution', in M. Cornwall (ed.), *The Last Years of Austria-Hungary: A Multi-National Experiment in Early Twentieth-Century Europe*, Exeter, 167–96.

Geyer, D., 1987, *Russian Imperialism: The Interaction of Domestic and Foreign Policy 1860–1914*, Leamington Spa, Hamburg and New York.

Kappeler, A., 2001, *The Russian Empire: A Multiethnic History*, Harlow.

Jelavich, C. and Jelavich, B., 1977, *The Establishment of the Balkan National States 1804–1920*, Seattle, WA.

Judson, P.M., 2016, *The Habsburg Empire: A New History*, Cambridge, MA and London.

MacFie, A.L., 1998, *The End of the Ottoman Empire 1908–1923*, London and New York.

Marin, I., 2013, *Contested Frontiers in the Balkans: Ottoman and Habsburg Rivalries in Eastern Europe*, London and New York.

Mason, J.W., 1997, *The Dissolution of the Austro-Hungarian Empire 1867–1918*, 2nd edn, London and New York.

May, A.J., 1968 [1951], *The Hapsburg Monarchy 1867–1914*, New York.

McCarthy, J., 2000, *The Ottoman Peoples and the End of Empire*, London.

Palairet, M., 1997, *The Balkan Economies c. 1800–1914: Evolution without Development*, Cambridge.

Porter, I. and Armour, I.D., 1991, *Imperial Germany 1890–1918*, London and New York.

Rogger, H., 1983, *Russia 1881–1917*, London and New York.

Roshwald, A., 2001, *Ethnic Nationalism and the Fall of Empires: Central Europe, the Middle East and Russia 1914–1923*, London and New York.

Rudolph, R.L. and Good, D.F. (eds), 1992, *Nationalism and Empire: The Habsburg Monarchy and the Soviet Union*, New York.

Seton-Watson, H., 1967, *The Russian Empire 1801–1917*, Oxford.

Wolff, L., 1994, *Inventing Eastern Europe: The Map of Civilization on the Mind of the Enlightenment*, Stanford, CA.

Nationalism and Transnationalism

Alter, P., 1994, *Nationalism*, 2nd edn, London.

Anderson, B., 1991, *Imagined Communities: Reflections on the Origin and Spread of Nationalism*, revised edition, London.

Baycroft, T., 1998, *Nationalism in Europe 1789–1945*, Cambridge.

Beller, S., 2005, 'Commentary: Central Europe Is Elsewhere', *Austrian History Yearbook*, XXXVI, 208–18.

Brunnbauer, U., 2018, 'Emigrants and Countries of Origin: The Politics of Emigration in Southeastern Europe until the First World War', in T. Snyder and K. Younger (eds), *The Balkans as Europe 1821-1914*, Rochester, NY, 78–109.

Gellner, E., 1983, *Nations and Nationalism*, Oxford.

Hobsbawm, E.J., 1992, *Nations and Nationalism since 1780: Programme, Myth, Reality*, 2nd edn, Cambridge.

Magocsi, P.R., 2005, 'In Step or Out of Step with the Times? Central Europe's Diasporas and Their Homelands in 1918 and 1989', *Austrian History Yearbook*, XXXVI, 167–89.

Naimark, N.M., 2001, *Fires of Hatred: Ethnic Cleansing in Twentieth-Century Europe*, Cambridge, MA.

Poliakov, L., 1974, *The Aryan Myth: A History of Racist and Nationalist Ideas in Europe*, translated by Edmund Howard, New York.

Ther, P., 2001, 'A Century of Forced Migration: The Origins and Consequences of "Ethnic Cleansing"', in P. Ther and A. Siljak (eds), *Redrawing Nations: Ethnic Cleansing in East-Central Europe 1944–1948*, Lanham, MD, 43–72.

Ther, P., 2013, 'Caught in Between: Border Regions in Modern Europe', in O. Bartov and E.D. Weitz (eds), *Shatterzone of Empires: Coexistence and Violence in the German, Habsburg, Russian and Ottoman Borderlands*, Bloomington, IN, 485–501.

Turda, M. and Weindling, P.J., 2007, 'Eugenics, Race and Nation in Central and Southeast Europe 1900–1940: A Historiographical Overview', in M. Turda and P.J. Weindling (eds), *Blood and Homeland: Eugenics and Racial Nationalism in Central and Southeast Europe 1900–1940*, Budapest and New York, 1–20.

Vick, B., 2006, 'Language and Nation: National Identity and the Civic-Ethnic Typology', in T. Baycroft and M. Hewitson (eds), *What Is A Nation? Europe 1789–1914*, Oxford and New York, 155–70.

Zahra, T., 2017, *The Great Departure: Mass Migration from Eastern Europe and the Making of the Free World*, reprint edition, New York.

Origins of the First World War

Bridge, F.R., 1972, *From Sadowa to Sarajevo: The Foreign Policy of Austria-Hungary 1866–1914*, London.

Bridge, F.R., 1983, *1914: The Coming of the First World War*, London.

Cornwall, M., 1995, 'Serbia', in K. Wilson (ed.), *Decisions for War, 1914*, London, 55–96.

Cornwall, M. (ed.), 2020, *Sarajevo 1914: Sparking the First World War*, London.

Hewitson, M., 2004, *Germany and the Causes of the First World War*, Oxford and New York.

Joll, J. and Martel, G., *The Origins of the First World War*, 3rd edn, Harlow.

Lynn, J., 2015, *Serbia and the Balkan Front: The Outbreak of the First World War*, London.

Mombauer, A., 2002, *The Origins of the First World War: Controversies and Consensus*, London and Toronto.

Spring, D.W., 1988, 'Russia and the Coming of War', in R.J.W. Evans and H. Pogge von Strandmann (eds), *The Coming of the First World War*, Oxford, 57–86.

Stevenson, D., 1996, *The Arming of Europe and the Making of the First World War*, Princeton, NJ.

Wawro, G., 2014, *A Mad Catastrophe: The Outbreak of World War I and the Collapse of the Habsburg Empire*, New York.

Williamson, S.R., Jr., 1991, *Austria-Hungary and the Origins of the First World War*, London.

The First World War

Calder, K., 1976, *Britain and the Origins of the New Europe 1914–1918*, Cambridge.

Chernev, B., 2011, 'The Brest-Litovsk Moment: Self-Determination Discourse in Eastern Europe before Wilsonianism', *Diplomacy & Statecraft*, XXII, #3 (September), 369–87.

Chernev, B., 2017, *Twilight of Empire: The Brest-Litovsk Conference and the Remaking of East-Central Europe 1917–1918*, Toronto.

Gerwarth, R., 2017, *The Vanquished: Why the First World War Failed to End 1917–1923*, London.

Gumz, J.E., 2009, *The Resurrection and Collapse of Habsburg Serbia 1914–1918*, Cambridge and New York.

Herwig, H.H., 1997, *The First World War: Germany and Austria-Hungary 1914–1918*, London, New York, Sydney and Auckland.

Liulevicius, V.G., 2000, *War Land on the Eastern Front: Culture, National Identity and German Occupation in World War I*, Cambridge.

Seton-Watson, H. and Seton-Watson, C., 1981, *The Making of a New Europe: R.W. Seton-Watson and the Last Years of Austria-Hungary*, London.

Stevenson, D., 2004, *Cataclysm: The First World War as Political Tragedy*, New York.

Stone, N., 1975, *The Eastern Front 1914–1917*, New York.

Watson, A., 2014, *Ring of Steel: Germany and Austria-Hungary at War 1914–1918*, London.

The Russian Revolutions

Figes, O., 1996, *A People's Tragedy: The Russian Revolution 1891–1924*, London.

Fitzpatrick, S., 1994, *The Russian Revolution*, 2nd edn, Oxford.

Pipes, R. (ed.), 1996, *The Unknown Lenin: From the Secret Archive*, New Haven, CT and London.

Service, R., 2005, *A History of Modern Russia from Nicholas II to Vladimir Putin*, Cambridge, MA.

Peace settlement of 1919–23

Adamthwaite, A., 1980, *The Lost Peace: International Relations in Europe 1918–1939*, London.

Baron, N. and Gatrell, P., 2004, 'Introduction', in N. Baron and P. Gatrell (eds), *Homelands: War, Population and Statehood in Eastern Europe and Russia 1918–1924*, London, 1–9.

Carsten, F.L., 1972, *Revolution in Central Europe 1918–1919*, Aldershot.

Dugdale, B.E.C. and Bewes, W.A., 1926, 'The Working of the Minority Treaties', *Journal of the British Institute of International Affairs*, V, #2 (March), 79–95.

Geiss, I., 1998, 'Armistice in Eastern Europe and the Fatal Sequels: Successor States and Wars 1918–23', in H. Cecil and P.H. Liddle (eds), *At the Eleventh Hour: Reflections, Hopes and Anxieties at the Closing of the Great War, 1918*, Barnsley, 237–54.

Goldstein, E., 2002, *The First World War Peace Settlements 1919–1925*, London.

Keylor, W.R. (ed.), 1997, *The Legacy of the Great War: Peacemaking 1919*, New York.

Mair, L.P., 1928, *The Protection of Minorities: The Working and Scope of the Minorities Treaties under the League of Nations*, London.

Sharp, A., 1978, 'Britain and the Protection of Minorities at the Paris Peace Conference, 1919', in A.C. Hepburn (ed.), *Minorities in History*, London, 170–8.

Sharp, A., 1991, *The Versailles Settlement: Peacemaking in Paris 1919*, Basingstoke and London.

Sharp, A., 1996, 'The Genie That Would Not Go Back Into the Bottle: National Self-Determination and the Legacy of the First World War and the Peace Settlement', in S. Dunn and T.G. Fraser (eds), *Europe and Ethnicity: World War I and Contemporary Ethnic Conflict*, London and New York, 10–29.

Wolff, L., 2020, *Woodrow Wilson and the Reimagining of Eastern Europe*, Stanford, CA.

Eastern Europe in the interwar period

Berend, I.T., 1998, *Decades of Crisis: Central and Eastern Europe before World War Two*, Berkeley, CA.

Chirot, D., 1989, 'Ideology, Reality and Competing Models of Development in Eastern Europe between the Two World Wars', *East European Politics and Societies*, III, #3 (Fall), 378–411.

Hehn, P.N., 2002, *A Low Dishonest Decade: The Great Powers, Eastern Europe and the Economic Origins of World War II 1930–1941*, New York.

Kaiser, D.E., 1980, *Economic Diplomacy and the Origins of the Second World War: Germany, Britain, France and Eastern Europe 1930–1939*, Princeton, NJ.

Lee, S.J., 2000, *The European Dictatorships 1918–1945*, 2nd edn, London.

Macartney, C.A., 1968 [1934], *National States and National Minorities*, New York.

Macartney, C.A. and Palmer, A.W., 1962, *Independent Eastern Europe*, London and New York.

Prażmowska, A.U., 2000, *Eastern Europe and the Origins of the Second World War*, London.

Rothschild, J., 1974, *East Central Europe between the Two World Wars*, Seattle, WA.

Seton-Watson, H., 1967 [1962], *Eastern Europe between the Wars 1918–1941*, 3rd edn, New York.

East European authoritarianism and fascism

Blinkhorn, M., 1990, 'Introduction: Allies, Rivals or Antagonists? Fascists and Conservatives in Modern Europe', in M. Blinkhorn (ed.), *Fascists and*

Conservatives: The Radical Right and the Establishment in Twentieth-Century Europe, London, 1–13.

Blinkhorn, M., 2000, *Fascism and the Right in Europe 1919–1945*, Harlow and Toronto.

Codreanu, C.Z., 1976 [1936], *For My Legionaries (The Iron Guard)*, Madrid.

Eatwell, R., 1997, *Fascism: A History*, New York.

Fischer, B.J. (ed.), 2007, *Balkan Strongmen: Dictators and Authoritarian Rulers of Southeast Europe*, West Lafayette, IN.

Griffin, R., 1993, *The Nature of Fascism*, London.

Haynes, R. and Rady, M. (eds), 2011, *In the Shadow of Hitler: Personalities of the Right in Central and Eastern Europe*, London and New York.

Knox, M., 1994, 'Conquest, Foreign and Domestic, in Fascist Italy and Nazi Germany', *Journal of Modern History*, LVI, #1 (March), 1–57.

Knox, M., 2000, *Common Destiny: Dictatorship, Foreign Policy and War in Fascist Italy and Nazi Germany*, Cambridge.

Laqueur, W. (ed.), 1976, *Fascism: A Reader's Guide: Analyses, Interpretations, Bibliography*, Berkeley, CA.

Larsen, S.U., Hagtvet, B. and Myklebust, J.P. (eds), 1980, *Who Were the Fascists? Social Roots of European Fascism*, Oslo.

Morgan, P., 2003, *Fascism in Europe 1918–1945*, London.

Mosse, G.L. (ed.), 1979, *International Fascism: New Thoughts and Approaches*, London and Beverly Hills.

Paxton, R.O., 1998, 'The Five Stages of Fascism', *Journal of Modern History*, LXX, #1 (March), 1–23.

Payne, S.G., 1995, *A History of Fascism 1914–1945*, London.

Riefenstahl, L., 2001 [1935], *Triumph of the Will: Triumph des Willens: das Dokument der Reichstparteitag 1934*, Bloomington, IL.

Roberts, D.R., 2006, *The Totalitarian Experiment in Twentieth-Century Europe: Understanding the Poverty of Great Politics*, New York and London.

Robinson, R.A.H., 1989, *Fascism in Europe 1919–1945*, London.

Sugar, P.F. (ed.), 1971, *Native Fascism in the Successor States 1918–1945*, Santa Barbara, CA.

Vágó, B., 1976, 'Fascism in Eastern Europe', in W. Laqueur (ed.), *Fascism: A Reader's Guide: Analyses, Interpretations, Bibliography*, Berkeley, CA, 229–53.

Weber, E., 1964, *Varieties of Fascism: Doctrines of Revolution in the Twentieth Century*, New York.

Weber, E., 1965, 'Introduction', in H. Rogger and E. Weber (eds), *The European Right: A Historical Profile*, London, 1–28.

Woolf, S.J. (ed.), 1981, *Fascism in Europe*, London.

Stalinist Russia and East European Communism to 1941

Allworth, E. (ed.), 1971, *Soviet Nationality Problems*, New York.

Applebaum, A., 2004, *Gulag: A History*, New York.

Conquest, R., 1986, *The Harvest of Sorrow: Soviet Collectivization and the Terror-Famine*, London.

Conquest, R., 1992, *The Great Terror: A Reassessment*, London.

Courtois, S. et al. (eds), 1999, *The Black Book of Communism: Crimes, Terror, Repression*, Cambridge, MA.

Furet, F., 1999, *The Passing of an Illusion: The Idea of Communism in the Twentieth Century*, translated by Deborah Furet, Chicago, IL and London.

Hosking, G., 1992, *A History of the Soviet Union 1917–1991*, final edition, London.

Jackson, G.D., Jr., 1966, *Comintern and Peasant in Eastern Europe 1919–1930*, New York and London.

Kenez, P., 2006, *A History of the Soviet Union from the Beginning to the End*, 2nd edn, New York.

Khrushchev, N., 1971, *Khrushchev Remembers*, translated by Strobe Talbot, with an introduction, commentary and notes by Edward Crankshaw, London.

Martin, T., 2001, *The Affirmative Action Empire: Nations and Nationalism in the Soviet Union 1923–1939*, Ithaca, NY.

McCauley, M., 1993, *The Soviet Union 1917–1991*, 2nd edn, London.

McDermott, K. and Agnew, J., 1997, *The Comintern: A History of International Communism from Lenin to Stalin*, New York.

Pipes, R., 2001, *Communism: A History*, New York.

Read, C., 2001, *The Making and Breaking of the Soviet System: An Interpretation*, Basingstoke and New York.

Rees, T. and Thorpe, A. (eds), 1998, *International Communism and the Communist International 1919–1943*, Manchester.

Seton-Watson, H., 1960, *The Pattern of Communist Revolution: A Historical Analysis*, revised edition, London.

Eastern Europe in the Second World War

Alexievich, S., 2017, *The Unwomanly Face of War*, translated by R. Pevear and L. Volokhonsky, London.

Bartov, O., 1994, *Hitler's Army: Soldiers, Nazis and War in the Third Reich*, Oxford.

Bell, P.M.H., 1986, *The Origins of the Second World War in Europe*, London and New York.

Browning, C.R., 2004, *The Origins of the Final Solution: The Evolution of Nazi Jewish Policy Sept. 1939–March 1942*, with contributions by Jürgen Matthäus, Lincoln, NE.

Chickering, R., Förster, S. and Greiner, B. (eds), 2005, *A World at Total War: Global Conflict and the Politics of Destruction 1937–1945*, Cambridge.

Churchill, W.S., 1954, *The Second World War*, vol. 6: *Triumph and Tragedy*, London.

Dallin, A., 1981, *German Rule in Russia 1941–1945: A study of Occupation Policies*, 2nd edn, London.

Drapac, V. and Pritchard, G., 2017, *Resistance and Collaboration in Hitler's Empire*, London.

Förster, S., 2007, 'Total War and Genocide: Reflections on the Second World War', *Australian Journal of Politics & History*, LIII, #1 (March), 68–83.

Fritz, S.G., 2011, *Ostkrieg: Hitler's War of Extermination in the East*, Lexington, KY.

Gross, J., 1998, 'War as Revolution', in N. Naimark and L. Gibianskii (eds), *The Establishment of Communist Regimes in Eastern Europe 1944–1949*, Boulder, CO, 17–40.

Harvey, E., 2003, *Women and the Nazi East: Agents and Witnesses of Germanization*, New Haven, CT and London.

Heinemann, I., 2013, 'Defining "(Un)Wanted Population Addition": Anthropology, Racist Ideology and Mass Murder in the Occupied East', in A. Weiss-Wendt and

R. Yeomans (eds), *Racial Science in Hitler's New Europe 1938–1945*, Lincoln, NE and London, 35–59.

Mastný, V., 1976, *Russia's Road to the Cold War: Diplomacy, Warfare and the Politics of Communism 1941–1945*, New York.

Mazower, M., 2008, *Hitler's Empire: Nazi Rule in Occupied Europe*, London.

Overy, R., 1997, *Russia's War*, London.

Plokhy, S., 2010, *Yalta: The Price of Peace*, New York.

Smith, W.D., 1986, *The Ideological Origins of Nazi Imperialism*, Oxford.

Snyder, T., 2010, *Bloodlands: Europe between Hitler and Stalin*, New York.

Ther, P., 2001, 'A Century of Forced Migration: The Origins and Consequences of "Ethnic Cleansing"', in P. Ther and A. Siljak (eds), *Redrawing Nations: Ethnic Cleansing in East-Central Europe 1944–1948*, Lanham, MD, Boulder, CO, New York and Oxford, 43–72.

Weiss-Wendt, A. and Yeomans, R. (eds), 2013, *Racial Science in Hitler's New Europe 1938–1945*, Lincoln, NE and London.

Wright, G., 1968, *The Ordeal of Total War 1939–1945*, New York.

The Cold War

Gaddis, J.L., 1997, *We Now Know: Rethinking Cold War History*, Oxford and New York.The Cold War

Gaddis, J.L., 2005, *The Cold War: A New History*, New York.

McCauley, M., 2003, *The Origins of the Cold War 1941–1949*, 3rd edn, London and New York.

Westad, O.A., 2018, *The Cold War: A World History*, London.

Wilson Center Digital Archive. http://digitalarchive.wilsoncenter.org/document/11 6224

Communist Eastern Europe 1945–89

Applebaum, A., 2012, *Iron Curtain: The Crushing of Eastern Europe 1945–1956*, London.

Berend, I.T., 1996, *Central and Eastern Europe 1944–1993: Detour from the Periphery to the Periphery*, Cambridge and New York.

Berend, I.T., 2009, *From the Soviet Bloc to the European Union: The Economic and Social Transformation of Central and Eastern Europe since 1973*, Cambridge and New York.

Bren, P. and Neuburger, M.C. (eds), 2012, *Communism Unwrapped: Consumption in Cold War Eastern Europe*, Oxford and New York.

Brzezinski, Z.K., 1967, *The Soviet Bloc: Unity and Conflict*, 2nd edn, Cambridge.

Connelly, J., 2000, *Captive University: The Sovietization of East German, Czech and Polish Higher Education 1945–1956*, Princeton, NJ.

Fejtö, F., 1974, *A History of the People's Democracies: Eastern Europe since Stalin*, translated from the French by Daniel Weissbrot, Harmondsworth.

Fowkes, B., 2000, *Eastern Europe 1945–1969: From Stalinism to Stagnation*, Harlow.

Gati, C., 1990, *The Bloc That Failed: Soviet-East European Relations in Transition*, London.

Hammond, T.T., 1975, 'The History of Communist Takeovers', in T.T. Hammond and R. Farrell (eds), *The Anatomy of Communist Takeovers*, New Haven, CT and London, 1–45.

Keep, J.L.H., 1995, *Last of the Empires: A History of the Soviet Union 1945–1991*, Oxford and New York.

Lendvai, P., 1971, *Anti-Semitism in Eastern Europe*, London.

McDermott, K. and Stibbe, M. (eds), 2006, *Revolution and Resistance in Eastern Europe: Challenges to Communist Rule*, Oxford and New York.

McDermott, K. and Stibbe, M. (eds), 2010, *Stalinist Terror in Eastern Europe: Elite Purges and Mass Repression*, Manchester.

Naimark, N. and Gibianskii, L. (eds), 1998, *The Establishment of Communist Regimes in Eastern Europe 1944–1949*, Boulder, CO.

Pittaway, M., 2004, *Eastern Europe: States and Societies 1945–2000*, London and New York.

Plokhy, S., 2018, *Chernobyl: History of a Tragedy*, London.

Rothschild, J., 1989, *Return to Diversity: A Political History of East Central Europe since World War II*, Oxford.

Ryback, T.W., 1990, *Rock Around the Bloc: A History of Rock Music in Eastern Europe and the Soviet Union*, New York.

Schöpflin, G., 1993, *Politics in Eastern Europe 1945–1992*, Oxford and Cambridge, MA.

Seton-Watson, H., 1956, *The East European Revolution*, 3rd edn, New York.

Stokes, G., 1996, *From Stalinism to Pluralism: A Documentary History of Eastern Europe since 1945*, 2nd edn, New York.

Swain, G. and Swain, N., 2003, *Eastern Europe since 1945*, 3rd edn, Basingstoke and New York.

Todorova, M., Dimou, A. and Troebst, S. (eds), 2014, *Remembering Communism: Private and Public Recollections of Lived Experience in Southeast Europe*, Budapest.

White, S., 2001, *Communism and Its Collapse*, London.

Zeman, Z.A.B., 1991, *The Making and Breaking of Communist Europe*, revised edition, Oxford and Cambridge, MA.

The revolutions of 1989 and their causes

Betts, P., 2019, '1989 at Thirty: A Recast Legacy', *Past and Present*, 244, #1 (August), 271–305.

Breslauer, G.W., 2002, *Gorbachev and Yeltsin as Leaders*, Cambridge and New York.

Brown, A., 1997, *The Gorbachev Factor*, Oxford and New York.

Brown, A., 2020, *The Human Factor: Gorbachev, Reagan and Thatcher and the End of the Cold War*, Oxford and New York.

Brown, J.F., 1991, *Surge to Freedom: The End of Communism in Eastern Europe*, Durham, NC.

Brown, J.F., 1994, *Hopes and Shadows: Eastern Europe after Communism*, Durham, NC.

Doder, D., 1986, *Shadows and Whispers: Power Politics Inside the Kremlin from Brezhnev to Gorbachev*, London.

Engel, J.A. (ed.), 2009, *The Fall of the Berlin Wall: The Revolutionary Legacy of 1989*, New York.

Galeotti, M., 1997, *Gorbachev and His Revolution*, New York.

Garton Ash, T., 1990, *We the People: The Revolution of '89 Witnessed in Warsaw, Budapest, Berlin and Prague*, London.

Gorbachev, M., 1988, *Perestroika: New Thinking for Our Country and the World*, new updated edition, London.

Gorbachev, M. and Mlynář, Z., 2003, *Conversations with Gorbachev: On Perestroika, the Prague Spring and the Crossroads of Socialism*, New York and Chichester.

Kenney, P., 2002, *A Carnival of Revolution: Central Europe 1989*, Princeton, NJ.

Kotkin, S., 2009, *Uncivil Society: 1989 and the Implosion of the Communist Establishment*, with a contribution by J.T. Gross, New York.

Kramer, M., 2009, 'The Myth of a No-NATO Enlargement Pledge to Russia', *The Washington Quarterly*, XXXII, #2 (April), 39–61.

Kramer, M., 2011, 'The Demise of the Soviet Bloc', *Journal of Modern History*, LXXXIII, #4 (December), 788–854.

Lévesque, J., 1997, *The Enigma of 1989: The USSR and the Liberation of Eastern Europe*, Berkeley, CA.

McCauley, M., 1998, *Gorbachev*, Harlow and New York.

McCauley, M. (ed.), 1998, *The Soviet Union under Gorbachev*, New York.

Okey, R., 2004, *The Demise of Communist Eastern Europe: 1989 in Context*, London and New York.

Plokhy, S., 2018, *Chernobyl: History of a Tragedy*, London.

Saranskaya, S. et al., 2010, 'Chronology of Events', in S. Savranskaya, T. Blanton and V. Zubok (eds), *Masterpieces of History: The Peaceful End of the Cold War in Europe*, Budapest, xix–xliv.

Sarotte, M.E., 2009, *1989: The Struggle to Create Post-Cold War Europe*, Princeton, NJ and Oxford.

Stokes, G., 1993, *The Walls Came Tumbling Down: The Collapse of Communism in Eastern Europe*, New York and Oxford.

Stokes, G., 2012, *The Walls Came Tumbling Down: Collapse and Rebirth in Eastern Europe*, 2nd edn, Oxford.

Tismaneanu, V. (ed.), 1999, *The Revolutions of 1989*, London and New York.

Post-Communist Eastern Europe

Berglund, S., Ekman, J. and Aarebrot, F.H. (eds), 2004, *The Handbook of Political Change in Eastern Europe*, 2nd edn, Cheltenham and Northampton, MA.

Borneman, J., 1997, *Settling Accounts: Violence, Justice and Accountability in Postsocialist Europe*, Princeton, NJ.

Cohen, S.J., 1999, *Politics Without a Past: The Absence of History in Post-Communist Nationalism*, Durham, NC.

Dawisha, K. and Parrott, B. (eds), 1997, *Democratic Changes and Authoritarian Reactions in Russia, Ukraine, Belarus and Moldova*, Cambridge and New York.

Dawisha, K. and Parrott, B. (eds), 1997, *Politics, Power and the Struggle for Democracy in South-East Europe*, Cambridge and New York.

Duke, V. and Grime, K., 1994, 'Privatization in East-Central Europe: Similarities and Contrasts in Its Application', in C.G.A. Bryant and E. Mokrzycki (eds), *The New Great Transformation? Change and Continuity in East-Central Europe*, London and New York, 144–70.

Garton Ash, T., 1999, The *Uses of Adversity: Essays on the Fate of Central Europe*, Cambridge.

Glenny, M., 1993, The *Rebirth of History: Eastern Europe in the Age of Democracy*, 2nd edn, London.

Grabbe, H., 2006, *The EU's Transformative Power: Europeanization through Conditionality in Central and Eastern Europe*, Basingstoke and New York.

Hamm, P., King, L.P. and Stuckler, D., 2012, 'Mass Privatization, State Capacity and Economic Growth', *American Sociological Review*, LXXVII, #2 (April), 295–324.

Haughton, T., 2017, 'Central and Eastern Europe: The Sacrifices of Solidarity, the Discomforts of Diversity, and the Vexations of Vulnerabilities', in D. Dinan, N. Nugent and W.E. Paterson (eds), *The European Union in Crisis*, London, 253–68.

Himka, J.-P. and Michlic, J.B. (eds), 2013, *Bringing the Dark Past to Light: The Reception of the Holocaust in Postcommunist Europe*, Lincoln, NE.

Hockenos, P., 1993, *Free to Hate: The Rise of the Right in Post-Communist Eastern Europe*, New York.

Kenney, P., 2006, *The Burdens of Freedom: Eastern Europe since 1989*, Black Point, NS and Fernwood, NY.

Kramer, M., 2003, 'The Collapse of East European Communism and the Repercussions within the Soviet Union (Part 1)', *Journal of Cold War Studies*, V, #4 (Fall), 178–256.

Kramer, M., 2004, 'The Collapse of East European Communism and the Repercussions within the Soviet Union (Part 2)', *Journal of Cold War Studies*, VI, #4 (Fall), 3–64.

Kramer, M., 2005, 'The Collapse of East European Communism and the Repercussions within the Soviet Union (Part 3)', *Journal of Cold War Studies*, VII, #1 (Winter), 3–96.

Mark, J., 2010, *The Unfinished Revolution: Making Sense of the Communist Past in Central-Eastern Europe*, New Haven and London.

Marples, D.R., 2004, *The Collapse of the Soviet Union 1985–1991*, Harlow.

Michnik, A., 2011, *In Search of Lost Meaning: The New Eastern Europe*, edited by Irena Grudzińska Gross, Berkeley, CA.

Millar, J.R. and Wolchik, S.L. (eds.), 1994, *The Social Legacy of Communism*, Washington, DC, Cambridge and New York.

Plokhy, S., 2014, *The Last Empire: The Final Days of the Soviet Union*, London.

Pond, E., 2006, *Endgame in the Balkans: Regime Change European Style*, Washington, DC.

Poulton, H., 1989, *Minorities in the Balkans*, London.

Pridham, G. and Vanhanen, T. (eds), 1994, *Democratization in Eastern Europe: Domestic and International Perspectives*, London and New York.

Ramet, S.P., 1995, *Social Currents in Eastern Europe: The Sources and Consequences of the Great Transformation*, 2nd edn, Durham, NC.

Ramet, S.P., 1997, *Whose Democracy? Nationalism, Religion and the Doctrine of Collective Rights in Post-1989 Eastern Europe*, Lanham, MD.

Rosenberg, T., 1995, *The Haunted Land: Facing Europe's Ghosts after Communism*, London.

Rupnik, J., 2014, 'From the Revolutions of 1989 to Democracy Fatigue in Eastern Europe', in J. Rupnik (ed.), *1989 as a Political World Event: Democracy, Europe and the New International System in the Age of Globalization*, London and New York, 56–71.

Schöpflin, G., 2000, *Nations, Identity, Power: The New Politics of Europe*, London.

Tismaneanu, V., 1998, *Fantasies of Salvation: Democracy, Nationalism and Myth in Post-Communist Europe*, Princeton, NJ.

Todorova, M. and Gille, Z. (eds), 2012, *Postcommunist Nostalgia*, New York.

Vaduchová, M.A., 2005, *Europe Undivided: Democracy, Leverage and Integration after Communism*, Oxford and New York.

White, S., Batt, J. and Lewis, P.G. (eds), 1993, *Developments in East European Politics*, Basingstoke.

Wilson, A., 2005, *Virtual Politics: Faking Democracy in the Post-Soviet World*, New Haven.

Wolchik, S.L. and Curry, J.L. (eds), 2008, *Central and East European Politics: From Communism to Democracy*, Lanham, MD.

II: Individual people and countries

Albanians, inc. Kosovo/Kosova

Fischer, B.J., 1984, *King Zog and the Struggle for Political Stability in Albania*, Boulder, CO.

Fischer, B.J., 1999, *Albania at War 1939–1945*, West Lafayette, IN.

Halliday, J., 1986, *The Artful Albanian: The Memoirs of Enver Hoxha*, London.

Judah, T., 2000, *Kosovo: War and Revenge*, New Haven and London.

Kapllani, G., 2009, *A Short Border Handbook*, translated by Anne-Marie Stanton-Ife, London.

Malcolm, N., 1998, *Kosovo: A Short History*, Basingstoke and London.

Marmullaku, R., 1975, *Albania and the Albanians*, Hamden, CT.

Vickers, M., 1999, *The Albanians: A Modern History*, revised edition, London and New York.

Vickers, M. and Pettifer, J., 2000, *Albania: From Anarchy to a Balkan Identity*, 2nd edn, New York.

Austria

Beller, S., 2006, *A Concise History of Austria*, Cambridge and New York.

Jedlicka, L., 1966, 'The Austrian Heimwehr', *Journal of Contemporary History*, I, #1 (April), 127–44.

Jelavich, B., 1987, *Modern Austria: Empire and Republic 1815–1986*, Cambridge.

Kirk, T., 2003, 'Fascism and Austrofascism', in G. Bischof, A. Pelinka and A. Lassner (eds), *The Dollfuss/Schuschnigg Era in Austria: A Reassessment*, New Brunswick, NJ and London, 10–31.

Lewis, J., 1990, 'Conservatives and Fascists in Austria 1918–34', in M. Blinkhorn (ed.), *Fascists and Conservatives: The Radical Right and the Establishment in Twentieth Century Europe*, London, 98–117.

Pick, H., 2000, *Guilty Victim: Austria from the Holocaust to Haider*, London and New York.

Baltic Peoples: Estonians, Latvians and Lithuanians

Eksteins, M., 2000, *Walking since Daybreak: A Story of Eastern Europe, World War II and the Heart of the Twentieth Century*, New York.

Kalnins, M., 2015, *Latvia: A Short History*, London.

Kasekamp, A., 2018, *A History of the Baltic States*, 2nd edn, London.

Kirby, D., 1995, *The Baltic World 1772–1993: Europe's Northern Periphery in an Age of Change*, London and New York.

Lieven, A., 1994, *The Baltic Revolution: Estonia, Latvia, Lithuania and the Path to Independence* , 2nd edn, New Haven and London.

Lukša, J., 2009, *Forest Brothers: The Account of an Anti-Soviet Lithuanian Freedom Fighter 1944–1948*, translated by Laima Vincė, Budapest and New York.

Misiunas, R. and Taagepera, R., 1993, *The Baltic States: Years of Dependence 1940–1990*, expanded & updated edition, London.

Plakans, A., 2011, *A Concise History of the Baltic States*, Cambridge.

Purs, A., 2010, 'Soviet in Form, Local in Content: Elite Repression and Mass Terror in the Baltic States 1940–1953', in K. McDermott and M. Stibbe (eds), *Stalinist Terror in Eastern Europe: Elite Purges and Mass Repression*, Manchester and New York, 19–38.

Purs, A., 2012, *Baltic Facades: Estonia, Latvia and Lithuania since 1945*, London.

Rauch, G. von, 1970, *The Baltic States: The Years of Independence 1917–1940: Estonia, Latvia, Lithuania*, translated by Gerald Onn, Berkeley and Los Angeles, CA.

Taagepera, R., 1993, *Estonia: Return to Independence*, Boulder, CO.

Taylor, N., 2018, *Estonia: A Modern History*, London.

Vardys, V.S., 1963, 'The Partisan Movement in Postwar Lithuania', *Slavic Review*, XXII, #3 (September), 499–522.

Vardys, V.S. and Sedaitis, J.B. (eds), 1997, *Lithuania: The Rebel Nation*, Boulder, CO.

Weiss-Wendt, A., 2009, *Murder without Hatred: Estonians and the Holocaust*, Syracuse, NY.

Belorussians

Marples, D.R., 1999, *Belarus: A Denationalized Nation*, Amsterdam.

Nolte, H.-H., 2005, 'Partisan War in Belorussia 1941–1944', in R. Chickering, S. Förster and B. Greiner (eds), *A World at Total War: Global Conflict and the Politics of Destruction 1937–1945*, Cambridge, 261–76.

Wilson, A., 2012, *Belarus: The Last European Dictatorship*, New Haven, CT and London.

Zaprudnik, J., 1993, *Belarus: At a Crossroads in History*, Boulder, CO, San Francisco, CA and Oxford.

Bulgarians

Bell, J.D., 1977, *Peasants in Power: Alexander Stamboliski and the Bulgarian Agrarian National Union 1899-1923*, Princeton, NJ.

Crampton, R.J., 2005, *A Concise History of Bulgaria*, 2nd edn, Cambridge and New York.

Dimitrov, V., 2008, *Stalin's Cold War: Soviet Foreign Policy, Democracy and Communism in Bulgaria 1941–1948*, Basingstoke and New York.

Kassabova, K., 2008, *Street without a Name: Childhood and Other Misadventures in Bulgaria*, London.

McIntyre, R.J., 1988, *Bulgaria: Politics, Economics and Society*, London and New York.

Rothschild, J., 1959, *The Communist Party of Bulgaria: Origins and Development 1883–1936*, New York.

Todorov, T., 1999, *Voices from the Gulag: Life and Death in Communist Bulgaria*, translated by Robert Zaretsky, University Park, PA.

Todorov, T., 2001, *The Fragility of Goodness: Why Bulgaria's Jews Survived the Holocaust; A Collection of Texts*, Princeton, NJ.

Czechs and Slovaks

Agnew, H., 2004, *The Czechs and the Lands of the Bohemian Crown*, Stanford, CA.

Bischof, G., Karner, S. and Ruggenthaler, P. (eds), 2010, *The Prague Spring and the Warsaw Pact Invasion of Czechoslovakia in 1968*, Lanham, MD.

Bolton, J., 2012, *Worlds of Dissent: Charter 77, the Plastic People of the Universe and Czech Culture under Communism*, Cambridge, MA.

Bradley, J.F.N., 1991, *Politics in Czechoslovakia 1945–1990*, New York.

Bren, P., 2010, *The Greengrocer and His TV: The Culture of Communism after the 1968 Prague Spring*, Ithaca, NY.

Bren, P., 2013, 'Tuzex and the Hustler: Living It Up in Czechoslovakia', in P. Bren and M.C. Neuburger (eds), *Communism Unwrapped: Consumption in Cold War Eastern Europe*, Oxford and New York, 27–48.

Bruegel, J.W., 1973, *Czechoslovakia before Munich: The German Minority Problem and British Appeasement Policy*, Cambridge.

Bryant, C., 2007, *Prague in Black: Nazi Rule and Czech Nationalism*, Cambridge, MA.

Cornwall, M., 2011, 'The Czechoslovak Sphinx: "Moderate and Reasonable" Konrad Henlein', in R. Haynes and M. Rady (eds), *In the Shadow of Hitler: Personalities of the Right in Central and Eastern Europe*, London, 206–26.

Cornwall, M. and Evans, R.J.W. (eds), 2007, *Czechoslovakia in a Nationalist and Fascist Europe 1918–1948*, Oxford and New York.

Długoborski, W., 2002, *The Tragedy of the Jews of Slovakia 1938–1945: Slovakia and the 'Final Solution of the Jewish Question'*, Oświęcim and Banska Bystrica.

Dubcek, A., 1993, *Hope Dies Last: The Autobiography of Alexander Dubcek*, edited and translated by J. Hochman, London.

El Mallakh, D., 1979, *The Slovak Autonomy Movement 1935–1939: A Study in Unrelenting Nationalism*, New York.

Felak, J.R., 1994, *'At the Price of the Republic': Hlinka's Slovak People's Party 1929–1938*, Pittsburgh, PA.

Frommer, B., 2005, *National Cleansing: Retribution against Nazi Collaborators in Postwar Czechoslovakia*, Cambridge and New York.

Havel, V. et al., 1985, *The Power of the Powerless: Citizens against the State in Central-Eastern Europe*, London.

Havel, V., 1987, *Living in Truth*, edited by J. Vladislav, London and Boston, MA.

Havel, V., 2008, *To the Castle and Back*, Toronto.

Hoensch, J., 1987, 'Slovakia: "One God, One People, One Party!"', in R. Wolff and J. Hoensch (eds), *Catholics, the State and the European Radical Right 1919–1945*, New York, 159–77.

Holy, L., 1996, *The Little Czech and the Great Czech Nation: National Identity and the Post-Communist Social Transformation*, Cambridge and New York.

Jelinek, Y.A., 1976, *The Parish Republic: Hlinka's Slovak People's Party 1939–1945*, Boulder, CO.

Josko, A., 1973, 'The Slovak Resistance Movement', in V.S. Mamatey and Luža (eds), *A History of the Czechoslovak Republic 1918–1948*, Princeton, NJ, 362–84.

Judt, T., 1992, 'Metamorphosis: The Democratic Revolution in Czechoslovakia', in I. Banac (ed.), *Eastern Europe in Revolution*, Ithaca, NY and London, 96–116.

Kirschbaum, S.J., 2005, *A History of Slovakia: The Struggle for Survival*, 2nd edn, New York.

Korbel, J., 1959, *The Communist Subversion of Czechoslovakia 1938–1948: The Failure of Coexistence*, London.

Korbel, J., 1977, *Twentieth-Century Czechoslovakia: The Meanings of Its History*, New York.

Kovály, H.M., 1986 [1973], *Under a Cruel Star: A Life in Prague 1941–1968*, Harmondsworth.

Kusin, A.V., 1971, *The Intellectual Origins of the Prague Spring: The Development of Reformist Ideas in Czechoslovakia 1956–1967*, Cambridge.

Lorman, T.A., 2011, 'The Christian Social Roots of Jozef Tiso's Radicalism 1887–1939', in R. Haynes and M. Rady (eds), *In the Shadow of Hitler: Personalities of the Right in Central and Eastern Europe*, London and New York, 245–60.

Lukes, I., 1996, *Czechoslovakia between Stalin and Hitler: The Diplomacy of Edvard Beneš in the 1930s*, New York and Oxford.

Luža, R., 1973, 'The Czech Resistance Movement', in V.S. Mamatey and R. Luža (eds), *A History of the Czechoslovak Republic 1918–1948*, Princeton, NJ, 343–61.

Mamatey, V.S. and Luža, R. (eds), 1973, *A History of the Czechoslovak Republic 1918–1948*, Princeton, NJ.

Margolius, I., 2006, *Reflections of Prague: Journeys through the 20th Century*, Chichester and Hoboken, NJ.

McRae, R., 1997, *Resistance and Revolution: Václav Havel's Czechoslovakia*, Ottawa.

Mlynář, Z., 1980, *Night Frost in Prague: The End of Humane Socialism*, New York.

Musil, J. (ed.), 1995, *The End of Czechoslovakia*, Budapest.

Myant, M., 1989, *The Czechoslovak Economy 1948–1988: The Battle for Economic Reform*, Cambridge and New York.

Olivová, V., 1972, *The Doomed Democracy: Czechoslovakia in a Disrupted Europe 1914–1938*, London.

Orzoff, A., 2009, *Battle for the Castle: The Myth of Czechoslovakia in Europe 1914–1948*, New York.

Sayer, D., 1998, *The Coasts of Bohemia: A Czech History*, Princeton, NJ.

Shawcross, W., 1990, *Dubcek: Dubcek and Czechoslovakia 1918–1990*, London.

Šimečka, M., 1984, *The Restoration of Order: The Normalization of Czechoslovakia 1969–1976*, translated by A.G. Brian, London.

Šimečka, M., 2002, *Letters from Prison*, selected and translated by Gerald Turner, Prague.

Stein, E., 1997, *Czecho/Slovakia: Ethnic Conflict, Constitutional Fissure, Negotiated Breakup*, Ann Arbor, MI.

Teich, M., Kováč, D. and Brown, M.D. (eds), 2011, *Slovakia in History*, Cambridge and New York.

Ward, J.M., 2013, *Priest, Politician, Collaborator: Jozef Tiso and the Making of Fascist Slovakia*, Ithaca, NY and London.

Wheaton, B. and Kavan, Z., 1991, *The Velvet Revolution: Czechoslovakia 1988–1991*, Boulder, CO.

Whipple, T. (ed.), 1991, *After the Velvet Revolution: Václav Havel and the New Leaders of Czechoslovakia Speak Out*, London.

Wiskemann, E., 1967, *Czechs and Germans: A Study of the Struggle in the Historic Provinces of Bohemia and Moravia*, 2nd edn, London.

Zahra, T., 2008, *Kidnapped Souls: National Indifference and the Battle for Children in the Bohemian Lands 1900–1945*, Ithaca, NY.

Žák, V., 1995, 'The Velvet Divorce: Institutional Foundations', in J. Musil (ed.), *The End of Czechoslovakia*, Budapest, London and New York, 245–68.

Zeman, Z., 1976, *The Masaryks: The Making of Czechoslovakia*, London.

Finns

Alapuro, R., 1988, *State and Revolution in Finland*, Berkeley, CA.

Edwards, R., 2006, *White Death: Russia's War on Finland 1939–40*, London.

Kirby, D., 2006, *A Concise History of Finland*, Cambridge.

Kirby, D., 2011, 'A Scandinavian Erratic amidst the Ruins of Empire: The Finnish Case 1918–1944', in R. Haynes and M. Rady (eds), *In the Shadow of Hitler: Personalities of the Right in Central and Eastern Europe*, London and New York, 138–52.

Rintala, M., 1962, *Three Generations: The Extreme Right in Finnish Politics*, Bloomington, IN.

Screen, J.E.O., 2014, *Mannerheim: The Finnish Years*, London.

Singleton, F., 1998, *A Short History of Finland*, revised and updated by A.F. Upton, Cambridge and New York.

Upton, A., 1980, *The Finnish Revolution 1917–1918*, Minneapolis, MN.

Former Soviet Union

Fisher, A.W., 1978, *The Crimean Tatars*, Stanford, CA.

Goldman, M.I., 2008, *Petrostate: Putin, Power, and the New Russia*, Oxford and New York.

Lucas, E., 2008, *The New Cold War: Putin's Russia and the Threat to the West*, New York.

McCauley, M., 2001, *Bandits, Gangsters and the Mafia: Russia, the Baltic States and the CIS since 1991*, Harlow.

Odom, W.E., 1998, *The Collapse of the Soviet Military*, New Haven and London.

Politkovskaya, A., 2004, *Putin's Russia: Life in a Failing Democracy*, New York.

Suny, R.G., 1998, *The Soviet Experiment: Russia, the USSR and the Successor States*, New York.

Williams, B., 2001, *The Crimean Tatars: The Diaspora Experience and the Forging of a Nation*, Leiden.

Yavlinsky, G., 2019, *The Putin System: An Opposing View*, New York.

Germans

Ahonen, P., 2003, *After the Expulsion: West Germany and Eastern Europe 1945–1990*, Oxford and New York.

Bendersky, J.W., 2007, *A Concise History of Nazi Germany*, 3rd edn, Lanham, MD.

Bruce, G., 2011, *The Firm: The Inside Story of the Stasi*, New York.

Burleigh, M., 2001, *The Third Reich: A New History*, New York.

Burleigh, M., 2002 [1988], *Germany Turns Eastward: A Study of Ostforschung in the Third Reich*, Basingstoke and Oxford.

Burleigh, M. and Wippermann, W., 1991, *The Racial State: Germany 1933–1945*, Cambridge and New York.

Craig, G.A., 1980, *Germany 1866–1945*, New York.

Fulbrook, M., 1991, *The Fontana History of Germany 1918–1990: The Divided Nation*, London.

Fulbrook, M., 1995, *Anatomy of a Dictatorship: Inside the GDR 1949–1989*, Oxford.

Fulbrook, M. (ed.), 1997, *German History since 1800*, London.

Fulbrook, M., 2005, *The People's State: East German Society from Hitler to Honecker*, New Haven, CT.

Funder, A., 2002, *Stasiland: Stories from Behind the Berlin Wall*, London.

Garton Ash, T., 1994, *In Europe's Name: Germany and the Divided Continent*, London.

Garton Ash, T., 1997, *The File: A Personal History*, London.

Ingrao, C.W. and Szabo, Franz A.J. (eds), 2008, *The Germans in the East*, West Lafayette, IN.

Kershaw, I., 2000, *The Nazi Dictatorship: Problems and Perspectives of Interpretation*, 4th edn, London.

Leonhard, W., 1957, *Child of the Revolution*, translated by C.M. Woodhouse, London.

Major, P. and Osmond, J. (eds), 2002, *The Workers' and Peasants' State: Communist Society in East Germany under Ulbricht 1945–71*, Manchester.

Overy, R.J., 1996, *The Nazi Economic Recovery 1932–1938*, 2nd edn, Cambridge and New York.

Overy, R.J., 2002, *War and Economy in the Third Reich*, Oxford.

Ross, C., 2000, *Constructing Socialism at the Grass-Roots: The Transformation of East Germany 1945–65*, Basingstoke.

Stibbe, M., 2006, 'The SED, German Communism and the June 1953 Uprising: New Trends and New Research', in K. McDermott and M. Stibbe (eds), *Revolution and Resistance in Eastern Europe: Challenges to Communist Rule*, Oxford and New York, 37–55.

Williamson, D.G., 2003, *Germany since 1815: A Nation Forged and Renewed*, London.

Zatlin, J.R., 2007, *The Currency of Socialism: Money and Political Culture in East Germany*, Washington, DC, Cambridge and New York.

Greeks

Clogg, R., 1992, *A Concise History of Greece*, Cambridge.

Close, D.H., 1995, *The Origins of the Greek Civil War*, London and New York.

Koliopoulos, J.S. and Veremis, T.M., 2002, *Greece: The Modern Sequel: 1831 to the Present*, New York.

Llewellyn Smith, M., 1998, *Ionian Vision: Greece in Asia Minor 1919–1922*, London.

Mazower, M., 1993, *Inside Hitler's Greece: The Experience of Occupation 1941–1944*, New Haven, CT and London.

Michas, T., 2002, *Unholy Alliance: Greece and Milošević's Serbia*, College Station, TX.

Vatikiotis, P.J., 1998, *Popular Autocracy in Greece, 1936–1941: A Political Biography of General Ioannis Metaxas*, London and Portland, OR.

Woodhouse, C.M., 2002 [1976], *The Struggle for Greece 1941–1949*, with a new introduction by Richard Clogg, London.

Hungarians

Aczél, T. and Méray, T., 1960, *The Revolt of the Mind: A Case History of Intellectual Resistance Behind the Iron Curtain*, London.

Brust, L. and Stark, D., 1992, 'Remaking the Political Field in Hungary: From the Politics of Confrontation to the Politics of Competition', in I. Banac (ed.), *Eastern Europe in Revolution*, Ithaca, NY and London, 13–55.

Case, H., 2009, *Between States: The Transylvanian Question and the European Idea during World War II*, Stanford, CA.

Cesarani, D., 1997, *Genocide and Rescue: The Holocaust in Hungary*, Oxford and New York.

Congdon, L., Király, B.K. and Nagy, K. (eds), 2006, *1956: The Hungarian Revolution and War for Independence*, Boulder, CO, Highland Lakes, NJ and New York.

Deák, I., 2000, 'A Fatal Compromise? The Debate over Collaboration and Resistance in Hungary', in I. Deák, J.T. Gross and T. Judt (eds), *The Politics of Retribution in Europe: World War II and Its Aftermath*, Princeton, NJ, 39–73.

Gati, C., 1986, *Hungary and the Soviet Bloc*, Durham, NC.

Gati, C., 2006, *Failed Illusions: Moscow, Washington, Budapest and the 1956 Hungarian Revolt*, Washington, DC and Stanford, CA.

Fryer, P., 1986 [1956], *Hungarian Tragedy*, London.

Hanebrink, P.A., 2006, *In Defense of Christian Hungary: Religion, Nationalism and Antisemitism 1890–1944*, Ithaca, NY.

Hoensch, J.K., 1996, *A History of Modern Hungary 1867–1994*, 2nd edn, London.

Ignotus, P., 1975, 'The First Two Communist Takeovers of Hungary: 1919 and 1948', in T.T. Hammond and R. Farrell (eds), *The Anatomy of Communist Takeovers*, New Haven, CT and London, 385–98.

Janos, A.C., 1982, *The Politics of Backwardness in Hungary 1825–1945*, Princeton, NJ.

Kenedi, János, n.d. [1981], *Do It Yourself: Hungary's Hidden Economy*, London.

Kenez, P., 2006, *Hungary from the Nazis to the Soviets: The Establishment of the Communist Regime in Hungary 1944–1948*, New York.

Klimó, Á. von, 2018, *Remembering Cold Days: The 1942 Massacre of Novi Sad and Hungarian Politics and Society 1942–1989*, Pittsburg, PA.

Konrád, G., 1984, *Antipolitics: An Essay*, translated by Richard E. Allen, San Diego, CA.

Kontler, L., 2002, *A History of Hungary: Millennium in Central Europe*, Basingstoke and New York.

Kovács, J.M. and Trencsényi, B. (eds), 2019, *Brave New Hungary: Mapping the 'System of National Cooperation'*, Lanham, MD.

Lendvai, P., 2008, *One Day That Shook the Communist World: The 1956 Hungarian Uprising and Its Legacy*, translated by Ann Major, Princeton, NJ.

Lendvai, P., 2018, *Orbán: Hungary's Strongman*, Oxford and New York.

Litván, G. (ed.), 1996, *The Hungarian Revolution of 1956: Reform, Revolt and Repression 1953–1963*, London and New York.

Lomax, B., 1976, *Hungary 1956*, London.

Low, A.D., 1963, *The Hungarian Soviet Republic and the Paris Peace Conference*, Philadelphia, PA.

Macartney, C.A., 1937, *Hungary and Her Successors: The Treaty of Trianon and Its Consequences 1919–1937*, London.

Macartney, C.A., 1956–57, *October Fifteenth: A History of Modern Hungary*, 2 vols, Edinburgh.

Matthews, J.P.C., 2007, *Explosion: The Hungarian Revolution of 1956*, New York.

Nagy-Talavera, N.M., 1970, *The Green Shirts and the Others: A History of Fascism in Hungary and Rumania*, Stanford, CA.

Rady, M., 2008, 'Conclusory Essay: Hungary's War of Independence in 1956', in L. Péter and M. Rady (eds), *Resistance, Rebellion and Revolution in Hungary and Central Europe: Commemorating 1956*, London, 347–54.

Rady, M., 2011, 'Ferenc Szálasi: "Hungarism" and the Arrow Cross', in R. Haynes and M. Rady (eds), *In the Shadow of Hitler: Personalities of the Right in Central and Eastern Europe*, London, 261–77.

Rainer, J.M., 2009, *Imre Nagy: A Biography*, translated by L.H. Legters, London and New York.

Ránki, G., 1971, 'The Problem of Fascism in Hungary', in P.F. Sugar (ed.), *Native Fascism in the Successor States 1918–1945*, Santa Barbara, CA, 65–72.

Schöpflin, G., 1978, *The Hungarians of Romania*, London.

Swain, N., 1992, *Hungary: The Rise and Fall of Feasible Socialism*, London and New York.

Turda, Marius, 2013, '"If Our Race Did Not Exist, It Would Have to Be Created": Racial Science in Hungary 1940–1944', in A. Weiss-Wendt and R. Yeomans (eds), *Racial Science in Hitler's New Europe 1938–1945*, Lincoln, NE and London, 237–58.

Zeidler, M., 2011, 'Gyula Gömbös: An Outsider's Attempt at Radical Reform', in R. Haynes and M. Rady (eds), *In the Shadow of Hitler: Personalities of the Right in Central and Eastern Europe*, London, 121–37.

Jews

Bartov, O., 1997, *Murder in Our Midst: The Holocaust, Industrial Killing and Representation*, Oxford.

Beorn, W.W., 2018, *The Holocaust in Eastern Europe: At the Epicenter of the Final Solution*, London.

Browning, C.R., 1995, *The Path to Genocide: Essays on Launching the Final Solution*, Cambridge.

Cohn, N., 2006 [1967], *Warrant for Genocide: The Myth of the Jewish World-Conspiracy and the Protocols of the Elders of Zion*, new edition, London.

Gay, P., 1978, *Freud, Jews and Other Germans: Masters and Victims in Modernist Culture*, Oxford, New York, Toronto and Melbourne.

Gilbert, M., 1985, *The Holocaust: The History of the Jews of Europe during the Second World War*, New York.

Hilberg, R., 2003 [1963], *The Destruction of the European Jews*, 3rd edn; 3 vols, New Haven, CT.

Hundert, G.D. (ed.), 2008, *The YIVO Encyclopedia of Jews in Eastern Europe*, 2 vols, New Haven, CT.

Polonsky, A., 2012, *The Jews in Poland and Russia*, vol. 3: *1914 to 2008*, Oxford and Portland, OR.

Pringle, H., 2006, *The Master Plan: Himmler's Scholars and the Holocaust*, New York.

Tec, N., 1993, *Defiance: The Bielski Partisans*, New York.

Vital, D., 2001, *A People Apart: The Jews of Europe 1789–1939*, Oxford and New York.

Wistrich, R.S., 1992, *Antisemitism: The Longest Hatred*, New York.

Poles

Andreski, S., 1981, 'Poland', in S.J. Woolf (ed.), *Fascism in Europe*, London and New York, 171–90.

Ascherson, N., 1987, *The Struggles for Poland*, London.

Bardach, J. and Gleeson, K., 1998, *Man Is Wolf to Man: Surviving Stalin's Gulag*, Berkeley, CA.

Bernhard, M.H., 1993, *The Origins of Democratization in Poland: Workers, Intellectuals and Oppositional Politics 1976–1980*, New York.

Bethell, N., 1972, *Gomułka: His Poland and His Communism*, Harmondsworth.

Borodziej, W., 2006, *The Warsaw Uprising of 1944*, translated by Barbara Harshav, Madison, WI.

Borowski, T., 1976, *This Way for the Gas, Ladies and Gentlemen*, translated by Barbara Vedder, New York.

Chodakiewicz, M.J., 2004, *Between Nazis and Soviets: Occupation Politics in Poland 1939–1947*, Lanham, MD.

Davies, N., 1981, *God's Playground: A History of Poland*, vol. II: *1795 to the Present*, Oxford.

Garliński, J., 1991, *The Survival of Love: Memoirs of a Resistance Officer*, Oxford.

Garton Ash, T., 1983, *The Polish Revolution: Solidarity 1980–82*, London.

Gross, J.T., 1979, *Polish Society under German Occupation: The General Government 1939-1944*, Princeton, NJ.

Gross, J.T., 1998, *Revolution from Abroad: The Soviet Conquest of Poland's Western Ukraine and Western Belorussia*, Princeton, NJ.

Gross, J.T., 2003, *Neighbours: The Destruction of the Jewish Community in Jedwabne, Poland, 1941*, London.

Grudzińska-Gross, I. and Gross, J.T. (eds), 1981, *War Through Children's Eyes: The Soviet Occupation of Poland and the Deportations 1939–1941*, Stanford, CA.

Hunczak, T., 1967, 'Polish Colonial Ambitions in the Inter-War Period', *Slavic Review*, XXVI, #4 (December), 648–56.

Jakelski, L., 2017, *Making New Music in Cold War Poland: The Warsaw Autumn Festival 1956–1968*, Berkeley, CA.

Kaliski, B., 2006, 'Solidarity 1980-1: The Second Vistula Miracle?', in K. McDermott and M. Stibbe (eds), *Revolution and Resistance in Eastern Europe: Challenges to Communist Rule*, Oxford and New York, 119–36.

Kemp-Welch, A., 2008, *Poland under Communism: A Cold War History*, Cambridge and New York.

Korbel, J., 1963, *Poland between East and West: Soviet and German Diplomacy toward Poland 1919–1933*, Princeton, NJ.

Kossert, A., 2011, 'Founding Father of Modern Poland and Nationalist Antisemite: Roman Dmowski', in R. Haynes and M. Rady (eds), *In the Shadow of Hitler: Personalities of the Right in Central and Eastern Europe*, London and New York, 89–104.

Laba, R., 1991, *The Roots of Solidarity: A Political Sociology of Poland's Working-Class Democratization*, Princeton, NJ.

Lebow, K., 2013, *Unfinished Utopia: Nowa Huta, Stalinism and Polish Society 1949–56*, Ithaca, NY.

Lipski, J.J., 1985, *KOR: A History of the Workers' Defense Committee in Poland 1976–1978*, Berkeley, CA.

Lukas, R., 1997 [1986], *The Forgotten Holocaust: The Poles under German Occupation 1939–1945*, London.

Lukowski, J. and Zawadzki, H., 2019, *A Concise History of Poland*, 3rd edn, Cambridge.

Mazurek, M., 2013, 'Keeping It Close to Home: Resourcefulness and Scarcity in Late Socialist Poland', in P. Bren and M.C. Neuburger (eds), *Communism Unwrapped: Consumption in Cold War Eastern Europe*, Oxford and New York, 298–324.

Miłosz, C., 1985 [1953], *The Captive Mind*, translated by J. Zielonko, Harmondsworth.

Ost, D., 1990, *Solidarity and the Politics of Anti-Politics: Opposition and Reform in Poland since 1968*, Philadelphia, PA.

Pease, N., 2009, *Rome's Most Faithful Daughter: The Catholic Church and Independent Poland 1914–1939*, Athens, OH.

Perechodnik, C., 1996, *Am I a Murderer? Testament of a Jewish Ghetto Policeman*, edited and translated by Frank Fox, Boulder, CO.

Piotrowski, T., 1998, *Poland's Holocaust: Ethnic Strife, Collaboration with Occupying Forces and Genocide in the Second Republic 1918–1947*, Jefferson, NC.

Plach, E., 2006, *The Clash of Moral Nations: Cultural Politics in Piłsudski's Poland 1926–1935*, Athens, OH.

Polonsky, A., 1972, *Politics in Independent Poland 1921–1939: The Crisis of Constitutional Government*, Oxford.

Polonsky, A. (ed.), 1976, *The Great Powers and the Polish Question 1941-45: A Documentary Study in Cold War Origins*, London.

Richmond, T., 1996, *Konin: A Quest*, New York.

Rossino, A.B., 2003, *Hitler Strikes Poland: Blitzkrieg, Ideology and Atrocity*, Lawrence, KS.

Rothschild, J., 1966, *Piłsudski's Coup d'Etat*, New York.

Stachura, P.D. (ed.), 1998, *Poland between the Wars 1918–1939*, Basingstoke and New York.

Wandycz, P.S., 1984, *The Lands of Partitioned Poland 1795–1918*, 2nd edn, Seattle, WA.

Wandycz, P.S., 1990, 'Poland's Place in Europe in the Concepts of Piłsudski and Dmowski', *East European Politics & Societies*, IV/3 (Fall), 451–68.

Wat, A., 2003 [1988], *My Century: The Odyssey of a Polish Intellectual*, translated by R. Lourie, New York.

Weit, E., 1973, *Eyewitness: The Autobiography of Gomulka's Interpreter*, translated by M. Schofield, London.

Wynot, E.D., 1971, '"A Necessary Cruelty": The Emergence of Official Anti-Semitism in Poland 1936–39', *American Historical Review*, LXXVI, #4 (October), 1034–58.

Zajdlerowa, Z., 1989 [1946], *The Dark Side of the Moon*, new edition, edited by J. Coutouvidis and T. Lane, New York.

Zawodny, J.K., 1978, *Nothing but Honour: The Story of the Warsaw Uprising, 1944*, Stanford, CA.

Roma (Gypsies)

Achim, V., 2004, *The Roma in Romanian History*, Budapest and New York.

Crowe, D.M., 2007 [1995], *A History of the Gypsies of Eastern Europe and Russia*, Basingstoke.

Fonseca, I., 1996, *Bury Me Standing: The Gypsies and Their Journey*, New York.

Puxon, G., 1975, *Rom: Europe's Gypsies*, London.

Weiss-Wendt, A. (ed.), 2015, *The Nazi Genocide of the Roma: Reassessment and Commemoration*, reprint edition, New York and Oxford.

Romanians, inc. Moldova

Almond, M., 1992, *The Rise and Fall of Nicolae and Elena Ceauşescu*, London.

Behr, E., 1991, *Kiss the Hand You Cannot Bite: The Rise and Fall of the Ceauşescus*, New York.

Bucur, M., 2007, 'Carol II of Romania', in B.J. Fischer (ed.), *Balkan Strongmen: Dictators and Authoritarian Rulers of Southeast Europe*, West Lafayette, IN, 86–117.

Case, H., 2009, *Between States: The Transylvanian Question and the European Idea during World War II*, Stanford, CA.

Deletant, D., 1995, *Ceauşescu and the Securitate: Coercion and Dissent in Romania 1965–1989*, Armonk, NY.

Deletant, D., 2001, 'Bessarabia', in I.C.B. Dear and M.R.D. Foot (eds), *The Oxford Companion to World War II*, 2nd edn, Oxford, 101.

Deletant, D., 2006, *Hitler's Forgotten Ally: Ion Antonescu and His Regime, Romania 1940–1944*, New York.

Deletant, D., 2011, 'Ion Antonescu: The Paradoxes of His Regime 1940–44', in R. Haynes and M. Rady (eds), *In the Shadow of Hitler: Personalities of the Right in Central and Eastern Europe*, London, 278–94.

Eyal, J. and Smith, G., 1996, 'Moldova and the Moldovans', in G. Smith (ed.), *The Nationalities Question in the Post-Soviet States*, 2nd edn, London, 223–44.

Fischer-Galati, S., 1975, 'The Communist Takover of Rumania: A Function of Soviet Power', in T.T. Hammond and R. Farrell (eds), *The Anatomy of Communist Takeovers*, New Haven, CT and London, 310–20.

Georgescu, V. and Călinescu, M., 1991, *The Romanians: A History*, Columbus, OH.

Haynes, R., 2000, *Romanian Policy towards Germany 1936–40*, London.

Haynes, R., 2020, *Moldova: A History*, London.

Hitchens, K., 1994, *Rumania 1866–1947*, Oxford.

Iordachi, C., 2004, 'Charisma, Religion and Ideology: Romania's Interwar Legion of the Archangel Michael', in J.R. Lampe and M. Mazower (eds), *Ideologies and National Identities: The Case of Twentieth-Century Southeastern Europe*, Budapest and New York, 19–53.

Livezeanu, I., 1990, 'Fascists and Conservatives in Romania: Two Generations of Nationalists', in M. Blinkhorn (ed.), *Fascists and Conservatives: The Radical Right and the Establishment in Twentieth-Century Europe*, London, 218–40.

Livezeanu, I., 1995, *Cultural Politics in Greater Romania: Regionalism, Nation Building and Ethnic Struggle 1918–1930*, Ithaca, NY.

Massino, J., 2012, 'From Black Caviar to Blackouts: Gender, Consumption and Lifestyle in Ceauşescu's Romania', in P. Bren and M.C. Neuburger (eds), *Communism Unwrapped: Consumption in Cold War Eastern Europe*, Oxford and New York, 226–49.

Nagy-Talavera, N.M., 1970, *The Green Shirts and the Others: A History of Fascism in Hungary and Rumania*, Stanford, CA.

Roberts, H.L., 1951, *Rumania: Political Problems of an Agrarian State*, New York.

Roper, S.D., 2000, *Romania: The Unfinished Revolution*, Amsterdam and Abingdon.

Săndulescu, V., 2007, 'Sacralised Politics in Action: The February 1937 Burial of the Romanian Legionary Leaders Ion Moţa and Vasile Marin', *Totalitarian Movements & Political Religions*, VIII, #2 (June), 259–69.

Shafir, M., 1985, *Romania: Politics, Economics and Society: Political Stagnation and Simulated Change*, Boulder, CO.

Siani-Davies, P., 2005, *The Romanian Revolution of December 1989*, Ithaca, NY.

Solonari, V., 2009, *Purifying the Nation: Population Exchange and Ethnic Cleansing in Nazi-Allied Romania*, Baltimore, MD.

Solonari, V., 2015, 'Ethnic Cleansing or "Crime Prevention"? Deportation of Romanian Roma', in A. Weiss-Wendt (ed.), *The Nazi Genocide of the Roma: Reassessment and Commemoration*, reprint edition, New York and Oxford, 96–119.

Tismaneanu, V., 2003, *Stalinism for All Seasons: A Political History of Romanian Communism*, Berkeley, CA.

Weber, E., 1965, 'Romania', in H. Rogger and E. Weber (eds), *The European Right: A Historical Profile*, London, 501–74.

Weber, E., 1979, 'The Men of the Archangel', in G.L. Mosse (ed.), *International Fascism: New Thoughts and Approaches*, London and Beverly Hills, CA, 317–43.

South Slavs: Croats, Slovenes, Serbs, Bosniacs and Macedonian Slavs

Banac, I., 1988, *The National Question in Yugoslavia: Origins, History*, Politics, Ithaca, NY.

Banac, I., 1988, *With Stalin against Tito: Cominformist Splits in Yugoslav Communism*. Ithaca, NY.

Benderly, J. and Kraft, E. (eds), 1996, *Independent Slovenia: Origins, Movements, Prospects*, New York.

Bennett, C., 1995, *Yugoslavia's Bloody Collapse: Causes, Course and Consequences*, London.

Benson, L., 2004, *Yugoslavia: A Concise History*, revised edition, Basingstoke and New York.

Biondich, M., 2000, *Stjepan Radić, the Croat Peasant Party and the Politics of Mass Mobilization 1904–1928*, Toronto.

Cigar, N., 1995, *Genocide in Bosnia: The Policy of 'Ethnic Cleansing'*, College Station, TX.

Cohen, L.J., 1995, *Broken Bonds: Yugoslavia's Disintegration and Balkan Politics in Transition*, 2nd edn, Boulder, CO.

Danforth, L.M., 1995, *The Macedonian Conflict: Ethnic Nationalism in a Transnational World*, Princeton, NJ.

Djilas, A., 1991, *The Contested Country: Yugoslav Unity and Communist Revolution 1919–1953*, Cambridge, MA and London.

Djilas, M., 1957, *The New Class: An Analysis of the Communist System*, New York.

Djilas, M., 1962, *Conversations with Stalin*, New York.

Djokić, D. (ed.), 2003, *Yugoslavism: Histories of a Failed Idea 1918–1992*, London.

Djokić, D., 2011, '"Leader" or "Devil"? Milan Stojadinović, Prime Minister of Yugoslavia (1935–39) and His Ideology', in R. Haynes and M. Rady (eds), *In the Shadow of Hitler: Personalities of the Right in Central and Eastern Europe*, London, 153–68.

Ferfila, B., 2010, *Slovenia's Transition: From Medieval Roots to the European Union*, Lanham, MD.

Friedman, F., 1996, *The Bosnian Muslims: Denial of a Nation*, Boulder, CO.

Goldstein, I., 1999, *Croatia: A History*, Montreal.

Gow, J., 1997, *Triumph of the Lack of Will: International Diplomacy and the Yugoslav War*, London.

Hoare, M.A., 2013, *The Bosnian Muslims in the Second World War*, London.

Honig, J.W. and Both, H., 1997, *Srebrenica: Record of a War Crime*, New York.

Ingrao, C. and T.A. Emmert (eds), 2009, *Confronting the Yugoslav Controversies: A Scholars' Initiative*, Washington, DC and West Lafayette, IN.

Judah, T., 2000, *The Serbs: History, Myth and the Destruction of Yugoslavia*, 2nd edn, New Haven, CT.

Király, B.K., 1982, 'The Aborted Soviet Military Plans Against Tito's Yugoslavia', in W.S. Vucinich (ed.), *At the Brink of War and Peace: The Tito-Stalin Split in a Historic Perspective*, New York, 273–88.

Korb, A., 2015, 'Ustaša Mass Violence Against Gypsies in Croatia 1941–1942', in A. Weiss-Wendt (ed.), *The Nazi Genocide of the Roma: Reassessment and Commemoration*, reprint edition, New York and Oxford, 72–95.

Lampe, J.R., 2000, *Yugoslavia as History: Twice There Was a Country*, 2nd edn, Cambridge and New York.

Lederer, I.J., 1963, *Yugoslavia at the Paris Peace Conference: A Study in Frontiermaking*, New Haven, CT and London.

Malcolm, N., 1996, *Bosnia: A Short History*, updated edition, New York.

Morrison, K., 2009, *Montenegro: A History*, London.

Naimark, N.M. and Case, H. (eds), 2003, *Yugoslavia and Its Historians: Understanding the Balkan Wars of the 1990s*, Stanford, CA.

Pavlović, S., 2008, *Balkan Anschluss: The Annexation of Montenegro and the Creation of the Common South Slavic State*, West Lafayette, IN.

Pavlowitch, S.K., 2008, *Hitler's New Disorder: The Second World War in Yugoslavia*, New York.

Popov, N. and Gojović, D. (eds), 2000, *The Road to War in Serbia: Trauma and Catharsis*, Budapest and New York.

Poulton, H., 2000, *Who Are the Macedonians?*, 2nd edn, Bloomington, IN.

Magaš, B. and Žanić, I. (eds), 2001, *The War in Croatia and Herzegovina 1991–1995*, London.

Ramet, S.P., 2002, *Balkan Babel: The Disintegration of Yugoslavia from the Death of Tito to Ethnic War*, 4th edn, Boulder, CO.

Ramet, S.P., 2006, *The Three Yugoslavias: State-Building and Legitimation 1918–2005*, Washington, DC and Bloomington, IN.

Ramet, S.P. (ed.), 2007, *The Independent State of Croatia 1941–1945*, London and New York.

Ramet, S.P. and Pavlaković, V. (eds), 2005, *Serbia since 1989: Politics and Society under Milošević and After*, Seattle, WA.

Rusinow, D.I., 1977, *The Yugoslav Experiment 1948–1974*, Berkeley, CA and London.

Rusinow, D.I., 2008, *Yugoslavia: Oblique Insights and Observations*, edited and with a preface by G. Stokes, Pittsburgh, PA.

Silber, L. and Little, A., 1995, *The Death of Yugoslavia*, London.

Simms, B., 2001, *Unfinest Hour: Britain and the Destruction of Bosnia*, London.

Singleton, F., 1985, *A Short History of the Yugoslav Peoples*, Cambridge.

Subotić, J., 2009, *Hijacked Justice: Dealing with the Past in the Balkans*, Ithaca, NY.

Tanner, M., 1997, *Croatia: A Nation Forged in War*, New Haven, CT.

Thomas, R., 1999, *Serbia under Milošević: Politics in the 1990s*, London.

Thompson, M., 1992, *A Paper House: The Ending of Yugoslavia*, New York.

Ukrainians

Applebaum, A., 2018, *Red Famine: Stalin's War on Ukraine*, London.

Berkhoff, K.C., 2004, *Harvest of Despair: Life and Death in Ukraine under Nazi Rule*, Cambridge, MA and London.

Brandon, R. and Lower, W. (eds), 2008, *The Shoah in Ukraine: History, Testimony, Memorialization*, Bloomington, IN.

Horak, S.M., 1988, *The First Treaty of World War I: Ukraine's Treaty with the Central Powers of February 9, 1918*, Boulder, CO.

Kurkov, A., 2014, *Ukraine Diaries: Dispatches from Kiev*, London.

Magocsi, P.R., 1996, *A History of Ukraine*, Toronto.

Marples, D.R., 2007, *Heroes and Villains: Constructing National History in Contemporary Ukraine*, Budapest and New York.

Marples, D.R., 2011, 'Stepan Bandera: In Search of a Ukraine for Ukrainians', in R. Haynes and M. Rady (eds), *In the Shadow of Hitler: Personalities of the Right in Central and Eastern Europe*, London and New York, 227–44.

Motyl, A.J., 1980, *The Turn to the Right: The Ideological Origins and Development of Ukrainian Nationalism 1919–1929*, Boulder, CO.

Plokhy, S., 2015, *Gates of Europe: A History of Ukraine*, London.

Reid, A., 2003, *Borderland: A Journey through the History of Ukraine*, London.

Seibel, W., 2017, 'The European Union, Ukraine and the Unstable East', in D. Dinan, N. Nugent and W.E. Paterson (eds), *The European Union in Crisis*, London, 269–93.

Subtelny, O., 2009, *Ukraine: A History*, 4th edn, Toronto.

Wilson, A., 2005, *Ukraine's Orange Revolution*, New Haven and London.

Wilson, A., 2014, *Ukraine Crisis: What It Means for the West*, New Haven and London.

Index

p. X

1. 'backwardness' ?
3. 'test tube' ? 'Near abroad'?
4. 'illusory'
5. 'conceptual thinking' ?
7. overambitious .
~~11. 'tidal forest'~~ !

11/12 vid.

18 ? peasant + land ownership

24 vid.
28 hegemon ?
29. Nationalism / Patriotism — Difference?
34 October Rev. / communist state NO
36 Baltic ?   War / Revolution *

39 ? 'semi-autocracy' — NO
40 'inevitably'.
41 'pariah regime' !
45 Western perspective
51. ?
54 Constantinople ?